Microsoft Office 2013
ProjectLearn

GLEN COULTHARD

MICHAEL ORWICK

JUDITH SCHEEREN

MICROSOFT OFFICE 2013: PROJECTLEARN
Published by McGraw-Hill Education, 2 Penn Plaza, New York, NY 10121. Copyright © 2014 by McGraw-Hill
Education. All rights reserved. Printed in the United States of America. No part of this publication may be
reproduced or distributed in any form or by any means, or stored in a database or retrieval system, without the
prior written consent of McGraw-Hill Education, including, but not limited to, in any network or other electronic
storage or transmission, or broadcast for distance learning.

Some ancillaries, including electronic and print components, may not be available to customers outside the United States.

This book is printed on acid-free paper.

1 2 3 4 5 6 7 8 9 0 RMN/RMN 1 0 9 8 7 6 5 4 3

ISBN   978-0-07-351940-1
MHID   0-07-351940-5

Senior Vice President, Products & Markets: *Kurt L. Strand*
Vice President, Content Production & Technology
Services: *Kimberly Meriwether David*
Director: *Scott Davidson*
Senior Brand Manager: *Wyatt Morris*
Executive Director of Development: *Ann Torbert*
Development Editor II: *Alan Palmer*
Freelance Development Editor: *Barrett Lyon Winston*
Digital Development Editor II: *Kevin White*
Senior Marketing Manager: *Tiffany Russell*
Director, Content Production: *Terri Schiesl*

Content Project Manager: *Kathryn D. Wright*
Content Project Manager: *Janean A. Utley/Susan Lombardi*
Senior Buyer: *Carol A. Bielski*
Senior Designer: *Srdjan Savanovic*
Cover and Interior Design: *Maureen McCutcheon*
Cover Image: @ *Influx Productions/Getty Images*
Content Licensing Specialist: *Joanne Mennemeier*
Typeface: *10.5/13 Minion Pro*
Compositor: *Aptara®, Inc.*
Printer: *R. R. Donnelley*

Photo Credits: Recurring design image: 'chess piece' © Influx Productions/Getty Images; O-2: © Goodshoot/
Punchstock; W-2: JUPITERIMAGES/Comstock Premium/Alamy; W-60: Inti St. Clair/Getty Images; W-128:
C Squared Studios/Getty Images; W-180: Purestock/SuperStock; E-2: BananaStock/JupiterImages; E-64: © John
Lund/Marc Romanelli/Blend Images LLC; E-120: Yellow Dog Productions/Getty Images; E-158: Pixtal/AGE
Fotostock; P-2: Ingram Publishing; P-62: Purestock/SuperStock; P-128: Ben Meyer/Getty Images; A-2: Purestock/
SuperStock; A-52: Corbis; A-100: Comstock Images/Getty Images.

Library of Congress Cataloging-in-Publication Data

Coulthard, Glen J.
    Microsoft Office 2013 : ProjectLearn / Glen Coulthard, Michael Orwick, Judith Scheeren.
       pages cm
    "ProjectLearn Series"—Preface.
    Includes index.
    ISBN 978-0-07-351940-1 (alk. paper) — ISBN 0-07-351940-5 (alk. paper)
    1. Microsoft Office. 2. Business—Computer programs. I. Title.
    HF5548.4.M525C674 2014
    005.5—dc23
                             2013030885

The Internet addresses listed in the text were accurate at the time of publication. The inclusion of a website does
not indicate an endorsement by the authors or McGraw-Hill Education, and McGraw-Hill Education does not
guarantee the accuracy of the information presented at these sites.

Brief Contents

Contents

PROJECTLEARN MICROSOFT EXCEL 2013

CHAPTER 4
Working with Tables, Worksheets, and Workbooks E-158

PROJECTLEARN MICROSOFT ACCESS 2013

CHAPTER 1
Introduction to Access A-2

PROJECTLEARN MICROSOFT POWERPOINT 2013

Preface

The ProjectLearn Series from McGraw-Hill

The ProjectLearn series builds upon the authors' years of instructional design and teaching experience with Microsoft Office applications. Developed from the ground up through discussions with higher-education faculty and students, ProjectLearn presents innovative design features, engaging content, and proven pedagogy, never before compiled in a single application series. The project-based approach ensures that students focus on the end result and leave the tutorial with quality artifacts from each of the Office applications. These project artifacts are designed to impress reviewers and potential employers.

The ProjectLearn approach supports a simple to complex learning progression, and stresses relevance and context to better engage students with real-life applications. In our specific learning series, students are presented with a scenario or situation and asked to produce an outcome that demonstrates their mastery of specific learning objectives. The strength of this learn-by-doing approach is that students understand and appreciate how individual skills are utilized and combined in performing work-related tasks, such as producing a newsletter or expense budget. Students are constantly introduced to new skills by completing artifacts in each class, requiring both their attendance and performance. Our ProjectLearn approach ensures that mastering Microsoft Office skills will lead to more productive students and future employees.

Walkthrough

The ProjectLearn approach focuses on the end result. The book introduces Office skills step-by-step in the context of a scenario-based project. This approach not only helps students learn Microsoft Office skills but also demonstrates their importance, connecting Office 2013 skills with meaningful, relevant projects. After completing lessons, students have a portfolio of quality products designed not only to show their mastery of each lesson's skills but also to impress potential employers.

Chapter Features

Project and Situation

Each lesson is introduced with a situation relevant to today's student experience, from building a personal financial budget to working in the registrar's office at a college. Each scenario then requires the use of Microsoft Office 2013 to solve a problem or complete an assignment.

PROJECT

Building A Professional Handout

In this project, you will make changes to an existing document to better organize and display the information. Place the finished version of this document into your career portfolio and title it "Word: Professional Handout."

This chapter will provide you with the techniques and skills that you will use in producing almost any document, whether you are a professional, a student, or just looking for a way to enhance your job skills.

THE SITUATION

Dr. Shoret's Veterinary Clinic

A friend of yours works at a veterinary clinic. The vet has scratched out some notes on how pet owners should groom their dogs and given the notes to your friend. After typing the material into a file and organizing it a bit, she would like to improve its impact by making it look more professional. She has asked you to help her "fix it up," so the clinic can print it and give to customers to take away with them. Let's turn the original document she has created into something that will be a benefit to both the clinic and its customers.

Lessons Connected to Project Learning Objectives

Each lesson maps directly to a learning objective, so students and instructors can be sure they know the material when a chapter's project and exercises are complete.

chapter **1**

Introduction to Word

CHAPTER OBJECTIVES

After completing this chapter, you will be able to:

1.1 Select Text
1.2 Move Things Around
1.3 Use Character Formatting
1.4 Use Paragraph Formatting
1.5 Use Document Views
1.6 Use Font Color and Effects
1.7 Create Bulleted Lists
1.8 Use Find and Replace
1.9 Use Spelling, Grammar, and Readability Statistics

Microsoft Word is likely the most-used word processing program in the modern office. But exactly what is "word processing"? The true power of word processing allows you to control, adjust, and improve the way your document appears—and the way in which you communicate your message. To learn how to "process" your words into powerful documents, this chapter introduces some of the most commonly used and most-often needed techniques and shows you how to make changes to an existing document. Some of the changes will be subtle, some spectacular. Some of the changes will involve a single word or sentence. Other changes will involve the entire document. But all changes are done for the same purpose—to make your document demand attention.

Clear Pedagogical Approach Supports Learning

Each lesson presents skills in a step-by-step approach. First, a "Lesson Overview" presents key terms and other general information regarding the learning outcome for that particular skill. Next, a "Skills Preview" table lists the individual Microsoft Office 2013 skills the lesson covers, including keyboard shortcuts and navigation directions. The last section in each lesson is the application of this information, found in "Project Practice." These exercises build upon knowledge gained in earlier lessons, adding new skills one at a time.

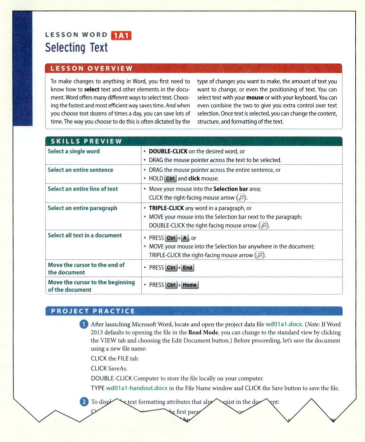

LESSON WORD `1A1`
Selecting Text

LESSON OVERVIEW

To make changes to anything in Word, you first need to know how to **select** text and other elements in the document. Word offers many different ways to select text. Choosing the fastest and most efficient way saves time. And when you choose text dozens of times a day, you can save lots of time. The way you choose to do this is often dictated by the type of changes you want to make, the amount of text you want to change, or even the positioning of text. You can select text with your **mouse** or with your keyboard. You can even combine the two to give you extra control over text selection. Once text is selected, you can change the content, structure, and formatting of the text.

SKILLS PREVIEW

Select a single word	• **DOUBLE-CLICK** on the desired word, or • DRAG the mouse pointer across the text to be selected.
Select an entire sentence	• DRAG the mouse pointer across the entire sentence, or • HOLD `Ctrl` and **click** mouse.
Select an entire line of text	• Move your mouse into the **Selection bar** area; CLICK the right-facing mouse arrow (⟋).
Select an entire paragraph	• **TRIPLE-CLICK** any word in a paragraph, or • MOVE your mouse into the Selection bar next to the paragraph; DOUBLE-CLICK the right-facing mouse arrow (⟋).
Select all text in a document	• PRESS `Ctrl`+`A`, or • MOVE your mouse into the Selection bar anywhere in the document; TRIPLE-CLICK the right-facing mouse arrow (⟋).
Move the cursor to the end of the document	• PRESS `Ctrl`+`End`
Move the cursor to the beginning of the document	• PRESS `Ctrl`+`Home`

PROJECT PRACTICE

1. After launching Microsoft Word, locate and open the project data file wd01a1.docx. (*Note*: If Word 2013 defaults to opening the file in the **Read Mode**, you can change to the standard view by clicking the VIEW tab and choosing the Edit Document button.) Before proceeding, let's save the document using a new file name:
CLICK the FILE tab.
CLICK SaveAs.
DOUBLE-CLICK Computer to store the file locally on your computer.
TYPE wd01a1-handout.docx in the File Name window and CLICK the Save button to save the file.

2. To display the text formatting attributes that already exist in the document:

Heads Up, Tip, and More Info Boxes

Throughout each chapter, boxed items call attention to important content that helps you successfully perform the tasks in each lesson. Look for "Heads Up" boxes to alert you to potential hidden pitfalls within Microsoft Office, "Tip" boxes for additional information about navigation or keyboard shortcuts, and "More Info" boxes for extra, detailed information related to a skill.

> **ⓘ MORE INFO**
>
> The Mini toolbar provides a shortcut to many of the common commands related to selecting text. The toolbar fades in and out depending how close the mouse is to the selected area. Its appearance can be controlled (turned on or off) via the **Backstage view**. Follow this path: FILE tab, Options, General. If the Show Mini Toolbar on Selection is turned on, it will activate when you select text.

> **💡 TIP**
>
> If the `Shift` key is held down, the arrow keys can be used to select text. This can be useful if you use another way of selecting text, but need to adjust your selection by a few characters. Just hold the `Shift` key down and each time you hit the arrow key, the selected text will adjust in that direction.
> The arrow keys on your keyboard may be grouped separately or they may share keys with the numeric pad. If your arrow keys are on the numeric pad, make sure you toggle the purpose of these keys using the

> **⚠ HEADS UP**
>
> When you click the Paste command (), be sure to hit the image of a Clipboard, and not the **drop-down** arrow. The drop-down arrow brings up a menu of pasting options that we are not using here.

Quizzes and Hands-On Exercises

Chapters are broken out into two projects, and each project contains its own quiz and two or three hands-on exercises. These hands-on exercises, called "Work It Out," assess a student's mastery of the material up to that point. In total, each chapter contains two multiple-choice quizzes and either four or six hands-on exercises to provide more opportunity for skill practice and understanding.

Chapter Summary

Word provides so many powerful features that many documents that once were fashioned only by professionals are now produced easily by almost anyone. Faculty, students, the self-employed, administrative personnel, and even the boss in the corner office can not only produce and edit the content they want, but they also can control the design and formatting as well. In addition to removing such barriers, Word has also proven to be one of the biggest cost-saving advantages for businesses of all sizes.

Besides entering, editing, and deleting text, Word allows you to adjust page margins, choose from a variety of font typefaces and styles, add special effects to text, and view all of your changes instantaneously. In this chapter, you learned to use the zoom controls and the advantages of different views. Copy, Paste, and Undo commands were demonstrated for changing the document structure and moving all types of elements around the document, without fear of making a mistake. The Find and Replace feature allowed you to make changes quickly and easily from one end of the document to the other. Even adding a drop cap to add interest is easy and adjustable. The built-in Spelling and Grammar tools, along with Readability Statistics, ensured that your writing was professional and targeted in both appearance and substance.

Chapter Key Terms

Backstage view, p. W-5	Italic, p. W-12	Readability statistics, p. W-43
Bold, p. W-13	Justify text, p. W-16	Ribbon, p. W-4
Center-align text, p. W-14	Landscape, p. W-56	Ruler, p. W-21
Click, p. W-4	Left-align text, p. W-4	Select, p. W-4
Deselect, p. W-5	Margins, p. W-16	Selection bar, p. W-4
Dialog box, p. W-12	Mouse, p. W-4	Show/Hide command, p. W-20
Double-click, p. W-4	Navigation pane, p. W-39	Size, p. W-4
Drag, p. W-3	Nonadjacent selection, p. W-14	Spelling and Grammar
Drop cap, p. W-31	Orientation, p. W-50	checker, p. W-43
Drop-down, p. W-10	Print, p. W-48	Status bar, p. W-22
Find, p. W-39	Print Preview pane, p. W-49	Text effects, p. W-31
Find and Replace, p. W-40	Proofing, p. W-43	Triple-click, p. W-4
Font typeface, p. W-4	Quick Access toolbar, p. W-8	Underline, p. W-13
Group, p. W-12	Read Mode, p. W-4	Zoom, p. W-20

On Your Own Exercise WD-1C-E1

This project provides the opportunity to practice the most important skills covered in this chapter, regardless of the project in which they were introduced. As the chapters progress, these comprehensive projects will become more challenging, building on all of the skills covered to that point.

Let's get started! In this project, you will create another professional handout—this time for a doctor's office or medical clinic. You can make your own decisions unless specifically told what to do. An idea of what the fin̶a̶l̶ may look like is shown Figure

End of Chapter Material

Each chapter ends with a brief chapter summary, a list of key terms, and two comprehensive chapter exercises, called "On Your Own." In these exercises, a student uses all the skills in the chapter to complete a unique project. Instructors may assign these as homework, and students may keep them for a portfolio piece.

Online Learning Center

Visit www.mhhe.com/office2013projectlearn

For Instructors

Instructors will find the following support materials at the online learning center:

- Instructor's manual
- Test bank
- PowerPoint slides
- Solution files

For Students

Students will find data files for the various projects and exercises throughout the book.

1:1 with Technology

ProjectLearn Lessons in SIMnet are 1:1 with the book to help students practice Office skills using SIMnet's interactive learning technology. Select auto-graded projects from the book are also available in SIMnet and allow students to master their skills and receive immediate feedback.

About the Authors

GLEN COULTHARD lives in British Columbia, Canada, where he is a full-time faculty member in the School of Business at Okanagan College. Glen holds a Bachelor of Commerce degree from the University of British Columbia and an MA in Educational Technology Leadership from George Washington University, and is currently completing his PhD in Learning Design and Technology at Purdue University. Having worked in education since 1988, Glen has taught in both continuing education and university degree programs, and he has worked as a curriculum and instructional designer for both McGraw-Hill and Pearson Education. When he is not teaching, developing e-learning, or writing textbooks, Glen helps corporate clients implement technology-based e-learning programs and performance support systems.

MICHAEL ORWICK, MBA, is a full-time faculty member with the School of Business at Okanagan College in Kelowna, British Columbia. In addition to teaching marketing, small-business management, and human resource management, Michael has been instructing computer classes in Microsoft Office for the past 10 years. Beginning his teaching career with private career schools, Michael focused on bettering his own instructional and technical skills by completing a well-recognized instructional diploma program and achieving the Microsoft Office Specialist Expert designation for both Word and Excel. Michael also has a background in broadcasting and has presented seminars for both academic and corporate clients.

JUDY SCHEEREN is a full-time faculty member, program director, and course coordinator in the computer technology department at Westmoreland County Community College in Youngwood, Pennsylvania. She has a Master's degree from the University of Pittsburgh, a certificate in online teaching and learning from the University of California, Hayward, and is a Quality Matters certified peer reviewer. During her career at WCCC she was named Teacher of the Year and was recognized as one of the "Fab Forty"—one of the 40 most influential people in the first 40 years of WCCC history. She is a member of the Achieving the Dream (AtD) core committee and is an integral part of the Academic Affairs Committee, having served as chair, and of several Middle States evaluation committees. In addition to teaching Microsoft Office applications in computer classes, she develops and teaches online courses and writes textbooks. Before coming to WCCC she had several years' experience in the computer industry with Fortune 500 companies.

Acknowledgments

Many thanks to the reviewers, symposium attendees, and survey respondents who provided advice and guidance throughout the development process for this series.

Darrell Abbey, Cascadia Community College

Sven Aelterman, Troy University

Nisheeth Agrawal, Calhoun Community College

Ted Ahlberg, Our Lady of the Lake University

Bobby Ahmed, Wilbur Wright College

Jack Alanen, California State University, Northridge

Doug Albert, Finger Lakes Community College

Farha Ali, Lander University

Karen Allen, Community College of Rhode Island

Don Allison, State University College, Oneonta

Rosalyn Amaro, Florida State College at Jacksonville

Chris Anderson, North Central Michigan College

Wilma Andrews, Virginia Commonwealth University

Damon Antos, American River College

Ralph Argiento, Guilford Tech Community College

Karen M. Arlien, Bismark State College

Abida Awan, Savannah State University

Ijaz Awan, Savannah State University

William Ayen, University of Colorado

Tahir Azia, Long Beach City College

Tahir Aziz, J. Sargeant Reynolds Community College

Frank Bagan, County College of Morris

Mark Bagley, Northwestern Oklahoma State University

Sheila Baiers, Kalamazoo Valley Community College

Susanne Bajt, William Rainey Harper College

Greg Ballinger, Miami Dade College

Carla Barber, University of Central Arkansas

Joyce Barnes, Coastal Carolina University

Carolyn Barren, Macomb Community College

Terry Beachy, Garrett College

Michael Beard, Lamar University, Beaumont

Anita Beecroft, Kwantlen Polytechnic University

Julia Bell, Walters State Community College

Paula Bell, Lock Haven University of Pennsylvania

Don Belle, Central Piedmont Community College

Jan Bentley, Utah Valley University

Nancy Bermea, Olympic College

Shantanu Bhagoji, Monroe College

Sai Bhatia, Riverside City College

Ann Blackman, Parkland College

Cindy Hauki Blair, West Hills College

Lois Blais, Walters State Community College

Olga Blinova, Hudson County Community College

Lisa Bock, Pennsylvania College of Technology

John Bodden, Trident Technical College

Gary Bond, New Mexico State University

Abigail Bornstein, City College of San Francisco

Carrie Boswell, Blue Ridge Community and Technical College

Eric Bothur, Midlands Technical College

Gina Bowers, Harrisburg Area Community College

Craig Bradley, Shawnee Community College

Gerlinde Brady, Cabrillo College

Jo Ann Brannen, Abraham Baldwin Agricultural College

Janet Bringhurst, Utah State University

Susan Bristow, University of Arkansas—Fayetteville

Cathy Brotherton, Riverside City College

Annie Brown, Hawaii Community College

Menka Brown, Piedmont Technical College

Shawn Brown, KCTCS Ashland Community College

Sylvia Brown, Midland College

Cliff Brozo, Monroe College

James Buck, Gateway Technical College

Barbara Buckner, Lee University

Sheryl Starkey Bulloch, Columbia Southern University

Kate Burkes, Northwest Arkansas Community College

Angela Butler, Mississippi Gulf Coast Community College, Gautier

Richard Cacace, Pensacola Junior College

Ric Calhoun, Gordon College

Carolyn Calicutt, Saint Louis Community College, Forest Park

Anthony Cameron, Fayetteville Technical Community College

Eric Cameron, Passaic County Community College

Janet Campbell, Dixie State College

Joel Campbell, Delta College

James Carrier, Guilford Tech Community College, Jamestown

Cesar Augustus Casas, St. Thomas Aquinas College

Bernard Castro, Cumberland County College

Emre Celebi, Louisiana State University, Shreveport

Jim Chaffee, The University of Iowa Tippie College of Business

Debra Chapman, University of South Alabama

Ketsia Chapman, Centura College Online

Stephen Cheskiewicz, Keystone College

Mark Choman, Luzerne County Community College

Kungwen "Dave" Chu, Purdue University, Calumet-Hammond

Carin Chuang , Purdue University, North Central

Richard Clare, Keiser University, Lakeland

Steve Clements, Eastern Oregon University

Robert Cloninger, University of Arkansas, Fort Smith

Sandra Cobb, Kaplan University

Phillip Coleman, Western Kentucky University

Andrea Compton, St. Charles Community College

Janet Conroy-Link, Holy Family College

Ronald Conway, Bowling Green State University

Judy Cook, East Central College

Margaret Cooksey, Tallahassee Community College

Kay Cooley, Western Wyoming College

Kim Copley, Mount West Technical College

Larry Corman, Fort Lewis College

Kim Cosby, Salt Lake Community College

Shannon Cotnam, Pitt Community College

Missie Cotton, North Central Missouri College

Lee Cottrell, Bradford School

John Coverdale, Norco College

Charles Cowell, Tyler Junior College

Diane Coyle, Montgomery County Community College

Elaine Crable, Xavier University

Ronnie Creel, Troy University

Martin Cronlund, Anne Arundel Community College

Doug Cross, Clackamas Community College

Kelli Cross, Harrisburg Area Community College

Geoffrey Crosslin, Kalamazoo State University

Randolph Cullum, KCTCS Ashland Community College

Donald Cunningham, Minneapolis Business College

Penny Cypert, Tarrant County College—NE Campus

Janet Czarnecki, Brown Mackie College

Harry Dalmaso, Onondaga Community College

Betty Dalton, Tarrant County College

Don Danner, San Francisco State University

Michael Danos, Central Virginia Community College

JD Davis, Southwestern College

Elaine Day, Johnson & Wales University

Jennifer Day, Sinclair Community College

Ralph De Arazoza, Miami Dade College

Lucy Decaro, College of Sequoias

Corey DeLaplain, Keiser University—E Campus

Carrie Delcourt, Black Hawk College

Edward Delean, Nova Community College Alexandria

J. Demaio, Brookdale Community College

Joy DePover, Minneapolis Community & Technical College

Charles DeSassure, Tarrant County Community College

John Detmer, Del Mar College

Thomas Dillon, James Madison University

Michael Discello, Pittsburgh Technical Institute

Mike Diss, Indiana University/Purdue University—Fort Wayne

Tracy Dobbs, Navarro College

Veronica Dooly, Asheville-Buncombe Technical Community College

Gretchen Douglas, SUNY Cortland

Robert Doyle, New Mexico State University

Evelyn Dubois, Baton Rouge Community College

Michael Dunkelbarger, Alamance Community College

Donna Dunn, Beaufort County Community College

Yves Durand, Keiser University—E Campus

Stacia Dutton, SUNY Canton

Joseph Dvorak, Community College of Allegheny County, Boyce

Heidi Eaton, Elfin Community College

Thomas Edmunds, Raritan Valley Community College

Nick Edwards, Mt. Empire Community College

Issam El-Achkar, Hudson County Community College

Bruce Elliot, Tarrant County College NW

Kim Ellis, Virginia Western Community College

Timothy Ellis, Schoolcraft College

Glenda Elser, New Mexico State University

Emanuel Emanouilidis, Kean University

Bernice Eng, Brookdale Community College

Joanne Eskola, Brookdale Community College

Susan Eyre, Metropolitan State University

Valerie Farmer, Community College of Baltimore County

Deb Fells, Mesa Community College

Jean Finley, Asheville-Buncombe Technical Community College

George Fiori, Tri County Technical College Pendleton

Alan Fisher, Walters State Community College

Margaret Fisher, Florida State College, Kent Campus

Brian Fox, Santa Fe College

Mark Frydenberg, Bentley University

Susan Fuschetto, Cerritos College

Samuel Gabay, Zarem/Golde ORT Technical Institute

Lois Galloway, Danville Community College

Saiid Ganjalizadeh, The Catholic University of America

Kurt Garner, Pitt Community College

Patricia Garrett, Florida State College, Kent Campus

Richard Garrett, Tyler Junior College

Summer Garrett, Saint Johns River State College, Saint Augustine

Marilyn Gastineau, University of Louisiana, Lafayette

Kathleen George, Becker College

Tom Gerace, Tulane University

Bish Ghosh, Metropolitan State College Denver

Debra Giblin, Mitchell Technical Institute

Linda Gibson, Piedmont Technical College

Amy Giddens, Central Alabama Community College

Anita Gilkey, Sinclair Community College

Tim Gill, Tyler Junior College

Sheila Gionfriddo, Luzerne County Community College

Susan Glen, New Mexico Military Institute

Mel Goetting, Shawnee State University

Mostafa Golbaba, Langston University Tulsa

Deborah Graham, Davenport University

Jennifer Grant, Metropolitan State University

Joseph Greer, Midlands Technical College

Kerry Gregory, Virginia Commonwealth University

Terry Griffin, Midwestern State University

Deb Gross, Ohio State University

Ruth Guthrie, Cal Poly Pomona

Angel Gutierrez, Montclair State University

Lidan Ha, Coppin State University

Norm Hahn, Thomas Nelson Community College

Lewis Hall, Riverside City College

Norma Hall, Manor College

Rachelle Hall, Glendale Community College

Kevin Halvorson, Ridgewater College

Patti Hammerle, Indiana University/Purdue University, Indianapolis

Hyo-Joo Han, Georgia Southern University

John Haney, Snead State Community College

Keith Hansen, University of South Carolina Upstate

Dorothy Harman, Tarrant County College—NE

Ashley Harrier, Hillsborough Community College, Plant City

Marie Hartlein, Montgomery County Community College

Shohreh Hashemi, University of Houston—Downtown

Michael Haugrud, Minnesota State University, Mankato

Mary Heikkinen, Lake-Sumter Community College

Julie Heithecker, College of Southern Idaho

Terri Helfand, Chaffey College

Jean Hendrix, University of Arkansas, Monticello

Gerry Hensel, University of Central Florida, Orlando

Katherine Herbert, Montclair State University

Lisa Marie Heyward, Manor College

Marilyn Hibbert, Salt Lake Community College

Jan Hime, University of Nebraska, Lincoln

Kristen Hockman, University of Missouri—Columbia

Emily Holliday, Campbell University

Mary-Carole Hollingsworth, Georgia Perimeter College

Terri Holly, Indian River State College

Timothy Holston, Mississippi Valley State University

Ralph Hooper, University of Alabama

Kim Hopkins, Weatherford College

Wayne Horn, Pensacola Junior College

Christine Hovey, Lincoln Land Community College

Mark Huber, University of Georgia

Susan Hudgins, East Central University

Jeff Huff, Missouri State University—West Plains

Debbie Huffman, North Central Texas College

Laura Hunt, Tulsa Community College

Maggie Hutchison, Flagler College—St. Augustine

Bobbie Hyndman, Amarillo College

Nt Izuchi, Quinsigamond Community College

Sherry Jacob, Jefferson Community College

Denise Jefferson, Pitt Community College

Linda Johnsonius, Murray State University

Robert Johnston, Heald College

Barbara Jones, Golden West College

Carla Jones, Middle Tennessee State University

Margie Jones, Central Virginia Community College

Irene Joos, Ela Roche College

Dee Joseph, San Antonio College

Jon Juarez, Dona Ana Community College, Las Cruces

Beverly Kahn, Suffolk University

Richard Kalman, Atlantic Cape Community College

Leticia Kalweit, Bryant & Stratton College

Jan Kamholtz, Bryant & Stratton College

M. Keele, Three Rivers Community College

Debby Keen, University of Kentucky

Judith Keenan, Salve Regina University

Jan Kehm, Spartanburg Community College

Gary Kern, Monroe Community College

Crystal Kernodle, North Arkansas University

Olivia Kerr, El Centro College

Annette Kerwin, College of DuPage

Manzurul Khan, College of the Mainland

Karen Kidder, Tri State Business Institute

Hak Joon Kim, Southern Connecticut State University, New Haven

Chuck Kise, Brevard Community College, Palm Bay

Richard Klein, Clemson University

Todd Kline, Mineral Area College

Linda Kliston, Broward College

Paul Koester, Tarrant County College, NE Campus

Kurt Kominek, Northeast State Community College

Thaddeus Konar, University of Oregon

Diane Kosharek, MATC Madison

Ruth Kurlandsky, Cazenovia College

Tom Kurtz, Baker College

Cherylee Kushida, Santa Ana College

Lana LaBruyere, Mineral Area College

Anita Laird, Schoolcraft College

Marjean Lake, LDS Business College

Kin Lam, Medgar Evers College

Connie Lance, Aims Community College

Jeanette Landin, Empire College

Robert La Rocca, Keiser University

Vicky Lassiter, Wayne Community College

Deborah Layton, Eastern Oklahoma State College

Art Lee, Lord Fairfax Community College

Ingyu Lee, Troy University

Kenneth Lee, Delaware Valley College

Kevin Lee, Guilford Tech Community College

Leesa Lee, Western Wyoming College

Thomas Lee, University of Pennsylvania

Denise Leete, Pennsylvania College of Technology

Linda Lemley, Pensacola State College

Sherry Lenhart, Terra Community College

Sue Lewis, Tarleton State University

Jane Liefert, Middlesex Community College

Renee Lightner, Florida State College, Kent Campus

Nancy Lilly, Central Alabama Community College, Alexander City

Mary Locke, Greenville Technical College

Maurie Lockley, University of North Carolina, Greensboro

Lisa Lopez, Spartanburg Community College

Haibing Lu, San Diego Mesa College

Frank Lucente, Westmoreland County Community College

Linda Lynam, Central Missouri State University

Lynne Lyon, Durham Technical Community College

Rebecca MaCafee, Hillsborough Community College

Elaine Macalister, Oakton Community College

Matthew Macarty, University of New Hampshire

Tanya Macneil, American InterContinental University

Winston Maddox, Mercer County Community College

Rob Major, Babson College

Rajiv Malkan, Lone Star College

Mary Lou Malone, Ohio University

Lynn Mancini, Delaware Technical Community College, Wilmington

Suzanne Marks, Bellevue Community College

Juan Marquez, Mesa Community College

Carlos Martinez, California State University—Fresno

Santiago Martinez, Fast Train College

Roberta Mae Marvel, Casper College

Lana Mason, Wayne Community College

Lynn Mason, Lubbock Christian University

Sandy McCormack, Monroe Community College

Martha McCreery, Rend Lake College

Sue McCrory, Missouri State University

Brian McDaniel, Palo Alto College

Theresa McDonald, Texarkana College

Jacob McGinnis, Park University

Norma McKenzie, El Paso Community College, Valle Verde

Bill McMillan, Madonna University—Livonia

David McNair, Mount Wachusett Community College

William Mee, Suffolk University

Peter Meggison, Massasoit Community College

Linda Mehlinger, Morgan State University

Gabriele Meiselwitz, Towson University

Mike Michaelson, Palomar College

Michael Mick, Purdue University—Calumet-Hammond

Debby Midkiff, Huntington Junior College of Business

Jenna Miley, Bainbridge College

Dave Miller, Monroe County Community College

Diane Miller, James A. Rhodes State College

Nancy Miller, Herzing University

Shayan Mirabi, American InterContinental University

John Molluzzo, Pace University

Shari Monson, Black Hawk College

Christine Moore, College of Charleston

Rodney Moore, Holland College

Diane Morris, Tyler Junior College

Michael Morris, Southeastern Oklahoma State University

Nancy Morris, Hudson Valley Community College

Steven Morris, Middle Tennessee State University

Carmen Morrison, North Central State College

Rodger Morrison, Troy University Montgomery

Gary Mosley, Southern Wesleyan University

Tamar Mosley, Meridian Community College

Carol Mull, Greenville Technical College

Melissa Munoz, Dorsey Business School

Warner Myntti, Ferris State University

Lisa Nademlynsky, Johnson & Wales University

Shirley Nagg, Everest Institute

Anozie Nebolisa, Shaw University

Barbara Neequaye, Central Piedmont Community College

Julie Neighbors, Chattahoochee Technical College

Angeline Nelson, Heald College

Melissa Nemeth, Indiana University/Purdue University, Indianapolis

John Newman, Coppin State University

Eloise Newsome, Northern Virginia Community College, Woodbridge

Fidelis Ngang, HCC, Central College

Minh Nguyen, Harrisburg Area Community College

Doreen Nicholls, Mohawk Valley Community College

Brenda Nickel, Moraine Park Technical College

Brenda Nielsen, Mesa Community College

Phil Nielson, Salt Lake Community College

Jose Nieves, Lord Fairfax Community College

Suzanne Nordhaus, Lee College

Ronald Norman, Grossmont College

Michael Brian Ogawa, University of Hawaii, Manoa

Jan Osteen, Trinity Valley Community College

Shelley Ota, Leeward Community College

Youcef Oubraham, Hudson County Community College

Lucy Parakhovnik, California State University, Northridge

Betty Parham, Daytona State College

Michelle Parker, Indiana University/Purdue University, Indianapolis

Rex Parr, Aims Community College

Patricia Partyka, Schoolcraft College

Denise Passero, Fulton Montgomery Community College

Tanya Patrick, Clackamas Community College

James Gordon Patterson, Paradise Valley Community College

Joanne Patti, Community College of Philadelphia

Kevin Pauli, University of Nebraska

Jeanette Peavler, Diablo Valley College

Lisa Perez, San Joaquin Delta College

Mike Peterson, Central Oregon Community College

Michael Picerno, Baker College

Janet Pickard, Chattanooga State Community College

Walter Pistone, Palomar College

Jeremy Pittman, Coahoma Community College

Carolyn Poe, Montgomery College, Lonestar

Morris Pondfield, Towson University

Joyce Porter, Weber State University

James Powers, University of Southern Indiana

Seth Powless, University of Toledo

Brenda Price, Bucks County Community College

Janet Prichard, Bryant University

Lisa Prince, Missouri State University

Melissa Prinzing, Orange Coast College

Yolanda Pritchard, Pitt Community College

Barbara Purvis, Centura College

Ram Raghuraman, Joliet Junior College

Patricia Rahmlow, Montgomery County Community College

Annette Rakowski, Bergen Community College

Harold Ramcharan, Shaw University

Syed Q. Raza, Talladega College

Sheri Renner, Spokane Community College

Michelle Reznick, Oakton Community College

David Richwine, Indian River State College—Central

Terry Rigsby, Hill College

Laura Ringer, Piedmont Technical College

Shaunda Roach, Oakwood University

Marti Robertson, Patrick Henry Community College

Vicki Robertson, Southwest Tennessee Community College

Linda Robinson, Weatherford College

Monty Robinson, Black Hills State University

Linda Rogers, Dixie State College

Terry Rooker, Germanna Community College, Fredericksburg

Seyed Roosta, Albany State University

Rebecca Ropp, Kellogg Community College

Randy Rose, Pensacola State College

Sandra Roy, Mississippi Gulf Coast Community College, Gautier

Kathleen Ruggieri, Lansdale School of Business

Cynthia Rumney, Middle Georgia Tech College

Candace Ryder, Colorado State University

Gloria Sabatelli, Butler County Community College

Sonya Sample, Greenville Technical College

Ramona Santamaria, Buffalo State College

Diane Santurri , Johnson & Wales University

June Sarbacker, MATC, Truax

Kellie Sartor, Lee College

Theresa Savarese, San Diego City College

Judith Scheeren, Westmoreland County Community College

William Schlick, Schoolcraft College

Helen Schneider, University of Findlay

Larry Schulze, San Antonio College

Paul Schwager, East Carolina University

Karen Sarratt Scott, University of Texas—Arlington

Michael Scroggins, Missouri State University

Vicky Seehusen, Metropolitan State College—Denver

Pat Serrano, Scottsdale Community College

Judy Settle, Central Georgia Technical College

John Seydel, Arkansas State University

Anci Shah, HCC—Central College

D'Anna Shaver, Tarrant County College—NE

Abul Sheikh, Abraham Baldwin Agricultural College

Lal Shimpi, Saint Augustine's College

Odus Shoemake, Lee College

Joanne Shurbert, NHTI Concord Community College

Sheila Sicilia, Onondaga Community College

Rafiq Siddiqui, Hudson County Community College

Pam Silvers, Asheville-Buncombe Technical Community College

Steve Singer, Kapiolani Community College

Atin Sinha, Albany State University

Beth Skipper, Lake-Sumter Community College

Mary Jo Slater, College of Beaver County

Cheryl Slavik, Computer Learning Services

Bonnie Sue Specht Smith, Fresno City College

Kristi Smith, Allegany College of Maryland

Thomas Michael Smith, Austin Community College

Anita Soliz, Palo Alto College

Don Southwell, Delta College

Mimi Spain, Southern Maine Community College

Candice Spangler, Columbus State Community College

V Sridharan, Clemson University

Diane Stark, Phoenix College

Jason Steagall, Bryant & Stratton College

Clarence Stokes, American River College

Sharron Storms, MATC, Madison

Linda Stoudemayer, Lamar Institute of Technology

Fred Strickland, Troy University Montgomery

Lynne Stuhr, Trident Technical College

Song Su, East Los Angeles College

Bala Subramanian, Kean University

Liang Sui, Daytona State College—Daytona Beach

Angela Sullivan, Joliet Junior College

David Surma, Indiana University—South Bend

Anita Sutton, Germanna Community College

Dana Swanson, Remington Colleges Inc.

Beverly Swisshelm, Cumberland University

Lo-An Tabar-Gaul, Mesa Community College

Alden Talbot, Weber State University

Kathleen Tamerlano, Cuyahoga Community College

Margaret Taylor, College of Southern Nevada

Debbie Telfer, Colorado Technical University

Jodie Temple, Drake College of Business

Mike Tetreault, McHenry County College

Fran Thomas, North Georgia Technical College

Sandra Thomas, Troy University

Joyce Thompson, Lehigh Carbon Community College

Astrid Todd, Guilford Technical Community College

Byron Todd, Tallahassee Community College

Kim Tollett, Eastern Oklahoma State College

Catherine Torok, Garrett College

Debora Towns, College of Central Florida Ocala

Tom Trevethan, ECPI College of Technology

David Trimble, Park University

Chen-Chen Tsao, Kalamazoo Valley Community College

Cheryl Turgeon, Asnuntuck Community College

Angela Unruh, Central Washington University

Cathy Urbanski, Chandler Gilbert Community College

Jose Valdes, Institute of Business & Medical Careers

Jack Van Arsdale, Monmouth University

Mark Vancleve, Fresno City College

Mary Grace Vaughn, El Paso Community College—Valle Verde

Kathleen Villarreal, Apollo University of Phoenix

Michelle Vlaich-Lee, Greenville Technical College

Bonita Volker, Tidewater Community College, Virginia Beach

Martin Wagner, Indiana University/Purdue University, Indianapolis

Dennis Walpole, University of South Florida

Merrill Warkentin, Mississippi State University

Kristy Wasmundt, Keiser University—E Campus

Sharon Wavle, Tompkins Cortland Community College

Rebecca Webb, Northwest Arkansas Community College

Sandy Weber, Gateway Technical College

Karen Welch, Tennessee Technology Center

Marcia Welch, Highline Community College

Lynne Weldon, Aiken Tech College

Lorna Wells, St. Louis Community College

Bradley West, Sinclair Community College

Stu Westin, University of Rhode Island

Billie Jo Whary, McCann School of Business & Technology—Sunbury

Cindy White, University of Tennessee—Martin

Melinda White, Seminole State College

Reginald White, Black Hawk College

Lissa Whyte-Morazan, Brookline College

Janet Wiggins, University of Central Missouri

Sophia Wilberscheid, Indian River State College

Amy Williams, Abraham Baldwin Agricultural College

G. Jan Wilms, Union University—Jackson

Arlene Wimbley, Oakwood University

Kathy Winters, University of Tennessee, Chattanooga

Diana Wolfe, Oklahoma State University, Oklahoma City

Veryl Wolfe, Clarion University of Pennsylvania

Kwok Wong, Fayetteville State University

Nancy Woodard, Moraine Valley Community College

Dezhi Wu, Southern Utah University

Kevin Wyzkiewicz, Delta College

Lily Xiao, Gardner-Webb University

Paul Yaroslaski, Dodge City Community College

Annette Yauney, Herkimer County Community College

Seong No Yoon, Savannah State University

Bahram Zartoshty, California State University, Northridge

Mary Ann Zlotow, College of DuPage

Laurie Zouharis , Suffolk College

Matthew Zullo, Wake Tech Community College

TECHNICAL EDITORS

We would like to thank our technical editors who helped shape the manuscript every step of the way.

Eric Bothur, Midlands Technical College

Gerlinde Brady, Cabrillo College

Diane Coyle, Montgomery County Community College

Sylvia Gholston, Chattahoochee Technical College

Ranida Harris, Indiana University Southeast

Terri Holly, Indian River State College

Kate LeGrand, Broward College

Brenda Nielsen, Mesa Community College

Phil Nielson, Salt Lake Community College

Matthew Probst, Ivy Tech Community College

Beverly Swisshelm, Cumberland University

Lorna Wells, Salt Lake Community College

Laurie Zouharis, Suffolk Community College

ProjectLearn
Microsoft Office
Introduction

1 The Microsoft
Office Environment

The Microsoft Office Environment

CHAPTER OBJECTIVES

After completing this chapter, you will be able to:

1.1 Create File Folders

1.2 Create, Save, and Handle Files

1.3 Copy and Use the Clipboard

1.4 Navigate with the Quick Access Toolbar

1.5 Use View and Zoom Controls

1.6 Use Backstage View and Options

To make the best use of any Microsoft application, you should have an understanding of how it handles files and folders. You should also have an idea of what makes the Office products so valuable, not just each one on its own, but as a group of applications. Microsoft Office provides seamless interaction between the different programs so that you can quickly move information from one to the other. For example, a chart built in Excel can easily be placed in a PowerPoint presentation.

Another one of the advantages of using the various Office applications is that although each one is designed for a different and specific use, the style of the user interface has purposely been repeated across all applications. The use of the tabs and ribbons and the placement of many common commands are similar in each of the applications. For this reason, once you learn how to move around the screen and the ribbons in one application, you already have a good understanding of how to use another. Table MO1.1 provides a summary of common terms and commands used in Microsoft Office.

It is this commitment to integration of style and design that makes Word, Excel, PowerPoint, Access, and Outlook (although Outlook is not part of this book) so easy to learn and to use.

TABLE MO1.1 Common terms and commands

Terminology	Action
Click	Pressing and releasing the left mouse button.
Right-click	Pressing and releasing the right mouse button.
Drag	Pressing and holding the left mouse button, and then sliding the mouse to a different location and releasing the mouse button.
File	A document
Folder	A place to store files and other folders

PROJECT

Introduction

Before you create projects with any of the Office applications, you will practice working with the basic components common to all the programs. This chapter provides an overview of creating and saving files and folders. You will discover how the Clipboard works in and between applications. The Quick Access toolbar is a time-saving feature you can adjust or customize for your needs. Each application has its own ways of viewing your work depending on your actions. Zooming the screen in and out will also help you gain the best vantage point for your work. You will also be introduced to the Backstage view and how its options control the functions inside the program.

Handling Files, Folders, and Clipboard

One of the greatest advantages of Microsoft Office is that the collection of the most popular office applications are interconnected in many ways. The screen is set up in a similar manner and uses ribbons to group related commands. MS Office works with the Windows application to allow you to create and control files and folders across applications. In this project, you will create, copy, delete, paste, and move files and folders using Windows. Because all MS Office programs operate on top of Windows, you can access files and folders no matter what program you are currently using. The Clipboard (which operates within Windows) allows you to copy and paste material from one application to another, such as Word, Excel, or PowerPoint.

PROJECT FILE: *Available at* www.mhhe.com/office2013projectlearn

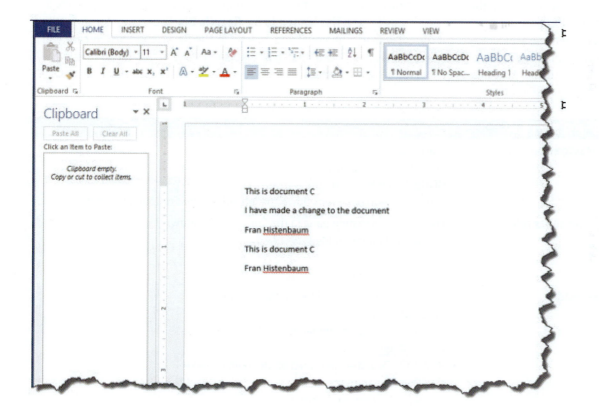

File Folders

LESSON OVERVIEW

When working on a project, you place all the documents you gather or produce for a project in one folder. When you need to access any information about the project, you open that folder. In this lesson, you will discover how to create **folders** on the computer and how to organize them for easy location. When creating folders, they automatically file alphabetically, or you can sort them by other criteria such as date or size.

Adding to the efficiency of MS Office is the ability to create folders inside of folders. Inside the folder for a major project, you can have smaller folders for the various project components. Also, it is easy to move a folder from one location to another or to copy the entire contents of a folder to another location.

It is simple to rename a folder to keep it current with its contents. Once you rename it, the folder again sorts alphabetically by its new name. You can display your list of fold-ers in different views such as large icons, extra-large icons, or even just a list. Using the **Navigation pane** and expand and collapse arrows, you can view the **folder tree** to see how one folder connects to another.

One of the greatest time-savers is the right-click short-cut menu. These **context-sensitive menus** are available from almost anyplace inside a Microsoft product. Just right-clicking on a folder displays a shortcut menu with the most common options that apply to a folder. When right-clicking somewhere else, you are presented with a different shortcut menu with options that apply to the current position of the mouse.

If a folder is no longer needed, you can easily delete it. This sends it to the **Recycle Bin**. Your computer stores the material you "delete" in the Recycle Bin just in case you need it later, or made a mistake in getting rid of it in the first place.

SKILLS PREVIEW

Locate the Navigation pane	• Start your computer. CLICK the Desktop tile. DOUBLE-CLICK the Computer icon. The Navigation pane runs down the left side of the Computer window.
Open the Documents folder	• Locate the Navigation pane in the Computer window. Locate the Libraries folder. CLICK Documents, or • CLICK the Documents shortcut on the desktop.
Create a new folder	• CLICK the HOME tab and locate the New group. CLICK New folder. Type the name of the folder in the New Folder box. PRESS Enter , or • RIGHT-CLICK in the blank area of the main window. CHOOSE New from the menu. CLICK Folder from the submenu. Type the name of the folder in the New Folder box. PRESS Enter .
Rename a folder	• RIGHT-CLICK on the folder to display a shortcut menu. CLICK Rename to open the naming box on the folder. Type the new name. PRESS Enter , or • CLICK on the folder. CLICK the HOME tab and locate the Organize group. CLICK Rename. Type the new name. PRESS Enter .

Delete a folder	• RIGHT-CLICK on the folder.
	  CHOOSE Delete, or
	• CLICK on the folder.
	  CLICK the HOME tab and locate the Organize group.
	  CLICK the Delete button.

Expand a folder	• Move your cursor to the Navigation pane. CLICK the expand arrow ▷ on the left of the folder.
Collapse a folder	• Move the cursor to the Navigation pane. CLICK the collapse arrow ◢ next to the folder.

PROJECT PRACTICE

1. Start the computer to open the Start window (see Figure MO1.1).

   CLICK the Desktop tile.

   DOUBLE-CLICK the Computer icon on the desktop.

   Locate the Libraries icon in the Navigation pane (see Figure MO1.2).

   CLICK Documents to open the current list of folders.

FIGURE MO1.1   Windows 8 Start window

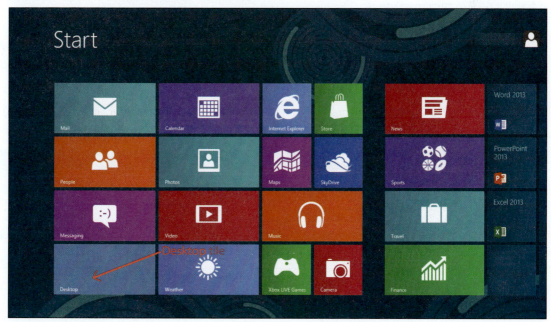

2. CLICK the HOME tab and locate the New group (see Figure MO1.2).

   CLICK New Folder to create a new folder in the main window.

   The new folder is waiting for you to enter a name for it.

   TYPE MyLessons

   PRESS Enter.

   (*Result:* The new folder takes its alphabetical place in the main window listing.)

FIGURE MO1.2 Navigation pane, Libraries, and Documents folder

3 DOUBLE-CLICK on the MyLessons folder to open it.

The folder is empty.

Use a shortcut to create another folder here inside the MyLessons folder.

RIGHT-CLICK in any white area of the main window.

CHOOSE New.

CHOOSE Folder.

TYPE **Word** to name the folder.

PRESS Enter .

(*Result:* A folder named Word has been created inside the folder called MyLessons.)

> ### MORE INFO
>
> You can see the current folder in the Address bar near the top of the window.
>
>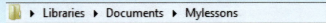
>
> Notice that the current folder is on the end of the line of folder names. You can jump to any folder along that line by clicking on it in the Address bar.

4 Using the same procedure create four more folders inside the MyLessons folder:

MyExcel

MyPowerPoint

MyAccess

MyOutlook

5 Now rename the Word folder to match the style of the others.

RIGHT-CLICK on the Word folder to display a shortcut menu.

CLICK Rename to open the naming box on the folder.

TYPE **MyWord**

PRESS Enter .

(*Result:* The folder named Word has been renamed MyWord.)

6 CLICK the VIEW tab to open the View ribbon and locate the Layout group.

Let your mouse hover over the Extra large icons button.

This shows what the main window would look like in Extra large icons.

Hover over Medium icons to preview what that would look like (try others if you like).

This ability to see the effects without actually clicking on the command is called Live Preview.

Move the cursor back to the main window to return to the original List view.

CLICK in a blank area in the main window to close the View ribbon.

7 You will not need the folder called MyOutlook so you can delete it.

RIGHT-CLICK on the MyOutlook folder to display the context-sensitive menu.

CHOOSE Delete to remove the folder.

8 Move your cursor to the Navigation pane.

CLICK Documents to move back to that folder.

CLICK the expand arrow () at the left of the image next to Documents.

CLICK the expand arrow next to My Documents.

CLICK the expand arrow next to MyLessons.
(*Result:* Now you can see the entire flow of the folders including the first one you created called MyLessons and the ones you created inside it. This is referred to as a folder tree.)

CLICK MyLessons in the Navigation pane to display the folders within it on the main window.

9 CLICK the collapse arrow (◢) next to Documents.

This will collapse all the folders (branches of the tree) below the Documents level.

The contents of the MyLessons folder remain in the main window.

DOUBLE-CLICK on MyExcel to open it.

The words "This folder is empty" are displayed and the folder tree opens on the left.

10 Move to the Address bar.

CLICK Documents to change what displays in the main window.

This does not affect what displays in the Navigation pane.

Navigating around your folders is easy when you use a combination of the Navigation pane, the Address bar, and the main window.

DOUBLE-CLICK MyLessons in the main window.

11 Your screen should look similar to Figure MO1.3. Obviously the number of folders differs from what is shown in the text.

FIGURE MO1.3 Completion of Lesson Microsoft Office 1A1

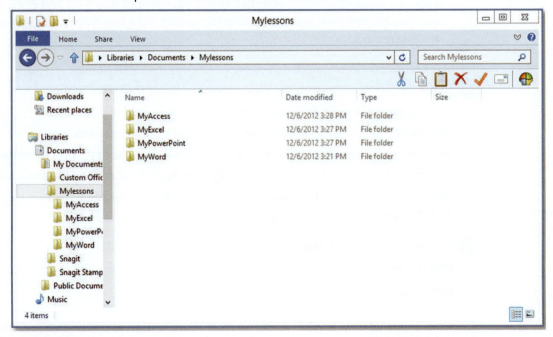

Creating, Saving, and Handling Files

LESSON OVERVIEW

Each document you create is called a **file**. It could be text, a photograph, an image, a spreadsheet, music, or many other things. Files are generally stored inside folders so you can organize and locate them easily. This part of the project allows us to create a simple file and **save** (store) it in a folder. Once you save it, you can reopen it to change it, copy it, move it, and even delete it. When saving a file, you can save it in a folder on your computer or on SkyDrive (a storage capability that allows you to create an account so you can access the file from another computer or device by logging into your account).

When you first save a file, it is given a file name. By default, the file has a name based on the text found in the first line of the document (which is likely the title of the document). You can easily change it when you first save it, or later. Save files in different formats using the **Save As** command.

Move files from folder to folder by **dragging** them from one place to another. When a file is opened and any type of change is made to the contents, a message pops up when you close the file, asking you if you want to save the new changes.

When you double-click to open a file, the computer recognizes the type of file it is and opens the program (called an application) that created it. So, if you open an Excel file, the computer opens Excel first, and then opens the file within it. The same happens to files created in Word, Access, and PowerPoint.

SKILLS PREVIEW

Create a file	• Open an application (such as Word). CLICK Blank document. Enter something in the screen (text, image, table).
Save a file	• CLICK the FILE tab. CLICK Save As from the menu down the left-hand side of the screen. CLICK Computer (or SkyDrive if you wish to save the files there). CLICK My Documents. CHOOSE the name and file type. CLICK Save.
Move (drag) a file	• CLICK and hold on the file icon. DRAG the file to the new location. Release the mouse.
Rename a file	• CLICK on the file. CLICK the HOME tab and locate the Organize group. CLICK Rename. Type the new name. PRESS Enter, or • RIGHT-CLICK on the file. CHOOSE Rename. TYPE the new file name.

PROJECT PRACTICE

1 Open Microsoft Word.

CLICK Blank document to create a new, blank document.

TYPE **This is document A**

PRESS Enter.

TYPE *Your Name*

2 To save this simple document as a file inside a folder created in the previous lesson:

CLICK the FILE tab.

CLICK Save As from the menu down the left-hand side of the screen.

CLICK Computer under the large Save As column.

CLICK My Documents from the list beneath the Computer column (see Figure MO1.4).

(*Result:* The Save As window appears, opening the Documents folder and inserting the first sentence of the newly created file as the suggested File name [see Figure MO1.5]. Because documents often have titles at the top of the page, Word suggests the first line as a file name to save time.)

FIGURE MO1.4 Saving a file to the computer in the My Documents folder

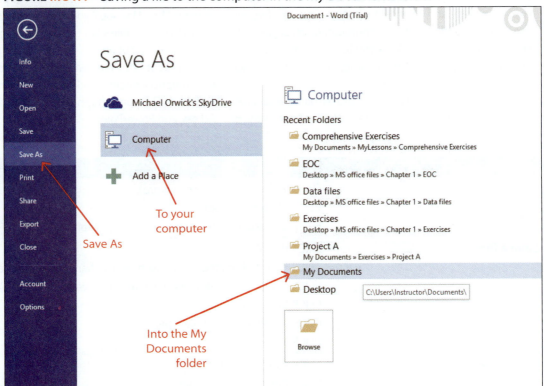

> ⓘ **MORE INFO**
>
> Saving to Computer places the files on the hard drive. You can only access the file when you are using or connected to that computer. Saving to SkyDrive saves your files to a secure Internet site that allows you to access your files from any Internet connection. SkyDrive requires you to create an account. It is not part of the scope of this book.

---

3 The name of the document is fine for your purposes.

Notice the Save as type (just below the file name) says "Word Document."

That means the file will save in the latest MS Word formatting.

CLICK the Save button at the bottom-right corner of the screen.

(*Result:* The file is saved, and you are returned to the document.)

CLICK the FILE tab.

CLICK Close to close the file without closing the program.

FIGURE MO1.5 The Save As window

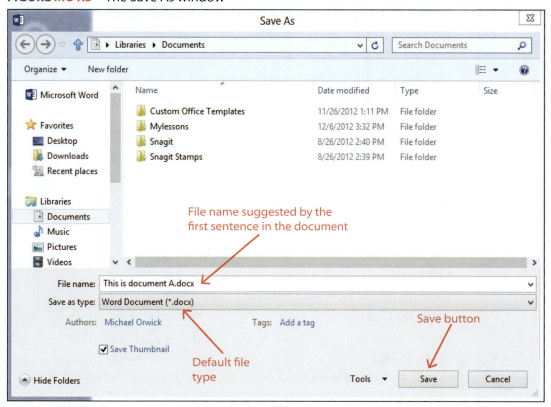

4 CLICK the FILE tab to reveal the list of Recent Documents (lists will vary).

You could open the **This is document A** file by clicking on it under Recent Documents.

CLICK Computer to open the computer folders.

CLICK My Documents to open the Documents folder.
Notice that the file you saved sits outside of the MyLessons folder.

You can move the file to the MyLessons folder.

DRAG the file on top of the MyLessons folder.

A small message appears telling you what will happen when you release the mouse.

When it says Move to MyLessons, release the mouse.
(*Result:* The file **This is document A** is moved to the MyLessons folder.)

5 DOUBLE-CLICK the MyLessons folder.

The **This is document A** file is now here.

Because this is a Word file, move it into the empty folder named MyWord.

DRAG the **This is document A** file to the MyWord folder.

DOUBLE-CLICK the MyWord folder to see the file has now been moved there.

6 DOUBLE-CLICK the **This is document A** file to open it.

DOUBLE-CLICK under your name to force Word to place the cursor there.

TYPE **I have made a change to the document**

CLICK the Close button (✕) in the top right-hand corner of the screen to close Word.

Because the open document was changed, Word asks you if you would like to save it before closing.

CLICK Save.
(*Result:* The file is saved and Word is closed.)

7 You do not have to open Word (or any application) first and then open a file. When you open a file, it automatically opens the application that was used to create it.

DOUBLE-CLICK the Documents shortcut on the desktop.

DOUBLE-CLICK MyLessons to open the folder.

DOUBLE-CLICK MyWord to open the folder.

DOUBLE-CLICK This is document A to open the file.
(*Result:* Word opens and the file opens as well.)

8 To change the first sentence to read "This is document B":

Change the A in the first line to B. CLICK the FILE tab.

CLICK Save As.

CLICK Computer.

CLICK MyWord.

Change the File name to read This is document B

CLICK Save.

Close the current file (CLICK the FILE tab and CHOOSE Close).

CLICK the FILE tab.

CLICK Computer.

CLICK MyWord.
(*Result:* Both files now appear in the MyWord folder as show in Figure MO1.6.)

FIGURE **MO1.6**   MyWord folder with two new files inside

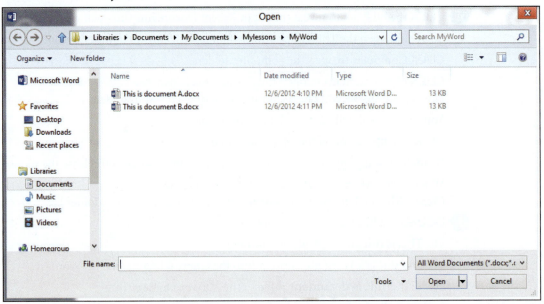

9 DOUBLE-CLICK This is document A to open the file.

This is the first file you created (the text says, "This is document A").

Notice the very top of the screen (called the Title bar) shows the name of the file that is currently open.

PRESS Ctrl + O (a shortcut to the Open command).

CLICK This is document B to open that file.

Both files are now open in separate windows.

10 Your screen should look similar to Figure MO1.7. Close both documents to return to the MyWord folder.

FIGURE MO1.7 Completion of Lesson Microsoft Office 1A2

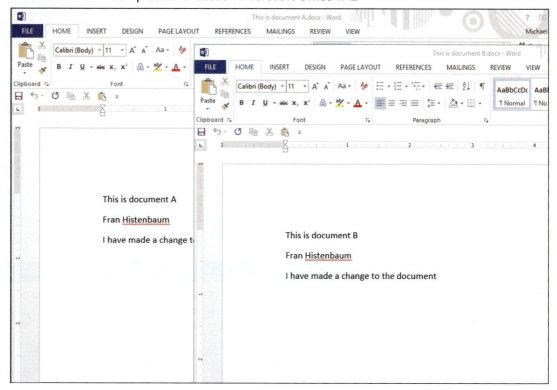

Copying and Using Clipboard

LESSON OVERVIEW

When you create files, you can easily move or copy them. When you copy something, whether it is a file, a folder, text, image, or a table, it is sent to the **clipboard**. Because the clipboard exists in the Windows operating system, you can retrieve it from any running program until the computer is shut down. This allows you to **copy** an image from Word and **paste** it into PowerPoint. You can copy a table from Excel and paste it into Word. This flexibility permits you tight control over how things are organized on your computer.

Anything that can be copied can also be **cut**. This also copies it into the clipboard but removes it from its original location. The ability of the clipboard to function across applications makes it much easier to provide consistent information and images within any program you use.

The clipboard saves a great deal of time. Without even opening a file, you can copy it and paste it into another folder. In fact, you can copy a folder (which includes all the folders and files inside it) and paste it to another location. All the contents of the original folder copy and paste in the new location. This can make sharing files with others effortless.

SKILLS PREVIEW

Copy a file	• CLICK the file to select it. CLICK the HOME tab and locate the Clipboard group. CLICK Copy, or • RIGHT-CLICK on the file. CHOOSE Copy from the shortcut menu.
Paste a file into another folder	• Copy the file. DOUBLE-CLICK the other folder to open it. CLICK the HOME tab and locate the Clipboard group. CLICK Paste, or • Copy the file. DOUBLE-CLICK the other folder to open it. RIGHT-CLICK inside the folder main window. CLICK Paste from the shortcut menu.
Copy or cut text	• Select the text you wish to copy or cut. RIGHT-CLICK on the selected area. CLICK Copy or Cut, or • Select the text you wish to copy or cut. CLICK the HOME tab and locate the Clipboard group. CLICK the Copy button or Cut button icon, or • Select the text you wish to copy or cut. PRESS Ctrl + C (to copy) or Ctrl + X (to cut).
Paste text	• Copy or cut the text. RIGHT-CLICK in the new location. CHOOSE Paste, or • Copy or cut the text. CLICK the mouse in the new location. CLICK the HOME tab and locate the Clipboard group. CLICK the Paste icon (not the word *paste*), or • Copy or cut the text. Move the cursor to the new location. CLICK in the new location. PRESS Ctrl + V.

Paste from the Clipboard pane	• CLICK the Launch button in the Clipboard group. The Clipboard pane lists all the text (or images) that are copied or cut. CLICK the text you desire on the Clipboard pane and insert it into the current location of the cursor.
Clear the Clipboard	• CLICK the Launch button in the Clipboard group. CLICK Clear All.

PROJECT PRACTICE

1 Locate and open the MyLessons folder in the Documents folder of your computer.

Open the MyWord folder.

CLICK on the **This is document A** file.

CLICK the HOME tab and locate the Clipboard group.

CLICK Copy (copying can also be done using the right-click shortcut menu).

2 Once a file is copied, it can be moved easily to another folder.

CLICK the Up One Level arrow () at the left of the Address bar.

DOUBLE-CLICK MyPowerPoint to open that folder.

CLICK the HOME tab and locate the Clipboard group.

The Clipboard options have changed because there is nothing to copy, but there is something to paste.

CLICK Paste.

(*Result:* This "pastes" a copy of the **This is document A** file in the MyPowerPoint folder.)

> **TIP**
>
> The actual Clipboard, while available in almost any application, does not "live" inside of Word, PowerPoint, Excel, or any Office program. It exists in the Windows application that is running your computer. This is why it is possible to copy and paste without Word or any program being open. This is also why you can copy and paste from one folder to another or even from one application to another. For example, you can copy something from Word and paste it in PowerPoint or Excel—and the other way around.

3 You can also move files without copying them first.

Locate the Documents folder icon in the Navigation pane.

CLICK the Expand button.

Locate the My Documents folder icon in the Navigation pane.

CLICK the Expand button.

Locate the MyLessons folder icon in the Navigation pane.

CLICK the Expand button.

DRAG the **This is document A** file from the main window to the MyExcel folder icon in the Navigation bar (see Figure MO1.8).

(*Result:* The file is removed from the MyPowerPoint folder and is now in the MyExcel folder.)

FIGURE MO1.8 Moving a document to the MyExcel folder

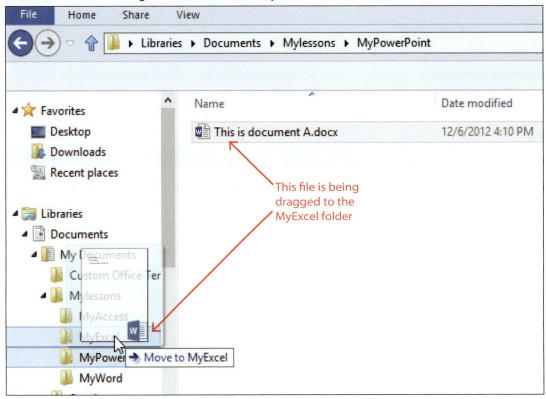

4 CLICK on the MyExcel folder icon in the Navigation pane.

DOUBLE-CLICK the **This is document A** file to open it.

Select the entire text in the first sentence "This is document A."

TYPE **This is document C**

Save the file as **Document C**.

(*Result:* The original document, **This is document A**, remains in the folder. A new document, **Document C**, will appear in that folder as well. Check the Title bar to see the name of the open document.)

5 Select your name (the second line of text).

RIGHT-CLICK on the selected area to display the shortcut menu.

CLICK the Cut command.

Although the sentence is cut from the document, it still exists on the Clipboard.

DOUBLE-CLICK below the last sentence to force Word to place the cursor there.

RIGHT-CLICK on the cursor to display the shortcut menu.

CLICK the first Paste button to paste your name in place.

⚠️ **HEADS UP**

The shortcut menu brought up three options for pasting. Consider if you had copied text from another document and it was in a different font and font size: The first option (Keep Source Formatting) would paste the text in place with the formatting from the other document (the source). The second option (Merge Formatting) would paste the new text, but it would be changed to match the formatting of the current document. The third option (Keep Text Only) will paste the text in without any formatting. Notice that after each option there is a letter in parentheses. You could press that key to choose the paste option.

6 DOUBLE-CLICK your mouse in the line below your name.

CLICK the HOME tab (if it is not already selected) and locate the Clipboard group.

CLICK the drop-down arrow under the word *Paste*.

The same three options appear.

As you hover over each option, Word displays a preview of what it would look like if pasted.

Once you copy (or cut) something into the Clipboard, you can paste it as many times as you wish.

CLICK back in the document to turn the Paste command off.

7 Select the first sentence of the document.

PRESS `Ctrl` + `C` (a shortcut to the Copy command) to copy it to the Clipboard.

Move to the line below your name.

PRESS `Ctrl` + `V` (a shortcut to the paste command) to paste in the last thing copied or cut to the Clipboard.

8 CLICK the Launch button in the Clipboard group to launch the Clipboard pane (see Figure MO1.9).

Notice there are two items on the Clipboard. The top one is the latest one, and that is why it was the one that was pasted.

When you have more than one thing copied to the Clipboard, you can choose which one to paste.

CLICK your name in the Clipboard pane to force Word to paste it into the document.

FIGURE MO1.9 Launching the Clipboard pane

9 Clipboard keeps gathering up the things you copy.

CLICK the Clear All button in the Clipboard pane to remove all material in the Clipboard.

RIGHT-CLICK your mouse on the new line below all the text in the document.

Notice the Paste Options are "grayed out" and cannot be used because the Clipboard is empty.

10 Your document should now appear similar to Figure MO1.10. Close the Clipboard pane and save the file.

FIGURE MO1.10 Completion of Lesson Microsoft Office 1A3

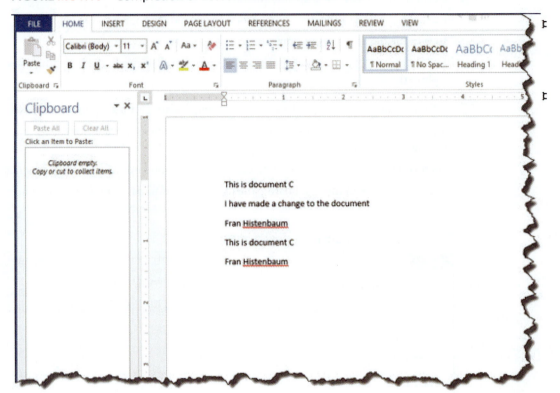

MULTIPLE-CHOICE QUIZ

Select the best choice in the following questions to review the project concepts. Good luck!

1. Files can be stored inside
   a. folders.
   b. other files.
   c. the Navigation pane.
   d. All of these are correct.

2. Once a folder or file is renamed
   a. a copy of the original file is stored in the Clipboard.
   b. it is automatically resorted alphabetically by the new name.
   c. it defaults to the first line of text in the document.
   d. None of these is correct.

3. When deleted, files are sent to the Recycle Bin and they
   a. will be deleted when the computer is shut down.
   b. can be restored if you need them.
   c. are sent to SkyDrive.
   d. None of these is correct.

4. When you right-click your mouse, it activates
   a. a context-sensitive menu.
   b. the Mini toolbar.
   c. the Save feature.
   d. All of these are correct.

5. Clicking, holding the mouse, and moving a file or folder to another location is called
   a. moving.
   b. sliding.
   c. dropping.
   d. None of these is correct.

6. A folder can be renamed by
   a. right-clicking on the folder.
   b. double-clicking on the folder name.
   c. using the HOME tab and Organize group.
   d. All of these are correct.

7. When text is cut from a document, it is
   a. sent to the Recycle Bin.
   b. copied to the Clipboard.
   c. deleted from the computer.
   d. None of these is correct.

8. The Clipboard exists
   a. within Word and Excel.
   b. within all MS Office applications.
   c. within the Windows operating system.
   d. None of these is correct.

9. When something is copied from Excel, it can be pasted into
   a. Word.
   b. Access.
   c. PowerPoint.
   d. All of these are correct.

10. Anything that is copied onto the Clipboard will
    a. be deleted when the computer is shut off.
    b. not remain available until it is cleared.
    c. copied in the Recycle Bin.
    d. None of these is correct.

In this exercise, you will create folders and copy files. You will alter a file and save it. You will also move files from one folder to another and rename the files. When completed, your screen should look similar to Figure MO1.11.

FIGURE MO1.11   Work It Out MO-1A-E1: completed

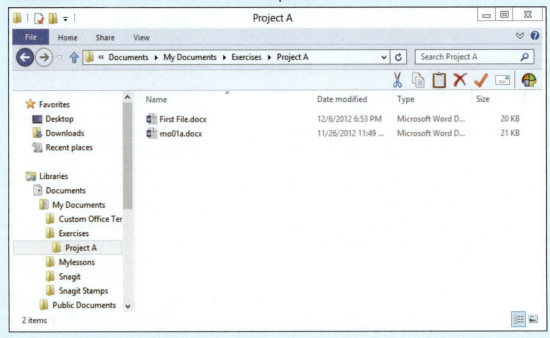

1. Open the Documents folder.

2. Create a new folder called **Exercises**.

3. Open the Exercises folder and create another folder inside it called **Project A**.

4. Locate the files associated with this lesson and copy the file named **mo01a.docx**.

5. Move to the Project A folder and paste **mo01a.docx** there.

6. Open **mo01a.docx** (in the Project A folder). Change the title of the document from "Random Text" to **First File**. Close the file and choose Save. Note: There will be two files now.

7. Use the Navigation pane to expand the Documents folder, the My Documents folder, and the Exercise folder to show the Project A folder.

8. Drag the file **mo01a.docx** onto the Navigation pane and move it to the Exercises folder.

9. Open the Exercises folder and rename the file as **First File**.

10. Drag the **First File** up to the Project A folder.

In this exercise, you will create a file and place it in a folder. You will alter it, save it, rename it, and move it to other folders. When completed, your screen should look similar to Figure MO1.12.

FIGURE MO1.12 Work It Out MO-1A-E2: completed

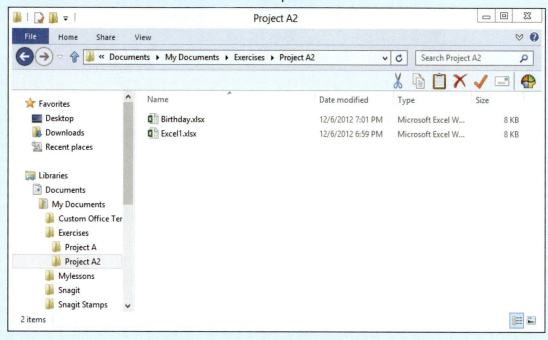

1. Open the Documents folder if necessary. Open the Exercises folder. Create a new folder called **Project A2**.

2. Open Microsoft Excel and create a new (blank) workbook. Type **My First Workbook** in the first cell and press Enter.

3. Go to the FILE tab and save the file to your Computer > My Documents > Exercises folder with the name of **Excel1**. Close Excel.

4. Copy the file **Excel1** and then paste it in the same Exercises folder. Notice it is automatically renamed **Excel1 – Copy**.

5. Open the **Excel1 – Copy** file. In the cell below the text, type your birthday using this format mm/dd/yyyy (if your birthday was February 7, 1998, you would type 02/07/1998). Press Enter.

6. Go to the FILE tab and use the Save As command to save the file in the Exercises folder as **Birthday**. Close Excel.

7. Delete the file **Excel1 – Copy**.

8. Drag both the **Excel1** and the **Birthday** files into the Project A2 folder.

9. Use the expand arrows in the Navigation window to open the following folder tree:
   Documents > My Documents > Exercises > Project A2

10. Check the window with Figure MO1.12. Close the window.

In this exercise, you will create folders and copy files. You will alter a file and save it. You will also move files from one folder to another and rename the files. When completed, your screen should look similar to Figure MO1.13.

FIGURE MO1.13   Work It Out MO-1A-E3: completed

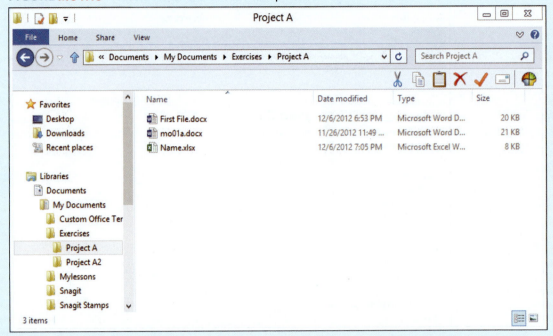

1. Open the Documents folder. Open the Exercises folder. Open the folder called Project A2.

2. Open the file called **Birthday** (created in the previous exercise).

3. In cell A3 (the third one down the first column), type your name. Press Enter.

4. Save the file in the Project A2 folder as **Name**. Close Excel.

5. In the Address bar click on Libraries to move to that folder.

6. Using the Navigation pane and its Expand buttons, open the following folder tree:

    Documents > My Documents > Exercises > Project A2

7. Using the Navigation pane, move the file **Name** into the Project A folder.

8. Open the Project A folder and delete the file **Name**.

9. Open the Project A2 folder and delete the file **Birthday**.

10. Double-click the Recycle Bin icon on the desktop. Right-click on the **Name** file and restore it. Close the Recycle Bin window.

11. Right-click on the Recycle Bin icon and empty it.

12. Open the Project A folder to see that the **Name** file is restored.

Customizing the Workplace

Not everyone uses Office products for the same purposes. One might use Word to write a report while another may use it to produce a poster. Someone might use Excel to generate charts and projections for a business while another might use it to track personal finances. Because there are so many ways to use the Office applications, it is important to be able to make the environment as efficient as possible. Office provides numerous ways to adjust the view, change the zoom, access the most commonly used commands, and even change the default settings so you can save time. Learning how to make the most of the customizing features allows you to make your Office uniquely yours.

After completing this project, you will be able to:

• Use, position, and modify the Quick Access toolbar.

• Change the view and zoom magnification of the screen.

• Control the actions of Office products from the Backstage view.

PROJECT FILE: *Available at* **www.mhhe.com/office2013projectlearn**

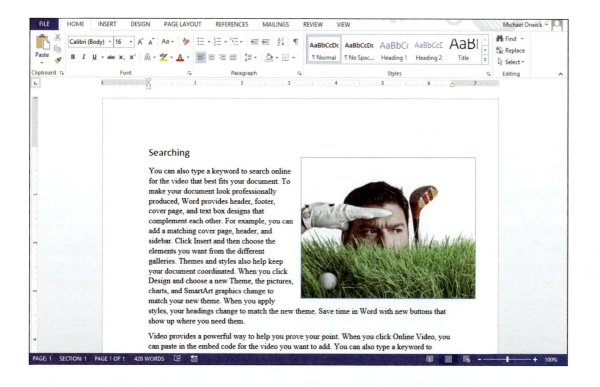

Quick Access Toolbar

LESSON OVERVIEW

The **Quick Access toolbar** is one of the most useful parts of your computer screen. Word, Access, Excel, and PowerPoint all feature this handy and easy-to-customize area. While the most commonly related commands are grouped on ribbons, it is common to find yourself on one ribbon when the command you need is on another ribbon. When you find a command that you use regularly, the Quick Access toolbar allows you to add that command to the toolbar so it remains on the screen no matter what ribbon is active.

While adding commands to the Quick Access toolbar is simple, so is removing them. This makes it easy to customize the toolbar for whatever project you are currently working on. When you move to another project, you can customize the commands you need for that in seconds.

You can even move the Quick Access toolbar below the Ribbon if it suits your purposes. By clicking More Commands, the Quick Access toolbar immediately sends you to the Customize window so you can see all the possible commands you can add. Here you can change the order of the commands on the toolbar. With one click, you can reset the Quick Access toolbar to its original settings.

SKILLS PREVIEW

Use the Quick Access toolbar	• Locate the Quick Access toolbar at the top-left corner of the screen. CLICK a button to perform the function.
Add a preset command to the Quick Access toolbar	• CLICK the drop-down arrow to the right of the Quick Access toolbar. CHOOSE the command you wish to add.
Add a command to the Quick Access toolbar from any ribbon	• RIGHT-CLICK the button you wish to add to the Quick Access toolbar. CHOOSE Add to Quick Access toolbar.
Remove a command from the Quick Access toolbar	• RIGHT-CLICK on the button you wish to remove from the Quick Access toolbar. CHOOSE Remove from Quick Access toolbar.
Change the location of the Quick Access toolbar	• CLICK the drop-down arrow to the right of the Quick Access toolbar. CHOOSE Show Below Ribbon (or if the toolbar is already below the ribbon, choose Show Above the Ribbon).
Change the order of buttons on the Quick Access toolbar	• CLICK the drop-down arrow to the right of the Quick Access toolbar. CHOOSE More Commands. CLICK the command you wish to move from the window on the right side. CLICK the up or down arrow on the right-hand side of the window.

PROJECT PRACTICE

1. Locate the files associated with this lesson. Open **mo01b1.xlsx**. This is an Excel file so it automatically opens the Excel application first, and then loads the file.

2. CLICK in the number below the city Weston.

   TYPE 38625

   PRESS Enter .

   You have changed the file. Now it is time to save the file.

   Move the mouse to the Quick Access toolbar (see Figure MO1.14).

   CLICK the Save button (🖫).

FIGURE MO1.14 Quick Access toolbar

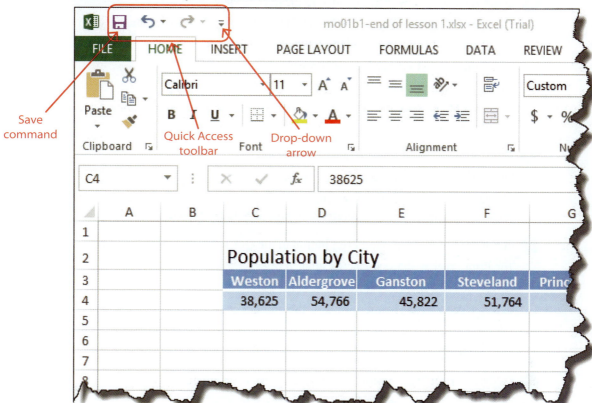

3 CLICK the drop-down arrow at the right of the Quick Access toolbar (see Figure MO1.15).

CHOOSE Print Preview and Print.

This inserts the Print Preview and Print button onto the Quick Access toolbar.

CLICK the Print Preview and Print button.
(*Result:* This one click does the same as clicking the FILE tab and choosing the Print button.)

FIGURE MO1.15 Adding to the Quick Access toolbar using the drop-down menu

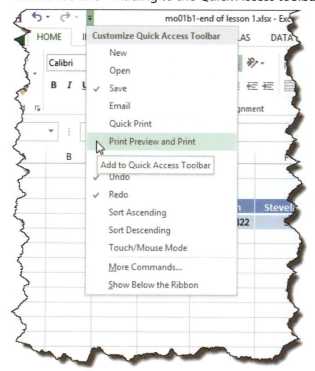

4 CLICK the Back arrow (⬅) to return to the normal view.

The title of the table ("Population by City") is not centered over the data.

CLICK and HOLD the mouse in the cell that says "Population."

DRAG the mouse to the cell above "Princeberg."

Locate the Alignment group.

CLICK the Merge & Center button (▦) (more on this command as you study Excel).
(*Result:* The title is centered across the table.)

5 This command could come in handy even if you were on another tab.

RIGHT-CLICK on the Merge & Center button.

CHOOSE Add to Quick Access toolbar.
(*Result:* The Merge & Center command is copied onto the Quick Access toolbar.)

6 CLICK the Print Preview and Print button in the Quick Access toolbar.

The Print Preview shows the newly aligned title.

CLICK the Back arrow to return to the normal view.

CLICK in cell C6 (one blank row below the number 38,625).

TYPE **Population from the 2011 census**

PRESS [Enter].

7 CLICK and HOLD the mouse to select the text you just entered.

DRAG the mouse to the right until it includes column G.

CLICK the Merge & Center button in the Quick Access toolbar to center the text.

8 The Quick Access toolbar can be moved around the screen to suit your needs.

CLICK the drop-down arrow next to the Quick Access toolbar.

CLICK Show Below the Ribbon to move it below the Ribbon.

CLICK the drop-down arrow again.

CLICK Show Above the Ribbon to return it to its original place.

9 CLICK the drop-down arrow on the Quick Access toolbar.

CLICK More Commands.

The Customize the Quick Access Toolbar window shows commands on the left side you can add to the current commands on the right (see Figure MO1.16).

CLICK Copy from the box on the left.

CLICK the Add button between the two boxes to add it to the Quick Access toolbar.

CLICK OK.
(*Result:* The Copy command is added to the Quick Access toolbar.)

10 RIGHT-CLICK on the Copy button in the Quick Access toolbar.

CHOOSE Remove from Quick Access toolbar.

RIGHT-CLICK on the Merge & Center button in the Quick Access toolbar.

CHOOSE Remove from Quick Access toolbar.

Do the same for the Print Preview and Print button in the Quick Access toolbar.

11 All the buttons added to the Quick Access toolbar are removed. Your screen should look similar to Figure MO1.17. Close and save the file.

FIGURE MO1.16   Customizing the Quick Access toolbar

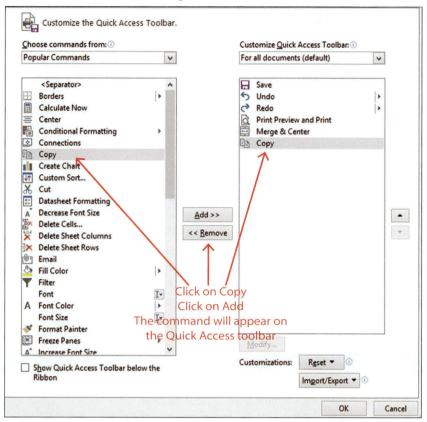

FIGURE MO1.17   Completion of Lesson Microsoft Office 1B1

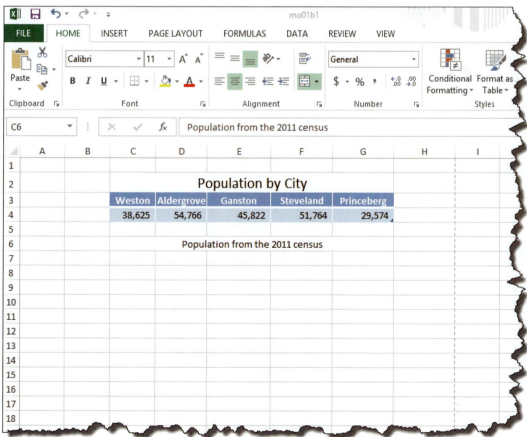

View and Zoom Controls

LESSON OVERVIEW

You can adjust the size and magnification window that contains the document, the tabs, and the ribbons. You can **minimize** any window to provide more room on the screen. When you minimize it, it moves to the Windows **taskbar** at the bottom of the screen. When ready, you can **maximize** the window again to see it. You can move or size a window without sending it to the taskbar.

The window of an application does not always show the entire document. You can **scroll** up or down a document quickly to view the rest of the document. There are also Ribbon Display Options that give you control over the ribbons in the window. The **Auto-hide Ribbon** provides the greatest possible view by hiding the Ribbon and tabs,

as well as expanding to fit the screen. Clicking on the top of the screen temporarily displays the tabs and ribbons. The **Show Tabs** option hides the Ribbon but leaves the tabs visible. When you click on a tab, the Ribbon appears. Once you complete a command, the Ribbon disappears.

You can change the **view** of a document, but it depends on which application is open. For example, Word provides Read Mode, Print Layout, and Outline views. Excel provides Normal, Page Break, and Page Layout views. It is also easy to change the **zoom** magnification to make the document larger or smaller. No matter how you change the view or the zoom, the printing of the document is not affected.

SKILLS PREVIEW

Minimize the window	• Locate the System Menu button on the left end of the Title bar. CLICK Minimize, or • CLICK the Minimize command on the right end of the Title bar.
Maximize the window	• If the window is open but not full screen, Locate the System Menu button in the Title bar. CLICK Maximize, or • CLICK the Maximize button on the right-hand end of the Title bar. • If the window is minimized to the Windows taskbar, CLICK the application icon on the Windows taskbar.
Move a window	• CLICK and HOLD the mouse on the Title bar. DRAG the window to the new location.
Size a window	• Move the mouse to one of the window borders until a two-headed arrow appears. DRAG the edge in, out, up, or down to resize the window. Release the mouse.
Scroll through a document	• DRAG the Scroll bar up and down. • CLICK just below (or after) the Scroll bar. • Roll the wheel on the mouse (if available) back (toward you) to scroll down or forward (away from you) to scroll up.
Change Ribbon Display Options	• Move the mouse to the right-hand end of the Title bar. CLICK the Ribbon Display Options button. CLICK your choice.
Change the view of a document	• CLICK the VIEW tab and locate the Views group. (Word, PowerPoint, and Access have similar controls.) Choose the desired view.
Adjust the zoom magnification	• CLICK the VIEW tab and locate the Zoom group. CLICK Zoom. CLICK to adjust to a preset magnification, or • DOUBLE-CLICK the Zoom level at the right-hand end of the Task bar. Choose the desired zoom.

1 Locate the files associated with this lesson. Open **mo01b2.xlsx**. This is an Excel file so it automatically opens the Excel application first, and then loads the file.

2 Locate the System menu button () in the top left-hand corner of the Title bar.

CLICK on that image to display a drop-down menu.

CHOOSE Minimize to shrink the window down to the Windows taskbar.

CLICK on the Excel icon in the Windows taskbar to restore the window to its former size.

PRESS `Alt` + `spacebar` as a shortcut to open the System menu.

CHOOSE Maximize to expand the window to the entire size of the screen.

CLICK on the System Menu button.

CHOOSE Restore to return to the original window size.

> **TIP**
>
> The Minimize, Maximize (along with the Restore, if the window is currently maximized), and Close buttons are also displayed on the far right-hand side of the Title bar. These shortcuts will perform the same actions as the commands in the System menu.

3 The System menu has two other commands (Move and Size) that can be performed more easily without the System menu.

Move the mouse to the Title bar (generally best if you choose a blank spot on the Title bar).

CLICK and HOLD the mouse.

DRAG the window to a different place on the screen.

RELEASE the mouse to leave the window in the new position.

Move the mouse to one of the window borders until a resizing arrow appears (⟷).

DRAG the edge to change the size of the window.

RELEASE the mouse to set the resizing.

4 Think of the Excel screen (or Word, PowerPoint, or Access) window as an actual "window" viewing a particular portion of the document.

To see more of the document, you need to move the "window."

CLICK in any of the data cells on the screen.

You can move the screen down by:

a. Dragging the scroll bar.

b. Clicking just below the scroll bar.

c. Rolling the wheel on the mouse (if available) back (toward you).

You can move up doing the opposite of any of these.

5 Move the mouse to the right end of the Title bar.

CLICK the Ribbon Display Options button (see Figure MO1.18).

CLICK Auto-hide Ribbon.

(*Result:* The ribbons are gone and the window now fills the screen for maximum visibility.)

CLICK anywhere along the top of the window to temporarily bring down the Tab and Ribbon.

CLICK on the main screen to hide the Tab and Ribbon.

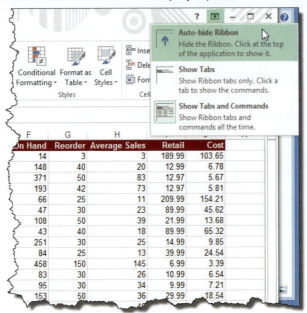

FIGURE MO1.18 Ribbon Display Options

6 CLICK the Ribbon Display Options button.

CLICK Show Tabs.
(*Result:* The ribbons are gone but the tabs remain.)

CLICK on any tab to reveal the ribbon.

CLICK on the main screen to hide the Ribbon.

7 CLICK the Ribbon Display Options button.

CLICK Show Tabs and Commands.
(*Result:* The screen returns to the normal tabs and ribbons display.)

8 CLICK the VIEW tab and locate the Workbook Views group.

CLICK the Page Break Preview to see what would print on page one and what would be on page two.

CLICK Page Layout to see rulers down the left-hand side and across the top of the page.

This view also shows a header across the top (Checking the View) that shows when you print.

CLICK Normal view.

 MORE INFO

The different Office applications have different types of views available from their View ribbon. Word, PowerPoint, and Access provide different views because the programs are so different in purpose.

---

9 Locate the Show group.

CLICK the Formula bar box to uncheck it (the Formula bar disappears).

Uncheck the Gridlines box (the gridlines between the columns and rows disappear).

Uncheck the Headings box (the column and row headings disappear).

CLICK all three of the check boxes to show them again.

10 Locate the Zoom group.

CLICK the Zoom button to display preset magnifications.

CHOOSE 200%.

CLICK OK to make the screen zoom to 200%.

CLICK the Zoom button again.

CHOOSE 50%.

CLICK OK to reduce the zoom factor to 50%.

11 There are zoom controls along the Status bar (far bottom right of the screen).

CLICK on the Zoom Level (the 50% button).

CHOOSE 100% from the Zoom magnification menu.

CLICK OK.

12 Return to Normal View.

13 All Microsoft Office products have similar view and zoom controls. You have not made any changes to this file, so there is no need to save it. Your screen should look similar to Figure MO1.19.

FIGURE MO1.19 Completion of Lesson Microsoft Office 1B2

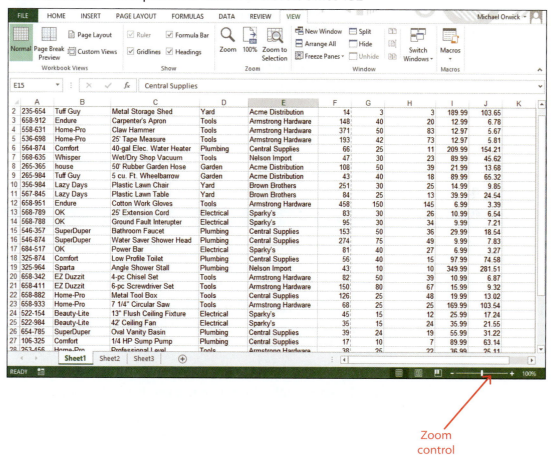

Zoom control

Backstage View and Options

LESSON OVERVIEW

One of the greatest things about the Office applications is that they are highly customizable. The FILE tab takes you to the **Backstage view**. From here, you can add or change the properties of a document. You can change the way the spell checking feature runs. You can set the application to a different language. You can decide where to save files and how often the **autosave** backs up your work. You can customize the Quick Access toolbar and the ribbons to contain the commands you most often use. You can even change the order of the commands.

Backstage view also allows you to create new documents or search for **templates** (a model of a document you can adjust for your use). From the Backstage view, you can open or save documents quickly. It also provides a Print page to control your printer and display the document as it will print via the Print Preview.

The **Word Options** menu allows to you turn on, turn off, and adjust the settings on hundreds of default options from the **Mini toolbar** to show measurements in inches, centimeters, or millimeters.

SKILLS PREVIEW

Enter Backstage view	• CLICK the FILE tab. CHOOSE from the Backstage view menu.
Change user name and initials	• CLICK the FILE tab. CLICK Options. CLICK General. Locate User name. Type in desired name. Locate Initials. Type in desired initials.
Change options	• CLICK the FILE tab. CLICK Options. Make desired changes.

PROJECT PRACTICE

1. Locate the files associated with this lesson. Open **mo01b3.docx**. This is a Word file so it automatically opens the Word application first, and then loads the file.

2. CLICK the FILE tab to open the Backstage view (see Figure MO1.20).

   The Info page provides information on the document.

   On the right-hand side, the properties list the size of the file, the number of pages, and other details.

   CLICK on Add a title.

   TYPE **Searching the Internet**

   You just gave the document a title. (Note: This does not change the file name.)

FIGURE MO1.20 Backstage view

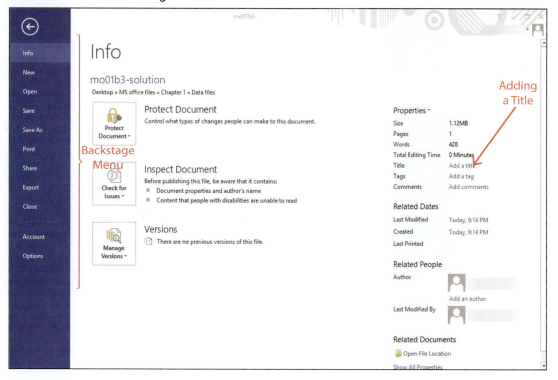

3 CLICK New from the Backstage menu (see Figure MO1.20).

Here you can see what templates are available within the Microsoft application you are using.

CLICK in the Search box.

TYPE **cards** and CLICK Search.

The program searches for card templates (business cards, greetings cards, etc.).

4 CLICK Open from the menu on the left-hand side.

Here you can open recent documents (which can save time).

You can open from folders and files stored on your computer.

5 CLICK Save from the menu on the left-hand side. If this is the first time the document is saved, the Save As dialog box appears.

Enter a name for the document and CLICK Save.

The document is saved and returns to normal view.

CLICK the FILE tab to return to the Backstage view.

CLICK Save As.

This allows you to save the current document under another name.

6 CLICK Print from the menu on the left-hand side.

This opens the Print and Print Preview window (see Figure MO1.21).

On the right-hand side is the Print Preview.

On the left are the print options.

The print controls differ depending on which application you are using, but they are all found via the Backstage view.

FIGURE MO1.21 Print and Print Preview window

7. CLICK Options from the menu on the left (the other options are not discussed here).

The General Option window is displayed (see Figure MO1.22).

This is where Word controls most of its behaviors.

Note the check boxes show what is currently active.

The Mini toolbar is not discussed here, but if you found it a distraction while working in Word, you could uncheck the box to turn it off.

Check the box to turn it back on.

8. Locate the User name window below Personalize your copy of Microsoft Office.

CLICK in the window.

TYPE *your name*

CLICK in the Initials window.

TYPE *your initials*

Now, when you save files or add comments to a file, Word will use your name and initials.

9. CLICK Display from the Word Options menu.

Again you see that some options are turned on and some are turned off.

Hover the mouse over the Information symbol (ⓘ) after Show highlighter marks.

This displays an information box with more information on the feature.

10. CLICK Save to see how Word decides where to save.

Locate the Save documents area.

Locate the spinner for the Save AutoRecover information every 10 minutes.

CLICK the button arrow of the spinner to change it to 9 minutes.

This automatically saves your work every 9 minutes.

FIGURE MO1.22 Word Options

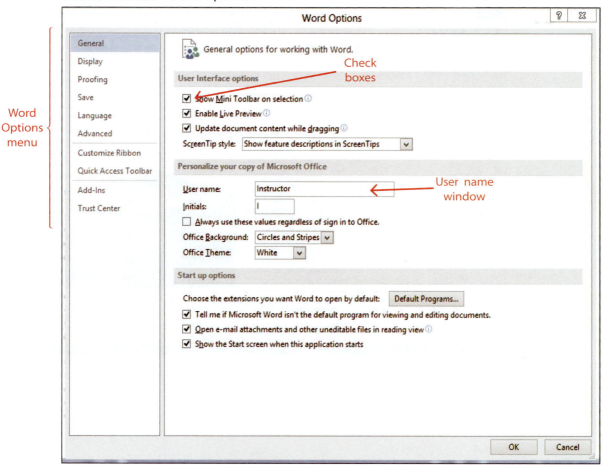

11 CLICK Proofing to see options such as AutoCorrect and Spell Checking.

CLICK Language to see the default language and other languages available.

CLICK Customize Ribbon to see why certain commands appear on specific ribbons.

CLICK Quick Access toolbar to see the option page you used a few lessons ago.

CLICK Advanced and scroll about halfway down to find the Display area.

CLICK the drop-down next to Show measurements in units of.

You can change to metric, Microsoft's Points, or the old typewriter's Pica.

Ensure Inches is selected.

12 CLICK OK to close the Options window. This returns you to the normal view of the document.

While we did not change many settings, it is helpful to know where you can go to customize Word, Excel, PowerPoint, or Access to suit your needs. You document should appear similar to Figure MO1.23. Do not save the file before closing.

13 CLOSE the Word application.

FIGURE MO1.23 Completion of Microsoft Office 1B3

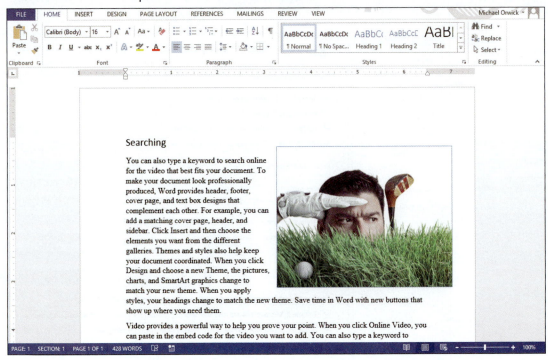

MULTIPLE-CHOICE QUIZ

Select the best choice in the following questions to review the project concepts.

1. The Quick Access toolbar is available
   a. no matter which ribbon is active.
   b. in all office applications.
   c. for customizing.
   d. All of these are correct.

2. To add a command to the Quick Access toolbar
   a. double-click on the command.
   b. right-click on the command.
   c. drag the command to the Quick Access toolbar.
   d. None of these is correct.

3. Remove a command from the Quick Access toolbar by
   a. right-clicking on the command in the Quick Access toolbar.
   b. dragging the command off the Quick Access toolbar.
   c. clicking the drop-down on the Quick Access toolbar and choosing Remove.
   d. None of these is correct.

4. Clicking the (☐) command on the Title bar will
   a. maximize the window.
   b. open the normal view.
   c. size the window.
   d. None of these is correct.

5. Move a window by
   a. double-clicking the Title bar.
   b. clicking on the text and dragging.
   c. right-clicking on the Title bar and dragging.
   d. None of these is correct.

6. You can scroll down a document by
   a. dragging the scroll bar.
   b. clicking above or below the scroll bar.
   c. rolling the mouse wheel up or down.
   d. All of these are correct.

7. There are preset zoom magnifications of
   a. 50%.
   b. 150%.
   c. page width.
   d. None of these is correct.

8. Which of these is **NOT** one of the Backstage view menu choices?
   a. Share
   b. Print
   c. Account
   d. None of these is correct.

9. On the Backstage view's Print page, you can
   a. see the Print Preview.
   b. change page orientation.
   c. set the number of copies.
   d. All of these are correct.

10. Using the Backstage view, you can change the units of measurement
    a. in the Proofing options.
    b. in the Advanced options.
    c. in the General options.
    d. None of these is correct.

In this exercise, you will add commands to the Quick Access toolbar, adjust the view and the zoom magnification of the document, and change some of the options in the Backstage view. When completed, your screen should look similar to Figure MO1.24.

FIGURE MO1.24 Work It Out MO-1B-E1: completed

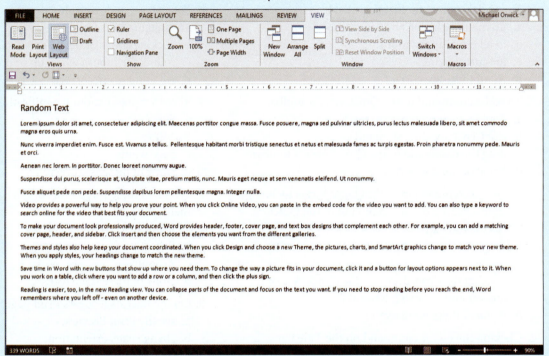

1. Open Word. Locate and open the file **mo01b1.docx**. Save the file as **mo01b1.hw1.docx**.

2. Go to the **PAGE LAYOUT** tab and add the Margins command to the Quick Access toolbar.

3. Move the Quick Access toolbar to below the Ribbon.

4. Change the view of the document to Web Layout.

5. Set the zoom magnification to 90%.

6. Using the Backstage view, General Word Options, change the Office Theme to Dark Gray.

7. Using the Backstage view, Save Word Options, set Word to AutoRecover every 6 minutes.

8. Your document should look similar to what is shown in Figure MO1.24.

9. Because many of the settings you adjusted will remain after you close the file, return all the settings back as they were:

   a. Return view to Print Layout.

   b. Return zoom to 100% (if it doesn't occur automatically).

   c. Return the Quick Access toolbar to above the Ribbon.

   d. Remove the Margins command from the Quick Access toolbar.

   e. Return the Office Theme setting to White.

   f. Return the AutoRecover to 10 minutes.

10. Save the file and close Word.

HANDS-ON EXERCISE: WORK IT OUT MO-1B-E2

In this exercise, you will add commands to the Quick Access toolbar, adjust the view and the zoom magnification of the document, and change some of the options in the Backstage view. When completed, your screen should look similar to Figure MO1.25.

FIGURE MO1.25 Work It Out MO-1B-E2: completed

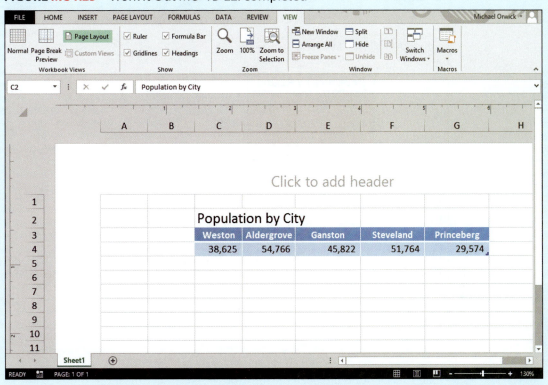

1. Open Excel. Locate and open the file **mo01b2.xlsx**. Save the file as **mo01b2.hw2.xlsx**.

2. Go to the INSERT tab and add the Table command to the Quick Access toolbar.

3. Using the Quick Access toolbar drop-down, add the Quick Print command.

4. Change the view of the document to Page Layout.

5. Set the zoom magnification to 130%.

6. Using the Backstage view, Info, change the title of the document to **Population in MacKenzie County**.

7. Using the Backstage view, General Excel Options, change the User name to *your name*.

8. Your document should look similar to what is shown in Figure MO1.25.

9. Because many of the settings you adjusted will remain after you close the file, return all the settings back as they were:

   a. Return view to normal.

   b. Return zoom to 100% (if it doesn't occur automatically).

   c. Remove the Table and Quick Print commands from the Quick Access toolbar.

10. Save the file and close Excel.

HANDS-ON EXERCISE: WORK IT OUT MO-1B-E3

In this exercise, you will add commands to the Quick Access toolbar, adjust the view and the zoom magnification of the document, and change some of the options in the Backstage view. When completed, your screen should look similar to Figure MO1.26.

FIGURE MO1.26 Work It Out MO-1B-E3: completed

1. Open Excel. Locate and open the file **mo01b3.xlsx.** Save the file as **mo01b3.hw3.xlsx.**

2. Go to the VIEW tab and add the Zoom command to the Quick Access toolbar.

3. Using the Quick Access toolbar drop-down and More Commands, add the Copy command.

4. Move the Copy command on the Quick Access toolbar so it appears before the Zoom command.

5. Using the Zoom command in the Quick Access toolbar, change the zoom to 200%.

6. Using the Backstage view, Info, change the title of the document to **Revenues by Region**.

7. Using the Ribbon Display Options, auto-hide the Ribbon.

8. Your document should look similar to what is shown in Figure MO1.26.

9. Because many of the settings you adjusted will remain after you close the file, return all the settings back as they were:

   a. Return to Show Tabs and Commands.

   b. Return zoom to 100% (if it does not occur automatically).

   c. Remove the Copy and Zoom commands from the Quick Access toolbar.

10. Save the file and close Excel.

Chapter Summary

This chapter is vital to prepare you for the integration of the Office applications. To better understand the environment that Microsoft Office works in, you first create folders. We examined how folders can be put inside other folders, just as you could inside a filing cabinet. This allows you to keep specific files inside a folder that you will store inside a more general folder. We also saw how easy it is to copy, move, and delete folders and files. Of course, you can restore your deleted items from the Recycle Bin.

This chapter showed how Clipboard is a powerful tool to copy, paste, and move elements around a document. The Clipboard can even store entire files and folders to move or paste in another folder. Perhaps its most useful property is Clipboard's functionality between applications. You can copy something from one program and paste it in another program.

One of the greatest time-saving features is the Quick Access toolbar. Because it sits above (or below) the Ribbon, you can access it anytime, no matter what ribbon is currently active. And to make the Quick Access toolbar even more useful, customize the commands or reorder them to suit your current project.

Each application offers its own views, so you can change the way the screen appears. This also includes the ability to zoom in or zoom out from your document by changing the magnification level. There are many ways to quickly access the Zoom commands.

The Backstage view provides many controls to adjust and customize the way the application behaves through its Options page. The Backstage view also displays a menu of pages that control printing, saving, opening files, and searching for new templates. All these skills are fundamental to making the best of the features offered in Microsoft Office 2013.

Chapter Key Terms

Auto-hide Ribbon, p. O-28	Folders, p. O-4	Save, p. O-9
Autosave, p. O-32	Folder tree, p. O-4	Save As, p. O-9
Backstage view, p. O-32	Maximize, p. O-28	Scroll, p. O-28
Clipboard, p. O-14	Minimize, p. O-28	Show Tabs, p. O-28
Context-sensitive menu, p. O-4	Mini toolbar, p. O-32	Taskbar, p. O-28
Copy, p. O-14	Navigation pane, p. O-4	Templates, p. O-32
Cut, p. O-14	Paste, p. O-14	View, p. O-28
Dragging, p. O-9	Quick Access toolbar, p. O-24	Word Options, p. O-32
File, p. O-9	Recycle Bin, p. O-4	Zoom, p. O-28

On Your Own Exercise: MO-1C-E1

This project will provide the opportunity to practice the most important skills covered in this chapter, regardless of the lesson in which they were introduced. The example shown in Figure MO1.27 is only a guideline of how the final project may appear.

Open the Documents folder. Open the MyLessons folder. Create a folder called Comprehensive Exercises. Locate the files associated with this chapter and copy **mo01cp1a.docx**. Paste the file into the Comprehensive Exercises folder.

Open the **mo01cp1a.docx** file. Save it in the Comprehensive Exercises folder as **comp1a.docx**. Click on the photograph and copy it. Move to the bottom of the text and paste the picture.

Add the Paste command from the HOME ribbon to the Quick Access toolbar. Open the Customize Quick Access Toolbar and using the More Commands, add the Copy and Cut commands. Move the Copy and Cut commands ahead of the Paste command. Move the Quick Access toolbar below the Ribbon.

Change the Ribbon Display Options to show just the tabs. Set the zoom to Page Width. Change the view to Outline. Click the Close Outline View button.

FIGURE MO1.27 Comprehensive Exercise MO-1C-E1: completed

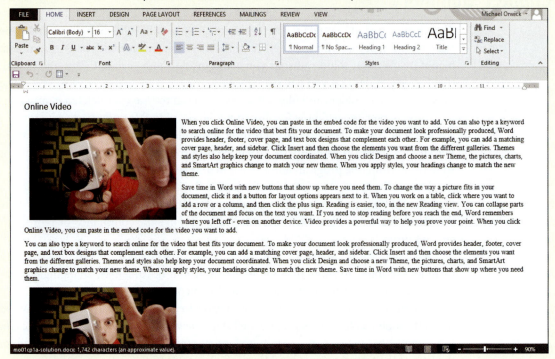

FIGURE MO1.27 Comprehensive Exercise MO-1C-E1: completed

Go to the Backstage view and Save As **comp1acopy.docx**. Using the Backstage view, give the document a title of **Online Video**. Change the user name to *your name* and the initials to *your initials*. Save this file and close Word.

On Your Own Exercise: MO-1C-E2

This project provides the opportunity to practice the most important skills covered in this chapter, regardless of the lesson in which they were introduced. The example shown in Figure MO1.28 is only a guideline of how the final project may appear.

FIGURE MO1.28 Comprehensive Exercise MO-1C-E2: completed

Open the Documents folder. Open the MyLessons folder. Open the Comprehensive Exercises folder. Create a folder here called Final Exercise. Using the Navigation pane and the expand arrows, locate the files associated with this lesson and move **mo01cp2b.xlsx** into the Final Exercise file.

Open the Final Exercise folder and open the **mo01cp2b.xlsx** file. Click and hold the mouse and slide across both columns and all nine rows. Copy this selection. Click in cell D3. Paste the selection into this cell. Press **Esc** to turn off the copy process.

Save this file in the Comprehensive Exercises folder as **comp1b.xlsx**.

Change the Ribbon Display Options to Show Tabs. On the DATA tab, add the Insert Function command to the Quick Access toolbar. Using the drop-down arrow, add Sort Ascending to the Quick Access toolbar. Click in cell D4. Click the Sort Ascending command (it will sort the table you just copied).

Go to Backstage view and then go to the Excel Options page and change the user name to *your name*. Return to the document. Increase the zoom to 130%. The document should appear similar to Figure MO1.28. Save the file and close Excel.

ProjectLearn Microsoft
Word 2013

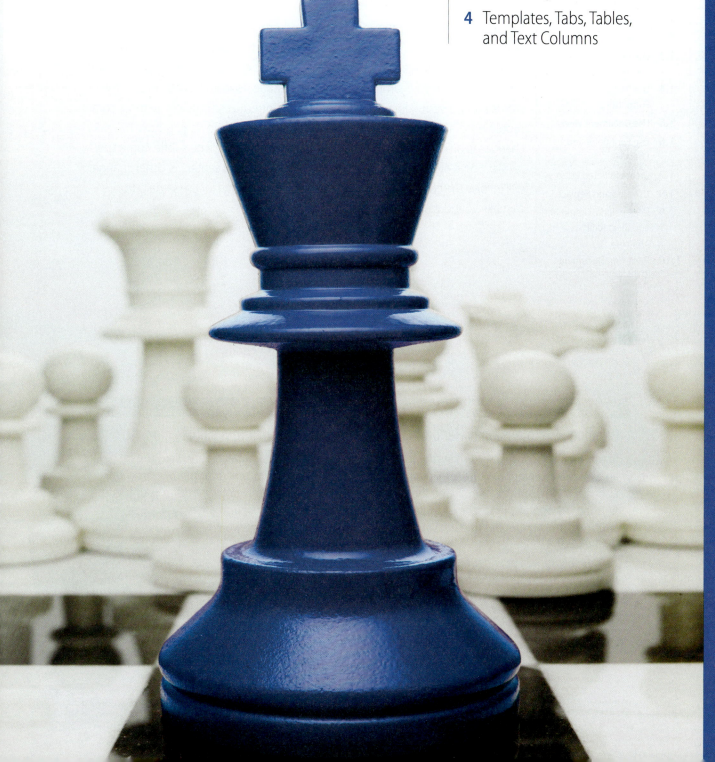

Introduction to Word

Microsoft Word is likely the most-used word processing program in the modern office. But exactly what is "word processing"? The true power of word processing allows you to control, adjust, and improve the way your document appears—and the way in which you communicate your message. To learn how to "process" your words into powerful documents, this chapter introduces some of the most commonly used and most-often needed techniques and shows you how to make changes to an existing document. Some of the changes will be subtle, some spectacular. Some of the changes will involve a single word or sentence. Other changes will involve the entire document. But all changes are done for the same purpose—to make your document demand attention.

PROJECT

Building A Professional Handout

In this project, you will make changes to an existing document to better organize and display the information. Place the finished version of this document into your career portfolio and title it "Word: Professional Handout."

This chapter will provide you with the techniques and skills that you will use in producing almost any document, whether you are a professional, a student, or just looking for a way to enhance your job skills.

THE SITUATION

Dr. Shoret's Veterinary Clinic

A friend of yours works at a veterinary clinic. The vet has scratched out some notes on how pet owners should groom their dogs and given the notes to your friend. After typing the material into a file and organizing it a bit, she would like to improve its impact by making it look more professional. She has asked you to help her "fix it up," so the clinic can print it and give to customers to take away with them. Let's turn the original document she has created into something that will be a benefit to both the clinic and its customers.

Editing the Professional Handout

In the first project, you will concentrate on getting the material in the document to look the way you want and to ensure that it is consistently structured and formatted. This will involve moving material, changing the way the headings appear, and adjusting the view of the document so you can see it best and work more efficiently when making these changes.

PROJECT FILE: *Available at* **www.mhhe.com/office2013projectlearn**

PROJECT OBJECTIVES

After completing this project, you will be able to:

- Select text using the mouse and the keyboard and navigate the document.

- Rearrange text with Copy and Paste, Cut and Paste, **Drag** and Drop, and Undo.

- Modify text formatting: typeface, style, size, bold, underline, and text justification.

- Control page margins, line spacing, indenting, and hyphenating in a document.

- Change the view, show/hide, and zoom factor options of a document.

How to groom a dog

Introduction

Regularly grooming your dog can keep him free of parasites and improve his general appearance as well. During grooming you also has the opportunity to check the condition of the dog's skin, eyes, ears, coat and teeth. Deciding on how often to groom your dog is up to you, however, Dr. Short recommends that it should be at least once a week.

Brushing can be a pleasant routine for the dog as well as the owner. You should have a specific place you wish to do the brushing. A table or chair will suffice. Lift the dog up onto the table or chair and talk to him. Reassure that all is well. It is important that you and your dog remain calm. Let the dog sniff the tools you will use. Doing this will allow the dog to associate the tools with a pleasant experience.

Required Tools

Tools you will need to brush and groom include comb, brush, nail clippers and scissors.

How to Start

Selecting Text

LESSON OVERVIEW

To make changes to anything in Word, you first need to know how to **select** text and other elements in the document. Word offers many different ways to select text. Choosing the fastest and most efficient way saves time. And when you choose text dozens of times a day, you can save lots of time. The way you choose to do this is often dictated by the type of changes you want to make, the amount of text you want to change, or even the positioning of text. You can select text with your **mouse** or with your keyboard. You can even combine the two to give you extra control over text selection. Once text is selected, you can change the content, structure, and formatting of the text.

SKILLS PREVIEW

Select a single word	• **DOUBLE-CLICK** on the desired word, or • DRAG the mouse pointer across the text to be selected.
Select an entire sentence	• DRAG the mouse pointer across the entire sentence, or • HOLD Ctrl and **click** mouse.
Select an entire line of text	• Move your mouse into the **Selection bar** area; CLICK the right-facing mouse arrow (⟋).
Select an entire paragraph	• **TRIPLE-CLICK** any word in a paragraph, or • MOVE your mouse into the Selection bar next to the paragraph; DOUBLE-CLICK the right-facing mouse arrow (⟋).
Select all text in a document	• PRESS Ctrl + A , or • MOVE your mouse into the Selection bar anywhere in the document; TRIPLE-CLICK the right-facing mouse arrow (⟋).
Move the cursor to the end of the document	• PRESS Ctrl + End
Move the cursor to the beginning of the document	• PRESS Ctrl + Home

PROJECT PRACTICE

1 After launching Microsoft Word, locate and open the project data file **wd01a1.docx**. (*Note*: If Word 2013 defaults to opening the file in the **Read Mode**, you can change to the standard view by clicking the VIEW tab and choosing the Edit Document button.) Before proceeding, let's save the document using a new file name:

CLICK the FILE tab.

CLICK SaveAs.

DOUBLE-CLICK Computer to store the file locally on your computer.

TYPE **wd01a1-handout.docx** in the File Name window and CLICK the Save button to save the file.

2 To display the text formatting attributes that already exist in the document:

CLICK the mouse pointer into the first paragraph of the document body.

(*Result*: On the HOME tab in the **Ribbon,** as shown in Figure WD1.1, you can see that the **font type-face** for the paragraph is Verdana, the font **size** is 10 points, and the text is aligned to the left margin, or **left-aligned**. You will also notice formatting marks within the text. These are visible when the Show/Hide button is turned on.)

FIGURE WD1.1 Formatting options for the current selection

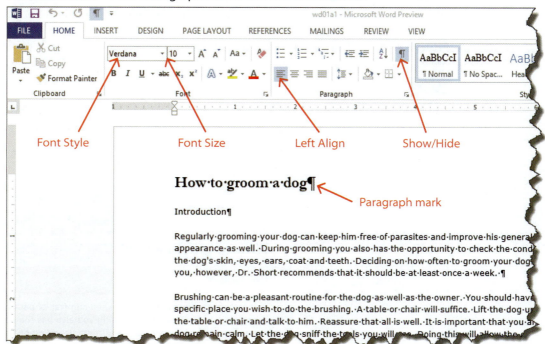

③ The fastest way to select a single word is to double-click anywhere in the word. Let's use the word *opportunity* in the first paragraph:

DOUBLE-CLICK on the word *opportunity* to select the word, including the blank space behind it.

CLICK anywhere in the document to **deselect** the text.

> **MORE INFO**
>
> The Mini toolbar provides a shortcut to many of the common commands related to selecting text. The toolbar fades in and out depending how close the mouse is to the selected area. Its appearance can be controlled (turned on or off) via the **Backstage view**. Follow this path: FILE tab, Options, General. If the Show Mini Toolbar on Selection is turned on, it will activate when you select text.

④ To select the entire paragraph that contains the word *opportunity*:

TRIPLE-CLICK any word in the paragraph.
(*Result:* Triple-clicking automatically selects the entire paragraph including the spaces after it.)

CLICK anywhere to deselect the text before proceeding.

⑤ To quickly select the entire sentence that contains the word *opportunity*:

PRESS Ctrl and hold it down.

CLICK on the word *opportunity*.

(*Result:* The entire sentence containing the word *opportunity* is selected. This includes the space after the sentence.)

CLICK anywhere to deselect the text before proceeding.

⑥ Another fast way to select text is to use the Selection bar shown in Figure WD1.2

MOVE your mouse to the left of the text, in the left-hand margin of the document until the cursor changes to a right-facing arrow (see Figure WD1.2).

CLICK once beside a line of text to select the entire line.
(*Result:* The entire line is selected regardless of where a sentence might begin or end.)

FIGURE WD1.2 The Selection bar area of the screen

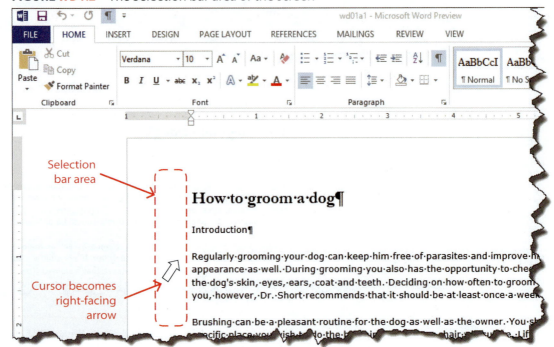

7. To select more than one line of text:

CLICK and DRAG the mouse pointer downward in the Selection bar area to select multiple lines
(*Note:* You can use this method to select lines of text in both up or down directions.)

8. To select an entire paragraph from the Selection bar area:

DOUBLE-CLICK your mouse next to any paragraph.
(*Note:* This is one of the quickest methods for selecting an entire paragraph.)

> **TIP**
>
> If the **Shift** key is held down, the arrow keys can be used to select text. This can be useful if you use another way of selecting text, but need to adjust your selection by a few characters. Just hold the **Shift** key down and each time you hit the arrow key, the selected text will adjust in that direction.
>
> The arrow keys on your keyboard may be grouped separately or they may share keys with the numeric pad. If your arrow keys are on the numeric pad, make sure you toggle the purpose of these keys using the **Num Lock** key, usually located in the top left-hand corner of the numeric pad.

9. To select everything in a document:
PRESS **Ctrl** + **A**

10. No matter how large your document is, you can move to the beginning or end of it instantly.
To move to the end (bottom) of a document:
PRESS **Ctrl** + **End**
To move to the start (top) of a document:
PRESS **Ctrl** + **Home**

11 While you have practiced selecting text in many different ways, the document itself has not changed and should appear similar to Figure WD1.3 (although you probably are viewing only one page at a time.) Before proceeding, save the **wd01a1-handout.docx** file.

FIGURE WD1.3   Completion of Lesson Word 1A1

LESSON WORD 1A2
Moving Things Around

LESSON OVERVIEW

As you write and modify documents in Word, you will frequently need to move words, sentences, and paragraphs within your document, and even to other documents. You may also need to move or reposition pictures, charts, and tables. You can choose from a number of ways to modify the placement of these elements and impact the overall structure of your document. Word allows you to copy and paste, cut and paste, or simply drag and drop elements around the document. However, the way you choose to move these elements is typically dependent on what you want to move, how far you want to move it, and how much you have to move.

SKILLS PREVIEW

Copy selected text	• PRESS Ctrl + C , or • CLICK the HOME tab and locate the Clipboard group, CLICK Copy (⎙).
Cut selected text	• CLICK the HOME tab and locate the Clipboard group, CLICK Cut (✂).
Paste selected text	• CLICK the HOME tab and locate the Clipboard group, CLICK Paste (📋), or • CLICK mouse into desired location and PRESS Ctrl + V .
Drag and drop selected text	• CLICK into selection and hold left mouse button down, DRAG to the desired location and release left mouse button.
Undo previous actions	• CLICK the Undo command (↺) in the **Quick Access toolbar**, or • PRESS Ctrl + Z .

PROJECT PRACTICE

1 Word provides several methods for moving and copying text. Let's practice using some of these methods to modify the structure of our document. To begin, ensure that **wd01a-handout.docx** is open.

2 To move text using the Drag and Drop method:

SELECT the entire paragraph on Bathing including the title and the paragraph marker (¶) at the end of the paragraph.

DRAG the selected paragraph so that the mouse pointer's insertion point appears in front of the title "Nail-Clipping."

RELEASE the mouse button to finish the drag and drop operation (see Figure WD1.4).
(*Result:* Because you included the title and paragraph marker in the selection, you should not need to make any adjustments to spacing.)

TIP

When performing a drag and drop, you will see a faint dotted line attached to the mouse pointer, which indicates that it has a "package" to move (or copy). This faint dotted line is the insertion point. When you let go of the mouse button, the "package" is deposited or inserted into the selected location.

---

the routine. Get in a comfortable position. Work quietly and quickly. While cutting, be
careful·not·to·cut·too·close·to·the·quick.··If·you·do,··there·will·be·some·bleeding·and·some·
pain·for·the·dog.··If·you·do·have·an·accident,·apply·pressure·to·the·wound·to·stop·the·
bleeding.··¶

Bathing¶

Occasionally,·your·dog·will·need·a·bath.··It·is·best·to·use·the·bath·tub·to·bathe·your·dog,·or·
if·it·is·warm·outside,·do·it·outdoors·using·the·waterhose.··If·using·the·bath·tub,·use·warm·
water.··Gradually·wet·the·dog·all·over.··Using·a·dog·shampoo,·cover·the·dog·and·gently·
scrub.··Be·careful·around·the·dog's·eyes,·ears·and·mouth.··Rinse·thoroughly.··It·is·wise·to·
have·newspapers·on·the·floor·to·catch·the·dripping·water.··Rub·the·dog·down·to·remove·
most·of·the·water.··He·will·dry·naturally·on·his·own.··¶ ← Highlighted text includes
the paragraph marker.

Cleaning·Ears¶

Cleaning·your·dog's·ears·is·an·important·part·of·the·grooming·routine.··Long·eared·dogs·
have·more·problems·than·short·eared.··Check·for·parasites,·scratches,·dirt,·etc.··For·just·a·
routine·cleaning·you·will·need·some·mineral·oil·and·some·cotton·swabs.··It·is·advised·to·

3 To move text long distances within a document, use the Clipboard.

To copy text into the Clipboard:

SELECT the two sections "Nail-Clipping" and "Bathing" and be sure to include both the titles and
last paragraph marker in your selection.

CLICK the HOME tab and locate the Clipboard group (Figure WD1.5).

CLICK the Copy command ( ).
(*Result:* This step copies the selected text to the Clipboard. Once it is placed into the Clipboard, you
can paste the data as many times as you like and wherever you want within Word, or even to another
application.)

FIGURE WD1.5   The Clipboard group and the Undo command

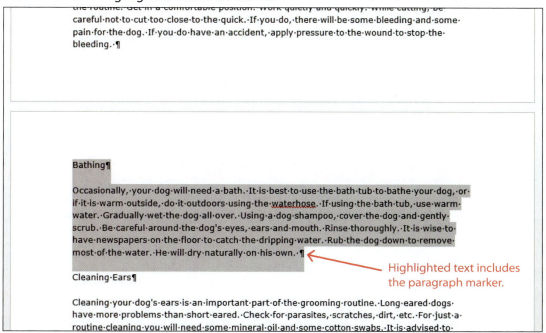

4 To paste text from the Clipboard into the document, first place the cursor at the desired location:

PRESS `Ctrl` + `End` to move to the last page.

Position the cursor (i.e., insertion point) in front of the title "Eye Care."

To paste the copied data:

CLICK the Paste command () (see Figure WD1.5).

(*Result:* This step pastes the data at the insertion point. Remember that the data remains in its original location, as well. The Copy and Paste method is most useful when you want the same material, perhaps a slogan or logo, to appear in more than one place in the document.)

⚠ HEADS UP

When you click the Paste command (📋), be sure to hit the image of a Clipboard, and not the **drop-down** arrow. The drop-down arrow brings up a menu of pasting options that we are not using here.

5 If you decide you do not want these sections in their new places, you can undo what you just did.

To undo actions in Word:

CLICK the Undo command (↶) in the Quick Access toolbar (see Figure WD1.5).

(*Result:* This step removes the text that was inserted into the document using the Paste command. Once the Undo command is used, the Redo command (↷) becomes active. Clicking on this will redo what was just undone.)

💡 TIP

Each time you click the Undo command (↶), Word will undo the next most recent action. To select multiple undo operations, you can click the drop-down arrow attached to the Command button to view and select an entire history of steps.

6 If you just want to move text from one place to another, without leaving the copied text in its original place, use the Cut and Paste method.

To use the Cut and Paste method for moving text:

SELECT the same two sections as before ("Nail-Clipping" and "Bathing").

CLICK the Cut command (✂).

(*Result:* The selected text is removed from the document and placed onto the Clipboard.)

7 Position the cursor (i.e., insertion point) in front of the title "Eye Care."

PRESS `Ctrl` + `V` as the shortcut for the Paste command.

(*Note:* The Cut and Paste method "cuts" the selected data from the document and "pastes" it to the desired location.)

8 Your final project document should appear similar to Figure WD1.6, if displayed using the two-page viewing magnification. Before proceeding, save the wd01a1-handout.docx file.

FIGURE WD1.6 Completion of Lesson Word 1A2

How to groom a dog¶

Introduction¶

Regularly grooming your dog can keep him free of parasites and improve his general appearance as well. During grooming you also has the opportunity to check the condition of the dog's skin, eyes, ears, coat and teeth. Deciding on how often to groom your dog is up to you, however, Dr. Short recommends that it should be at least once a week. ¶

Brushing can be a pleasant routine for the dog as well as the owner. You should have a specific place you wish to do the brushing. A table or chair will suffice. Lift the dog up onto the table or chair and talk to him. Reassure that all is well. It is important that you and your dog remain calm. Let the dog sniff the tools you will use. Doing this will allow the dog to associate the tools with a pleasant experience. ¶

Required Tools¶

Tools you will need to brush and groom include comb, brush, nail clippers and scissors. ¶

How to Start¶

Begin by brushing ~~again~~ the grain (so to speak). This helps to loosen dead hair and to stimulate the skin. It is important to have the proper brush. Generally, short bristles are for short and medium haired dogs and long bristles is for long haired dogs. Use a flannel cloth to bring out the shine in your dog's coat after brushing. ¶

If you dog is a long haired dog, some matting of the hair may occur. Matted hair can occur from burs, food, tar and other sticky substances. Matted hair is not only unsightly but can also irritate the dog. Try combing gently to remove the mat. If it is too tight or large, you may just need to cut it off. The fur will grow back in time. Always use blunt end scissors to cut. Matting of the hair can be avoided or lessened with proper and frequent brushing. ¶

If you want to give your dog's coat a trim, it is important to know the specific way according to the type. Dr. Short reminds us that most short haired dogs need little or no trimming. However, longer haired types need frequent trimming to keep a kept appearance. Except for the occasional trim at home, it may be necessary for you to take your dog to a professional groomer, depending on the type. Use blunt scissors or clippers. Be sure to have your dog relaxed and in a position that is easy for you to use. It is also important to realize that in the summer months, a shorter cut may do fine, but ~~because~~ of sunburn if your dog spends any time out of doors. ¶

Cleaning Ears¶

Cleaning your dog's ears is an important part of the grooming routine. Long eared dogs have more problems than short eared. Check for parasites, scratches, dirt, etc. For just a routine cleaning you will need some mineral oil and some cotton swabs. It is advised to restrain the dog in some way before you begin. Start by dropping a few drops of mineral oil

in the dog's ears. Take the cotton swab and gently stoke the inside of the ear. Do not enter the ear canal. Do this until the ear is clean. ¶

Bathing¶

Occasionally, your dog will need a bath. It is best to use the bath tub to bathe your dog, or if it is warm outside, do it outdoors using the ~~waterhose~~. If using the bath tub, use warm water. Gradually wet the dog all over. Using a dog shampoo, cover the dog and gently scrub. Be careful around the dog's eyes, ears and mouth. Rinse thoroughly. It is wise to have newspapers on the floor to catch the dripping water. Rub the dog down to remove most of the water. He will dry naturally on his own. ¶

Nail Clipping¶

It is wise to start clipping nails during the puppy stage so your dog becomes accustomed to the routine. Get in a comfortable position. Work quietly and quickly. While cutting, be careful not to cut too close to the quick. If you do, there will be some bleeding and some pain for the dog. If you do have an accident, apply pressure to the wound to stop the bleeding. ¶

Eye Care¶

Care of the eyes is essential. When you notice foreign matter in or around your dog's eyes, take a soft cloth and wipe from the outer corner towards the inner corner. Apply ointment if irritation is present. ¶

Dental¶

Lastly, it is very important to care for your dog's teeth. After the first year of life a dog begins to develop tartar. You can combat this with dog biscuits as well as brushing, if your dog allows. ¶

Summary¶

As you can see, grooming your dog can be a very pleasant and productive part of ~~you~~ life as well as your dog's life. Dr. Short advises that if anything seems amiss while grooming, you should always have it checked out by a licensed veterinarian. ¶

¶

LESSON WORD 1A3

Character Formatting

LESSON OVERVIEW

Each character of text can have its own formatting in Word. How text appears can have a big impact on how it is read. By controlling the style of the typeface and its size, and by adding emphasis with bolding, underlining, and **italics**, you can make certain words or sentences stand out from the rest. While many of these commands are contained on the ribbon, we will also introduce the Launch button that opens up the **dialog boxes** for almost every ribbon **group**. These dialog boxes provide more control and more precise adjustments than the shortcuts found in the ribbon groups.

SKILLS PREVIEW

Change font typeface	• CLICK the HOME tab and locate the Font group. SELECT desired font from the Font drop-down list (Times New Ro ▾).
Change font size	• CLICK the HOME tab and locate the Font group. SELECT desired point size from the drop-down list (14 ▾).
Change alignment of selected text	• CLICK the HOME tab and locate the Paragraph group. SELECT desired alignment from the alignment command. 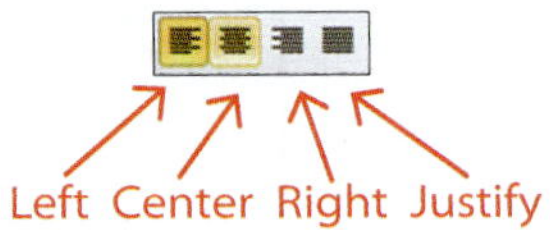 Left Center Right Justify
Add bold, italics, or underline to selected text	• CLICK the HOME tab and locate the Font group. CLICK any of the formatting commands (B I U), or • PRESS Ctrl+B to bold, PRESS Ctrl+I to italicize, PRESS Ctrl+U to underline.
Open Font dialog box (or any group's dialog box)	• CLICK the HOME tab and locate the Font group. CLICK the Launch button ( ).

PROJECT PRACTICE

1. To begin, ensure that **wd01a-handout.docx** is open.

2. To change all the font style in the document at once (except for the title "How to groom a dog":
   CLICK the insertion point at the beginning of the word Introduction.
   PRESS Shift and hold it down.
   PRESS Ctrl+End to move the selection to the end of the document.
   CLICK the HOME tab and locate the Font group (see Figure WD1.7).
   CLICK the Font drop-down arrow.
   SELECT **Times New Roman** from the Font list.
   (*Result:* The entire selection changes to Times New Roman. Any text that was not selected, however, is not changed. Are you seeing the importance of being able to select text efficiently?)

3 You can make more changes while the text is still selected.

To change the font size to 14 points:

CLICK the Font Size drop-down arrow (see Figure WD1.7)

SELECT **14** from the Font Size list.

(*Result:* This selection instantly changes the font size of the selected text to 14 points.)

FIGURE WD1.7 Font commands on the Home Ribbon

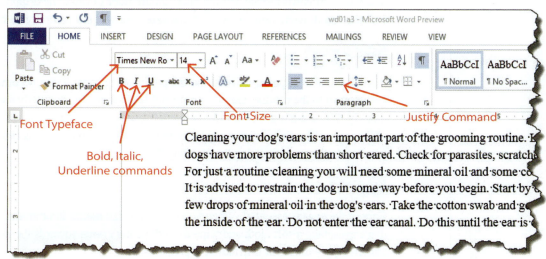

4 Section tiles are important, so let's enhance one with bold, underline, and a different font:

Select the first title, "Introduction."

CLICK the HOME tab and locate the Font group (see Figure WD1.7).

CLICK the Bold command (**B**).

CLICK the Underline command (**U**).

CLICK the Font drop-down arrow (Times New Ro ▾).

SELECT Arial from the Font list.

CLICK anywhere in the document to deselect the text and better see the results.

5 To save even more time, you can enhance more than one section title at a time:

SELECT "Required Tools."

PRESS **Ctrl** and hold it down.

SELECT the following lines:

"How to Start"

"Cleaning Ears"

"Bathing"

"Nail-Clipping"

"Eye Care"

"Dental"

"Summary"

When finished, release the **Ctrl** key. Your screen should now appear similar to Figure WD1.8.

Apply Bold, Underline, and Arial as before. All selected titles will change at the same time.

FIGURE WD1.8   Selecting nonadjacent elements for formatting

thoroughly. It is wise to have newspapers on the floor to catch the dripping water. Rub the dog down to remove most of the water. He will dry naturally on his own. ¶

Nail-Clipping¶

It is wise to start clipping nails during the puppy stage so your dog becomes accustomed to the routine. Get in a comfortable position. Work quietly and quickly. While cutting, be careful not to cut too close to the quick. If you do, there will be some bleeding and some pain for the dog. If you do have an accident, apply pressure to the wound to stop the bleeding. ¶

Eye Care¶

Care of the eyes is essential. When you notice foreign matter in or around your dog's eyes, take a soft cloth and wipe from the outer corner towards the inner corner. Apply ointment if irritation is present. ¶

Dental¶

6 Let's make changes to the main title of the document.

To **center-align** the title:

CLICK your mouse on any character in the document title.

CLICK the HOME tab and locate the Paragraph group.

CLICK Center command (≡) (or press `Ctrl` + `E`).

SELECT the title.

CLICK the Font drop-down arrow.

CHOOSE Arial.

CLICK anywhere in the document to deselect the text and better see the results (see Figure WD1.9). (*Result:* By centering one character in the title, Word automatically centers everything in that line. It couldn't center just one character without affecting the rest.)

7 The ribbon commands are usually just shortcuts to controls found in dialog boxes that offer more options. Let's use the ribbon to emphasize one of the most important sentences in the document:

SELECT the last 17 words of the document (starting with "…if anything seems amiss…").

CLICK the HOME tab and locate the Font group.

CLICK the Launch button (⌐).

Locate the Effects section of the dialog box.

CHOOSE Small caps and CLICK OK. (*Result:* The last portion of the final sentence has now been emphasized to add impact.)

8 Your final project document should appear similar to Figure WD1.9, if displayed using the 1×3 Pages viewing magnification. Before proceeding, save the **wd01a1-handout.docx** file.

FIGURE WD1.9 Completion of Lesson Word 1A3

Paragraph Formatting

LESSON OVERVIEW

To give the document a more finished appearance, you can **justify** the paragraph alignment as seen in most magazines and books. One of the most powerful capabilities of a word processor is the ability to modify (change) the appearance of paragraphs or the entire document at once. Paragraphs may be aligned to the left, right, or justified to line up against both **margins**. You can adjust print margins to provide a tidy on-screen appearance for your document, as well as for printing. You can adjust the line-spacing indentation and even add automatic hyphenation to a document. Word provides presets for many of these features, so you do not have to make these adjustments to every new document.

SKILLS PREVIEW

Change page margins	• CLICK the PAGE LAYOUT tab and locate the Page Setup group. CLICK Margins command. CHOOSE preset margins.
Create custom margins	• CLICK the PAGE LAYOUT tab and locate the Page Setup group. CLICK Margins command. CHOOSE Custom Margins and select desired margins.
Set line spacing	• CLICK the HOME tab and locate the Paragraph group. CLICK Launch button (⌐). CLICK on Line Spacing and select desired spacing, or • CLICK the HOME tab and locate the Paragraph group. CLICK the Paragraph Spacing command (↕≣▾) and choose preset options.
Add paragraph indenting	• CLICK the HOME tab and locate the Paragraph group. CLICK Launch button (⌐). CLICK the drop-down arrow below Special and select desired indenting option.
Hyphenate a document	• CLICK the PAGE LAYOUT tab and locate the Page Setup group. CLICK the hyphenation command (b꜀ᵃ Hyphenation). CHOOSE Automatic.

PROJECT PRACTICE

1 To begin, ensure that **wd01a-handout.docx** is open.

2 Currently the document text is left-aligned.

To align the document text to both the left and right margins (called *justified text*):

PRESS `Ctrl`+`A` to select all of the text in the document.

CLICK the HOME tab and locate the Paragraph group.

CLICK the Justify command (≡) or PRESS `Ctrl`+`J`.

This is also called block justification because paragraphs appear to be rectangular blocks of text.

Deselect the text.

3 Let's increase the margins on the document to add more white space.

To adjust the size of the page margins in a document:

CLICK the PAGE LAYOUT tab and locate the Page Setup group.

CLICK the Margins command drop-down arrow (Figure WD1.10).

SELECT Normal from the menu.

(*Result:* This automatically adjusts all margins in the document to 1 inch.)

FIGURE WD1.10 PAGE LAYOUT tab with Margins command

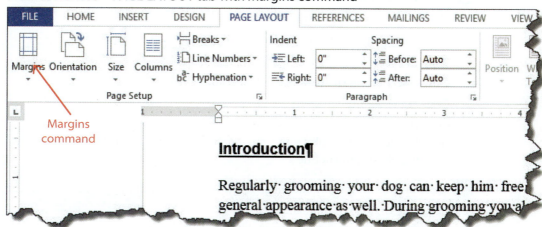

4 Sometimes the preset margin choices don't work well. Return to displaying the Margin command menu.

To set your own margins:

SELECT Custom Margins from the menu.

TYPE **1.25** in the Top, Bottom, and Right spin boxes.

TYPE **1.5** in the Left margin box.

CLICK the OK command button after you have finished entering the values.

(*Result:* The page margins you input now take effect on the entire document.)

5 To adjust the line spacing:

SELECT the entire document.

CLICK the HOME tab and locate the Paragraph group.

CLICK the Launch button in the Paragraph group.

CLICK the drop-down arrow under Line spacing.

CHOOSE Single.

CLICK OK.

(*Result:* The entire document has changed from its original 1.15 spacing to single spacing.)

MORE INFO

Clicking on the Line and Paragraph Spacing command ( ) in the Paragraph group provides quick access to many of the common line and paragraph settings.

---

6 To add indentation to a document:

SELECT the entire document.

CLICK the Launch button in the Paragraph group.

In the Indentation section:

CLICK the drop-down arrow beneath Special.

CHOOSE First line.

CLICK OK.

(*Result:* Every paragraph in the document is now indented by the default value of 0.5 inches, including the document title.)

7 These indents don't really add much to the layout. Let's put things back the way they were.

CLICK the Undo ( ) command.

(*Result:* Everything returns to the previous indentation.)

8 Justified text can create unnatural spaces between words. Hyphenating can reduce that.

To hyphenate a document:

CLICK the PAGE LAYOUT tab and locate the Page Setup group.

CLICK the Hyphenation command (bc Hyphenation).

CHOOSE Automatic.

(*Result:* The entire document hyphenates instantly without you having to select any specific text. A quick look down the right-hand margin of the text shows that Word has found about six or seven words that it could hyphenate.)

MORE INFO

As you can tell by the drop-down hyphenation menu, you can also walk through the document and manually insert hyphens if you wish (automatic hyphenation may not be perfect). You can also adjust hyphen settings, such as how many consecutive lines should be hyphenated and how large the hyphen zone should be.

---

9 Your final project document should appear similar to Figure WD1.11, if displayed using the 1×3 Pages viewing magnification. Before proceeding, save the wd01a1-handout.docx file.

FIGURE WD1.11 Completion of Lesson Word 1A4

Getting the Best View

LESSON OVERVIEW

Another great advantage of word processing using Word is the ability to adjust the screen view and magnification to best suit your needs and preferences. You can **zoom** in to enlarge the text and to see more detail in graphics and tables, or you can zoom out to see the entire page or even multiple pages at the same time. Word also provides formatting marks (invisible, by default) that you can display to help you organize the structure and formatting of text, and the overall design of your document.

SKILLS PREVIEW

View formatting marks	• CLICK the HOME tab and locate the Paragraph group. CLICK the **Show/Hide** button (¶) on or off.
Turn ruler on or off	• CLICK the VIEW tab and locate the Show group. CLICK the Ruler (☑ Ruler) on or off.
Adjust zoom factor	• CLICK the plus (to magnify) or minus (to demagnify), or • DRAG the Zoom Slider button right or left. De-magnify Slider Magnify
Change modes of View	• CLICK the VIEW tab and locate the Views group, CHOOSE VIEW, or • CHOOSE desired view from the View controls located in the status bar. Read Mode Print Layout Web Layout
View preset zooms	• CLICK the VIEW tab and locate the Zoom group. CHOOSE One Page, Multiple Pages, or 100%, or • CLICK the VIEW tab and locate the Zoom group. CLICK Zoom command (🔍) to open Zoom dialog box and select desired zoom factor.

PROJECT PRACTICE

1 Word provides helpful formatting marks and symbols that can assist you when editing and positioning elements in your document. By default, these marks and symbols are hidden, but we have used files with them turned on to help us move text. You can easily toggle their display on or off using the Show/Hide command. To begin, ensure that **wd01a-handout.docx** is open.

2 To toggle the formatting marks on and off:

CLICK the HOME tab and locate the Paragraph group.

CLICK the Show/Hide command (¶) to turn it off (see Figure WD1.12).
(*Result:* You will see a much cleaner page with the various formatting marks turned off.)

FIGURE WD1.12 The Show/Hide button

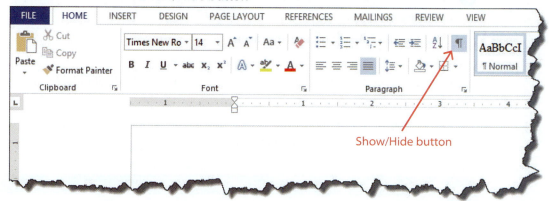

Show/Hide button

3 Another helpful feature for editing and positioning text and graphics is the document **ruler**.

To turn on the ruler:

CLICK the **VIEW** tab and locate the Show group.

CLICK the Ruler check box (☑ Ruler) (see Figure WD1.13).

(*Result:* With a check mark selection in this option, two rulers are actually displayed: the horizontal ruler across the top of the document and the vertical ruler along the left-hand side.)

FIGURE WD1.13 Displaying rulers in the document area

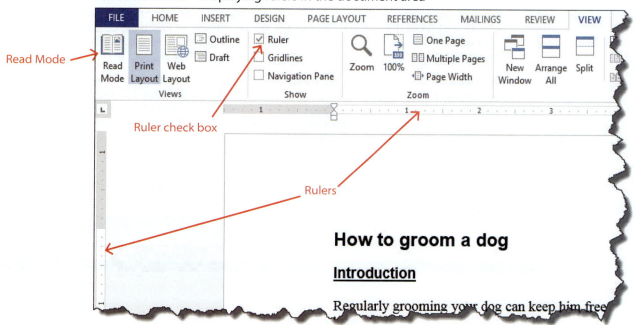

Read Mode

Ruler check box

Rulers

4 The Read Mode allows you to proofread your document with the least amount of distraction. To turn on the Read Mode view:

CLICK the **VIEW** tab and locate the Document Views group.

CLICK the Read Mode command (▦) (Figure WD1.13).

(*Result:* The full-screen Read Mode shown in Figure WD1.14 eliminates all of the controls and commands on the screen and displays the document's text in an easy-to-read viewing mode—great for proofreading, and it automatically resizes for reading on portable devices.)

5 Three methods allow you to exit the Read Mode(see Figure WD1.14):

CLICK the VIEW tab.

CHOOSE Edit Document from the menu,

or

CLICK the Print Layout button along the bottom right-hand side of the screen,

or

PRESS [Esc] to return to the Print Layout view. Other views in the Document Views group have specific uses that will be discussed in other projects.

> **MORE INFO**
>
> The Read Mode view does not display the document as it will print. Instead, it is used primarily for reading on devices other than a desktop computer and for proofreading (as opposed to editing or printing) purposes. Do not confuse this mode with the Print Layout mode or Print Preview.

FIGURE WD1.14   Displaying Read Mode

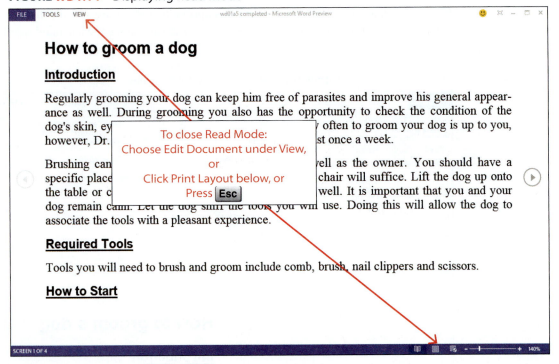

> **TIP**
>
> Rather than switching to the Document Views group on the VIEW tab, you can select a view mode using the buttons on the **Status bar**, located in the bottom right-hand corner of the Word window (see Figure WD1.15) next to the zoom controls. Hold your mouse over each button to display a helpful tooltip that tells you which view mode it activates.

6 When you need a closer look at your document, you can magnify your document using the zoom controls on the Status bar:

Locate the Zoom control in the bottom right-hand corner of the Status bar (Figure WD1.15).

CLICK the Zoom In command (the plus sign) three times to increase zoom 10 percent each time.

To return the magnification level to the previous setting,

CLICK the Zoom Out command (the minus sign) three times.

FIGURE WD1.15 Zoom control bar

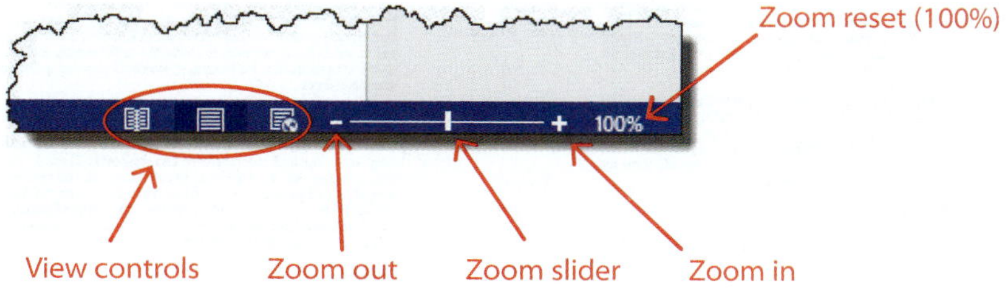

Zoom reset (100%)

View controls   Zoom out   Zoom slider   Zoom in

7 To change the magnification level quickly:

DRAG the Zoom slider (Figure WD1.15) to the right to increase the magnification or to the left to decrease magnification.

You can also click to the right or left of the Zoom slider button on the Zoom slider bar to change the magnification. No matter how you zoom, it does not impact the font size or printing of the document in any way.

8 To quickly see two pages side by side:

CLICK the VIEW tab and locate the Zoom group.

CLICK Multiple Pages.

(*Result:* Two pages appear side by side as shown in Figure WD1.16.)

9 To return to the normal 100 percent zoom:

CLICK on the Zoom Reset line appearing midway on the Zoom slider bar seen in Figure WD1.15 (this line marks the 100 percent position)

or

CLICK the 100% command in the Zoom group.

(*Result:* The screen returns to the 100 percent size.)

FIGURE WD1.16 Multiple Pages zoom showing side-by-side pages

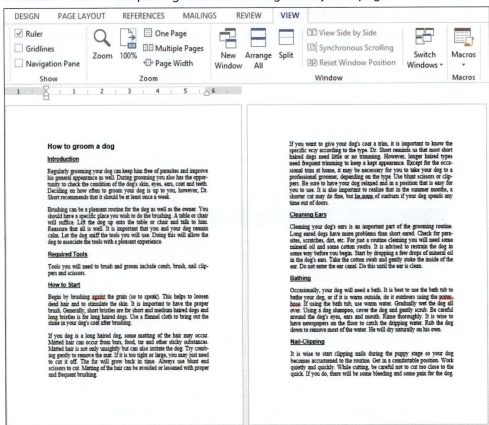

10 To use a preset magnification view:

CLICK the Zoom factor indicator (the percentage to the right of the plus sign, see Figure WD1.15)

This opens the Zoom dialog box (see Figure WD1.17).

CLICK the Many pages button (Figure WD1.17).

SELECT the *1×3 pages* option (hover your mouse to see the names of the options).

CLICK the OK button to accept the changes.

FIGURE WD1.17 The Zoom dialog box

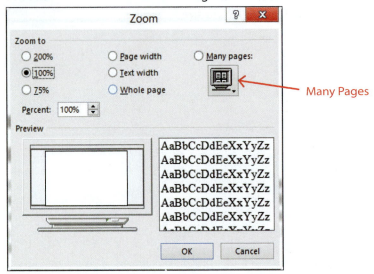

11 Your document window should now appear similar to Figure WD1.18. Before proceeding, save the **wd01a1-handout.docx** file.

FIGURE WD1.18 Completion of Lesson Word 1A5

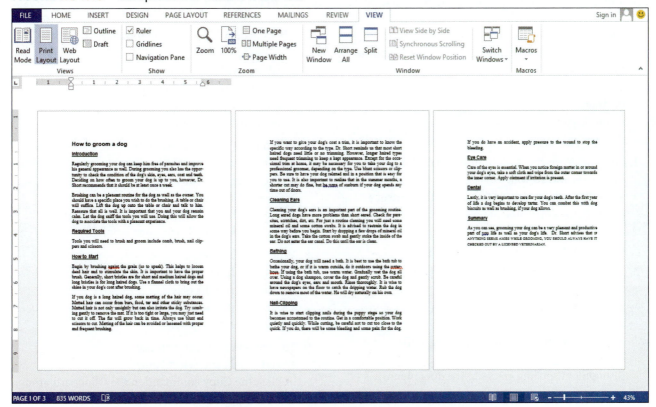

MULTIPLE-CHOICE QUIZ

Select the best choice in the following questions to review the project concepts. Good luck!

1. Clicking and holding your mouse on a selected section of text, and then moving the text to another location is called
   a. double-clicking.
   b. dragging.
   c. modifying.
   d. copying.

2. Holding down the `Ctrl` button and clicking your mouse on a word will
   a. position the mouse at the end of the sentence.
   b. select the entire line of text.
   c. copy the word to the clipboard.
   d. select the entire sentence.

3. Holding down the `Ctrl` button and pressing the letter `A` will
   a. select the entire document.
   b. select the entire paragraph.
   c. move the cursor to the beginning of the document.
   d. highlight spelling errors in the document.

4. Which of the following is NOT one of Word's text justification options?
   a. Align Right
   b. Align to Page
   c. Align Left
   d. Justify

5. The preset margin choice called "Normal" sets the page margins at
   a. 1 inch all around.
   b. 0.75 inch all around.
   c. 1 inch left and right, 0.75 inch top and bottom.
   d. 0.75 inch left and right, 1 inch top and bottom.

6. Clicking on a tab across the top of the screen activates a
   a. ribbon with groups of commands.
   b. ribbon with drop-down menu choices.
   c. command.
   d. None of these is correct.

7. When the zoom factor is set to 75%, it shows the page of the document at
   a. the actual size when printed.
   b. 75% of the space on the screen.
   c. 75% of the horizontal space of the screen.
   d. 75% of the actual size when printed.

8. When text is copied, it is
   a. copied onto the Clipboard.
   b. deleted from its place.
   c. pasted into the next place the mouse is clicked.
   d. All of these are true.

9. To copy selected text, you can
   a. right-click and select Copy.
   b. click the Copy command in the Clipboard group.
   c. press `Ctrl` + `C`.
   d. All of these are correct.

10. Dragging the Zoom slider to the left will
    a. decrease the magnification level.
    b. increase the magnification level.
    c. enlarge the viewing window.
    d. None of these is correct.

In this exercise, you will open an existing document and make some changes to prepare it for printing. You will be provided with specific tasks, but not step-by-step instructions. The final document is shown in Figure WD1.19.

FIGURE WD1.19 Work It Out WD-1A-E1: completed

1. Locate and open the exercise data file **wd01a-ex01.docx**. Save the file as **wd01a-hw01.docx**.

2. Change all the text in the document to Arial, 12 point size.

3. Set the page margins of the document to the following:

   Left margin = 2"

   Right margin = 1.5"

   Top and bottom margins = 1.0"

4. Fully justify the text of the entire document so that both left and right margins form straight vertical lines.

5. Move the first sentence of the document (beginning with "Developed by the President's") below the document title ("Making a Commitment"). Leave a blank line above and below the sentence you have just moved.

6. Reduce the size of the text for the author's credits (the same sentence you just moved) to 10 points.

7. Change the font of the document title to Verdana, 16 point size.

8. Modify the remaining headings of the document so they are all underlined and bold.

9. Automatically hyphenate the document.

10. Save and then close the document file.

In this exercise, you will open an existing document and make some changes to prepare it for printing. You will be provided with specific tasks, but not step-by-step instructions. The final document is shown in Figure WD1.20.

FIGURE WD1.20 Work It Out WD-1A-E2: completed

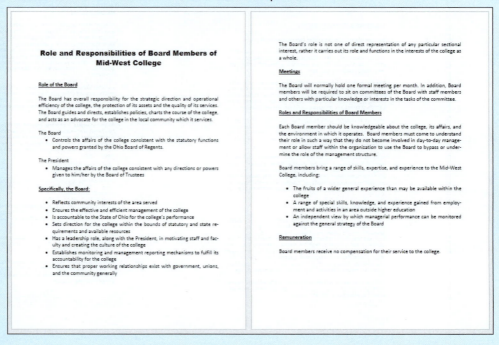

1. Locate and open the exercise data file **wd01a-ex02.docx**. Save the file as **wd01a-hw02.docx**.

2. Select the text of the entire document and change the text's font typeface to Calibri, point size 14.

3. Change the alignment of the entire document so that it is justified between the left and right margins, also called *block justification*.

4. Select the title, which starts with "Role and Responsibilities of Board."
   Change the font typeface to Arial Black with a point size of 18. Center the text.

5. Move the third paragraph, which starts with "The President" (and includes the bulleted sentence and blank line below it), to directly in front of the fifth paragraph that starts with "The Board has overall."

6. Set the page margins to 1-inch all around.

7. Hyphenate the entire document.

8. Apply boldface and underlines to the document subtitles:
   Role of the Board
   Specifically, the Board:
   Meetings
   Roles and Responsibilities of Board Members
   Remuneration

9. Drag the entire paragraph (including the blank paragraph marker after it) that starts with "The Board has overall responsibility for" above the third paragraph (the first bulleted paragraph that starts with the title "The Board"). Refer to the finished example for clarification.

10. Save and then close the document file.

HANDS-ON EXERCISE: WORK IT OUT WD-1A-E3

In this exercise, you will open an existing document and make changes to prepare it for printing. You will be provided with specific tasks, but not step-by-step instructions. The final document is shown in Figure WD1.21.

FIGURE WD1.21 Work It Out WD-1A-E3: completed

1. Locate and open the exercise data file **wd01a-ex03.docx**. Save the file as **wd01a-hw03.docx**.

2. Change the font of the entire document to Arial Narrow, point size 12.

3. Adjust the left margin to 2 inches.

4. Change the justification to left-aligned.

5. Use the automatic feature to hyphenate the document.

6. Change the existing subheadings ("Introduction," "Top Vulnerabilities to Windows Systems," "Immediate Attention," and "Sources") to Arial Black.

7. Cut and paste the section "Top Vulnerabilities to Windows Systems" (including the heading, the bulleted list, and the extra blank line below it) from the first page to the second page in front of the heading "Sources."

8. Add a title to the top of the document by typing **Attacks on Operating Systems**.

9. Make this new title Arial Black, 18 points in size and ensure it is on its own line as seen in Figure WD1.21.

10. Save and then close the document file.

Finishing Touches for the Handout

You will prepare this project for printing by adding final touches such as font color, drop caps, and text effects—all of which add energy to the document's appeal. You will also find your way around the document with the Find command. Combining Find with Replace, you can correct some wording along the way. Then, to reduce chances of an error slipping through, you will use the Spelling and Grammar checking feature to remove mistakes and analyze the level of the writing. When that is all done, you are ready to print.

PROJECT FILE: *Available at* **www.mhhe.com/office2013projectlearn**

After completing this project, you will be able to:

- Change font color, insert a drop cap, and use Text Effects.

- Create and control bulleted and numbered lists.

- Use Find and Replace to search and correct a document.

- Use Spelling and Grammar check and analyze Readability Statistics.

- Print a document using various options.

Font Color and Effects

LESSON OVERVIEW

Word provides easy ways to add energy to your document's appearance. With the increase in color printing available to so many, writers can utilize the expressive nature of colors to increase impact. Word also allows for time-tested techniques such as **drop caps** to provide a professional appearance to any document. One of Word's greatest advantages is that many of these features include preset options that can save you time and take advantage of professional designers. Among these are the set of **Text Effects** that will instantly intensify the visual interest of a document title or heading.

SKILLS PREVIEW

Add Text Effects	• CLICK the HOME tab and locate the Font group. CLICK Text Effects (A) button and choose the desired preset effect.
Adjust Text Effects	• CLICK the HOME tab and locate the Font group. CLICK Text Effects (A). SELECT the effect you wish to adjust: Outline, Shadow, Reflection, or Glow. CHOOSE from preset options or set your own adjustments.
Insert a Drop Cap into a paragraph	• CLICK the INSERT tab and locate the Text group. CLICK the Drop Cap button (A≣ Drop Cap ▾). CHOOSE the desired style.
Adjust Drop Cap settings	• CLICK the INSERT tab and locate the Text group. CLICK the Drop Cap button (A≣ Drop Cap ▾). SELECT Drop Cap Options and adjust the font, lines to drop, or distance from text.
Change color of Drop Cap	• DOUBLE-CLICK on the Drop Cap to select it. CLICK the Font Color button. CHOOSE desired color.
Change color of selected text	• CLICK the HOME tab and locate the Font group. CLICK the Font Color button. CHOOSE desired color.

PROJECT PRACTICE

1 Word has many built-in formatting commands that can add instant energy to your document. One of the easier to use is Text Effects. Locate and open the project data file **wd01b1.docx**. Save the file as **wd01b1-handout2.docx**.

2 To add text effects to this document title:

SELECT the title, "How to groom a dog."

CLICK the HOME tab and locate the Font group.

CLICK Text Effects command (A) to show the drop-down list (see Figure WD1.22).

SELECT Gradient Fill—Blue, Accent 1, Reflection.

CLICK the Bold command.

CLICK the Center command.

(*Result:* This changes the text color to blue with a faded reflection beneath the title. Also, the entire title is bolded and centered across the document.)

3 Let's add more effects to the title using the Text Effects command.

SELECT the title, "How to groom a dog."

CLICK on the Text Effects command.

CLICK on the Glow option.

CHOOSE Orange, 8 pt glow, Accent color 2.

(*Result:* The title now includes a glow. Don't worry about the blue and orange colors; you will fix them later.)

 MORE INFO

The Text Effects command has many other choices and each choice has many options such as outline, shadow, reflection, and glow. Each of these options also has options. Word allows you to create your own combination of text effects. Feel free to experiment.

FIGURE WD1.22   Applying Text Effects

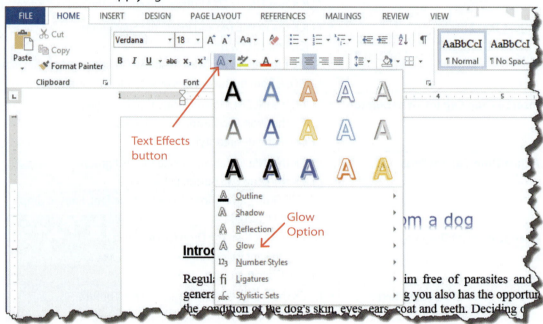

4 Another dramatic feature is a drop cap at the beginning of a paragraph. To prepare the document for this enhancement, let's remove the section title "Introduction":

SELECT the entire line with the word *Introduction*.

PRESS [Delete] (sometimes labeled [Del] on your keyboard).

(*Result:* This step removes the section title permanently, unlike the Cut command, which removes the selection but puts a copy on the Clipboard. Fortunately, you can undo a mistaken deletion.)

5 To insert a drop cap into a paragraph:

Position the cursor anywhere within the first paragraph.

CLICK the **INSERT** tab and locate the Text group.

CLICK the Drop Cap command (see Figure WD1.23).

SELECT Dropped.

(*Result:* Notice that the first letter of the paragraph becomes much larger and "drops" down a few lines. By default, this command drops the letter down three lines and wraps the text around it, as shown in Figure WD1.23.)

FIGURE WD1.23 Inserted drop cap and Drop Cap dialog box

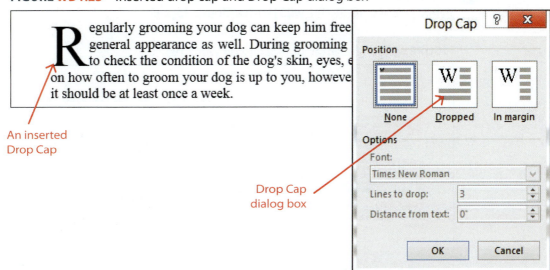

An inserted
Drop Cap

Drop Cap
dialog box

6 You can adjust the Drop Cap settings very easily.
With your cursor still in the first paragraph:

CLICK the Drop Cap command.

SELECT the Drop Cap Options.

SELECT 4 in the Lines to drop spin box (click the top arrow once).

CLICK OK.
(*Result:* The drop cap now drops four lines. When you increase the number of lines to drop, Word will enlarge the first letter to fill the space.)

7 Let's change the color of the font in the document's headings. This can be very effective if used sparingly. To change the color of text:

Select all the headings in this document (they are bold and underlined).

CLICK the HOME tab and locate the Font group.

CLICK the Font Color command (**A ▾**) drop-down arrow.

CHOOSE Red.
(*Result:* All the headings in the document are now changed to that color.)

8 Let's change the color of the title and the drop cap to match the headings.

Select the title "How to groom a dog."

Notice the Font Color button has retained the last color change made. You don't have to drop down the menu and choose red again.

CLICK the Font Color command (not the drop-down list).
(*Result:* The title retains all the other attributes of the text effects, but the font and the reflection change to Red.)

9 To change the color of the drop cap:

DOUBLE-CLICK the single letter "R" to select it.

CLICK the Font Color command.
(*Result:* Again, the same color as before is applied to the drop cap.)

10 Your document should now appear similar to Figure WD1.24, if displayed using multiple pages. Before proceeding, save the **wd01b1-handout2.docx** file.

FIGURE WD1.24   Completion of Lesson Word 1B1

How to groom a dog

Regularly grooming your dog can keep him free of parasites and improve his general appearance as well. During grooming you also has the opportunity to check the condition of the dog's skin, eyes, ears, coat and teeth. Deciding on how often to groom your dog is up to you, however, Dr. Short recommends that it should be at least once a week.

Brushing can be a pleasant routine for the dog as well as the owner. You should have a specific place you wish to do the brushing. A table or chair will suffice. Lift the dog up onto the table or chair and talk to him. Reassure that all is well. It is important that you and your dog remain calm. Let the dog sniff the tools you will use. Doing this will allow the dog to associate the tools with a pleasant experience.

Required Tools

Tools you will need to brush and groom include comb, brush, nail clippers and scissors.

How to Start

Begin by brushing against the grain (so to speak). This helps to loosen dead hair and to stimulate the skin. It is important to have the proper brush. Generally, short bristles are for short and medium haired dogs and long bristles is for long haired dogs. Use a flannel cloth to bring out the shine in your dog's coat after brushing.

If you dog is a long haired dog, some matting of the hair may occur. Matted hair can occur from burs, food, tar and other sticky substances. Matted hair is not only unsightly but can also irritate the dog. Try combing gently to remove the mat. If it is too tight or large, you may just need to cut it off. The fur will grow back in time. Always use blunt end scissors to cut. Matting of the hair can be avoided or lessened with proper and frequent brushing.

If you want to give your dog's coat a trim, it is important to know the specific way according to the type. Dr. Short reminds us that most short haired dogs need little or no trimming. However, longer haired types need frequent trimming to keep a kept appearance. Except for the occasional trim at home, it may be necessary for you to take your dog to a professional groomer, depending on the type. Use blunt scissors or clippers. Be sure to have your dog relaxed and in a position that is easy

for you to use. It is also important to realize that in the summer months, a shorter cut may do fine, but be ware of sunburn if your dog spends any time out of doors.

Cleaning Ears

Cleaning your dog's ears is an important part of the grooming routine. Long eared dogs have more problems than short eared. Check for parasites, scratches, dirt, etc. For just a routine cleaning you will need some mineral oil and some cotton swabs. It is advised to restrain the dog in some way before you begin. Start by dropping a few drops of mineral oil in the dog's ears. Take the cotton swab and gently stoke the inside of the ear. Do not enter the ear canal. Do this until the ear is clean.

Bathing

Occasionally, your dog will need a bath. It is best to use the bath tub to bathe your dog, or if it is warm outside, do it outdoors using the waterhose. If using the bath tub, use warm water. Gradually wet the dog all over. Using a dog shampoo, cover the dog and gently scrub. Be careful around the dog's eyes, ears and mouth. Rinse thoroughly. It is wise to have newspapers on the floor to catch the dripping water. Rub the dog down to remove most of the water. He will dry naturally on his own.

Nail-Clipping

It is wise to start clipping nails during the puppy stage so your dog becomes accustomed to the routine. Get in a comfortable position. Work quietly and quickly. While cutting, be careful not to cut too close to the quick. If you do, there will be some bleeding and some pain for the dog. If you do have an accident, apply pressure to the wound to stop the bleeding.

Eye Care

Care of the eyes is essential. When you notice foreign matter in or around your dog's eyes, take a soft cloth and wipe from the outer corner towards the inner corner. Apply ointment if irritation is present.

Dental

Lastly, it is very important to care for your dog's teeth. After the first year of life a dog begins to develop tartar. You can combat this with dog biscuits as well as brushing, if your dog allows.

Bulleted Lists

LESSON OVERVIEW

One of the best ways to draw attention to an important set of items is to create a list. Word makes it easy to generate a vertical list using either bullets or numbers. Each list can be modified to include its own indentation and bullet styles. Although almost any image can be used to create bullets, Word generally considers the use of images and symbols separate from the use of numbers. A bulleted list has many more options than a numbered list. These options allow you to instantly use preset bullets or to create your own style.

SKILLS PREVIEW

Create a bulleted list	• SELECT the vertical text you wish to bullet. CLICK the HOME tab and locate the Paragraph group. CLICK the Bullets drop-down menu (☰▾).
Change bullet style	• CLICK the HOME tab and locate the Paragraph group. CLICK the Bullets drop-down menu (☰▾). CHOOSE from the bullet library.
Define your own bullet	• CLICK the HOME tab and locate the Paragraph group. CLICK the Bullets drop-down menu (☰▾). CHOOSE Define New Bullet. CHOOSE Symbol. SELECT the desired font. CLICK the desired image.
Insert numbered bullets	• SELECT the vertical text you wish to bullet. CLICK the HOME tab and locate the Paragraph group. CLICK the Numbered Bullets drop-down menu (☰▾).
Change numbered bullet style	• CLICK the HOME tab and locate the Paragraph group. CLICK the Numbered Bullets drop-down menu (☰▾) CHOOSE from the bullet library, or CHOOSE Define New Number Format and choose from the available options.
Change the indent of a bulleted list	• CLICK Increase Indent (☲), or CLICK Decrease Indent (☲).

PROJECT PRACTICE

1 To begin, ensure that **wd01b-handout2.docx** is open.

2 Let's make the items needed for dog grooming stand out using a bulleted list under the section marked "Required Tools." First, let's change the horizontal list into a vertical list.

CLICK your mouse in front of the word "comb."

PRESS Enter.

Add a colon immediately after the word "include."

Delete the period after the word "scissors."

(*Result:* The list is now separated from the introductory sentence.)

3 To create a bulleted list:

SELECT the new line (comb, brush, nail clippers, and scissors).

CLICK the HOME tab and locate the Paragraph group (see Figure WD1.25).

CLICK the Bullets command (▤ ▾).

(*Result:* A bullet and default indentations are applied to the sentence.)

4 To move each of the individual items into separate bullets:

INSERT `Enter` after each word (comb, brush, nail clippers, and scissors).

Delete extra spaces, commas, and the extra word "and" using Figure WD1.25 as a guide. Change any items that may have automatically capitalized themselves back into lowercase words.

FIGURE WD1.25   Inserting bullets

5 To adjust the amount of indentation quickly:

SELECT the entire bulleted list.

CLICK the Increase Indent command (▤) (Figure WD1.25) twice.
(*Result:* Each time you click the command, the indentation of the list is increased. Each time you click the Decrease Indent command (▤), the list moves to the left.)

6 To change the image of bullets:

SELECT the entire bulleted list.

CLICK the Bullets drop-down arrow.

CHOOSE the bullet that looks like a check mark.
(*Result:* All the bullets instantly change to check marks. If you had selected only one bullet, only that bullet would have been affected.)

7 Let's look for a more appropriate image to use as a bullet. Each font style has its own set of characters that can be inserted. Be sure the entire bulleted list is still selected.

To define a different image as a bullet:

CLICK the Bullets drop-down menu.

CHOOSE Define New Bullet.

CHOOSE Symbol.

CLICK the drop-down button next to Fonts.

CHOOSE Webdings from the list.

Along the bottom row for this font is a tiny dog (you may have to scroll down).

CLICK on the dog.

PRESS OK, twice.

(*Result:* The check marks are replaced with the dog-shape bullets.)

8 When the order of the list is important, use numbered bullets. Let's move to the "Bathing" section of the document and create a numbered list there.

CLICK in front of the word "Gradually."

PRESS Enter.

CLICK in front of the words "It is wise to have newspapers."

PRESS Enter.

CLICK anywhere in the newly created paragraph that begins with "Gradually wet the dog."

CLICK the Numbering command ().

Separate the bullets the same way as you did earlier (using Figure WD1.26 as a guide). Because these bullets are complete sentences, ensure each one starts with a capital letter and ends with a period.

FIGURE WD1.26 Numbered bullets

Bathing

Occasionally, your dog will need a bath. It is best to use the bath tub to bathe your dog, or if it is warm outside, do it outdoors using the waterhose. If using the bath tub, use warm water.

1. Gradually wet the dog all over.
2. Using a dog shampoo, cover the dog and gently scrub.
3. Be careful around the dog's eyes, ears and mouth.
4. Rinse thoroughly.

Numbered list

It is wise to have newspapers on the floor to catch the dripping water. Rub the dog down to remove most of the water. He will dry naturally on his own.

9 To check out the options available for numbered lists:

CLICK the Numbering drop-down menu.

CLICK the drop-down arrow on the Numbering command.

Here you can choose from predesigned numbering lists or even define your own format. You can also control the numbering value if you want to continue numbering from a previous list or set your own starting number value.

10 Your document should now appear similar to Figure WD1.27, if displayed using the Multiple Pages view. Before proceeding, save the **wd01b1-handout2.docx** file.

FIGURE WD1.27 Completion of Lesson Word 1B2

Find and Replace

LESSON OVERVIEW

Because the words you type into a word processing program are really just a string of characters and symbols, it is easy for Word to search for unique combinations of text in your documents. Not only can you locate text instantly (using the **Find** command), but you can also ask Word to replace the found text with a new word (or group of words) in a single command. This feature improves your productivity and efficiency in working with any word processing application.

SKILLS PREVIEW

Find a word(s) in a document	• CLICK the HOME tab and locate the Editing group. CLICK the Find button (🔍). TYPE in the word(s) you are looking for. The **Navigation pane** opens showing where the word(s) appear.
Replace a word(s) in a document	• CLICK the HOME tab and locate the Editing group. CLICK the Replace button (🔤). TYPE the word(s) you want to be replaced in the "Find what" window. TYPE the replacement word(s) in the "Replace with" window. CLICK Replace or Replace All.
Modify search criteria	• CLICK the HOME tab and locate the Editing group. CLICK the Replace button (🔤). CLICK the More button. CHOOSE the options you wish to use (such as Match case, Find whole words only).
Add formatting to search and/or replace criteria	• CLICK the HOME tab and locate the Editing group. CLICK the Replace button (🔤). CLICK the More button. CLICK Format or Special buttons and select from the options available.

PROJECT PRACTICE

1. The Find command can help you locate a certain word (or string of words) instantly no matter what size the document. This can save time and improve accuracy. To begin, ensure that **wd01b-handout2.docx** is open.

2. Move the cursor to the top of the document because Word searches from the location of the cursor "down" through the document.

   To find a specific string of text in a document:

   CLICK the HOME tab and locate the Editing group.

   CLICK the Find command (🔍).

   TYPE mineral oil into the Search Document text box.
   (*Result:* Word quickly locates and highlights the occurrences of the text in the document. To move to the actual location of the word, click on one of the matches in the Navigation window.)

3 You want to replace the word *type* with the word *breed*. First use the Find feature to see if there are any problems with such a replacement.

CLICK the HOME tab and locate the Editing group.

CLICK the Find command ().

TYPE **type** into the Search Document text box.

(*Result:* Word quickly locates the occurrences of the word in the document.)

> ⚠️ **CAUTION**
>
> Notice that the second occurrence found for the word *type* is actually the plural word *types*. This is not a problem as *types* would become *breeds*. By default, Word will find the string of letters even if it occurs within the middle of a word (e.g., it would locate *type* in the word *stereotypes* if it were in the document. Changing it would result is the new word *stereobreeds*.) Therefore, you must be careful in finding and replacing text, especially when making document-wide changes.

4 Let's replace the word *type* with *breed*. Ensure the cursor is at the top of the document.

To automatically replace a string of text:

CLICK the HOME tab and locate the Editing group.

CLICK the Replace command (). (See Figure WD-1.28.)

TYPE **type** into the Find what window, if it isn't already there from the last search.

PRESS [Tab] to move to the next text box.

TYPE **breed** into the Replace with window.

CHOOSE Replace All.

(*Result:* Word tells you that it completed its search of the document and found the word *type* and replaced it with the word *breed* three times.)

CLICK OK.

CLICK CLOSE

FIGURE WD1.28 The Find and Replace dialog box

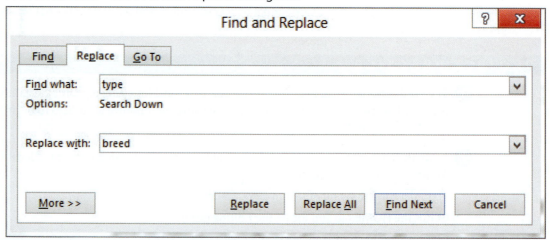

> ℹ️ **MORE INFO**
>
> Notice the command buttons at the bottom of the **Find and Replace** dialog box in Figure WD1.28. The Replace button allows you to replace each occurrence of the word one at a time (so you can be sure each one is correct). The Replace All button lets you replace all occurrences of the word. And, the Find Next button asks Word to simply locate the next occurrence of the word. The More >> button provides advanced options and Cancel closes the dialog box.

5 The correct spelling of the veterinarian should be Dr. Shoret, not Dr. Short. Check again to see if changing all occurrences of *short* to *Shoret* would work.

Use the Find feature to locate the occurrences of *short* in the document (see Figure WD1.29).

You'll notice that although the occurrences of *Dr. Short* show up, so does the word *short* in reference to short-haired dogs and short bristles. Therefore, you will not be able to use the Replace All feature as you did in the previous step because short-haired dogs will become "Shoret-haired dogs."

FIGURE WD1.29 Find results for the word *short*

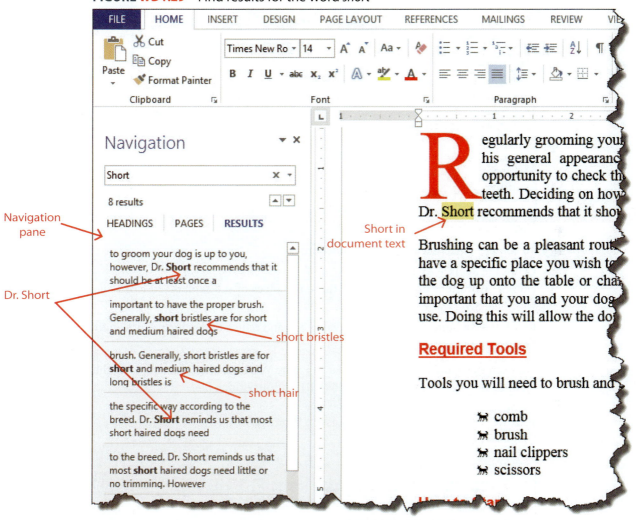

6 You can modify your Find requirements to find the word *Short* only when it starts with a capital letter (as in the doctor's name).

Start the Replace feature as before, to find *Short* and replace with *Shoret* (be sure to type in the capital "S") as in Figure WD1.30.

To modify search criteria:

CLICK the More >> button in the Find and Replace dialog box.

CLICK the check box next to Match case.

Now Word will search only for instances of the word *Short* that match the case typed in (that is, with a capital first letter.)

FIGURE WD1.30 Correcting the misspelling of a person's name

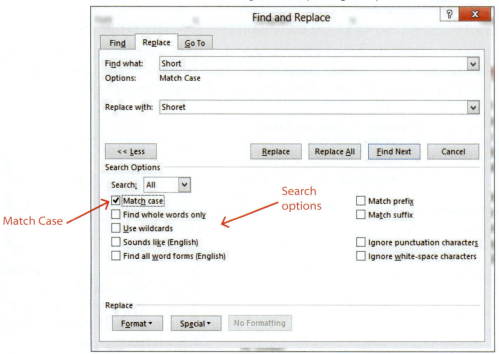

⑦ To complete the Find and Replace function:

CLICK the Replace All button.

(*Result:* Word tells us that it found three instances of the capitalized word *Short* and replaced it with *Shoret*.)

CLICK the OK button to remove the dialog box and return to the document window.

CLICK CLOSE.

Your screen should now appear similar to Figure WD1.31, once again showing the Multiple Pages view. Before proceeding, save the **wd01b1-handout2.docx** file.

FIGURE WD1.31 Completion of Lesson Word 1B3

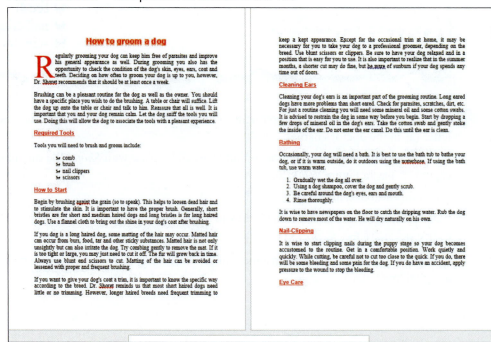

Spelling, Grammar, and Readability Statistics

LESSON OVERVIEW

Word provides excellent tools to help you write more clearly and accurately. Allowing Word to check both the spelling and grammar of your writing can improve the readability and professionalism of your document. You can even ask Word to offer spelling and grammar suggestions as you type.

When Word doesn't recognize a word, it underlines it with a wavy red line. When Word suspects a grammar error, it underlines it with a wavy green line. When Word suspect the wrong word may have been used (contextual spelling), it underlines it with a wavy blue line. This allows you to make corrections if needed.

Furthermore, Word can analyze your document to identify how easy it is to read and assign a grade level to your sentence structure and writing style. This makes it simple to evaluate your writing to see if it matches your intended audience.

SKILLS PREVIEW

Check spelling in a document	• CLICK the REVIEW tab and locate the **Proofing** group. CLICK **Spelling and Grammar** button (ABC✓). CHOOSE the appropriate action for each error: Change, Change All, Ignore, Ignore All, or Add to dictionary.
Setting proofing options	• CLICK the FILE tab. SELECT Options. CLICK Proofing and adjust or activate desired settings in the "When correcting spelling and grammar in Word" section. CLICK OK.
Check grammar in a document	• CLICK the FILE tab. SELECT Options. CLICK Proofing and ensure Check Grammar with Spelling box is checked. CLICK OK and run Spell check.
Analyze Readability Statistics	• CLICK the FILE tab. SELECT Options. CLICK Proofing and ensure Show Readability Statistics is turned on. CLICK OK and run Spell check.

PROJECT PRACTICE

① To begin, ensure that **wd01b-handout2.docx** is open.

② To adjust settings for spelling, grammar, and readability:

CLICK the FILE tab to display the Backstage view shown in Figure WD1.32.

SELECT Options.

CLICK Proofing.

LOCATE the section marked "When correcting spelling and grammar in Word" (see Figure WD1.33).

SELECT any empty check boxes to ensure that all five check boxes are selected.

CLICK OK.

FIGURE WD1.32 Selecting the Options command in Backstage view

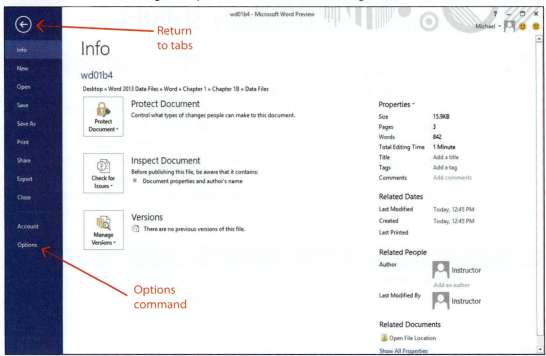

FIGURE WD1.33 Setting options for proofing your document

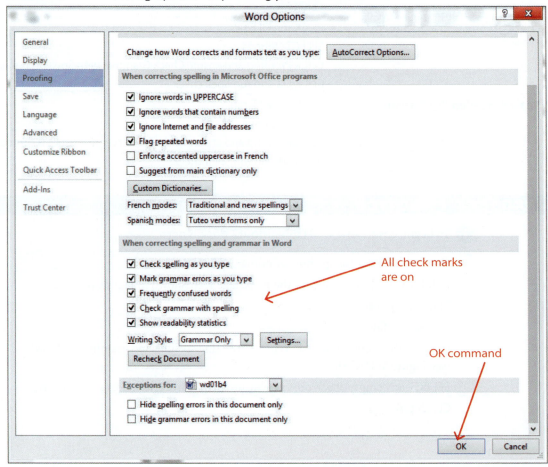

3 Ensure your cursor is at the top of the document.

To begin the Spelling and Grammar check:

CLICK the REVIEW tab and locate the Proofing group.

CLICK the Spelling and Grammar command as shown in Figure WD1.34 (or PRESS [F7]).
(*Result:* The Spelling and Grammar pane will appear with words or phrases appearing in the pane. Remember, one of the settings you selected in the Proofing options was to "Check grammar with spelling," so this will do both.)

FIGURE WD1.34   The Spelling and Grammar button on the REVIEW ribbon

Spelling &
Grammar Check

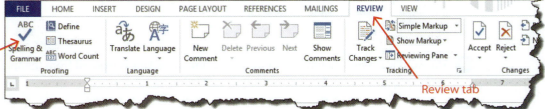

4 The word *Shoret* is not recognized by the dictionary (see Figure WD1.35). Because it is spelled correctly, let's add it to Word's dictionary.

To add a word to the dictionary:

CLICK Add to add this word to Word's Dictionary
(*Result:* By adding this name into Word's dictionary, it will recognize it in the future and not flag it as a spelling error.)

FIGURE WD1.35   The Spelling and Grammar Checker

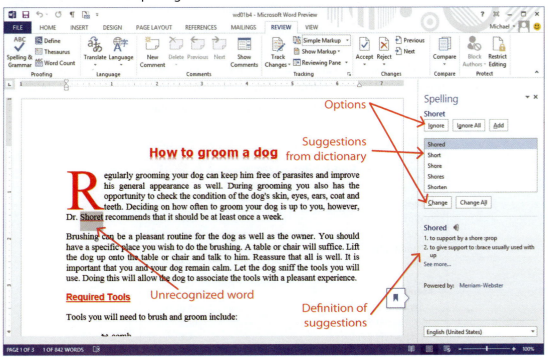

5 The next problem is *againt*. It should be the word *against*. That is one of Word's suggestions.

To replace a flagged word to one of the suggested words:

Ensure the correct suggestion is selected.

CLICK Change.

6 The two words *be ware* appear in blue underline. Although both are words on their own, Word's contextual spelling function (which you turned on in step 2) suspects that the word *beware* might be more appropriate. Word is correct.

CLICK Change.

7 The word *waterhose* should be two words. Be sure *water hose* is selected from the spelling suggestions.

CLICK Change.

8 Word uses its grammar function to suggest the word *you* should be *your*. Again, it is correct.

CLICK Change.

9 Once Word has completed its spelling and grammar check, it will display the **Readability Statistics** (see Figure WD1.36) because you turned this option on at the beginning of this lesson.

Some of the data, such as counts and averages, is obvious. Other statistics are not as obvious.

The higher the Flesch Reading Ease index is (it goes as high as 100.0), the easier the document is to read. The Flesch-Kincaid Grade Level indicates this document is written around a Grade 5 level. This helps the writer determine if the complexity of the writing is proper for the target audience.

CLICK OK, when finished analyzing the Readability Statistics.

FIGURE WD1.36   The Readability Statistics evaluation window

Readability Statistics	
Counts	
Words	833
Characters	3594
Paragraphs	30
Sentences	64
Averages	
Sentences per Paragraph	4.0
Words per Sentence	12.5
Characters per Word	4.1
Readability	
Passive Sentences	3%
Flesch Reading Ease	80.6
Flesch-Kincaid Grade Level	5.1

MORE INFO

You can also make quick changes to individual spelling and grammar errors. Simply place your mouse on top of a word that appears with a wavy underline, and then right-click the word to display a shortcut menu of suggested corrections. Make your choices from that shortcut menu.

10 Your document should now appear similar to Figure WD1.37, if displayed using the Multiple Pages view. Before proceeding, save the **wd01b1-handout2.docx** file.

FIGURE WD1.37 Completion of Lesson Word 1B4

How to groom a dog

Regularly grooming your dog can keep him free of parasites and improve his general appearance as well. During grooming you also has the opportunity to check the condition of the dog's skin, eyes, ears, coat and teeth. Deciding on how often to groom your dog is up to you, however, Dr. Shoret recommends that it should be at least once a week.

Brushing can be a pleasant routine for the dog as well as the owner. You should have a specific place you wish to do the brushing. A table or chair will suffice. Lift the dog up onto the table or chair and talk to him. Reassure that all is well. It is important that you and your dog remain calm. Let the dog sniff the tools you will use. Doing this will allow the dog to associate the tools with a pleasant experience.

Required Tools

Tools you will need to brush and groom include:

- comb
- brush
- nail clippers
- scissors

How to Start

Begin by brushing against the grain (so to speak). This helps to loosen dead hair and to stimulate the skin. It is important to have the proper brush. Generally, short bristles are for short and medium haired dogs and long bristles is for long haired dogs. Use a flannel cloth to bring out the shine in your dog's coat after brushing.

If you dog is a long haired dog, some matting of the hair may occur. Matted hair can occur from burs, food, tar and other sticky substances. Matted hair is not only unsightly but can also irritate the dog. Try combing gently to remove the mat. If it is too tight or large, you may just need to cut it off. The fur will grow back in time. Always use blunt end scissors to cut. Matting of the hair can be avoided or lessened with proper and frequent brushing.

If you want to give your dog's coat a trim, it is important to know the specific way according to the breed. Dr. Shoret reminds us that most short haired dogs need little or no trimming. However, longer haired breeds need frequent trimming to

keep a kept appearance. Except for the occasional trim at home, it may be necessary for you to take your dog to a professional groomer, depending on the breed. Use blunt scissors or clippers. Be sure to have your dog relaxed and in a position that is easy for you to use. It is also important to realize that in the summer months, a shorter cut may do fine, but beware of sunburn if your dog spends any time out of doors.

Cleaning Ears

Cleaning your dog's ears is an important part of the grooming routine. Long eared dogs have more problems than short eared. Check for parasites, scratches, dirt, etc. For just a routine cleaning you will need some mineral oil and some cotton swabs. It is advised to restrain the dog in some way before you begin. Start by dropping a few drops of mineral oil in the dog's ears. Take the cotton swab and gently stoke the inside of the ear. Do not enter the ear canal. Do this until the ear is clean.

Bathing

Occasionally, your dog will need a bath. It is best to use the bath tub to bathe your dog, or if it is warm outside, do it outdoors using the water hose. If using the bath tub, use warm water.

1. Gradually wet the dog all over.
2. Using a dog shampoo, cover the dog and gently scrub.
3. Be careful around the dog's eyes, ears and mouth.
4. Rinse thoroughly.

It is wise to have newspapers on the floor to catch the dripping water. Rub the dog down to remove most of the water. He will dry naturally on his own.

Nail-Clipping

It is wise to start clipping nails during the puppy stage so your dog becomes accustomed to the routine. Get in a comfortable position. Work quietly and quickly. While cutting, be careful not to cut too close to the quick. If you do, there will be some bleeding and some pain for the dog. If you do have an accident, apply pressure to the wound to stop the bleeding.

Eye Care

Printing Your Document

LESSON OVERVIEW

When you have the content and formatting of a document just the way you like, it is time to specify the various options for printing it. While some of these **print** options may be limited by the capabilities of your printer, most of the options described here are standard. When you are ready to proceed, you can choose to print one page, print all pages in the document, print a specific range of pages, or simply preview the document on-screen, which may help to identify visible errors before wasting paper.

SKILLS PREVIEW

Activate Print Preview	• CLICK the FILE tab. SELECT Print from menu. Preview appears on the right-hand side of screen.
Print a document	• CLICK the FILE tab (or PRESS **Ctrl** + **P**). SELECT Print from menu. CLICK the Print button.
Set number of copies to print	• CLICK the FILE tab. SELECT Print from menu. SELECT desired number of copies in the Copies box. CLICK the Print button.
Print current page only	• CLICK the FILE tab. SELECT Print from menu. CLICK Print All Pages button. CHOOSE Print Current Page. CLICK the Print button.
Print specific pages	• CLICK the FILE tab. SELECT Print from menu. TYPE the pages you wish to print in the Pages box using commas to separate pages and dashes to select a range (1,5 or 3-6). CLICK the Print button.
Print to a different printer	• CLICK the FILE tab. SELECT Print from menu. SELECT Printer from the Printer drop-down menu. CLICK the Print button.
Print on both sides of paper	• CLICK the FILE tab. SELECT Print from menu. CLICK Print One Sided. CLICK Manually Print on Both Sides. CLICK the Print button.

1 To begin, ensure that **wd01a-handout2.docx** is open.

2 To view the print options:

CLICK the FILE tab to display Backstage view (see Figure WD1.38).

SELECT Print from the menu.

(*Result:* This step brings up the **Print Preview pane**, also shown in Figure WD1.38).

FIGURE WD1.38 The Print Page showing the settings and the Print Preview pane

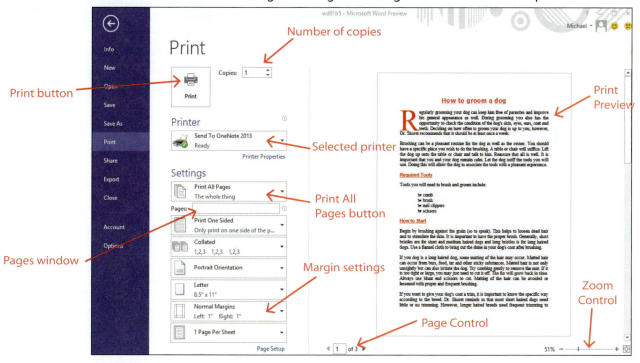

3 Be sure the printer is turned on.

To send your document to that printer:

CLICK the Print button.

(*Result:* The printer will print one copy of the entire three-page document to the default printer.)

4 Word offers many options and controls for customizing how you print documents.

To print more than one copy of the current page:

SELECT **2** in the Copies box.

CLICK the drop-down arrow on the Print All Pages button (Figure WD1.38).

CHOOSE the Print Current Page option.

CLICK the Print button.

(*Result:* Word sends two copies of the first page of the document to the printer.)

 MORE INFO

Many of the buttons on the Print page will change their names to reflect their current setting. For example, the Print Pages button appears as Print All Pages at first (that is Word's default option). But if you drop-down the menu and choose another option, the name on the button will retain the last action as its new name. So in our example, after choosing the Print Current Page option, the Print All Pages button will appear as Print Current Page until another option is chosen.

5 You do not have to print pages in order.

To select a custom print range:

CLICK the mouse into the Pages box (Figure WD1.38).

TYPE **1,3** (including the comma).

CLICK the Print button.

(*Result:* The comma tells Word to print page 1 and page 3, but to skip page 2.)

TABLE WD1.1   Print Options

Print Option	Result of Printing
Print All Pages	Every page of the document will print.
Print Selection	Only areas that you have selected with your mouse will print.
Print Current Page	Only the page displayed in the Preview window will print.
Custom Print	Only the specific pages or range of pages will print.

6 To print to a different printer:

CLICK the Printer drop-down button (see Figure WD1.39, although your list may differ).

CHOOSE the printer you wish to use.

CLICK the Print button.

FIGURE WD1.39   Selecting a target printer

TABLE WD1.2   Controls available from the Settings drop-down options

Settings Buttons	Resulting Options
Print All Pages	Print all pages, current page, specific page or pages, printing only odd or even pages.
Print One Sided	Choose to print the document one-sided or double-sided.
Collated	If more than one copy is requested, you can decide if you want the pages collated or not.
Portrait Orientation	Changes the **orientation** of the page to portrait or landscape.
Letter	Changes how the printer will print depending on the size of the paper in the printer.
Normal Margins	Allows you to access the Page Margins again. This button would say "Custom Margins" if we had used our own margin settings.
1 Page Per Sheet	Automatically resizes the document during printing to allow for printing more than one page per sheet. Options include 2, 4, 6, and more pages per sheet.

7 This document would be much easier to handle if it were two pages that could be printed on one double-sided handout.

To modify the margin settings from the Print Preview page:

CLICK the Margins Settings button (which may read "Normal Margins" or "Custom Margins").

CHOOSE Narrow.

(*Result:* The Page Control indicator shows that this document now fits on two pages.)

8 To view the next page in the Print Preview pane:

CLICK the Next Page arrow at the bottom of the Print Preview pane (see Figure WD1.38).

(*Result:* You will now see a preview of the second page. This document fits nicely on two pages with the Narrow margin setting.)

9 To print the final version of this document:

SELECT 1 in the Copies spin box.

CLICK Print One Sided button.

SELECT Print on Both Sides (it may say "Manually Print on Both Sides" depending on the configuration of your printer.

CLICK the Print button.

(*Result:* The document will print out on two pages and the screen will return to the HOME tab.)

MORE INFO

If you want, you can change the settings to Manually Print on Both Sides. This means that after you print one side, you can feed the same page back into the printer, so it can print the next page on the other side. This usually takes a little practice to ensure you are feeding the paper correctly the second time.

---

10 Your document should now appear similar to Figure WD1.40 if displayed using the Multiple Pages view. Before proceeding, save the wd01a1-handout2.docx file.

FIGURE WD1.40 Completion of Lesson Word 1B5

MULTIPLE-CHOICE QUIZ

Select the best choice in the following questions to review the project concepts. Good luck!

1. The icon on the HOME tab that looks like a pair of binoculars is the
   a. replace command.
   b. find command.
   c. magnify command.
   d. None of these is correct.

2. One of the fastest ways to move your cursor to the top of a document is to
   a. double-click the ruler at the top of the screen.
   b. hold down the `Ctrl` button and double-click.
   c. press `Shift` + `Home`.
   d. press `Ctrl` + `Home`.

3. The Find and Replace dialog box can be set so that it will find
   a. only words with matching case.
   b. only words in bold.
   c. only words one at a time.
   d. All of these are correct.

4. By default, Word searches a document from
   a. the top of the document to the bottom.
   b. the current place of the cursor to the top of the document.
   c. the current place of the cursor to the bottom of the document.
   d. None of these is correct.

5. Spell check controls and options are found
   a. by clicking the FILE tab, clicking Options, and clicking Proofing.
   b. by right-clicking the REVIEW tab.
   c. by right-clicking on the Spelling and Grammar command.
   d. All of these are correct.

6. Spelling and Grammar check can be started quickly by
   a. right-clicking on a page and choosing Run Spell Check.
   b. pressing the `F7` key.
   c. pressing `Ctrl` + `Shift`.
   d. All of these are correct.

7. The Print Preview window can be opened by
   a. pressing `Alt` + `P`.
   b. clicking Print on the HOME tab.
   c. clicking on the FILE tab and choosing Print.
   d. right-clicking in the border of a document and choosing Print.

8. The orientation of a page can be changed from
   a. the Print Preview pane.
   b. the PAGE LAYOUT tab.
   c. double-clicking the gray area of the ruler.
   d. All of these are correct.

9. To print just the first, fourth, fifth, and eighth pages of a document, you would use which of these for the custom range?
   a. 1-4, 5-8
   b. 1,4,5-8
   c. 1,4-5,8
   d. 1,4:5,8

10. Word can analyze your document and identify
    a. how many sentences are duplicates.
    b. the number of active sentences in a document.
    c. the grade level of the writing.
    d. All of these are correct.

In this exercise, you will open an existing document and make changes to prepare it for printing. You will be provided with specific tasks, but not step-by-step instructions. The final document is shown in Figure WD1.41

FIGURE WD1.41   Work It Out WD-1B-E1: completed

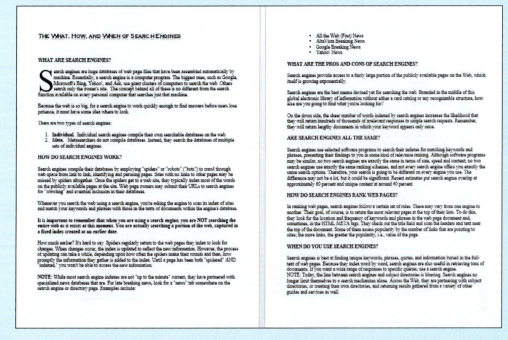

1. Locate and open the project data file **wd01b-ex01.docx**. Save the file as **wd01b-hw01.docx**.

2. Apply a text effect to the title (Gradient Fill – Gray). Add Tight Reflection, touching to the title using the additional Text Effects options. Change font color to black.

3. Insert a drop cap into the third paragraph, which starts with "Search engines are huge." Make this drop cap drop four lines into the text.

4. Locate the list of four news sources just above the heading "What Are the Pros and Cons of Search Engines." Turn these into a bulleted list with square bullets. Indent them to the 1.25-inch mark (the bullets themselves will be at the 1-inch mark).

5. The word *Web* has been misspelled a few times as the word *wed*. Correct these errors by using Find and Replace.

6. Set the proofing options so that Word will check spelling and grammar as you type, check grammar with spelling, and show readability statistics.

7. Run the Spelling and Grammar check. Make the following corrections, while ignoring all others:

   Change the spelling mistake *datbases* to *databases*.

   Change the spelling mistake *oftin* to *often*.

   Change the contextual spelling mistake *shear* to *sheer*.

   Change the spelling mistake *relevent* to *relevant*.

   Change the grammar mistake *Search engines is* to *Search engines are*.

8. Set the margins of the document to 1-inch for top and bottom margins and 0.75-inches for left and right margins.

9. Set the document to print two copies.

10. Save and close the document file.

In this exercise, you will open an existing document and make changes to prepare it for printing. You will be provided with specific tasks, but not step-by-step instructions. The final document is shown in Figure WD1.42.

FIGURE WD1.42   Exercise Work It Out WD-1B-E2: completed

1. Locate and open the exercise data file **wd01b-ex02.docx**. Save the file as **wd01b-hw02.docx**.

2. Change the font of the title to Tahoma, point size 18. Center the title across the page.

3. Apply the following text effect to the title: *Fill – White, Outline – Accent 2, Hard Shadow – Accent 2.*

4. Insert a drop cap into the first paragraph below the title, which starts with "Up until recently." Set the drop cap to drop two lines.

5. Use the Find and Replace feature to:

   Find the words *home based* and replace them all with *home-based.*

   Find the word *cellar* and replace it with *basement.*

6. Locate the two lists under the heading "Is a Home Based Business Right for You?" Change both lists to be bulleted lists using check marks as bullets. Increase the indent of both lists to the 1-inch mark (the bullets will be at the 0.75 inch mark).

7. In the Proofing section of the Word Options window, ensure that all of the proofing options are selected in the *When correcting spelling and grammar in Word* section.

8 Run the Spelling and Grammar check. Make the following corrections, while ignoring all others:

Change the grammar mistake *finds* to *find*.

Change the spelling mistake *seperate* to *separate* twice.

Change the spelling mistake *spose* to *spouse*.

Change the grammar mistake *you has* to *you have*.

Examine and accept the Readability Statistics.

9 Set the document to print on both sides of the paper.

10 Save and close the document file.

HANDS-ON EXERCISE: WORK IT OUT WD-1B-E3

In this exercise, you will open an existing document and make changes to prepare it for printing. You will be provided with specific tasks, but not step-by-step instructions. The final document is shown below in Figure WD1.43.

FIGURE WD1.43 Work It Out WD-1B-E3: completed

Preparing a Plain Text Resume

Preparing your resume for e-mail is really an easy process. Anyone creating a resume should take the extra few minutes needed to generate a plain text version while still at the computer. Most word processors and resume-writing programs will let you save a file to plain text. The next step, altering the format, is simple.

Please note that these instructions assume that your resume is in MS Word for Windows. If your resume is in another word processing application or on a different computer platform like Macintosh, you may need to consult your word processing manual for specific instructions.

Step 1: Save Your Resume as a Text Only document. After converting your resume to Text Only, what appears in your document window is your resume stripped of any fancy formatting. You is now ready to make a few final adjustments before posting it online:

Step 2: Check keywords. Make sure you have all the keywords that define your job qualifications.

Step 3: Delete any references to "page two," "Continued," or your name or head on page 2. You are making your resume appear as one continuous electronic document.

Step 4: Use all CAPS for words that need special emphasis. For the best overall effect, use all caps sparingly and judiciously, highlighting only what you really want to have stand out.

Step 5: Replace each bullet point with a standard keyboard symbol. Suggested replacements are:

- Dashes (-)
- Plus signs (+)
- Single or Double Asterisks (*) (**)

Use the Space Bar, not the Tab Key, to place a single space immediately after each symbol (and before the words). Allow the lines to wrap naturally at the end of a line. Don't put a forced return (don't push the Return or Enter key) if it's not the end of the statement and don't indent the second line of a statement with the Space Bar.

Step 6: Use straight quotes in place of curly quotes. To do this, select the text that includes the quotes you want to change. Click Format in your tool bar and select AutoFormat. Click the Options button, and make sure Replace Straight Quotes With Smart Quotes is not selected under both the AutoFormat and AutoFormat As You Type tabs. Then click OK to exit the AutoFormat box, and your curly quotes will be changed to straight quotes.

Step 7: Rearrange text if necessary. Do a line-by-line review of your document to make sure there are no odd-looking line wraps, extra spaces, or words scrunched together in the body, making adjustments accordingly. This may require inserting commas between items that were once in columns and are now in paragraph format because tabs and tables disappeared when the document was converted to Text Only.

Now that you have the ***Plain Text Resume for Posting***, it takes just a few more steps to create a perfect ***Plain Text Resume for E-mailing***. Again, if you take the time to do this now, you will save yourself a lot of time later.

Step 8. Limit line lengths. Because each e-mail software has its own the length of lines, your message may not look as good when it is read by a potential employer. To avoid this problem, limit each line to no more than 65 characters, including spaces. To do this:

1. Open MS Word, click Open, select the file named "ResTextOnly.txt," and click Open. **Warning: If you open the resume document by clicking on its icon in the directory, it will be opened in Notepad -- not what you want right now.**
2. Select the entire document and change the font to Courier, 12 pt.
3. Go to File in your toolbar and click Page Setup. Set the left margin at 1 inch and the right margin at 1.75 inches. (Yahoo e-mail users set your right margin at 2.5 inches.)

Step 9: Save as Text Only with Line Breaks. To save changes you made in Step 8, you must convert your Text Only document one more time by doing the following:

- With your Text Only resume document open, click File in your tool bar and select Save As.
- Type in a new name for this document in File Name, such as "ResTextBreak."
- Directly under this is the Save As Type pull-down menu. From this list, select "Text Only with Line Breaks (*.txt)."
- Click Save to perform the conversion.
- Now close the document and exit MS Word.
- Reopen the resume document (ResTextBreak.txt) by clicking on its icon in the directory. That will open it as a Notepad document.

Step 10: Copy the entire text in your ResTextBreak.txt document that you've opened in Notepad, and paste it in the body of the e-mail message.

Before sending your resume to an employer, run a test by sending it to yourself and to a friend to see how it looks after going through the Internet. This will help you identify any additional formatting problems you need to correct before you start sending it out to possible employers.

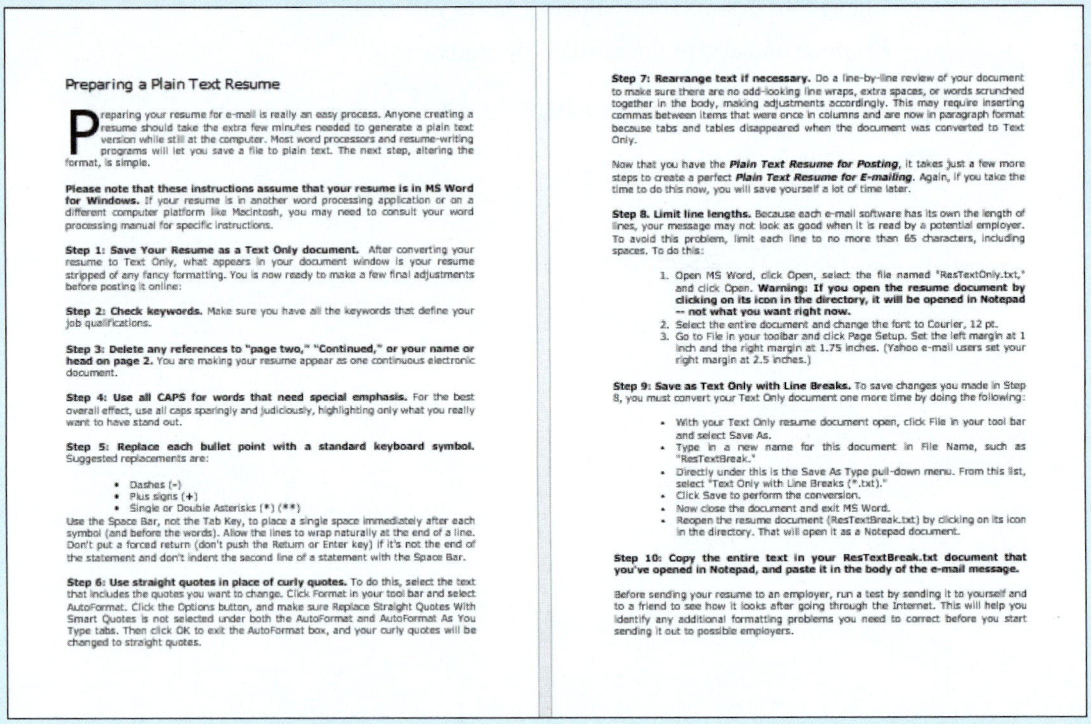

1. Locate and open the exercise data file **wd01b-ex03.docx**. Save the file as **wd01b-hw03.docx**.
2. Align the text for the entire document to be (block) justified.
3. Apply the following text effect to the title: *Fill – Black, Text 1, Shadow*. Add the Glow effect *Blue, 5 pt. glow, Accent color 5*.
4. Insert a drop cap into the first paragraph, which starts with "Preparing your resume for e-mail." Set the *Lines to drop* to 4.
5. Find and replace the word *email* with the word *e-mail*.
6. Locate *Step 5 in the document*. Change the vertical list (Dashes, Plus signs, Single or Double Asterisks) to a bulleted list with round black dots as bullets.
7. Indent this list so the bullets sit at the 0.75-inch mark.
8. Run the Spelling and Grammar check. Make the following corrections, while ignoring all others:

   Change the spelling *anothr* to *another*.

   Change the grammar mistake *You is* to *You are*.

   Change the spelling mistake *Eter* to *Enter*.

   Change the grammar mistake *Step 8.* to *Step 8:*.

   Review and accept the readability statistics.
9. Set the document to print in **Landscape** orientation.
10. Save and then close the document file.

Chapter Summary

Word provides so many powerful features that many documents that once were fashioned only by professionals are now produced easily by almost anyone. Faculty, students, the self-employed, administrative personnel, and even the boss in the corner office can not only produce and edit the content they want, but they also can control the design and formatting as well. In addition to removing such barriers, Word has also proven to be one of the biggest cost-saving advantages for businesses of all sizes.

Besides entering, editing, and deleting text, Word allows you to adjust page margins, choose from a variety of font typefaces and styles, add special effects to text, and view all of your changes instantaneously. In this chapter, you learned to use the zoom controls and the advantages of different views. Copy, Paste, and Undo commands were demonstrated for changing the document structure and moving all types of elements around the document, without fear of making a mistake. The Find and Replace feature allowed you to make changes quickly and easily from one end of the document to the other. Even adding a drop cap to add interest is easy and adjustable. The built-in Spelling and Grammar tools, along with Readability Statistics, ensured that your writing was professional and targeted in both appearance and substance.

Chapter Key Terms

Backstage view, p. W-5
Bold, p. W-13
Center-align text, p. W-14
Click, p. W-4
Deselect, p. W-5
Dialog box, p. W-12
Double-click, p. W-4
Drag, p. W-3
Drop cap, p. W-31
Drop-down, p. W-10
Find, p. W-39
Find and Replace, p. W-40
Font typeface, p. W-4
Group, p. W-12

Italic, p. W-12
Justify text, p. W-16
Landscape, p. W-56
Left-align text, p. W-4
Margins, p. W-16
Mouse, p. W-4
Navigation pane, p. W-39
Nonadjacent selection, p. W-14
Orientation, p. W-50
Print, p. W-48
Print Preview pane, p. W-49
Proofing, p. W-43
Quick Access toolbar, p. W-8
Read Mode, p. W-4

Readability statistics, p. W-43
Ribbon, p. W-4
Ruler, p. W-21
Select, p. W-4
Selection bar, p. W-4
Show/Hide command, p. W-20
Size, p. W-4
Spelling and Grammar checker, p. W-43
Status bar, p. W-22
Text effects, p. W-31
Triple-click, p. W-4
Underline, p. W-13
Zoom, p. W-20

On Your Own Exercise WD-1C-E1

This project provides the opportunity to practice the most important skills covered in this chapter, regardless of the project in which they were introduced. As the chapters progress, these comprehensive projects will become more challenging, building on all of the skills covered to that point.

Let's get started! In this project, you will create another professional handout—this time for a doctor's office or medical clinic. You can make your own decisions unless specifically told what to do. An idea of what the finished project may look like is shown Figure WD1.44.

FIGURE WD1.44 Professional Handout: Sample of finished version

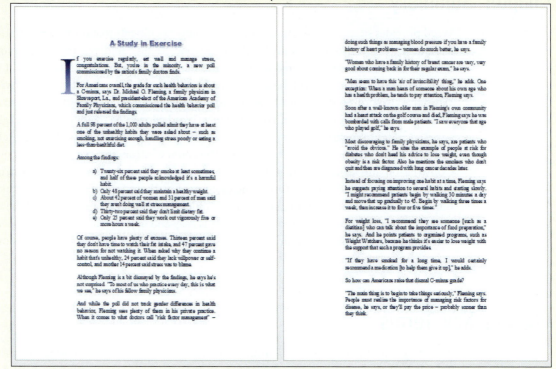

Open the file **wd01cp1.docx** and save it as **wd01cp1-handout.docx**. Change the font of the document to something easier to read and use an 11 or 12 point size. Add the title of **A Study in Exercise**. Add a few text effects to the title to make it stand out. Justify the body of the text. Move the paragraph starting with "Of course, people have plenty" in front of the paragraph that begins with "Although Fleming is a bit dismayed." Maintain the proper spacing between the paragraphs.

Turn the five indented lines below the phrase "Among the findings:" into a numbered list. Use a numbering format that is different from the default. Place a drop cap in the first paragraph and use the In Margin setting. Make sure the drop cap has the same text effect as the title.

Use Find and Replace to change all the occurrences of *females* to *women*. Correct the spelling and grammar errors throughout the document. Set it to print three copies using both sides of the paper. Save and close the document, unless directed to print it by your instructor.

On Your Own Exercise WD-1C-E2

This project provides the opportunity to practice the most important skills covered in this chapter, regardless of the project in which they were introduced. As the chapters progress, these comprehensive projects will become more challenging, building on all of the skills covered to that point.

Let's get started! In this project, you will create another professional handout—this time for a Building Supply Store. You can make your own decisions unless specifically told what to do. An idea of what the finished project may look like is shown Figure WD1.45.

FIGURE WD1.45 Building Store Handout: Sample of finished version

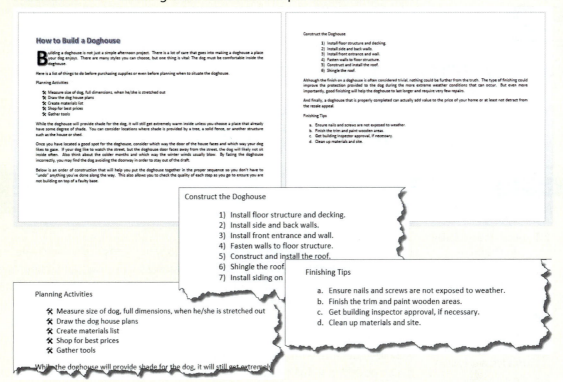

After launching Microsoft Word, locate and open the project data file **wd01cp2.docx**. Save the document as **wd01cp2-handout.docx**. Change the font to Calibri, 13 point. Add a title to the document: **How to Build a Doghouse**. This title should have a text effect and an outline effect added to it.

Justify the text for an even edge on both margins, and hyphenate the document. Move the first paragraph (starts with "Here is a list of things") beneath the second paragraph (starts with "Building a doghouse is not just").

Locate the five sentences after the heading "Planning Activities" and convert them to a vertical bulleted list using a different symbol as bullet. Change the paragraph directly after the heading "Construct the Doghouse" into seven numbered steps (using numbered bullets) in a vertical list. Increase the indent of this list so the bullets sit at 0.75 inches on the ruler. Change the final list (under the heading "Finishing Tips") to a numbered list using lower-case letters as shown in the insert on Figure WD1.45.

Insert a drop cap into the first paragraph. Change the color and effects of the drop cap to match the title's effects. Correct all spelling and grammar errors. Set the document to print using both sides of the paper. Change the orientation of the document to Landscape.

Save and close the document, unless directed to print it by your instructor.

2

Writing a
Research Paper

One of the most important things you will do with Microsoft Word is create and manage large documents. Reports, plans, professional applications, and many more documents likely will be required of you as soon as you enter a new job or start your postsecondary education.

Word 2013 has many built-in and easy to customize features for organizing long documents. Creating a cover page can be done manually or you can use one of Word's built-in designs. With a few modifications, you can make it your own. Page numbers can be added to the header or footer of a page to help readers find their way. Page numbers can be controlled and will automatically renumber themselves when you add or delete material and pages. While Word automatically creates new pages as needed, you can decide precisely where pages end and begin with what is called **hard page breaks**. For even more control, **section breaks** provide the ability to format an entire section of a document without affecting the other sections. **Headers and footers** are the areas at the top and bottom of a page that repeat throughout the document.

Other powerful features for use in larger documents include the ability to designate text as **headings** of various levels. These headings can use identical styles throughout the document and be easily updated or changed. These headers are also key in producing an automatic **table of contents** that can be updated in a flash when pages are added or deleted. **Footnotes** and **endnotes** provide the additional details to a document, and Word will automatically renumber them and keep them on the correct page as the document develops. The citation of material is controlled through Word's **Manage Sources** feature, providing shortcuts for citing material and also allowing you to build a bibliography formatted for the writing styles of APA, MLA, Chicago, Harvard, or other styles.

PROJECT
Writing a Research Document

In this project, you will add functional features and research references to an existing proposal. Place the finished version of this document into your career portfolio and title it "Word: Research Document."

This chapter will help you develop the ability to add the structure required for longer, professionally reviewed reports. This set of skills is needed at any level of professionalism from student to chief executive officer.

THE SITUATION
Peritia College Education Proposal

Peritia College is planning to offer Associate of Arts and Associate of Applied Science in Business Management degrees at off-campus centers. A proposal of the plan has been written. To prepare it for printing, you have been asked to add a cover page, page numbers, headers and footers, a table of contents, and, most importantly, references for the research that was done.

Generating and Modifying a Cover Page

To begin, you will work on ensuring an existing proposal has the proper functional features. This will entail creating a cover page, inserting page numbers, applying section breaks, and adding headers and footers to the report. Also, once these features are included, you will learn to format them and control how they operate across a multi-page document.

PROJECT FILE: *Available at* **www.mhhe.com/office2013projectlearn**

PROJECT OBJECTIVES

After completing this project, you will be able to:

- Generate and modify a cover page.

- Insert and format page numbers.

- Control page and section breaks to format the document.

- Create page headers and footers.

- Edit headers and footers and control them across multiple sections.

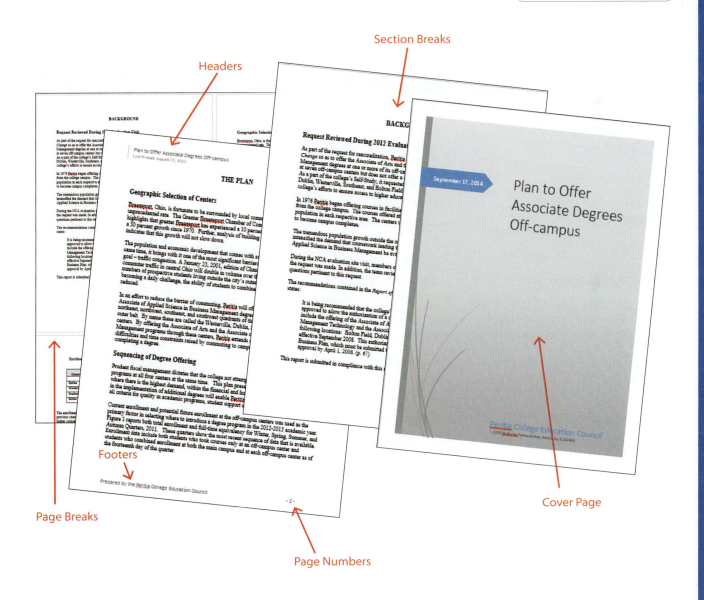

Headers

Section Breaks

Page Breaks

Footers

Page Numbers

Cover Page

Generating and Modifying a Cover Page

LESSON OVERVIEW

The first impression any report makes is from the cover page. You can labor long hours trying to get just the right impact for that first impression, or you can let Word provide direction with its automatic **Cover Pages** feature. These cover pages are professionally designed so you can select the one with the layout, information, and color scheme that best suit the work you are presenting. But that's just the beginning. You can make these preset designs your own by modifying the elements quickly and easily.

The preset cover page provides **placeholders** to allow you to format and control each element separately.

Common placeholders include: Title, Author, Abstract, Company Name, and Address. Word also uses a **Date Picker** to insert a date on a cover page. This feature allows you to pick the date from a calendar to reduce the chance of error.

Placeholders will automatically fill with information that is provided within the properties of the document. If you wish to change the text in a placeholder, just click on it and add your new text. When you change from one cover page to another, any information you have entered (or is generated by the document properties) will automatically fill the appropriate placeholder on the new cover page design.

SKILLS PREVIEW

Customize the Status bar	• RIGHT-CLICK on the Status bar. CHOOSE the options you wish to activate.
Insert a cover page	• CLICK the INSERT tab and locate the Pages group. CLICK Cover Page (📄 Cover Page ▾). CHOOSE the desired style.
Change a cover page to another style	• CLICK the INSERT tab and locate the Pages group. CLICK Cover Page (📄 Cover Page ▾). CHOOSE the new style. The page will instantly change to the new style.
Modify a placeholder	• CLICK into the placeholder. TYPE the new information.
Remove unneeded placeholders	• CLICK on the unwanted placeholder to activate it. CLICK the dots on the tab (⠿ Phone) to select the placeholder itself. PRESS Delete on the keyboard.
Use the Date Picker placeholder	• CLICK the Date arrow to display a calendar. CLICK to the desired month and day.
Insert a placeholder	• CLICK the INSERT tab and locate the Text group. CLICK Quick Parts. CHOOSE Document Property. CHOOSE the desired placeholder.

1 When an existing file is opened, the Status bar (after a brief delay) will provide general, but important information such as the number of pages, the word count, and if any proofing errors were found in the document. To see the Status bar information, locate and open the project data file **wd02a1.docx**. Save the file as **wd02a1-associatesdegree.docx**.

> ### *i* MORE INFO
>
> The spell checking process can be started by clicking the "Proofing errors were found" button in the Status bar. This will activate the Spelling pane as discussed in Lesson B4 of Chapter 1.

2 To add or remove (customize) what shows on the Status bar:

RIGHT-CLICK the mouse anywhere along the Status bar (see Figure WD2.1).

The items that are "checked" will appear along the Status bar when they are available.

CLICK Formatted Page Number to activate it (if it isn't).

CLICK Section to activate it (if it isn't).

CLICK away from the menu to return to the main window.

FIGURE WD2.1 Status bar information with Customize Status Bar menu

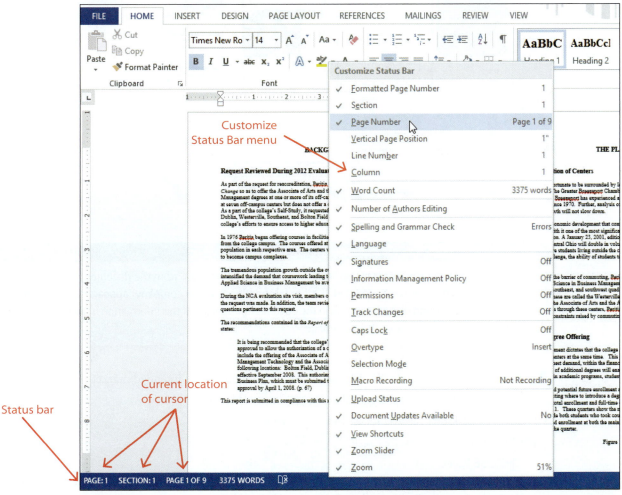

3 This document needs a cover page. It does not matter where your cursor is for this action. A cover page will always appear at the beginning of the document.

To insert a cover page:

CLICK the INSERT tab and locate the Pages group.

CLICK Cover Page (Cover Page).

CHOOSE Grid from the menu (see Figure WD2.2).

(*Result:* A cover/title page is inserted at the beginning of the document. It contains placeholders for you to fill in specific information.)

FIGURE WD2.2 Cover Page menu of predesigned cover pages

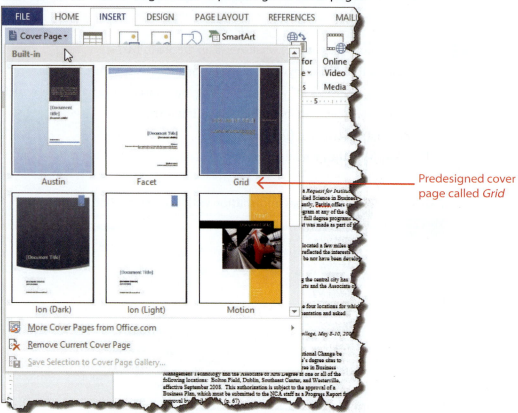

Predesigned cover page called *Grid*

4 You decide that this style of cover page is not quite right for the intended market.

To change one cover page to another (in this case to Facet):

CLICK the INSERT tab and locate the Pages group.

CLICK Cover Page (Cover Page).

CHOOSE Facet.

(*Result:* The first cover page is replaced by the new one. This new design is better because it includes the author's name: Peritia College Education Council.)

5 This cover page offers many placeholders for information. Placeholders are automatically formatted to match the style of the cover page. Let's fill in a few of them.

CLICK on the Abstract placeholder and type:

A business plan to offer the associate of arts and the associate of applied science in business management degrees at off-campus centers.

CLICK on the Company Address placeholder and type:

2200 Endicore Parkland Ave, Kentucky, IL 61943

6 Let's remove the unneeded placeholder.

To delete a placeholder:

CLICK on the Company Name placeholder (see Figure WD2.3) to activate the field.

CLICK the dots on the tab that says Company (Company) to select the placeholder itself.

PRESS Delete on the keyboard.

(*Result:* The placeholder is gone. This will prevent the placeholder from appearing when the document is printed.)

FIGURE WD2.3 Cover page with various placeholders

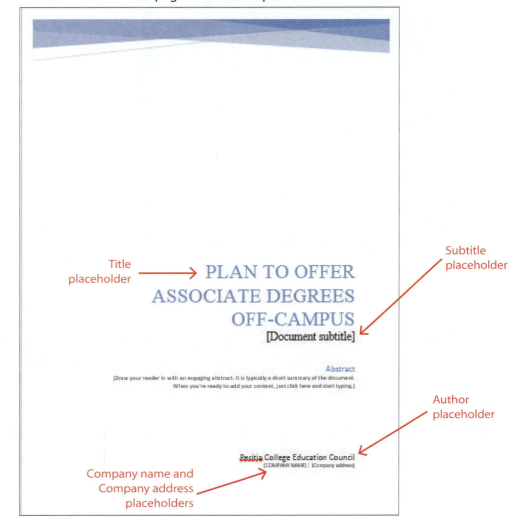

7 This cover page is good, but it doesn't provide a placeholder for the date.

CLICK the INSERT tab and locate the Pages group.

CLICK Cover Page ( ).

CHOOSE Whisp.

(*Result*: The cover page instantly changes to the new design, but all the information you have just entered remains and is adjusted to meet the new style and formatting.)

8 This cover page offers a date placeholder. It uses an advanced feature of Word called Date Picker (see Figure WD2.4). This allows you to select a date from a calendar menu.

CLICK the drop-down arrow to display a calendar. (Note: You could type a date in directly, if you desired.)

CLICK ahead to September 2014 (or whatever year you wish).

CLICK 17 to insert the date of September 17, 2014.

FIGURE WD2.4 Date Picker

HEADS UP

If the controls that are built in to the placeholders prevent you from making the changes you desire, you can turn them off. To turn off these controls, RIGHT-CLICK on the placeholder and select the Remove Content Control command. But remember the controls cannot be turned on again—the placeholder will have to be inserted (see the accompanying Tip).

9 Once again, remove the unneeded placeholders (Company Name and Document Subtitle).

To change the font size in a placeholder:

SELECT the text in the Author placeholder to bring up the Mini toolbar.

CLICK the Size arrow.

CHOOSE **20**.

10 Your document should appear similar to Figure WD2.5 when in the Multiple Pages view. Save the file.

FIGURE WD2.5   Completion of Lesson Word 2A1

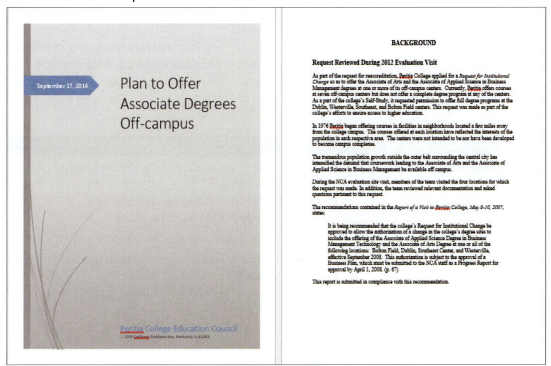

Inserting Page Numbers

LESSON OVERVIEW

One of the most important functional features you can add to a document is **page numbers**. This allows readers to easily find their way and relate specific passages or comments to others. Page numbers are contained in the header and footers of the document. The **Header & Footer view** opens access to headers and footer so you can insert, delete, and format page numbers without affecting the main body of the text. While in this specialized view, the main body text is grayed out and cannot be edited. In return, while working in the main body text of a document, the headers and footers are grayed out and cannot be edited.

Other than the page numbers, material in the headers and footers will be the same on each page of the document. Often the first page of a document is kept clear of page numbers by using the **Different First Page** option. With this option, the first page of the document is treated separately from the rest of the pages. It can include different text or, as is most common, the header and footer can be left blank.

Page numbers can be inserted using predesigned styles and separate formatting. They can appear at the top of the page, the bottom of the page, at the current location of the cursor, and even in the page margins.

Word will automatically number the pages for you. If you later add or delete pages anywhere in the document, Word automatically renumbers the pages for you. Once inserted properly, you don't have to worry about page numbers again—Word does the work.

SKILLS PREVIEW

Insert page numbers	• CLICK the INSERT tab and locate the Header & Footer group. CLICK Page Number. Choose the location of the page number. Choose the style of page number.
Open the Header & Footer view	• DOUBLE-CLICK anywhere in the blank area above or below the main text area.
Close the Header & Footer view	• DOUBLE-CLICK anywhere in the main body of a document to close the Header & Footer view, or • CLICK the Close Header & Footer button (▣) in the right-hand corner of the Header & Footer ribbon.
Control the Different First Page option	• Open the Header & Footer view. Locate the Options group. CLICK the check box to turn the option on or off.
Remove existing page numbers	• CLICK the INSERT tab and locate the Header & Footer group. CLICK the Page Number button. CHOOSE Remove Page Numbers.
Change the formatting of a page number	• Open the Header & Footer view. CLICK the DESIGN tab and locate the Header & Footer group. CLICK on the Page Number button. CHOOSE Format Page Numbers. CLICK the Number Format drop-down arrow. CHOOSE the desired format. CLICK the OK button.
Add text to a page number location	• Open the Header & Footer view. Move the cursor to the desired position. Type the desired text. PRESS the space bar once. CLICK the INSERT tab and locate the Header & Footer group. CLICK the Page Number command. CLICK Current Position. CHOOSE the desired format.

1 Page numbers are important to most professional documents. To begin, ensure that **wd02a1-associatesdegree** is open. Save it as **wd02a2-associatesdegree.docx**.

2 To insert page numbers:

CLICK the INSERT tab and locate the Header & Footer group.

CLICK Page Number.

CLICK Top of Page to reveal the page number styles for the top of the page.

CHOOSE Plain Number 3.

(*Result:* You are moved past the cover page and the page numbers are inserted into the top of the rest of the document. Also, the Ribbon changes to the DESIGN tab under Header & Footer Tools as in Figure WD2.6.)

FIGURE WD2.6   The Header & Footer tools

MORE INFO

When page numbers are inserted this way, the entire view of the document changes to Headers & Footers view. Automatic page numbers are placed into either a header or footer. The dotted line across the top shows the invisible separation between the "text" (or body of the document) and the header or footer (notice the text is now grayed out and not available for editing). While here, any changes you make will affect the page number on every page.

3 To turn off the Headers & Footers view and return to Normal view:

CLICK the Close Header & Footer button () in the right-hand corner of the Ribbon (Figure WD2.6). (*Result:* This returns the document to the Normal view with the page numbers slightly grayed out.) Notice that the cover page does not show a page number. That is quite common in document numbering, although not absolute. Examine the Status bar: While you are on what is numbered as page 1, you are actually on page 2 of 10 (this counter includes the cover page and all pages of the document, no matter how they are numbered).

HEADS UP

Be careful not to click the Close Program button at the top right-hand corner of the screen. That will start to close the program. Although they look similar, the Close Header & Footer button is clearly labeled to avoid confusion.

4 By default, the cover page is page 0 and the number does not show on the cover page.

DOUBLE-CLICK in the header area (on any page) to reenter the Header & Footer view.

Locate the Options group (Figure WD2.6).

Notice the Different First Page option is on (this is why no number shows on Page 0).

5 To move a page number to a different location on the page, it is best to remove the current numbers or you may end up with more than one set of page numbers.

To remove a page number:

CLICK the INSERT tab and locate the Header & Footer group.

CLICK the Page Number button.

CHOOSE Remove Page Numbers ().

6 To insert a new page number format:

CLICK the Page Number button.

CLICK Bottom of Page.

CHOOSE Accent Bar 2.

(*Result:* The new page numbers appear at the bottom of the page in a new format, and the Ribbon changes to the DESIGN tab under Header & Footer Tools.)

ℹ MORE INFO

The drop-down menu for page numbers allows you to choose predesigned formatting that places page numbers at the top, bottom, and even in the margins of your document. If you want a page number to appear in the position your cursor sits currently, choose the option Current Position.

---

7 To change the formatting of a page number:

CLICK the DESIGN tab under Header & Footer Tools and locate the Header & Footer group.

CLICK on the Page Number button to reveal the menu.

CHOOSE Format Page Numbers.

CLICK the Number Format drop-down arrow (see Figure WD2.7).

CHOOSE the second option (numbers with hyphens before and after them).

CLICK the OK button.

(*Result:* The placement and the style of the page numbering is the same, but the numbers themselves have hyphens added before and after them.)

FIGURE WD2.7 Page Number Format dialog box

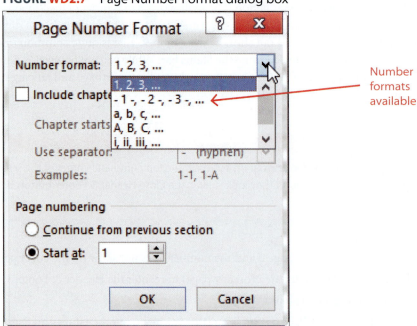

8 Let's put the page numbers in the margin of the document.

Once again, remove the current page numbers from the document.

CLICK the INSERT tab and locate the Header & Footer group.

CLICK the Page Number button.

CLICK Page Margins.

CHOOSE Circle, Right from the bottom of the list.

(*Result:* The new page numbers style appears in the right-hand margin. Although the style is new, it still includes the number format of hyphens before and after the number.)

9 If pages are added or deleted, automatic page numbering will adjust. Let's try it.

CLOSE the Headers & Footers view.

CLICK on the Show/Hide button (¶) to reveal the hidden formatting marks.

SELECT everything on the current Page 1, including the Page Break and paragraph mark next to it (see Figure WD2.8).

PRESS Delete on the keyboard.

(*Result:* The entire Background page is gone. The next page titled "The Plan" now becomes Page 1 and the rest of the document has adjusted its page numbers accordingly.)

FIGURE WD2.8 View showing page numbers in margin, Show/Hide turned on, and entire Page 1 selected

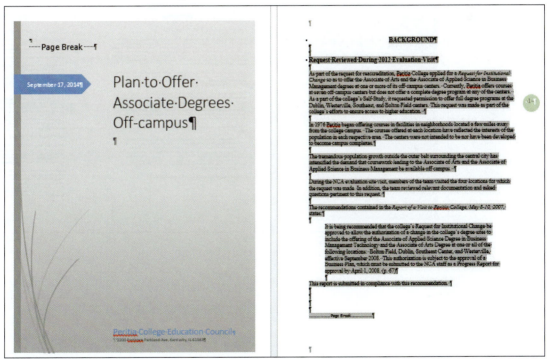

10 CLICK the undo command to return the deleted page to the document.

DESELECT the text.

CLICK the Show/Hide button (¶) off.

11 You can make custom changes to the page numbering and it will show on all page numbers. Remove the current page numbers from the document as done before.

To insert a page number at the cursor location:

DOUBLE-CLICK in the footer area of page 1 to activate the Header & Footer view.

PRESS [Tab] once to center the tab (this is a preset tab in headers and footers).

TYPE **You are now enjoying page**

PRESS the space bar once.

CLICK the INSERT tab and locate the Header & Footer group.

CLICK the Page Number command.

CLICK Current Position.

CHOOSE Plain Number to insert a plain number into the current cursor position.

Every page number in the document is now preceded with the phrase "You are now enjoying page." Also, notice the formatting of the hyphen before and after the number remains from your previous formatting choice.

12 Your document should appear similar to Figure WD2.9 when in the Multiple Pages view. Save the file.

FIGURE WD2.9   Completion of Lesson Word 2A2

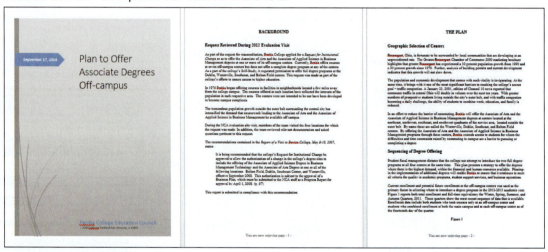

Inserting Breaks and Setting Sections

LESSON OVERVIEW

One of the great time-savers in word processing is the ability to enter text and information knowing you can edit it later. When you get to the end of a line or the bottom of a page, Word automatically starts a new line or new page. While you are constructing your document, it is best to let Word organize your pages for you. These are called **soft breaks**. Because they are "soft," as you add or delete material, Word can adjust and re-create new breaks as it needs to.

A **page break** will force a new page to begin. This way you can control what will appear at the top of a certain page. A **section break** will separate the previous part of the document from the following part by creating a new section that can be controlled and formatted (including page numbers) without having any effect on the other sections. You can create as many sections as you wish. The **next page section break** creates a page break along with the section break.

Page numbers can be formatted and controlled across sections in a number of ways. The numbering can simply continue by using the **Continue from Previous Section** command. Or you can use the **Start at** control to set the page number yourself. The **Format Page Numbers** function allows you to choose from numbers, letters, or Roman numeral formats.

Headers and footers are elements that appear on each page of the document. Page numbers are part of headers or footers. The Different First Page option allows you to have a different header or footer on the first page of a section.

SKILLS PREVIEW

Insert page break	• CLICK your mouse where you would like to insert the page break. CLICK the INSERT tab and locate the Pages group. CLICK Page Break, or • CLICK your mouse where you would like to insert the page break. PRESS `Ctrl` and `Enter` at the same time.
Insert a next page section break	• CLICK your mouse where you would like to insert the next page section break. CLICK the PAGE LAYOUT tab and locate the Page Setup group. CLICK on Breaks to bring down a menu. SELECT Next Page under the Section Breaks area.
Delete a page or section break	• CLICK the mouse in front of the dotted line(s) so that the cursor shows up at the far left of the break. CLICK `Delete`.
Continue page numbering from previous section	• CLICK the INSERT tab and locate the Header & Footer group. CLICK Page Number. CLICK Format Page Numbers. SELECT Continue from Previous Section. CLICK OK.
Turn Different First Page option on or off	• Open the Header & Footer view. GO TO Options group. CLICK the check box to turn the Different First Page option on or off.
Format page numbers differently in a section	• CLICK the cursor into the section you would like to change. CLICK the INSERT tab and locate the Header & Footer group. CLICK Page Number. CLICK Format Page Numbers. CLICK the drop-down arrow in the Number Format window. SELECT the desired option.

PROJECT PRACTICE

1 By default, as you type in more text, Word will create its own breaks. Lines will break to start new lines and pages will break to start new pages. These are called soft breaks because they will change automatically as material is added or deleted from the document. You can force the document to break where you want by using hard breaks. To begin, ensure that **wd02a2-associatesdegree.docx** is open. Save it as **wd02a3-associatesdegree.docx**.

2 Locate the text "Figure 1" at the bottom of page 2 (3 of 10) of the document.

To ensure that the label ("Figure 1") always appears on the same page as the table that follows, you will insert a page break here.

To insert a Page Break:

CLICK your mouse directly before the text "Figure 1."

CLICK the INSERT tab and locate the Pages group.

CLICK Page Break.
(*Result:* The text is moved to the next page.)

MORE INFO

Turn the Show/Hide button on to see the invisible formatting marks. Notice the Page Break symbol with single dotted lines before and after it. This was inserted where the cursor was—right before the words "Figure 1." The page break moved everything after it to the next page.

Note: To delete a hard break, click your mouse in front of the dotted line so that the cursor shows up at the far left of the break. Then click Delete .

3 This document already has page numbers inserted. Go to page 5 (6 of 10).

Insert your cursor before the heading "Student and Academic Support Services."

This part of the plan should begin on its own page and should be its own section with its own page numbering. This will require a next page section break.

To insert a next page section break:

CLICK the PAGE LAYOUT tab and locate the Page Setup group.

CLICK on Breaks to bring down a menu of breaks (notice a page break is also available here).

SELECT Next Page under the Section Breaks area (see Figure WD2.10).
(*Result:* The text moves to the next page, as it did before, but the "next page" is also the beginning of a new section.)

FIGURE WD2.10 Page Break and Section Break drop-down menus

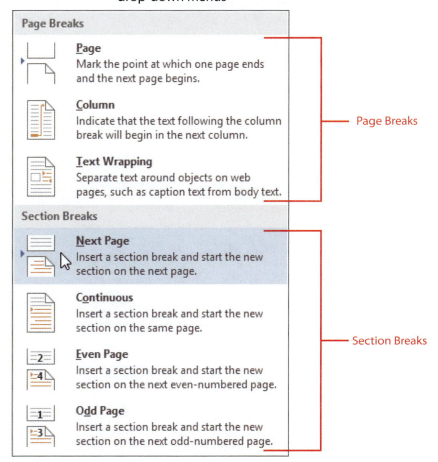

MORE INFO

Turning the Show/Hide button on will show that the Section Break (Next Page) marker has two dotted lines rather than the single dotted line of a Page Break symbol.

Your cursor is now at the top of the next page. However, if you check the Status bar, you will see that the cursor is on Page 0 of Section 2 (page 7 of 10). The page numbers start over again at the new section. Since the Different First Page command is still on, the page number does not show on this first page of this new section.

4 Creating sections allows you to treat each section of the document separately from the other sections. While it has many applications, we will concentrate on its effect on page numbers.

Turn the Show/Hide command off to provide a cleaner view of the screen.

With your cursor in section 2:

CLICK the INSERT tab and locate the Header & Footer group.

CLICK Page Number.

CLICK Format Page Numbers.

SELECT Continue from Previous Section.

CLICK OK.

(*Result:* The page number in the Status bar shows that what was "Page 0 of Section 2" is now "Page 6 of Section 2." The numbering of the document has been continued from the previous Section.)

5 To show a page number on Page 6, you will need to turn off the Different First Page setting.

DOUBLE-CLICK in the footer area of Page 6 to activate the Header & Footer view.

GO TO Options group.

CLICK to remove and turn off Different First Page.
(*Result:* The page number now appears on the first page of the new section.)

This does not make the cover page show a page number because the cover page is in Section 1. Your changes were made to Section 2 (see Figure WD2.11).

FIGURE WD2.11 Document now in two sections

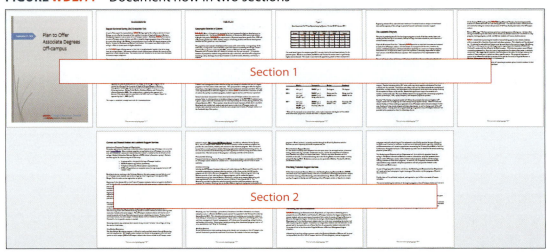

6 Let's assume that Section 2 of the document is to have page numbers different from Section 1.

With your cursor somewhere in Section 2:

CLICK the INSERT tab and locate the Header & Footer group.

CLICK Page Number.

CLICK Format Page Numbers.

CLICK the drop-down arrow in the Number Format window.

SELECT the A, B, C, … option.

CLICK the Start at button.

Ensure the spinner says "A."

CLICK OK.
(*Result:* The page numbering for Section 2 is now in an A, B, C, format.)

7 Return to the top of Page 1, Section 1, Page 2 of 10. You want to add a blank page (perhaps to add a table of contents, later) between the cover page and Page 1.

To insert a blank page:

CLICK your mouse in front of the heading "Background" on Page 1, Section 1.

To insert a page break using a keyboard shortcut:

PRESS `Ctrl` and `Enter` at the same time (this is a shortcut for a page break).

8 Now you notice that the blank page is Page 1. It is not likely that this page will be given a number in the document, so you would like the current Page 2 (3 of 11) to become Page 1. To do so, you will replace the new page break with a section break.

Turn the Show/Hide command on.

CLICK after the Page Break symbol on the newly created blank page.

PRESS `Enter` to separate one break from the other.

CLICK the PAGE LAYOUT tab and locate the Page Setup group.

CLICK on Breaks.

SELECT Next Page under the Section Breaks area to insert a section break right after the page break.

CLICK in front of the Page Break symbol and delete it.

CLICK into the heading "Background."

The Status bar shows you that you are now on Page 0 of Section 2. The cover page and the blank page are Section 1, you are in Section 2, and the pages marked with A, B, C, are Section 3 (see Figure WD2.12).

FIGURE WD2.12 Document now in three sections

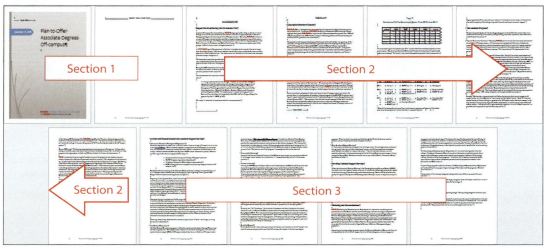

9 Let's clean up the page numbering for these first two sections.

While your cursor is in Section 2:

CLICK the INSERT tab and locate the Header & Footer group.

CLICK Page Number.

CLICK Format Page Numbers.

CLICK the Start at button.

CLICK the spinner to 1.

CLICK OK.

10 DOUBLE-CLICK in the Footer area of the Page 1, Section 2 to activate the Header & Footer view.

CLICK Different First Page to turn it off.

CLICK Link to Previous to turn off any connection to the page numbers in Section 1.

(*Result:* The page number 1 shows up on this page. It is Page 1 of Section 2.)

11 On the blank page, click into the footer where the page number is showing.

CLICK on Page Number.

SELECT Remove Page Numbers.

Delete the text left behind in the footer.

(*Result:* This removes page numbers from Section 1 without affecting those in Section 2 or 3.)

12 Your document should appear similar to Figure WD2.13 when in the Multiple Pages view. Save the file.

FIGURE WD2.13   Completion of Lesson Word 2A3

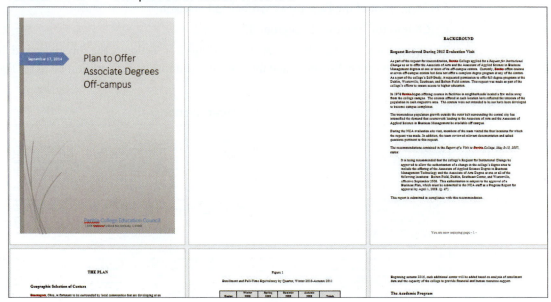

LESSON WORD 2A4
Headers and Footers

LESSON OVERVIEW

Headers and footers provide guidance to the reader as they convey general information about the document on each page. The title of the document, the author, and the date are the most common elements. Word provides predesigned header and footer layouts for easy insertion of high-quality features. When using a predesigned header or footer, data from the document properties and the cover page (if already created) will automatically show up in placeholders in the header or footer. You can add more information if you wish.

While predesigned layouts are fast, you can also create your own customized headers and footers by opening the Header & Footer view and adding text or by using the Blank design option. The Header & Footer view locks the rest of the document from editing, but allows you to add your own information. Anything added into the header or footer of one page will instantly appear on the other pages of the document.

The elements of a header or footer can be modified to different font styles and sizes just like text anywhere else in the document. Making changes to one header or footer will automatically make the same changes to all the headers or footers.

Each header or footer has a default setting for aligning elements. When a header or footer is opened, you can leave the text left-aligned, or by pressing the Tab button once, you can center the text in the header or footer. Pressing the Tab button again will move the text to a right-aligned format.

SKILLS PREVIEW

Insert a predesigned header (or footer) into a document	• CLICK the INSERT tab and locate the Header & Footer group. CLICK the Header (or Footer) button. SELECT the desired style.
Insert a custom header (or footer) into a document	• CLICK the INSERT tab and locate the Header & Footer group. CLICK the Header (or Footer) button. SELECT the Blank style. Type in your desired text.
Adjust the font in a header (or footer)	• CLICK into the header text. CLICK the HOME tab and locate the Font group. Adjust the font size, color, or style.
Align elements within a header (or footer)	• Open the Header & Footer view. CLICK the cursor into the element (text or page number) you wish to align. PRESS the Tab button once to align to center. PRESS the Tab button again to right-align.

PROJECT PRACTICE

1. You would like to add a header to the pages of the document. A header is text that is repeated on each page. For the top of the page (header), it is common to include the title of the document. To begin, ensure that **wd02a3-associatesdegree.docx** is open. Save the file as **wd02a4-associatesdegree.docx**.

2. To insert a header into a document:
   CLICK on Page 1 of Section 2 (3 of 11).
   CLICK the INSERT tab and locate the Header & Footer group.
   CLICK the Header button.
   SELECT the Sideline style from the drop-down menu.

(*Result:* The title, which is contained in the document properties, appears in a placeholder on each page of the document except for the cover page, which still has the Different First Page command turned on for Section 1.)

3 The font size of the header is a little large for the rest of the text. Let's make it fit better.

To resize the font in an automatic style header (or footer):

CLICK into the header text on any of the pages where it appears.

CLICK the HOME tab and locate the Font group.

CLICK the drop-down menu for font size.

CHOOSE font size 12.

DOUBLE-CLICK the body text to turn the Header & Footer view off.

FIGURE WD2.14 Document in Header & Footer view

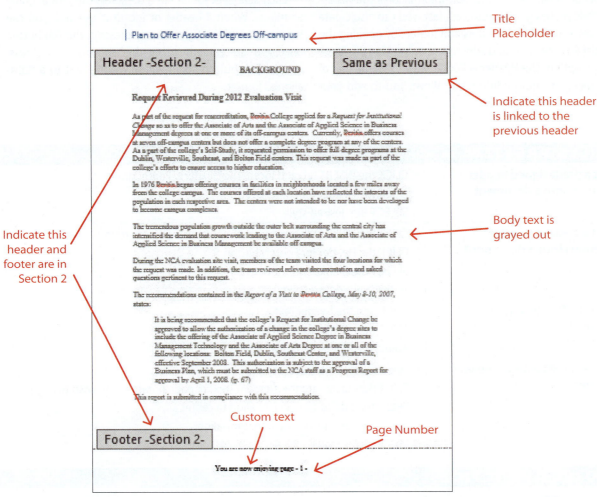

4 The style of header that you choose uses blue font color. When printed, it will appear faded. Let's change that.

Open the Header & Footer view.

CLICK into the title text to open the placeholder.

CLICK the HOME tab and locate the Font group.

CLICK the Font Color button to open the color palette.

CHOOSE Automatic (or Black, Text 1).

5 Now you would like to add the name of the author into the footer of the page. Since the existing page numbers already appear in the footer, along with additional text, you will be customizing your own footer.

To modify text into a footer:

CLICK outside the placeholder.

CLICK the Go to Footer button in the Navigation group.

CLICK in front of the current footer text.

PRESS `Tab` to align the footer to the right margin.

SELECT the current text (without the page number as in Figure WD2.15).

PRESS `Delete`.

FIGURE WD2.15 Selecting only the text in the footer—not the page number

6 Let's add text to the footer that is left-aligned.

CLICK the cursor to the far left of the footer.

TYPE **Prepared by the Peritia College Education Council**.

PRESS `Delete`.

(*Result:* This text crossed the center of the footer, which moved the page number to a line below. By pressing delete, you have removed the spacing problem.)

 MORE INFO

Headers and footers have three built-in tab positions to make aligning easy. When you first create a custom header or footer, the cursor sits at the left-hand margin. Any text typed here will be left-aligned. If you press `Tab` once, the cursor moves to the center of the header or footer and text typed here will be centered. Press `Tab` again and the cursor moves to the right-hand margin. All text typed here will be right-aligned.

---

7 The text that was inserted into the footer used the current font of the document (Times New Roman), but the header was part of an automatic style that used Calibri Light. Because the footer text was typed in, it is not inside a placeholder.

To change the font of a footer:

SELECT the text of the footer (ignoring the page number) to bring up the Mini toolbar.

CLICK the Font drop-down arrow (see Figure WD2.16).

CHOOSE Calibri Light.

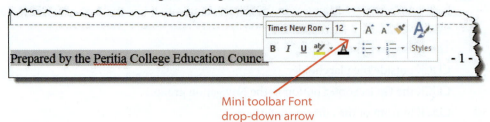

Mini toolbar Font
drop-down arrow

8 The page number font is also different from the rest of the footer. Let's fix that.

SELECT Page Number (it is actually not text, but a field).

CLICK the HOME tab and locate the Font group.

CLICK the Font drop-down arrow.

CHOOSE Calibri Light.

DOUBLE-CLICK the body of the document to exit the Header & Footer view.

MORE INFO

Word allows you to put a different header or footer on odd and even pages. To activate this option, open the Header & Footer view and locate the Options group. CLICK the Different Odd & Even Pages option to turn it on. Now you can add even more flexibility to what is contained in the headers and footers.

9 Your document should appear similar to Figure WD2.17 starting at Page 1 of Section 2. Save the file.

FIGURE WD2.17   Completion of Lesson Word 2A4

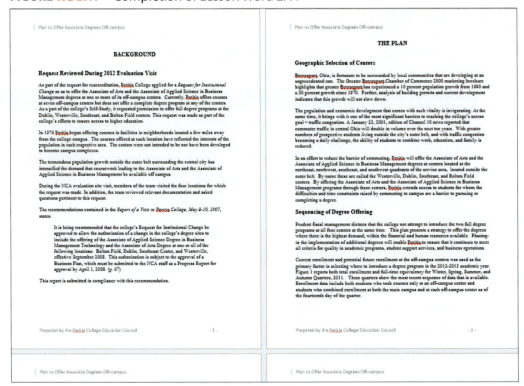

Managing and Controlling Headers and Footers

LESSON OVERVIEW

Headers and footers can be a little challenging to control. When changes are made to one, it will change all the others (even across sections) unless you have set them up properly. By default, all headers and footers are linked to the header or footer before them by the **Link to Previous** control. You can turn the Link to Previous control off to separate headers and footers that are in different sections so each one can have its own material or settings.

Page numbers can be set to continue across a section break with the Continue from Previous Section setting. This permits you to change headers and footers from one section to the other while leaving the page numbering to work automatically across all pages.

Occasionally you may need more or less room around a header or footer. You can change the default header and footer margin of a half inch by adjusting the settings of the **Header from Top** or the **Footer from Bottom** controls.

You can insert the date into a header or footer with the **Date & Time** feature. You can choose from various formats for the date field. You can also set the field to **Update Automatically**. When this feature is used, every time the file is opened, the date field will update to the new date.

The **Remove Header** (or footer) button allows you to quickly delete a header or footer.

SKILLS PREVIEW

Disconnect one header (or footer) from the header (or footer) before it	• Open the Header & Footer view. CLICK into the header (or footer) that you want to disconnect from the previous header (or footer). Locate the Navigation group. CLICK the Link to Previous button to turn it off.
Remove a header (or footer)	• Open the Header & Footer view. CLICK into the header (or footer) that you want to remove. Locate the Header & Footer group. CLICK the Header (or footer) button. CHOOSE Remove Header (or footer).
Set Page Numbers to continue from a previous section	• DOUBLE-CLICK into the footer containing the page numbers you wish to change. Locate the Header & Footer group. CLICK the Page Number button. CHOOSE Format Page Number from the menu. CHOOSE Continue from previous section. CLICK OK.
Adjust the spacing around a header (or footer)	• DOUBLE-CLICK into the header (or footer) you wish to adjust. Locate the Position group. CLICK the spinner in the Header (or footer) from Top or the Header (or footer) from Bottom as desired.
Insert the date or time into a header (or footer)	• Open the Header & Footer view. CLICK the mouse where you wish to insert the date or time. Locate the Insert group. CLICK Date & Time. CHOOSE the format you desire. CHOOSE Update Automatically (if desired). CLICK OK.
Add text in front of a placeholder	• CLICK in front of the placeholder. TYPE the desired text.

1 The document header appears on the blank page (the second page of the document, which will be used for a table of contents). You can't delete that header without deleting all the related headers in the document because they are all linked. But because your document is divided into three invisible sections, you can control each section separately. To begin, ensure that **wd02a4-associatesdegree. docx** is open. Save the file as **wd02a5-associatesdegree.docx**.

2 To disconnect the header in Section 1 from the header in Section 2:

Open the header on Page 1, Section 2 and locate the Navigation group.

CLICK the Link to Previous button to turn it off so it is no longer connected to the previous header.

Locate the Navigation group.

CLICK the Previous button to move to the previous header.

Locate the Header & Footer group.

CLICK the Header button.

CHOOSE Remove Header.

(*Result:* The header is gone from Section 1, but it remains in place for the rest of the document.)

 MORE INFO

The Link to Previous connection applies to both headers and footers by default. The reason the footer is not showing on the blank page is because it had been previously unlinked when we set up the page numbers.

---

3 Generally, the first page of the body of a document does not display headers or footers.

To remove headers or footers from the first page of a section:

CLICK into the header on Page 1, Section 2.

CLICK the Different First Page option to turn it on.

The header and footer is gone from this page.

You are free to add any content into these headers or footers now. The content will not appear on any other page.

DOUBLE-CLICK on the body text to turn the Header & Footer view off.

4 Our document uses different page numbering from Section 2 to Section 3. You now decide the page numbers should be continuous across the entire report.

To set page numbers to continue from a previous section:

DOUBLE-CLICK into the footer on Page A, Section 3.

Locate the Header & Footer group.

CLICK the Page Number button (see Figure WD2.18).

CHOOSE Format Page Numbers.

CHOOSE the same Number format as is used in the rest of the document (-1-, -2-, -3-,…).

CHOOSE Continue from previous section.

CLICK OK.

(*Result:* The page numbers of the entire document are identical in format and the numbering continues across Sections 2 and 3.)

FIGURE WD2.18 Page Number Format options

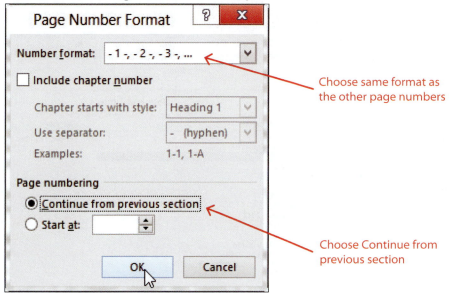

5. You would like to add a few more professional touches to the headers, but you will need more room in the headers. By default, headers and footers start 0.5" from the edge of the paper.

   To adjust the margins around a header or footer:

   DOUBLE-CLICK into the header on Page 2, Section 2 and locate the Position group.

   CLICK the Spinner in the Header from Top control to 0.4".
   (*Result:* The header moves closer to the top of the page.)

6. This slightly smaller header margin provides room to add another line of text to the header.

   To insert another line in a header or footer:

   DOUBLE-CLICK into the header on Page 2, Section 2.

   DOUBLE-CLICK the mouse after the Title text (outside of the placeholder).

   PRESS the **Enter** key.
   (*Result:* The cursor is moved below the current text and is ready for you to type.)

7. Rather than typing the date into this spot, let Word do the work.

   To insert the date:

   In the **DESIGN** tab under Header & Footer Tools locate the Insert group.

   CLICK Date & Time (see Figure WD2.19).

   CHOOSE the third option that shows the long date (for example, July 22, 2014).

   CLICK OK.
   (*Result:* That date is automatically inserted.)

FIGURE WD2.19   Date & Time dialog box

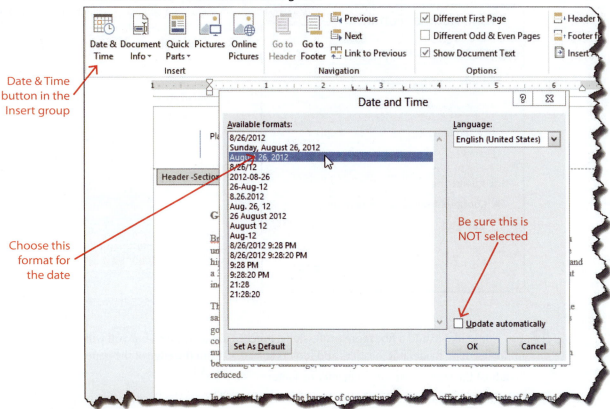

Date & Time button in the Insert group

Choose this format for the date

Be sure this is NOT selected

8 The date that has just been inserted is static and will not change.

It is decided that because this document is dated on the cover page, the dates inside should reflect the last time the document was printed. You would like to insert a date field that will automatically update each time the file is opened.

CLICK the Undo command to remove the date.

To insert a date that will update automatically:

Locate the Insert group.

CLICK Date & Time.

CHOOSE the same option as before.

CLICK the Update Automatically command to turn it on (Figure WD2.19).

CLICK OK.

(*Result:* That date is automatically inserted. It is actually a placeholder for the date field. If you open this file tomorrow, tomorrow's date will replace the current date.)

9 The date field has used the original formatting of the header and is too large. Let's fix that.

SELECT the entire text of the date.

CLICK the HOME tab and locate the Font group.

CLICK the Size button and set it to 10.

CLICK the Color button and set it to Automatic.

10 To complete the date and time notification:

CLICK in front of the newly inserted date field. (It will appear difficult to do, but just click to the left of the date field and what is typed there will appear outside of the placeholder.)

TYPE **Last Printed:**

PRESS the space bar once.

(*Result:* That date is preceded by "Last Printed:" and will appear on each page of the document.)

11 Your document should appear similar to Figure WD2.20 when in the Multiple Pages view, Page 2, Section 2. Save your file.

FIGURE WD2.20 Completion of Lesson Word 2A5

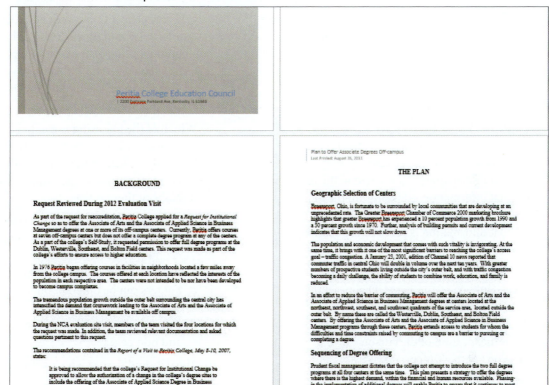

MULTIPLE-CHOICE QUIZ

Select the best choice in the following questions to review the project concepts. Good luck!

1. The area of the screen that tells users which page the cursor is on and which section the cursor is in is called the
   a. Navigation pane.
   b. Overview.
   c. Selection bar.
   d. Status bar.

2. The choice of a predesigned cover page should be determined by
   a. its appropriateness for the intended reader.
   b. the contrast of colors.
   c. which placeholders are available.
   d. the font styles.

3. Sometimes cover pages fill in placeholders automatically. This is because
   a. that information is contained in the file name.
   b. that information is taken from the first sentence in the document.
   c. that information is part of the document properties.
   d. None of these is correct.

4. By default, page numbers will appear
   a. at the bottom of the page.
   b. at the top of the page.
   c. at the location of the cursor.
   d. None of these is correct.

5. Which of these is NOT correct?
   a. Page numbers can be inserted into the location of the cursor.
   b. Page numbers can be set to start at zero.
   c. Page numbers can be restarted within one section.
   d. Page numbers can be placed in the margin.

6. When Word starts a new page in a document, it is called a
   a. Next page break.
   b. Section break.
   c. hard break.
   d. soft break.

7. When a section break is added, existing page numbers will continue across the break
   a. until you change the formatting.
   b. only if you format it that way.
   c. if you turn off the Link to Previous command.
   d. None of these is correct.

8. Which of the following is true?
   a. Headers must be created from built in styles.
   b. Headers must be the same on all pages.
   c. Headers cannot be the same as footers.
   d. None of these is true.

9. Which of the following is NOT true?
   a. Headers can be linked to previous, but footers cannot.
   b. Page numbers can be placed into a header.
   c. Footers can be different on the first page of each section.
   d. Both headers and footers can be different on even and odd pages.

10. The date and time can be inserted into a header or footer and
    a. be set to automatically update.
    b. formatted to show the day of the week as well as the date.
    c. custom text added before or after it.
    d. All of these are correct.

HANDS-ON EXERCISE: WORK IT OUT WD-2A-E1

In this exercise, you will open an existing document and add professional touches such as a cover page, page numbers, section breaks, headers, and footers. You will be provided with specific tasks, but not step-by-step instructions. The final document is shown in Figure WD2.21.

FIGURE WD2.21   Work It Out WD-2A-E1: completed

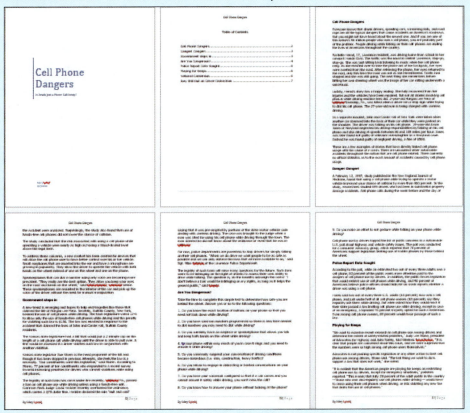

1. Locate and open the exercise data file **wd02a-ex01.docx**. Save the file as **wd02a-hw01.docx**.

2. Insert a cover page using the built-in Sideline style. Pick a date of August 7, 2014 and format the date to match the exercise example.

3. Delete the Company placeholder. In the Subtitle placeholder, type: **Is Death Just a Phone Call Away?**

4. Insert page numbers into the bottom of the pages using built-in Accent Bar 2 style.

5. Format the page numbers to be capital Roman numerals.

6. Insert a page break on page V, just before the heading "National Consensus." This will move the heading to the next page so it is on the same page as its text.

7. Insert a next page section break immediately after the Table of Contents. Eliminate any unneeded page breaks of paragraph markers between the Table of Contents and the next page of text.

8. Eliminate all page numbers in Section 1 (the cover page and Table of Contents page). Format Section 2 so that no page number appears on the first page of Section 2, but that Word recognizes it as Page I.

9. Insert a custom header into Section 2 that says **Cell Phone Dangers**. Center the header. Ensure the header does not show on Page I of Section 2.

10. Insert a footer into Section 2 that says **By Mary Lyzakj**. Left-align the footer. Ensure the footer does not show on Page I of Section 2.

    Save and then close the document file **wd02a-hw01.docx**.

HANDS-ON EXERCISE: WORK IT OUT WD-2A-E2

In this exercise, you will open an existing document and add professional touches such as a cover page, page numbers, section breaks, headers, and footers. You will be provided with specific tasks, but not step-by-step instructions. The final document is shown in Figure WD2.22.

FIGURE WD2.22   Work It Out WD-2A-E2: completed

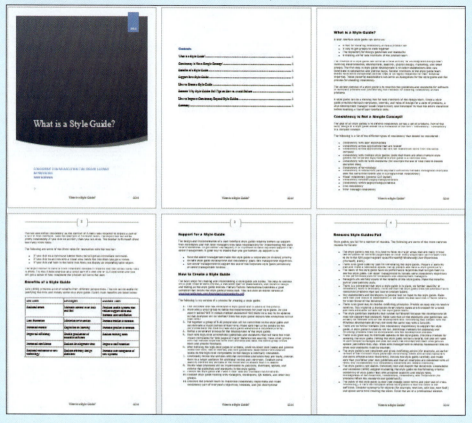

1. Locate and open the exercise data file **wd02a-ex02.docx**. Save the file as **wd02a-hw02.docx**.

2. Insert a cover page using the built-in Ion (Dark) style.

3. In the Year placeholder, type: **2014**. Delete the Company Name and Company Address placeholders.

4. In the Document Subtitle placeholder, type: **Consistent communication can create lasting impressions**.

5. In the Author placeholder, type: **Gary Northsen**.

6. Create a next page section break between the Table of Contents page and the start of the text. Eliminate any extra breaks or paragraph markers between the two pages.

7. Insert page numbers at the top of the page using built-in Brackets 2 style. Ensure the page numbers do not appear in Section 1, nor on the first page of Section 2. The first page of Section 2 should be page 1.

8. Insert a page break in front of the heading "Support for a Style Guide" and also in front of "Reasons Style Guides Fail" to move that heading to the next page.

9. Insert a custom footer into the document with the title centered and the year right-aligned. Ensure that Page 1 of Section 2 shows the footer, but not the header.

10. Save and then close the document file **wd02a-hw02.docx**.

HAND-ON EXERCISE: WORK IT OUT WD-2A-E3

In this exercise, you will open an existing document and add professional touches such as a cover page, page numbers, section breaks, headers, and footers. You will be provided with specific tasks, but not step-by-step instructions. The final document is shown in Figure WD2.23.

FIGURE WD2.23 Work It Out WD-2A-E3: completed

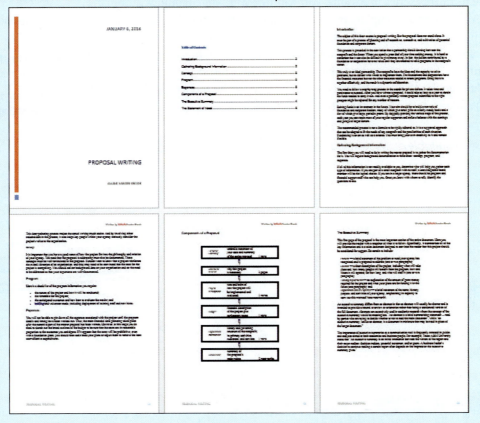

1. Locate and open the exercise data file **wd02a-ex03.docx**. Save the file as **wd02a-hw03.docx**.

2. Insert a cover page using the Semaphore style. Pick the date January 6, 2014.

3. Enter the document title as **Proposal Writing**. Delete all other placeholders.

4. Create a next page section break between the Table of Contents and the Introduction. Delete any unneeded breaks or paragraph markers.

5. Insert a built-in footer using the Semaphore style. Ensure the footer does not show up on the first three pages of the document (cover page, table of contents, and the first page of text).

6. Insert page breaks immediately before the headings:
   "Components of a Proposal,"
   "The Executive Summary,"
   "The Statement of Need."

7. Adjust the footer so it is 0.3" from the bottom of the page.

8. Insert a custom header that says **Written by Alaine Vander Brook**. Right-align the header and change the font size of this header to 11 point.

9. Ensure the header does not show up on the cover page, contents page, or the first page of text.

10. Save and then close the document file **wd02a-hw03.docx**.

Unifying the Document

This project is all about pulling a research paper or business report together to print and distribute it. In this series of lessons, you will uncover some fabulous automatic features that Word uses to complete the most tedious tasks instantly. These features include creating, modifying, and updating headings throughout the document and generating a table of contents in just seconds. Footnotes and endnotes can be entered that will renumber themselves when new ones are added. And perhaps best of all: Word will keep track of the sources you used in preparing the report (books, articles, websites, etc.) and produce a bibliography and citations with a click of the mouse.

PROJECT OBJECTIVES

After completing this project, you will be able to:

- Create and apply headings.
- Generate a table of contents.
- Add footnotes and endnotes.
- Organize the sources used in researching the document.
- Insert automatic citations and bibliographies.

PROJECT FILE: *Available at* www.mhhe.com/office2013projectlearn

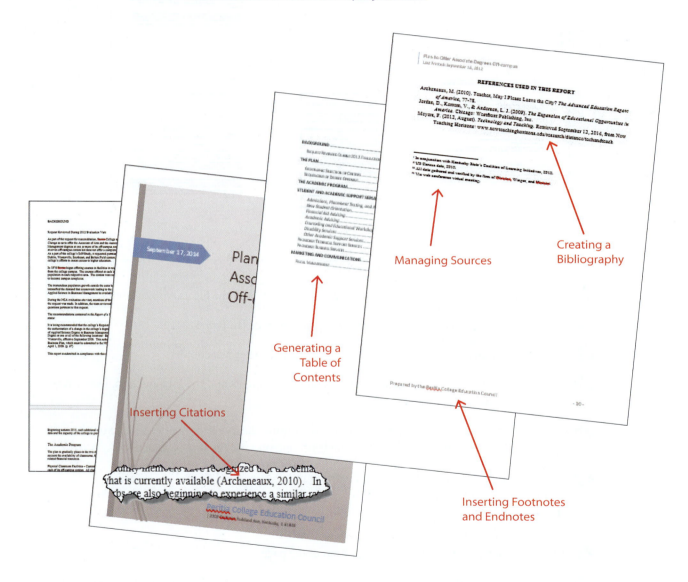

Creating a Bibliography

Managing Sources

Generating a Table of Contents

Inserting Citations

Inserting Footnotes and Endnotes

Creating and Applying Headings

LESSON OVERVIEW

The use of headings (not to be confused with headers) is important in the organization of a report. These section titles quickly indicate the topic that is being discussed in the paragraphs following it. While we often create headings, Word allows us to assign a format and a level of importance to these headings. Once in place, changes to the font, size, styles, or spacing of a heading can instantly change all the similar headings in the document. This consistency helps readers to categorize information as they are reading it, and to reference specifics much quicker when referring to the document.

Word uses simple terms to keep headings in order. Heading 1 is considered the most important and should be applied to the major headings in a document. Heading 2 is used for subheadings that are part of a Heading 1 section. By default Word uses three levels of headings, although you can create more, if you wish.

There are two types of **heading styles** in this lesson: paragraph headings and character headings. A **paragraph style** heading will format the entire paragraph in which it is included. A **character style** heading will only affect the actual characters you have selected.

Headings can be **modified** in a number of ways. Once a heading is changed, all headings in the document will instantly change to match the modifications. You can easily create your own heading style using the **New Style** button.

By designating document titles using Word's headings feature, you can apply, control, and adjust all the headings in a document instantly. The body text of a document is assigned a heading called **Normal**. Any changes made to the Normal style will automatically format the body of the document without changing the text that has been designated as headings.

SKILLS PREVIEW

Apply a predesigned heading	• CLICK into the text you wish to make a heading. CLICK the HOME tab and locate the Styles group. SELECT the heading style from the palette, or • CLICK into the title you wish to make a heading. CLICK the HOME tab and locate the Styles group. CLICK the Styles Launch button (⬓). CHOOSE the desired style from the menu.
Modify a heading style	• CLICK the HOME tab and locate the Styles group. CLICK the Styles Launch button (⬓). CLICK the drop-down arrow of the desired heading. CHOOSE Modify. Make the desired changes. CLICK OK.
Modify a heading to match the formatting in a document	• Make the changes you wish to text in the document. CLICK the Styles Launch button (⬓). CLICK the drop-down next to the desired heading. CHOOSE Update Heading 2 to Match Selection.
Create a new style heading	• CLICK the Styles Launch button (⬓). SELECT New Style (⬓) from the bottom of the Styles box. Give the style a name in the Name window. Give the style a type in the Style type window. Make the desired formatting changes. CLICK OK.

Change the body text of an entire document without affecting other headings	• CLICK the HOME tab and locate the Styles group. CLICK the Launch button (⌐⌐). CLICK the Normal style drop-down button. CHOOSE Modify. Make the desired changes. CLICK OK.

PROJECT PRACTICE

1. This document contains major section titles such as "Background," and smaller section titles such as "Geographic Selection of Centers." Some are centered, and some are italic. By setting these titles as headings, you can control and change them quickly without having to bounce around the document. After launching Microsoft Word, locate and open the project data file **wd02b1.docx**. Save the file as **wd02b1-associatesdegree.docx**.

2. First, let's concentrate on the main headings.

   CLICK into the title "Background" on Page 1, Section 2.

   CLICK the HOME tab and locate the Styles group.

   CLICK on Heading 1 (see Figure WD2.24).

   (*Result:* The title takes on the preset style of a Heading 1: Times New Roman, 14 point, bold, left aligned.)

FIGURE WD2.24 The Styles group

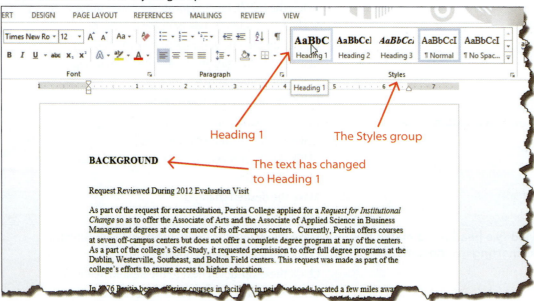

3. Set the following titles as Heading 1:

   "The Plan" (page 2, Section 2)

   "The Academic Program" (Page 4, Section 2)

   "Student and Academic Support Services" (Page 6, Section 3)

   "Marketing and Communications" (Page 8, Section 3)

4 The predesigned heading format isn't exactly what you want. Let's modify it.

CLICK the HOME tab and locate the Styles group.

CLICK the Styles Launch button ( ) (see Figure WD2.25).

CLICK the drop-down arrow next to Heading 1.

CHOOSE Modify.

CLICK the Center button to center the text.

CLICK the Format button (Format ▾).

CHOOSE Font.

CHOOSE All Caps in the Effects section of the dialog box.

CLICK OK twice.

Close the Styles box.

(*Result*: You have changed the Heading 1 setting and it has reformatted all the Heading 1 selections to match.)

FIGURE WD2.25 The Styles menu

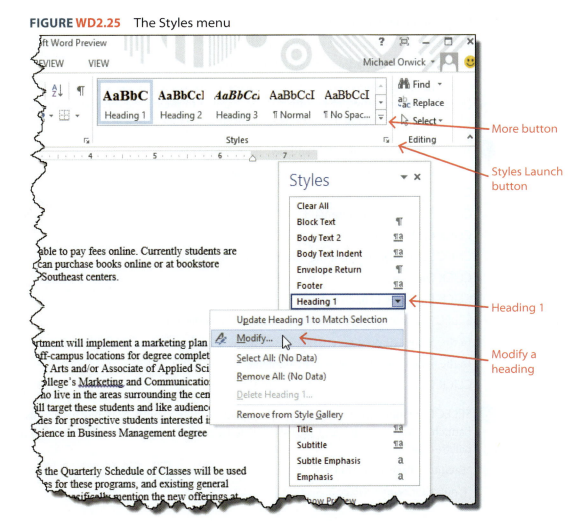

TIP

The Ribbon displays only a few of the most common styles, but by clicking the More button (Figure WD2.25), you can open the styles palette to display many more styles. On the palette, each style is shown displaying the formatting assigned to it. If a style is in Arial font, blue text, and underlined, the thumbnail will be in Arial font, blue text, and underlined.

5 Using the previous process, mark the following text as Heading 2:

"Request Reviewed During 2002 Evaluation Visit"

"Geographic Selection of Centers"

"Sequencing of Degree Offering"

"Fiscal Management"

6 There is a fast way to modify a heading style that allows you to visualize the changes as you make them.

SELECT any of the Heading 2 text (let's use the first one): "Request Reviewed During 2002 Evaluation Visit."

CLICK the HOME tab.

CLICK the Center button to center the text across the page.

CLICK the Font Color button.

SELECT Blue, Accent 1.

Increase the font size to 14 point.

CLICK the Styles Launch button ( ).

CLICK the drop-down next to Heading 2.

CHOOSE Update Heading 2 to Match Selection.

Close the Styles box.

(*Result:* The formatting of Heading 2 has changed to match the formatting changes you just made. Also, the other Heading 2 selections have instantly changed to match.)

7 You can create your own style and save it for future use.

SELECT the text "Physical Classroom Facilities" on Page 4, Section 2.

CLICK the HOME tab.

CLICK the Underline command.

CLICK the Font Launch button ( ).

CHOOSE Small Caps from the Effects area of the dialog box.

CLICK OK.

CLICK the Styles Launch button.

SELECT New Style ( ) from the bottom of the Styles box.

In the Name window, type: **Standout**. That will be the name of this new style.

In the Style type window, select Character.

CLICK OK.

8 SELECT the following text and apply the Standout style to both. You may have to use the Styles Launch button to locate your new style (listed alphabetically), if it doesn't show up in the preset palette of styles.

"Faculty" (Page 4, Section 2)

"Course Offerings" (Page 5, Section 2)

9 The body text also has a style. Click your mouse into it and you will see it is called Normal.

To change the Normal style in a document:

CLICK the HOME tab and locate the Styles group.

CLICK the Launch button (⌐).

CLICK the Normal style drop-down button.

CHOOSE Modify.

CLICK the Font drop-down arrow.

CHOOSE Calibri from the menu.

CLICK OK.

(*Result:* The text of the entire document body changes to Calibri.)

10 You decide that the change is not what you wanted. To change a Normal style back to its original style, you have two choices: You can follow the previous procedure and set the Normal style to Times New Roman or:

CLICK the Undo command.

(*Result:* The body text of the document returns to Times New Roman.)

11 Your document should appear similar to Figure WD2.26 when in the Multiple Pages view. Save the file **wd02b1-associatesdegree.docx**.

FIGURE WD2.26 Completion of Lesson Word 2B1

Table of Contents

LESSON OVERVIEW

Every long document needs a table of contents. Word can make a **Table of Contents** in less than a second. You don't have to wait until you complete the document preparation because Word can **update the table** of contents just as quickly as it created it. Not only will Word create and format an accurate and appealing table of contents, but the entries on the table of contents also will be **hyperlinked** so you can click on the heading and Word will immediately move to that point of the document.

Word creates a table of contents by using headings. Word scans the document for headings and builds the table based on what it finds. Although you can adjust how Word does this, by default, Word will put each Heading 1 at the highest level in the table of contents. Text that is set as Heading 2 or Heading 3 will be relegated to a lower level.

Word provides predesigned tables of contents so you can create one instantly. You can build your own **custom table of contents** and add, remove, or modify options such as tab leaders, levels shown, and general formatting. There are many more options you can control that are beyond the scope of this lesson and provide even more control for the advanced user.

Word's automatic table of contents feature looks like text, but it is actually a field. This is what makes it so easy to update. It is also easy to remove a table of contents by clicking the Table of Contents button and choosing **Remove table of contents**.

SKILLS PREVIEW

Insert a predesigned table of contents	• CLICK the REFERENCES tab and locate the Table of Contents group. CLICK the Table of Contents button. CHOOSE the desired format.
Use hyperlinking from the table of contents	• HOLD the `Ctrl` button. CLICK the desired entry in the table of contents.
Return from a followed hyperlink	• HOLD the `Alt` button. PRESS the `←` arrow.
Update a table of contents	• CLICK into the Table of Contents field. CLICK the Update Table tab. CHOOSE the desired update option, or • RIGHT-CLICK into the Table of Contents field. CHOOSE Update field. CHOOSE the desired update option.
Remove a table of contents	• CLICK the REFERENCES tab and locate the Table of Contents group. CLICK Remove Table of Contents.
Create a custom table of contents	• CLICK the Table of Contents button. CHOOSE Custom Table of Contents. Make the desired choices. CLICK OK.

1 It is important that you know that Word builds its tables of contents (generally) by searching the document for text that has had the Heading formatting applied to it. Now you see another advantage of using headings. Locate and open the file **wd02b1-associatesdegree.docx**. Save it as **wd02b2-associatesdegree.docx**.

2 CLICK the cursor to the top of the blank page of the document.

CLICK the REFERENCES tab and locate the Table of Contents group.

CLICK the Table of Contents button (see Figure WD2.27).

CHOOSE Automatic Table 2.

(*Result:* An entire table of contents was created showing Heading 1s aligned left with Heading 2s indented slightly.)

FIGURE WD2.27 Table of Contents menu

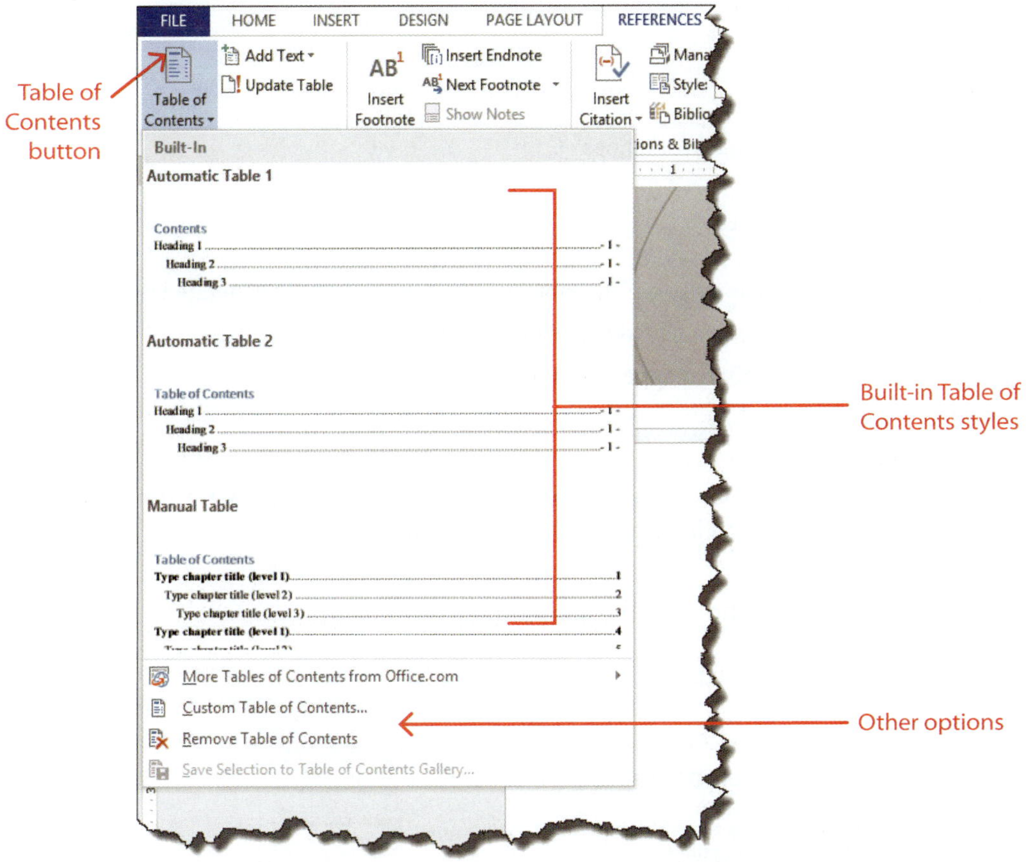

Table of Contents button

Built-in Table of Contents styles

Other options

HEADS UP

Sometimes the Table of Contents function does not recognize all the attributes of a style. For example, although the Heading 1 style included All Caps, the text that was not in uppercase before the Heading 1 style was applied may not appear in capitals in the table of contents, although it does appear in uppercase in the document.

3 Notice that the page numbers in the Table of Contents refer to the formatted page numbers you assigned, not the actual page in the document. You can easily move from the table of contents to a specific place in the document:

HOLD the **Ctrl** button down.

CLICK the entry "THE ACADEMIC PROGRAM."

(*Result:* The cursor moves to that point of the document. Each entry in the Table of Contents is hyperlinked to its corresponding place in the document.)

HOLD the **Alt** button down.

PRESS the **←** to return to your previous location (the Table of Contents).

4 The Table of Contents can handle more than just two levels of headings. Use the previous method to move the cursor to the "STUDENT AND ACADEMIC SUPPORT SERVICES" location.

Set the following text as Heading 3:

"Admissions, Placement Testing, and Registration"

"New Student Orientation"

"Financial Aid Advising"

"Academic Advising"

"Counseling and Educational Workshops"

"Disability Services"

"Other Academic Support Services"

5 CLICK to the Table of Contents page. The table is NOT text, but a field generated by Word.

CLICK into the Table of Contents field (see Figure WD2.28).

CLICK the Update Table tab that appears at the top of the table.

CHOOSE Update entire table.

CLICK OK.

(*Result:* The entire Table of Contents has updated itself to include the new Heading 3s that were just assigned. They are indented a little farther than the Heading 2 entries.)

FIGURE WD2.28 Updating a table of contents

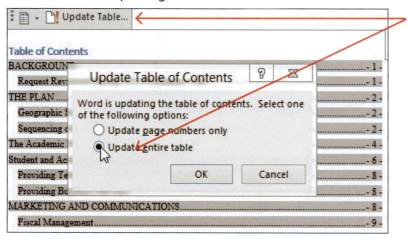

Click the Update Table button then choose the Update entire table option

6 To insert a different Table of Contents, you must first remove the existing one.

To remove a table of contents:

CLICK the REFERENCES tab and locate the Table of Contents group.

CLICK Remove Table of Contents (refer to Other Options in Figure WD2.27).

7 CLICK the Table of Contents button.

CHOOSE Custom Table of Contents (refer to Other Options in Figure WD2.27).

CLICK the drop-down next to Tab leader (see Figure WD2.29).

SELECT the dashed line (instead of the current dotted line).

CLICK OK.

(*Result:* The Table of Contents is re-created using the dashed line. Also note that this custom table does not include its own title. You would have to type your own title atop the table.)

FIGURE WD2.29   Updating a table of contents

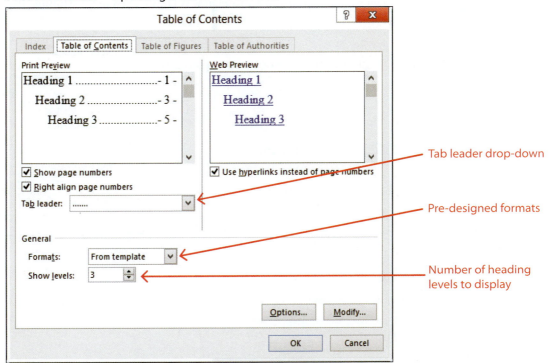

8 Remove the Table of Contents again:

CLICK the Table of Contents button.

CHOOSE the Custom Table of Contents again.

CLICK the drop-down next to Formats.

CLICK Classic and view it in the Print Preview window above.

CLICK the drop-down next to Formats.

CHOOSE Formal.

CLICK OK.

9 CLICK the cursor above the Table of Contents.

Insert a few blank lines.

CLICK the HOME tab.

TYPE **Table of Contents**.

Center the text.

Bold the text (if needed).

10 Your document should appear similar to Figure WD2.30 when in the Multiple Pages view. Save the file.

FIGURE WD2.30 Completion of Lesson Word 2B2

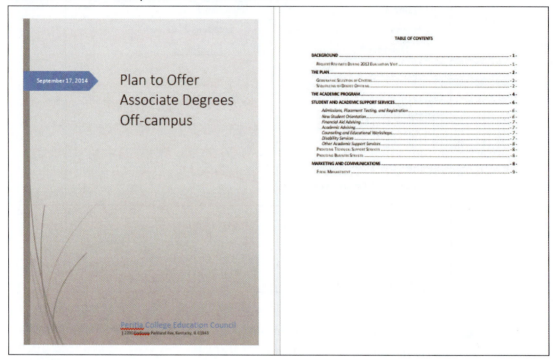

Adding Footnotes and Endnotes

LESSON OVERVIEW

Footnotes are used to add information or clarification to a document without interrupting the flow of the writing. Often including this information in the body of the text would make the sentence too long or overly complicated for the reader. Some writers prefer notes at the bottom of the page (footnotes), while others prefer them at the end of the chapter or document (endnotes). Word makes either very simple.

Inserting a **footnote** automatically creates a superscript marker (superscript means the marker is elevated as the "2" is in $E=MC^2$) and opens a related area at the bottom of the page ready for you to type your note. Inserting an **endnote** does the same except the note that is opened appears at the end of the document. The placing of footnotes

and endnotes can be changed to tuck footnotes closer to the body of text (**below text**) and to move endnotes to the **end of chapter** or **end of section**.

Editing a footnote or endnote is as easy as clicking the mouse into the note and making changes. Word will automatically renumber notes to keep them in order and located on the correct page, even if you add or delete material to the document.

You can instantly **convert** notes from one form to the other. Footnotes can be converted to endnotes and vice versa with just a few mouse clicks. Some document styles prefer footnotes to endnotes, while others may not allow footnotes. No matter how they are entered, they can quickly be changed.

SKILLS PREVIEW

Insert a footnote (or endnote)	• CLICK the mouse into the text where you wish to add a footnote (or endnote) marker. CLICK the REFERENCES tab and locate the Footnotes group. CLICK Insert Footnote (or endnote) to open a footnote (or endnote). TYPE the desired note.
Edit a footnote (or endnote)	• CLICK into the footnote at the bottom of the page (or the endnote at the end of the document). Make your typing or formatting changes.
Locate footnotes (or endnotes) quickly	• CLICK the REFERENCES tab and locate the Footnotes group. CLICK Next Footnote (AB¹ Next Footnote) or endnote. CLICK Show Notes (Show Notes) to move to the actual notes associated with that footnote (or endnote).
Quickly view the content of footnote (or endnote)	• Hover the mouse over the footnote (or endnote) marker in the text. The note's content will appear in a window next to the mouse.
Change the automatic numbering of a footnote (or endnote)	• CLICK the Footnotes Launch button (⌐). CLICK the Number format drop-down arrow. CHOOSE the desired format. CLICK Apply.
Move footnotes from the bottom of the page to just below the text	• CLICK the Footnotes Launch button (⌐). Ensure the Footnotes button is selected. CLICK the Footnotes drop-down arrow. CHOOSE Below text. CLICK Apply.
Convert footnotes to endnotes	• CLICK the Footnotes Launch button (⌐). CLICK the Convert button. CHOOSE Convert all footnotes to endnotes. CLICK OK.
Convert endnotes to footnotes	• CLICK the Footnotes Launch button. CLICK the Convert button (Convert...). CHOOSE Convert all endnotes to footnotes. CLICK OK.

1 Locate and open the file **wd02b2-associatesdegree.docx**. Save it as **wd02b3-associatesdegree.docx**.

2 Move the cursor to Page 1, Section 2.

Locate the first sentence in the third paragraph that begins with "The tremendous population."

CLICK after the word *growth*.

CLICK the REFERENCES tab and locate the Footnotes group.

CLICK Insert Footnote to insert the footnote marker and open a footnote.

TYPE **US Census data, 2010**.

(*Result*: A footnote is created with the number[1] both in the text and in the footnote area.)

3 Let the mouse hover over the footnote marker in the text and the content of the footnote appears next to the cursor.

CLICK the cursor after the period of the last sentence of the page's first paragraph that ends with "access to higher education."

CLICK Insert Footnote.

TYPE **In conjunction with Kentucky State's Coalition of Learning Initiatives, 2012**.

(*Result*: As shown in Figure WD2.31, although the new footnote was added after the first one, since it was inserted earlier in the document, it receives marker number 1 while the existing footnote was renumbered to 2.)

FIGURE WD2.31   Footnote markers and notes

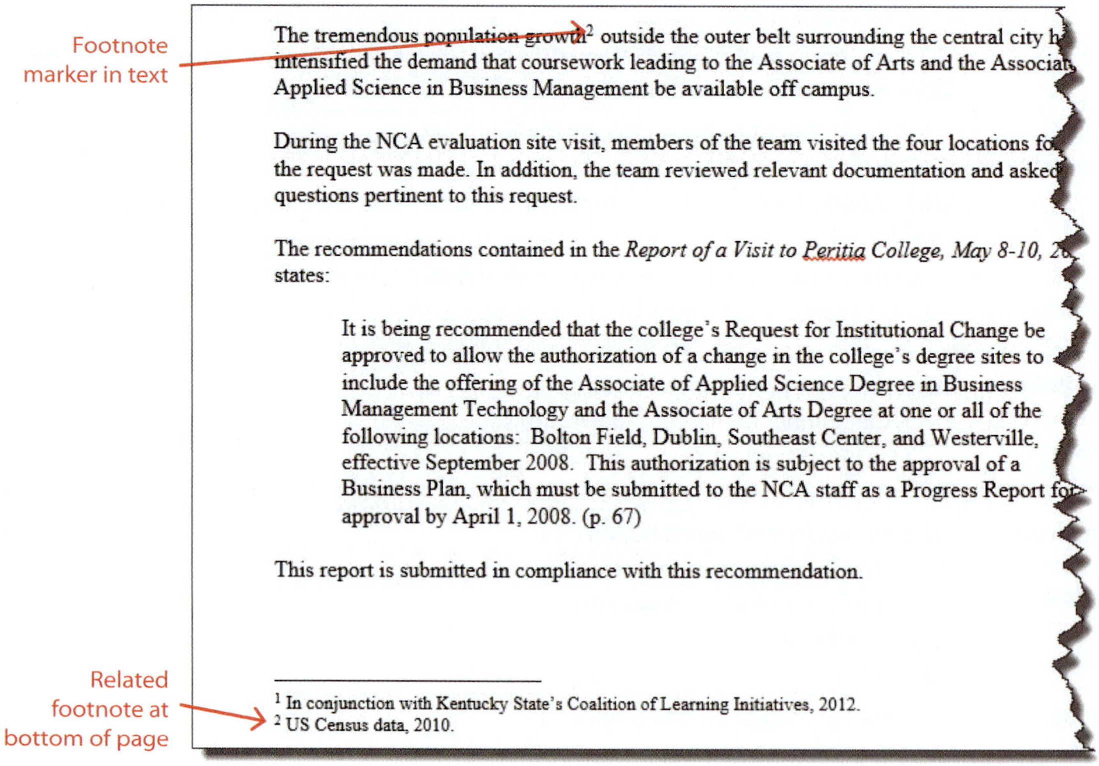

Footnote marker in text →

The tremendous population growth[2] outside the outer belt surrounding the central city h intensified the demand that coursework leading to the Associate of Arts and the Associat Applied Science in Business Management be available off campus.

During the NCA evaluation site visit, members of the team visited the four locations fo the request was made. In addition, the team reviewed relevant documentation and asked questions pertinent to this request.

The recommendations contained in the *Report of a Visit to Peritia College, May 8-10, 2* states:

It is being recommended that the college's Request for Institutional Change be approved to allow the authorization of a change in the college's degree sites to include the offering of the Associate of Applied Science Degree in Business Management Technology and the Associate of Arts Degree at one or all of the following locations: Bolton Field, Dublin, Southeast Center, and Westerville, effective September 2008. This authorization is subject to the approval of a Business Plan, which must be submitted to the NCA staff as a Progress Report fo approval by April 1, 2008. (p. 67)

This report is submitted in compliance with this recommendation.

_____

Related footnote at bottom of page →

[1] In conjunction with Kentucky State's Coalition of Learning Initiatives, 2012.
[2] US Census data, 2010.

4 Move the cursor to the top of the document.

CLICK the REFERENCES tab and locate the Footnotes group.

CLICK Next Footnote ([AB] Next Footnote) to move to the first footnote.

CLICK Show Notes (Show Notes) to move to the actual notes associated with that footnote.

5 Some styles prefer to keep all the notes at the end of the chapter or document.

CLICK to Page 2, Section 2, after the sentence that ends with "30 percent growth since 1970."

(Hint: Use the Search function to locate those words.)

CLICK the REFERENCES tab and locate the Footnotes group.

CLICK Insert Endnote.

TYPE **All data gathered and verified by the firm of Blouten, Winger, and Hausen**.

6 Return to the top of the document.

CLICK the Show Notes button.

Because there are two types of notes (footnotes and endnotes) you must choose.

CHOOSE View endnote area.

CLICK OK to see the endnote at the end of the document.

7 To change the formatting of the automatic numbering:

CLICK the Footnotes Launch button (⬚).

CLICK the Number format drop-down arrow (see Figure WD2.32).

CHOOSE the uppercase Roman numerals.

CLICK Apply.

(*Result:* The Roman numerals of the endnotes have changed from lowercase to uppercase.)

FIGURE WD2.32 Footnote and Endnote dialog box

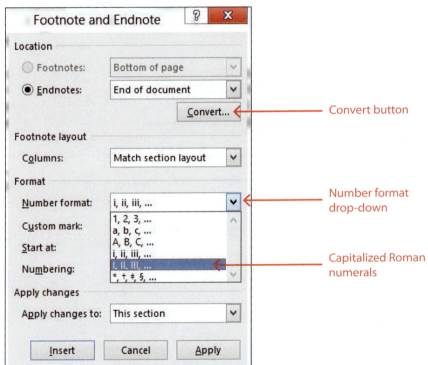

Convert button

Number format drop-down

Capitalized Roman numerals

ⓘ **MORE INFO**

The location of footnotes and endnotes can be changed. In the case of the endnotes, they could appear at the end of the document or at the end of a section. Footnotes can appear at the button of the page (just above the footer area) or below text (just below the last line of text on a page).

8 CLICK into Page 5, Section 2, in the first sentence, right after the words "January 2012 meeting."

CLICK Insert Footnote.

TYPE **Via web conference virtual meeting**.

CLICK the Footnotes Launch button.

Ensure the Footnotes button is selected.

CLICK the Footnotes drop-down arrow.

CHOOSE Below text.

CLICK Apply.

(*Result:* The footnote has moved up the page and now sits directly below the last line of text.)

9 Now you decide that all of the notes in the document should have been endnotes.

CLICK the Footnotes Launch button.

CLICK the Convert button (Convert...).

CHOOSE Convert all footnotes to endnotes.

CLICK Close.

Close the dialog box.

10 Move the cursor to the last page of the document to see all the notes in one place.

To quickly see the text that is associated with an endnote (or footnote):

DOUBLE-CLICK on a Roman numeral in the endnotes.

(*Result:* Word moves the cursor to the location of the endnote in the document.)

11 The last page of your document should appear similar to Figure WD2.33. Save the file.

FIGURE WD2.33   Completion of Lesson Word 2B3

Organizing References

LESSON OVERVIEW

When submitting a document, it is important to include the sources of information used in creating the document. Word streamlines this tedious task with its **Manage Sources** button. This allows you to enter the information of the sources you used into the actual file. Once entered, that information is saved for you to use, update, and apply into both citations and a bibliography (created in the next lesson).

You can choose a **writing style** such as **APA**, **MLA**, **Chicago**, and more to direct Word on how it should format the data you have entered. With just the click of a mouse, Word will adjust the punctuation and formatting of citations and bibliographies to suit whatever style you have chosen.

Each **source type** of information (book, lecture, article from a periodical, website, report, and more) has its own set of fields that you fill in so that Word can create the proper formatting when producing a citation or bibliography. The Source Manager displays a preview of how Word will arrange the information depending on which style has been selected.

While the Source Manager defaults to show just the recommended bibliography fields, you can **show all bibliography fields** if you wish to include more information. Whether the extra fields are shown or not, if you enter information into them, Word will save them.

SKILLS PREVIEW

Enter a source into the Source Manager	• CLICK the REFERENCES tab and locate the Citations & Bibliography group. CLICK the Manage Sources button (Manage Sources). CLICK New. CLICK the Type of Source drop-down arrow. CHOOSE the source type that is applicable. TYPE the information. CLICK OK.
View all the bibliography fields	• CLICK the REFERENCES tab and locate the Citations & Bibliography group. CLICK the Manage Sources button (Manage Sources). CLICK New or Edit to open an entry. CLICK the Show All Bibliography Fields button. Scroll to see all the fields.
Edit an existing source	• CLICK the REFERENCES tab and locate the Citations & Bibliography group. CLICK the Manage Sources button (Manage Sources). CLICK on an entry in the list (Current or Master). CLICK Edit. Make the desired changes. CLICK OK.
Change the writing style	• CLICK the REFERENCES tab and locate the Citations & Bibliography group. CLICK the Style drop-down arrow. CHOOSE the desired style.
Preview the style of citations or bibliography	• CLICK the REFERENCES tab and locate the Citations & Bibliography group. CLICK Manage Sources (Manage Sources). The Preview window appears at the bottom of the Source Manager.
Sort entries on the Current and Master Lists	• CLICK the REFERENCES tab and locate the Citations & Bibliography group. CLICK Manage Sources (Manage Sources). CLICK the Sort by Author drop-down arrow. CHOOSE the manner of sort you desire.

1 Most professional documents require that the sources of information be cited. This can be done quickly within Word. And once information is added, it can be managed in many useful ways. Locate and open the file **wd02b3-associatesdegree.docx**. Save it as **wd02b4-associatesdegree.docx**.

2 You have used a couple of sources in researching the report. You will let Word manage. Entering the names of the authors can be a little tricky, so let's concentrate on that step first.

CLICK the REFERENCES Tab and locate the Citations & Bibliography group.

CLICK the Manage Sources button (see Figure WD2.34).

CLICK New.

CLICK the Type of Source drop-down arrow.

CHOOSE Book.

CLICK Edit on the Author line.

Add the following into the corresponding Bibliography Fields:

Last: **Jordan**

First: **Dorry**

CLICK the Add button to add this author to the list.

Add the following into the corresponding Bibliography Fields:

Last: **Korrem**

First: **Vijat**

CLICK the Add button to add this author to the list.

CLICK OK.

(*Result:* Both names are listed alphabetically in the writing style selected.)

FIGURE WD2.34 The Source Manager, Create Source, and Edit Name dialog boxes

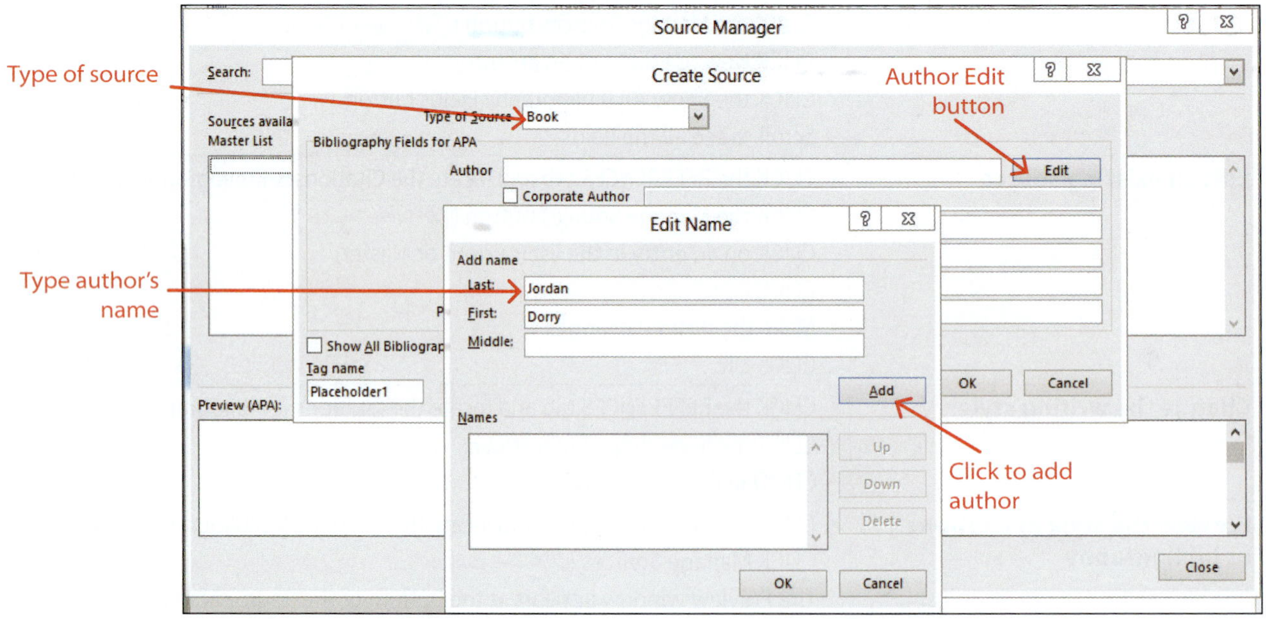

3 Now let's add the rest of the information by filling in the correct fields.

Title: **The Expansion of Educational Opportunities in America**

Year: **2008**

City: **Chicago**

Publisher: **Westfront Publishing, Inc.**

CLICK OK to return to the Source Manager window.

(*Result:* The entries appears on both the lists. The Master List is stored on your computer and will be available with every document you open. The Current List is stored in this document's file.)

4 Notice how the Preview in the Source Manager displays how the citation and the bibliography entry will appear (see Figure WD2.35). This format is based on the chosen style, which appears in parenthesis above the preview window.

CLICK New.

CLICK the Type of Source drop-down arrow.

CHOOSE Web site.

CLICK Corporate Author (meaning no individual author is credited) to open the Corporate Author field.

Add the information into the appropriate fields:

Corporate Author: **New Teaching Horizons**

Name of Web Page: **Technology and Teaching**

Name of Web Site: **New Teaching Horizons**

Year: **2012**

Month: **August**

URL: **www.newteachinghorizons.edu/research/distance/techandteach**

FIGURE WD2.35 The Source Manager's Preview pane

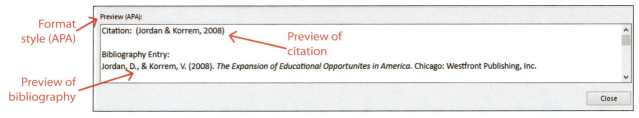

5 Websites can be a great resource, but they can be changed quickly without notice. You should include information on when you accessed the site.

CLICK the Show All Bibliography Fields check box.

Fill in the information as follows using today's actual date (these dates are examples):

Year Accessed: *2014*

Month Accessed: *September*

Day Accessed: *12*

CLICK OK.

 MORE INFO

Many more bibliography fields are available, but only certain ones are recommended for ensuring enough information for citing and listing in a bibliography. They are the only ones that appear when the Show All Bibliography Fields button is off. When the Show All Bibliography Fields button is on, these fields can still be identified by red asterisks.

TABLE WD2.1 Common fields used by the Source Manager

Field	Information
Type of Source	Choose book, website, article, etc., to generate the required fields.
Author	The name of each author. It is recommended to use the edit button to avoid errors in style.
Corporate Author	Many organizations issue material that is authored by a combination of people and not intended to belong to any one author.
Title	Usually the title of the article or web page. Not to be confused with the name of the periodical or the journal.
Year	The year of copyright. The year the work was published.
City	The city in which the work was published.
Publisher	The name of the publishing company or organization.
Pages	The specific pages that contain the information being used as a source.
URL	The actual web address of the specific page being referenced.
Name of the Web Site	For example, the URL for *The New York Times* is www.nytimes.com, but the name of the website is "The New York Times."
Name of Web Page	If you got your information from the health page of *The New York Times*, you would enter "Health."

6 CLICK New.

Add a Journal Article using the following information:

Author: **Maurice Archeneaux**

Title: **Teacher, May I Please Leave the City?**

Journal Name: **The Advanced Education Report of America**

Year: **2010**

Pages: **77-78**

CLICK OK.

CLICK Close.

7 Notice that the Style button in the Citations & Bibliography group is set to APA by default (see Figure WD2.36).

CLICK the drop-down arrow.

This list includes other writing styles such as Chicago (mostly in newspapers and journalism) and MLA (mostly in the fields of English and foreign language).

CHOOSE MLA.

CLICK Manage Sources.

The preview window will show the new formatting of the citation and bibliography entry using the rules of MLA.

FIGURE WD2.36 Reference writing styles

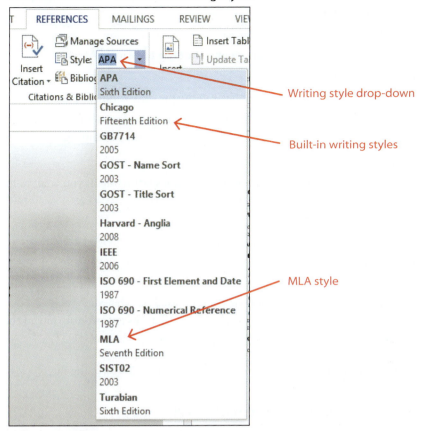

Writing style drop-down

Built-in writing styles

MLA style

8 With the Source Manager dialog box still open, let's edit an error in one of the sources.

CLICK on "Jordan, Dorry," etc. in the Current List window.

CLICK Edit.

In the Author field, CLICK Edit and add the following author:

Lawrence James Anderson

CLICK OK.

Correct the year of publication to **2009**.

CLICK OK.

CLICK Yes to the warning that this source exists in both the Master and Current List.

💡 **TIP**

Word will adjust the formatting of citations and bibliographies from one writing style to another without you having to reenter the material. The information you entered, even if it is not used in the style you've chosen, is never lost.

9 Notice that the preview shows (in MLA style) the authors' names listed in complete form including Anderson's middle name.

CLICK Close to exit the Source Manager.

In the Citations & Bibliography group, change the style back to APA:

CLICK Manage Sources.

CLICK the "Jordan, Dorry" entry to display it in the preview window.

Notice the authors are shown by last name and initials only. Anderson has both a first and middle initial displaying. This is how Word instantly restructures the formatting based on the style you have selected.

10 By default, Word sorts the list of sources by the author's last name. If you want to locate an entry from a long list, you can adjust the list order.

CLICK the Sort by Author drop-down arrow.

CHOOSE Sort by Year so the list reorders itself.

CLICK into the Search field of the Source Manager.

TYPE please.

As you type, the list (both lists, in fact) sorts itself based on what you enter.

(*Result:* You can locate a source by any string of text that was entered into any of the fields.)

CLICK Close.

11 The Source Manager should appear similar to Figure WD2.37. Save the file.

FIGURE WD2.37 Completion of Lesson Word 2B4

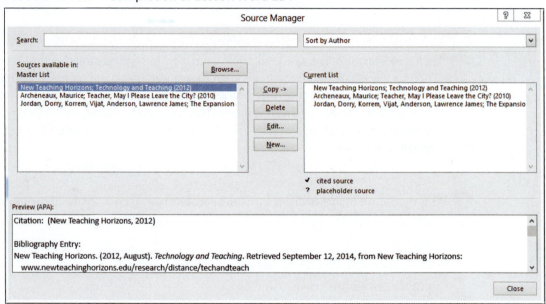

Inserting Citations & Bibliography

LESSON OVERVIEW

Citations and bibliographies are intimately related. A **citation** is an in-line reference indicating from where the specific information was taken. A **bibliography** (also commonly known as Works Cited or, simply, **References**) is a list of the actual documents and sources used in the research of the document. The in-line citation is a short reference that allows the reader to locate the entry in the bibliography. This provides readers with the ability to locate the source for themselves for further study or for substantiating the claims made in the report.

Because the bibliography is a list of material used in writing the document, only sources that have been cited in the document text should be listed in the bibliography. The **Source Manager** displays which sources have been cited by placing a check mark next to them in the Current List of sources.

Citations and bibliographies have specific formats based on the writing style of the document. When you select one of these styles (APA, MLA, and such) Word will adjust the formatting of both the citation and the bibliography entry appropriately.

The writer can **edit the citation** to include things such as the **page numbers**, but you can even **edit the source** directly from the citation in the text.

Bibliographies can be created instantly (similar to a table of contents). After changes have been made to sources, you can **update a bibliography** to show the latest changes.

SKILLS PREVIEW

Insert a citation	• CLICK the mouse in the location you wish. CLICK the REFERENCES tab and locate the Citations & Bibliography group. CLICK Insert Citation to open the Current List of sources. CHOOSE the desired source.
Edit a citation	• RIGHT-CLICK on the citation field. CHOOSE Edit Citation. Make the desired changes.
Edit a source from a citation	• RIGHT-CLICK on the citation field. CHOOSE Edit Source. Make the desired changes.
Ensure each source has been cited in the document	• CLICK the REFERENCES tab and locate the Citations & Bibliography group. CLICK Manage Sources (Manage Sources). Word will place a check mark next to each source that has been cited in the document.
Generate a bibliography	• CLICK the REFERENCES tab and locate the Citations & Bibliography group. CLICK the Bibliography button. CHOOSE the style of bibliography desired.
Update a bibliography	• RIGHT-CLICK in the bibliography field. CHOOSE Update field.
Adjust the formatting of a bibliography	• SELECT the entire text of the bibliography. RIGHT-CLICK inside the selected text. CHOOSE Font or Paragraph depending on the changes you would like to make. Make the desired changes.
Remove a generated bibliography	• SELECT the entire table including the title. RIGHT-CLICK in the selected area. CHOOSE Cut.

1 Locate and open the file **wd02b4-associatesdegree.docx**. Save the file as **wd02b5-associatesdegree.docx**.

2 On Page 4, Section 2, locate the sentence that begins with the words "Minimal labs."

CLICK the mouse immediately after the word "labs."

PRESS the space bar once.

CLICK the REFERENCES tab and locate the Citations & Bibliography group.

CLICK Insert Citation to open the Current List of sources (created in the last lesson and displayed in alphabetical order by author).

CHOOSE "New Teaching Horizons."

(*Result:* Word inserts the APA style in-line citation from the information that was entered into the Source Manager.)

3 On Page 3, section 2, locate the sentence that ends with "is greater than what is currently available."

CLICK the mouse before the period.

PRESS the space bar once.

CLICK Insert Citation to open the Current List of sources (created during the previous lesson).

CHOOSE "Archeneaux, Maurice" to insert that citation.

See Figure WD2.38 to see how the citations appear.

FIGURE WD2.38   Citations inserted into the text

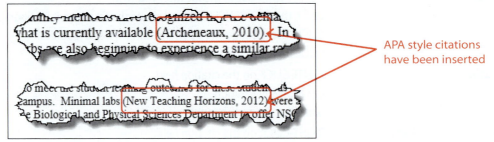

APA style citations have been inserted

4 CLICK the REFERENCES tab and locate the Citations & Bibliography group.

CLICK Manage Sources.

Notice in Figure WD2.39 that the Current List has check marks next to two of the entries.

These check marks indicate that two of the three sources have been cited in the document.

When complete, all entries that you are claiming to be a source for the document must be cited somewhere in the document—or else deleted from this list because they were not actually used.

FIGURE WD2.39   The Current List in the Source Manager
                   showing the cited sources

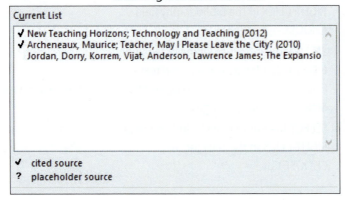

5 Let's add the final reference.

On Page 1, Section 2, you will insert two citations for the same source.

Locate the sentence that ends with "…Southeast, and Bolton Field centers."

CLICK the mouse before the period.

PRESS the space bar once.

CLICK Insert Citation.

CHOOSE "Jordan, Dorry, Korrem, et al."

Locate the sentence that ends with "to become campus complexes."

CLICK the mouse before the period.

Insert the same citation for Jordan, Dorry, Korrem, et al.

6 On Page 3, Section 2, locate the in-line citation for Archeneaux.

RIGHT-CLICK on the citation field.

CHOOSE Edit Citation.

CLICK into the Pages window.

TYPE 77-78.

CLICK OK.

(*Result:* The citation has been edited to include the specific page numbers.)

7 You realize that the source "New Teaching Horizons" has an error. You can make a change to that source directly from the citation.

Locate the citation "New Teaching Horizons" on Page 4, Section 2.

CLICK on the citation.

CLICK the drop-down arrow.

CHOOSE Edit Source.

CLICK off the Corporate Author button.

CLICK the Edit button next to the Author window.

CLICK on the only entry in the Names window.

CLICK Delete.

Enter this information into the appropriate fields:

Last: Meyers

First: Florence

CLICK OK twice.

CLICK Yes to the warning window.

(*Result:* The corrected citation now shows in the citation field.)

8 Move the mouse to the very end of the document above the endnotes.

INSERT a page break to create a new, blank last page.

CLICK the REFERENCES tab and locate the Citations & Bibliography group.

CLICK the Bibliography button.

CHOOSE Works Cited.

(*Result:* An automatic bibliography has been inserted into the document as in Figure WD2.40. The terms *Bibliography, References,* and *Works Cited* are interchangeable in meaning, but some styles prefer one.)

FIGURE WD2.40 The built-in bibliography using the Works Cited style

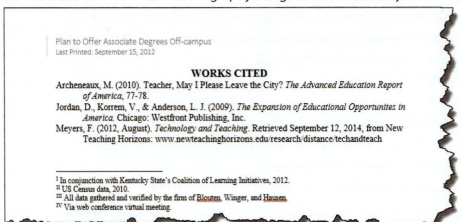

Plan to Offer Associate Degrees Off-campus
Last Printed: September 15, 2012

WORKS CITED

Archeneaux, M. (2010). Teacher, May I Please Leave the City? *The Advanced Education Report of America,* 77-78.

Jordan, D., Korrem, V., & Anderson, L. J. (2009). *The Expansion of Educational Opportunites in America.* Chicago: Westfront Publishing, Inc.

Meyers, F. (2012, August). *Technology and Teaching.* Retrieved September 12, 2014, from New Teaching Horizons: www.newteachinghorizons.edu/research/distance/techandteach

—————————

[I] In conjunction with Kentucky State's Coalition of Learning Initiatives, 2012.
[II] US Census data, 2010.
[III] All data gathered and verified by the firm of Blouten, Winger, and Hausen.
[IV] Via web conference virtual meeting.

9 The Works Cited is automatically formatted in APA style because that was the style selected in the Citations & Bibliography group. It is not uncommon for APA style to require that bibliographies be double-spaced. That is easy to do.

SELECT the entire text of the Works Cited field (except the title).

RIGHT-CLICK in the selected text.

CHOOSE Paragraph.

In the Spacing section of the dialog box:

CLICK the Line Spacing drop-down arrow.

CHOOSE Double.

CLICK OK.

(*Result:* The Works Cited section is now double spaced. You can click after the title "Works Cited" and add a blank line to improve the spacing, if you like.)

TIP

To remove a bibliography, you need to select the entire table including the title. Then RIGHT-CLICK in the selected area and choose Cut from the Shortcut menu.

---

10 Let's insert our own custom bibliography.

DELETE the current bibliography.

CLICK the mouse at the top of the last page.

TYPE **REFERENCES USED IN THIS REPORT**.

PRESS ENTER twice.

CLICK the REFERENCES tab and locate the Citations & Bibliography group.

CLICK the Bibliography button.

CHOOSE Insert Bibliography.

SELECT the title of the bibliography and apply bold and center the text.

11 The final pages of your document should now appear similar to Figure WD2.41. Save your file.

FIGURE WD2.41 Completion of Lesson Word 2B5

MULTIPLE-CHOICE QUIZ

Select the best choice in the following questions to review the project concepts. Good luck!

1. When you make changes to a Heading 2 style
   a. all Heading 2 text will change.
   b. all text in the document will change.
   c. all headings will change.
   d. None of these is correct.

2. A character style will
   a. change the style of all characters in a paragraph.
   b. change the style of the paragraph containing the selected characters.
   c. format the character of any text.
   d. None of these is correct.

3. An automatic Table of Contents generates itself based on the
   a. order of the document.
   b. levels of the TOC settings.
   c. text designated as headings.
   d. All of these is correct.

4. By default, each entry into an automatic Table of Contents is
   a. hyperlinked to its location in the text.
   b. set to level one.
   c. highlighted in bold.
   d. All of these are correct.

5. Footnotes are indicated in text by
   a. markers that are superscript.
   b. tiny numbers that are subscript.
   c. Roman numerals.
   d. None of these is correct.

6. Footnotes can be located
   a. in-line with text.
   b. at the end of the chapter.
   c. at the bottom of the page.
   d. All of these are correct.

7. Endnotes can appear
   a. at the end of a page.
   b. at the end of a section.
   c. at the end of a paragraph.
   d. None of these is correct.

8. Which of the following is NOT a writing style supported by Word?
   a. Chicago
   b. Turabian
   c. MLA
   d. ISO 9000

9. In-line citations can be inserted through which shortcut?
   a. Right-click and select Insert Citation
   b. Selecting text and double-clicking
   c. Ctrl + Shift + C
   d. None of these is correct.

10. A bibliography is generated by the
    a. headings within the document.
    b. citations inserted in the document.
    c. information in the Source Manager.
    d. None of these is correct.

In this exercise, you will open an existing document and add unifying features such as document headings, table of contents, footnotes, endnotes, research sources, citations, and a bibliography. You will be provided with specific tasks, but not step-by-step instructions. The final document is shown in Figure WD2.42.

FIGURE WD2.42   Work It Out WD-2B-E1: completed

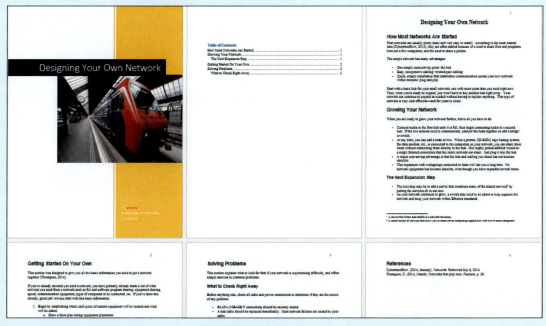

1. Locate and open the project data file **wd02b-ex01.docx**. Save the file as **wd02b-hw01.docx**.

2. Change the following subtitles to Heading 1 styles:

   "How Most Networks Are Started"

   "Growing Your Network"

   "Getting Started On Your Own"

   "Solving Problems"

   Change the following subtitles to Heading 2 styles:

   "The Next Expansion Step"

   "What to Check Right Away"

3. Modify Heading 2 so that it is Arial, 14 point.

4. Create a Table of Contents on Page 1 of Section 1 using Automatic Table 2.

5. Add the following footnotes:

   After the phrase "…combines many of the shared services…"

   Footnote: **A select bundle of services that allow you to share server computing capabilities with two or more computers.**

   After the phrase "…add a bridge"

   Footnote: **A device that filters data traffic at a network boundary.**

6 Using the APA writing style add the following source into the Source Manager:

Web site:

Corporate Author: **Cybermindflow**

Name of Web Page: **Networks**

Year: **2014**

Month: **January**

Year Accessed: **2014**

Month Accessed: **July**

Day Accessed: **6**

7 Using APA writing style add the following source into the Source Manager:

Article in a periodical:

Author: **Clarence Thompson**

Title: **Networks that play nice**

Periodical Title: **Fastzam**

Year: **2014**

Month: **March**

Pages: **26**

8 Insert in-line citations at the following places:

"…according to the most current data…"

Insert: **Cybermindflow**

"…need to put a network together."

Insert: **Clarence Thompson**

9 Create new blank page and insert a bibliography using the References format.

10 Save and close the document file **wd02b-hw01.docx**.

In this exercise, you will open an existing document and add unifying features such as document headings, table of contents, footnotes, endnotes, research sources, citations, and a bibliography. You will be provided with specific tasks, but not step-by-step instructions. The final document is shown in Figure WD2.43.

FIGURE WD2.43 Work It Out WD-2B-E2: completed

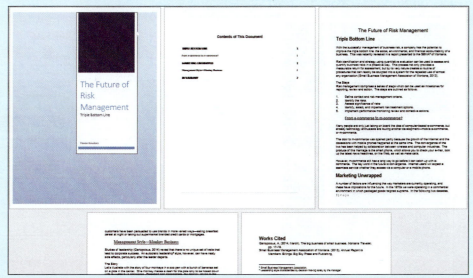

1. Locate and open the exercise data file **wd02b-ex02.docx**. Save the file as **wd02b-hw02.docx**.

2. Apply Heading 1 to the following subtitles:
   "Triple Bottom Line"
   "Marketing Unwrapped"
   "In Summary"
   Apply Heading 2 to the following subtitles:
   "From e-commerce to m-commerce?"
   "Management Style—Monkey Business"

3. Modify the Normal style to Arial font.

4. Generate a Table of Contents on Page 1, Section 1 using the custom table of contents and the Classic format. Create a centered and bold title of 14 point size with the words **Contents of This Document** above the table.

5. Locate the abbreviation "SBMA" on Page 1, Section 2. Insert an endnote after the abbreviation. The endnote should appear at the end of the document and say:
   Small Business Management Association.

6. Locate the term "autocratic leadership" on page 2, Section 2. Insert an endnote after the term. The endnote should appear at the end of the document and say:
   Leadership style characterized by decision making solely by the manager.

7. Change the number format of the endnotes to lowercase letters (a, b, c,…)

8. Locate the sentence on Page 1, Section 2 that ends with "use of almost any organization." Insert an APA style citation from the Small Business Management Association.

   Locate the phrase "Studies of leadership…" on Page 2, Section 2. Insert an APA style citation from Anthony Garlopolous after the word "leadership".

9. Create a new page at the end of the document and insert a bibliography using the Works Cited model.

10. Save and close the **wd02b-hw02.docx** document file.

In this exercise, you will open an existing document and add unifying features such as document headings, table of contents, footnotes, endnotes, research sources, citations, and a bibliography. You will be provided with specific tasks, but not step-by-step instructions. The final document is shown in Figure WD2.44.

FIGURE WD2.44   Work It out WD-2B-E3: completed

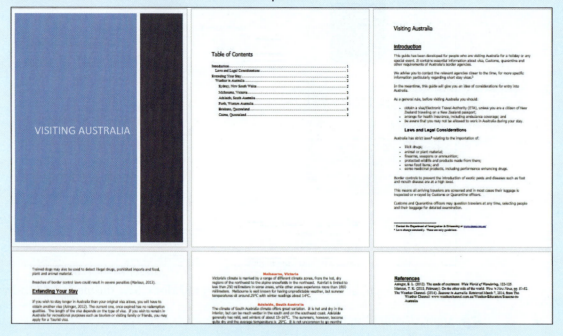

1. Locate and open the exercise data file **wd02b-ex03.docx**. Save the file as **wd02b-hw03.docx**.

2. Locate the sentence on Page 1, Section 2 that ends with "regarding short stay visas." Insert this footnote: **Contact the Department of Immigration & Citizenship at www.immi.gov.au/**

   Locate the phrase "Australia has strict laws…" on Page 1, Section 2. Insert this footnote: **Laws change constantly. These are only guidelines**.

3. On Page 2, Section 2, locate the phrase "extenuating circumstances" and insert the following endnote: **Contact the citizenship representative for your home country**.

4. Convert all the notes in the document to footnotes.

5. Apply Heading 1 to the following subtitles:

   "Introduction"

   "Extending Your Stay"

   Apply Heading 2 to the following subtitles:

   "Laws and Legal Considerations"

   "Weather in Australia"

6 Modify Heading 3 so that it is Verdana font, 11 point, Red color, bold, and centered. Apply the new style to the following subtitles:

"Sydney, New South Wales"

"Melbourne, Victoria"

"Adelaide, South Australia"

"Perth, Western Australia"

"Brisbane, Queensland"

"Cairns, Queensland"

7 Generate a custom Table of Contents on Page 1, Section 1. Ensure the three levels show.

8 Insert a citation from The Weather Channel after the subtitle "Weather in Australia."

Insert a citation from Azinger after the phrase "…you will have to obtain another visa."

Insert a citation from Marious after the phrase "…could result in severe penalties."

9 Generate a bibliography using the References model.

10 Save and then close the wd02b-hw03.docx document file.

Chapter Summary

Word provides so many powerful features that many documents that were once fashioned only by professionals are now produced easily by almost anyone. Faculty, students, the self-employed, administrative personnel, and even the boss in the corner office can not only produce and edit the content they want, but they can also control the design and formatting. In addition to removing such barriers, Word has also proven to be a big cost-saving advantage for businesses of all sizes.

This chapter concentrated on the functions used to prepare a long document for presentation or printing. Creating a cover page that matches the tone of the content is easy. Adding page numbers to the document and controlling the formatting of those numbers provides flexibility for the writer. Hard breaks such as page breaks and section breaks allow you to control where pages end and where new sections begin. The inclusion of headers and footers adds clarity to a document as well as a unification of style across pages.

The application of headings to a document has many advantages. Once applied, modifications to the style of a heading instantly change all existing headings of the same style throughout the document. Headings are also vital to creating an automatic table of contents—one of Word's greatest timesavers. To further improve the precision of writing, footnotes or endnotes can be inserted effortlessly and will reorder themselves automatically with changes to the document.

Perhaps the most welcome of all features is the Manage Sources function. While researching a report, the Source Manager allows you to enter the detailed information normally gathered for a bibliography and store it directly into the document file. From here, the Source Manager allows you to insert citations into the document immediately as well as generate a perfect bibliography in a fraction of a second. Both the citations and the bibliography can be formatted into almost any of the common writing styles.

Chapter Key Terms

Align within a header or footer, p. W-79

APA, p. W-107

Below text, p. W-103

Bibliography, p. W-113

Character style, p. W-93

Chicago style, p. W-107

Citations, p. W-113

Common fields used by the Source Manager, p. W-110

Content of footnote, p. W-103

Continue from previous section, p. W-73

Convert endnotes to footnotes, p. W-103

Convert footnotes to endnotes, p. W-103

Cover page, p. W-62

Custom header or footer, p. W-79

Custom table of contents, p. W-93

Date & Time, p. W-83

Date Picker, p. W-62

Delete hard breaks, p. W-74

Different First Page, p. W-68

Different odd and even pages, p. W-82

Document properties, p. W-62, W-64, W-79, W-80

Edit a footnote, p. W-63

Edit the citation, p. W-113

Edit the source, p. W-113

End of chapter, p. W-103

End of section, p. W-103

Endnote, p. W-60, W-103

Footer from bottom, p. W-83

Footnote, p. W-60, W-103

Format page numbers, p. W-73

Hard page breaks, p. W-60

Header and Footer view, p. W-68

Header from top, p. W-83

Headers and footers, p. W-60

Heading styles, p. W-93

Headings, p. W-60

Hyperlink, p. W-98

Link to Previous, p. W-83

Manage Sources, p. W-60, W-107

Mini toolbar, p. W-66, W-81, W-82

MLA, p. W-107

Modify, p. W-93

New Style, p. W-93

Next page section break, p. W-73

Normal, p. W-93

Page break, p. W-73

Page numbers, p. W-68, W-113

Paragraph style, p. W-93

Placeholder, p. W-62

Remove a bibliography, p. W-113

Remove content control, p. W-66

Remove Header or footer, p. W-83

Remove table of contents, p. W-98

References, p. W-113

Section break, p. W-60, W-73

Show all bibliography fields, p. W-107

Soft breaks, p. W-73

Sort entries to Current and Master Lists, p. W-107

Source Manager, p. W-113

On Your Own WD-2C-E1

This project provides the opportunity to practice the most important skills covered in this chapter, regardless of the project in which they were introduced. As the chapters progress, these comprehensive projects will become more challenging, building on all of the skills covered to that point.

Let's get started! In this project, you will take an existing document and prepare it for printing. You will be given general guidance, but not specific instructions. The finished document may look like the one shown in Figure WD2.45.

FIGURE WD2.45   Professional Handout: Sample of finished version

Locate and open the data file **wd02cp1.docx**. Save the file as **wd02cp1-ex1.docx**.

Add a cover page to the document that includes the title, subtitle, author, and date. Set the date to the current date. In the subtitle add **A discussion of the Invisible Barrier to Women in the Workplace**. Delete any other placeholders.

Insert a page break before "Concerns with Correction" to move it to the next page. Set up a section break so there is a blank page after the cover page. The blank page (and the cover page) should be a separate section from the rest of the document. Set up page numbering so that the numbers do not display on the cover page or the blank page or on page 1 of the document.

Create a header with the title of the document. Create a footer with the author's name and a date that automatically updates. The headers and footers should not appear on page 1 (page 3 of 6). Apply Heading 1 styles to each of the short subtitles. On the blank page, generate an automatic table of contents.

Add endnotes to the following phrases:

Sentence	Endnote
"…a fantasy novel, the idea of 'affirmative action' "	An active effort to improve the employment or educational opportunities of members of minority groups and women.
"…consider the health field."	Includes medical, dental, physiotherapy, and other related areas of work.
"…evidence of discrimination."	In this case using illegal criteria in the hiring process.

Add the following sources into the document's Source Manager using the APA style:

1. From the website Merriam-Webster Dictionary, the page *Affirmative Action*. The year of the page is copyright 2014 and the URL is http://www.merriam-webster.com/dictionary/affirmative%20action

2. From the book *A Level Playing Field Cannot Be Tilted* by Jacob Martin. Printed by Paraline Publishing, Ltd., in 2005 in New York City. The points used are from pages 81–82.

3. *Personal Communication* between the author, Russell Madden, and a number of employees in the health field. These communications occurred on April 11, 2013. (Hint: This source would be entered as an interview entitled Personal Communication.)

Add the following citations into the document (including one at the end of an endnote):

Sentence	Citation
"…tend to be more highly compensated."	Jacob Martin
"…accept only part-time positions."	Personal Communication
"…minority groups and women."	Merriam-Webster

Insert a bibliography using APA style and the Works Cited built-in style.

On Your Own WD-2C-E2

This project provides the opportunity to practice the most important skills covered in this chapter, regardless of the project in which they were introduced. As the chapters progress, these comprehensive projects will become more challenging, building on all of the skills covered to that point.

Let's get started! In this project, you will take an existing document and prepare it for printing. You will be given general guidance, but not specific instructions. The finished document may look like the one shown in Figure WD2.46.

FIGURE WD2.46   Professional Handout: Sample of finished version

Locate and open the data file **wd02cp2.docx**. Save the file as **wd02cp1-ex2.docx**.

Insert a cover page that displays the title, authors, and date. You can create any of these placeholders if you like, but remove any other placeholders.

Insert page numbers into the right-hand margin of the document. Ensure no page number shows on the cover page. Format the following subtitles as Heading 1: "Overview," "Tire Town Superstore," "Blue Zone Coffee," "Sunshine Farm Bakery," "Davison Family Foods Ltd.," "Piper Dairy Products," "Our Mandate." Format the other subtitles as Heading 2. Use breaks to ensure the pages look organized. Modify Heading 2 to be 12 point size and a dark blue.

Insert a footer that includes the title of the document and the authors. The footer should not appear on the cover page. Create a header that shows the date centered across the page and matches the font of the footer.

Add the following to the Source Manager: Sunshine Farm Economic Development Commission Annual Report. It is from 2013 and has no identifiable author. It was printed in Minoka and published by Austin Printing.

Add endnotes to the following phrases:

Sentence	Endnote
"…five outstanding businesses"	As selected by the Sunshine Farm Marketing Group, 2014.
"…browse in the brewery's Beer Bin."	Contact Sunshine Farm Breweries via e-mail: sfbrewbeer@sunshinefarm.com.
"…fluid milk production plant."	A process that combines the operations of separation, pasteurization, and homogenization.

Add the following citations into the document:

Sentence	Citation
"…Purity Law of 1516,"	Bavarian Beer
"…to a healthier lifestyle."	Foester, Belinda
"…create new employment and wealth."	Sunshine Farm Economic…

Edit the Foester citation to include the page number of 45. Convert the endnotes to footnotes.

Create a blank page after the cover page and insert a table of contents using the Formal format. Correct the page numbering so it doesn't show on the table of contents page and so that the overview appears on page 1. Create a new "last page" and generate an automatic bibliography on that page using the References model.

3

Enhancing Your Documents

One of the greatest advantages of Microsoft Word is the amazing flexibility the program offers. The value of a word processor can be seen in just a few minutes, but this type of processing can include much more than just words. Bringing pictures and graphics together with text can produce striking results such as posters, flyers, and signs that communicate important messages in a professional manner—and in the blink of an eye.

Sometimes a message is emphasized by including other elements. This chapter provides you with the tools to add some muscle to your message. The right images can strengthen the significance of the information. Catching the reader's eye is frequently the hardest part of relaying a valuable idea. Remember: although the right words are important, "a picture can be worth a thousand words."

Combining the appropriate visual touches together with just the right amount of text is a balancing act. With a word processor, you can work toward that balance one step at a time. This chapter focuses on a step-by-step approach to create an effective message without changing the original idea. This process allows you to weigh the effectiveness of each addition to ensure that good balance.

PROJECT

Creating a Marketing Poster

In this project, you will take an existing event and the same information from a previous year, but you will rev it up to make it much more appealing. This document can be added to your career portfolio and called "Word: Marketing Poster."

The result of this chapter will be more than just an effective poster. It will allow you to explore some of Word's most appealing visual features, which can be useful in many different types of documents.

THE SITUATION

Carmando College Career Fair

You have been asked to help the Student Alumni Association promote its career fair. This event provides one of the best opportunities for students and potential employers to meet and learn about each other. This event has a long history, and the old signage has been seen so many times people tend to overlook it. You have been given new information, but in the form of the old poster. Your expertise in designing a fresh and appealing poster will help the alumni get the message out to as many students as possible.

Designing a Marketing Poster

PROJECT OBJECTIVES

After completing this project, you will be able to:

- Insert and adjust photographs.
- Create text boxes.
- Add and control borders and shading.
- Insert and format shapes.

"It's not just *what* you say—it's *how* you say it." Effective communication is often more than just the right words. Thankfully, Word provides powerful tools to enhance your message with images, clip art, photos, borders, text boxes, and even predesigned styles. Once you start to investigate the possibilities, you will find that you can produce professional-quality signs and posters suitable for most any organization, club, school, team, or business. The ability to showcase this type of design will add an impressive aspect to your portfolio of projects.

PROJECT FILE: *Available at* www.mhhe.com/office2013projectlearn

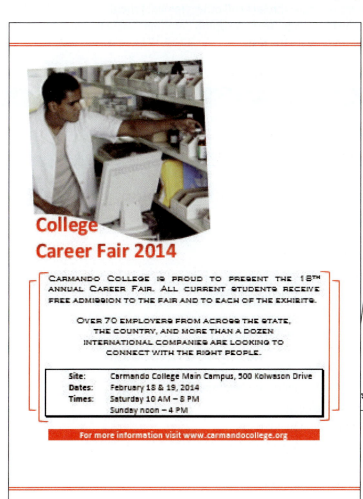

Inserting and Adjusting Photographs

LESSON OVERVIEW

Taking an existing message and making it appear new again is one of the ways Word allows you to use your creativity. Even if you feel your creativity is limited, you will soon find that, because Word offers complete control over most of the elements, you can experiment freely—and even more important, quickly. Word provides many built-in styles, but you ultimately have the ability to let your imagination guide you.

The first step to inserting a picture into a document is to find one. Word's **Online Pictures** allows you to search Office.com's Clip Art library and other sources of royalty-free images using **keywords**. Once you locate the right image and insert it into your document, you can resize the image, move it, rotate it, flip it, and even use the **Layout dialog box** to set the precise size and positioning.

Sometimes you do not need the entire picture and Word allows you to crop the unwanted portion. You can use the **Crop to shape** feature to crop the picture inside a **shape**. The **Layout Options** feature allows you to decide how the text and other elements should wrap around the image. **Text wrapping** determines how the image blends with the text.

SKILLS PREVIEW

Search using Online Pictures	• CLICK the INSERT tab and locate the Illustrations group. CLICK Online Pictures. TYPE what you are looking for (keyword) into Office.com Clip Art window.
Insert an online picture	• CLICK the thumbnail image to select it. DOUBLE-CLICK the image (or click the Insert button) to insert it in the document.
Resize an inserted image	• CLICK on the image to select it. CLICK and hold any of the sizing handles. DRAG the image to the desired size.
Set precise height and width of an image	• CLICK on the image to select it. CLICK the FORMAT tab under Picture Tools. Locate the Size group. Adjust the Height or Width spinners, or • CLICK the Size Launch button. CLICK the SIZE tab (if necessary). Set the Height and Width spinners to the desired size.
Rotate an image	• CLICK on the image to select it. CLICK and hold the rotation handle (⟳). DRAG the image to the desired rotation, or • CLICK on the image to select it. CLICK the FORMAT tab under Picture Tools. CLICK the Size Launch button. Locate the Size group. CLICK the SIZE tab (if necessary). Adjust the spinner to the desired rotation.
Flip an image	• CLICK the image to select it. CLICK the FORMAT tab under Picture Tools. Locate the Arrange group. CLICK the Rotate Objects button (Rotate ▾). SELECT Flip Horizontal or Flip Vertical.

Crop a picture to a shape	• CLICK the image to select it. CLICK the FORMAT tab under Picture Tools. Locate the Size group. CLICK the drop-down arrow of the Crop button (⊞). CLICK Crop to Shape. SELECT the desired shape.
Set text wrapping around a picture	• CLICK the image to select it. CLICK the FORMAT tab under Picture Tools. Locate the Arrange group. CLICK Wrap Text. Choose the type of wrapping you desire, or • CLICK the image to select it. CLICK the Layout Options button (⊡) that appears next to the image. Choose the type of wrapping you desire.
Set the absolute position of an image	• CLICK on the image to select it. CLICK the FORMAT tab under Picture Tools. Locate the Size group. CLICK the Size Launch button. CLICK the Position tab (if necessary). Set the Horizontal and Vertical alignments.

PROJECT PRACTICE

1 Locate the file **wd03a1.docx**. Open it and save it as **wd03a1-collegeposter**. Zoom out so you can see the entire page. Ensure the mouse pointer is at the top of the document.

2 To search for and insert an image (in this case a photograph):

CLICK the INSERT tab and locate the Illustrations group.

CLICK Online Pictures.

TYPE **medical** into Office.com Clip Art window.

PRESS ENTER to open the results shown in small images called thumbnails.

Scroll down to find the image shown in Figure WD3.1. (Your results may differ from the figure as the clip art is constantly changing.)

CLICK the image to select it.

DOUBLE-CLICK the image (or click the Insert button) to insert it in the document.

MORE INFO

You can insert more than one image at a time. Select the first image by clicking on it. Then hold the **Ctrl** button down as you click on other images. When you release the **Ctrl** button, all of the images will remain selected. Click the Insert button and all the images will be pasted into your document.

FIGURE WD3.1 Office.com Clip Art search window

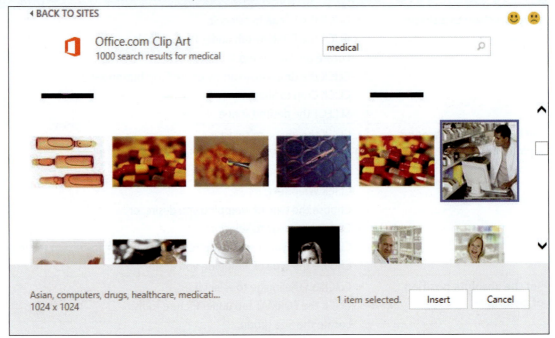

3. The image is too large, but you will fix that. Notice the eight small boxes around the outline of the image (see Figure WD3.2). These are called sizing handles. They allow you to quickly change the size and proportions of the image.

CLICK and HOLD your mouse on the bottom-right sizing handle.

DRAG the bottom-right sizing handle toward the top left-hand corner of the photo until your mouse is approximately halfway to the top left-hand corner.
Release the mouse.
(*Result:* The image has been reduced in size.)

4. While the image is still selected (the sizing handles are visible), the PICTURE TOOLS tab is activated and the Format ribbon is displayed. From here we can make absolute size choices.
Locate the Size group.

💡 **TIP**

When dragging images or objects around the screen, automatic alignment guides will show up when the edge of the object touches "obvious" aligning points such as the page margin, edge of the page, or horizontal or vertical center of the page. These can make accurate alignment quick and easy.

CLICK the Shape Height spinner until it reads 4.2".
(*Result:* The Shape Width spinner should change to 4.2" automatically.)

5. While the FORMAT tab under Picture Tools is still active:

Locate the Arrange group.

CLICK the Rotate Objects button (Rotate ▾).

SELECT Flip Horizontal.
(*Result:* The photograph is now facing into the poster rather than away from it.)

6 With the image still selected, notice the rotation control at the top of the image (Figure WD3.2).

CLICK and HOLD on the rotation handle (⟳) and tilt the picture to the left a bit.

To set the rotation to precise measurements:

Locate the Arrange group.

CLICK the Rotate Objects button.

SELECT More Rotation Options to open the Layout dialog box.

(Notice that from your previous actions, the height and width are 4.2".)

CLICK the Rotation spinner until it reads 357° of rotation.

CLICK OK.

FIGURE WD3.2 Photograph chosen from Office.com clip art search.

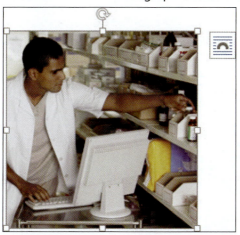

7 Locate the Size group on the FORMAT tab under Picture Tools.

CLICK the drop-down arrow of the Crop button (▣).

HOVER your mouse on the Crop to Shape options.

SELECT Flowchart: Document image (the seventh image on the first row of Flowchart shapes).
(*Result:* Notice how the image has been cropped or "clipped" to fit the shape you selected.)

8 While the image is still selected:

CLICK the Layout Options box (▤) that is on the right-hand side of the image (Figure WD3.2).

SELECT Tight.

SELECT Fix position on page.

Under the With Text Wrapping choices:

DESELECT the image to hide the Layout Options box.

DRAG the image toward the top left-hand side of the poster until it matches the position in Figure WD3.3.

9 To ensure it is in the exact position:

CLICK on the image to activate the FORMAT tab under Picture Tools.

Locate the Size group.

CLICK the Launch button to open the Advanced Layout dialog box.

CLICK the Position tab.

The settings should be as follows:

Horizontal: Absolute position −0.42" to the right of Column.

Vertical: Absolute position 0.8 below Page.

Ensure the Allow overlap is turned on.

CLICK OK.

10 Be sure the image is selected.

Locate the Picture Styles group.

CLICK the Picture Border drop-down arrow.

SELECT Black, Text 1. (This description is only visible when the mouse hovers over it.) (*Result:* A thin black border is added around the image.)

11 Your document should appear similar to Figure WD3.3. Save your file.

FIGURE WD3.3 Completion of Lesson Word 3A1

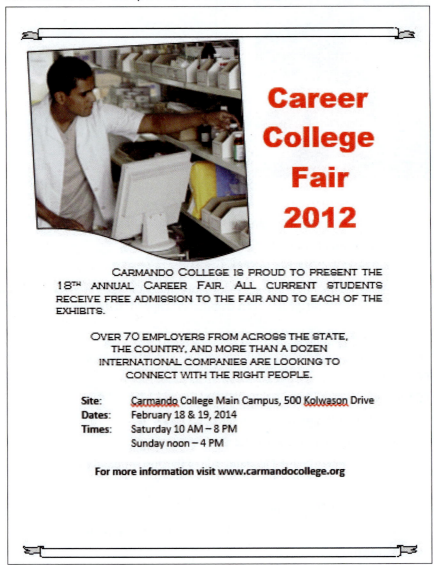

Creating Text Boxes

LESSON OVERVIEW

You can add images in text and wrap text around the image, but there are many times when it is better (and easier) to add text in a **text box**. These boxes can be drawn any size and easily moved around the page. Control the text inside a text box and format it without affecting anything else on the page. This feature makes text boxes ideal for use in signs and posters.

Once you draw a text box, you enter and format text in the same way you format text on a page. You can center it within the text box, you can apply a different font or font size, you can change the color of the text and add bold, italics, and such, but the only element that is affected is inside the text box.

Apply special formatting such as **gradient font** color to the contents of a text box. You can control the color inside a text box using **Shape Fill** to change the default color of white to any color. You can even set it to **No Fill** so the document can be seen through the text box. You can change the **Shape Outline** to be a different style (solid line, dotted line, etc.) or a different color. When you change the outline to **No Outline**, the text in the text box appears to hover on its own.

Just like any object or image, a text box can have its text wrapping, adjusted to force document text to wrap in many different ways. Text boxes can also be precisely sized and placed (as can any image or object) on a page by using the **Horizontal** and **Vertical** settings and Size controls in the Layout dialog box.

SKILLS PREVIEW

Draw a text box	• CLICK the INSERT tab and locate the Text group. CLICK Text Box. SELECT Draw Text Box. DRAG the crosshair cursor to draw the box.
Select all the text inside a text box	• CLICK into the text box. PRESS `Ctrl` + `A`.
Change text color in a text box	• Select the text in the text box. CLICK the HOME tab and locate the Font group. CLICK the Font Color drop-down button. Choose the desired color.
Add gradient shading to text	• Select the text in the text box. CLICK the Font Color drop-down button again. CLICK the Gradient button. Choose the desired gradient.
Wrap text around a text box	• CLICK the text box to select it. CLICK the FORMAT tab under Drawing Tools. CLICK the Wrap Text button. Choose the wrapping that is desired.
Adjust the Fill of a text box	• CLICK the text box to select it. CLICK the FORMAT tab under Drawing Tools. Locate the Shape Styles group. CLICK Shape Fill. Choose color, no fill, or other options.

Adjust the Outline of a text box	• CLICK the text box to select it.
	CLICK the FORMAT tab under Drawing Tools.
	Locate the Shape Styles group.
	CLICK Shape Outline.
	Choose color, no outline, weight, or other options.
To set the precise position of a text box	• CLICK the text box to select it.
	Locate the Size group.
	CLICK the Position tab.
	Set the Horizontal or Vertical alignment.

PROJECT PRACTICE

1. Because you are using a file from an old poster, you should update it a bit. Ensure that **wd03a1-collegeposter** is open. Save it as **wd03a2-collegeposter**.

2. To delete the large text "Career College Fair 2012" in the top right-hand corner of the document: PRESS the Enter button enough times to move the main text under the photograph (see Figure WD3.4).

FIGURE WD3.4   Large text is deleted and remaining text is moved to below the image

3 CLICK the INSERT tab and locate the Text group.

CLICK Text Box.

SELECT Draw Text Box.

Move the cursor anywhere on the screen (we will move the text box to its correct location later).

DRAG to draw a Text Box about 2 inches wide and 1 inch long (use the rulers to help).
(*Results:* When you release the mouse, a box appears.)

4 Once created, the text box has a flashing cursor inside and is ready for you to enter text.

TYPE **College**.

PRESS Enter.

TYPE **Career Fair 2014**.

Adjust the font to Calibri, 36 pt. size, bold.

> **TIP**
>
> If the text does not fit in the text box properly, drag the sizing handles on the text box until it does. Be sure the text box is just big enough to display all the text.

5 SELECT all the text in the text box (click into the text box and PRESS `Ctrl` + `A`).

CLICK the HOME tab and locate the Font group.

CLICK the Font Color drop-down button.

SELECT Red.

6 CLICK the Font Color drop-down button again.

CLICK the Gradient button.

SELECT Linear Down from the Dark Variations. (The descriptions are only visible when the mouse hovers over them.)

7 With the text box still selected:

CLICK the FORMAT tab under Drawing Tools.

CLICK the Wrap Text button.

SELECT Tight.

8 With the text box still selected:

Locate the Shape Styles group.

CLICK Shape Fill.

SELECT No Fill.

CLICK Shape Outline.

SELECT No Outline.

9 Drag the text box to the position shown in Figure WD3.5.
The absolute position is:
Horizontal: −0.41" to the right of the Column.
Vertical: 4.14" below Page.
Add spacing as required to move the text "Carmando College is proud…" so it is just below the text box as in Figure WD3.5.

10 Your document should appear similar to Figure WD3.5. Save your file.

College
Career Fair 2014

CARMANDO COLLEGE IS PROUD TO PRESENT THE 18TH ANNUAL CAREER FAIR. ALL CURRENT STUDENTS RECEIVE FREE ADMISSION TO THE FAIR AND TO EACH OF THE EXHIBITS.

OVER 70 EMPLOYERS FROM ACROSS THE STATE, THE COUNTRY, AND MORE THAN A DOZEN INTERNATIONAL COMPANIES ARE LOOKING TO CONNECT WITH THE RIGHT PEOPLE.

Site: Carmando College Main Campus, 500 Kolwason Drive
Dates: February 18 & 19, 2014
Times: Saturday 10 AM – 8 PM
             Sunday noon – 4 PM

For more information visit www.carmandocollege.org

Page Borders and Shading

LESSON OVERVIEW

Word provides built-in borders you can add to a document. Under the Borders and Shading dialog box there are Borders, Page Borders, and Shading controls. When you apply **Borders** to blocks of text, your options include single lines, double lines, dotted lines, fancy lines, and even art. You can change the width of the lines used as borders and adjust the color. This is particularly useful for text that contains important details such as event times or business hours.

Page borders are designs you apply to single pages or all pages in a document. You can change color, width, and design to find just the right accent. As with borders, you can determine if the page border should be on all four sides or any combination of top, bottom, left, and right.

Shading allows you to add a color or pattern to a block of text. This can be done separately or combined with a border. Adding color to shade key information can make it quick to spot and easy to remember.

SKILLS PREVIEW

Insert a page border	• CLICK the DESIGN tab and locate the Page Background group. CLICK Page Borders. Choose the type of border you desire (style, color, art, and width). CLICK OK.
Remove a page border	• CLICK the DESIGN tab and locate the Page Background group. CLICK Page Borders. Locate the Settings controls. CLICK None. CLICK OK.
Change the color of a border	• CLICK the DESIGN tab and locate the Page Background group. CLICK Page Borders. CLICK the Color drop-down arrow. SELECT the desired color. CLICK OK.
Change the width of a border	• CLICK the DESIGN tab and locate the Page Background group. CLICK Page Borders. CLICK the Width drop-down arrow. SELECT the desired thickness. CLICK OK.
Remove borders from selected sides of the page	• CLICK the DESIGN tab and locate the Page Background group. CLICK Page Borders. Locate the Preview pane. CLICK on the preview diagram to remove a border. CLICK on the preview diagram to apply a border. CLICK OK.
Apply a (nonpage) border	• SELECT the text you wish to border. CLICK Page Borders. CLICK the BORDERS tab. CHOOSE the type of border that is desired. CLICK the Apply to drop-down arrow. CHOOSE Paragraph or Text. CLICK OK.

Apply shading to text	• SELECT the text you wish to shade. CLICK Page Borders. CLICK the SHADING tab. CLICK the Fill drop-down arrow. SELECT the color or pattern you desire. CLICK the Apply to drop-down arrow. SELECT Paragraph or Text. CLICK OK.

PROJECT PRACTICE

1 Ensure that **wd03a2-collegeposter** is open. Save it as **wd03a3-collegeposter**.

2 You should change the horizontal banners that occupy the top and bottom of the poster. You cannot click on them because they are part of the page border. To get rid of them:

CLICK the DESIGN tab and locate the Page Background group.

CLICK Page Borders to open the Borders and Shading dialog box.
(*Result:* Because these borders are already in place, the dialog box opens with the PAGE BORDER tab already selected. The Setting has Box selected, and the Art window shows the banner. Notice on the Preview, the horizontal banners appear at the top and the bottom.)

3 To remove an existing page border:

Locate the Setting controls.

CLICK None.

CLICK OK.

4 CLICK Page Borders.

Locate the Setting controls.

CLICK Box.

Locate the Style controls.

SCROLL down to the double underline.

CLICK on the double underline.

Ensure that the Preview shows the border on all four sides of the page and that the settings get applied to the whole document.

CLICK OK.

5 The border surrounds all the elements of the poster. It would be more effective if it matched the highlight color of red.

CLICK Page Borders.

CLICK the Color drop-down arrow.

SELECT Red.

(*Result:* The existing border has turned to red as seen in Figure WD3.6)

CLICK OK.

FIGURE WD3.6   The Borders and Shading dialog box

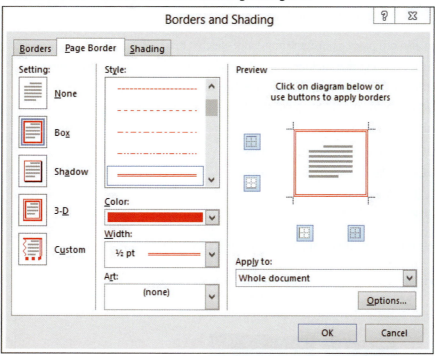

6 To make this border a little more effective, it could be thicker.

CLICK Page Borders.

CLICK the Width drop-down arrow (it is currently at ½ pt.).

SELECT 1½ pt.

CLICK OK.

7 Page borders do not have be on all four sides.

CLICK Page Borders.

The Preview window shows the border as it is (on all four sides).

CLICK on the left-hand border to remove it (or click the left-hand border indicator).

CLICK on the right-hand border to remove it (or click the right-hand border indicator).

CLICK OK.

8 Try some shading to add impact to the website address.

SELECT the text that says "For more information visit."

CLICK Page Borders.

CLICK the SHADING tab.

CLICK the Fill drop-down arrow.

SELECT Red from the Standard Colors.

CLICK the Apply to drop-down arrow.

SELECT Paragraph.

CLICK OK.

9 While the red shading draws attention, the black font is a little hard to read. To fix that:

SELECT the text that has the red shading.

CLICK the HOME tab and locate the Font group.

CLICK the Font Color drop-down arrow.

SELECT White, Background 1.

10 You also can place a border around any selected text.

SELECT the text that includes the information about Site, Dates, and Times.

CLICK the DESIGN tab and locate the Page Background group.

CLICK Page Borders to bring up the Borders and Shading dialog box.

CLICK the BORDERS tab.

CLICK Shadow in the Setting controls.

CLICK the Apply to drop-down arrow.

SELECT Paragraph.

CLICK OK.

11 Your document should appear similar to Figure WD3.7. Save your file.

FIGURE WD3.7   Completion of Lesson Word 3A3

Adding and Formatting Shapes

LESSON OVERVIEW

To add visual impact to your poster (or any document, for that matter), Word provides over 150 different shapes. From a line or an arrow to an explosion or a hand-drawn scribble, with lots of circles, rectangles, and triangles in between, Word's library of shapes is both extensive and adjustable. You can draw these shapes with a click and drag of your mouse. Once drawn, you can fill them with color or shading, or you can remove the fill altogether. You can move shapes around the screen and wrap text around them.

If necessary, shapes can be flipped to face the other direction. This can be useful if you want to create one shape facing right, then copy it, paste it, and flip to have a mirrored shape facing the other way. Shapes can be controlled just as text boxes are with **outline colors**, **fill colors**, **outline width**, and **precise size and positioning** from the Layout dialog box.

SKILLS PREVIEW

Insert a shape	• CLICK the INSERT tab and locate the Illustrations group. CLICK Shapes to drop down a palette of shapes. CHOOSE the desired shape. DRAG the crosshair cursor to draw the shape.
Insert a symmetrical shape	• CLICK the INSERT tab and locate the Illustrations group. CLICK Shapes to drop down a palette of shapes. CHOOSE the desired shape. PRESS and hold the **Shift** button. DRAG the crosshair cursor to draw the shape.
Adjust the color of a shape	• SELECT the shape. CLICK the FORMAT tab under Drawing Tools. Locate the Shape Styles group. CLICK Shape Outline (✏). SELECT the desired color.
Change the fill of a shape	• SELECT the shape. CLICK the FORMAT tab under Drawing Tools. Locate the Shape Styles group. CLICK Shape Fill (🎨). SELECT the desired color.
Set the weight (thickness) of a shape outline	• SELECT the shape. CLICK the FORMAT tab under Drawing Tools. Locate the Shape Styles group. CLICK Shape Outline. CLICK Weight. CHOOSE the desired thickness.
Flip a shape	• SELECT the shape. CLICK the FORMAT tab under Drawing Tools. Locate the Arrange group. CLICK the Rotate Objects drop-down arrow. CLICK Flip Horizontal (or Flip Vertical).

1 You will concentrate on adding a subtle touch to this poster by inserting and formatting a simple shape. Ensure that **wd03a3-collegeposter** is open. Save it as **wd03a4-collegeposter**.

2 CLICK the INSERT tab and locate the Illustrations group.

CLICK Shapes to drop down a palette of shapes.

Under Basic Shapes:

CLICK Left Bracket.
(*Result:* The Shape palette disappears and the cursor becomes a thick crosshair image.)

3 DRAG the crosshair down to draw a shape similar to the blue bracket to the left of the text (Figure WD3.8).

DRAG the middle-left sizing handle left to widen the image (if necessary).

FIGURE WD3.8   Placement of the Left Bracket shape

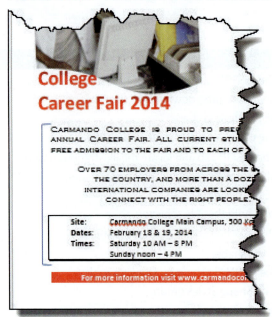

4 You can use the Shape Layout dialog box to ensure precise positioning and size of all shapes.

SELECT the shape (if necessary) to activate the FORMAT tab under Drawing Tools.

Locate the Size group.

CLICK the Size Launch button.

CLICK the Size tab (if necessary).
The size of the shape should be:
3.44 inches high and 0.22 inch wide.

CLICK the POSITION tab.
The position of the shape should be:
Horizontal = Absolute position –0.23" to the right of Column.
Vertical = Absolute position 0.22" below Line.

CLICK OK.

5 With the shape still selected (the FORMAT tab under Drawing Tools is visible), you can change the color and make the line a little thinner.

Locate the Shape Styles group.

CLICK Shape Outline (⬚).

SELECT Red.

CLICK Shape Outline again.

CLICK Weight.

SELECT ¼ pt.

6 Using the same steps as before, draw another left bracket (slightly smaller) as shown in Figure WD3.9.

The precise size and position of this shape are as follows:

2.99 inches high and 0.17 inch wide.

Horizontal = Absolute position –0.48" to the right of Column.

Vertical = Absolute position 0.17 below Line.

CLICK OK.

FIGURE WD3.9 Placement of the smaller Left Bracket shape

7 To have matching shapes on the other side of the text area, rather than draw and adjust them again, you can take advantage of those you have already created.

SELECT the first shape you created.

COPY the shape (PRESS Ctrl + C or use the HOME tab and Copy command).

PASTE the shape (Ctrl + V).

(*Result:* The pasted shape shows up next to the original shape. It remains selected.)

8 DRAG the shape to the position shown in Figure WD3.10.

CLICK the FORMAT tab under Drawing Tools.

Locate the Arrange group.

CLICK the Rotate Objects drop-down arrow.

CLICK Flip Horizontal.

The size of this shape will not change.

The precise positioning of this shape will be:

Horizontal = 6.5 to the right of Column.

Vertical = 0.2 below Line.

CLICK OK.

FIGURE WD3.10   Placement of bracket on the right

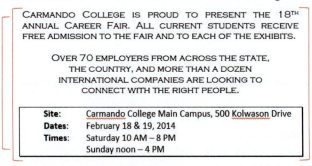

CARMANDO COLLEGE IS PROUD TO PRESENT THE 18TH ANNUAL CAREER FAIR. ALL CURRENT STUDENTS RECEIVE FREE ADMISSION TO THE FAIR AND TO EACH OF THE EXHIBITS.

OVER 70 EMPLOYERS FROM ACROSS THE STATE,
THE COUNTRY, AND MORE THAN A DOZEN
INTERNATIONAL COMPANIES ARE LOOKING TO
CONNECT WITH THE RIGHT PEOPLE.

Site:	Carmando College Main Campus, 500 Kolwason Drive
Dates:	February 18 & 19, 2014
Times:	Saturday 10 AM – 8 PM
	Sunday noon – 4 PM

For more information visit www.carmandocollege.org

9 Using this process, copy the smaller bracket from the left side of the text and paste a copy of it to the right of the newly positioned bracket so all brackets are symmetrical.

Remember to flip the shape horizontally.

The size of the shape will not change.

The precise positioning of this shape will be:

Horizontal = 6.79 to the right of Column.

Vertical = 0.17 below Line.

10 Your document should appear similar to Figure WD3.11. Save your file.

College
Career Fair 2014

CARMANDO COLLEGE IS PROUD TO PRESENT THE 18TH
ANNUAL CAREER FAIR. ALL CURRENT STUDENTS RECEIVE
FREE ADMISSION TO THE FAIR AND TO EACH OF THE EXHIBITS.

OVER 70 EMPLOYERS FROM ACROSS THE STATE,
THE COUNTRY, AND MORE THAN A DOZEN
INTERNATIONAL COMPANIES ARE LOOKING TO
CONNECT WITH THE RIGHT PEOPLE.

Site:	Carmando College Main Campus, 500 Kolwason Drive
Dates:	February 18 & 19, 2014
Times:	Saturday 10 AM – 8 PM
	Sunday noon – 4 PM

For more information visit www.carmandocollege.org

MULTIPLE-CHOICE QUIZ

Select the best choice in the following questions to review the project concepts. Good luck!

1. After you select an image, how do you add a border around the image?
   a. Right-click and choose Borders
   b. Double-click and choose Borders from the menu
   c. Click Picture Border and choose the color
   d. Click the Layout Options button and choose Borders

2. When using the Office.com's Clip Art feature to search for an image, a pane of small images appears. These are called
   a. thumbnails.
   b. drop-downs.
   c. file types.
   d. illustrations.

3. You can rotate an image by
   a. right-clicking on the image and clicking Rotate.
   b. going to the PAGE LAYOUT tab and clicking Arrange.
   c. dragging the green rotation handle on the image.
   d. using the Picture Tools, FORMAT tab, Adjust control.

4. Deleting an unwanted part of an image is called
   a. cutting.
   b. editing.
   c. compressing.
   d. erasing.

5. When an image is dragged around the screen, Word
   a. tracks its precise horizontal and vertical positions.
   b. constantly refreshes the image.
   c. leaves an invisible copy of the image in its original place to enable Undo.
   d. All of these are correct.

6. To remove an existing page border
   a. right-click on the border and choose Delete.
   b. click "Remove border" in the Borders and Shading dialog box.
   c. click "None" in the Borders and Shading dialog box.
   d. None of these is correct.

7. To fit an image inside a shape, you can
   a. right-click an image and select Fit to shape.
   b. right-click an image, click Cut, then right-click and select Crop to shape.
   c. go to Picture Tools, FORMAT tab, click Fit to shape.
   d. None of these is correct.

8. To select two or more images for inserting at the same time
   a. click on each image one at a time.
   b. hold down the **Ctrl** button when clicking the images.
   c. hold down the **Shift** button when clicking the images.
   d. All of these are correct.

9. To draw a perfectly symmetrical shape
   a. hold the **Alt** key down as you draw.
   b. use the right mouse key to draw.
   c. hold the **Shift** key down as you draw.
   d. All of these are correct.

10. Clicking on text inside a text box, and then pressing **Ctrl** + **A** will
    a. select all the text inside the text box.
    b. select all the text in the document.
    c. select the outline of the text box.
    d. None of these is correct.

HANDS-ON EXERCISE: WORK IT OUT WD-3A-E1

In this exercise, you will open an existing poster and add visual elements to make it more appealing. Text boxes, shapes, and photographs add so much to the impact of a poster. The final document is shown in Figure WD3.12.

FIGURE WD3.12   Work It Out WD-3A-E1: completed

1 Open file **wd03a-ex01.docx**. Save it as **wd03a-hw01.docx** (all of the "0" are zeros).

2 Insert a text box (using Figure WD3.12 as a guide) and type:

Curio

Bravanda

Stoh-Meyer

Calistooga

Remingblooms

Walker

Obrendo

Garcia

Set the font to Calibri, 20 pt., and bold.

3 Using shapes, insert Arc to the right of the background as show in Figure WD3.12. The precise size is Height 8.9" and Width 1.48". The precise position is:

Horizontal: Absolute position 5.75" to the right of Column.

Vertical: Absolute position –0.17" below Paragraph.

4 Change the Shape Outline to Orange, Accent 2, Lighter 40%.

5 Copy the shape. Paste it into the document. Flip the shape vertically. Drag it to match its top with the bottom of the first shape, so they appear to be one continuous line. The precise position of the pasted shape is:

Horizontal: Absolute position 5.75" to the right of Column.

Vertical: Absolute position –0.2" below Paragraph.

6 Select both shapes (click on one, then hold **Shift** and click the other). Copy them and paste them into the document.

7 Flip the shapes Horizontal (while they are still both selected). Drag the shapes into the opposite position on the left side of the poster. The precise position of the top shape is:

Horizontal: Absolute position –0.68" to the right of Column.

Vertical: Absolute position –0.16" below Paragraph.

The precise position of the lower shape is:

Horizontal: Absolute position –0.68" to the right of Column.

Vertical: Absolute position –0.18" below Paragraph.

8 Use Office.com's Clip Art search feature to locate the image (type in **fashion model**) shown in Figure WD3.12. Resize the image to a height of 3.0".

9 Add a black border around the image.

10 Crop the image into an oval shape and drag into the position shown in Figure WD3.12.

11 Save and then close the document file.

In this exercise, you will open an existing poster and include visual elements to make it more appealing. Text boxes, shapes, and photographs add so much to the impact of a poster. The final document is shown in Figure WD3.13.

FIGURE WD3.13 Work It Out WD-3A-E2: completed

1. Open the exercise data file **wd03a-ex02.docx**. Save it as **wd03a-hw02**.

2. Insert a circle (oval shape) that is exactly 6.5" by 6.5". Center on the poster (let the automatic alignment guides help you).

3. Remove the fill from the circle. Ensure the circle is colored Dark Blue, Text 2.

4. Using Office.com's Clip Art, search (using **heartbeat**) and insert the center image from Figure WD3.13. Set the Layout Options to In Front of Text. Resize and position it to match the figure (the center of the poster). The size is 3.9" high, 5.2" wide.

5. Using Office.com's Clip Art, find the other three images (using **weights**). The image of the man should be sized to 2.3" high by 2.3" wide. The image of the three people should be sized to 2.4" high by 3.0" wide. The image of the woman should be sized to 2.7" high by 2.16" wide.

6. All three of the images just inserted should be cropped to the shape of a Rounded Rectangle. Using the Layout Options button, set to In Front of Text. Move them to the approximate spots as shown in Figure WD3.13.

7 Using Office.com's Clip Art, find the final picture (using **business card**). Insert the image into the proper place and size it to 2.8" square. Set the Layout Options to In Front of Text.

8 Draw a text box in the blank spot of the business card in the image you have just inserted. Type in the following as shown in Figure WD3.13 (center the text within the text box):

Anderson Fitness

(555) 451-2252

www.a-fitness.com.

9 Turn the text box outline to "no outline" and the fill color to "no fill" so that only the text shows. You may have to resize the text box to allow all the text to show.

10 Create a large text box at the top of the page and, using Vivaldi font size 60, type **Anderson Fitness**. Center the text. Be sure the text box is large enough to display all the text. Drag it to the proper position (centered across the page) and make the same changes (no fill, no outline) to this text box so that only the text shows.

11 Save and then close the document file.

In this exercise, you will open an existing poster and include visual elements to make it more appealing. Text boxes, shapes, and photographs add so much to the impact of a poster. The final document is shown in Figure WD3.14.

FIGURE WD3.14   Work It Out WD-3A-E3: completed

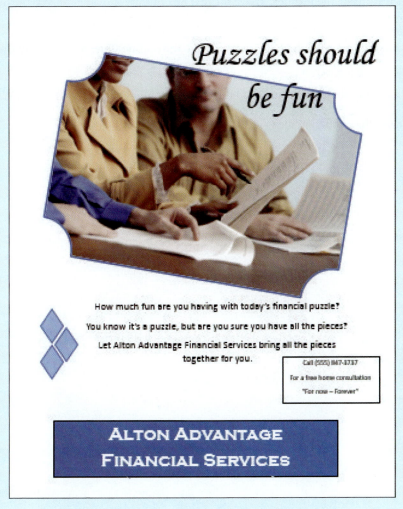

① Open **wd03a-ex03.docx**. Save the file as **wd03a-hw03**.

② Locate the Office.com's Clip Art photograph shown in Figure WD3.14 (using **consultant**). Crop the photograph to the Plaque shape (basic shape). Rotate the photo a bit as shown.

③ Insert a text box that overlaps onto the photograph. Type **Puzzles should be fun** into the text box. Make the font Monotype Corsiva and 55 pt. size. Center the text within the text box.

④ Add a border to the shape. Make it Blue, Accent 5. Increase the weight of the outline to 3 pt.

⑤ Set the text box to No fill, No outline. Be sure the text doesn't block out anything important in the photograph.

⑥ Insert a text box with no fill. Using Calibri font, 16 pt., centered text, type:

How much fun are you having with today's financial puzzle?

You know it's a puzzle, but are you sure you have all the pieces?

Let Alton Advantage Financial Services bring all the pieces together for you.

Drag and resize the text box until it matches Figure WD3.14.

7 Insert another text box (no fill, no outline) and using Calibri font, 11 pt., type:

Call (555) 847-3737

for a free home consultation

"For now–Forever"

Center the text inside the text box. Leave the text box outline showing. Ensure the outline fits nicely around the text.

8 Insert a diamond shape 0.7" high, 0.5" wide. Make the outline Blue, Accent 5. Fill the shape with Blue, Accent 1, light 40%.

9 Copy the diamond shape twice and drag the copies into position to match Figure WD3.14.

10 Save and close the document file.

Adding Power to the Poster

This chapter began by taking the raw information from an old design. After adding a photograph, a text box, borders, shading, and shapes, the visual attractiveness of the poster is vastly improved. In this project, you will be working with Clip Art, grouping elements, and learning about layering of elements to strengthen the message of the poster. People rarely have a lot of time to read a poster, so Word provides many ways to accentuate various details in different ways. This helps the readers to separate vital information for quick understanding and to store it much easier in their minds.

PROJECT FILE: *Available at www.mhhe.com/office2013projectlearn*

PROJECT OBJECTIVES

After completing this project, you will be able to:

- Insert pictures, layer, and nudge.

- Search for Clip Art, insert, and format.

- Search with Internet sources (Bing) and add built-in text boxes.

- Group objects, text box format control.

Inserting Pictures, Layering, and Nudging

LESSON OVERVIEW

While the Office.com Clip Art library is a great place to search for pictures and illustrations, sometimes the picture you want is right on your own computer. Word allows you to add pictures to any document as easily as any other image. After clicking **Pictures** in the Illustrations group, Word opens a window that allows you to browse your computer to find the right file.

Once pictures (or any objects) are inserted, you can use the **Layer** feature to set one image in front of or behind another. The **Bring Forward** and **Send Backward** buttons allow you to work in as many layers as you need.

You have cropped an image to fit a shape, but here you will learn to **crop** an image to get rid of areas you no longer need. When you need to make small changes in the position of an image, Word allows you to **nudge** the image by selecting it and using the arrow keys. The higher the zoom factor, the smaller the increments of movement produced by each arrow key.

After cropping an image, Word provides a **Compress Pictures** feature that not only compresses the file size of inserted pictures, but also permits you to delete any cropped areas of the pictures. You will not see a difference because the pictures are compressed to match the size to which you have set them.

SKILLS PREVIEW

Insert a picture from your computer	• CLICK the INSERT tab and locate the Illustrations group. CLICK Pictures. Locate the image on your computer. CLICK Insert.
Use the Layout Options button	• CLICK on an image to select it. CLICK the Layout Options button (⬚). Set the text wrapping of the image, anchor it to neighboring text, or fix its position on the page, or CLICK See more… to activate the Layout dialog box.
Crop unneeded portions of a picture	• CLICK the image to select it. CLICK the top half of the Crop button. DRAG the cropping handles to remove the unneeded portion of the picture. CLICK away to complete the crop.
Compress pictures and delete cropped area	• CLICK the image to select it. CLICK the FORMAT tab under Picture Tools and locate the Adjust group. CLICK the Compress Pictures button (⬚). Ensure the desired settings are active. CLICK OK.
Layer objects	• CLICK the image or object to select it. CLICK the FORMAT tab under Picture Tools. Locate the Arrange group. CLICK the Send Backward drop-down arrow. CLICK Send to Back to layer the image "behind" another. CLICK the Bring Forward drop-down arrow. CLICK Bring to Front to layer the image "in front" of another.
Nudge objects	• SELECT the image or object. PRESS the arrow keys (↑ ↓ → ←) to move the object in small increments.

1 Open the file **wd03b1.docx**. Use the Save As command to save it as **wd03b1-collegeposter**.

2 You have inserted a photograph that you located from Office.com. But Word can also insert photographs that reside on your computer.

CLICK the INSERT tab and locate the Illustrations group.

CLICK Pictures.

Locate the data files used for this exercise and notice the image files (.jpg extensions).

CLICK the file named "Spine."

CLICK Insert.

3 This image is far too big. Adjust it as you did the previous photograph. The FORMAT tab under Picture Tools automatically opens when a picture is inserted.

Locate the Arrange group.

CLICK Wrap Text.

SELECT In Front of Text.

4 Adjust the size to 4.6" high and 3.68" wide.

CLICK the Layout Options button (⬜).

CLICK Fix position on page so that it isn't linked to any text.

DRAG the image to the position shown on Figure WD3.15.

Horizontal: Absolute position 3.56" to the right of Column.

Vertical: Absolute position 0" below Margin.

FIGURE WD3.15 Position of the second picture

5 Locate the Size group.

CLICK the top half of the Crop button.

DRAG the bottom-center cropping handle up until it is just below the round stand that holds the model of the spine (Figure WD3.16 shows the cropping).

CLICK the Crop button to complete the crop.

6 Although an image is resized and cropped, the file size and the cropped area of the picture remain. This allows for future editing. Because you are sure you don't need to make any further changes, compress the picture.

CLICK the image to select it.

CLICK the FORMAT tab under Picture Tools and locate the Adjust group.

CLICK the Compress Pictures button ().

Uncheck the box next to Apply only to this picture (so you can compress all the pictures at once). Ensure the Delete cropped areas of pictures is selected.

CLICK OK.

> **TIP**
>
> Previously you clicked on the drop-down arrow of the Crop button (in the lower half of the button), which provided a choice of cropping options. This time, by clicking the top half of the crop button, you activate the simple crop tool without the other options.

7 Notice the newest image sits on top of the first picture. This is called layering. To move the new image "beneath" (technically, behind) the original one:

CLICK to select the new image.

CLICK the FORMAT tab under Picture Tools.

Locate the Arrange group.

CLICK the Send Backward drop-down arrow (see Table WD3.1 for details).

CLICK Send to Back to layer the new image "behind" the original image.

TABLE WD3.1 The Layer commands in the Arrange group and their functions

Layer Command	Function
Bring Forward	Brings the selected image forward one layer.
Bring to Front	Brings the selected image all the way to the front layer no matter how many layers exist.
Bring in Front of Text	Since text is not an image and cannot be controlled by the other commands, this allows you to bring the selected image in front of existing text.
Send Backward	Sends the selected image back one layer.
Send to Back	Sends the selected image all the way to the back layer no matter how many layers exist.
Send Behind Text	Since text is not an image and cannot be controlled by the other commands, this allows you to send the selected image behind existing text.
Selection pane	Opens a pane that lists all the objects in the document. You can click on any one to select it. This is very useful when you (a) cannot click on an object because it is behind another one and (b) find yourself "moving" objects when you try to select them.

8 CLICK the Rotate Objects button.

CLICK More Rotation Options.
In the SIZE tab locate the Rotate control.
Set it to 3°.
CLICK OK.

9 Now do some final nudging of the new image so the top of it is level with the original image.
Ensure the new image is selected.

PRESS the up arrow key (↑) to nudge the image up until it is level with the original image.

> **TIP**
>
> You can use any of the arrow keys to nudge objects. The amount of space that each nudge moves the image is dependent on the zoom factor. If you are zoomed out (low zoom factor), each nudge will move the image farther and faster. To get smaller increments for more detailed movement, zoom the page in (increase zoom factor). This will allow you to do more refined work.

10 Your document should appear similar to Figure WD3.16. Save your file.

FIGURE WD3.16   Completion of Lesson Word 3B1

Inserting and Formatting Clip Art

LESSON OVERVIEW

Clip art and photographs are searched for in the same way. **Clip art** is generally regarded as illustrations such as cartoons and drawings. The clip art used in Word is part of the Office.com Clip Art library. It is royalty-free and available for anyone to add impact to a document. Clip art can be resized, dragged, and positioned the same way photographs can.

Among the shapes Word contains is a small group titled **callouts**. These shapes are similar to the dialog and thought balloons seen in comic strips and comic books. Due to their nature, they automatically assume that you want to add text to them. Text inside these callouts is controlled just as the text inside a text box. These shapes have a yellow handle that allows you to direct the dialog in any direction you wish.

SKILLS PREVIEW

Search Online Pictures	• CLICK the INSERT tab and locate the Illustrations group. CLICK Online Pictures. Type a keyword or keywords into the Bing Image Search window. PRESS Enter.
Insert an online picture	• CLICK the thumbnail of the image you want. DOUBLE-CLICK, or CLICK Insert to insert it into the document.
Adjust the shape of shapes	• CLICK the INSERT tab and locate the Illustrations group. CLICK Shapes. SELECT the shape you want. DRAW the shape. DRAG the yellow shape handle to adjust the shape.
Add text to a callout	• CLICK the INSERT tab and locate the Illustrations group. CLICK Shapes. SELECT the callout you want. DRAW the callout. Enter text at the flashing cursor.

PROJECT PRACTICE

1 Open the file **wd03b1-collegeposter**. Save it as **wd03b2-collegeposter**.

2 CLICK the INSERT tab and locate the Illustrations group.

CLICK Online Pictures.

TYPE **holding balloons** into the Office.com Clip Art window.

PRESS Enter.

CLICK the image "A bear dressed as a doctor, holding balloons" to select it.

CLICK Insert.

3 The inserted image is not sized appropriately.

Using the Layout Options button:

SET the Text Wrapping to In Front of Text.

Size the image to 0.8" high and 0.49" wide.

CHOOSE Fix position on page.

4 Move the image to the position shown in Figure WD3.17.

The precise position is:

Horizontal: Absolute position 5.87" to the right of Column.

Vertical: Absolute position 8.16" below Page.

FIGURE WD3.17 Position the "bear" clip art

5 CLICK the INSERT tab and locate the Illustrations group.

CLICK Shapes.

CHOOSE Oval Callout (near the bottom of the palette).

6 DRAG the crosshair cursor to draw a callout as you see it in Figure WD3.17.

Use the Size group to set the height as 0.7" and the width to 1.3".

(*Result:* Callouts are special shapes that automatically show a flashing cursor for you to enter text.)

7 Using the Shape Styles group:

SET the Shape Fill to White.

SET the Shape Outline to Black.

REDUCE the weight of the Shape Outline to ½ pt.

8 CLICK the HOME tab and locate the Font group.

CLICK the Font color to Black (do not choose automatic).
Center the text in the shape, if necessary.

TYPE Free Parking.

9 While the shape is still selected, you can adjust the pointer so it points at the bear.

CLICK and hold the yellow handle of the shape.

DRAG it to point right at the bear's head.

10 Your document should appear similar to Figure WD3.18. Save your file.

FIGURE WD3.18   Completion of Lesson Word 3B2

Searching Internet Sources

LESSON OVERVIEW

Word allows you to search more than just Microsoft's extensive library for images. Built into Word is a **Bing Image Search** feature. This allows you to access the Internet to locate the right image for your document.

In this lesson you will dig down for more detailed work. You will combine an Internet image with a text box to create an image that when properly aligned will be professional in its message and appearance. The **automatic alignment guides** will make the positioning fast and accurate.

By applying bullets inside a text box, you will create a small image that conveys a strong message that is unrelated to the main message of the poster but is likely important to a prospective student considering the career fair.

The overall message is almost complete. The final added touches provide more details for those who have already seen the poster once but now are paying more attention as they consider its message.

SKILLS PREVIEW

Search for an image using Bing	• CLICK the INSERT tab and locate the Illustrations group. CLICK Online Pictures. CLICK into the Bing Image Search window. TYPE the keyword or keywords you desire. PRESS Enter .
Size and position an image without the Ribbon	• RIGHT-CLICK on the image to bring up a shortcut menu. CLICK Size and Position to open the Layout dialog box. CLICK SIZE tab. Set the precise size, or CLICK the Position tab. Set the precise positioning of the image.
Insert a text box with built-in style	• CLICK the INSERT tab and locate the Text group. CLICK Text Box. CHOOSE from the built-in text box styles. TYPE in your text.
Insert bullets into a text box	• CLICK into the text box. CLICK the HOME tab and locate the Paragraph group. CLICK Bullets. TYPE your text.
Adjust the indent of bullets inside a text box	• CLICK into the text box. CLICK into the bulleted text. CLICK the HOME tab and locate the Paragraph group. CLICK Bullets. CLICK Decrease (or Increase) Indent.

1 Open the file **wd03b2-collegeposter**. Save it as **wd03b3-collegeposter**.

2 CLICK the INSERT tab and locate the Illustrations group.

CLICK Online Pictures.

CLICK into the Bing Image Search window.

TYPE **medical education**.

Mouse over pictures to locate one titled Medical Education Evolution and CLICK on "Medical Education Evolution" to select it.

DOUBLE-CLICK to insert it.

HEADS UP

When you use Internet search engines such as Bing, you are no longer searching Microsoft's library of images and there is little (if any) control over the content of the images. That leads to the possibility of inappropriate images being located. Also, note that the Bing Image Search in Word warns you about copyright issues and attempts to restrict images to those licensed under Creative Commons. When that warning appears, you can click the X to close the message and get a better view of the thumbnails. If you decide to click the Show All Web Results button, then you will find images included that are not licensed. You assume the responsibility of complying with the applicable laws.

---

3 CLICK the Layout Options button next to the picture.

CLICK In Front of Text.

CLICK to hide the Layout Options button.

4 RIGHT-CLICK on the picture to bring up a shortcut menu.

CLICK Size and Position to launch the Layout dialog box.

Be sure the Lock aspect ratio check box is checked.

SET the size of the picture to 0.7" tall and 1.05" wide.

CLICK OK.

5 DRAG the image to the bottom of the document and to the right.

Stop when the automatic alignment guide shows it is aligned with the right end of the "For more information…" text (see Figure WD3.19).

FIGURE WD3.19 Automatic alignment guide showing the image is lined up with the text box above it

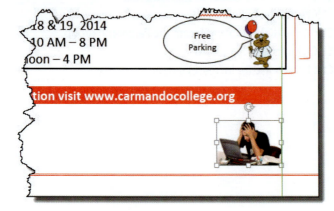

6 ZOOM in to 120% to get a good view of the bottom of the screen.

CLICK the INSERT tab and locate the Text group.

CLICK Text Box.

CLICK the Simple Text Box from the Built-in styles.

7 The text box appears with filler text that is already selected and ready to be replaced.

TYPE **Student Assistance**.

PRESS Enter.

CLICK the HOME tab and locate the Paragraph group.

CLICK Bullets.

CLICK Decrease Indent (once).

TYPE:

Academic

Financial

Counselling

8 SET the text wrapping to In Front of Text.
SET the Shape fill to No Fill.
SET the Shape Outline to No Outline.

9 DRAG the sizing handles of the text box so it is small enough to just hold the text.

CLICK the border that appears around the image.

DRAG to the position shown in Figure WD3.20.

10 Your document should appear similar to Figure WD3.20. Save your file.

FIGURE WD3.20 Completion of Lesson Word 3B3

Grouping Objects

LESSON OVERVIEW

Word proves it is much more than just a word processor with its ability to allow you to layer and **group** objects to create lasting impressions and designs. The skills you have acquired so far in creating text boxes and drawing and adjusting shapes now are brought together in the creation of a logo.

Grouping objects allows you to move them around a document as if they were one object. They do not lose proportion or position in relation to each other as they are dragged around. Once grouped, you can even set text wrapping controls for the newly created object.

Ungrouping objects is simple to do and allows you to adjust and edit each individual object again. Once that is done, they can be grouped again.

This is one of the most exciting features of Word. Grouped objects copied and pasted into other graphic programs can be used as corporate logos and trademarks.

SKILLS PREVIEW

Place a shape on top of another	• CLICK on each shape. CLICK the Layout Options button. Ensure all shapes are set to In Front of Text. DRAG one shape on top of the other.
Duplicate the characteristics of an existing text box	• CLICK on the original text box. PRESS Ctrl + C to copy the text box. PRESS Ctrl + V to paste the new text box. MOVE it to its desired location. REPLACE the old text with your new text.
Adjust the internal margins of a text box	• RIGHT-CLICK on the border of the text box. CLICK Format Shape to open the Format Shape pane. CLICK the Layout & Properties button (⊞). CLICK Text Box. ADJUST the left, right, top, bottom margins.
Grouping objects	• CLICK one object to select it. HOLD the Shift button. CLICK another object to select it (as many objects as you wish as long as you hold the Shift button). RELEASE the Shift button. CLICK the FORMAT tab under Drawing Tools and locate the Arrange group. CLICK the Group Objects button (⊞ ▾). CLICK Group.

1 Open the file **wd03b3-collegeposter**. Save it as **wd03b4-collegeposter**.

2 Move the cursor to the bottom of the page and zoom to 140%.

3 CLICK the INSERT tab and locate the Illustrations group.
CLICK Shapes.
CHOOSE Oval.
DRAG the cursor to draw an oval that is 0.8" high and 1.76" wide.

4 SET the fill to No Fill.
SET the Shape Outline to Red.
SET the Shape Outline weight to 1 pt.

5 DRAW a text box 0.3" high and 1.4" wide.
TYPE Carmando into the text box.
CENTER the text inside the box.
MAKE the font Arial Black, 16 pt.

6 The font doesn't fit into the text box. Youcan adjust the interior settings of the text box.
While the text box is selected:
RIGHT-CLICK on the border of the text box.
CLICK Format Shape to open the Format Shape pane on the right.
CLICK the Layout & Properties button (▦).
CLICK Text Box.
CLICK the Left margin, Right margin, Top margin, and Bottom margin spinners to zero.
(*Result:* The entire word "Carmando" should now fit in the text box. You have reduced the default margins inside the text box to zero.)

7 While the Format Shape pane is open, you can make other changes.
CLICK Fill and Line (◇).
CLICK Fill and set it to No fill.
CLICK Line and set it to No line.
CLOSE the Format Shape pane.
DRAG the text box so it fits into the top half of the oval (top image in Figure WD3.21).

FIGURE **WD3.21**   Positioning of first and second text boxes

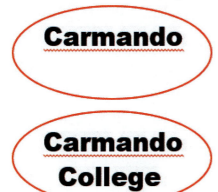

8 You can use a keyboard shortcut to copy that text box, so you don't have to create a new one and make all the same formatting changes.

CLICK the text box to select it.

MOVE the cursor away from the text box.

HOLD `Ctrl` and move the cursor toward the text box.

When the cursor becomes a right-facing white arrow with a plus sign () CLICK the left mouse button.

DRAG the cursor below the text box.

RELEASE the mouse button.

RELEASE the `Ctrl` button.

(*Result:* A copy of the text box will appear. Position it directly below the first text box.)

9 DOUBLE-CLICK the new text box to select the text.

TYPE: **College**.

CLICK away.

DRAG the text boxes to a position similar to that shown on the bottom image of Figure WD3.21.

10 You can group the three elements (two text boxes and one shape) into one, so it can be moved around the page without coming apart.

CLICK one text box to select it.

HOLD the `Shift` button.

CLICK the other text box to select it (continue holding the `Shift` button).

CLICK the edge of the shape to select it.

RELEASE the `Shift` button as all three are now selected.

CLICK the FORMAT tab under Drawing Tools and locate the Arrange group.

CLICK the Group Objects button (⊞▾).

CLICK Group.

> ### *i* MORE INFO
>
> If you need to change any object that has been grouped, you can ungroup them by following the same procedure and clicking Ungroup. This can also be done by right-clicking the edge of the grouped object, clicking Group, and choosing Ungroup. Once ungrouped, objects can be separated and adjusted individually. When completed, just group them again.

11 DRAG the newly grouped object to the left.

Use the automatic alignment guide to help you align it to the left end of the "For more information…" text.

12 Your document should appear similar to Figure WD3.22. Save the file.

FIGURE **WD3.22** Completion of Lesson Word 3B4

MULTIPLE-CHOICE QUIZ

Select the best choice in the following questions to review the project concepts. Good luck!

1. To change the thickness of a shape outline, you would adjust the
   a. style.
   b. size.
   c. line.
   d. weight.

2. As you are dragging the mouse to draw a shape, you can produce a perfectly symmetrical shape by
   a. holding down the **Shift** button.
   b. holding down the **Alt** button.
   c. right-clicking the mouse.
   d. double-clicking the shape when complete.

3. The Online Pictures button allows you to locate and insert images from all EXCEPT
   a. Clip Art from Office.com.
   b. Bing Image Search.
   c. your SkyDrive.
   d. pictures from your computer.

4. Images can be resized by
   a. dragging the sizing handles.
   b. right-clicking and using the Size and Position shortcut.
   c. using the Height and Width controls in the Size group.
   d. All of these are correct.

5. Sending one image behind or in front of another is called
   a. layering.
   b. adjusting.
   c. in Front of Text.
   d. None of these is correct.

6. You can nudge an object in small increments by
   a. right-clicking on the object border.
   b. clicking and holding it while you press the space bar.
   c. clicking and holding the mouse while using the arrow keys.
   d. None of these is correct.

7. When using keywords for a search you can
   a. use only one word at a time.
   b. use more than one word.
   c. restrict it to only photographs.
   d. All of these are correct.

8. To group objects, you can
   a. hold **Shift** and click each object.
   b. select objects, then right-click and group.
   c. insert a text box around the objects.
   d. None of these is correct.

9. When Absolute position of an object is set from the Layout dialog box, it can be to the right of
   a. right column.
   b. column margin.
   c. page.
   d. in front of text.

10. When objects are "grouped," they will
    a. stay together when moved.
    b. stay in position relative to each other.
    c. allow you to set text wrapping for the entire group.
    d. All of these are correct.

HANDS-ON EXERCISE: WORK IT OUT WD-3B-E1

In this exercise, you will open an existing poster and include visual elements to make it more appealing. By adding and controlling shapes, fill, and color, you can make a document with a basic image into something that catches the eye. The final document is shown in Figure WD3.23.

FIGURE WD3.23   Work It Out WD-3B-E1: completed

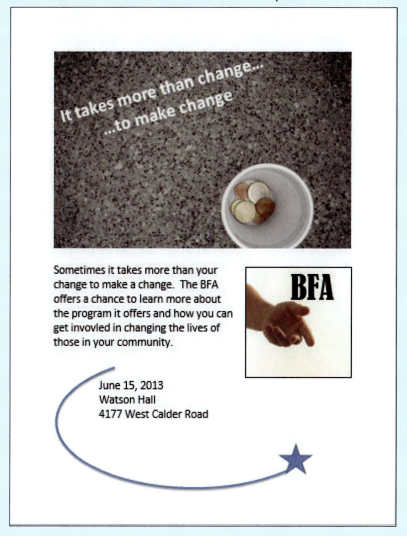

1. Open file **wd03b-ex01.docx**. Save it as **wd03b-hw01.docx**. Ensure you cursor is at the very top of the document.

2. Search Online Pictures for clip art for "charity" and insert the image seen at the top of Figure WD3.23. Align the image to the top margin.

3. Insert a text box as seen in Figure WD3.23. Use Calibri, 28 pt. Type:
   It takes more than change…(Enter **) …to make change**.

4. Adjust the text box for a snug fit around the text, then set it to no fill, no outline.

5. Change the font to white and make it bold. Rotate the text box 345° and move it to the spot shown in Figure WD3.23

6 Search Clip Art for the smaller image in Figure WD3.23 using the keyword "reaching." Size the image to 2.3" high and 2.3" wide. Set text wrap to square. Move the image so it is aligned with the right-hand edge of the first (larger) image. Put a picture border of black around the "reaching" image.

7 Draw another text box that is 0.7" high and 1.3" wide (no fill, no outline). Type **BFA** into it. Make the font Bernard MT Condensed and 48 pt. Using the Format Shape pane, reset all the interior margins of the text box to zero so the text shows. Move it to the position shown in Figure WD3.23.

8 Insert a shape (Arc) that is 2.8" high and 6" wide. Rotate it 180°. Use the Shape Styles drop-down menu to apply the Intense Line – Accent 1 theme. Drag the yellow shape handles to give it more curve on both ends to match Figure WD3.23. Move into position to wrap around the address.

9 Insert a symmetrical shape (star) that is 0.6" high and 0.7" wide. Move it so it connects to the end of the arc.

10 Your document should appear similar to Figure WD3.23. Save the file.

In this exercise, you will open an existing poster and include visual elements to make it more appealing. Text boxes, shapes, and photographs add so much to the impact of a poster. The final document is shown in Figure WD3.24.

FIGURE WD3.24 Work It Out WD-3B-E2: completed

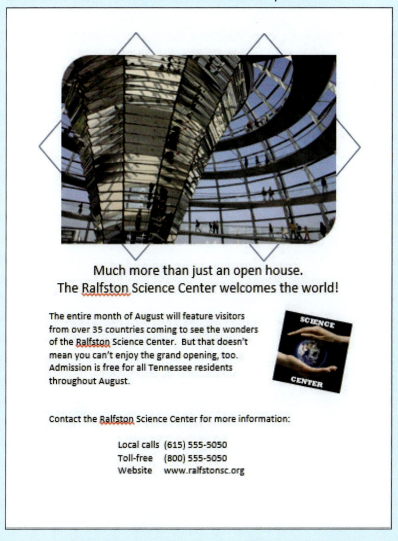

1. Open the file **wd03b-ex02.docx**. Save it as **wd03b-hw02.docx**.

2. Move the cursor to the top of the document. Locate the folder for the files used in this exercise and insert the photograph "building." Size the photograph to 4" high by 6" wide. Locate the Arrange group and click the Position button. Choose the Position in Top Center with Square Text Wrapping option.

3. Search for the photograph shown in Figure WD3.24 using the keywords "hands holding earth." Resize it to 1.5" high and 1.5" wide. Set the text wrapping to square.

4. Create a text box with no outline and no fill to fit on the top of this new image. Type in the word **SCIENCE**. Turn the text to white. Use Rockwell Extra Bold font at 11 pt. size. Fit it neatly atop the logo as shown in Figure WD3.24.

5. Create a second text box identical to the first one. Type in the word **CENTER** in the same font style and size as before. Fit it nearly to the bottom of the logo as shown in Figure WD3.24.

6. Group the original photograph with both of the new text boxes. Set the text wrapping to square.

7. Rotate the newly created logo 11°.

8. Insert a shape (diamond) that is 4.8" high and 3.5" wide. Place it over the left-hand half of the main picture as shown in WD3.24 and resize the diamond if necessary. Set it to No fill.

9. Center the telephone numbers.

10. Copy the diamond shape. Paste it into the document. Place it behind the right-hand half of the main picture. Layer both shapes so they are beneath the main picture.

11. Your document should appear similar to WD3.24. Save your file.

In this exercise, you will open an existing poster and include visual elements to make it more appealing. Text boxes, shapes, and photographs add so much to the impact of a poster. The final document is shown in Figure WD3.25.

FIGURE **WD3.25**   Work It Out WD-3B-E3: completed

1. Create a blank document. Save it as **wd03b-hw03.docx**.

2. Search and insert (all at once) the four pictures of teachers from Clip Art (use *teachers* as the keyword). Resize each one to 2.8" high. Set the text wrapping for them all to In Front of Text. Arrange them in the positions shown in Figure WD3.25

3. Looking at the photos in Figure WD3.25, starting at the top left and moving clockwise, set the rotations as: 346°, 13°, 0°, and 352°.

4. Use the Bring to Front and Send to Back controls to layer them as shown in Figure WD3.25

5. Insert a text box with no fill, no outline at the top of the images that says **Making a difference** in Calibri font, 36 pt. as shown in Figure WD-3.25. Copy that text box and paste it into the document. Replace the text with **Every day**.

6. Create another text box using the built-in style of Austin Pull Quote or a similar style. Type the first line **Tell the Teacher** in 24 pt. The rest of the text is in 20 pt. Type **The national "Tell the Teacher" campaign reminds students and parents to take some time to tell your teacher how much you appreciate what they do**. Resize the text box to display all the text and the upper and lower border as shown in Figure WD-3.25.

7. Search Clip Art (using the keywords "star shape") to find the star shown in Figure WD3.25 Insert it into the document.

8. Set the star to text wrapping of In Front of Text. Resize the star to 1.7" square. Copy the star and place the three stars as shown in Figure WD3.25.

9. Rotate the top star 70°. Rotate the lowest star 188°. Layer the middle star so it is behind the photograph.

10. Your document should appear similar to WD3.25. Save your file.

Chapter Summary

To look at a word processor such as Word for only its word processing is to miss some of its most compelling attributes. Word's ability to integrate text boxes, illustrations, photographs, and shapes seamlessly into a document has been made so simple that even a novice writer can do so. Finding the right image is easy with Word's "keyword" search system, which searches Microsoft's online library of photos and illustrations and can also be used to search Bing and other sources. Creating and controlling text boxes allows the writer to manipulate specific portions of text without affecting the rest of the document.

The use of images in a document can be a very powerful way not only to attract the reader's attention, but also to add an emotional involvement between the reader and the words. By providing such a vast set of controls such as size, shape, color, rotation, and text wrapping, Word allows the writer to consider any number of combinations to ensure the document is making the most effective use of the reader's time.

Chapter Key Terms

Automatic alignment
   guides, p. W-163
Bing Image Search, p. W-163
Borders, p. W-139
Bring Forward, p. W-156
Callouts, p. W-160
Clip art, p. W-160
Compress picture, p. W-156
Crop, p. W-156
Crop to shape, p. W-130
Fill colors, p. W-143
Gradient font, p. W-135
Group, p. W-166

Horizontal, p. W-135
Keywords, p. W-130
Layer, p. W-156
Layout dialog box, p. W-130
Layout Options, p. W-130
No Fill, p. W-135
No Outline, p. W-135
Nudge, p. W-156
Online Pictures, p. W-130
Outline colors, p. W-143
Outline width, p. W-143
Page borders, p. W-139
Pictures, p. W-156

Precise size and
   positioning, p. W-143
Send Backward, p. W-156
Shading, p. W-139
Shape, p. W-130
Shape Fill, p. W-135
Shape Outline, p. W-135
Text box, p. W-135
Text wrapping, p. W-130
Ungrouping, p. W-166
Vertical, p. W-135

On Your Own WD-3C-E1

This project provides the opportunity to practice the most important skills covered in this chapter, regardless of the project or lesson in which they were introduced. The example shown in Figure WD3.26 is only a guideline of how the final project may appear.

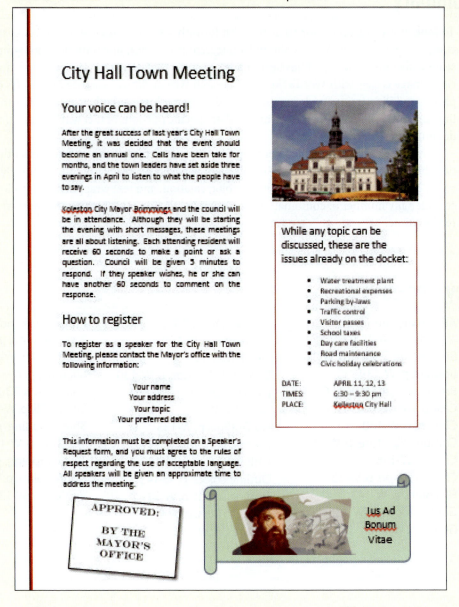

After launching Microsoft Word, open the project data file **wd03cp1.docx**. Save the document as **wd03cp1-Townhall.docx**.

The photograph at the top was located by searching the keywords "town hall."

Below the picture is a text box using Calibri font, 15 pt. with bold where needed. The outline of the text box is Red, Accent 2.

The founding father was located by searching the keyword "explorer" through Office.com Clip Art. The image is flipped and layered over a shape (scroll). Another text box is added with the Latin slogan **Ius Ad Bonum Vitae**. Group all three objects.

The page has just a left side border.

The stamp of approval by the mayor is created in a text box. Use the font Engravers MT, size 13 pt. To give the impression of it being stamped, it has been rotated slightly and a shadow was added using Shape Effects.

Save and then close the document, unless directed to print it by your instructor. Exit Microsoft Word.

On Your Own WD-3C-E2

This project provides the opportunity to practice the most important skills covered in this chapter, regardless of the project or lesson in which they were introduced. The example shown in Figure WD3.27 is only a guideline of how the final project may appear.

FIGURE WD3.27 On Your Own WD-3C-E2: completed

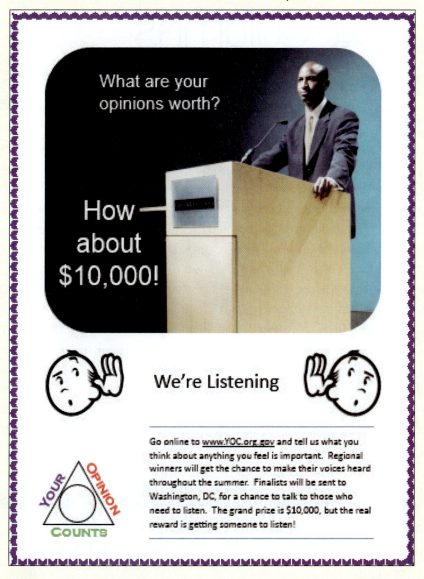

After launching Microsoft Word, open a blank document and save it as wd03cp2-YOC.docx.

This poster starts with an online picture that can be found using the keywords businessman speaking. The text layered in front of the picture is done in text boxes.

This poster has a border (using art) and a Clip Art image (keyword: *listening*) and the image has been copied and flipped.

The main text box uses a built-in style that was adjusted slightly with the text size (14 pt.), color (black), and font style (Calibri).

The logo in the bottom corner is created by two shapes (triangle and circle—both symmetrical) and three text boxes. Two of the text boxes have been rotated. All the text boxes and the shapes have been grouped and moved to their current position.

Save and then close the document, unless directed to print it by your instructor. Then exit Microsoft Word.

Templates, Tabs, Tables, and Text Columns

As an organization seeks to develop its own identity, Microsoft Word can be one of its most important assets. Even home-based businesses can utilize the prede-signed templates to create professional-looking material such as letterheads and memos. With a few clicks, you can customize a template to suit and support the unique personality of the organization. When alterations are complete, a user can save a template as a custom template to be used by anyone in the organization.

Ensuring clarity in a document is often a function of its form as much as the words themselves. Using tabs and tables can greatly increase the effectiveness of a memo or a letter by organizing data and text in clean rows or columns. Features such as Table Styles and Quick Tables bring professional designs right into a docu-ment without having to ponder colors, border styles, fonts, and other enhance-ments. Plus, everything is customizable so you can create your own style.

Changing the format of the text to draw attention to specific areas can improve a document's ap-pearance and effectiveness. When most of a document is in one column, formatting a small section into two (or more) columns allows the reader to more easily understand the document in smaller chunks of information.

PROJECT

Creating, Saving, and Using a Corporate Memo and Letterhead Template

In this project, you will turn a Word tem-plate for both a memo and a letterhead into a unique, reusable document for a growing accounting firm. While general Word templates are great, customizing them to suit the needs of the organiza-tion makes them even better.

When you complete the lessons in this chapter, you will have a memo and letterhead that can be used as part of your portfolio to display not only cus-tomizing of a template, but also the use of tabs, tables, and text columns.

THE SITUATION

Remerson and Black Accounting

Your job with the accounting firm of Remerson and Black has been quite ex-citing so far, and a new assignment may lead to even more opportunities. The company seeks to expand and wants to create a new image in its written documents. Using your skills in Word, you will generate a unified persona for the company on both internal memos and outgoing letterhead.

Designing Corporate Memos and Letterhead

PROJECT OBJECTIVES

After completing this project, you will be able to:

- Locate, download, and modify templates.

- Insert built-in or custom watermarks.

- Use existing and customized tabs.

- Apply advanced control to tabs and tab types.

One of the most exciting advantages Word provides companies is the ability to create their own style for written communications. With the help of built-in templates and a few creative twists, you can give a unique polish to the documents you produce for your company, organization, charity, project, or group. This project introduces the use of templates for kick-starting your creative flair. You will also add your own design ideas to a document and save it as a template. Adding personalization with watermarks and custom tabs allows you to generate memos and letterheads that are distinctively your own yet consistent throughout the organization.

PROJECT FILE: *Available at* **www.mhhe.com/office2013projectlearn**

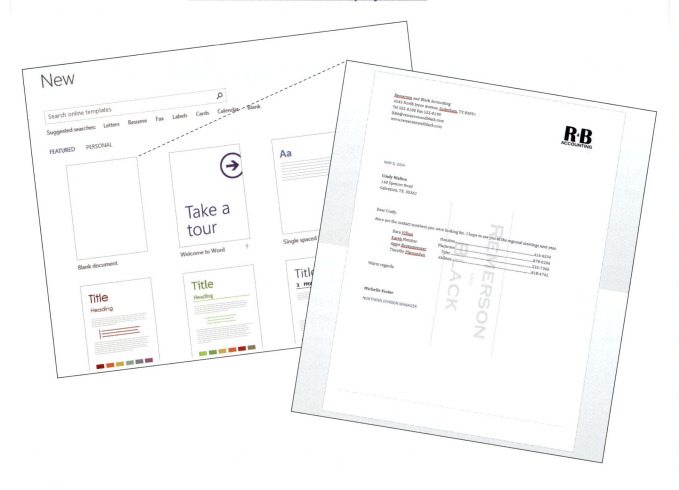

Introduction to Templates

LESSON OVERVIEW

One of the fastest ways to produce a professional document is to use Word's **template** library. A template is a predesigned document that includes the most common elements of the document. Word provides templates for letters, memos, business cards, invitations, reports, résumés, newsletters, and many other common documents. Microsoft's library of templates holds thousands of examples.

The placeholders contain hints and directions to what type of information should be typed into them. Simply click on a placeholder and add the appropriate information: address, phone number, website, or text.

You can customize templates by adding your own information or deleting placeholders. This customized document can be saved as a **custom template** to be used over and over throughout the organization.

Sometimes the template serves as a great way to start your own creation. Rather than begin with a blank page, opening a template provides ideas for design elements, styles, and colors.

SKILLS PREVIEW

Insert a template	• Open Word.
	  CLICK on the desired template.
	  CLICK Create, or, if Word is already open,
	• CLICK the FILE tab.
	  CLICK New.
	  CLICK on the desired template.
	  CLICK Create.

Search for a template	• CLICK the FILE tab.
	  CLICK New.
	  CLICK the Suggested searches, or
	  TYPE your choice into Search online templates.
	  CLICK on your choice.
	  CLICK Create.

Fill in the template placeholders	• CLICK the cursor on the placeholder. TYPE your text.

Save a custom template	• CLICK the FILE tab.
	  CLICK Save As.
	  CLICK Computer.
	  CLICK Custom Word Templates.
	  CLICK the Save as type drop-down arrow.
	  CHOOSE Word Template.
	  TYPE the file name you wish for this template.
	  CLICK Save.

Open a custom template	• Open Word.
	  CLICK Open Other Documents.
	  CLICK Computer.
	  CLICK Custom Word Templates.
	  DOUBLE-CLICK on the file you wish.

1 When you start Word without opening an existing file, the Backstage view displays the most recently opened files and a choice of templates (models that can be used to start a new document). Open Word.

FIGURE **WD4.1**   The opening page of Word

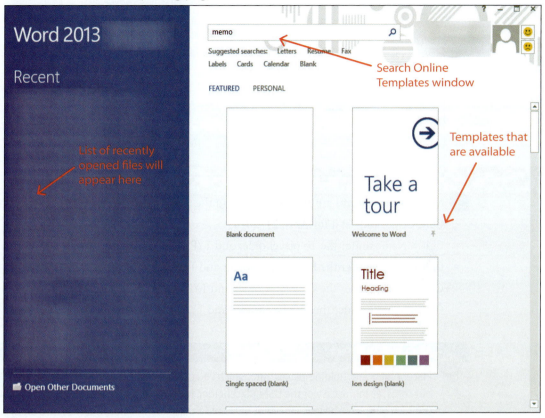

2 Scroll down the opening page (see Figure WD4.1) to see the many options of templates: blank document, letterhead, reports, blogs, greeting cards, newsletters, business cards, résumés, and more. The one you are looking for (memo) is not there.

CLICK into the Search Online Templates window.

TYPE **memo**.

PRESS Enter for a list of memo templates.

CLICK on Business memo (Red and Black design) to enlarge the thumbnail (see Figure WD4.2).

CLICK the Create button.

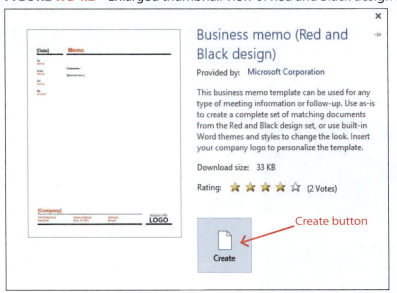

Create button

3 Many of the features are already in place in the template. You can quickly fill in some.

CLICK Date and set it for April 21, 2014.

CLICK Name under the To placeholder and TYPE **Darlene Florence**.

CLICK Name under the From placeholder and TYPE *your own name*.

CLICK Name under the CC placeholder and TYPE **Terry Haslack**.

CLICK Subject under the Re placeholder and TYPE **Vacation request**.

 MORE INFO

Placeholders are "holding places" into which you can type text. Many placeholders are actually text boxes, but some, as in the case of the Date placeholder, have other characteristics and capabilities. They are very useful in templates because they not only hold a place on the page, but they also often provide hints as to what could be inserted into them. In some cases, such as with a letter template, putting your name in the proper placeholder at the top of the letter will automatically fill out your name in the placeholder at the bottom of the letter. If unneeded, you can remove placeholders by clicking on them and pressing the [Delete] key.

---

4 Move to the bottom of the page. These elements are part of the footer.

DOUBLE-CLICK in the footer area to activate the footer view.

Make the following changes:

Company: **Remerson and Black Accounting**

Tel: **555-0188**

Fax: **555-0190**

Street Address City, ST Zip : **4545 North Joyce Avenue**

PRESS [Enter].

TYPE **Soderham, TX 83091**

Website: **www.remersonandblack.com**

Email: **r&b@remersonandblack.com**

5 CLICK on "replace with LOGO."

CLICK the Change Picture button (the icon at the right).

In the Insert Pictures window, locate From a file.

CLICK the Browse button next to it.

Locate the files used for this lesson.

CLICK the R and B logo (it is a PNG file).

CLICK Insert.

RESIZE the logo to 0.8" high (see Figure WD4.3).

CLOSE the footer view.

FIGURE WD4.3   Close-up of the bottom of the memo

6 Back in the Normal view, delete the word *Comments* , the "Re" section, and the colon.

CLICK on Start text here.

TYPE **Thanks for the early request for vacation time. It gets really crazy next month when most of the requests start coming in.**

PRESS **Enter** .

TYPE **I am happy to inform you that your vacation time has been approved. You will be on vacation starting July 14. You are expected back at work on July 29, 2014.**

PRESS **Enter** .

TYPE **Have a great vacation**.

7 This memo is ready to print. But now is a great time to use this template as a basis for your own template. This means you won't have to make all those changes each time you use it.

DELETE the text you have just written.

DELETE the names you typed under the To, From, and CC sections (be careful to delete just the names and not the spaces after them or you will lose a line).

CLICK into the main part of the memo and PRESS **Enter** after the word "light.".

8 Now the document is ready to be saved as a template for future use. This all depends on how you save the file.

CLICK the FILE tab.

CLICK Save As.

CLICK Computer.

CLICK Custom Word Templates (see Figure WD4.4).

CLICK the Save as type drop-down arrow.

CHOOSE Word Template.

(Notice the location of this file changes to Custom Word Templates. You can store all your templates here. This will make them easier to find.)

TYPE **RB-memo** In the File Name window.

CLICK Save (Word will add the dotx extension to signify it is a template).

CLOSE Word.

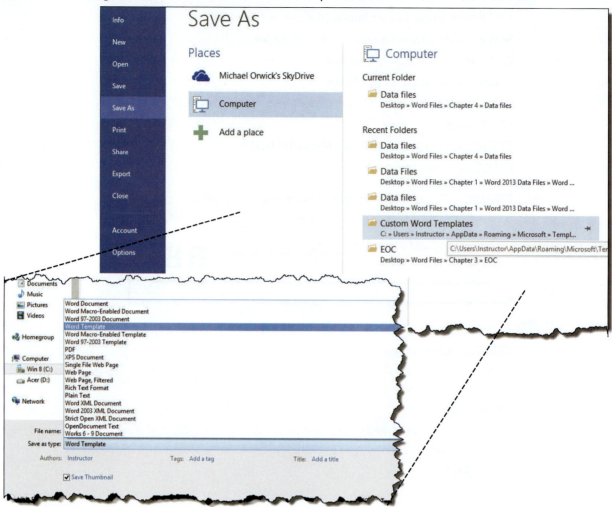

⑨ To find that template the next time you want to use it:

Open Word (ignore the fact that the Recent list shows the file).

CLICK Open Other Documents in Backstage view.

CLICK Computer.

CLICK Custom Word Templates to open the folder with all your custom templates (there will likely be just one there). The folder structure shown may differ on your computer.

DOUBLE-CLICK on "RB-memo."

The file opens with all the company information in place just waiting for you to enter your new information. The folder structure shown on your machine may vary from the example.

⑩ CLICK the Date placeholder and change it to October 29, 2014.

Fill in the following:

To: **Lawrence**

From: **Karen**

CC: **Kathy**

Re: **Halloween**

CLICK into the body of the memo.

TYPE **When leaving the office on Halloween, please remember to leave all exterior lights on as well as the main office lights and the staff room light. Have a safe weekend. See you Monday.**

11 To save this as a memo (not as a template because the RB-memo is already a template), be sure to put it into the right folder.

CLICK the FILE tab.

CLICK Save As.

CLICK Computer.

CLICK the folder you wish to save to (you can use the data folder for this project).

CLICK the Save as type drop-down arrow.

CHOOSE Word Document (not Word Template).

TYPE Lawrence-Halloween lights

CLICK Save.

12 The memo you just created is saved as a document. The template you created is saved in the Custom Word Templates folder for future use. The document remains on the screen. It should be similar to Figure WD4.5. Save the file as wd04a1-memo.docx and close the file.

FIGURE WD4.5 Completion of Lesson Word 4A1

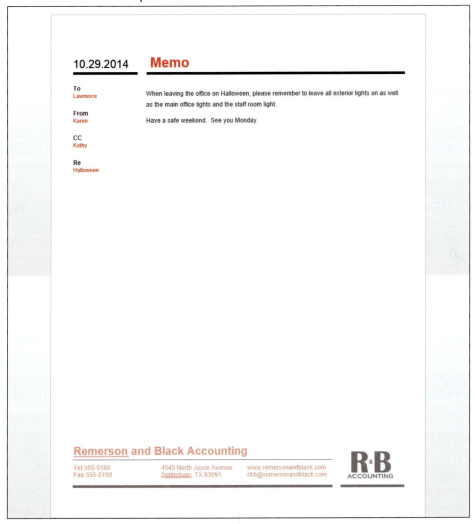

Watermarks

LESSON OVERVIEW

A **watermark** is an image that appears to be woven into the paper itself. And at one time, it was. Adding a watermark to a document used to be quite expensive. It was a symbol of luxury and was often used on the stationery of upscale hotels or very successful businesses. Now it is simple to add a watermark to any document using Word.

You can create a **picture watermark** or a logo that sets your document apart from others and becomes uniquely your own. In many cases, a **text watermark** is all that is required. Adding simple text such as the word *Confidential* or *Draft* across the background of the page makes all readers aware of the singular value of a document.

Word has built-in watermarks for the most common uses, but also allows you to customize the watermark. Once inserted, you can resize or reposition a watermark to suit your needs. Watermarks will appear on each page of your document as they become part of the header. Word also provides a simple process to remove a watermark.

To add a final touch of personalization to your document, this lesson also explains the process of replacing a logo inside a template placeholder. A watermark and a custom logo make an effective statement about your company.

SKILLS PREVIEW

Replace logo placeholder with logo	• CLICK on Replace with LOGO placeholder. CLICK the Change Picture button (the icon at the right). CLICK Browse on the Insert Pictures window. Locate the logo file. CLICK Insert.
Insert a built-in watermark	• CLICK the DESIGN tab and locate the Page Background group. CLICK Watermark. CHOOSE the premade watermark you desire.
Insert a custom picture watermark	• CLICK the DESIGN tab and locate the Page Background group. CLICK Watermark. CLICK Custom Watermark. CHOOSE Picture watermark. CLICK Select Picture. CLICK Select Picture to open the Insert Pictures window. SEARCH for an image using Office.com Clip Art or Bing, or CLICK Browse next to From a file, if the picture is on your computer. Locate the file. CLICK OK.
Insert a custom text watermark	• CLICK the DESIGN tab and locate the Page Background group. CLICK Watermark. CLICK Custom Watermark. CHOOSE Text watermark. CLICK the Text drop-down menu. CHOOSE the built-in text you desire, or TYPE the text you wish into the Text drop-down box.

SKILLS PREVIEW

Resize or move a watermark	• CLICK the INSERT tab and locate the Header & Footer group. CLICK Edit Header. CLICK the watermark to select it. Adjust as you desire. CLOSE the Header and Footer view.
Remove a watermark	• CLICK the DESIGN tab and locate the Page Background group. CLICK Watermark. CLICK Remove Watermark.

PROJECT PRACTICE

1. You will start with a new template for this lesson. Open Word.

2. CLICK into the Search Online Templates window.

   TYPE letterhead.

   PRESS Enter.

   SCROLL down to locate the Letterhead (Timeless Design) template.

   DOUBLE-CLICK it to download and insert it into your document.

3. TYPE the appropriate company information into the placeholders:

   Company: **Remerson and Black Accounting**

   Street Address City, ST ZIP Code : **4545 North Joyce Avenue, Soderham, TX 83091**

   Tel: **555-0188**

   Fax: **555-0190**

   Email: **R&b@remersonandblack.com**

   Website: **www.remersonandblack.com**

4. CLICK the Replace with LOGO text box (this is not the same type of placeholder as in the previous lesson).

   You could delete it and insert your own, but use the same text box to make the logo approximately the same size as this one.

   RIGHT-CLICK in the text box.

   CLICK Change Picture.

   Locate the From a file option.

   CLICK Browse.

   Locate the folder that contains the files for this lesson.

   INSERT the R and B Logo.

   RESIZE it to 0.8" high (that should be approximately 1.19" wide).

5. Much of the document consists of placeholders. To make the watermark feature function properly, ensure your cursor is on actual text (such as "Dear" or "Warm regards").

   CLICK the DESIGN tab and locate the Page Background group.

   CLICK Watermark.

   CLICK Confidential 1 and the word appears to be stamped diagonally across the page, behind the text (see Figure WD4.6).

6 Save this letterhead as a template for confidential communication.

CLICK on Watermark again.

CLICK on Remove Watermark.
(*Result:* The watermark has been removed.)

7 Add a new watermark.

CLICK Watermark.

CLICK Custom Watermark (if it is not available, be sure your cursor is on actual text).

CHOOSE Text watermark.

CLICK the drop-down arrow on the Text (likely showing ASAP).

CLICK DO NOT COPY.

CLICK OK.

8 Remove the watermark.

CLICK Watermark again.

CLICK Custom watermark to return to the Printed Watermark dialog box.

CHOOSE Picture watermark.

CLICK Select Picture to open the Insert Pictures window.

You could search for an image using Office.com Clip Art or Bing as you have before. But the picture for this lesson is located on your computer.

CLICK Browse next to From a file.

SELECT the Remerson and Black PNG file (not the logo).

CLICK Insert.

CLICK OK (see Figure WD4.7).

FIGURE WD4.7 Letterhead with company name as watermark

TIP

Watermarks are inserted into a document as part of the header. If you wish to adjust the watermark (such as moving or rotating it), you need to open the Header & Footer view. That can be done from the INSERT tab and the Header & Footer group. Once there, click Header, choose Edit Header, and click on the watermark. You can also enter the header by double-clicking in the header area (top margin) of the page.

9 This watermark is too large and tends to overwhelm the page. To change the size:

CLICK the Watermark button.

CLICK Custom Watermark to open the Printed Watermark dialog box.

CLICK the drop-down arrow next to Scale (it currently says Auto).

CHOOSE 50%.

CLICK OK.

10 The watermark is now smaller and less distracting. Because you are just creating another company template, you do not want to enter any more information. Save your file to the Custom Word Templates (as you did in the previous lesson).

CLICK the FILE tab.

CLICK Save As.

CLICK Computer.

CLICK Custom Word Templates.

CLICK the Save as type drop-down arrow.

CHOOSE Word Template.

TYPE RB-letterhead in the File name window.

CLICK Save (Word will add the dotx extension to signify it is a template).

11 Your file should appear similar to Figure WD4.8. If you are continuing to work, leave the file open. If you are leaving Word, close the file.

Remerson and Black Accounting
4545 North Joyce Avenue, Soderham, TX 83091
Tel 555-0188 Fax 555-0190
R&b@remersonandblack.com
www.remersonandblack.com

CLICK HERE TO SELECT A DATE

[Recipient Name]
[Recipient Street Address, City, ST ZIP Code]

Dear [Recipient],

If you're ready to write, just click here and go to it!

Or, if you want to customize the look of your letter, you can do that in almost no time...

On the Design tab of the ribbon, check out the Themes, Colors, and Fonts galleries to preview different looks from a variety of choices. Then just click to apply one you like.

Have company-branded colors and fonts? No problem. You can add your own combination. To add your own logo just right-click the placeholder logo, and then click Change Picture.

If you love the look (and who wouldn't?), see other templates under File, New that coordinate with this letter, including a résumé and a report. So, you can quickly create a professional, branded look for your documents.

Warm regards,

Instructor

[YOUR TITLE]

Setting and Customizing Tabs

LESSON OVERVIEW

One of the best ways to organize information on a page is to line it up. **Tabs** allow you to arrange rows of text or data into straight vertical lines. Word has default tabs set at every half inch across the page. Each time you press the `Tab` button, the cursor moves 0.5" to the right. If you need to move backward along the **default tabs**, hold the `Shift` button down while you press `Tab`. Each time, this moves the cursor backward to the tab on its left.

Sometimes the default tabs are not what you need. Word allows you to set **custom tabs** by setting the **Tab Selection button** to your choice of tab and then clicking along the ruler to set the tab. You can apply a different set of tabs to every row of text. If you would like to set a tab to more than one row, just select the text first and apply a tab setting; all the selected text assumes the tabs you place on the ruler.

When you need to move a custom tab to a different place on the ruler, simply drag it to the new location and release the mouse.

SKILLS PREVIEW

Use default tabs	• PRESS `Tab`. This will move the cursor 0.5" to the right. Each time `Tab` is pressed, the cursor will move to the next tab on the right.
Go to the previous tab	• PRESS `Shift` + `Tab`. If you have pressed `Tab` at least once, each time you press `Shift` + `Tab`, the cursor will move backward one tab setting.
Set custom tabs on the ruler	• Ensure the horizontal ruler is displayed. CLICK the Tab Selection button until it displays the Left tab image (L). CLICK once along the ruler to insert a tab.
Move a tab along the ruler	• Locate the tab marker you wish to move. DRAG it along the ruler to the desired location. Release the mouse.
Apply a new tab to specific text	• SELECT the text for which you wish to set a tab. SET the tab on the ruler. All the selected text will be given the new tab setting.

PROJECT PRACTICE

1 You will use one of your new templates for this exercise. Locate and open **RB-letterhead.dotx**. Save the file as **wd04a3-contact_letter.docx**. Remember to save the file as a Word document, not a template.

2 To get the letter ready to go, fill in the following placeholders:

Set the date to **May 8, 2014**

Recipient Name: **Cindy Walton**

Recipient Street Address, City, ST, ZIP Code:

148 Spencer Road

Galveston, TX 35362

SELECT the name and address you just entered.

CLICK the HOME tab and locate the Paragraph group.

CLICK the Line and Paragraph Spacing button.

REMOVE both the Space Before Paragraph and the Space After Paragraph.

This will allow the address to fit together without the extra lines between.

3 TYPE Dear Cindy,

CLICK into the body of the letter to highlight the entire text.

TYPE Here are the contact numbers you were looking for. I hope to see you at the regional meetings next year.

PRESS Enter.

4 If your name is not already located in the Your Name placeholder, CLICK the Your Name placeholder.

TYPE your name.

CLICK YOUR TITLE.

TYPE NORTHERN DIVISION MANAGER.

5 CLICK the mouse into the first line below the sentence that begins with "Here are the contact…"

TYPE Dave Villian

PRESS Tab.

TYPE Houston

PRESS Tab.

TYPE 414-6536

PRESS Enter.

MORE INFO

Word's default tabs are every 0.5". Each time you press Tab, the cursor moves 0.5" to the right. When the Show/Hide button is on, tabs appear as tiny arrow images (→).

---

6 Following the same pattern of pressing Tab between each element, enter two more lines of text:

Karen Fletcher (Tab) Plainview (Tab) 878-0206

Aggie Borenniesser (Tab) Tyler (Tab) 535-7366

SELECT these contact numbers (the three lines you've added) and remove the space before and after the paragraph.

7 Notice that the third name was longer than the default tab of 0.5" so it spilled over. When you pressed Tab, it moved to the next default location. You can use the ruler to insert custom tabs to line things up.

SELECT all three lines of contact information.

CLICK the mouse on the 2" mark on the horizontal ruler (see Figure WD4.9).

Word inserts a custom tab marker on the ruler.

FIGURE WD4.9 Placing a custom tab on the horizontal ruler

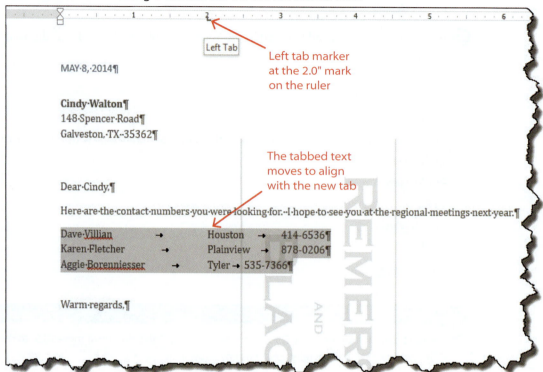

HEADS UP

 Once you insert your own (custom) tabs, the existing default tabs between the left margin and your custom tab will disappear. For example, if you set a custom tab at the 2.0" mark, the default tabs at 0.5", 1.0", and 1.50" will be cleared away.

8 While the three lines of text are still selected:

CLICK the mouse at the 3" mark on the horizontal ruler.

Now the next column of information lines up with that tab.

Word has inserted a left tab marker at the 3" mark.

9 Now you decide that the tab for the phone numbers is too close to the city names.

While the three lines of text are still selected move the mouse to the ruler:

DRAG the 3" tab over to the 4" mark (see Figure WD4.10).

RELEASE the mouse.

CLICK away to deselect the text.

FIGURE WD4.10   Dragging a tab marker along the horizontal ruler

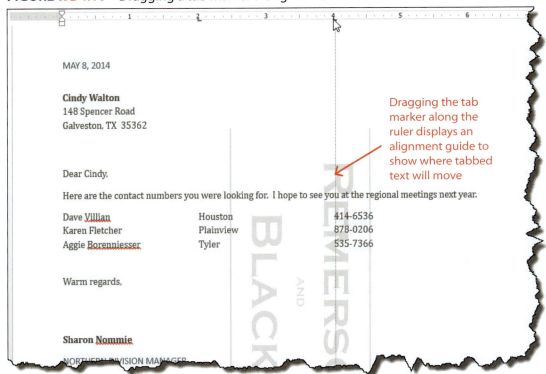

Dragging the tab marker along the ruler displays an alignment guide to show where tabbed text will move

10 CLICK the mouse into the phone number 414-6536.

CLICK the mouse at the 3.5" mark on the ruler.

Notice how this change only affected the single line of text (because the others were not selected).

Now that line has a tab at 3.5" and at 4".

DRAG the 3.5" tab off the ruler.

This will delete that tab and the phone number moves to the 4" tab.

11 Your document should look similar to Figure WD4.11. Save the document as **wd04a3-contact_letter.docx**.

FIGURE WD4.11   Completion of Lesson Word 4A3

Advanced Ruler and Tab Control

LESSON OVERVIEW

While the most common tab is the Left tab, Word offers seven types of tabs (see Table WD4.1). Each time you click the Tab Selection button, it changes to another type of tab that you can apply to the ruler. When you get to the end of the seven types of tabs, it starts over again with the Left tab.

No matter what type of tab you select, it is set onto the horizontal ruler with a click of the ruler. Drag it to move it along the ruler. If you want to **remove a tab**, drag it off the ruler and release the mouse.

The ruler offers a quick way to insert, move, and remove tabs, but much more control is available from the **Tabs dialog box**. This provides additional options such as the ability to enter an exact placement for a tab (e.g., 3.15"), apply the **tab alignment** (left, center, right, decimal, etc.), and set a **leader** for the tab (dots, dashes, underline, etc.).

The Tabs dialog box allows you to make these changes to existing tabs or to create new tabs and apply these characteristics at the same time. You can **Clear all tabs** at once from the entire document using the Tabs dialog box.

SKILLS PREVIEW

Apply a Center tab to the ruler	• CLICK the Tab Selection button until it displays the Center tab image (⊥). CLICK on the ruler to set the Center tab in place.
Apply a Right tab to the ruler	• CLICK the Tab Selection button until it displays the Right tab image (⊐). CLICK on the ruler to set the Right tab in place.
Use the Tabs dialog box to set tabs	• CLICK the HOME tab and locate the Paragraph group. CLICK the Paragraph launch button. CLICK the Tabs button at the bottom left of the dialog box. TYPE the tab into the Tab stop position box (e.g., 2.25" will place a tab at the 2.25" position on the ruler). CLICK Set (if you wish to continue to enter more tabs), or, CLICK OK to set the tab and close the dialog box.
Use the Tabs dialog box to set tab alignment	• CLICK the HOME tab and locate the Paragraph group. CLICK the Paragraph launch button. CLICK the Tabs button at the bottom left of the dialog box. If it is a current tab: CLICK on the tab you wish to change to select it. In the Alignment section, choose the type of tab you want. If you are entering a new tab: TYPE the tab into the Tab stop position box. CLICK the Alignment type you desire. CLICK Set (if you wish to continue to enter another tab), or, CLICK OK to set the tab and close the dialog box.

Set a leader for a tab	• CLICK the HOME tab and locate the Paragraph group. CLICK the Paragraph launch button. CLICK the Tabs button at the bottom left of the dialog box. If it is a current tab: CLICK on the tab you wish to change to select it. In the Leader section, choose the type of leader you want. If you are entering a new tab: TYPE the tab into the Tab stop position box. CLICK the Leader type you desire. CLICK Set (if you wish to continue to enter another tab), or, CLICK OK to set the tab and close the dialog box.
Remove a tab	• Locate the tab marker on the ruler. DRAG the tab down off the ruler. Release the mouse, or • CLICK the HOME tab and locate the Paragraph group. CLICK the Paragraph launch button. CLICK the Tabs button at the bottom left of the dialog box. CLICK to select the tab you want to remove. CLICK Clear.
Clear all tabs	• SELECT the text. CLICK the HOME tab and locate the Paragraph group. CLICK the Paragraph launch button. CLICK the Tabs button at the bottom left of the dialog box. CLICK Clear All.

PROJECT PRACTICE

1. Ensure that **wd04a3-contact_letter.docx** is open. Save it as **wd04a4-contact_letter.docx**.

2. Insert Custom Tabs.

   SELECT all three lines of tabbed text.

   See Figure WD4.12 and locate the Tab Selection button, which by default shows a Left tab (⌞).

   CLICK it once to change to a Center tab (⊥).

   MOVE the mouse to the 2.5" mark of the ruler.

   CLICK to insert the Center tab at that mark.

   DRAG the 2" marker off the ruler to delete it.

   The column of text with the city names is now centered at the 2.5" mark.

FIGURE WD4.12   The location of the Tab Selector button

TABLE WD4.1   Types of tabs available in Word

Tab Type	Effect on Text
Left	Aligns text to the left of the tab position
Center	Centers text beneath the tab position
Right	Aligns text to the right of the tab position
Decimal	Aligns numbers vertically by the decimal point
Bar	Inserts a vertical bar at the tab position
First Line Indent	Sets the indent of the first line of a paragraph
Hanging Indent	Indents the rest of the paragraph but leaves the first sentence at the margin

3 CLICK the Tab Selector button once more to change it to a Right tab.

CLICK the ruler at the 6" mark.

DRAG the 4" tab down and off the ruler.

The last column now moves to the right-aligned tab at the 6" mark.

4 While there are many things you can do with tabs directly on the ruler, even more can be done in the Tabs dialog box (see Figure WD4.13). Ensure the three lines of tabbed text are selected.

CLICK the HOME tab and locate the Paragraph group.

CLICK the Paragraph launch button.

CLICK the Tabs button at the bottom left of the dialog box.

FIGURE WD4.13 Close-up of the Tabs dialog box

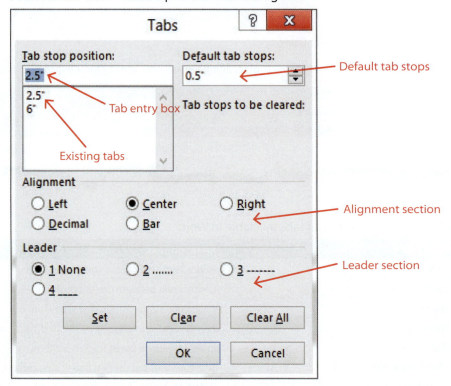

TIP

The Tabs dialog box can also be displayed by double-clicking on any tab marker on the horizontal ruler. If there is no marker to double-click, the Tabs dialog box will still display, but a tab marker appears on the ruler where you double-clicked. This shortcut is best to use only if an existing tab is in place.

5 Notice the 2.5" and 6" tabs are displayed in the Tab stop position. Next to that is the Default tab stops spinner control and it is set to 0.5". That is why the tabs stop at 0.5" by default. (You could adjust the default by changing this setting.)

Currently the 2.5" tab is highlighted in the entry box.

The Alignment shows it is a Center tab.

CLICK the 6" tab and it shows it is a Right tab.

6 Locate the Leader section of the Tabs dialog box.

CLICK Leader style 2.

That applies a dotted leader to the 6" tab.

CLICK OK.

Now there is a dotted line "leading" to the text at the 6" tab (see Figure WD4.14).

FIGURE WD4.14   The result of adding a leader to a tab

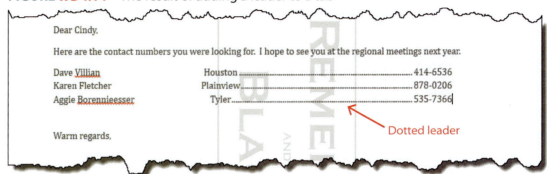

Dear Cindy,

Here are the contact numbers you were looking for. I hope to see you at the regional meetings next year.

Dave Villian	Houston	414-6536
Karen Fletcher	Plainview	878-0206
Aggie Borennieesser	Tyler	535-7366

Warm regards,

Dotted leader

7 Add another contact and see how the tabs work.

CLICK the mouse at the end of the phone number 535-7366.

PRESS `Enter`.

TYPE Timothy Plamondon (`Tab`) Abilene (`Tab`) 818-4742

 MORE INFO

Each line of text can have its own set of tabs. When you move to the end of an existing line and press `Enter` to start a new line, the tabs from the existing line are carried down to the new line.

---

8 SELECT all four lines of the tabbed information.

CLICK the Paragraph launch button.

CLICK the Tabs button.

In the Tab stop position window (currently shows tab 2.5"):

TYPE 0.6

SET the Alignment to Left.

Leave the Leader at None.

CLICK the Set button to set this tab into the document.

CLICK OK.

9 Now the tab you created directly from the Tabs dialog box is in place (you can see it on the ruler).

CLICK in front of each name and press `Tab` once.

They all move up to the new 0.6" tab.

CLICK the Show/Hide button to see what the tab keys look like on the screen.

Each time `Tab` is pressed, it shows as a right-facing arrow.

10 Your document should look similar to Figure WD4.15. Save the file **wd04a4-contact_letter.docx**. Close Word.

FIGURE WD4.15   Completion of Lesson Word 4A4

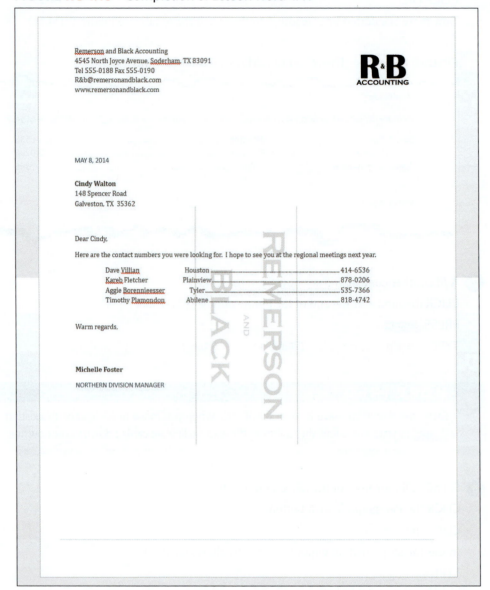

Remerson and Black Accounting
4545 North Joyce Avenue, Soderham, TX 83091
Tel 555-0188 Fax 555-0190
R&b@remersonandblack.com
www.remersonandblack.com

R&B
ACCOUNTING

MAY 8, 2014

Cindy Walton
148 Spencer Road
Galveston, TX 35362

Dear Cindy,

Here are the contact numbers you were looking for. I hope to see you at the regional meetings next year.

Dave Villian	Houston	414-6536
Kareb Fletcher	Plainview	878-0206
Aggie Borennieesser	Tyler	535-7366
Timothy Plamondon	Abilene	818-4742

Warm regards,

Michelle Foster

NORTHERN DIVISION MANAGER

MULTIPLE-CHOICE QUIZ

Select the best choice in the following questions to review the project concepts. Good luck!

1. If Word is already open, you can find the Template Search window by
   a. clicking the INSERT tab and clicking Templates.
   b. right-clicking on a blank page and selecting Templates.
   c. clicking the FILE tab and clicking New.
   d. All of these are correct.

2. Templates have precreated boxes for you to type information into. These are called
   a. drop-downs.
   b. tabs.
   c. placeholders.
   d. None of these is correct.

3. When Word saves a custom template, it is
   a. saved in your export file.
   b. copied to the SkyDrive.
   c. saved in Custom Word Templates.
   d. All of these are correct.

4. Word has many predesigned text watermarks including
   a. Do not copy.
   b. ASAP.
   c. Draft.
   d. All of these are correct.

5. When a picture watermark is being inserted, it
   a. can be searched using Bing Image Search.
   b. must be filed on your computer.
   c. must be in black and white.
   d. None of these is correct.

6. The Tab Selection button is
   a. directly below the horizontal ruler.
   b. found by right-clicking the ruler.
   c. directly above the vertical ruler.
   d. None of these is correct.

7. The default position for tabs is
   a. every 1 inch.
   b. a half inch ahead of the cursor location.
   c. every 0.5 inch along the ruler.
   d. None of these is correct.

8. To remove a tab from the ruler, you can
   a. right-click the marker and select Delete.
   b. hold the **Ctrl** button when clicking the marker.
   c. double-click the marker on the ruler.
   d. None of these is correct.

9. To locate the Tabs dialog box, you can
   a. click the HOME tab, click the Paragraph launch button.
   b. double-click the ruler margin.
   c. select the tabs and use the Mini toolbar.
   d. All of these are correct.

10. Which of these is not one of Word's tab styles?
    a. Left tab
    b. Dot tab
    c. Bar tab
    d. Hanging indent

In this exercise, you will open a template and fill in the appropriate placeholders. You will insert a corporate logo as a watermark and insert and apply left, right, and center tabs to text. These additions will turn a generic template into a document that is specific to your corporation. The final document is shown in Figure WD4.16.

FIGURE WD4.16 Work It Out WD-4A-E1: completed

1. Open Word. Locate and create (insert) the template for "Letter confirming receipt of applicant reference letter." Save the file as **wd04a-ex01.docx** (all the "0" in the file name are zeros).

2. Replace the placeholders in the first address block using the following information:

   Your Name: *your name* and **CEO** on the line below.

   Company Name: **Bowkropp Industries**

   Street Address: **25 – 9500 Pleasant Street**

   City, ST ZIP Code: **Evanville, Oregon 97588**

   Date: **June 17, 2014**

3 Replace the placeholders in the Recipient address block with any information you desire. You may use the information provided in Figure WD4.16. Notice the recipient's name and your name automatically fill in the appropriate places in the letter.

4 Replace the applicant name, job title, and phone number with the following:

Applicant name: **Julie Walls**

Job title: **Sales Representative**

Phone number: **555-0144**

5 Locate the files associated with this exercise and insert the Bowkropp Logo as a watermark. Leave the Scale on Auto and the Washout turned on.

6 Insert a tabbed list after the paragraph that ends with the words "…will be kept confidential." Using Figure WD4.16 as a guide, insert the following using a Left tab at 0.9", a Left tab at 3.0", and a Right tab at 5.75". (Hint: You can press **Shift** + **Enter** at the end of each line to move down without adding the extra space. Or you can select the text later and use the Line and Spacing button to remove the space before and after a paragraph.)

Jefferson County	**July 12**	**Jason Michaels**
Harney County	**July 17**	**Monte Haskins**
Deschutes County	**July 24**	**Missy Nakagawa**
Grant County	**July 31**	**Angela Golocek**

7 The Right tab should be set to include a dashed leader (leader option 3).

8 Insert a Center tab at 5.5" and ensure all the tabbed material moves accordingly. Remove the Right tab that is currently at 5.75".

9 Drag the tab from 3.0" to 2.6". Move the Center tab at 5.5" to 5.0". Ensure all the tabbed material moves accordingly. Reinsert the leader lines to match Figure WD4.16.

10 Space the list as shown in Figure WD4.16.

11 Save the file as **wd04a-hw01.docx** and close the document.

In this exercise, you will open a template and fill in the appropriate placeholders. You will insert a corporate logo as a watermark and save it as a template that can be used by anyone in the company. These additions will turn a generic template into a document that is specific to your corporation. The final document is shown in Figure WD4.17.

FIGURE WD4.17   Work It Out WD-4A-E2: completed

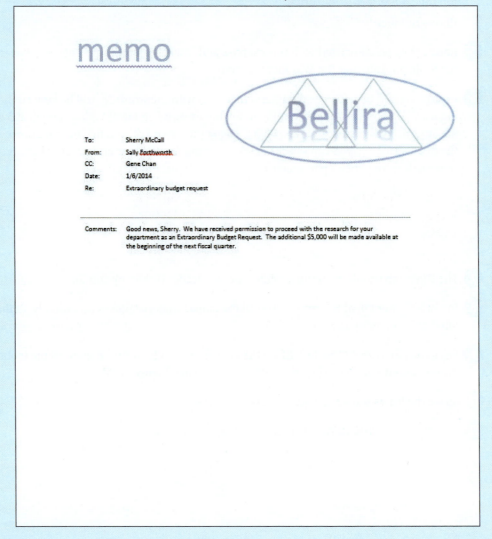

1. Open Word. Enter **memo** into the Template Search box. Locate and create (insert) the template for Memo (Simple design). If the Document Properties appear at the top of the document, close them by clicking the X on the right-hand side of the screen next to the words "Required field." Save the file as **wd04a-ex02.docx** (all the "0" in the file name are zeros).

2. Locate the files associated with this lesson and using the watermark feature, add the Bellira Logo to the document. Do not use the Washout setting.

3. Resize the logo to 1.6" high and 4.16" wide. Drag the logo to the approximate place shown in Figure WD4.17.

4. Change the color of the word *memo* to Blue, Accent 1. Close the header view.

5 Delete the Company name placeholder. Delete the Your comments placeholder. Save this file as a custom template called **Bellira-memo.dotx**. Close the file.

6 Locate and open the Bellira-memo custom template. If the Document Properties appear, close them.

7 Insert the following information into the appropriate placeholders:

To: **Sherry McCall**

From: *your name*

CC: **Heather Laine**

Date: **January 6, 2014**

Re: **Extraordinary budget request**

8 Next to the word *Comments*, TYPE

Good news, Sherry. We have received permission to proceed with the research for your department as an Extraordinary Budget Request. The additional $5,000 will be made available at the beginning of the next fiscal quarter.

9 Save the file as **wd04a-hw02.docx**. Close the document file.

In this exercise, you will open a template and fill in the appropriate placeholders. You will insert a corporate logo as a watermark and insert and apply Left, Right, and Center tabs to text. These additions will turn a generic template into a document that is specific to your corporation. The final document is shown in Figure WD4.18.

FIGURE WD4.18   Work It Out WD-4A-E3: completed

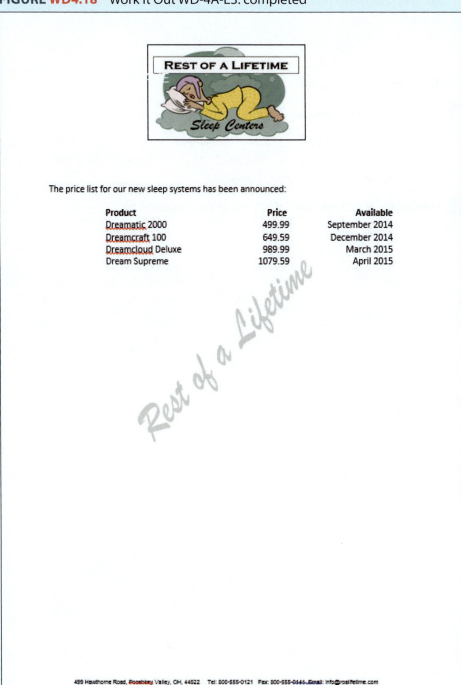

1. Open Word. Enter **letterhead** into the Template Search box. Locate and create (insert) the template for Corporate letterhead. Save the file as **wd04a-hw03.docx** (all the "0" in the file name are zeros).

2. Customize this document by changing the left and right margins to 1". Turn on the Show/Hide button, select the paragraph markers, and change the font to Calibri, 12 pt. Click before the first paragraph and press **Enter** 10 times to move the cursor down the page.

3. Right-click on the Company Name text box and change the picture to the Rest of Lifetime Logo (it is located in the files associated with this lesson). Resize the logo to 1.6" high and 2.58" wide (the width is proportionally controlled).

4. Change the information at the bottom of the page to the following:

   499 Hawthorne Road, Pooshkey Valley, OH 44522

   Tel: 800-555-0121

   Fax: 800-555-0141

   Email: info@roalifetime.com

   Change the font size if necessary so all information fits on one line.

5. Type in the sentence as shown in Figure WD4.18: **The price list for our new sleep systems has been announced:**

6. Leave a blank line, then insert the following text and tabs:

First line: **Tab type and position**	Left tab: 1.5"	Center tab: 4.5"	Right tab: 6.2"
Text to type (in boldface):	**Product**	**Price**	**Available**
Rest of the lines: **Tab type and position**	Same	Decimal tab: 4.5"	Same
Text to type	**Dreamatic 2000**	**499.99**	**September 2014**
	Dreamcraft 100	**649.59**	**December 2014**
	Dreamcloud Deluxe	**989.99**	**March 2015**
	Dream Supreme	**1079.59**	**April 2015**

7. Drag the Left tab at the 1.5" position back to the 1.0" position. Drag the Center tab at the 4.5" mark to the 4.0" position. Change the Decimal tab from 4.5" to 4.0". Drag the Right tab from the 6.2" position to the 6.0" mark. Ensure all tabbed material moves accordingly.

8. Insert a Text watermark that says **Rest of a Lifetime**. Use the font Brush Script MT, 48 pt. Use the semitransparent setting.

9. Save the file as **wd04a-hw03.docx**. Close the document file.

Inserting Tables and Controlling Columns

Maintaining control over how text and data are organized on a page is vital to ensuring effectiveness. Word provides many ways to manage the formatting and positioning of these elements. The use of tables is one of the most efficient methods because you can format the contents of a table separately from the rest of the document. Table Styles is a powerful feature that instantly gives an existing table a professional-looking format. Quick Tables actually inserts a mock table with design and data—easy to replace and adjust. You can add or delete rows or columns in a table cleanly and quickly; sort the data in tables alphabetically or numerically in ascending or descending order; and add formulas to a table to quickly total, count, multiply, average, and more. Outside of a table, another way to control text in a document is to arrange it into multiple columns. Word can effortlessly create balanced columns from existing text and change the number of columns and size of margins to suit the document.

After completing this project, you will be able to:

- Insert tables and use Table Styles.

- Adjust table appearance and use Quick Tables.

- Add rows, columns, and formulas to a table; sort a table.

- Format and control text in columns.

PROJECT FILE: *Available at* www.mhhe.com/office2013projectlearn

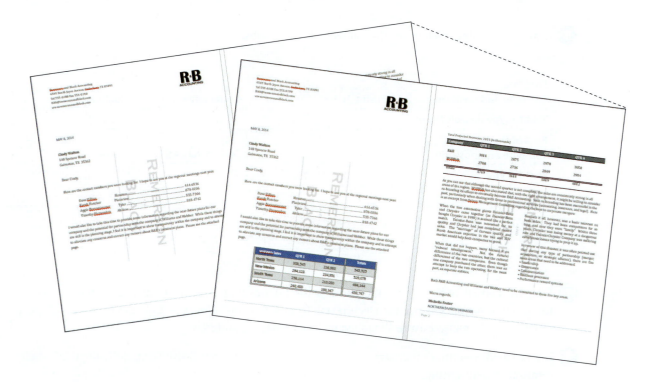

Inserting Tables and Using Table Styles

LESSON OVERVIEW

The use of **tables** in a document is often overlooked. While tabs can help set up crisp alignment of information, they are best used for a limited number of rows. When you place information in tables, it is easy to move text and data, it is simple to add another row or column, and you can sort the table instantly.

When you insert a table in a document, Word allows you to decide how many columns and rows the table should have and the table is automatically sized and centered on the page. With the predesigned **Table Styles**, any table instantly has a professional and effective appearance.

Each table consists of **rows** and **columns** that create **cells** similar to Excel and other spreadsheet software. Click into any cell and enter your text. Moving from one cell to another or even inserting new columns or rows can be done swiftly. Resize rows and columns for width or height by simply dragging the border lines; or use Word's **Autofit** feature to size them automatically.

You will begin to see how the **Table Control button** allows you to control almost every aspect of the table's attributes and appearance.

SKILLS PREVIEW

Insert a table	• CLICK the INSERT tab and locate the Tables group. CLICK Table. MOVE the mouse down the grid until it highlights the type of table you desire (2×3, 6×5, etc.). CLICK to insert the table.
Apply Table Styles	• SELECT the table. CLICK the DESIGN tab and locate the Table Styles group. CLICK the More button to see the entire palette of table styles. Hover on a style to see the live preview display on the table in your document. CLICK the style of table you desire.
Enter text into a table	• CLICK into a cell of the table. TYPE your text.
Move from one cell to another	• PRESS the [Tab] button to move to the next cell. PRESS [Shift]+[Tab] to move to the previous cell, or • CLICK the mouse into the desired cell.
Add a row to the bottom of a table	• CLICK the mouse into the very last cell of the table. PRESS [Tab] to create another row below.
Insert a row above	• CLICK the LAYOUT tab under Table Tools and locate the Rows & Columns group. CLICK Insert Above to create a new row above the rest of the table.
Adjust the column width	• DRAG the line between two columns left or right to adjust the width, or • DOUBLE-CLICK the line between two columns to automatically match the width of the column to display the largest entry in that column.
Adjust the row height	• DRAG the line between two rows up or down to adjust the height, or • DOUBLE-CLICK the line between two rows to automatically match the height to display the largest entry in that row.
Center a table across the page	• CLICK the Table Control box.

1 The file for this project includes a second page that was not included in the first, so be sure to open file **wd04b1.docx**. Save it as **wd04b1-professional_letter.docx**.

2 Insert a table below the text on the first page.

CLICK the mouse one line below the text on the first page.

CLICK the **INSERT** tab and locate the Tables group.

CLICK Table.

MOVE the mouse down and across the grid until it highlights a 3×3 table (see Figure WD4.19).

CLICK to insert the table.

FIGURE WD4.19   The Insert Table selection menu

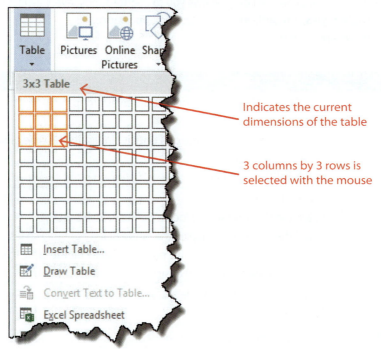

Indicates the current dimensions of the table

3 columns by 3 rows is selected with the mouse

3 CLICK the **DESIGN** tab under Table Tools (if it is not already selected).

Locate the Table Styles group.

Let the mouse hover over the various styles for a moment and the newly inserted table will display the style in the document.

CLICK Plain Table 1.

This simple table style makes the table easy to see.

4 The cursor should automatically flash in the first cell of the table. Pressing **Tab** moves the cursor from one cell to the next.

TYPE **South Texas**

PRESS **Tab** .

TYPE **256,114**

PRESS **Tab**

TYPE **210,030**

PRESS **Tab** to move to the next row of the table.

TIP

Pressing **Tab** is the quickest way to move ahead in a table because your hands do not have to leave the typing position, but it only moves the cursor ahead. You can move backward by pressing **Shift** + **Tab** . You can move the cursor ahead in a table by using the arrow keys (→ ← ↑ ↓). This allows you to move in any direction. If you need to move to a cell that is not adjacent to the cell you are currently in, you can simply click the mouse into that cell.

5 Using the same technique as in the last step, insert the following:

North Texas (**Tab**) 308,545 (**Tab**) 236,980 (**Tab**)

New Mexico (**Tab**) 294,128 (**Tab**) 234,951 (**Tab**)

6 To add another row for the last entry, with the cursor at the end of the last entry:

CLICK **Tab** to create another row with the same style as the rest of the table.

TYPE Arizona (**Tab**) 260,400 (**Tab**) 198,347

7 Add a Table Style.

CLICK the DESIGN tab under Table Tools and locate the Table Styles group.

CLICK the More button to display the palette of Table Styles.

CLICK Grid Table 4, Accent 5.

The table instantly changes to match the style.

TIP

If the palette of styles extends down the screen and interferes with your view of the table in the document, you can make the palette smaller. The bottom right-hand corner has a sizing handle shown by three little dots. When you place the mouse above it, the cursor becomes a two-headed arrow. The palette can then be dragged up the screen to allow you to see the document (this applies to almost every selection palette in Word). You can access all the styles by using the scrolling bar on the right side of the palette.

Sizing handle

Sizing cursor

8 The table has a style that obviously enhances the heading row across the top.

To add a row to a table, ensure your cursor is somewhere in the first row of the table.

CLICK the LAYOUT tab under Table Tools and locate the Rows & Columns group.

CLICK Insert Above to create a new row above the rest of the table.

In this row add the following headings to the appropriate column:

WillWeb Sales

QTR 1

QTR 2

9 The table currently sits across the entire page. This makes some of the columns much wider than they have to be. You can adjust the size of the columns and rows.

HOVER the cursor on the line between the first and second columns.

DRAG the line to about the 1.5" mark on the ruler to use manual adjustment.

DOUBLE-CLICK on the line between the second and third columns to use the AutoFit feature.

CLICK UNDO so you can try an even easier feature.

HOVER the mouse over the top of the second column until the cursor becomes a black arrow facing downward (see Figure WD4.20 for the column selection arrow).

CLICK and HOLD the mouse.

DRAG it over to the third column to select both columns.

DOUBLE-CLICK the very last borderline of the table (at the right of the third column).

This automatically sizes all the selected columns.

FIGURE WD4.20 The column selection arrow

Column selection arrow

WillWeb Sales	QTR 1	QTR 2
South Texas	256,114	210,030
North Texas	308,545	236,980
New Mexico	294,128	234,951
Arizona	260,400	198,347

> ### MORE INFO
>
> Double-clicking on a table border automatically resizes the column to fit the largest text in the column. The AutoFit feature on the LAYOUT tab under Table Tools offers more options and control. Once you click the cursor anywhere in a table, the AutoFit drop-down displays three options. AutoFit Contents adjusts the columns of the entire table to fit the content inside them (similar to double-clicking). AutoFit Window stretches the table evenly across the document page (as it does when a table is first inserted). Fixed Column Width protects the column widths from changing when the table is moved or adjusted otherwise (you can still adjust them).

10 To adjust the height of the column manually:

Locate the line below the first row (the heading row).

DRAG it down to about twice its height.

RELEASE the mouse.

11 To center the table across the page:

HOVER the mouse over the table to display the Table Control button ( ).

CLICK it to select the entire table.

CLICK the HOME tab and locate the Paragraph group.

CLICK the Center button to center the table across the page.

12 Your document should look similar to Figure WD4.21. Save your file before continuing.

FIGURE WD4.21   Completion of Lesson Word 4B1

Remerson and Black Accounting
4545 North Joyce Avenue, Soderham, TX 83091
Tel 555-0188 Fax 555-0190
R&b@remersonandblack.com
www.remersonandblack.com

R&B
ACCOUNTING

MAY 8, 2014

Cindy Walton
148 Spencer Road
Galveston, TX 35362

Dear Cindy,

Here are the contact numbers you were looking for. I hope to see you at the regional meetings next year.

Dave Villian	Houston	414-6536
Kareb Fletcher	Plainview	878-0206
Aggie Borennieesser	Tyler	535-7366
Timothy Plamondon	Abilene	818-4742

I would also like to take this time to provide some information regarding the near-future plans for our company and the potential for partnership with the company of Williams and Webber. While these things are still in the planning stage, I feel it is important to show transparency within the company and to attempt to alleviate any concerns and correct any rumors about R&B's imminent plans. Please see the attached page.

WillWeb Sales	QTR 1	QTR 2
South Texas	256,114	210,030
North Texas	308,545	236,980
New Mexico	294,128	234,951
Arizona	260,400	198,347

Adjusting Table Appearance

LESSON OVERVIEW

You can make tables look great with just a click on the Table Styles palette, but you can also create your own designs or make a slight change to one of the Table Styles. To make changes, Word provides a specific cursor image that appears when you work on a table. The **column selection arrow** allows you to select one column or more than one adjacent column for formatting separately from the rest of the table. The **cell/row selection arrow** allows you to select one particular cell, or the entire row of cells, to make formatting changes.

If you change the dimensions of a table (usually by dragging an outside border), you will lose the symmetrical design of the cells or columns. Word offers two features to snap the table back into symmetry—**distribute columns evenly** and **distribute rows evenly**. You can align the text or data inside each cell horizontally to the left, right, or center, as well as to the top, bottom, or middle of the cell.

Customize the shading (fill) of a cell (or an entire column and row) to match the style of your document. You can change the color, width, and style of **table borders**. You can add these changes to all the borders of a table or use the **Border Painter button** to apply the changes to just the borders you wish.

Word offers **Quick Tables**. This feature provides not only a professional design, but also mock data that is easy for you to delete or replace to create your own table.

SKILLS PREVIEW

Select a column in a table	• MOVE the cursor to the top of a column in the table. MOVE the cursor until it becomes a black down-facing arrow. CLICK to select the column.
Select a row in a table	• MOVE the cursor to the left of a row in the table. MOVE the cursor until it becomes a black right-facing arrow. CLICK once to select the cell. CLICK twice to select the row.
Distribute columns evenly in a table	• RIGHT-CLICK the Table Control button (left-hand corner of the table) to open the shortcut menu. CHOOSE Distribute Columns Evenly.
Distribute rows evenly in a table	• RIGHT-CLICK the Table Control button (left-hand corner of the table) to open the shortcut menu. CHOOSE Distribute Rows Evenly.
Align text in a cell of a table	• CLICK into the cell. CLICK the LAYOUT tab under Table Tools and locate the Alignment group. CLICK the alignment you desire.
Align contents of cells in a table	• Using the solid black selection arrow, select the columns or rows you want to align. CLICK the LAYOUT tab under Table Tools and locate the Alignment group. CLICK the alignment you desire.
Change the shading (fill) of a cell	• SELECT the cell (or entire row or column, if desired). CLICK the HOME tab and locate the Paragraph group (or use the Mini toolbar and the Shading button). CLICK the Shading drop-down arrow. CHOOSE the desired color.

Alter the borders of a table	• SELECT the table (using the Table Control button). CLICK the DESIGN tab under Table Tools and locate the Borders group. CLICK Borders. SELECT Borders and Shading. USE the drop-down arrows to choose the style of line, the color of the lines, and the width of the line. In the Style box, SELECT the style of line. • In the Preview, CLICK the borders you wish to change. CLICK OK, or • After selecting the options for the border, CLICK OK. CLICK the Border Painter button (in the Borders group). DRAG the mouse (that now looks like a fine paintbrush) down the borders you wish to change. CLICK the Border Painter button (or PRESS the Esc key) to turn the painter off.
Insert a Quick Table	• PLACE the mouse where you would like to insert the table. CLICK the INSERT tab and locate the Tables group. CLICK Table. CLICK Quick Tables. CHOOSE the style of table you wish to use.

PROJECT PRACTICE

1 Ensure the file **wd04b1-professional_letter.docx** is open. Save it as **wd04b2-professional_letter.docx**.

2 To change the attributes of a column in a table, DRAG the left-hand border of the table about an inch to the left.

HOVER the mouse over the first column until the mouse turns to a downward-facing solid black arrow.

CLICK to select the column.

USE the Mini toolbar to change the font of that column to Calibri, 12 pt.

3 HOVER the mouse over the second column until the mouse becomes a downward-facing solid black arrow.

CLICK and HOLD the cursor.

DRAG the mouse to the third column to select both the second and third columns.
Change the font to Calibri, 12 pt.

> **MORE INFO**
>
> The down-facing black arrow that appears over a table column is called the column selection arrow. Clicking once on a column selects the entire column. You can click and hold while sliding across to select more adjacent columns. The right-facing black arrow that appears over a cell is the cell/row selection arrow. Clicking once in a cell selects that particular cell. Clicking twice in any cell selects the entire row.

4 Locate the Table Control button ().

RIGHT-CLICK the Table Control button to bring up a shortcut menu specific to the table.

CLICK Distribute Columns Evenly.

Because you had selected the entire table, all the columns are now equal width.

5 Using the solid black selection arrow, select the second and third columns.

CLICK the LAYOUT tab under Table Tools and locate the Alignment group.

CLICK the Align Center button to align those cells to the center.

CLICK into the cell that says "WillWeb Sales" (do not select the cells below it).

CLICK the Align Center button (see Figure WD4.22).

FIGURE WD4.22   The Text Alignment buttons in the Alignment group

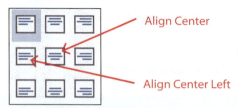

Align Center

Align Center Left

6 DRAG the bottom line of the table down about ½ inch.

RIGHT-CLICK the Table Control button.

CLICK Distribute Rows Evenly.
Notice that the alignment of all the text adjusts to remain in the horizontal and vertical center of the cells.

7 HOVER the mouse just inside the left of the cell that says "South Texas" until a right-facing black arrow appears (the cell or row selection arrow).

DRAG down to select all four cells.

CLICK the LAYOUT tab under Table Tools (if necessary) and locate the Alignment group.

CLICK the Align Center Left button (see Figure WD4.22).
(*Result:* The regions align vertically center, but remain aligned to the left.)

8 HOVER the mouse just inside the left of the heading row to display the black right-facing arrow.

DOUBLE-CLICK to select the entire row.

CLICK the HOME tab and locate the Paragraph group (or use the Mini toolbar and the Shading button).

CLICK the Shading drop-down arrow.

CHOOSE Blue.
Deselect the table to see the changes.

9 SELECT the table (use the Table Control box).

CLICK the DESIGN tab under Table Tools and locate the Borders group.

CLICK Borders.

SELECT Borders and Shading from the bottom of the menu.

In the Style box, SELECT the double line.

CLICK OK.

CLICK the Border Painter button (in the Borders group).

DRAG the mouse (that now looks like a fine paintbrush) down the left-hand outside border of the table.

DRAG it across the bottom border and up the right-hand side border (see Figure WD4.23).

CLICK the Border Painter button (or PRESS the Esc key) to turn the painter off.

FIGURE WD4.23 Table with new borders drawn with the Border Painter

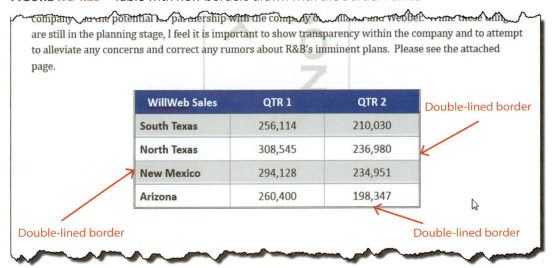

10 MOVE to page two of the document.

CLICK the mouse one line above the first paragraph of page two.

CLICK the INSERT tab and locate the Table group.

CLICK Table.

CLICK Quick Tables.

CHOOSE With Subheads 2 to insert a predesigned table.

11 The table is too long for your purposes, but the formatting is excellent.

SELECT all the rows (using the right-facing white arrow) from the first occurrence of "Pine College" down to the bottom (including "Source"). If necessary, change the table structure so it is similar to Figure WD4.25

RIGHT-CLICK in the selected area.

CHOOSE Cut.

REPLACE the text and data in the various cells as shown in Figure WD4.24.

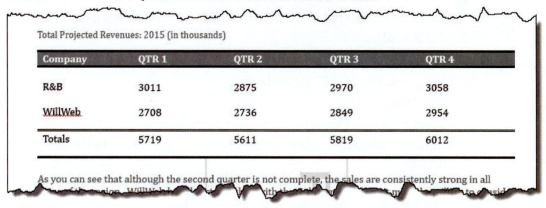

Total Projected Revenues: 2015 (in thousands)

Company	QTR 1	QTR 2	QTR 3	QTR 4
R&B	3011	2875	2970	3058
WillWeb	2708	2736	2849	2954
Totals	5719	5611	5819	6012

As you can see that although the second quarter is not complete, the sales are consistently strong in all

12 Your document should look similar to Figure WD4.25. Do not worry if it spills over to three pages. That will be addressed in another lesson. Save it before proceeding.

FIGURE **WD4.25** Completion of Lesson Word 4B2

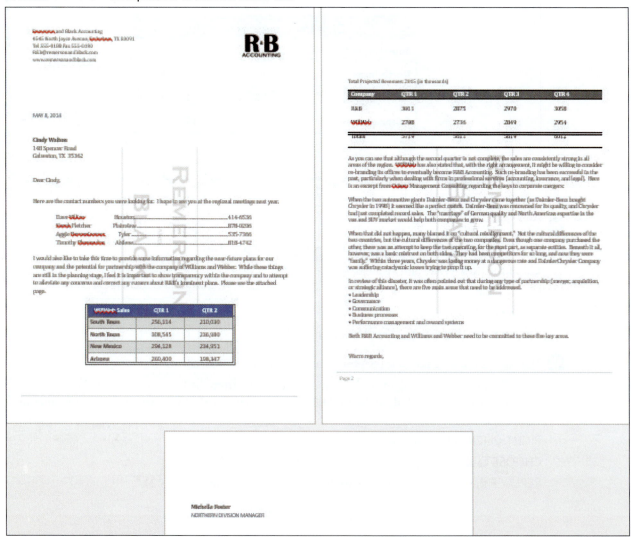

Adding Columns and Formulas and Sorting Tables

LESSON OVERVIEW

Once you create tables, they offer great flexibility. You can quickly **insert a column** or **insert a row** anywhere in a table—the middle, end, top, or bottom. If you find you have too many columns or rows, the **Delete Columns** and **Delete Rows** commands remove the columns or rows and instantly reformat the table to a perfectly balanced table.

Although not nearly as flexible as Excel and other spreadsheet software, Word does allow you to insert **formulas** into tables. This allows you to quickly sum, multiply, average, count, and perform other functions on data across cells in the table. You can choose the **number format** that Word applies to the result.

Once you add data or text to a table, you can sort it quickly in ascending or descending order. When Word sorts in one column, it automatically sorts the adjacent columns so the information is not jumbled. If your table has a **header row** with column titles, you can remove them from the sorting so they remain at the top of the table.

SKILLS PREVIEW

Add (insert) a column to a table	• HOVER the mouse at the top of the line between two columns. CLICK the Add Column button (the plus sign).
Add (insert) a row to a table	• HOVER the mouse at the far left of the line between two rows CLICK the Add Row button (the plus sign).
Delete a row or column from a table	• SELECT the row or column. RIGHT-CLICK on the selected area. CHOOSE Delete Columns (or Rows) from the menu.
Insert a formula into a cell	• CLICK the cursor into the cell where you wish to insert the formula. CLICK the LAYOUT tab under Table Tools and locate the Data group. CLICK Formula. CHOOSE the formula options: Sum, Count, Average, etc. CHOOSE the number format. CLICK OK.
Sort a table	• CLICK into the column you wish to use for the sort. CLICK the LAYOUT tab under Table Tools and locate the Data group. CLICK the Sort button. SET the sort criteria in the Sort dialog box. CHOOSE Ascending or Descending. CLICK OK.

PROJECT PRACTICE

1. Ensure the file **wd04b2-professional_letter.docx** is open. Save it as **wd04b3-professional_letter.docx**.

2. To add a column to a table, HOVER the mouse at the top of the line between the first and second columns of the first table.

   CLICK the Add Column button (see Figure WD4.26) to add (insert) a new column.

   Deselect the table to see the new column better.

   (*Result:* The inserted column is based on the characteristics of the existing columns.)

FIGURE WD4.26 The Add Column button

concerns and correct any rumors about R&B's imminent plans. Please see t

Add Column button

WillWeb Sales	QTR 1	QTR 2
South Texas	256,114	210,030
North Texas	308,545	236,980
New Mexico	294,128	234,951
Arizona	260,400	198,347

3 SELECT the new column (with the column selection arrow).

RIGHT-CLICK on the selected area to bring up the shortcut menu.

CLICK Delete Columns.

Because only one column was selected, that is the column that will disappear.

4 HOVER the mouse on the left-hand border between "North Texas" and "New Mexico."

CLICK the Add Row button (the plus sign) to insert a new row.

Deselect the table to see the new row better.

Notice the banded color pattern (one row blue, then one row white) of the new row is the same as the rest of the table.

5 DOUBLE-CLICK the new row (with the cell/row selection arrow) to select it.

RIGHT-CLICK on the selected area to bring up the shortcut menu.

CLICK Delete Rows.

Because only one row was selected, that is the row that will disappear.

6 HOVER the mouse at the right-hand corner of the top border.

CLICK the Add Column button to add a new column to the right of the table.

CLICK into the first new blue cell (on the top of the new row).

TYPE **Totals**

7 CLICK into the cell below the word *Totals*.

CLICK the LAYOUT tab under Table Tools and locate the Data group.

CLICK Formula (it will be inserted at your cursor's location).

The Formula dialog box defaults to SUM and locates numbers to its left (see Figure WD4.27).

CLICK OK to total the numbers in that row.

Do the same to the remaining empty cells.

FIGURE WD4.27 The Formula dialog box

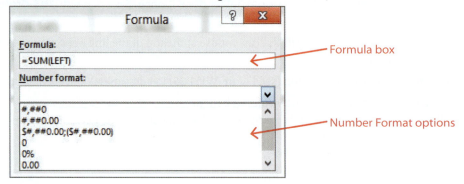

Formula

Formula:
=SUM(LEFT)

Formula box

Number format:

Number Format options

#,##0
#,##0.00
$#,##0.00;($#,##0.00)
0
0%
0.00

8 To sort the table alphabetically by region:

CLICK into the column with the names of the regions.

CLICK the LAYOUT tab under Table Tools and locate the Data group.

CLICK the Sort button.

The Sort dialog box opens to allow you to make choices (see Figure WD4.28).

Ensure the following settings:

Sort by box: WillWeb Sales

Type: Text

Using: Paragraphs

And sort in Ascending order.

CLICK OK.

(*Results:* The data has been sorted alphabetically by the name of the region.)

FIGURE WD4.28   The Sort dialog box and its options

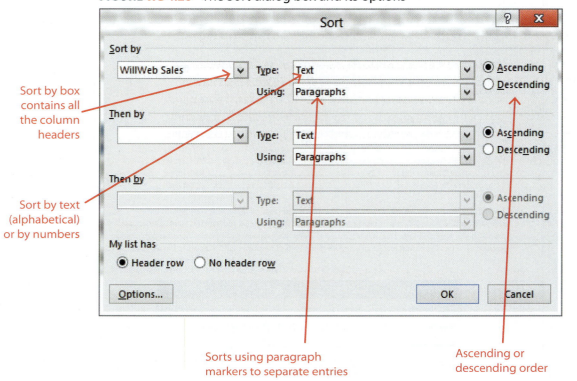

Sort by box contains all the column headers

Sort by text (alphabetical) or by numbers

Sorts using paragraph markers to separate entries

Ascending or descending order

9 CLICK the Sort button again.

Change the settings to the following:

Sort by: Totals

Type: Number

Using: Paragraphs

Descending

CLICK OK.

(*Results:* The table is sorted by the amount of sales from highest to lowest.)

10 The first page of your document should look similar to Figure WD4.29. Save the file before proceeding.

FIGURE WD4.29   Completion of Lesson Word 4B3

Remerson and Black Accounting
4545 North Joyce Avenue, Soderham, TX 83091
Tel 555-0188 Fax 555-0190
R&b@remersonandblack.com
www.remersonandblack.com

MAY 8, 2014

Cindy Walton
148 Spencer Road
Galveston, TX 35362

Dear Cindy,

Here are the contact numbers you were looking for. I hope to see you at the regional meetings next year.

Dave Villian	Houston	414-6536
Kareb Fletcher	Plainview	878-0206
Aggie Borennieesser	Tyler	535-7366
Timothy Plamondon	Abilene	818-4742

I would also like to take this time to provide some information regarding the near-future plans for our company and the potential for partnership with the company of Williams and Webber. While these things are still in the planning stage, I feel it is important to show transparency within the company and to attempt to alleviate any concerns and correct any rumors about R&B's imminent plans. Please see the attached page.

WillWeb Sales	QTR 1	QTR 2	Totals
North Texas	308,545	236,980	545,525
New Mexico	294,128	234,951	529,079
South Texas	256,114	210,030	466,144
Arizona	260,400	198,347	458,747

Working in Columns

LESSON OVERVIEW

Adding **columns** to a document draws attention to one section by setting it apart from the rest of the text. Often, slightly more text can fit on each page if it is set into columns. While you can start with a blank page and set it to multiple columns, it is generally easier to create your text first, then apply columns to the text you desire.

Technically, all text is in columns. What might be considered "no columns" is actually one column that fills the space from margin to margin. To change from one column to multiple columns requires that you insert a **continuous section break**. This break is just like other section breaks, except that it does not create a new page—it continues on the same page. You can add this break manually, but when you select existing text and change it to multiple columns, Word automatically inserts the continuous section break before and after the selected text.

Text that is "in columns" often looks more effective when it is justified. **Justified columns** display straight margins down both the left-hand and right-hand sides of each column. You can also add a **line between columns**. This improves the visual separation of columns for the reader.

Adjust the **width of columns** and the margins between them by entering measurements in the **Columns dialog box** or drag the column margins along the horizontal ruler. Also, you can use a **column break** to force text to move from one column to the next. This allows you to avoid breaking columns in the middle of a paragraph.

SKILLS PREVIEW

Change an entire document to more than one column	• CLICK the PAGE LAYOUT tab and locate the Page Setup group. CLICK Columns. SELECT the number of columns from the menu or CLICK More Columns to make custom-sized columns.
Create columns using existing text	• SELECT the text you want to turn into columns. CLICK the PAGE LAYOUT tab and locate the Page Setup group. CLICK Columns. SELECT the number of columns from the menu or CLICK More Columns to make custom-sized columns.
Change from a single column to multiple columns as you enter text	• LEAVE the cursor at the point where you wish to change from one column to more columns. CLICK the PAGE LAYOUT tab and locate the Page Setup group. CLICK Breaks. CLICK Continuous to insert a continuous section break. CLICK Columns. SELECT the number of columns from the menu or CLICK More Columns to make custom-sized columns.
Change from multiple columns to a single column as you enter text	• LEAVE the cursor at the point where you wish to change from multiple columns to one column. CLICK the PAGE LAYOUT tab and locate the Page Setup group. CLICK Breaks. CLICK Continuous to insert a continuous section break. CLICK Columns. SELECT one.
Insert a line between columns	• CLICK the PAGE LAYOUT tab and locate the Page Setup group. CLICK Columns. CLICK the Line between check box to insert a line. CLICK OK.

Adjust column or column margin width	• CLICK inside the column. DRAG the column margin on the horizontal ruler to increase or decrease the width of the margin.
Justify the text in columns	• SELECT the entire text you wish to justify. CLICK the HOME tab and locate the Paragraph group. CLICK the Justify button (or use **Ctrl** + **J**).
Insert a column break	• CLICK the cursor in front of the word you would like to move to the next column. CLICK the Breaks button in the Page Setup group. CLICK Column to insert a column break.

PROJECT PRACTICE

1 Ensure the file **wd04b3-professional_letter.docx** is open. Save it as **wd04b4-professional_letter.docx**.

2 Change text to two columns.

MOVE to the end of the document. Notice there are two lines on the third page.

Inserting columns is easier if the text already exists.

SELECT the three paragraphs starting with "When the two automotive…" and ending with "…performance reward systems."

CLICK the PAGE LAYOUT tab and locate the Page Setup group.

CLICK Columns.

SELECT Two to change the text to two columns.

HEADS UP
Converting one-column (often called "no columns") text into columns generally allows slightly more text to fit in the same amount of space. Here, after applying two columns to a section of the text, the document adjusts and fits on just two pages.

3 CLICK the Columns button again.

CLICK More Columns to open the Columns dialog box.

The settings are as shown in Figure WD4.30.

CLICK the Line between check box to insert a line between the two columns.

CLICK OK.

FIGURE WD4.30 Columns dialog box with two-column presets

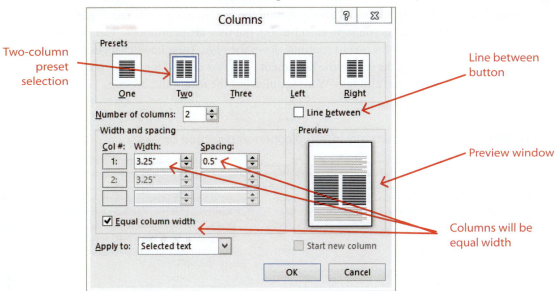

Two-column preset selection

Line between button

Preview window

Columns will be equal width

4️⃣ CLICK inside the left-hand column.

Notice the horizontal ruler displays the column widths and the size of the margin between them.

DRAG the left-hand column's right margin (shown on the ruler) to the left (to about the 3" mark).

This decreases the width of that column.

DRAG the far right-hand margin of the right column to the left about 0.5".

This increases the width of the right-hand margin.

CLICK UNDO twice to return to the previous settings.

5️⃣ SELECT the entire text in the two columns.

CLICK the HOME tab and locate the Paragraph group.

CLICK the Justify button (▤) or PRESS **Ctrl** + **J**.

This will justify the text in both columns without affecting the rest of the document.

6️⃣ With the sharp justified columns, you no longer need the line between the columns.

CLICK anywhere within the columns.

CLICK the PAGE LAYOUT tab and locate the Page Setup group.

CLICK the Columns button.

CLICK More Columns.

CLICK the Line between check box to deselect that option.

CLICK OK.

7 TURN the Show/Hide button on (¶).

Notice that Word has placed special breaks around the section in columns (see Figure WD4.31). These are section breaks (as you have used before), but they are continuous. This means they do not start a new page but allow the text to continue down the page. This allows changes to be made to this section without affecting the rest of the document. This was needed for Word to apply two columns to just the selected text; it is also how Word justified just the text in this section.

TURN the Show/Hide button off.

FIGURE WD4.31 Automatically inserted continuous section breaks

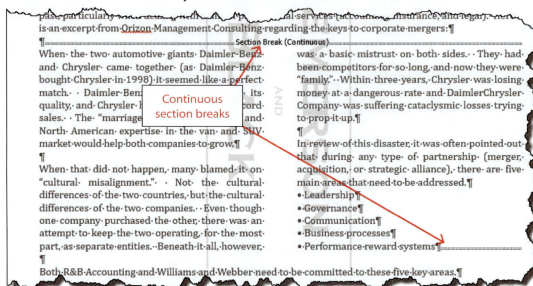

8 SELECT the text in the columns.

CLICK the Columns button.

CLICK Three to change the columns from two to three.

Notice the last bullet ("Performance reward systems…") is too long for the column.

CLICK the Columns button.

CLICK Two.

9 CLICK the cursor in front of the sentence that begins with "Beneath it all, however…"

CLICK the Breaks button in the Page Setup group.

CLICK Column to insert a column break.

This forces the first column to break at that point and moves the text to the next column.

TURN the Show/Hide button on to see how that break looks.

10 Your document should be similar to Figure WD4.32. Turn the Show/Hide button off. Save the file and close Word.

Severson and Black Accounting
4545 North Joyce Avenue, Galveston, TX 83093
Tel 555-0188 Fax 555-0198
R&b@reversonandblack.com
www.reversonandblack.com

R·B
ACCOUNTING

MAY 6, 2014

Cindy Walton
148 Spencer Road
Galveston, TX 35362

Dear Cindy,

Here are the contact numbers you were looking for. I hope to see you at the regional meetings next year.

Dave Wilson	Houston	414-6536
Kevin Fletcher	Plainview	878-0206
Aggie Bereanicosger	Tyler	535-7366
Timothy Plasencian	Abilene	818-4742

I would also like to take this time to provide some information regarding the near-future plans for our company and the potential for partnership with the company of Williams and Webber. While these things are still in the planning stage, I feel it is important to show transparency within the company and to attempt to alleviate any concerns and correct any rumors about R&B's imminent plans. Please see the attached page.

Wil/Web Sales	QTR 1	QTR 2	Totals
North Texas	308,545	236,980	545,525
New Mexico	294,128	234,951	529,079
South Texas	256,114	210,030	466,144
Arizona	260,400	198,347	458,747

Total Projected Revenue 2015 (in thousands)

Company	QTR 1	QTR 2	QTR 3	QTR 4
R&B	3011	2875	2970	3058
Wil/Web	2708	2736	2849	2954
Totals	5719	5611	5819	6012

As you can see that although the second quarter is not complete, the sales are consistently strong in all areas of the region. Wil/Web has also stated that, with the right arrangement, it might be willing to consider re-branding its offices to eventually become R&B Accounting. Such re-branding has been successful in the past, particularly when dealing with firms in professional services (accounting, insurance, and legal). Here is an excerpt from Orion Management Consulting regarding the keys to corporate mergers:

When the two automotive giants Daimler-Benz and Chrysler came together (as Daimler-Benz bought Chrysler in 1998) it seemed like a perfect match. Daimler-Benz was renowned for its quality, and Chrysler had just completed record sales. The "marriage" of German quality and North American expertise in the van and SUV market would help both companies to grow.

When that did not happen, many blamed it on "cultural misalignment." Not the cultural differences of the two countries, but the cultural differences of the two companies. Even though one company purchased the other, there was an attempt to keep the two operating, for the most part, as separate entities.

Beneath it all, however, was a basic mistrust on both sides. They had been competitors for so long, and now they were "family." Within three years, Chrysler was losing money at a dangerous rate and DaimlerChrysler Company was suffering cataclysmic losses trying to prop it up.

In review of this disaster, it was often pointed out that during any type of partnership (merger, acquisition, or strategic alliance), there are five main areas that need to be addressed.
- Leadership
- Governance
- Communication
- Business processes
- Performance reward systems

Both R&B Accounting and Williams and Webber need to be committed to these five key areas.

Warm regards,

Michelle Foster
NORTHERN DIVISION MANAGER

Page 2

MULTIPLE-CHOICE QUIZ

Select the best choice in the following questions to review the project concepts. Good luck!

1. A table can be inserted by
   a. right-clicking and choosing Insert Table.
   b. clicking the INSERT tab, clicking Design, choosing Tables.
   c. clicking the PAGE LAYOUT tab and clicking Tables.
   d. None of these is correct.

2. In a table, when a row and column intersect, it is called a
   a. cell.
   b. tab.
   c. placeholder.
   d. None of these is correct.

3. Double-clicking a border between two columns will
   a. use Auto-fit to adjust the width.
   b. make both columns the same width.
   c. select the column for formatting.
   d. All of these are correct.

4. The Table Control button allows you to
   a. distribute rows evenly.
   b. apply border styles.
   c. delete the table.
   d. All of these are correct.

5. Quick Tables
   a. applies preset styles to existing tables.
   b. creates a table in which you can replace data.
   c. inserts a totals function.
   d. All of these are correct.

6. The column/row selection arrow appears as a
   a. thick white arrow.
   b. left-facing black arrow.
   c. small crosshair.
   d. None of these is correct.

7. When a Quick Tables style is applied, it
   a. cannot be adjusted.
   b. allows customization.
   c. automatically centers the table.
   d. None of these is correct.

8. When a formula is inserted into a table, it
   a. defaults to SUM.
   b. works with numbers to its left.
   c. adjusts to the appropriate number format.
   d. All of these are correct.

9. To apply columns to just one part of a document without creating a new page, you must
   a. insert a continuous section break.
   b. insert a column break.
   c. insert a column break, then a section break.
   d. None of these is correct.

10. When multiple columns are applied to a portion of a document, it can
    a. have a line between the columns.
    b. draw attention to the column portion.
    c. be justified separately from the rest of the document.
    d. All of these are correct.

In this exercise, you will open an existing letter and insert a Quick Table, then edit the information for your purposes. Using the Table Styles and borders and shading control, you will adjust the table to match it to the design of the letter. The final document is shown in Figure WD4.33.

FIGURE WD4.33   Work It Out WD-4B-E1: completed

flemington fulmans

8000 – Timaheel Boulevard
Rialto, CA 93244
phone: (808) 555-0077
e-mail: flemingtonfulmans.com

November 7, 2012

David Larosa
Clestals Fashions
336 Reid Street
Folgan, Minnesota 41415

Dear David:

Thank you for your interest in our new line of clothing. Keeping with our tradition of previewing our newest creations during small-town charity events, we have established the following schedule of cities and towns in your region. Let me present a personal invitation for you to attend as my guest for any of these shows.

City or Town	Jan	Feb	March	April
Ladny	21	18	16	18
Newfield	-	-	10	14
Rolling Hills	15	9	12	17
Wentor	16	10	-	10

These events are truly "small town" in nature. The organizing bodies are mostly volunteer, and the presentations are usually filled with little irregularities that would not occur at the industrial-level shows. It is truly one of the most endearing attributes of these shows.

If you would like to attend, please contact our office, and an official invitation will be sent to you with all the pertinent information. I look forward to seeing you.

Marsha Fulmans,

Promotions Director
Flemington Fulmans Fashions

1. Locate and open the file **wd04b-ex1.docx**. Save it as **wd04b-hw01.docx**.

2. Using Quick Tables, insert a Matrix table into the space between the first and the second paragraphs. Delete the bottom row. Delete the last column.

3. Replace the "City or Town" column with the following four places:

Rolling Hills

Wentor

Newfield

Ladny

4 Replace the column headings ("Point A," "Point B," etc.) with the following:

Jan

Feb

March

April

5 Replace the existing data in the table with the data below:

Jan	Feb	March	April
15	9	12	17
16	10	–	10
–	–	10	14
21	18	16	18

6 To match the table with the green theme of the company logo, use the Table Styles to apply List Table 7 Colorful – Accent 6 to the table.

7 Sort the table in alphabetical order by the "City or Town" column.

8 Paint a border style along the top and bottom of the table. Use Double solid lines, ½ pt., Green Accent 6.

9 Center the table across the page.

10 Save and close the file.

In this exercise, you will open an article and change it to a two-column format. You will add a line between the columns and a column break to create a balanced document. You will also insert a table and enter data. After applying a table style, you will sort the table, then add a few new rows into the table. The final document is shown in Figure WD4.34.

FIGURE WD4.34   Work It Out WD-4B-E2: completed

1. Locate and open the file **wd04b-ex02.docx**. Save it as **wd04b-hw02.docx**.

2. Leave the title as one column, but change the rest of the document to two columns. Place a line down between the columns.

3. Insert a 2×8 table on the blank line just above the words "Almost 30 years before…" Ensure there is a blank line both above and below the table.

4. Enter the following data:

City	Summer Average
Tampa	83
Phoenix	93
New Orleans	83
Miami	84
Las Vegas	90
Dallas	85
Austin	84

5 Use the Table Styles to format the table to Grid Table 6 Colorful – Accent 6.

6 AutoFit both columns of the table. Center the data in column 2. Center the table in the column.

7 Sort the table in order of temperature from the hottest to the coolest.

8 Add a row between "Dallas" and "Miami." Insert **Walla Walla** for the city and **85** for the temperature. Add a row between "Miami" and "Austin." Insert **Houston** for the city and **84** for the temperature.

9 Move to the second page and insert a column break at the start of the paragraph that begins with "Today's city is known… ."

10 Save and close the file.

In this exercise, you will open a short one-page document and add a table with important information for the reader. You will adjust the table's color scheme and style to clearly communicate the price changes over the past decade. You will add to the table and sort the data. The clean and concise table breaks the document into two parts as the text that follows is moved into two columns to provide a different view for the reader. The final document is shown in Figure WD4.35.

FIGURE **WD4.35**   Work It Out WD-4B-E3: completed

Shopping for Your Home

Buying a home isn't easy. It's even harder if you are moving to a new city. We know and we understand. There *is* an easier way to buy a home, however, and if you have to relocate — *to do that too*. At HomeHelp we offer our specialized, unique consumer-oriented services to assist you in consummating your home purchase transaction as rapidly and as advantageously as possible. Our goal is to save you needless time, effort, frustration and expense associated with this important purchase and investment.

Our goal at HomeHelp is to empower you, the buyer, during the home purchase process. Your purchase and move to your next home, whether it be your first, or fifth, is one of the most important transactions of your lifetime. It isn't just a matter of money and financial commitment. People don't just invest in homes — they live in them. Homes are where memories are created and families are raised. We share this view of its importance. Looking back, we can see how the housing markets have changed. The following prices are all in thousands of dollars.

Year	Bungalow	Rancher	Split-level	Duplex	Condo
2010	210	255	268	160	165
2005	240	290	290	180	173
2000	194	230	260	148	155
Averages	215	258	273	163	164

Today, "traditional" real estate brokerage is dead. The state of the art in brokerage services for the home buyer is Buyer Brokerage. This is the answer to the question of how to ensure that both parties to a transaction receive the same level of effective, confidential representation and service both need and deserve. Let us show you how to control your own inside track and maximize the potential for solid, value-added services.

The days of hoarding important real estate decision-making information are over. Welcome to the information explosion! You, the home buying consumer, now have direct, virtually unlimited access to information on available homes via your desktop computer to our property listings and directories with a simple mouse click.

Looking for information on Shopping for Your Home, Financing, Preparing the Offer, Negotiation Strategies, and Getting to Closing? Want to know more about home inspections, radon gas, balloon mortgages, lead paint, mortgage insurance, land surveys, title searches, and ARMS, to name a few? Then you've come to the right place. Be sure to visit our Virtual Library of Home Buying Information. Valuable Info, Tools, Checklists and FAQs will be found here.

You would think that such a valuable service as ours would be an expensive addition to an already costly transaction. The good news is that participating in the HomeHelp experience will not result in any additional cost.

We also recognize the importance, the necessity, of creating a "good match" between buyer and agent. Following agent selection, HomeHelp will stay on as an intermediary, a referral advocate, to help assure that you are completely satisfied and at ease with the selected agent.

① Locate and open **wd04b-ex03.docx**. Save it as **wd04b-hw03.docx**.

② Move to the empty line between the second and third paragraphs. Insert a 5×3 table. Be sure there is a blank line above and below the table. Enter the following data:

Year	Bungalow	Split-level	Duplex	Condo
2000	194	260	148	155
2005	240	290	180	173

3 Apply the List Table 6 Colorful – Accent 5 format to the table. Leave column one as it is, but AutoFit the remaining four columns.

4 Add a column between "Bungalow" and "Split-level." Enter the following data:

Rancher
230
290

5 Add another row to the buttom of the table with the following data:

2010	210	255	268	160	165

6 Select the table and distribute the columns evenly. Center all text in the table. Center the table across the page.

7 Sort the table by year from 2010 down to 2000. Turn the Banded Rows feature off. Add a total row. Use the Table Styles Options to add a total row.

8 Add an Averages row to the bottom and add a blank row to the bottom and insert a formula beneath each column to average the price of each type of home.

9 Apply two columns to the text that follows the table. Justify that text.

10 Save and close the file.

Chapter Summary

This chapter explores the built-in capabilities of Word and how the program assists you in creating fast and attractive documents or using the preset templates as a starting point for your own designs. Customizing professional documents may include developing a unique corporate look, including a watermark and logo, and saving it as your own template to be used again and again.

Understanding how to use tabs and tables provides great control over your documents. Left tabs, Right tabs, Decimal tabs, Center tabs, and more allow you to organize and line up text in ways that make it much easier and more effective to read. Tables offer even more absolute control over the arrangement of text or data. You can format tables with fill colors, borders, even no borders. You can adjust the width and height of rows and columns and the alignment of text. Word's powerful Table Styles and Quick Tables apply professional style to any table in an instant. Although not a spreadsheet program, Word allows you to insert formulas into a table such as sum, average, product, and count.

Changing a document from the common one column into two or more columns adds flexibility to the design and improves the attractiveness of a document. Word inserts automatically balanced columns or allows you to adjust the settings. This includes the ability to enter a column break to control precisely where one column ends and the next begins.

Optimizing your use of Word gives you the power to generate professional letterhead, memos, and other documents as much a part of your company's identity as its logo.

Chapter Key Terms

Autofit, p. W-213
Border Painter button, p. W-218
Cell/row selection arrow, p. W-218
Cells, p. W-213
Clear all tabs, p. W-199
Column break, p. W-227
Column selection arrow, p. W-218
Columns (table), p. W-213
Columns (text), p. W-227
Columns dialog box, p. W-227
Continuous section break, p. W-227
Custom tabs, p. W-194
Custom template, p. W-182

Default tabs, p. W-194
Delete columns, p. W-223
Delete rows, p. W-223
Distribute columns evenly, p. W-218
Distribute rows evenly, p. W-218
Formulas, p. W-223
Header row, p. W-223
Insert a column, p. W-223
Insert a row, p. W-223
Justified columns, p. W-227
Leader, p. W-199
Line between columns, p. W-227
Number format, p. W-223
Picture watermark, p. W-188

Quick Tables, p. W-218
Rows, (table), p. W-213
Tab alignment, p. W-199
Tab Selection button, p. W-194
Table borders, p. W-218
Table Control button, p. W-213
Table Styles, p. W-213
Tables, p. W-213
Tabs, p. W-194
Tabs dialog box, p. W-199
Template, p. W-182
Text watermark, p. W-188
Watermark, p. W-188
Width of columns, p. W-227

On Your Own WD-4C-E1

This project provides the opportunity to practice the most important skills covered in this chapter, regardless of the project or lesson in which they were introduced. Here, you will create a corporate memo, a letterhead, and a calendar, all branded with the corporate logo. The example shown in Figure WD4.36 is only a guideline of how the final project may appear.

FIGURE WD4.36   On Your Own WD-4C-E1: completed

After launching Microsoft Word, locate and open the template for a calendar (One Page Family Photo Calendar).

Locate the files associated with this lesson and insert the Semanine Pure Water logo on the calendar. Add or replace a graphic that represents fresh, pure water. Add some generic text into any placeholders to make the calendar seem a part of the marketing effort of Semanine Pure Water. Save this file as **wd04cp1a.docx**.

Locate the template for Memo (Professional design). Place (replace, depending on the template) the Semanine Pure Water logo on the memo. Save this document as a custom template.

Fill in the Memo heading (To, From, etc.). You may use the text and table data from Figure WD4.36 if you desire. Insert a table (this was a 3×6 table) and apply a Table Style to the table. The style should work well with the blue color in the logo.

The table should be clean and clear with the columns adjusted to fit the data. Center the table across the page. Save this document as **wd04cp1b.docx**.

Locate and create the letterhead template Real estate agent letterhead. Insert the Semanine Pure Water logo as a watermark in the center of the document. Change the company name to Semanine Pure Water. Insert a picture (using a Bing Image Search) of a glass of water above the company name.

Change the address information and the name of the service representative. Insert the date and follow the example of Figure WD4.36. The first list is built using a center tab at 3.0" and another center tab at 5.0" for the heading. The product information uses a decimal tab at 3.0" and another decimal tab at 5.0".

The table consists of imaginary sales numbers from the four divisions of the company. The table style is chosen to include blue as it helps to match the branding of the company. The table is adjusted to fit the data and to be centered on the page. The data in the second column is right-aligned. There is a formula inserted beneath the sales figures to total the sales to date.

The bottom of the letterhead has been adapted to read "Residential and Commercial."

Save this file as **wd04cp1c.docx**. Close the file. These three files form the basis of Semanine Pure Water's image branding.

On Your Own WD-4C-E2

This project provides the opportunity to practice the most important skills covered in this chapter, regardless of the project or lesson in which they were introduced. Starting with a template for an annual report, insert data into a table, reformat the table, and insert formulas to total the table. Using tabs, create a schedule for events throughout the upcoming year. Insert a watermark and manipulate its size and placement on the page and insert the full-color logo on the last page of the document. The entire document could be saved as a custom template to be used in the future. The example shown in Figure WD4.37 is only a guideline of how the final project may appear.

FIGURE WD4.37   On Your Own WD-4C-E2: completed

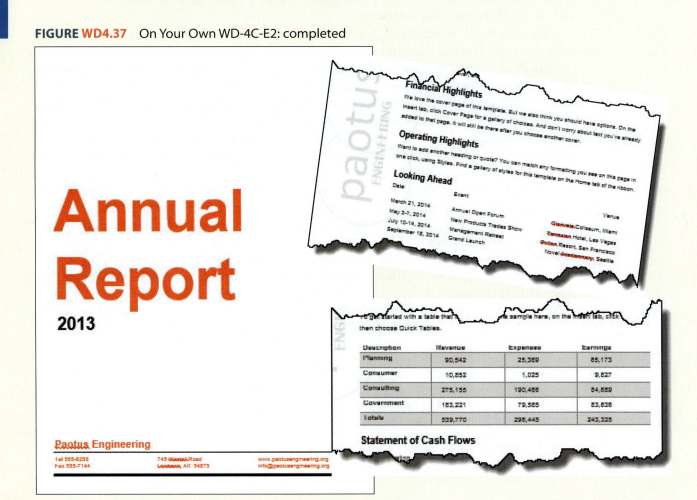

Open the template for Annual Report (Red and Black Design). Save the file as **wd04-cp2.docx**. There are eight pages, but you will change just a few.

On the cover page, change the appropriate information such as the company name and make up phone numbers, address, and website information.

Move to page 3 of 8 (page 1, section 2). Locate the files associated with this lesson and insert a watermark using the Paotus Engineering logo. Enter the header and rotate the logo 90 degrees. Resize and place the logo in the margin of the report. Note: If the logo appears on the first two pages of the report, enter the headers for those pages (being sure they are not linked to the previous one) and delete the logo.

Next, delete the placeholder text under the Looking Ahead heading and use a left tab at 1.5" and a right tab at 5.5" to enter the following information:

Date	Event	Venue
March 21, 2014	Annual Open Forum	Glenvale Coliseum, Miami
May 3 – 7	New Products Trade Show	Terrazian Hotel, Las Vegas
July 10 – 14, 2014	Management Retreat	Polton Resort, San Francisco
September 18, 2014	Grand Launch	Novel Acedeminary, Seattle

On page 5 of 8 (page 3, section 2) enter the following data into the table. Insert a formula into the "Totals" row to sum all three columns. Use the Grid Table 2 – Accent 6 from Table Styles to format the table. Distribute all columns evenly.

Description	Revenue	Expenses	Earnings
Planning	90,542	25,369	formula
Consumer	10,852	1,025	formula
Consulting	275,155	190,466	formula
Government	163,221	79,585	formula
Totals	formula	formula	formula

On the last page, insert the Paotus Engineering logo into the marked area. Resize the logo to 0.8" high and 1.38" wide.

Save and then close the document, unless directed to print it out by your instructor. Then, exit Microsoft Word.

ProjectLearn Microsoft
Excel 2013

Introduction to Excel

Microsoft Office Excel is a spreadsheet software program that enables you to store, manipulate, and chart numeric data. Researchers, statisticians, and businesspeople use spreadsheets to analyze and summarize mathematical, statistical, and financial data. Closer to home, you can use Excel to create a budget for your monthly living expenses, analyze returns in the stock market, develop a business plan, or calculate your student loan payments.

Excel 2013 enables you to create and customize worksheets, chart sheets, and reports. A **worksheet** is divided into vertical columns and horizontal rows. The rows are numbered and the columns are labeled from A to Z, then AA to AZ, and so on to column XFD. The intersection of a column and a row is called a **cell**. Each cell is given a cell address consisting of its column letter followed by its row number (for example, B4 or FX400). A **chart sheet** displays a chart graphic that is typically linked to data stored in a worksheet. When the data is changed, the chart is updated automatically to reflect the new information. Charts may also appear embedded in a worksheet, alongside their data.

Related worksheets and chart sheets are stored together in a single disk file called a **workbook**. You can think of an Excel workbook file as a three-ring binder with tabs at the beginning of each new page or sheet. In this chapter, you learn to create, modify, save, format, and print an Excel worksheet containing text, numbers, dates, formulas, and functions.

PROJECT

Building a Financial Budget

In this project, you will use Excel to navigate and create a simple worksheet application for personal budgeting. Specifically, you will enter text, numbers, formulas, and functions, and then format and prepare the budget for printing. Place the finished version of this workbook into your portfolio and title it "Excel-Personal Financial Budget."

This chapter will lead you through the techniques and skills required to produce and format almost any type of worksheet, whether you are a professional, a student, or someone seeking to enhance your job skills.

THE SITUATION

Personal Financial Planning 101

It's Monday at 8:30 a.m., and you're sitting in Personal Financial Planning 101, listening to your friend tell you about her amazing weekend. Besides the overnight trip and concert she attended, she describes in detail the fabulous restaurant she and her friends visited. However, all you can think about is the money she must have spent. How could she have so much disposable income? You realize it's time to get your personal finances in order, beginning with a monthly budget. Fortunately, your professor just mentioned how you can use Excel 2013 to track your expenses. Time to get serious about financial planning and start using Excel!

Creating a Financial Budget

In this project, you will construct a personal financial budget to introduce you to some of the core functionality of Excel 2013, including entering and editing data, creating formulas, and working with workbooks and worksheets. Although this project may be completed successfully without any previous experience using Excel, you should be comfortable working within Windows and the Microsoft Office environment.

PROJECT FILE: *Available at www.mhhe.com/office2013projectlearn*

PROJECT OBJECTIVES

After completing this project, you will be able to:

- Move around a worksheet effectively, and select cells and cell ranges.

- Enter text, numbers, and dates into worksheet cells.

- Construct simple formula expressions for performing calculations.

- Use Excel's Quick Analysis feature to insert totals for a table of values.

- Perform basic editing functions, such as editing, inserting, and deleting cells.

- Copy and move worksheet data, and extend a data series within a cell range.

- Display and hide cell formulas for auditing and printing purposes.

- Start a new workbook based on a professionally designed template.

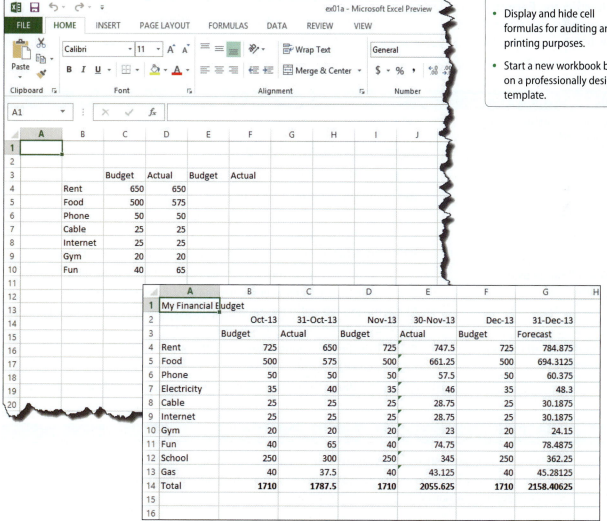

LESSON OVERVIEW

The Excel **application window** acts as a container for your workbook files containing worksheets and charts. It also provides the Windows icons, File menu, Ribbon, Name box, Formula bar, and Status bar. Each worksheet's **document window** includes its own scroll bars, sheet tabs, and Tab Scrolling arrows. Figure EX1.2 in the Project Practice section highlights several of these components.

The **cell pointer** is the cursor used to select a cell in the worksheet using either the mouse or keyboard. When you open a new workbook, the Sheet1 worksheet tab is active and the cell pointer is positioned in cell A1. As you move the cell pointer around the worksheet, Excel displays the current cell address in the **Name box**, directly above column A. The contents of the selected cell are displayed in the **Formula bar**, appearing to the right of the Name box.

A **cell range** can be a single cell or rectangular block of cells. Each cell range has a beginning cell address in the top left-hand corner and an ending cell address in the bottom right-hand corner. To refer to a cell range in Excel, you separate the two cell addresses using a colon. For example, the range B2:C4 references the six selected cells shown here. Notice that the current or active cell, B2 as shown in the Name box, does not appear shaded within the selection outline.

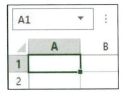

SKILLS PREVIEW

Navigate a worksheet using the keyboard	• ↑, ↓, ←, and → arrow keys • Home, End, PgUp, and PgDn • Ctrl + Home to move to cell A1. • F5 (GoTo) key to move to a specific cell.
Select a cell range using the keyboard	• SELECT the top-left cell in the desired range. PRESS and HOLD Shift. PRESS an arrow key (or any combination of the navigation keys listed above).
Select a cell range using the mouse	• CLICK the top-left cell in the desired range and hold down the mouse button. DRAG the mouse pointer over the desired cells in the range, or • CLICK the top-left cell in the desired range. Shift +CLICK the mouse pointer over the cell in the bottom-right corner.
Select multiple cell ranges using the mouse	• SELECT the first cell range using one of the above methods. PRESS and HOLD Ctrl. CLICK and DRAG the mouse pointer over the additional cell ranges desired.

PROJECT PRACTICE

1. When you launch Microsoft Excel 2013, an opening or welcome screen (Figure EX1.1) appears showing you a list of recently opened workbooks, along with several template options to use in creating new workbooks.

FIGURE EX1.1 The Excel 2013 welcome screen

Recently opened workbooks will appear in a list

To start a new workbook, double-click this template

2 To display a new blank workbook:

CLICK the Blank workbook option.

(*Result:* An empty worksheet appears with cell A1 selected on the Sheet1 tab. Figure EX1.2 highlights some primary components that make up the Excel application window.)

FIGURE EX1.2 The Excel 2013 application window

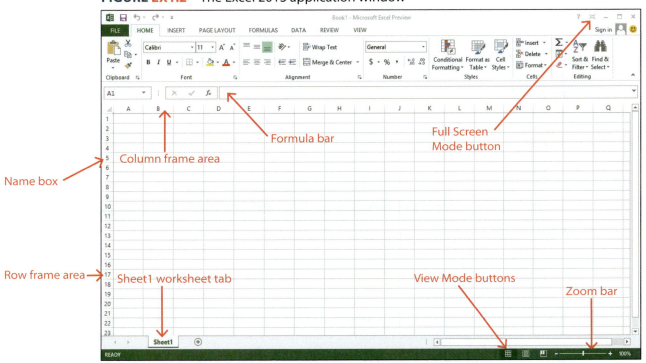

Name box

Column frame area

Formula bar

Full Screen Mode button

Row frame area

Sheet1 worksheet tab

View Mode buttons

Zoom bar

3 To view how many columns and rows there are in a typical worksheet:

PRESS Ctrl + → to scroll to the furthest right column, XFD.

PRESS Ctrl + ↓ to scroll down to the bottom row, 1048576.

4 To return to cell A1:

PRESS Ctrl + Home.

5 To begin working on your project, locate and open the project data file **ex01a.xlsx**. On the File menu tab, use the Save As command to save the file as **ex01a-budget.xlsx**. (*Note:* You may need to choose a place to store the workbook file, such as "SkyDrive" or "Computer," and then browse to the desired folder location.)

6 Notice in the bottom right-hand corner of the Status bar, the zoom factor is set to 100 percent. To increase the zoom factor:

CLICK the Zoom In button (➕) until 120% is achieved.

(*Result:* Your screen should now appear similar to Figure EX1.3. Depending on your screen's resolution, you may see more or fewer columns and rows than those shown in the screen graphic.)

FIGURE EX1.3 Zooming the worksheet window

	A	B	C	D	E	F
3			Budget	Actual	Budget	Actual
4		Rent	650	650		
5		Food	500	575		
6		Phone	50	50		
7		Cable	25	25		
8		Internet	25	25		
9		Gym	20	20		
10		Fun	40	65		

Zoom factor is set to 120%

7 Let's practice selecting a cell range using both the mouse and keyboard:

CLICK cell C3.

(*Result:* Notice that "C3" appears in the Name box and "Budget" appears in the Formula bar, ready for editing.)

8 Before copying or formatting worksheet content, you must first select the cell data. For short ranges, the easiest method is to use the mouse. Using the mouse, click in cell C3 and hold down the mouse button as you perform the following instruction:

DRAG across the cell range from C3 to C10.

(*Result:* You may notice that the current or active cell is still C3; therefore, the contents in the Name box and Formula bar remain the same as in the previous step. Also, the column letter and row numbers in the frame area should now appear highlighted.)

9 While this method works well for short ranges, long columns or rows of numbers can be difficult to drag across using the mouse. Therefore, another method for selecting cells is to use the keyboard shortcuts. To begin:

PRESS [→] to select cell D3 (or CLICK cell D3).

PRESS and HOLD [Shift].

PRESS [Ctrl]+[↓] to move to the bottom of the column.
(*Result:* The [Shift] key is used to select multiple cells in a cell range; the [Ctrl]+[↓] key combination is used to move to the last filled cell in a column. If you have a column of data covering hundreds of rows, this method is far more efficient than dragging across the data using the mouse.)

> **TIP**
>
> If you still prefer using the mouse, you can click the first cell in the top left-hand corner of the desired cell range, scroll down or across the worksheet, and then [Shift]+CLICK on the last (or bottom right-hand) cell to select the entire range. When you are asked to DRAG the mouse pointer to select cells, you must first click in the top left-hand cell of the range, hold down the mouse button, and then drag the cell pointer across the desired cells.

10 Some times you will need to make multiple selections on the worksheet that do not fit nicely into a rectangular block of cells. For example, in this step, you select non-adjacent rows in the budget using the mouse. Do the following:

SELECT cell B5

DRAG across the cell range from B5 to D5.

PRESS and HOLD [Ctrl].

DRAG across the cell range from B9 to D9.

RELEASE [Ctrl].
(*Result:* Your screen should now appear similar to Figure EX1.4.)

FIGURE EX1.4 Selecting multiple cell ranges

	A	B	C	D	E	F	G
1							
2							
3			Budget	Actual	Budget	Actual	
4		Rent	650	650			
5		Food	500	575			
6		Phone	50	50			
7		Cable	25	25			
8		Internet	25	25			
9		Gym	20	20			
10		Fun	40	65			
11							
12							

11 Before proceeding, return to cell A1:

PRESS [Ctrl]+[Home]

12 Even though no changes have been made to this workbook, save your file before proceeding to the next lesson.

> **HEADS UP**
>
> From here on, we will use the instruction SELECT cell A1 or SELECT the cell range B6:B9, rather than directing you to use the mouse or keyboard. You are free to use whichever method you feel most comfortable with to select the required cells.

Entering Text, Numbers, and Dates

LESSON OVERVIEW

Text labels are used for titles, headings, and other descriptive information in a worksheet. Although a typical cell displays fewer than nine characters (depending on its width and the selected font size), it can store thousands of words. With longer entries, text spills over the column border into the next cell, if it is empty. If the adjacent cell is not empty, the text is truncated at its right border. In this graphic, the text in cell D1 spills over into the empty columns E, F, and G. Fortunately, Excel allows you to increase a cell's column width, or wrap text to display within its borders.

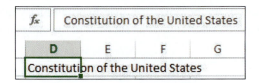

Numbers are used in performing calculations, preparing reports, and creating charts. You can enter a raw or unformatted number, such as 3.141593, or a formatted number, such as 37.5% or $24,732.33. Note that phone numbers and U.S. zip codes are not treated as numeric values, because they are never used in performing calculations. By default, numbers (and date values) are right-aligned in a cell, as opposed to text, which is left-aligned. Notice in this graphic that Excel's Formula

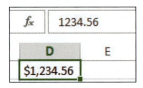

bar stores and displays the raw numeric value, without currency symbols and commas.

Unlike text labels that spill over cell boundaries, numeric and date values cannot display in a column that is too narrow. You will know that a column is too narrow if you see the cell filled with a # symbol, as shown here. In this case, you must either change the formatting of the cell (i.e., remove some formatting elements) or increase the width of the column.

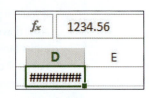

Date values are often used as column headings, but they mostly appear in row entries such as invoice transactions. You must enter date values using one of the date formats recognized by Excel, such as mm/dd/yyyy (10/31/2013) or dd-mmm-yy (31-Oct-13). In the Formula bar (shown here), Excel displays the stored date value using the mm/dd/yyyy format, but the worksheet cell shows the formatted date as it was entered. You can also use date values to perform arithmetic calculations, such as finding out how many days have elapsed between two calendar dates.

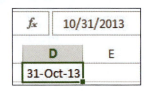

SKILLS PREVIEW

Enter text into a cell	• TYPE *your text*. • PRESS `Enter` or CLICK another cell.
Enter a number into a cell	• TYPE *a number*, such as $1,234.56, 0.789, or 5.275%. • PRESS `Enter` or CLICK another cell.
Enter a date into a cell	• TYPE *a date*, such as 31-Mar-13. • PRESS `Enter` or CLICK another cell.

1 Ensure that **ex01a-budget.xlsx** is open.

2 To add a title to the worksheet:

SELECT cell A1.

TYPE **My Personal Financial Budget**.

PRESS Enter .

(*Result:* Notice that the text is deposited into cell A1, but it spills over into columns B and C. Also, the cell pointer moves down to the next row automatically when Enter is pressed, which makes entering long lists of data much easier. If you do not want the cell pointer to advance downward, use the mouse to click the Enter button (✔) in the Formula bar instead.)

3 To add a new category to our budget:

SELECT cell B11.

TYPE **School**.

PRESS → to move the cell pointer to the right.

TYPE **250**.

PRESS → .

TYPE **300**.

PRESS Enter .

(*Result:* Numeric values are entered right-aligned with the cell border, as opposed to text, which is left-aligned by default.)

4 Add another category, but this time you'll use formatted numbers:

SELECT cell B12.

TYPE **Gas**.

PRESS → to move the cell pointer to the right.

TYPE **$40.00**.

PRESS → .

TYPE **$37.50**.

PRESS Enter .

5 To view the results:

SELECT cell D12.

(*Result:* Notice in the Formula bar that the value stored in the worksheet cell is 37.5, but the value displayed in the cell is formatted as $37.50.)

6 To enter dates at the top of each "Budget" column, do the following:

SELECT cell C2.

TYPE **Oct-2013**.

SELECT cell E2.

TYPE **Nov-2013**.

PRESS Enter .

(*Result:* The monthly date values are entered into the two cells, formatted using the mmm-yy format.)

7 For practice, you should enter the "Actual" column dates using a different format:

SELECT cell D2.

TYPE **31-Oct-13**.

SELECT cell F2.

TYPE **30-Nov-13**.

PRESS [Enter].

(*Result:* The date values are entered into the two cells, formatted using the dd-mmm-yy format.)

8 To display the actual stored value for the first date entered:

SELECT cell C2.

(*Result:* When you look in the Formula bar for cell C2, as shown in Figure EX1.5, the date value stored is 10/1/2013, even though the formatted data in the worksheet appears as Oct-13. As you can see, the formatted value displayed in the worksheet is not necessarily identical to the actual value that is stored in the cell.)

9 Select the date values in the other cells and refer to the Formula bar to view their actual stored contents. As you can see, a cell's stored value is not always identical to the value that is displayed in the worksheet. This feature is especially important to note when dealing with the rounding of numeric values.

10 Save your file before proceeding to the next lesson.

FIGURE EX1.5 Entering text, numbers, and date values

	A	B	C	D	E	F	G
1	My Personal Financial Budget						
2			Oct-13	31-Oct-13	Nov-13	30-Nov-13	
3			Budget	Actual	Budget	Actual	
4		Rent	650	650			
5		Food	500	575			
6		Phone	50	50			
7		Cable	25	25			
8		Internet	25	25			
9		Gym	20	20			
10		Fun	40	65			
11		School	250	300			
12		Gas	$40.00	$37.50			
13							
14							

C2 — f_x — 10/1/2013 ← Stored value

Displayed value

Entering Formulas and Using AutoSum

LESSON OVERVIEW

You use formulas to perform calculations, such as adding a column of numbers or calculating a mortgage payment. A **formula** is an expression that begins with an equal sign (=) and contains numbers, cell references, and/or mathematical operators. The basic operators ("+" for addition, "−" for subtraction, "/" for division, and "*" for multiplication) and rules of precedence from your high school algebra textbook also apply to Excel. As a refresher, Excel calculates a formula according to the acronym BEDMAS: Brackets (or parentheses) first, Exponents second, Division and Multiplication operators (from left to right) third, and Addition and Subtraction (again from left to right) last.

Using Excel's **AutoCalculate** feature, you can view the calculated results (e.g., AVERAGE, COUNT, and SUM, as well as MIN and MAX) of a selected range of values in the **Status bar**, as shown in the graphic below. This feature is useful for checking the result of a calculation, without having to actually store its value in the worksheet. To store the calculated result, use the AutoSum button ($\sum$ ▾) on the HOME tab. With the **AutoSum** feature, Excel reviews the surrounding cells, guesses at the range you want to sum, and then places a SUM function (described in the next chapter) into the active cell.

AVERAGE: 20   COUNT: 3   SUM: 60

SKILLS PREVIEW

Enter a formula into a cell	• TYPE = (an equal sign). • TYPE a formula, such as b1+d1.
Enter the SUM function using the AutoSum feature	• SELECT an empty cell next to a column or row of values. CLICK the HOME tab and locate the Editing group. CLICK the AutoSum button ($\sum$ ▾).

PROJECT PRACTICE

1. Ensure that ex01a-budget.xlsx is open.

2. You will now create a formula to keep the budgeted values the same month to month. For example, rather than typing or copying the values from column C, you will use a formula in column E that simply duplicates the values. Do the following:

   SELECT cell E4.

   TYPE =c4.

   PRESS Enter.

   (*Result:* You should now see the value stored in cell C4 displayed in cell E4.)

3. You can also use the mouse to enter a formula. Ensure that cell E5 is selected and then:

   TYPE =

   CLICK cell C5.

   CLICK Enter button (✔) in the Formula bar.

   (*Result:* Notice that the cell you selected in building the formula appeared with a dashed marquee surrounding the cell. This highlighting is especially useful when building more complex formulas.)

4. Rather than entering the rest of the formulas in the column, you can use the fill handle to copy the formula from cell E5 downward. Ensure that cell E5 is selected and then:

   POSITION the mouse pointer over the small square in the lower right-hand corner of the cell pointer, until it changes shape to a plus sign.

   DRAG from cell E5 to cell E12.

   (*Result:* Your screen should appear similar to Figure EX1.6.)

FIGURE EX1.6   Copying formulas using the fill handle

	A	B	C	D	E	F	G
1	My Personal Financial Budget						
2			Oct-13	31-Oct-13	Nov-13	30-Nov-13	
3			Budget	Actual	Budget	Actual	
4		Rent	650	650	650		
5		Food	500	575	500		
6		Phone	50	50			
7		Cable	25	25			
8		Internet	25	25			
9		Gym	20	20			
10		Fun	40	65			
11		School	250	300			
12		Gas	$40.00	$37.50			
13							
14							

⑤ RELEASE the mouse button to complete the copy and fill operation.

⑥ Let's see how the formulas work:

SELECT cell C4.

TYPE 725.

PRESS Enter.

(*Result:* Notice that the value in cell E4 is automatically updated to reflect the new rent value.)

⑦ Time to challenge your understanding! Imagine that each of your actual values for November (column F) increased 15 percent from the previous month (column D). Rather than typing in these values manually, enter a formula to input all of the calculations at once. The formula you will enter takes the previous month's actual value and then multiplies it by (1+15%). There are many different ways to enter this expression, but you will use this format. To begin, specify the cells that will accept the new formula:

SELECT the cell range F4:F12.

⑧ Ensure that F4 appears in the Name box, denoting it as the active cell. Then:

TYPE =d4*(1+15%).

(*Result:* Notice that cell D4 is highlighted in the worksheet so that you may quickly confirm that this is the desired cell.)

⑨ If you press Enter now, the formula is deposited into the active cell of the selected range. However, you want to deposit the formula into all of the selected cells. To do so:

PRESS Ctrl + Enter.

(*Result:* The formula is entered correctly into all of the cells, without having to use the fill handle.)

⑩ You may use Excel's AutoCalculate feature to temporarily view the results of one or more calculations. By default, Excel displays results for the sum, average, and count calculations in the Status bar. To illustrate:

SELECT the cell range E4:E12.

(*Result:* Your Status bar should now display the following results.)

AVERAGE: 186.1111111   COUNT: 9   SUM: 1675

11 You can also use the AutoSum feature to insert these results into a worksheet cell. Let's sum the four budget columns. To begin, prepare the "Totals" row:

SELECT cell B13.

TYPE Total.

SELECT the cell range C13:F13.

12 To launch the command:

CLICK the HOME tab and locate the Editing group.

CLICK the AutoSum button (∑ ▾).

(*Result:* As shown in Figure EX1.7, Excel inserts the SUM function into the four selected cells to total the values at the bottom of each column.)

13 Save your file before proceeding to the next lesson.

FIGURE EX1.7 Using the AutoSum button to total columns

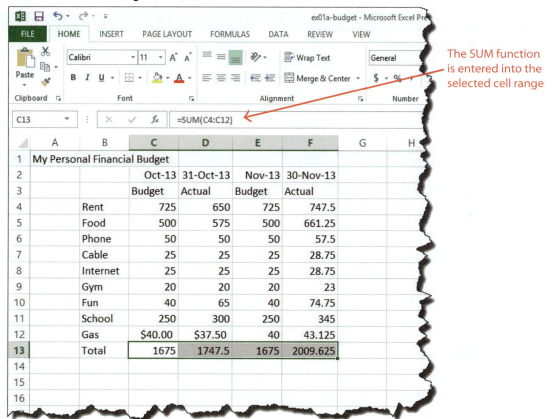

Inserting Quick Totals

LESSON OVERVIEW

Excel provides a fast method for analyzing and summarizing values in your worksheet, including totaling a row or column of values. The **Quick Analysis** feature provides options for formatting, charting, totaling, creating tables, and inserting sparklines based on the values stored in a selected range. When you highlight a range of cells, a Quick Analysis button (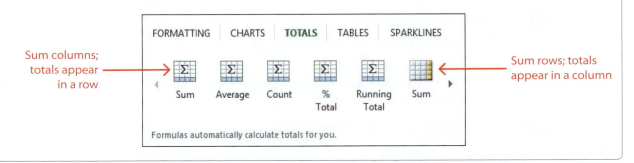) appears in the bottom right-hand corner of the range for accessing the Quick Analysis options. In this lesson, you will practice selecting the Totals option shown below for quickly summarizing worksheet values.

SKILLS PREVIEW

Insert row and column totals for the selected cell range using the Quick Analysis tool	• SELECT the cell range that you want to analyze. CLICK the Quick Analysis button (). CLICK the Totals option. CHOOSE the desired totaling option (e.g., Sum).

PROJECT PRACTICE

1 Ensure that **ex01a-budget.xlsx** is open.

2 For comparison purposes, you will now use Excel's Quick Analysis feature to calculate the same column totals that you entered in the previous lesson using AutoSum. To begin:
SELECT the cell range C13:F13, if it is not already selected.
PRESS Delete to remove the previous totals.

3 To use Excel's Quick Analysis feature, first select the cell range that you wish to summarize:
SELECT the cell range C4:F12.

4 By hovering the mouse pointer over the selected range, the Quick Analysis button () appears:
CLICK the Quick Analysis button ().
CLICK the Totals option, as shown in Figure EX1.8.

FIGURE EX1.8 The Quick Analysis Totals option

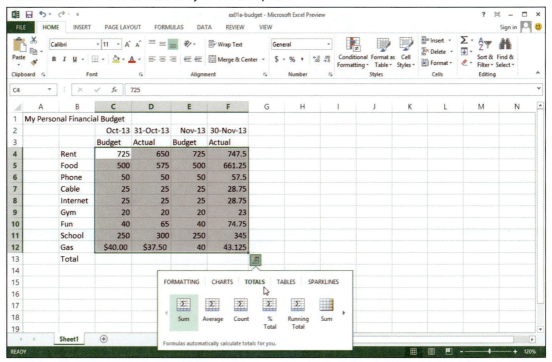

5 Hover the mouse over the various Totals options (e.g., SUM, AVERAGE, and COUNT) to see the results in your worksheet. To enter the SUM function for totaling each column:

CLICK the Sum option button (□).

(*Result:* The same totals shown in Figure EX1.7 are now displayed in boldface font.)

> **i MORE INFO**
>
> The Quick Analysis feature provides easy access to many different calculation and analysis options, which you will use throughout this text. This lesson serves as a simple introduction.

6 Save your file before proceeding to the next lesson.

Editing, Inserting, and Deleting Cell Data

LESSON OVERVIEW

What if you type a label, a number, or a formula into a cell and then decide it needs to be changed? Your ability to edit a worksheet effectively is an extremely valuable skill. In many jobs, you will be asked to modify and maintain existing worksheets, rather than create new ones. Fortunately, Excel provides several features for editing and erasing data that has already been entered. Besides working with existing content, you can insert new, empty cells in the middle of a range. When you make changes that affect the structure of the worksheet (e.g., inserting and deleting cells), Excel will attempt to correct any formulas that reference those cells affected by the changes.

SKILLS PREVIEW

Edit a cell's contents	• PRESS BackSpace to correct typographical or spelling errors. • TYPE a new entry on top of an existing cell to overwrite and replace its contents. • PRESS F2 (or double-click in a cell) to perform **in-cell editing**. • CLICK in the Formula bar to enter Edit mode, in which you can insert and delete the desired data.
Erase the contents of a cell or cell range	• SELECT the cell or cell range that you want to erase. PRESS Delete.
Remove a cell's contents and other attributes	• SELECT the cell or cell range that you want to erase. CLICK the HOME tab and locate the Editing group. CLICK the Clear button (✐ ▾).
Insert a cell or cell range	• SELECT the cell or cell range where empty cells should be inserted. CLICK the HOME tab and locate the Cells group. CLICK the Insert Cells command.
Delete a cell or cell range	• SELECT the cell or cell range to be deleted. CLICK the HOME tab and locate the Cells group. CLICK the Delete Cells command.

PROJECT PRACTICE

1. Ensure that **ex01a-budget.xlsx** is open.

2. The worksheet title, "My Personal Financial Budget," is stored in cell A1. While you could always type a new entry over the top of the existing contents, let's edit the text to remove the word *Personal*. To begin, you will switch from Ready mode to Edit mode:

   DOUBLE-CLICK cell A1.

   (*Result:* Excel displays a flashing cursor within the cell contents and the word *EDIT* appears in the bottom left-hand portion of the Status bar to signify that you have entered Edit mode. You can also select the cell and press F2, instead of double-clicking on the cell to enter Edit mode.)

3. To select the word within the cell area:

   DOUBLE-CLICK *Personal*.

   (*Result:* The cell should now appear similar to the graphic shown. You can use the standard cursor movement and editing keys at this point.)

◢	A	B	C	D	E	F
1	My Personal Financial Budget					
2			Oct-13	31-Oct-13	Nov-13	30-Nov-13
3			Budget	Actual	Budget	Actual

4 PRESS `Delete` twice to remove the word *Personal* and the trailing space.

PRESS `Enter` to save your changes.

5 To insert space for two additional categories between "Phone" and "Cable":

SELECT the cell range B7:F8.

CLICK the HOME tab and locate the Cells group.

CLICK Insert Cells command.

(*Result:* The two selected rows are pushed downward to make room for the new empty rows, as shown in Figure EX1.9.)

FIGURE EX1.9 Inserting cells within a range

	A	B	C	D	E	F	G
1	My Financial Budget						
2			Oct-13	31-Oct-13	Nov-13	30-Nov-13	
3			Budget	Actual	Budget	Actual	
4		Rent	725	650	725	747.5	
5		Food	500	575	500	661.25	
6		Phone	50	50	50	57.5	
7							
8							
9		Cable	25	25	25	28.75	
10		Internet	25	25	25	28.75	
11		Gym	20	20	20	23	
12		Fun	40	65	40	74.75	
13		School	250	300	250	345	
14		Gas	$40.00	$37.50	40	43.125	
15		Total	1675	1747.5	1675	2009.625	
16							

6 Let's practice removing one of the empty rows:

SELECT the cell range B8:F8.

CLICK the HOME tab and locate the Cells group.

CLICK Delete Cells command.

(*Results:* The selected cells are removed and the data previously in row 8 has moved up to row 7.)

7 Now, complete the new budget category in row 7 with the following information:

SELECT cell B7.

TYPE Electricity.

PRESS `→`.

TYPE 35.

PRESS `→`.

TYPE 40.

8 You can use the fill handle to copy the column formulas to the two remaining cells:

SELECT the cell range E6:F6.

DRAG the fill handle downward one row.
(*Result:* The formulas are copied to the row for "Electricity." Also note that the Totals in cell D14 and F14 are updated automatically.)

9 The Clear command allows you to remove cell contents, formatting, and other special attributes. In this step, you will remove the numeric formatting applied to the "Gas" values. Do the following:

SELECT the cell range C13:D13.

CLICK the HOME tab and locate the Editing group.

CLICK the Clear drop-down button (🧽 ▾).

CHOOSE Clear Formats from the menu shown here.

10 Your screen should appear similar to Figure EX1.10. Save your file before proceeding to the next lesson.

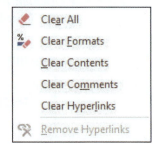

FIGURE EX1.10   Editing and modifying worksheet data

	A	B	C	D	E	F	G
1	My Financial Budget						
2			Oct-13	31-Oct-13	Nov-13	30-Nov-13	
3			Budget	Actual	Budget	Actual	
4		Rent	725	650	725	747.5	
5		Food	500	575	500	661.25	
6		Phone	50	50	50	57.5	
7		Electricity	35	40	35	46	
8		Cable	25	25	25	28.75	
9		Internet	25	25	25	28.75	
10		Gym	20	20	20	23	
11		Fun	40	65	40	74.75	
12		School	250	300	250	345	
13		Gas	40	37.5	40	43.125	
14		Total	**1710**	**1787.5**	**1710**	**2055.625**	
15							

Copying, Moving, and Filling Data

LESSON OVERVIEW

Excel provides several tools for copying, moving, and pasting data that can reduce the number of repetitive entries you must make. For example, once you enter a formula to sum one column of values, you can duplicate that formula using Copy and Paste commands (or drag and drop) to sum the adjacent columns. Another method for extending the contents of a cell is to use the Fill commands. These commands are especially useful for extending a formula across a row or down a column. When using a mouse, Excel's **AutoFill** feature allows you to create a data series by simply dragging the **fill handle** for a selected range (as shown below). Whether a numerical progression (1, 2, 3…) or a row of date headings (Jan, Feb, Mar…), a series is any sequence of data that follows a pattern that may be extrapolated and extended. Excel 2013's new **Flash Fill** feature takes this one step further by reviewing your previous entries and then predicting how you want a column or row completed. This feature is a tremendous time-saver and reduces the potential for making data entry errors.

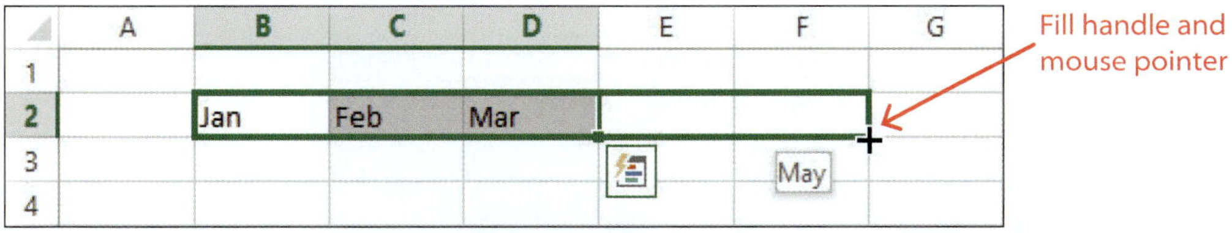

	A	B	C	D	E	F	G
1							
2		Jan	Feb	Mar			+
3						May	
4							

Fill handle and mouse pointer

SKILLS PREVIEW

Move data in a cell range using drag and drop	• SELECT the cell range that you want to move. DRAG the selected range by its border to the destination.
Copy data in a cell range using drag and drop	• SELECT the cell range that you want to copy. PRESS and HOLD Ctrl. DRAG the selected range by its border to the destination.
Copy or extend data in a cell range using the Fill command	• SELECT the cell range containing the data you want to extend, along with the target cells that you wish to fill. CLICK the HOME tab and locate the Editing group. CLICK the Fill drop-down button (⬇ ▾). CHOOSE the desired fill direction.
Copy or extend data in a cell range using the fill handle	• SELECT the cell range containing the data you want to extend. DRAG the **fill handle**, which is the small square appearing in the bottom right-hand corner of the selected range, to copy or extend the series.

PROJECT PRACTICE

1 Ensure that **ex01a-budget.xlsx** is open.

2 Let's practice moving and copying worksheet data. To begin, you will move the entire budget to the left by one column:

SELECT the cell range B2:F14.

3 POSITION the mouse pointer on one of the borders surrounding the selected range, until the mouse changes shape, as shown below.

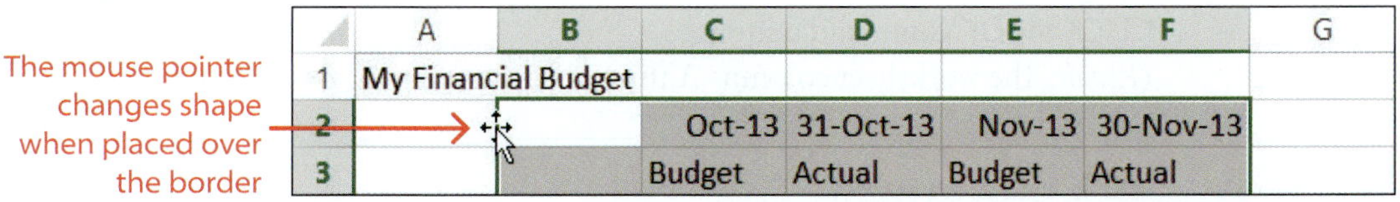

The mouse pointer changes shape when placed over the border

	A	B	C	D	E	F	G
1	My Financial Budget						
2			Oct-13	31-Oct-13	Nov-13	30-Nov-13	
3			Budget	Actual	Budget	Actual	

4 To complete the drag and drop operation:

CLICK and DRAG the selection to the left by one column.

RELEASE the mouse button when it is placed correctly.
(*Result*: The selected block of cells should now appear covering A2:E14. Remember that the appearance of # symbols in a column simply means the column is not wide enough to display the selected number or date formatting.)

5 Before adjusting the column widths, you will set up the December columns for forecasting purposes:

SELECT the cell range D2:E14.

CLICK the HOME tab and locate the Clipboard group.

CLICK the Copy button (🖺) to copy the contents to the Clipboard.
(*Result*: Notice that a dashed marquee appears surrounding the copied cells, as shown in Figure EX1.11.)

FIGURE EX1.11   Copying data to the Clipboard

	A	B	C	D	E	F	G
1	My Financial Budget						
2		Oct-13	#######	Nov-13	#######		
3		Budget	Actual	Budget	Actual		
4	Rent	725	650	725	747.5		
5	Food	500	575	500	661.25		
6	Phone	50	50	50	57.5		
7	Electricity	35	40	35	46		
8	Cable	25	25	25	28.75		
9	Internet	25	25	25	28.75		
10	Gym	20	20	20	23		
11	Fun	40	65	40	74.75		
12	School	250	300	250	345		
13	Gas	40	37.5	40	43.125		
14	Total	1710	1787.5	1710	2055.63		
15							
16							

6 To paste the copied cells:

SELECT cell F2 (which is the top left-most cell in the target or destination range).

CLICK the Paste button (📋) to paste the contents.

PRESS Esc to end the paste operation.
(*Result*: Notice that the dashed marquee disappears and that the Paste button is now disabled.)

7 Before proceeding, adjust the column widths:

SELECT the cell range A1:G1.

CLICK the HOME tab and locate the Cells group.

CLICK the Format button (🗔).

CHOOSE the Column Width command.

8 In the Column Width dialog box (shown here with 8.43 entered):

TYPE 12.

CLICK the OK command button.
(*Result*: The worksheet columns A through G should now appear wider.)

9 To replace the text labels used for column headings:

SELECT cell F2.

TYPE Dec-2013.

PRESS →.

TYPE 31-Dec-13.

PRESS Enter.

TYPE Forecast.

PRESS Enter.

10 To prepare a new forecasting formula, you should clear column G's results. Do the following:

SELECT the cell range G5:G13.

PRESS Delete to erase the cell contents.

(*Result:* Notice you did not include cells G4 and G14 in the selection to be deleted. If you deleted these cells by accident, click the Undo button (↶ ▾) in the Quick Access toolbar.)

11 You will now edit the formula expression in cell G4 and then copy it to the remaining cells. Assume that costs are forecasted to increase by 5 percent over November's actual values. To begin:

DOUBLE-CLICK cell G4.

12 Using the cursor movement (e.g., ← and →) and editing keys (e.g., Delete and BackSpace):

MODIFY the value 15% to read 5%.

PRESS Enter.

13 Previously you used the fill handle to copy values. In this step, you will practice using the Fill command, which is usually more efficient for a large number of cells (as opposed to the small cell range in this example):

SELECT the cell range G4:G13.

CLICK the HOME tab and locate the Editing group.

CLICK the Fill drop-down button (⬇ ▾).

CHOOSE Down from the menu shown here.

(*Result:* Notice that the top cell in the selected range contained the formula to be copied. Your screen should now appear similar to Figure EX1.12.)

14 Save your file before proceeding to the next lesson.

FIGURE EX1.12 Filling a column with a formula expression

	A	B	C	D	E	F	G	H
1	My Financial Budget							
2		Oct-13	31-Oct-13	Nov-13	30-Nov-13	Dec-13	31-Dec-13	
3		Budget	Actual	Budget	Actual	Budget	Forecast	
4	Rent	725	650	725	747.5	725	784.875	
5	Food	500	575	500	661.25	500	694.3125	
6	Phone	50	50	50	57.5	50	60.375	
7	Electricity	35	40	35	46	35	48.3	
8	Cable	25	25	25	28.75	25	30.1875	
9	Internet	25	25	25	28.75	25	30.1875	
10	Gym	20	20	20	23	20	24.15	
11	Fun	40	65	40	74.75	40	78.4875	
12	School	250	300	250	345	250	362.25	
13	Gas	40	37.5	40	43.125	40	45.28125	
14	Total	1710	1787.5	1710	2055.625	1710	2158.40625	
15								
16								

Displaying and Hiding Cell Formulas

LESSON OVERVIEW

By default, Excel displays only the results of a formula or function in a worksheet cell. But for documentation purposes, you may want to display and print the actual formula expressions. Refer to cell B4 in the graphics shown to differentiate between the two views: One displays the result of the formula, while the other displays the formula itself. This feature is also helpful when auditing and testing a worksheet for accuracy and validity.

◢	A	B	C
1			
2		10	
3		20	
4		30	
5			

◢	A	B
1		
2		10
3		20
4		=B2+B3
5		

SKILLS PREVIEW

Toggle (or switch) the display between showing and hiding cell formulas	• CLICK the FORMULAS tab and locate the Formula Auditing group. CLICK the Show Formulas button (⧄) to toggle on and off the display of formulas.

PROJECT PRACTICE

1 Ensure that **ex01a-budget.xlsx** is open.

2 To begin, move the cell pointer to cell A1:
PRESS `Ctrl` + `Home`.

3 To display the worksheet's formulas, as opposed to the resulting values:
CLICK the FORMULAS tab and locate the Formula Auditing group.
CLICK the Show Formulas button (⧄).
(*Result:* Excel should now display the worksheet's raw values and formula expressions. Notice that Excel stores the dates in row 2 as serial numbers; designating January 1, 1900, as day 1 and then adding 1 for each elapsed day since that date. In other words, 41,578 days elapsed between 01-Jan-1900 and 31-Oct-2013.)

4 If necessary, you can use the Zoom Out button (▬) in the Status bar to reduce the worksheet until all columns are displayed. Your screen should now appear similar to Figure EX1.13.

5 To return to the normal display, toggle the display of worksheet formulas off by doing the following: CLICK the Show Formulas button (🔣) again.

(*Result:* Notice that the columns have been returned to their normal widths, as appearing in Figure EX1.12 from the previous lesson.)

6 Save and close ex01a-budget.xlsx before proceeding to the next lesson.

FIGURE EX1.13   Displaying a worksheet's cell formulas

	A	B	C	D	E	F	G
1	My Financial Budget						
2		41548	41578	41579	41608	41609	41639
3		Budget	Actual	Budget	Actual	Budget	Forecast
4	Rent	725	650	=B4	=C4*(1+15%)	=D4	=E4*(1+5%)
5	Food	500	575	=B5	=C5*(1+15%)	=D5	=E5*(1+5%)
6	Phone	50	50	=B6	=C6*(1+15%)	=D6	=E6*(1+5%)
7	Electricity	35	40	=B7	=C7*(1+15%)	=D7	=E7*(1+5%)
8	Cable	25	25	=B8	=C8*(1+15%)	=D8	=E8*(1+5%)
9	Internet	25	25	=B9	=C9*(1+15%)	=D9	=E9*(1+5%)
10	Gym	20	20	=B10	=C10*(1+15%)	=D10	=E10*(1+5%)
11	Fun	40	65	=B11	=C11*(1+15%)	=D11	=E11*(1+5%)
12	School	250	300	=B12	=C12*(1+15%)	=D12	=E12*(1+5%)
13	Gas	40	37.5	=B13	=C13*(1+15%)	=D13	=E13*(1+5%)
14	Total	=SUM(B4:B13)	=SUM(C4:C13)	=SUM(D4:D13)	=SUM(E4:E13)	=SUM(F4:F13)	=SUM(G4:G13)
15							
16							

Managing Files and Using Templates

LESSON OVERVIEW

Excel 2013 allows you to save your workbook files locally or to the cloud using SkyDrive. For important workbooks (ones that you cannot risk losing), you should save your work every 10 minutes, or whenever you are interrupted, to protect against an unexpected power outage or other catastrophe. You can also specify a different file format for saving the workbook, such as an earlier version of Excel, Microsoft's XML Paper Specification (XPS), or Adobe's Portable Document Format (PDF). This is especially handy when you need to share a workbook with associates who haven't upgraded to the latest version of Office.

To create a new workbook, you can either start with a blank workbook (as you did in this project) or select a workbook template that provides preexisting data and design elements. A **template** is a time-saving utility that promotes consistency and professionalism. Many different types of templates are available, and you should review them to see if anything exists that you can customize to meet your current needs. You can also search online for templates by simply entering your search parameters into the Search online templates text box shown below.

Search for available templates online and download them to your computer

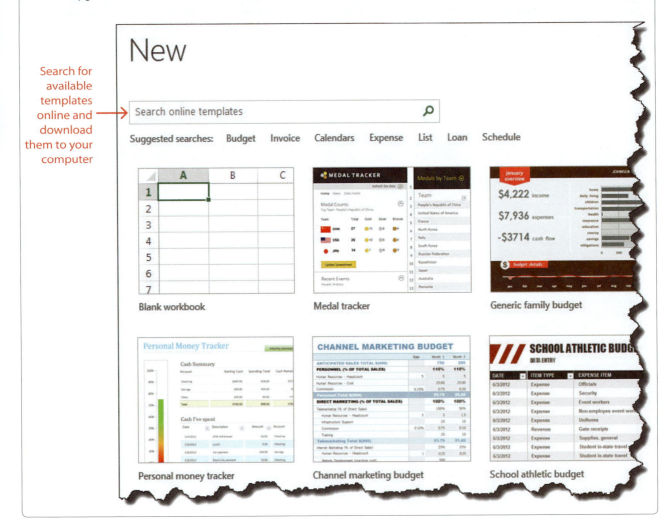

Save your work locally using a new file name or file type	• CLICK the FILE tab and CHOOSE the Save As command. SELECT Computer in the Places area. CLICK the Browse button (📁) in the Computer area. TYPE *file name* in the File name text box. SELECT a file type from the Save as type drop-down list box. CLICK the Save command button.
Save and send your workbook via email	• CLICK the FILE tab and CHOOSE the Share command. SELECT Email in the Share area. SELECT one of the options available for e-mailing, faxing, converting, or publishing your workbook to the web.
Create a new workbook using a template	• CLICK the FILE tab and CHOOSE the New command. SELECT a template by double-clicking or search for a new template online and then download the desired workbook.

PROJECT PRACTICE

1. Ensure that you have closed the workbook from the previous lesson or that you are starting with a new workbook after launching Excel.

2. Rather than create your own worksheet for personal financial budgeting, see what Microsoft has in the way of professionally designed workbook templates. Do the following:

   CLICK the FILE tab and CHOOSE the New command.

3. To view the budget templates available from Office.com:

   CLICK the Budget hyperlink appearing under the Search online templates text box.

   SCROLL through the resulting template options.

   (*Results:* Your screen should now appear similar to Figure EX1.14. Note that you need an Internet connection to view and download templates from Office.com, and the actual template options displayed here will change over time.)

FIGURE EX1.14 Viewing Office.com templates

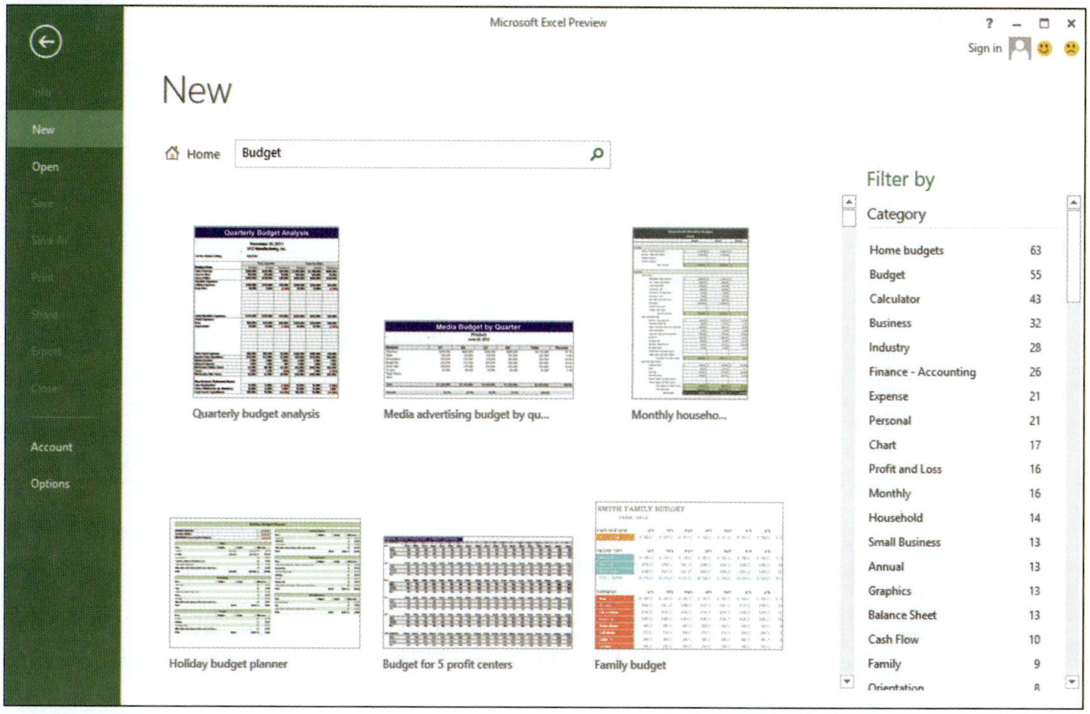

4 To filter the list of budget templates:

CLICK "Student" in the Filter by Category list area.

5 To view more information about a particular template:

CLICK the Monthly college budget template.

(*Result:* If you cannot find this template, click on another option. Your screen should appear similar to Figure EX1.15, but only if you selected the same budget. Notice that an image of the template appears, along with information regarding who provided the template, the download file size, the average user rating, and the number of votes it has received thus far.)

FIGURE EX1.15 Reviewing additional template information

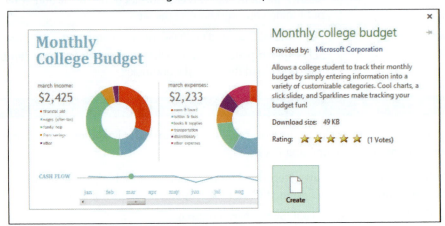

6 When you are ready to proceed:

CLICK the Create command button ( ).

(*Results:* The template is downloaded and opens in the Excel application window.)

7 Use the Zoom Out button ( ) in the Status bar to reduce the worksheet until more information is displayed. Your screen should now appear similar to Figure EX1.16. Notice that the template uses many Excel features that we have not yet covered. Therefore, some users may find templates a bit overwhelming. However, you should be aware that they are available and a great tool from which to learn and generate ideas.

FIGURE EX1.16 The Monthly College Budget workbook template

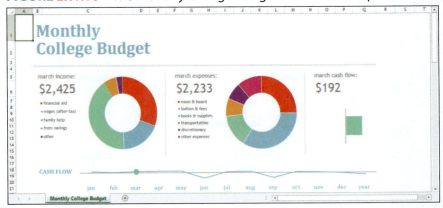

8 At this point, you would typically enter data into the blank template file. However, for our purposes, you may simply save the workbook as **ex01a-templatebudget.xlsx**.

9 Navigate the template and review the contents by clicking on cells and looking into the Formula bar to see their formulas or values. Once you are ready to proceed, you may close the workbook file(s) you have open and exit Microsoft Excel.

MULTIPLE-CHOICE QUIZ

Select the best choice in the following questions to review the project concepts. Good luck!

1. You hold down this key(s) to select multiple cell ranges using the mouse.

   a. `Alt`

   b. `Ctrl`

   c. `Shift`

   d. `Shift` + `Ctrl`

2. Excel displays the active or current cell address in the
   a. Name box.
   b. HOME tab.
   c. Formula bar.
   d. Status bar.

3. When you enter a date value, Excel justifies the entry automatically between the cell borders as
   a. centered.
   b. fully justified.
   c. left-aligned.
   d. right-aligned.

4. When a series of ######## appears in a cell, it typically means
   a. the value you entered is invalid.
   b. the formula you entered is incorrect.
   c. the column is too narrow to display the number or date.
   d. the column is too narrow to display all of the text.

5. Which is the correct formula for adding cells B4 and F7?
   a. @B4*F7
   b. =B4+F7
   c. +B4+F7
   d. =B4:F7

6. This feature allows you to view the sum of a range of values without entering a formula into a worksheet cell.
   a. AutoCalculate
   b. AutoComplete
   c. AutoTotal
   d. AutoValue

7. The AutoSum feature enters this function into a cell to sum a range of values.
   a. ADD
   b. PLUS
   c. SUM
   d. VALUE

8. By default, when you insert cells into a worksheet using the Insert Cells command, the existing cell contents are
   a. pushed up.
   b. pushed down.
   c. pushed left.
   d. removed.

9. To copy a cell or cell range using a drag and drop operation, you need to hold down this key(s).

   a. `Alt`

   b. `Ctrl`

   c. `Shift`

   d. You do not hold down a key.

10. To display cell formulas in a worksheet, you click the Show Formulas command button, which is located under which tab of the Ribbon?
    a. HOME
    b. FORMULAS
    c. REVIEW
    d. VIEW

In this exercise, you will create a new workbook file and practice fundamental worksheet skills, including entering labels, numbers, dates, and formulas. The final worksheet is shown in Figure EX1.17.

FIGURE EX1.17   Work It Out EX-1A-E1: completed

	A	B	C	D	E	F
1	Tip Top Dry Cleaning					
2	Today is:	30-Sep-13				
3			Jul-13	Aug-13	Sep-13	
4	Number of Staff		16	18	19	
5	Avg Hours Worked		36	42	38	
6	Avg Wage per Hour		$10	$11.50	$10.75	
7						
8	Total Wage Costs		$5,760	$8,694	$7,762	
9						
10						

1. Start a new blank workbook in Excel and then save the file as **ex01a-hw01.xlsx**.

2. Adjust the Zoom factor for the workbook to 120%.

3. Enter the title **Tip Top Dry Cleaning** into cell A1.

4. Complete the worksheet as it appears in Figure EX1.17, except for the cell range C8:E8. (*Note:* Depending on how your computer is configured, the worksheet's date values may appear formatted differently on your screen. Even though the monthly column titles display using the format mmm-yy, you must enter the date values using the format mmm-yyyy (e.g., Jul-2013) to ensure that Excel recognizes the year. Furthermore, the text labels in rows 4 through 8 are entered into column A, but their length requires that they spill over into column B.)

5. Rather than typing the values for row 8, start by constructing a formula in cell C8 that calculates the "Total Wage Costs." The formula should consist of the number of staff (cell C4) multiplied by the average hours worked (cell C5) multiplied by the average wage per hour (cell C6). Multiply the three cells together so that the result appears in cell C8 as a total value. (*Note:* Do not multiply the values stored within the cells; rather, multiply the cell addresses.)

6. Copy the formula in cell C8 to the next two columns using the fill handle. (*Result:* Your worksheet should now appear similar to Figure EX1.17.)

7. Save and then close the workbook file.

HANDS-ON EXERCISE: WORK IT OUT EX-1A-E2

In this exercise, you will assume the role of a market researcher and finalize the analysis of a questionnaire using formulas in Excel. The final worksheet is shown in Figure EX1.18.

FIGURE EX1.18 Work It Out EX-1A-E2: completed

	A	B	C	D	E	F	G
1	Survey Results						
2							
3	Number of Stores Carrying Each Brand						
4	Brand	YR 2012	Share	YR 2013	Share	Change	
5	For the Halibut	94	51.37%	86	44.33%	-0.085106	
6	Capetown Cod	60	32.79%	58	29.90%	-0.033333	
7	Magic Mackerel	25	13.66%	36	18.56%	0.44	
8	Fisherman's Delight	4	2.19%	14	7.22%	2.5	
9	Total Stores	183		194			
10							
11							

1. Locate and open the exercise data file **ex01a-ex02.xlsx**. Ensure that the file is not in Protected View mode and then save it as **ex01a-hw02.xlsx**.

2. The Kolander brand of frozen fish has recently been renamed to For the Halibut. Make this editing change in cell A5.

3. The Capetown Cod brand is mistakenly entered as Cape Cod. Make this editing change in cell A6.

4. In cell B9, use the AutoSum button (∑ ▾) on the HOME tab to sum the column values from B5:B8.

5. In cell D9, use the AutoSum button (∑ ▾) on the HOME tab to sum the column values from D5:D8.

6. Select the cell range B5:B8 and then use the Quick Analysis tool to calculate the percent share that each brand possesses for YR 2012. See Figure EX1.19 for assistance.

7. Select the cell range D5:D8 and perform the same calculation for YR 2013.

FIGURE EX1.19 Using the Quick Analysis tool to calculate the percent share

	A	B	C	D	E	F	G
1	**Survey Results**						
2							
3	**Number of Stores Carrying Each Brand**						
4	**Brand**	**YR 2012**	**Share**	**YR 2013**	**Share**	**Change**	
5	For the Halibut	94	**51.37%**	86			
6	Capetown Cod	60	**32.79%**	58			
7	Magic Mackerel	25	**13.66%**	36			
8	Fisherman's Delight	4	**2.19%**	14			
9	**Total Stores**	**183**		**194**			

FORMATTING   CHARTS   **TOTALS**   TABLES   SPARKLINES

Running Total   Sum   Average   Count   % Total   Running Total

Formulas automatically calculate totals for you.

Use the scroll arrows to select the "% Total" option for a row calculation

8 Now calculate the percentage change that resulted for each brand between 2012 and 2013. Construct a formula that performs the following calculation: (Brand Result in 2013 −Brand Result in 2012) / Brand Result in 2012. (*Hint:* Notice the use of parentheses or brackets in this pseudo-formula. Also, make sure to replace these words with the appropriate cell references.) To begin, enter a formula in cell F5 to calculate the percentage change for the For the Halibut brand using a technique of your choosing. Then, complete the rest of the column's entries. Check your work against Figure EX1.18.

9 Save and then close the workbook file.

HANDS-ON EXERCISE: WORK IT OUT EX-1A-E3

In this exercise, you will open an existing workbook and revise it to appear similar to Figure EX1.20. Several methods and features are applied, so make sure you follow the steps closely.

FIGURE EX1.20 Work It Out EX-1A-E3: completed

	A	B	C	D	E	F	G
1	Monthly Efficiency Report						
2	Date:	14-Feb-14					
3							
4	Vehicle	Revenue	Expenses	Profit	Miles	Profit/Mile	
5	Runner	15,326	4,109	11,217	3,120	3.5951923	
6	Wanderer	17,210	3,843	13,367	5,054	2.6448358	
7	Zephyr	9,845	2,766	7,079	2,449	2.8905676	
8	Rodeo	5,957	1,894	4,063	854	4.7576112	
9	Total	**48,338**	**12,612**	**35,726**	**11,477**		
10							
11							

1. Locate and open the exercise data file **ex01a-ex03.xlsx**. Ensure that the file is not in Protected View mode and then save it as **ex01a-hw03.xlsx**.

2. To begin, modify the text labels in the worksheet cells to match the contents of Figure EX1.20.

3. Insert cells from A3:F3 that will push down the existing content in line with row 4.

4. Enter the date using the proper formatting. (*Hint:* If you make a mistake, make sure you use the Clear All or Clear Format command before attempting a new formatted entry. Excel remembers the previous formatting that you applied.)

5. Now, insert the necessary cells for a new vehicle, named Rodeo. Enter the information for this new vehicle, referring to the existing vehicle data in the worksheet for guidance.

6. Enter formulas for calculating Profit (Revenue minus Expenses) in column D and Profit/Mile (Profit divided by Miles) in column F.

7. Use the Quick Analysis tool to calculate the column SUM for Revenue, Expenses, Profit, and Miles.

8. Check your work against Figure EX1.20.

9. Save and then close the workbook file.

Formatting and Printing the Budget

In this project, you will continue modifying the worksheet created in Project EXCEL 1A. By adjusting column widths and row heights in the worksheet, you can enhance its appearance for both viewing and printing—making it easier to read and understand. You will also modify the structure of a worksheet by inserting and deleting rows and columns. Lastly, you will apply several formatting options to polish and prepare the worksheet for printing.

PROJECT FILE: *Available at* **www.mhhe.com/office2013projectlearn**

PROJECT OBJECTIVES

After completing this project, you will be able to:

- Change the width and height of columns and rows to provide appropriate spacing.

- Modify the structure of a worksheet by inserting and deleting columns and rows.

- Enhance a worksheet's appearance using fonts, styles, and colors.

- Format the display of numeric and date values in the worksheet.

- Manipulate the alignment and rotation of text within cells for design and legibility.

- Highlight different areas in a worksheet using borders and shading.

- Prepare, configure, and send a worksheet to the printer.

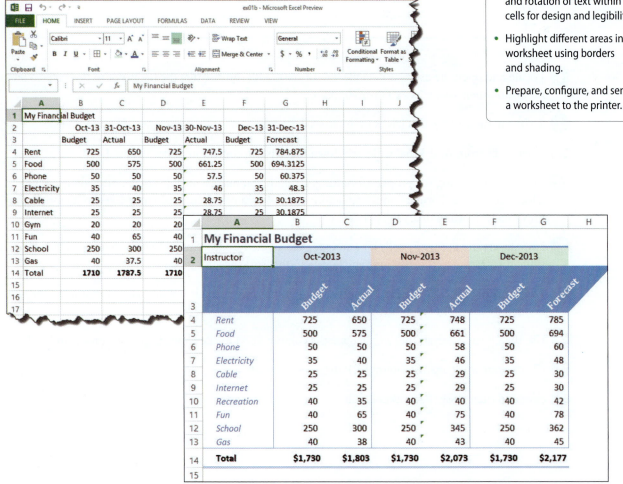

Changing Column Widths and Row Heights

LESSON OVERVIEW

Previously, you witnessed long text labels in a cell spill characters over the cell borders into adjacent columns. For numeric entries, the data cannot extend beyond a column's borders. Instead, a series of number signs (#) fill the cell when the column is not wide enough to display the formatted value. Fortunately, you can increase and decrease the width of your worksheet columns to allow for varying lengths of text labels, numbers, and dates. Excel can even calculate the best or AutoFit width for a column based on its existing entries. Similarly, you can change the height of any worksheet row to customize the borders and line spacing in a worksheet. What's more, a row's height is adjusted automatically when you increase or decrease the font size of information appearing in the row. Whereas a column's width is measured in characters, a row's height is measured in **points**, where 72 points is equal to one inch. The larger the font size that you select for a given cell, the larger its row height.

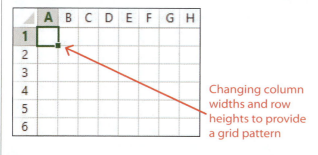

Changing column widths and row heights to provide a grid pattern

SKILLS PREVIEW

Adjust a column's width	• DRAG a column's right border in the column frame area, *or*
	• DOUBLE-CLICK a column's right border to find the best fit, *or*
	• SELECT a cell in the column that you want to format.
	CLICK the HOME tab and locate the Cells group.
	CLICK the Format button (▦).
	CHOOSE Column Width (*or* AutoFit Column Width).
	TYPE a *value*, such as 12, for the desired width.
Adjust a row's height	• DRAG a row's lower border in the row frame area, or
	• DOUBLE-CLICK a row's lower border to find the best height, *or*
	• SELECT a cell in the row that you want to format.
	CLICK the HOME tab and locate the Cells group.
	CLICK the Format button (▦).
	CHOOSE Row Height (*or* AutoFit Row Height).
	TYPE a *value*, such as 18, for the desired height.

1 After launching Microsoft Excel, locate and open the project data file **ex01b.xlsx**. On the File menu tab, use the Save As command to save the file as **ex01b-budget.xlsx**. Your worksheet should appear similar to Figure EX1.21.

FIGURE EX1.21 Opening and saving the ex01b-budget workbook

2 In this worksheet, the first column is distinct from the monthly columns. You can adjust the width of column A to better differentiate it and to provide some needed white space:

SELECT cell A1 (if it is not already selected).

CLICK the HOME tab and locate the Cells group.

CLICK the Format button (⊞).

CHOOSE Column Width from the menu.

(*Result:* The Column Width dialog box appears with the default width setting of 8.43, as shown.)

3 In the dialog box, enter the new width value in characters:

TYPE **12**.

PRESS **Enter** (or CLICK the OK command button).

(*Result:* The width of column A is modified to 12 characters, from its default size of 8.43.)

4 To change the width of several columns at once:

SELECT the cell range B1:G1.

CLICK the Format button ().

CHOOSE Column Width.

TYPE **10**.

PRESS Enter .

(*Result:* The widths for columns B through G are modified.)

5 To adjust the width of column A using the mouse:

POSITION the mouse pointer over column A's right borderline in the frame area.

CLICK and DRAG to the right until the tooltip reads "Width: 15.00" as shown.

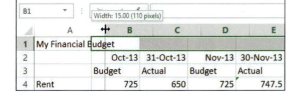

RELEASE the mouse button to complete the sizing operation.

(*Result:* Notice you did not have to worry about selecting the proper cell range first.)

6 To increase the height of row 2 using the mouse:

POSITION the mouse pointer over row 2's bottom borderline in the frame area.

CLICK and DRAG downward until the tooltip reads "Height: 21.00."

RELEASE the mouse button to complete the sizing operation

> **TIP**
>
> To size multiple columns or rows using the mouse, select the columns or rows first in the frame area and then size a single column or row in order to modify the entire selection.

7 Lastly, you should increase the height of row 14 to improve the readability:

SELECT cell A14 (although any cell within row 14 would suffice).

CLICK the Format button ().

CHOOSE Row Height.

TYPE **21**.

PRESS Enter .

(*Result:* The additional height provides some much needed separation between the budget categories and the "Total" row. Your screen should now appear similar to Figure EX1.22.)

8 Save your file before proceeding to the next lesson.

FIGURE EX1.22   Changing column widths and row heights

	A	B	C	D	E	F	G	H
1	My Financial Budget							
2		Oct-13	31-Oct-13	Nov-13	30-Nov-13	Dec-13	31-Dec-13	
3		Budget	Actual	Budget	Actual	Budget	Forecast	
4	Rent	725	650	725	747.5	725	784.875	
5	Food	500	575	500	661.25	500	694.3125	
6	Phone	50	50	50	57.5	50	60.375	
7	Electricity	35	40	35	46	35	48.3	
8	Cable	25	25	25	28.75	25	30.1875	
9	Internet	25	25	25	28.75	25	30.1875	
10	Gym	20	20	20	23	20	24.15	
11	Fun	40	65	40	74.75	40	78.4875	
12	School	250	300	250	345	250	362.25	
13	Gas	40	37.5	40	43.125	40	45.28125	
14	Total	1710	1787.5	1710	2055.625	1710	2158.4063	
15								
16								

Inserting, Deleting, and Hiding Columns and Rows

LESSON OVERVIEW

You insert and delete rows and columns to affect the structure of a worksheet. In doing so, however, you must be careful not to change other areas in your worksheet unintentionally. Deleting column B, for example, removes all of the data in the entire column, not just the cells that are currently visible on your screen. Instead of deleting a row or column, you can hide the row or column that you do not want displayed (as shown below). For example, you may want to hide sensitive data, such as salaries or commissions, from displaying in a particular report.

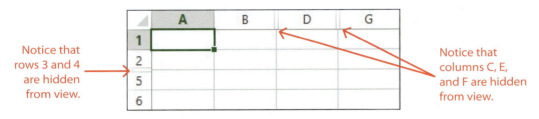

Notice that rows 3 and 4 are hidden from view.

Notice that columns C, E, and F are hidden from view.

SKILLS PREVIEW

Insert a column or row	• RIGHT-CLICK a column letter or a row number in their respective frame area. CHOOSE Insert, *or* • SELECT a cell in the column or row to be inserted. CLICK the HOME tab and locate the Cells group. CLICK the Insert drop-down button (⊞). CHOOSE Insert Sheet Columns (*or* Insert Sheet Rows).
Delete a column or row	• RIGHT-CLICK a column letter or a row number in their respective frame area. CHOOSE Delete, *or* • SELECT a cell in the column or row to be deleted. CLICK the HOME tab and locate the Cells group. CLICK the Delete drop-down button (⊞). CHOOSE Delete Sheet Columns (*or* Delete Sheet Rows).
Hide a column or row	• RIGHT-CLICK the desired column or row. CHOOSE Hide.
Unhide a column or row	• SELECT the rows or columns on both sides of the hidden row(s) or column(s), so that the hidden portion is in the middle. RIGHT-CLICK the frame area of the selected rows or columns. CHOOSE Unhide.

PROJECT PRACTICE

1 Ensure that **ex01b-budget.xlsx** is open.

2 To insert a new budget category between "Internet" and "Gym," do the following:

SELECT cell A10.

CLICK the HOME tab and locate the Cells group.

CLICK Insert drop-down button (⊞).

CHOOSE Insert Sheet Rows from the menu.

(*Result:* A new, empty row 10 is inserted, pushing down the previous contents in row 10 to row 11.)

3 To complete the entry, type the following data in row 10:

TYPE **Recreation**.

PRESS →.

TYPE **40**.

PRESS →.

TYPE **35**.

PRESS Enter.

(*Result*: Notice that Excel automatically copies the standard row formulas appearing in columns D through G to the new cells. Your worksheet should now appear similar to Figure EX1.23.)

FIGURE EX1.23 Inserting a new budget category

	A	B	C	D	E	F	G	H
1	My Financial Budget							
2		Oct-13	31-Oct-13	Nov-13	30-Nov-13	Dec-13	31-Dec-13	
3		Budget	Actual	Budget	Actual	Budget	Forecast	
4	Rent	725	650	725	747.5	725	784.875	
5	Food	500	575	500	661.25	500	694.3125	
6	Phone	50	50	50	57.5	50	60.375	
7	Electricity	35	40	35	46	35	48.3	
8	Cable	25	25	25	28.75	25	30.1875	
9	Internet	25	25	25	28.75	25	30.1875	
10	Recreation	40	35	40	40.25	40	42.2625	
11	Gym	20	20	20	23	20	24.15	
12	Fun	40	65	40	74.75	40	78.4875	
13	School	250	300	250	345	250	362.25	
14	Gas	40	37.5	40	43.125	40	45.28125	
15	Total	**1750**	**1822.5**	**1750**	**2095.875**	**1750**	**2200.6688**	
16								
17								

4 You can now delete the "Gym" category. To do so, use the right-click shortcut menu:

RIGHT-CLICK row 11 in the row frame area.

CHOOSE Delete from the menu shown.

5 Because the "Budget" values do not change for November and December, hide these columns temporarily. You will start by selecting the two columns:

CLICK column D in the column frame area.

PRESS and HOLD Ctrl.

CLICK column F in the column frame area.

RELEASE Ctrl.

(*Result*: The two columns should now appear highlighted and selected.)

6 To hide these columns from displaying in the worksheet:

CLICK the HOME tab and locate the Cells group.

CLICK the Format drop-down button (⊞).

CHOOSE Hide & Unhide command.

CHOOSE Hide Columns (as shown in Figure EX1.24).

(*Result*: The contents of the columns are hidden from display and the column letters should no longer appear in the column frame area.)

FIGURE EX1.24 Choosing to hide the selected columns

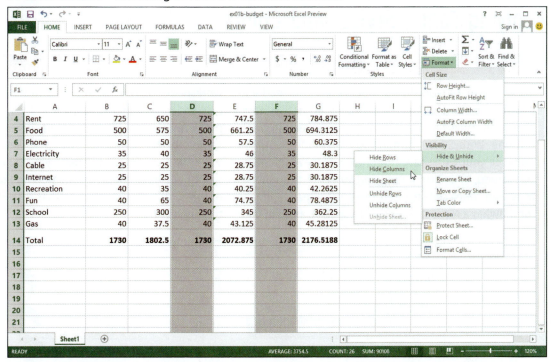

7 Before proceeding, you should unhide the columns for use in the next lesson. Using the mouse:
CLICK and DRAG across columns C, E, and G in the column frame area.
(*Result:* All three columns should appear highlighted and selected. Notice that you selected the columns on both sides of the hidden columns.)

8 To unhide the columns using the right-click context menu:
RIGHT-CLICK any of the selected column letters in the frame area (e.g., column E).
CHOOSE Unhide from the menu.
(*Results:* The columns are again displayed in the worksheet.)

9 Select cell A1 and then save your file before proceeding to the next lesson.

Applying Fonts, Styles, and Colors

LESSON OVERVIEW

Strive to create worksheets that are easy to read and pleasing to the eye. Clearly, a visually attractive worksheet will convey information better than an unformatted one. With Excel's formatting capabilities, you can enhance your worksheets for on-screen viewing, online publishing, or printing. Applying **fonts** to titles, headings, and other cells is often the most effective means for drawing a reader's attention to specific areas in your worksheet. You can also specify font styles, such as boldface and italic, adjust font sizes, and select colors. Excel's preformatted cell styles (shown here) provide some sample design combinations for your worksheets, but you may also choose to create your own. To keep your worksheets easy to read, remember to limit the number of fonts, styles, and colors so that they do not become too distracting.

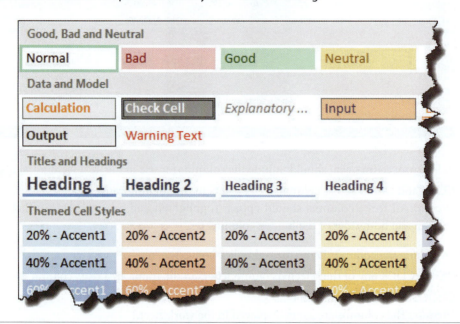

SKILLS PREVIEW

Apply character formatting to the selected cell range	• CLICK the HOME tab and locate the Font group. SELECT the desired formatting options using these buttons. 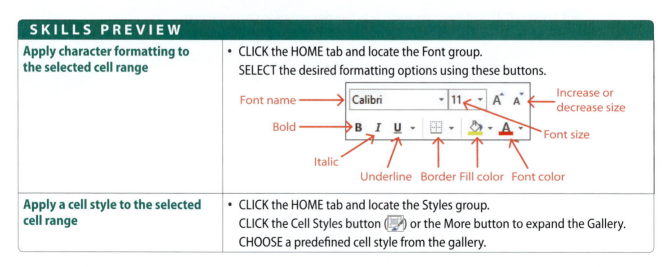
Apply a cell style to the selected cell range	• CLICK the HOME tab and locate the Styles group. CLICK the Cell Styles button (▨) or the More button to expand the Gallery. CHOOSE a predefined cell style from the gallery.

1 Ensure that **ex01b-budget.xlsx** is open.

2 Now for some fun! You can modify the appearance of this worksheet using font and style commands. To begin:

SELECT the cell range A1:B1.

CLICK the HOME tab and locate the Styles group.

CLICK the Cell Styles button (⬚) or the More button to expand the Gallery. (*Result:* The Cell Styles gallery appears.)

3 In the gallery, locate the Titles and Headings group. Then:

CLICK Heading 1. (*Result:* The title text is now formatted and underlined at the top of the worksheet.)

4 To call attention to the column headings:

SELECT the cell range A3:G3.

CLICK the Cell Styles button (⬚) or the More button to expand the Gallery.

5 In the gallery, locate the Themed Cell Styles group. Then:

CLICK Accent 1. (*Result:* The cells are formatted with a blue background and white lettering.)

6 To make the text stand out even more, ensure that the cell range A3:G3 remains selected and then locate the Font group on the HOME tab. Do the following:

CLICK the Bold button (**B**).

CLICK the Font drop-down list box (Calibri ⌄).

CHOOSE Cambria from the list box. (*Result:* The column headings should now appear quite distinct from the rest of the worksheet cells, as shown.)

	A	B	C	D	E	F	G	H
1	**My Financial Budget**							
2		Oct-13	31-Oct-13	Nov-13	30-Nov-13	Dec-13	31-Dec-13	
3		**Budget**	**Actual**	**Budget**	**Actual**	**Budget**	**Forecast**	
4	Rent	725	650	725	747.5	725	784.875	
5	Food	500	575	500	661.25	500	694.3125	

7 To apply a cell style to the "Total" row:

SELECT the cell range A14:G14.

CLICK the Cell Styles button (⬚) or the More button to expand the Gallery.

8 In the Titles and Headings group of the gallery:

CLICK Total. (*Result:* The contents of row 14 are now formatted with font attributes and cell borders.)

9 You can modify the category text in column A. Do the following:

SELECT the cell range A4:A13.

CLICK the Italic button (*I*) to italicize the text.

CLICK the Font Color drop-down button (**A** ▾).

10 In the drop-down color palette that appears:

HOVER your mouse over the top row of Theme Colors to display tooltips for the color names.

CLICK the Blue, Accent 5 color box.

(*Result:* The text color for the selected range is modified.)

11 Select cell A1 so that your worksheet appears similar to Figure EX1.25. Save your file before proceeding to the next lesson.

FIGURE EX1.25   Applying fonts and cell styles

	A	B	C	D	E	F	G	H
1	My Financial Budget							
2		Oct-13	31-Oct-13	Nov-13	30-Nov-13	Dec-13	31-Dec-13	
3		Budget	Actual	Budget	Actual	Budget	Forecast	
4	Rent	725	650	725	747.5	725	784.875	
5	Food	500	575	500	661.25	500	694.3125	
6	Phone	50	50	50	57.5	50	60.375	
7	Electricity	35	40	35	46	35	48.3	
8	Cable	25	25	25	28.75	25	30.1875	
9	Internet	25	25	25	28.75	25	30.1875	
10	Recreation	40	35	40	40.25	40	42.2625	
11	Fun	40	65	40	74.75	40	78.4875	
12	School	250	300	250	345	250	362.25	
13	Gas	40	37.5	40	43.125	40	45.28125	
14	Total	1730	1802.5	1730	2072.875	1730	2176.5188	
15								
16								

Formatting Numbers and Dates

Number formats, like those shown in this graphic, improve the appearance and readability of values in a worksheet by inserting dollar signs, commas, percentage symbols, and decimal places. Although a number or date may appear formatted on the worksheet, the underlying value that is stored in the cell (and seen in the Formula bar) does not change. Excel stores date and time entries as values and, therefore, allows you to customize their display as you do numbers.

Are you getting tired of selecting the same formatting commands over and over? Excel understands these frustrations and provides the **Format Painter** feature for copying formatting styles and attributes from one area of your worksheet to another. Not only does Format Painter help speed up formatting procedures, but it also ensures formatting consistency within your workbooks.

Now you can rest assured that all of your worksheet content is formatted using the same fonts, sizes, colors, alignments, and numeric styles.

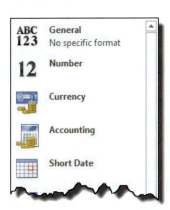

Apply number and date formatting to the selected cell range	• CLICK the HOME tab and locate the Number group. CLICK the Number Format drop-down button (General). CHOOSE a number or date style from the list, *or* • SELECT the desired style using these buttons. General — Number Format drop-down list box $ ▾ % , ←.0 .00 Accounting style · Percent style · Comma style · Increase or Decrease Decimals
Copy formatting from one cell range to another using the Format Painter	• SELECT a cell with the formatting you wish to copy. CLICK the HOME tab and locate the Clipboard group. CLICK the Format Painter button (✦). SELECT the cell or cell range to which you wish to apply the copied formatting.

① Ensure that **ex01b-budget.xlsx** is open.

② To format the numeric values in the worksheet so that they appear uniform:

SELECT the cell range B4:G13.

CLICK the HOME tab and locate the Number group.

CLICK the Comma Style button (,).

(*Result*: The numbers in the selected range are formatted using the comma style with two decimal places.)

3 To remove the decimals from displaying, ensure that the range remains selected and then:

CLICK the Decrease Decimal button (![Decrease Decimal icon]) twice.

(*Result:* The decimals are removed from the display and the values are rounded automatically.)

4 To format the total values in row 14:

SELECT the cell range B14:G14.

CLICK the Number Format drop-down button (![General drop-down]).

CLICK Currency in the list box.

(*Result:* The Currency style displays the dollar sign immediately next to the value, as opposed to the Accounting style, which left-aligns the symbol in the cell.)

5 To remove the decimals from displaying:

CLICK the Decrease Decimal button (![Decrease Decimal icon]) twice.

6 You will now format the budget dates appearing in row 2. To begin:

CLICK cell B2.

CLICK the Number Format drop-down button (![General drop-down]).

CLICK More Number Formats at the bottom of the list box.

(*Result:* The Format Cells dialog box appears, as shown in Figure EX1.26.)

FIGURE EX1.26 Displaying the Format Cells dialog box

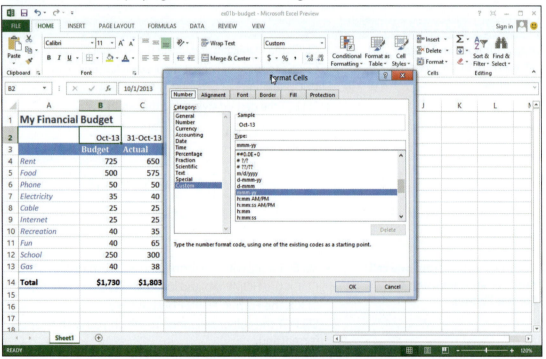

7 To display the date as Oct-2013, you will need to modify the formatting style to read mmm-yyyy. Do the following:

CLICK to the right of "mmm-yy" in the Type text box.

TYPE yy to append the text to the current style.

CLICK OK.

(*Result:* The date value in cell B2 should now read "Oct-2013.")

8 You will now copy this custom date format to the other Budget cells using the Format Painter. To begin, ensure that cell B2 is selected and then:

CLICK the HOME tab and locate the Clipboard group.

DOUBLE-CLICK the Format Painter button (🖌).

(*Result*: By double-clicking the Format Painter button (🖌), you lock it into position so that you may apply the formatting to multiple selections.)

9 To apply the copied formatting:

CLICK cell D2.

CLICK cell F2.

10 To turn off the Format Painter feature:

CLICK the Format Painter button (🖌) to toggle it off.

(*Result*: Your worksheet should now appear similar to Figure EX1.27.)

11 Save your file before proceeding to the next lesson.

FIGURE EX1.27   Applying numeric and date formatting

	A	B	C	D	E	F	G	H
1	**My Financial Budget**							
2		Oct-2013	31-Oct-13	Nov-2013	30-Nov-13	Dec-2013	31-Dec-13	
3		**Budget**	**Actual**	**Budget**	**Actual**	**Budget**	**Forecast**	
4	Rent	725	650	725	748	725	785	
5	Food	500	575	500	661	500	694	
6	Phone	50	50	50	58	50	60	
7	Electricity	35	40	35	46	35	48	
8	Cable	25	25	25	29	25	30	
9	Internet	25	25	25	29	25	30	
10	Recreation	40	35	40	40	40	42	
11	Fun	40	65	40	75	40	78	
12	School	250	300	250	345	250	362	
13	Gas	40	38	40	43	40	45	
14	**Total**	**$1,730**	**$1,803**	**$1,730**	**$2,073**	**$1,730**	**$2,177**	
15								
16								

Aligning, Merging, and Rotating Cells

LESSON OVERVIEW

By default, Excel aligns text labels against the bottom-left edge of a cell and values against the bottom-right edge, as shown. You can, however, change both the vertical and horizontal **cell alignment** for any type of data entered into the worksheet. Furthermore, you can indent the contents of a cell, rotate the contents (as shown in row 1), and merge or combine data across cells.

	A	B	C	D
1		2012	2013	2014
2	Widgets	100	125	130
3	Gadgets	300	307	319
4				

SKILLS PREVIEW

Align contents of the selected cell range horizontally and vertically	• CLICK the HOME tab and locate the Alignment group. SELECT the desired alignment options using these buttons. 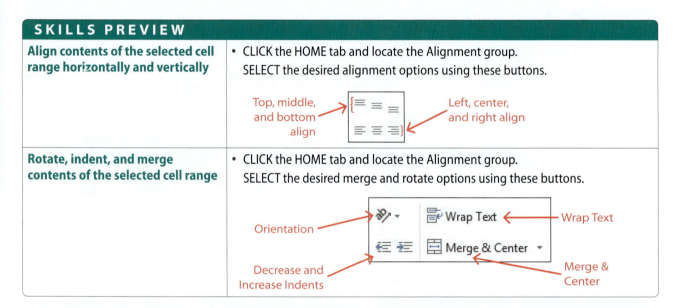
Rotate, indent, and merge contents of the selected cell range	• CLICK the HOME tab and locate the Alignment group. SELECT the desired merge and rotate options using these buttons.

Top, middle, and bottom align

Left, center, and right align

Orientation

Wrap Text — Wrap Text

Decrease and Increase Indents

Merge & Center — Merge & Center

PROJECT PRACTICE

1. Ensure that **ex01b-budget.xlsx** is open.

2. In continuing to format the budget worksheet, you can modify the alignment of the category text entries:

    SELECT the cell range A4:A14.

    CLICK the HOME tab and locate the Alignment group.

    CLICK the Align Right button (▤).
    (*Result*: The text entries should now appear right-aligned against the right cell border.)

3. Now change the vertical alignment of entries:

    SELECT the cell range A14:G14.

    CLICK the Middle Align button (▤).
    (*Result*: Remember that you increased the height of this row in a previous lesson. In such cases, you will often want to modify the vertical cell alignment to ensure a proper fit between cell borders.)

4 Rather than the two date entries above each column, use the merge and center command to display a single date. To begin:

SELECT cell C2, E2, and G2 (i.e., hold down the `Ctrl` key while clicking the cells one at a time).

PRESS `Delete` to remove the cell contents.

5 You will now merge and center the two cells above each month's "Budget" and "Actual" or "Forecast" columns. Do the following:

SELECT the cell range B2:C2.

CLICK the Merge & Center button ( ).

CLICK the Middle Align button ( ).

(*Result:* If you click the Merge & Center button's drop-down arrow by mistake, simply choose the Merge & Center command from the menu that appears. Once completed, the cell entry extends across two columns, although the cell is still referred to as B2 as shown below in the Name box.)

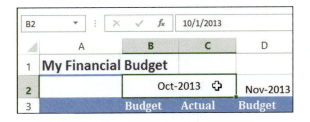

6 To extend this formatting to the other columns, first copy the formatting attributes to the Clipboard:

DOUBLE-CLICK the Format Painter button ( ).

(*Result:* Remember that double-clicking the Format Painter button ( ) locks it in the On position.)

7 Now, apply the formatting:

CLICK cell D2.

CLICK cell F2.

CLICK the Format Painter button ( ) to toggle it off.

(*Result:* The column headers should now appear merged and centered above their respective columns.)

8 To demonstrate the text orientation feature, you can rotate the column headings below the dates:

SELECT the cell range B3:G3.

CLICK Center button ( ).

CLICK the Orientation button ( ).

CHOOSE the Angle Counterclockwise command.

(*Result:* Notice that the row height automatically adjusts to fit the rotated text. Your screen should now appear similar to Figure EX1.28.)

TIP

Using the Alignment tab in the Format Cells dialog box, you can adjust the orientation angle (shown here) to better customize the appearance of rotated text. To view the alignment options, click the Dialog Box launcher ( ) for the Alignment group on the HOME tab.

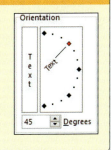

9 Return the cell pointer to cell A1 and save your file.

FIGURE EX1.28 Aligning and rotating cell contents

	A	B	C	D	E	F	G	H
1	My Financial Budget							
2		Oct-2013		Nov-2013		Dec-2013		
3		Budget	Actual	Budget	Actual	Budget	Forecast	
4	Rent	725	650	725	748	725	785	
5	Food	500	575	500	661	500	694	
6	Phone	50	50	50	58	50	60	
7	Electricity	35	40	35	46	35	48	
8	Cable	25	25	25	29	25	30	
9	Internet	25	25	25	29	25	30	
10	Recreation	40	35	40	40	40	42	
11	Fun	40	65	40	75	40	78	
12	School	250	300	250	345	250	362	
13	Gas	40	38	40	43	40	45	
14	Total	$1,730	$1,803	$1,730	$2,073	$1,730	$2,177	
15								

Adding Borders and Shading

LESSON OVERVIEW

As with the other formatting options, you use borders, patterns, shading, and colors to enhance a worksheet's readability. The **gridlines** that appear in the worksheet window are nonprinting lines, provided only to help you line up information. As shown in this example, borders are used to place printed gridlines on a worksheet and color shading is used to separate the contents into logical sections. These formatting options also enable you to create professional-looking invoice forms, memos, and tables.

	A	B	C	D
1		2012	2013	2014
2	Widgets	100	125	130
3	Gadgets	300	307	319
4	**Totals**	**400**	**432**	**449**
5				

SKILLS PREVIEW

Toggle the display of gridlines on a worksheet	• CLICK the VIEW tab and locate the Show group. CLICK the Gridlines check box to toggle the display on and off.
Apply borders to the selected cell range	• CLICK the HOME tab and locate the Font group. CLICK the Borders drop-down button (⊞ ▾). CHOOSE the desired border (*or* More Borders).
Apply colors or shading to the selected cell range	• CLICK the HOME tab and locate the Font group. CLICK the Fill Color drop-down button (🎨 ▾). CHOOSE the desired color (*or* More Colors).

PROJECT PRACTICE

1. Ensure that **ex01b-budget.xlsx** is open.

2. You can view the worksheet as it would print, without the cell gridlines:

CLICK the VIEW tab and locate the Show group.

CLICK the Gridlines check box to remove the check mark that appears.
(*Result:* The cell gridlines disappear and your worksheet should appear similar to the one shown in Figure EX1.29. Notice that it is somewhat difficult to determine which columns belong to a month.)

FIGURE EX1.29 Displaying the worksheet without gridlines

	A	B	C	D	E	F	G
1	My Financial Budget						
2			Oct-2013		Nov-2013		Dec-2013
3		Budget	Actual	Budget	Actual	Budget	Forecast
4	Rent	725	650	725	748	725	785
5	Food	500	575	500	661	500	694
6	Phone	50	50	50	58	50	60
7	Electricity	35	40	35	46	35	48
8	Cable	25	25	25	29	25	30
9	Internet	25	25	25	29	25	30
10	Recreation	40	35	40	40	40	42
11	Fun	40	65	40	75	40	78
12	School	250	300	250	345	250	362
13	Gas	40	38	40	43	40	45
14	**Total**	**$1,730**	**$1,803**	**$1,730**	**$2,073**	**$1,730**	**$2,177**
15							

3 You can add some printing cell borders to the worksheet:

SELECT the cell range B4:C13.

CLICK the HOME tab and locate the Font group.

CLICK the Borders drop-down button (⊞ ▾).

CHOOSE More Borders.

(*Results:* The Format Cells dialog box appears, as shown in Figure EX1.30, with the Border tab active.)

FIGURE EX1.30   Format Cells dialog box: Border tab

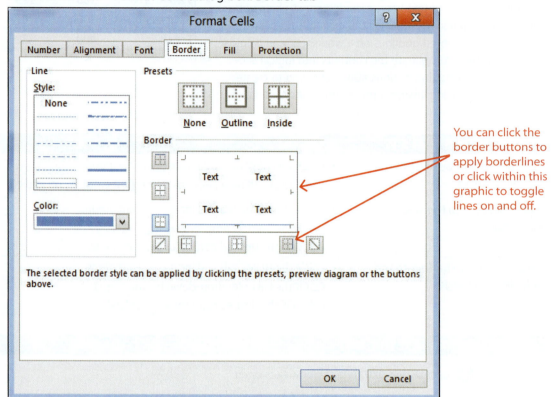

You can click the border buttons to apply borderlines or click within this graphic to toggle lines on and off.

4 In the Border area of the dialog box:

CLICK the Top Border button (⊞).

CLICK the Left Border button (⊞).

CLICK the Right Border button (⊞).

(*Results:* Notice that the Bottom Border button is already selected, due to the Total cell style that was selected in an earlier lesson for row 14.)

5 To finish applying formatting to this range:

CLICK the OK command button.

6 Repeat the steps in the previous two steps to add borders to the cell ranges D4:E13 and F4:G13.

7 Now you can add some finishing touches by color-coding the different months. Do the following:

SELECT cell B2.

CLICK the Fill Color drop-down button (🎨 ▾).

CLICK Blue, Accent 1, Lighter 80% from the palette.

8 For the remaining months:

SELECT cell D2.

CLICK the Fill Color drop-down button (🎨 ▾).

CLICK Orange, Accent 2, Lighter 80% from the palette.

SELECT cell F2.

CLICK the Fill Color drop-down button (🎨 ▾).

CLICK Green, Accent 6, Lighter 80% from the palette.

(*Results:* The monthly results are now easier to differentiate from one another.)

9 To finish the formatting, extend the title formatting in row 1:

SELECT the cell range A1:G1.

CLICK the Cell Styles button (📋) or the More drop-down button (▦) to expand the Gallery.

CLICK Heading 1 in the Titles and Headings group.

10 Increase the space between the category text and the cell border:

SELECT the cell range A4:A14.

CLICK the Increase Indent button (▤) twice.

(*Results:* Notice that the cell alignment changes to left-aligned and that the text is indented away from the cells' left border.)

11 To prepare for the next lesson:

SELECT cell A2.

CLICK the VIEW tab and locate the Show group.

CLICK the Gridlines check box to toggle the gridlines back on.

(*Results:* Your screen should now appear similar to Figure EX1.31.)

12 Save your file before proceeding to the next lesson.

FIGURE EX1.31 Adding borders and shading to the worksheet

	A	B	C	D	E	F	G	H	I
1	**My Financial Budget**								
2		Oct-2013		Nov-2013		Dec-2013			
3		Budget	Actual	Budget	Actual	Budget	Forecast		
4	Rent	725	650	725	748	725	785		
5	Food	500	575	500	661	500	694		
6	Phone	50	50	50	58	50	60		
7	Electricity	35	40	35	46	35	48		
8	Cable	25	25	25	29	25	30		
9	Internet	25	25	25	29	25	30		
10	Recreation	40	35	40	40	40	42		
11	Fun	40	65	40	75	40	78		
12	School	250	300	250	345	250	362		
13	Gas	40	38	40	43	40	45		
14	**Total**	**$1,730**	**$1,803**	**$1,730**	**$2,073**	**$1,730**	**$2,177**		
15									

Printing a Worksheet

LESSON OVERVIEW

Besides the **Normal view** that you have used thus far, Excel provides two additional views for adjusting the appearance of your worksheets. In **Page Layout** view (shown), the worksheet is displayed in a full-page WYSIWYG (What You See Is What You Get) window with margins, page breaks, and headers and footers. You can use this view to move through the workbook pages, zoom in and out on desired areas, and modify layout options. **Page Break Preview** offers another view mode for specifying the desired print area and for setting page breaks. Lastly, you can display a preview of how the worksheet will print using **Backstage view**, before actually sending it to the printer.

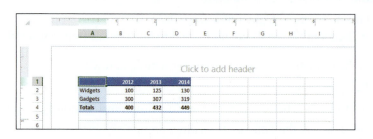

SKILLS PREVIEW

Change the display or view mode using the Ribbon	• CLICK the VIEW tab and locate the Workbook Views group. SELECT the desired view button. 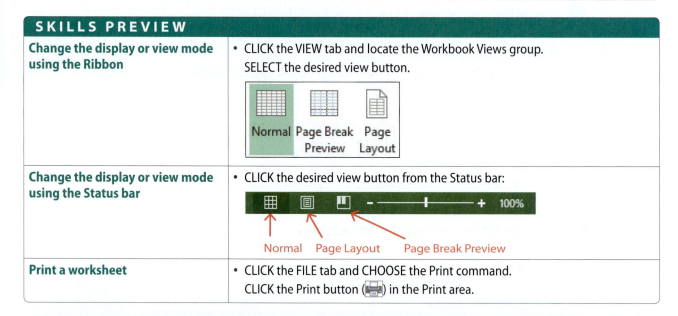
Change the display or view mode using the Status bar	• CLICK the desired view button from the Status bar:
Print a worksheet	• CLICK the FILE tab and CHOOSE the Print command. CLICK the Print button (🖶) in the Print area.

PROJECT PRACTICE

1 Ensure that **ex01b-budget.xlsx** is open.

2 To display the worksheet using the Page Layout view mode:

CLICK the VIEW tab and locate the Workbook Views group.

CLICK the Page Layout button (▤).

(*Result*: Your screen should now appear similar to Figure EX1.32. Notice that the column and row frame area has been enhanced with ruler markings, and that the worksheet page now looks like a printed page, complete with header and footer areas.)

FIGURE EX1.32   Displaying Page Layout view

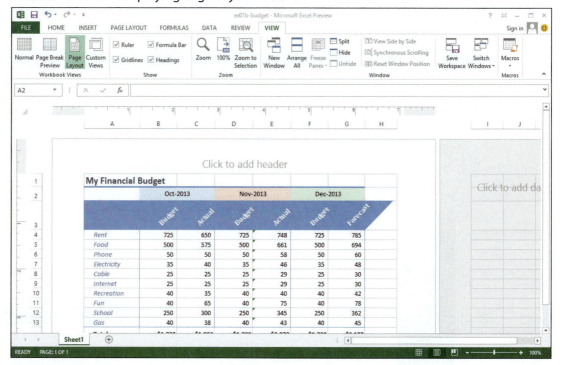

3. You can still edit and format content in the Page Layout view mode. For example:

SELECT cell A2.

TYPE *your name* (replace this with your own name).

PRESS Enter .

4. To adjust the cell formatting:

SELECT cell A2.

CLICK the HOME tab and locate the Alignment group.

CLICK the Middle Align button (≡).

(*Result:* You can perform most commands in Page Layout view. However, it is typically used for finalizing the layout of your worksheet right before printing.)

5. To return to Normal view:

CLICK the Normal button (▦) in the View area of the Status bar.

(*Result:* You may notice that Excel has added a dashed vertical line between columns H and I on your worksheet. This line, whose location and appearance is dependent on your default printer selection, displays the right margin of your worksheet's print range. Anything appearing to the right of this line will be printed on subsequent pages, given the current print configuration such as page orientation and margin settings.)

6. You can preview the print configuration settings and prepare the worksheet for printing:

CLICK the FILE tab and CHOOSE the Print command.

(*Result:* Your screen should now appear similar to Figure EX1.33. In addition to the preview area, review the Printer selection and the Settings area in the Backstage view. In this screen, notice that the Microsoft XPS Document Writer is selected, which sends the worksheet to a disk file. If you selected a black-and-white printer, the preview area would show a black-and-white image.)

7 To print your worksheet with the default settings:
CLICK the Print button ().

> ### MORE INFO
> In a later chapter, you will learn how to customize the various print options, select specific print ranges, create headers and footers, set page numbering and margins, and change the orientation of the printed page.

8 Save and then close the workbook file and exit Microsoft Excel.

FIGURE EX1.33 Previewing and printing a worksheet

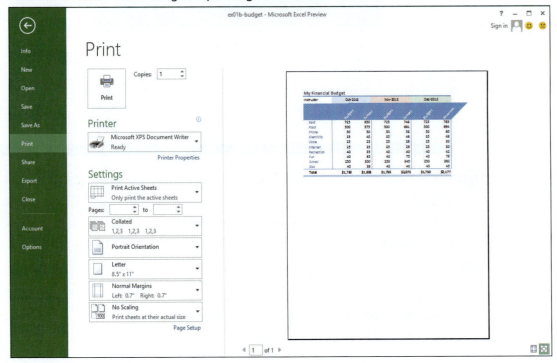

MULTIPLE-CHOICE QUIZ

Select the best choice in the following questions to review the project concepts. Good luck!

1. To change a column's width using the mouse, you position the mouse pointer into the column frame area until it changes to this shape.
   a. ⟷
   b. ✚
   c. ⧗
   d. ⬉

2. The height of a row is typically measured using these units.
   a. characters
   b. fonts
   c. picas
   d. points

3. To select an entire column in the worksheet for editing, inserting, or deleting
   a. double-click any cell within that column.
   b. double-click the column letter in the frame area.
   c. click the column letter in the frame area.
   d. choose the column in the FORMULAS tab.

4. Row 5 is hidden on your worksheet. To unhide the row, you must make the following selection before issuing the appropriate right-click shortcut command.
   a. rows 4 through 6
   b. rows 1 through 4
   c. row 4
   d. row 6

5. To change the text color of a cell entry
   a. click the Fill Color button.
   b. click the Font Color button.
   c. click the Text Color button.
   d. click the Line Color button.

6. The Orientation button ( ) is located in which Ribbon group?
   a. Font group of the HOME tab
   b. Show group of the VIEW tab
   c. Alignment group of the HOME tab
   d. Page Setup group of the HOME tab

7. The Format button in the Cells group of the HOME tab does not allow you to
   a. change the height of a row.
   b. hide columns or rows.
   c. AutoFit a column to its best-fit width.
   d. apply a predefined cell style.

8. When you choose the More Borders command for modifying cell borders, the following dialog box appears.
   a. Format Borders dialog box
   b. Format Cells dialog box
   c. Cell Borders dialog box
   d. More Borders dialog box

9. Which tab on the Ribbon contains the Gridlines checkbox for toggling the display of worksheet gridlines on and off?
   a. HOME tab
   b. PAGE LAYOUT tab
   c. FORMULAS tab
   d. VIEW tab

10. Which view displays the headers and footers on a page, while still allowing you to edit and format the worksheet?
    a. Normal view
    b. Page Layout view
    c. Page Break Preview
    d. Backstage view

HANDS-ON EXERCISE: WORK IT OUT EX-1B-E1

In this exercise, you will open an existing workbook, construct formulas, and make some structural and other enhancements to the worksheet. The final worksheet is shown in Figure EX1.34.

FIGURE EX1.34 Work It Out EX-1B-E1: completed

	A	B	C	D	E	F	G
1	Home Hardware Supply						
2							
3	Sales Rep	Location	Volume	Revenue	Commission	Paid	
4	Frances Hillman	East	$ 75	$ 75,000	$ 3,750	$ 71,250	
5	Randy Brewski	North	$ 82	$ 90,000	$ 4,500	$ 85,500	
6	Cecilia Adams	West	$ 50	$ 54,000	$ 2,700	$ 51,300	
7	Moira Walsh	East	$ 15	$ 16,500	$ 825	$ 15,675	
8	Bruce Towne	South	$ 85	$ 95,000	$ 4,750	$ 90,250	
9	Kela Henderson	North	$ 43	$ 52,000	$ 2,600	$ 49,400	
10	Camilla Edsell	West	$ 30	$ 34,000	$ 1,700	$ 32,300	
11	Tessa Huberty	South	$ 24	$ 26,500	$ 1,325	$ 25,175	
12	Rich Williams	East	$ 102	$ 112,000	$ 5,600	$ 106,400	
13	Jean Arston	West	$ 33	$ 36,000	$ 1,800	$ 34,200	
14	Presley Schuler	North	$ 36	$ 40,000	$ 2,000	$ 38,000	
15	Stevey Yap	South	$ 14	$ 15,000	$ 750	$ 14,250	
16							

1. Locate and open the exercise data file **ex01b-ex01.xlsx**. Ensure that the file is not in Protected View mode and then save it as **ex01b-hw01.xlsx**.

2. The sales rep names in column A are truncated by the location entries in column B. Therefore, adjust the width of column A to its best fit.

3. Adjust the widths for columns B through D to nine characters using the mouse. Then, adjust the widths for columns E through G to 11 characters wide using the Format command on the Ribbon.

4. Adjust the height of row 2 to 12.00 using the mouse. Adjust the height of rows 3 through 15 to 16.50 using the Ribbon.

5. Delete column C to remove the route information from the worksheet.

6. In column E, calculate the commission paid to the sales reps as 5 percent of revenue.

7. In column F, enter an expression that subtracts the commission from the revenue collected.

8. Format the title in cell A1 using the Title cell style.

9. Format the column headings in row 3 using the Accent6 cell style.

10. Center and middle-align the text labels in the cell range A3:F3. Apply boldface to the range.

11. Format the dollar values using the Accounting Number Format style with no decimal places.

12. Save and then close the workbook file.

In this exercise, you will open an existing workbook and use your formatting skills to make the worksheet appear similar to Figure EX1.35.

FIGURE EX1.35   Work It Out EX-1B-E2: completed

	A	B	C	D	E
1	Geeks-For-Hire				
2					
3	REVENUE	Jun-13	Jul-13	Aug-13	
4	Programming	12,400	13,100		
5	Service Calls	450	540		
6	Technical Support	225	330		
7	Total Revenue	$13,075	$13,970	$0	
8	EXPENSES				
9	Bank Charges	25	25		
10	Depreciation	2,400	2,400		
11	Payroll Costs	10,000	10,000		
12	Telephone	275	275		
13	Total Expenses	$12,700	$12,700	$0	
14	PROFIT	$375	$1,270	$0	
15					
16					

1 Locate and open the exercise data file ex01b-ex02.xlsx. Ensure that the file is not in Protected View mode and then save it as ex01b-hw02.xlsx.

2 Increase the width of column A to 18 characters. Adjust the width of columns B and C to 10 characters.

3 Adjust the row height for rows 3 through 12 to 17.25.

4 Apply the Heading 1 cell style to the cell range A1:C1.

5 Insert a new row 7 and then a new row 13. (Hint: Refer to Figure EX1.35 for assistance.)

6 Enter the text labels Total Revenue and Total Expenses into cells A7 and A13, respectively.

7 Enter the required formulas to sum the total revenues and total expenses for the two months.

8 Apply boldface to the "Total Revenue" and "Total Expenses" rows, and then select a text color of Dark Blue, Text 2, Lighter 40% from the color palette.

9 Apply the Heading 3 cell style to the cell range A3:C3 and to A8:C8.

10 Apply the Total cell style to the cell range A14:C14.

11 Enter the required formulas in row 14 to subtract the total expenses from the total revenue figures. For example, in Jun-13, you would enter a formula that subtracted 12,700 (Total Expenses) from 13,075 (Total Revenue).

12 Apply currency formatting with no decimal places to rows 7, 13, and 14.

13 Using Format Painter, copy the formatting from the cell range C1:C14 to column D, in preparation for entering values for next month. Change the width for column D to 10 characters.

14 Enter the monthly heading for Aug-2013 in column D, and then copy the formulas from rows 7, 13, and 14 to the new column. Your worksheet should now appear similar to Figure EX1.35.

15 Save and then close the workbook file.

HANDS-ON EXERCISE: WORK IT OUT EX-1B-E3

In this exercise, you will be asked to reproduce the worksheet appearing in Figure EX1.36. Fortunately the original data is stored in an existing workbook, so you can focus solely on the formatting tasks.

FIGURE EX1.36 Work It Out EX-1B-E3: completed

1. Locate and open the exercise data file **ex01b-ex03.xlsx**. Ensure that the file is not in Protected View mode and then save it as **ex01b-hw03.xlsx**.

2. To begin, insert three additional rows: one between the title and column headings (row 2), one between the column headings and USD currency table (row 4), and one between the USD and EUR currency tables (row 7).

3. Adjust the heights of rows 2, 4, and 7 to 7.5 points.

4. Adjust the width for column A to 11 characters, and the widths of columns B through J to 9 characters.

5. Remove the column for the INR currency exchange rate.

6. Merge and center the title across the top of the page, between columns A and I. Format the title to appear White on a Red, Accent 2 background, with a Cambria, 13-point, and boldface font style.

7. Format the column headings to appear White on an Olive Green, Accent 3 background in boldface. Center the column headings within their respective cells, as shown in Figure EX1.36.

8. Format cells A5 and A8 to appear boldface, and cells A6 and A9 to appear italic.

9. Format the currency tables to appear using the Number format 3 decimal places.

10. Apply an All Borders outline to the currency tables and then shade the USD and EUR values using the Olive Green, Accent 3, Lighter 80% background, as shown in Figure EX1.36.

11. Move the cell pointer to cell A1 and remove the gridlines from displaying on the worksheet.

12. View the worksheet in Page Layout view.

13. Save and then close the workbook file.

Chapter Summary

Microsoft Excel is an electronic spreadsheet program used extensively in business for performing statistical analyses, summarizing numerical data, and publishing reports. Over the past few decades, spreadsheet software has proven to be the most robust and indispensable power tool for knowledge workers. You create a worksheet in Excel by typing text, numbers, dates, and formulas into cells. Editing the contents of a worksheet is also an important skill because of the frequency with which most worksheets are reused and modified. Like most applications, Excel provides the standard Cut, Copy, and Paste commands for manipulating a worksheet's contents. You can also modify a worksheet's structure by inserting and deleting cells, rows, and columns. Especially important for presentation is your ability to adjust a worksheet's row heights and column widths and even hide (and unhide) rows and columns temporarily. To enhance the appearance of worksheets, Excel offers many features and shortcuts that help you apply formatting to cells. You can select from various character formatting commands to change a cell's font typeface and size or to apply boldface, italic, and character underlining to its contents. The readability of numbers and dates is improved when you format values using currency and percent symbols, commas, and decimal places. Furthermore, you can change the appearance of a cell by aligning its contents, surrounding it with borders, or filling it with color. After the worksheet is formatted with your preferences, you can use various options to customize its output and send it to the printer. Congratulations! You are well on your way to becoming a proficient user of Microsoft Excel.

Chapter Key Terms

Application window, p. E-4
AutoCalculate, p. E-11
AutoFill, p. E-19
AutoSum, p. E-11
Backstage view, p. E-52
Cell, p. E-2
Cell alignment, p. E-46
Cell pointer, p. E-4
Cell range, p. E-4
Chart sheet, p. E-2

Document window, p. E-4
Fill handle, p. E-19
Flash Fill, p. E-19
Fonts, p. E-40
Format Painter, p. E-43
Formula, p. E-11
Formula bar, p. E-4
Gridlines, p. E-49
In-cell editing, p. E-16
Name box, p. E-4

Normal view, p. E-52
Page Break Preview, p. E-52
Page Layout view, p. E-52
Points, p. E-33
Quick Analysis, p. E-14
Status bar, p. E-11
Template, p. E-24
Workbook, p. E-2
Worksheet, p. E-2

On Your Own Exercise EX-1C-E1

This exercise provides an opportunity to practice several important skills covered in this chapter. Specifically, you have been asked to help create a professional-looking workbook for your university bookstore. To begin, open the exercise data file **ex01c-ex01.xlsx** and then ensure that the file is not in Protected View mode before saving it as **ex01c-hw01.xlsx**. Your screen should appear similar to Figure EX1.37.

FIGURE EX1.37   Starting worksheet for the University Bookstore

	A	B	C	D	E	F	G	H
1	University Bookstore							
2	ISBN	Title	Cost	Markup	Price	On Hand	Value	
3	0-201-066	Algorithm:	54	0.38		42		
4	0-02-3955	Fiction 10(	62.4	0.4		1039		
5	0-256-033	Intermedi:	64.95	0.4		430		
6	0-13-5262	Law and B	76.2	0.5		110		
7	0-201-409	Legal Guid	58.95	0.63		78		
8	0-07-0347	Marketing	55.75	0.475		339		
9								
10								

Complete the following tasks to reproduce the formatted worksheet in Figure EX1.38.

- Modify the structure of the worksheet by adding a new, empty row 2. Adjust the widths for columns A through G.

- Enter formula expressions into columns E and G. Calculate the price of each book in column E as the cost multiplied by the markup factor (1 + markup). Once you have completed entering and copying this formula, calculate the total value of the inventory in column G by multiplying the price of each book by the number of units on hand.

- Enter two AutoSum formulas to sum the values at the bottom of the On Hand (column F) and Value (column G) columns.

- Insert a new row 7 and then enter the data displayed for "Japan: Culture and History," as shown in Figure EX1.38. Make sure to copy the appropriate formulas into cells E7 and G7.

- Format the numeric values in the worksheet to appear similar to Figure EX1.38.

- Apply cell styles to format the column headings and the "Total Amounts" row.

- Make any other changes that you see fit in order to match the worksheet shown in Figure EX1.38. Save and then close the workbook.

FIGURE EX1.38   University Bookstore inventory worksheet

	A	B	C	D	E	F	G	H
1			**University Bookstore**					
2								
3	ISBN	Title	Cost	Markup	Price	On Hand	Value	
4	0-201-06672-6	Algorithms	$54.00	38.00%	$74.52	42	$3,129.84	
5	0-02-395540-6	Fiction 100 Anthology	$62.40	40.00%	$87.36	1,039	$90,767.04	
6	0-256-03331-5	Intermediate Accounting	$64.95	40.00%	$90.93	430	$39,099.90	
7	0-18-123456-X	Japan: Culture and History	$72.50	35.20%	$98.02	100	$9,802.00	
8	0-13-526293-3	Law and Business Admin	$76.20	50.00%	$114.30	110	$12,573.00	
9	0-201-40931-3	Legal Guide to Multimedia	$58.95	63.00%	$96.09	78	$7,494.90	
10	0-07-034745-X	Marketing Research	$55.75	47.50%	$82.23	339	$27,876.39	
11	**Total Amounts**					2,138	$190,743.08	
12								
13								

On Your Own Exercise EX-1C-E2

To practice working with data and formulas, open the **ex01c-ex02.xlsx** data file and then ensure that the file is not in Protected View mode before saving it as **ex01c-hw02.xlsx**. Enter some sample grades into column D of the worksheet for both courses. Sum the "Grade" and "Out Of" columns for each of the course totals. In cell F4, construct a formula that calculates the percentage grade (i.e., grade achieved divided by possible points) and then copy the formula to the remaining cells. Enter another formula to calculate the average grade for both courses by adding together the Course Total percentages using parentheses and then dividing by two (rather than basing the result on the points earned and available). Check your worksheet calculations against the results shown in Figure EX1.39.

After you have finished building the worksheet, edit some of the grades in order to check the formulas for accuracy and completeness. Apply formatting to the headings and numeric values, and then remove the gridlines, so your worksheet appears similar to Figure EX1.39.

FIGURE EX1.39   Compiling a grade book

	A	B	C	D	E	F	G	H
1			My Grade Book					
2								
3	Business Computer Systems			GRADE	OUT OF	%		
4		assigment #1		27	30	90.00%		
5		mid-term test		100	120	83.33%		
6		assignment #2		42	45	93.33%		
7		final exam		88	100	88.00%		
8		Course Total		257	295	87.12%		
9								
10	Pacific Rim Studies			GRADE	OUT OF	%		
11		assigment #1		49	50	98.00%		
12		mid-term test		24	30	80.00%		
13		assignment #2		39	50	78.00%		
14		final exam		68	80	85.00%		
15		Course Total		180	210	85.71%		
16								
17	Average of Both Courses:					86.42%		
18								
19								

Summarizing Data in Excel

Summarizing data in a worksheet requires the use of formulas and functions, as well as a clear understanding of cells and ranges. While the term *cell range* is commonly used to describe a "from here to there" area on a worksheet, it can also reference a three-dimensional area, crossing multiple worksheets within a workbook. A new workbook contains three worksheets named Sheet1, Sheet2, and Sheet3, accessed by clicking their tabs appearing along the bottom of the document window. Think of each worksheet as a tear-off page on a paper notepad.

In this chapter, you learn that a cell range can be given a nickname, or **range name**, which can be used to facilitate entering formulas. For example, the formula expression =Revenue-Expenses is far easier to understand than =c5-c6. Working with cell references from more than one worksheet adds another level of complexity. For example, if the value for Revenue is stored on Sheet1 and the value for Expenses is stored on Sheet2, the formula using cell addresses would read =Sheet1!c5-Sheet2!c6. Notice that the worksheet name is separated from the cell address using an exclamation point (!). By default, range names already contain this information, making them far easier to remember than these cryptic expressions.

Since the earliest versions of Excel, users have been able to summarize their numerical data using graphs and charts. Although these graphics were acceptable for in-house business reports and school projects, they often lacked the depth and quality required by professional users. Until now. Excel 2013 provides the ability to create visually stunning worksheets and charts that are suitable for formal business presentations, color print slides, published reports, and web pages. In this chapter, you learn how to use formulas, functions, sparklines, and charts to bring life to your worksheet data.

PROJECT

Preparing a Sales Forecast

In this project, you will explore the power of using formulas and functions in preparing a sales forecasting worksheet. In addition to summing values, you will use Excel's built-in functions and charting features to summarize and present the data contained therein.

This chapter will provide you with the core skills required to use Excel productively in many situations. The skills introduced in this project will continue to be used and developed in later projects.

THE SITUATION

Gourmet Blenz Coffee Shop

John Mahoney is the owner of the Gourmet Blenz Coffee Shop in Madison, Wisconsin. Over the past six months, John has experimented in offering various blends to determine what products are most appealing to his customers. Unfortunately, the worksheet of monthly sales results that he has constructed provides lots of data, but not much information. He has asked for your help in summarizing the data and in extracting any identifiable trends.

Using Formulas and Functions in a Sales Forecast

This project introduces you to Excel's built-in functions for performing calculations. Do not let the word *function* conjure up visions of your last calculus class; functions are merely shortcuts that you use in place of entering lengthy and complicated formulas. As you will see, functions are incredible time-savers that can increase your productivity and efficiency in creating informative worksheets.

PROJECT FILE: *Available at* **www.mhhe.com/office2013projectlearn**

PROJECT OBJECTIVES

After completing this project, you will be able to:

- Define and apply names for cells and cell ranges.

- Understand the difference between absolute and relative cell addresses.

- Enter built-in functions by typing and by using the Insert Function dialog box.

- Use mathematical and statistical functions, including SUM, AVERAGE, and MEDIAN.

- Use the MIN and MAX functions to extract the lowest and highest values in a range and the COUNT function to count cell entries.

- Use date and time functions, including NOW and TODAY.

- Use the IF logical function for decision branching.

- Use the VLOOKUP and HLOOKUP functions to retrieve data from a list

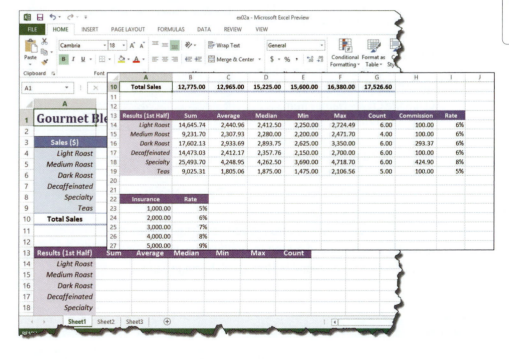

LESSON EXCEL 2A1
Working with Named Cell Ranges

LESSON OVERVIEW

By naming individual cells and groups of cells in a worksheet, you can make formulas much easier to read and construct. To name a selected cell range, you click in the Name box, located to the left of the Formula bar, and type a unique name with no spaces. Another method is to use the Define Name command on the FORMULAS tab in the Ribbon. Lastly, you can create range names automatically from the row and column headings appearing in a worksheet. Once created, you can modify and delete range names using the Name Manager dialog box or paste a list of range names into cells on the worksheet.

You can then refer to this list when you are building formula expressions or when you need to jump to a particular spot in the worksheet.

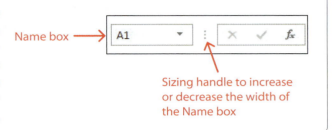

Name box →

Sizing handle to increase or decrease the width of the Name box

SKILLS PREVIEW

Name a cell range using the Name box	• SELECT the desired cell or cell range. CLICK in the Name box. TYPE *a range name*, such as "Profit." PRESS `Enter`.
Name a cell range based on adjoining row or column labels	• SELECT the desired cell or cell range, including the row and column labels (e.g., monthly headings or product names). CLICK the FORMULAS tab and locate the Defined Names group. CLICK the Create Names from Selection command. SELECT the location of the labels that you want to use for names, as shown in this dialog box.
Display the Name Manager dialog box for managing range names	• CLICK the FORMULAS tab and locate the Defined Names group. CLICK the Name Manager command. CLICK the New command button to add new range names, *or* CLICK the Edit command button to modify range names, *or* CLICK the Delete command button to delete range names.

PROJECT PRACTICE

1. After launching Microsoft Excel, locate and open the project data file **ex02a.xlsx**. On the FILE tab, use the Save As command to save the file as **ex02a-salesforecast.xlsx**. Your worksheet should appear similar to Figure EX2.1 before proceeding.

	A	B	C	D	E	F	G	H	I
1	**Gourmet Blenz Coffee Shop**								
2									
3	**Sales ($)**	**Jan**	**Feb**	**Mar**	**Apr**	**May**	**June**		
4	*Light Roast*	2,400	2,250	2,300	2,425				
5	*Medium Roast*			2,250	2,200				
6	*Dark Roast*	3,350	2,900	2,625	2,750				
7	*Decaffeinated*	2,700	2,650	2,300	2,150				
8	*Specialty*	4,325	3,690	4,150	4,200				
9	*Teas*		1,475	1,600	1,875				
10	**Total Sales**								
11									
12									
13	**Results (1st Half)**	**Sum**	**Average**	**Median**	**Min**	**Max**	**Count**		
14	*Light Roast*								
15	*Medium Roast*								
16	*Dark Roast*								
17	*Decaffeinated*								
18	*Specialty*								

Sheet1   Sheet2   Sheet3   (+)

2 To define a range name on the worksheet, you must first select the range and then apply the name:

SELECT the cell range B10:G10

CLICK in the Name box, which appears immediately above column A.

TYPE TotalSales (with no extra space between the two words).

PRESS Enter.

(*Result:* In the Name box, you should now see "TotalSales" appear, with the range still highlighted.)

3 You can use a shortcut for naming more cells in the worksheet:

SELECT the cell range B3:G9.

CLICK the FORMULAS tab and locate the Defined Names group.

CLICK the Create from Selection command.

(*Result:* The Create Names from Selection dialog box appears.)

4 Excel evaluates your selected cell range and provides the Top row recommendation in the dialog box. To accept this option and proceed:

CLICK OK.

5 Let's review what you've done in the previous steps:

CLICK the drop-down arrow attached to the Name box.

CHOOSE Feb from the list.

(*Result:* Notice that the cell range C4:C9 is selected and that the name "Feb" appears in the Name box. Whenever you need to reference this cell range, you can now use the range name "Feb.")

6 Using the same process, name the monthly sales results for each product:

SELECT the cell range A4:G9.

CLICK the Create Names from Selection command.

7 Ensure that the Left column check box is the only one enabled. Then:

CLICK OK to define the names.

8 To test these new range names:

CLICK the drop-down arrow for the Name box.

SELECT Medium_Roast from the list.

(*Result:* The cell range B5:G5 is highlighted. Notice that Excel places an underscore between the two words, Medium and Roast, in order to create an acceptable, single-word range name.)

9 To delete or modify a range name, you use the Name Manager dialog box. To begin:

CLICK the FORMULAS tab and locate the Defined Names group.

CLICK Name Manager command.

(*Result:* The Name Manager dialog box appears, as shown in Figure EX2.2, listing all of the defined range names and providing command buttons to help you manage the contents.)

FIGURE EX2.2 The Name Manager dialog box

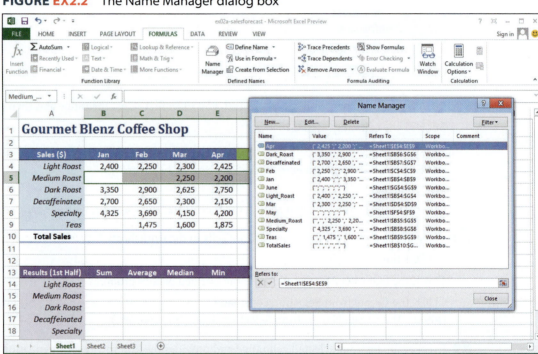

10 To delete the first range name you created:

SELECT TotalSales in the list box area.

CLICK the Delete command button.

(*Result:* A warning dialog box is displayed.)

11 CLICK OK to proceed with the deletion.

(*Result:* The "TotalSales" range name is removed from the workbook.)

12 As a final step, click the Close command button to close the Name Manager dialog box and then save your file.

LESSON EXCEL 2A2
Using Relative and Absolute Cell Addresses

LESSON OVERVIEW

You can enter two types of cell references into formulas: relative and absolute. The difference between the two types becomes especially important when you start copying and moving formulas in your worksheet. When copied, a **relative cell address** appearing in a formula will adjust itself automatically, because the cell reference is relative to where it sits in the worksheet. On the other hand, an **absolute cell address** always refers to an exact cell location in the worksheet.

The formulas that you have entered so far have all used relative cell references—Excel's default. To specify an absolute reference, you must precede each column letter and row number in a cell address with a dollar sign. For example, to make cell B5 an absolute cell reference, you type $B$5. A **mixed cell address**, on the other hand, locks only a portion of a cell address by inserting a dollar sign ($) before either the address's column letter or row number, such as B$5. Sometimes it helps to vocalize the word *absolutely* whenever you see a dollar sign in a cell address; you would read $B$5 as "absolutely column B and absolutely row 5."

SKILLS PREVIEW

Convert a relative cell address to an absolute or mixed cell address using a shortcut key	• POSITION the insertion point in (or after) the desired cell address (in the Formula bar or in a dialog box entry). PRESS **F4** (ABS key; ABS stands for absolute) repeatedly to toggle dollar signs before the column letter and row number.

PROJECT PRACTICE

1. Ensure that **ex02a-salesforecast.xlsx** is open.

2. You can use a formula to extend the sales values for each product by a specific growth factor. Do the following:

   SELECT cell F2.

   TYPE 5%.

   SELECT cell G2.

   TYPE 7%.

   PRESS Enter.

   (*Result:* You will use these cells, F2 and G2, to compute the forecasted sales in the columns below.)

3. To enter the forecasted sales growth formula for May:

   SELECT cell F4.

   TYPE =e4*(1+f2).

   PRESS Enter.

   (*Result:* The value 2,546 appears in cell F4.)

   >
   > **TIP**
   >
   > Although we direct you to type the formula, you may find it easier to use the mouse or keyboard cursor keys to select the cells specified (i.e., e4 and f2). Please use the method that is most comfortable for you.

4 Next, copy the formula to the rest of the cells in the column using the fill handle. Do the following:

SELECT cell F4.

DRAG the fill handle to cell F9.
(*Result:* Notice that the result is not what you may have expected, as shown here.)

	5%	7%
Apr	**May**	**June**
2,425	2,546	
2,200	#VALUE!	
2,750	#######	
2,150	#VALUE!	
4,200	#######	
1,875	#VALUE!	

5 Review the contents of each cell using the Formula bar, beginning with cell F5. Can you find the problem with the copied formula? Because you entered the formula using relative cell references, each cell address is adjusted (in this case, the rows are incremented) automatically when you copy it downward. So, instead of E5*(1+F2), it reads E5*(1+F3).

6 CLICK the Undo button (↶ ▾) in the Quick Access toolbar to undo the previous fill operation.

7 To lock the cell containing the growth factor (5%) in place, you must edit the formula to include an absolute cell reference. To begin:

SELECT cell F4.

8 Move the mouse pointer to the Formula bar and do the following:

POSITION the I-beam mouse pointer over F2 (preferably between the F and 2).

CLICK once to enter Edit mode.
(*Result:* If done properly, the cell addresses will change color and appear selected in the worksheet.)

9 While you could type the $ signs to precede the column letter and row number, you can use the keyboard shortcut instead:

PRESS **F4** (ABS) once.

CLICK the Enter button (✔) in the Formula bar.
(*Result:* Your formula should now read =E4*(1+$F$2).)

10 Use the fill handle to copy the formula to the remaining cells in the range F4:F9. Your screen should appear similar to Figure EX2.3 before proceeding. (*Result:* If you review the results, you'll notice that only the product row number changes in each formula and the F2 cell address remains locked and absolute in the column.)

FIGURE EX2.3 Using the fill handle to copy the revised formula

	A	B	C	D	E	F	G	H	I
1	**Gourmet Blenz Coffee Shop**								
2						5%	7%		
3	**Sales ($)**	**Jan**	**Feb**	**Mar**	**Apr**	**May**	**June**		
4	Light Roast	2,400	2,250	2,300	2,425	2,546			
5	Medium Roast			2,250	2,200	2,310			
6	Dark Roast	3,350	2,900	2,625	2,750	2,888			
7	Decaffeinated	2,700	2,650	2,300	2,150	2,258			
8	Specialty	4,325	3,690	4,150	4,200	4,410			
9	Teas		1,475	1,600	1,875	1,969			
10	**Total Sales**								
11									
12									
13	**Results (1st Half)**	**Sum**	**Average**	**Median**	**Min**	**Max**	**Count**		
14	Light Roast								
15	Medium Roast								
16	Dark Roast								
17	Decaffeinated								
18	Specialty								

Formula bar: =E4*(1+$F$2)

11 For the next column, use a range name for the monthly growth factor. Do the following:

SELECT cell G2.

CLICK in the Name box.

TYPE **JuneGrowth**.

PRESS [Enter].

(*Result:* You have now named cell G2 "JuneGrowth." Remember that range names use absolute cell references, and include the sheet name. Therefore, JuneGrowth refers to cell Sheet1!$G$2.)

12 To enter the growth formula for June:

SELECT cell G4.

TYPE **=f4*(1+JuneGrowth)**.

PRESS [Enter].

(*Result:* Notice that when you start typing "JuneGrowth," Excel displays a pop-up list, like the one shown here, of possible range names that you may want to insert. You can double-click one of these names or continue typing.)

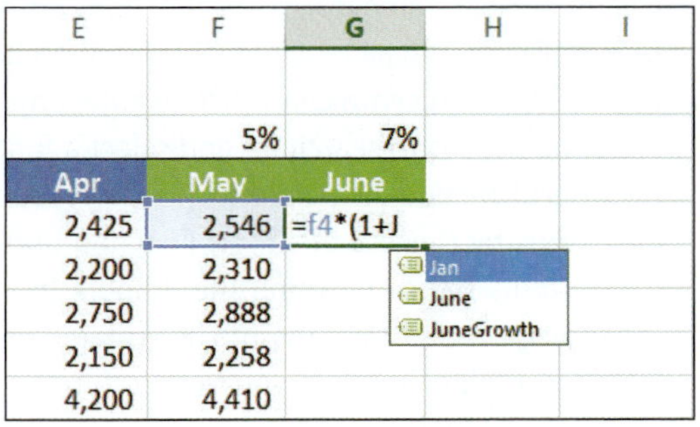

E	F	G	H	I
		5%	7%	
Apr	May	June		
2,425	2,546	=f4*(1+J		
2,200	2,310		Jan	
2,750	2,888		June	
2,150	2,258		JuneGrowth	
4,200	4,410			

13 Use the fill handle for cell G4 to copy the formula to the remaining cells in the range G4:G9. Your worksheet should now appear similar to Figure EX2.4.

14 Change the growth factors to 10% for May and 12% for June. Notice the increase in sales for each month that results from these two growth factors. Before proceeding, return the growth factor values to 5% and 7%.

15 Save your file.

FIGURE **EX2.4** Entering the forecasted growth formulas

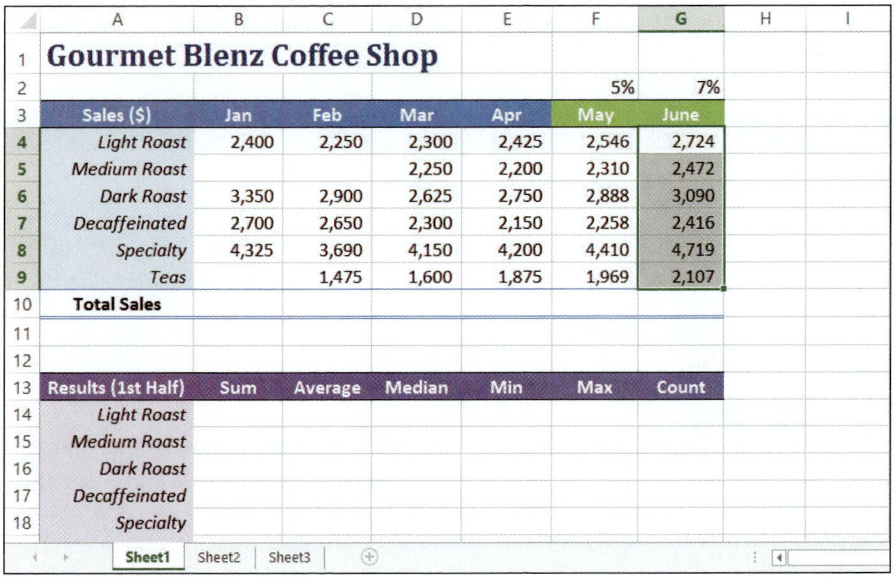

	A	B	C	D	E	F	G	H	I
1	**Gourmet Blenz Coffee Shop**								
2						5%	7%		
3	Sales ($)	Jan	Feb	Mar	Apr	May	June		
4	Light Roast	2,400	2,250	2,300	2,425	2,546	2,724		
5	Medium Roast			2,250	2,200	2,310	2,472		
6	Dark Roast	3,350	2,900	2,625	2,750	2,888	3,090		
7	Decaffeinated	2,700	2,650	2,300	2,150	2,258	2,416		
8	Specialty	4,325	3,690	4,150	4,200	4,410	4,719		
9	Teas		1,475	1,600	1,875	1,969	2,107		
10	Total Sales								
11									
12									
13	Results (1st Half)	Sum	Average	Median	Min	Max	Count		
14	Light Roast								
15	Medium Roast								
16	Dark Roast								
17	Decaffeinated								
18	Specialty								

Sheet1 | Sheet2 | Sheet3

Entering Built-in Functions, Starting with SUM

LESSON OVERVIEW

There are several methods for entering a function into a worksheet cell. You can type a function name, preceded by an equal sign (=), and then enter its **arguments** (labels, values, or cell references). Many functions are quite complex, however, and all require that you remember the precise order, called **syntax**, in which to enter arguments. An easier method is to search for and select a function from the Insert Function dialog box shown here. You access this dialog box by clicking the Insert Function button (f_x) in the Formula bar or by using the Ribbon. In addition to organizing Excel's **functions** into tidy categories, the Insert Function dialog box lets you view a function's syntax, along with a brief description.

In this lesson, you will use the **SUM** function to add values appearing in a range of cells. This built-in function saves you from having to enter long addition formulas, such as =A1+A2+A3...+A99. As you have already seen, the AutoSum button (Σ ▾) may also be used to insert the SUM function into a worksheet cell automatically.

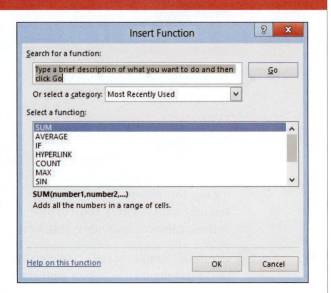

SKILLS PREVIEW

Use the SUM function to sum values in a cell range	• =**SUM**(*range*) where the range can be a cell range (e.g., A3:A8), individual cell addresses (e.g., A3, A5, A7), or a range name (e.g., SalesTax).

PROJECT PRACTICE

1 Ensure that **ex02a-salesforecast.xlsx** is open.

2 To demonstrate another method for summing values apart from using the AutoSum button (Σ ▾), you can type the SUM function into the Total Sales row in the worksheet. Do the following:

SELECT the cell range B10:G10.

TYPE =**sum(b4:b9)**.

PRESS Ctrl + Enter .

(*Result:* The function is entered into all cells in the selected range. Notice that you type the function using the cell range parameters for the active cell (B10), in this case summing the cell range B4:B9.)

3 You can also enter the SUM function using range names:

SELECT cell B14.

TYPE =**sum(Light_Roast)**.

PRESS Enter .

(*Result:* The cell range for Light_Roast sales, B4:G4, is summed.)

4 To double-check this result:

SELECT the cell range B4:G4.
(*Result:* Look into the AutoCalculate area of the Status bar. You should notice that the formatted value of 14,646 appears, which matches the rounded result of 14645.74 that appears in cell B14.)

5 Use the Insert Function dialog box to practice entering the SUM function for the Medium Roast sales. Do the following:

SELECT cell B15.

CLICK Insert Function button (𝑓𝑥) in the Formula bar.
(*Result:* The Insert Function dialog box appears, as shown on page E-72.)

6 Ensure that SUM is selected in the list box. (If you cannot find a function, type its name or description into the Search for a function text box and click the Go command button. Excel displays the closest functions to your request in the Select a function list box.) Do the following:

CLICK OK.

7 In the Function Arguments dialog box (see Figure EX2.5):

TYPE Medium_Roast in the Number1 range selection text box, overwriting any existing cell reference information.
(*Result:* When a proper range is entered, values from the range appear to the right of the range selection text box. If the range is valid, the result of the SUM operation appears below this area. Other helpful information is also presented in the dialog box.)

FIGURE EX2.5   The Function Arguments dialog box

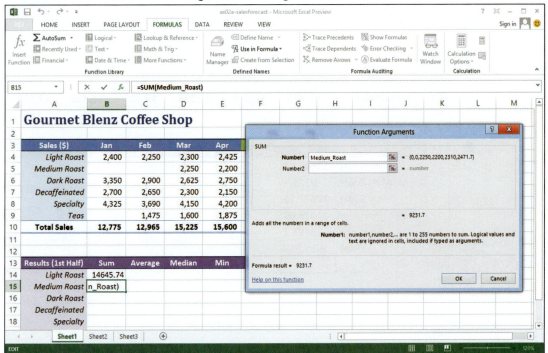

8 To insert the function into cell B15:

CLICK OK.
(*Result:* The value 9231.7 should now appear in the cell.)

9 For practice, insert the SUM function using a variation of the previous steps:

SELECT cell B16.

CLICK the FORMULAS tab and locate the Function Library group.

CLICK the Insert Function button (f_x).

10 In the Insert Function dialog box that appears:

SELECT Sum in the list box.

CLICK OK to proceed.

11 Rather than type the range name for the selected cells, use the mouse to select the cell range. Make sure the cell reference is highlighted in the Number1 range selection text box and move the dialog box, by dragging its Title bar, so that you can see row 6 in your worksheet. Do the following to enter the range to sum:

DRAG across the cell range B6:G6.

(*Result:* Notice the dialog box collapses so that you can better see your worksheet. As you drag across the range, the cell addresses are entered until you reach the last cell, when Excel replaces the range address with the range name "Dark_Roast." When you release the mouse button after the drag process, you are returned to the full version of the Function Arguments dialog box.)

12 To complete the entry:

CLICK OK.

13 On your own, enter the SUM function by typing and by using the Insert Function dialog box for cells B17, B18, and B19. Your completed worksheet should appear similar to Figure EX2.6.

14 Save your file.

FIGURE EX2.6   Summing values in the worksheet

	A	B	C	D	E	F	G	H	I
10	**Total Sales**	**12,775**	**12,965**	**15,225**	**15,600**	**16,380**	**17,527**		
11									
12									
13	**Results (1st Half)**	**Sum**	**Average**	**Median**	**Min**	**Max**	**Count**		
14	*Light Roast*	14645.74							
15	*Medium Roast*	9231.7							
16	*Dark Roast*	17602.13							
17	*Decaffeinated*	14473.03							
18	*Specialty*	25493.7							
19	*Teas*	9025.313							
20									
21									
22									
23									
24									
25									
26									
27									
28									

Sheet1 | Sheet2 | Sheet3

Calculating Average and Median Values

LESSON OVERVIEW

You use the **AVERAGE** function to compute the average value, sometimes called the arithmetic mean, for a range of cells. This function adds all the numeric values in a range and then divides the sum by the number of cells used in the calculation. The **MEDIAN** function, on the other hand, computes the middle value in a set of numbers. Both are useful statistical measures of center for a range of worksheet values.

SKILLS PREVIEW

Use the AVERAGE function to calculate the mean of a range	• **=AVERAGE(*range*)** where the range can be a cell range (e.g., A3:A8), individual cell addresses (e.g., A3, A5, A7), or a range name (e.g., SalesTax).
Use the MEDIAN function to calculate the median value for a range	• **=MEDIAN(*range*)** where the range can be a cell range (e.g., A3:A8), individual cell addresses (e.g., A3, A5, A7), or a range name (e.g., SalesTax).

PROJECT PRACTICE

1 Ensure that **ex02a-salesforecast.xlsx** is open.

2 Start by entering the AVERAGE function to calculate the average monthly sales for each product. Do the following:

SELECT cell C14.

TYPE **=average(Light_Roast)**.

PRESS [Enter].

(*Result:* The value, 2440.956, appears in cell C14.)

3 Remember that range names use absolute cell references. Therefore, you cannot copy this formula to the rest of the cells in the column. However, you can use the [Ctrl]+[Enter] shortcut with relative cell references, as follows:

SELECT the cell range C15:C19.

TYPE **=average(**.

4 You must now complete the function by selecting the cell range to average for the "Medium Roast" product category. Use the mouse to make the selection in this step. To do so:

DRAG across the cell range B5:G5.

(*Result:* Your screen should now appear similar to Figure EX2.7. Even though cells B5 and C5 are empty, you must include them in the selection because you will copy the formula down to the other product categories that do have values stored in those cells.)

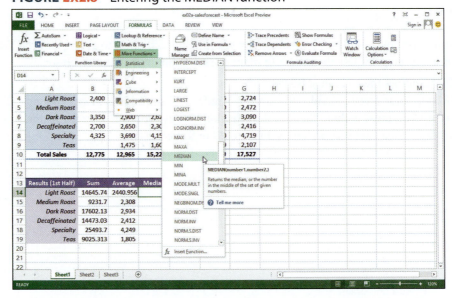

5 To complete the function and copy it to the other cells in the selection:

TYPE **)**.

PRESS **Ctrl** + **Enter** .

6 On your own, CLICK in the cell range C14:C19 and review the function entries and range arguments. Then, when you are ready to proceed:

SELECT cell D14.

7 Use the Function Arguments dialog box to help insert the MEDIAN function. Do the following:

CLICK the FORMULAS tab and locate the Function Library group.

CLICK the More Functions button.

CHOOSE Statistical.

CHOOSE Median from the list menu, as shown in Figure EX2.8.

FIGURE **EX2.8** Entering the MEDIAN function

8 With the default range selection, C14, highlighted:

CLICK the Collapse Dialog button (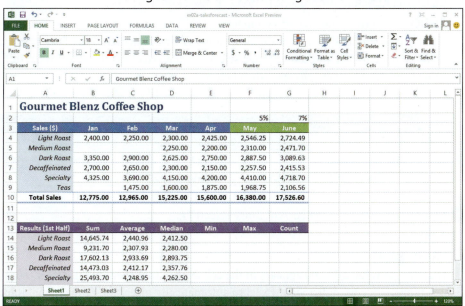) for the Number1 range selection text box.

SELECT the cell range B4:G4.

(*Result:* Notice that Light_Roast appears in the dialog box.)

9 To continue entering the function:

CLICK the Expand Dialog button ( ).

CLICK OK.

(*Result:* The value 2412.5 should now appear in cell D14. Because there are an even number of entries, the values are sorted from smallest to largest and the middle two numbers, 2400 and 2425, are added together and then divided by two to calculate the median.)

10 Complete the remaining cells in the column using whatever method you prefer for entering the MEDIAN function.

11 Format the values in the Results area to appear more uniform. Do the following:

SELECT the cell range B14 to G19.

CLICK the HOME tab and locate the Number group.

CLICK the Comma Style button ( ).

12 On your own, format the values in the cell range B4 to G10 to use the default Comma Style as well.

13 You can adjust the column widths to display the newly formatted values. To do so:

SELECT the cell range B14:G14.

CLICK the Format drop-down command in the Cells group.

CHOOSE Column Width.

TYPE 11 in the dialog box.

CLICK OK.

(*Result:* The widths for columns B through G are updated to 11 characters. Position the cell pointer in cell A1, and check to see that your screen appears similar to Figure EX2.9.)

14 Save your file.

FIGURE EX2.9   Entering functions and formatting the worksheet

Extracting MIN, MAX, and COUNT Values

LESSON OVERVIEW

You use the **MIN** and **MAX** functions to determine the minimum (lowest) and maximum (highest) values in a range of cells. These functions are useful in pulling information from your worksheet, such as the highest and lowest mark appearing in a teacher's grade book.

The **COUNT** function counts the number of cells in a range that contain numeric or date values, but ignores cells containing text labels. You can use this function to determine how many entries are present in a worksheet column.

SKILLS PREVIEW

Use the MIN function to extract the minimum or lowest value in a range	• **=MIN(*range*)** where the range can be a cell range (e.g., A3:A8), individual cell addresses (e.g., A3, A5, A7), or a range name (e.g., SalesTax).
Use the MAX function to extract the maximum or highest value in a range	• **=MAX(*range*)** where the range can be a cell range (e.g., A3:A8), individual cell addresses (e.g., A3, A5, A7), or a range name (e.g., SalesTax).
Use the COUNT function to count the number of values (i.e., numeric and date entries) in a range	• **=COUNT(*range*)** where the range can be a cell range (e.g., A3:A8), individual cell addresses (e.g., A3, A5, A7), or a range name (e.g., SalesTax).

PROJECT PRACTICE

1 Ensure that **ex02a-salesforecast.xlsx** is open.

2 To find the minimum monthly sales for the "Light Roast" product category, you can use the Auto-Sum button on the HOME tab. Do the following:

SELECT cell E14.

CLICK the HOME tab and locate the Editing group.

CLICK the AutoSum drop-down button (Σ ⌄).

CHOOSE Min from the drop-down menu.

(*Hint:* Make sure that you click the drop-down arrow attached to the button in order to display the menu. Notice by the automatic range selection that Excel assumes you want to find the minimum value from the adjacent cells, as shown below.)

		Sum	Average	Median	Min	Max	Count
12							
13	**Results (1st Half)**	Sum	Average	Median	Min	Max	Count
14	*Light Roast*	14,645.74	2,440.96	2,412.50	=MIN(B14:D14)		
15	*Medium Roast*	9,231.70	2,307.93	2,280.00	MIN(**number1**, [number2], ...)		
16	*Dark Roast*	17,602.13	2,933.69	2,893.75			

3 Rather than accepting the current range selection:

TYPE **b4:g4**.

PRESS Enter.

(*Result:* The value 2,250.00 appears in the cell. Notice that we didn't use the mouse to drag across the cell range, since we didn't want Excel to automatically insert the range name. Range names are very useful sometimes, but other times we need to have relative cell references in our formulas.)

4 Use the same method to find the maximum monthly sales value for the Light Roast blend:

SELECT cell F14.

CLICK the AutoSum drop-down button (Σ ▾).

CHOOSE Max from the drop-down menu.

TYPE **b4:g4**.

PRESS **Enter**.

(*Result:* The value 2,724.49 appears in the cell.)

5 Enter the COUNT function in the same manner:

SELECT cell G14.

CLICK the AutoSum drop-down button (Σ ▾).

CHOOSE Count Numbers from the drop-down menu.

TYPE **b4:g4**.

PRESS **Enter**.

(*Result:* The value 6.00 appears in the cell with a COUNT function.)

6 You can copy these functions to the remaining cells in the columns. Do the following:

SELECT the cell range E14:G19.

(*Result:* Notice that the three cells containing the MIN, MAX, and COUNT functions appear in the top row of the selected range.)

7 To fill the rest of the columns with these three functions:

CLICK the HOME tab and locate the Editing group.

CLICK the Fill button (⬇ ▾).

CHOOSE Down (⬇).

(*Result:* The functions are copied to the remaining cells. Notice that the COUNT function shows the number of months with numeric data included in the calculations.)

> **MORE INFO**
>
> The COUNT function has a second cousin named COUNTA. Whereas COUNT tallies the cells containing numbers and dates, **COUNTA** counts all nonblank cells. The primary difference, therefore, is that the COUNTA function includes text labels in its calculations.

---

8 CLICK in each of the cells and review the functions and range arguments entered. Your worksheet should now appear similar to Figure EX2.10.

9 Save your file.

FIGURE EX2.10 Filling a range with functions

	A	B	C	D	E	F	G	H	I
2						5%	7%		
3	Sales ($)	Jan	Feb	Mar	Apr	May	June		
4	Light Roast	2,400.00	2,250.00	2,300.00	2,425.00	2,546.25	2,724.49		
5	Medium Roast			2,250.00	2,200.00	2,310.00	2,471.70		
6	Dark Roast	3,350.00	2,900.00	2,625.00	2,750.00	2,887.50	3,089.63		
7	Decaffeinated	2,700.00	2,650.00	2,300.00	2,150.00	2,257.50	2,415.53		
8	Specialty	4,325.00	3,690.00	4,150.00	4,200.00	4,410.00	4,718.70		
9	Teas		1,475.00	1,600.00	1,875.00	1,968.75	2,106.56		
10	**Total Sales**	12,775.00	12,965.00	15,225.00	15,600.00	16,380.00	17,526.60		
11									
12									
13	Results (1st Half)	Sum	Average	Median	Min	Max	Count		
14	Light Roast	14,645.74	2,440.96	2,412.50	2,250.00	2,724.49	6.00		
15	Medium Roast	9,231.70	2,307.93	2,280.00	2,200.00	2,471.70	4.00		
16	Dark Roast	17,602.13	2,933.69	2,893.75	2,625.00	3,350.00	6.00		
17	Decaffeinated	14,473.03	2,412.17	2,357.76	2,150.00	2,700.00	6.00		
18	Specialty	25,493.70	4,248.95	4,262.50	3,690.00	4,718.70	6.00		
19	Teas	9,025.31	1,805.06	1,875.00	1,475.00	2,106.56	5.00		
20									

Sheet1 | Sheet2 | Sheet3

Entering Date Values Using NOW and TODAY

LESSON OVERVIEW

You use the NOW and TODAY functions to display the date and time in your worksheets. The **NOW** function returns the current date and time as provided by your computer's internal clock. The way the function's result appears in a cell (i.e., Jan-13, 11:00am, or 41234) is determined by the date and time formatting selected. Unlike the NOW function, the **TODAY** function provides only the current date. Neither of these functions requires an argument (but the parentheses must still be present).

SKILLS PREVIEW

Use the TODAY function to display the current date	• =TODAY()
Use the NOW function to display the current date and time	• =NOW()

PROJECT PRACTICE

1 Ensure that **ex02a-salesforecast.xlsx** is open.

2 To display the current date and time on a worksheet, do the following:

SELECT cell A2.

TYPE **The date & time:**.

PRESS →.

3 Now, enter the TODAY function to display the date:

TYPE **=today()**.

PRESS →.

4 With the cell pointer in cell C2, enter the NOW function to display the time:

TYPE **=now()**.

PRESS **Enter**.

(*Result:* In the next step, you will format the display of the time so that it appears in cell C2.)

5 To format the value returned by the NOW function:

SELECT cell C2.

CLICK the HOME tab and locate the Number group.

CLICK the Number Format drop-down list box.

SELECT Time from the list menu.

(*Result:* The current time should now appear using the format hh:mm:ss AM/PM. If you see "#" symbols in the cell, adjust the column width by dragging its column border to the right. Your entry should appear similar to the image shown here.)

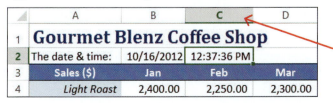

You may need to increase the width of the column to see the time formatting.

6 You can customize the display of the date value in cell B2. Do the following:

SELECT cell B2.

CLICK the HOME tab and locate the Number group.

CLICK the dialog box launcher () labeled as Number Format in the tooltip.
(*Result:* The Format Cells dialog box should now appear with Date selected in the Category list box.)

7 In the Format Cells dialog box:

SELECT Custom in the Category list box.

TYPE **ddd, mm-dd** in the Type text box.
(*Result:* Notice that the Sample area shows how the current cell entry will appear when formatted, as shown in Figure EX2.11. Review some of the other custom formats to see how the various symbol combinations are used.)

8 CLICK OK to apply the formatting.

9 Save your file.

FIGURE EX2.11 Creating a custom date format

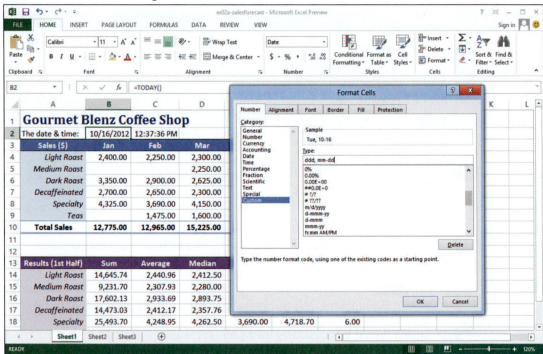

Making Decisions Using Logical Functions

LESSON OVERVIEW

You use the **IF** function when you need to employ conditional logic in your worksheets. The IF function lets you test for a condition and then, depending on the result, perform one of two calculations. **Conditional expressions** make use of the following **comparison operators**: equal (=), not equal (<>), less than (<), less than or equal to (<=), greater than (>), and greater than or equal to (>=). As you become more experienced in Excel, you will find many uses for the IF function in building dynamic, user-driven worksheets.

SKILLS PREVIEW

Use the IF function to test for a condition and perform a calculation based on the result	• **=IF(condition, true, false)** where *condition* is an expression to be evaluated as either true or false (e.g., b4>100) and, where *true* and *false* are the conditional entries or calculations that you want performed (e.g., "Over 100!" or b4*10%).

PROJECT PRACTICE

1. Ensure that **ex02a-salesforecast.xlsx** is open.

2. You've decided to pay your store manager an annual bonus based on the average monthly sales volume for each product. At the lowest level, the bonus per product will be $100. However, if the average monthly sales for any product is greater than $2,500, the bonus is calculated as 10 percent of the average monthly sales. To perform this calculation, you will use the IF function. To begin:

    SELECT cell H13.

    TYPE Commission.

    PRESS Enter .

3. To increase the width of the column to its best fit:

    POSITION the mouse pointer over the cell's right border in the column frame area.

    DOUBLE-CLICK the cell border.

    (*Result:* The column width is increased so that the word *Commission* can be viewed fully.)

4. To calculate the bonus for the Light Roast blend:

    SELECT cell H14.

    CLICK the FORMULAS tab and locate the Function Library group.

    CLICK the Logical command.

    SELECT IF from the list menu.

    (*Result:* The Function Arguments dialog box appears, as shown in Figure EX2.12.)

FIGURE EX2.12   Function Arguments dialog box for the IF function

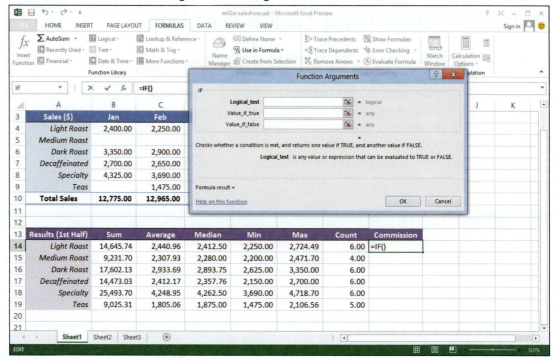

⑤ In the Logical_test text box, you enter the condition that you want to evaluate. In this exercise, you need to determine whether the average monthly sales volume for the Light Roast blend is greater than $2,500. To do so:

TYPE c14>2500.

PRESS Tab to move to the next text box.

(*Result:* Notice that the dialog box displays the answer to the logical expression, "= FALSE," to the right of the text box.)

⑥ In the Value_if_true text box, enter the expression you want to calculate if the value in cell C14 is greater than $2,500; in this case, multiply the sales by 10 percent. Do the following:

TYPE c14*10%.

PRESS Tab.

⑦ In the Value_if_false text box, enter the lowest bonus level:

TYPE 100.

(*Result:* Notice that the calculated result, = 100, is shown in the dialog box.)

⑧ CLICK OK to enter the function into cell H14.

(*Result:* The Formula bar for cell H14 should now read =IF(C14>2500,C14*10%,100).)

⑨ Using the fill handle, copy the function in cell H14 to the cell range H15:H19. Format the cell range to appear using the Comma style. (*Result:* Your screen should appear similar to Figure EX2.13.)

⑩ Save your file.

FIGURE EX2.13 Formatting the results of the IF function

	A	B	C	D	E	F	G	H	I
3	Sales ($)	Jan	Feb	Mar	Apr	May	June		
4	Light Roast	2,400.00	2,250.00	2,300.00	2,425.00	2,546.25	2,724.49		
5	Medium Roast			2,250.00	2,200.00	2,310.00	2,471.70		
6	Dark Roast	3,350.00	2,900.00	2,625.00	2,750.00	2,887.50	3,089.63		
7	Decaffeinated	2,700.00	2,650.00	2,300.00	2,150.00	2,257.50	2,415.53		
8	Specialty	4,325.00	3,690.00	4,150.00	4,200.00	4,410.00	4,718.70		
9	Teas		1,475.00	1,600.00	1,875.00	1,968.75	2,106.56		
10	Total Sales	12,775.00	12,965.00	15,225.00	15,600.00	16,380.00	17,526.60		
11									
12									
13	Results (1st Half)	Sum	Average	Median	Min	Max	Count	Commission	
14	Light Roast	14,645.74	2,440.96	2,412.50	2,250.00	2,724.49	6.00	100.00	
15	Medium Roast	9,231.70	2,307.93	2,280.00	2,200.00	2,471.70	4.00	100.00	
16	Dark Roast	17,602.13	2,933.69	2,893.75	2,625.00	3,350.00	6.00	293.37	
17	Decaffeinated	14,473.03	2,412.17	2,357.76	2,150.00	2,700.00	6.00	100.00	
18	Specialty	25,493.70	4,248.95	4,262.50	3,690.00	4,718.70	6.00	424.90	
19	Teas	9,025.31	1,805.06	1,875.00	1,475.00	2,106.56	5.00	100.00	
20									
21									

Sheet1　Sheet2　Sheet3　⊕

Retrieving Data Using Lookup Functions

LESSON OVERVIEW

Excel's Lookup & Reference functions enable you to find and extract data from a table or list. The most popular lookup function is **VLOOKUP**, which allows you to look up a value in a vertical list and then retrieve data from a column on the same row as the matching value. For example, in a teacher's grade book application, a student's ID number could be the lookup value used to retrieve the student's full name and email address from a large student list. The **HLOOKUP** function, while similar to VLOOKUP, is used to look up values in a horizontal list or cell range and then retrieve data from a row in the same column as the matching value.

SKILLS PREVIEW

Use the VLOOKUP function to retrieve data from a vertical list or table	• **=VLOOKUP(*lookup_value, table_array, col_index_number, range_lookup*)** where *lookup_value* is the value you wish to look up in the leftmost column of a cell range (also called a *table_array*), *col_index_number* is the column number containing the data you wish to retrieve, and *range_lookup* is a TRUE or FALSE switch to specify whether you require an exact match.
Use the HLOOKUP function to retrieve data from a horizontal list or table	• **=HLOOKUP(*lookup_value, table_array, row_index_number, range_lookup*)** where *lookup_value* is the value you wish to look up in the topmost row of a cell range (also called a *table_array*), *row_index_number* is the row number containing the data you wish to retrieve, and *range_lookup* is a TRUE or FALSE switch to specify whether you require an exact match.

PROJECT PRACTICE

1. Ensure that **ex02a-salesforecast.xlsx** is open.

2. In this lesson, you will create a product insurance table that will be used to select an insurance rate based on the average monthly dollar sales. To begin, re-create the range from A22:B27 shown in Figure EX2.14. To apply the heading formatting, use the Format Painter button ( ) to copy the formatting from row 13.

FIGURE EX2.14 Entering the product insurance table

	A	B	C	D	E	F	G	H	I
10	**Total Sales**	12,775.00	12,965.00	15,225.00	15,600.00	16,380.00	17,526.60		
11									
12									
13	**Results (1st Half)**	**Sum**	**Average**	**Median**	**Min**	**Max**	**Count**	**Commission**	
14	*Light Roast*	14,645.74	2,440.96	2,412.50	2,250.00	2,724.49	6.00	100.00	
15	*Medium Roast*	9,231.70	2,307.93	2,280.00	2,200.00	2,471.70	4.00	100.00	
16	*Dark Roast*	17,602.13	2,933.69	2,893.75	2,625.00	3,350.00	6.00	293.37	
17	*Decaffeinated*	14,473.03	2,412.17	2,357.76	2,150.00	2,700.00	6.00	100.00	
18	*Specialty*	25,493.70	4,248.95	4,262.50	3,690.00	4,718.70	6.00	424.90	
19	*Teas*	9,025.31	1,805.06	1,875.00	1,475.00	2,106.56	5.00	100.00	
20									
21									
22	**Insurance**	**Rate**							
23	1,000.00	5%							
24	2,000.00	6%							
25	3,000.00	7%							
26	4,000.00	8%							
27	5,000.00	9%							
28									

← Enter the data shown in the cell range from A22:B27.

Sheet1 Sheet2 Sheet3 ⊕

3 Add a new column beside "Commission" to display the appropriate product insurance rate, based on the average monthly sales. To begin:

SELECT cell I13.

TYPE Rate.

PRESS Enter.

4 To retrieve the appropriate rate for the Light Roast blend, you will use the VLOOKUP function because the rate table is organized vertically. Do the following:

SELECT cell I14.

CLICK the FORMULAS tab and locate the Function Library group.

CLICK the Lookup & Reference command.

SELECT VLOOKUP from the list menu.
(*Result:* The Function Arguments dialog box appears.)

5 In the Lookup_value text box, select the average monthly sales value for the Light Roast brand. This is the value that you want to look up in the rate table. Do the following:

TYPE c14.

PRESS Tab to move to the next text box.
(*Result:* Notice that the dialog box displays the cell's value to the right of the text box.)

6 In the Table_array text box, select the rate table that contains the insurance rates. Because you will copy this formula to appear next to the remaining products, make this selection absolute (since the table will always remain in this area of the worksheet). To begin:

SELECT the cell range A22:B27.

PRESS F4 (ABS) key once.

PRESS Tab.

7 In the Col_index_num text box, enter the column number containing the rate:

TYPE 2.

(*Result:* Notice that the first column contains the value to look up, so the second column contains the rate. Your Function Arguments dialog box should now appear similar to the one shown in Figure EX2.15.)

FIGURE EX2.15 Completing the VLOOKUP Function Arguments dialog box

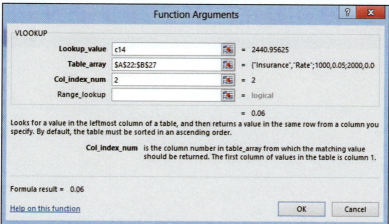

8 CLICK OK to enter the function into cell I14.
(*Result:* The resulting rate is .06 or 6%. Notice that the Formula bar for cell I14 should now read =VLOOKUP(C14,$A$22:$B$27,2). Lastly, the final parameter in the dialog box, Range_lookup, is optional and defaults to TRUE, which will return an exact match or the next closest value.)

> **TIP**
>
> If you omit the last match parameter, Excel assumes it to be TRUE, which will then return an exact match (if one is found) or the next closest value in the lookup table's first column or row. However, for this to work properly, your lookup table must be organized in ascending order!

9 Using the fill handle, copy the function in cell I14 to the cell range I15:I19. Format the cell range to appear using the Percent Style button.
(*Result:* Your screen should now appear similar to Figure EX2.16.)

10 Save your file.

FIGURE EX2.16 The completed workbook for Project Excel 2A

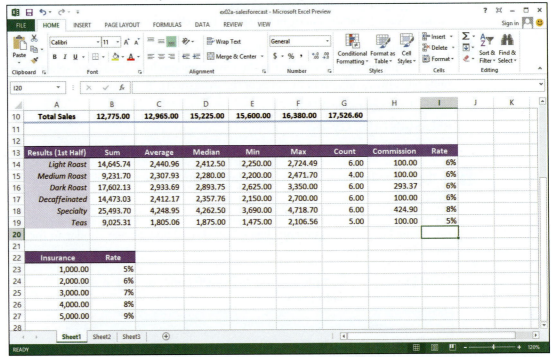

MULTIPLE-CHOICE QUIZ

Select the best choice in the following questions to review the project concepts. Good luck!

1. To define a range name for the currently selected cell, in what area do you type the desired name?
   a. Formula bar
   b. Status bar
   c. Function box
   d. Name box

2. Which of the following symbols precedes a column letter or row number in an absolute cell reference?
   a. &
   b. $
   c. @
   d. !

3. In Edit mode, which shortcut key do you press to toggle a cell address to being relative, absolute, or mixed?
   a. F2
   b. F3
   c. F4
   d. F5

4. Which is the correct expression for adding the values stored in the cell range from A1 to A20?
   a. =ADD(A1+A20)
   b. =AutoSUM(A1,A20)
   c. =SUM(A1+A20)
   d. =SUM(A1:A20)

5. Which is the correct expression for determining the average value of a range that is named "Units"?
   a. =AVERAGE(Units)
   b. =AVG(Units)
   c. =MEDIAN(Units)
   d. =SUM(Units/Count)

6. What does the COUNT function actually count?
   a. The number of cells in a range.
   b. The number of cells containing any type of data in a range.
   c. The number of cells containing only numeric or date values.
   d. The number of cells containing only text values.

7. Which of the following functions can be used to display both the date and time?
   a. =NOW()
   b. =THEN()
   c. =TODAY()
   d. =DATE&TIME()

8. Which of the following is the correct syntax for the IF function?
   a. =IF(condition, false, true)
   b. =IF(condition, true, false)
   c. =IF(true, false, condition)
   d. =IF(false, true, condition)

9. Which of the following is not a comparison operator that may be used in an IF function?
   a. >
   b. <=
   c. =
   d. /

10. Which of the following functions would you use to look up and retrieve a value from a horizontal table or cell range list?
    a. EXACTMATCH
    b. HLOOKUP
    c. MYLOOKUP
    d. VLOOKUP

HANDS-ON EXERCISE: WORK IT OUT EX-2A-E1

In this exercise, you will practice creating named cell ranges and use them in constructing formulas. The final worksheet is shown in Figure EX2.17.

FIGURE EX2.17   Work It Out EX-2A-E1: completed

	A	B	C	D	E	F
1	**Department of Domestic Affairs**					
2	Area	Employees	Percent			
3	Agriculture	987	7.77%			
4	Education	1,738	13.69%			
5	Forestry	2,361	18.59%			
6	Health	3,182	25.06%			
7	Revenue	2,805	22.09%			
8	Transportation	1,626	12.80%			
9	**Total**	**12,699**				
10						
11	Funding Source A	7725				
12	Funding Source B	4974				
13						
14						
15						
16						

1 Locate and open the exercise data file **ex02a-ex01.xlsx**. Save the file as **ex02a-hw01.xlsx**.

2 To begin, name cell B9 "Total" using the Name box.

3 Now use the existing worksheet labels in the cell range A3:A8 to define range names for the data stored in the cell range B3:B8. Make a few selections from the Name box to confirm that the range names were created properly.

4 In cell B9, use the AutoSUM button (Σ ·) to total the number of employees by using the SUM function.

5 You will now use the worksheet range names to create a simple addition formula. To proceed:
SELECT cell B11.
TYPE **=Education+Health+Revenue**.
PRESS Enter.

6 In cell B12, use the typing or pointing method to enter an expression that totals the remaining departments not included in the previous formula.

7 Now calculate the employment percentage for each department. Do the following:
SELECT cell C3.
TYPE **=b3/Total**.
(*Result:* Notice that we used b3 in the formula, rather than Agriculture. Since you will copy this formula in the next step, we cannot use an absolute cell reference for cell B3.)

8 Use the fill handle to copy the formula in cell B3 to the remaining cells in the range B4:B8.

9 Select the cell range C3:C8 and apply the Percent style number formatting. Then, increase the decimals to two points. After moving the cell pointer to A1, your screen should appear similar to Figure EX2.17.

10 Save and then close the workbook file.

HANDS-ON EXERCISE: WORK IT OUT EX-2A-E2

You will now practice using some of Excel's built-in functions to complete an existing worksheet. The final worksheet is shown in Figure EX2.18.

FIGURE EX2.18 Work It Out EX-2A-E2: completed

	A	B	C	D
1	**Tablet Sales by Day of the Week**			
2		**Apple**	**Samsung**	**Toshiba**
3	**Monday**	4,500	2,600	2,654
4	**Tuesday**	4,750	2,350	2,690
5	**Wednesday**	3,800	2,975	2,590
6	**Thursday**	3,426	2,845	2,810
7	**Friday**	3,375	2,497	2,678
8				
9	**Total**	19,851	13,267	13,422
10	**Average**	3,970	2,653	2,684
11	**Median**	3,800	2,600	2,678
12	**Minimum**	3,375	2,350	2,590
13	**Maximum**	4,750	2,975	2,810
14				
15				
16				

1. Locate and open the exercise data file **ex02a-ex02.xlsx**. Save the file as **ex02a-hw02.xlsx**.

2. Use the fill handle for cell A3 to drag down a series of weekdays to the cell range A4:A7.

3. Select the cell range A2:D7 and then create range names based on the labels in column A and row 2.

4. In the cell range B9:D9, use the AutoSUM button (Σ ▾) to sum the columns for the three manufacturers. Check your formulas to ensure that Excel entered the correct values.

5. In the cell range B10:D10, enter the AVERAGE function using the range names to calculate the average sales per manufacturer.

6. In the cell range B11:D11, enter the MIN function using the range names to extract the lowest sales from the week.

7. In the cell range B12:D12, enter the MAX function using the range names to extract the highest sales from the week.

8. Insert a new row 11, between "Average" and "Minimum," and enter the MEDIAN function to calculate the median values from the worksheet data. Lastly, label the new row "Median" as shown in Figure EX2.18.

9. Save and then close the workbook file.

In this exercise, you will open an existing workbook and complete it to appear similar to Figure EX2.19. You will be asked to create range names and enter several of Excel's built-in functions.

FIGURE EX2.19   Work It Out EX-2A-E3: completed

	A	B	C	D	E	F	G
1		Calculating Fuel Economy					
2	Make and Model	Fuel Capacity	MPG (City)	MPG (Hwy)			
3	Aston Martin XG7	23.5	14.0	20.0			
4	Chevrolet Corvette	19.1	18.0	27.0			
5	Ferrari F50	27.7	8.0	12.0			
6	Jaguar XJR	21.4	16.0	21.0			
7	Porsche 911	26.0	10.0	14.0			
8	Audi G8	17.2	19.0	32.0			
9	Average	22.5	14.2	21.0			
10							
11	Count	6.0					
12	Minimium	17.2	8.0	12.0			
13	Maximum	27.7	19.0	32.0			
14	Range	10.5	11.0	20.0			
15							
16	Worst MPG	8.0	This is not very good.				
17	Best MPG	32.0	This is excellent.				
18							

1. Locate and open the exercise data file **ex02a-ex03.xlsx**. Save the file as **ex02a-hw03.xlsx**.

2. In cell B11, enter the COUNTA function to count the number of cars appearing in column A, specifically the cell range A3:A8.

3. Name the cell range B3:B8 as **Capacity**. Then, name the cell range C3:C8 as **MPG_City** and D3:D8 as **MPG_Hwy**.

4. Using the range names you created in step 3, calculate the average of each column in row 9.

5. Using the range names, extract the minimum and maximum values from each column and place the results in rows 12 and 13.

6. In row 14, enter a formula that calculates the difference or range between the minimum and maximum values. Label this row **Range** in cell A14, and then format it to appear similar to the other values.

7. In row 16, enter a function to calculate the lowest gas mileage, regardless of city or highway driving. Label this row **Worst MPG** as shown in Figure EX2.19 and then format it to appear similar to the other values.

8. In row 17, enter a function to calculate the highest gas mileage, regardless of city or highway driving. Label this row **Best MPG**, and then format it to appear similar to the other values.

9. In cell C16, enter an IF function that tests whether the worst MPG in cell B16 is less than 10. If it is less than 10, type **"This is not very good."** If it is equal to or higher than 10, type **"This is not horrible."** (*Hint:* When entering the text entries in the IF function, include the quotation marks.)

10. In cell C17, enter an IF function that tests whether the best MPG in cell B17 is greater than 30. If it is greater than 30, type **"This is excellent."** If it is equal to or less than 30, type **"This is not very good."** (*Hint:* When entering the text entries in the IF function, include the quotation marks.)

11. Move the cell pointer to cell A1. Your workbook should now appear similar to Figure EX2.19.

12. Save and then close the workbook file.

Displaying Sparklines and Charts for Forecasting

PROJECT OBJECTIVES

After completing this project, you will be able to:

In this project, you will learn how to represent worksheet data visually. First, you will use sparklines, which are tiny in-cell graphics, to display simple trends. Then, you will create and embed a full-featured chart alongside your worksheet data. Lastly, you will use Excel's Page Layout view to help you select, position, and print the chart and worksheet.

PROJECT FILE: *Available at* **www.mhhe.com/office2013projectlearn**

- Insert sparklines to visually represent trends occurring within the worksheet data.

- Change the type of sparkline and formatting to best communicate key data points.

- Create an embedded chart and position it alongside your worksheet data.

- Select among various types of charts to discern the best way to present the data.

- View the worksheet in Page Layout view and then send it to the printer.

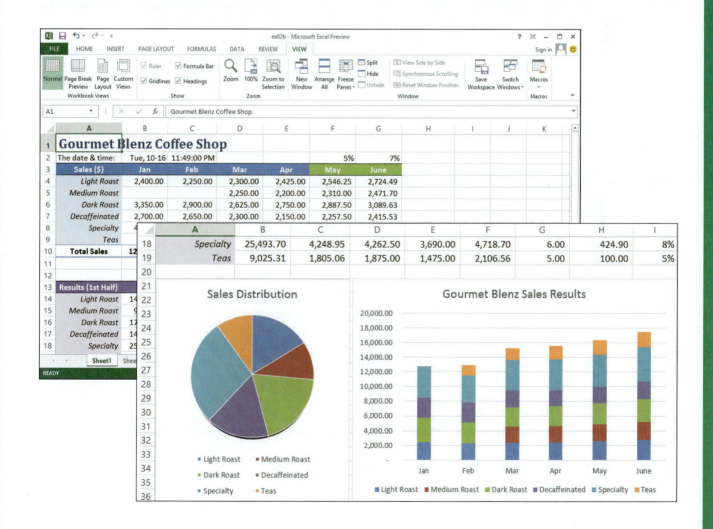

Adding Sparklines to Cells

LESSON OVERVIEW

To better show patterns and trends resulting from worksheet data, Excel lets you place tiny, word-sized charts, called **sparklines**, within cells. These in-cell graphics can help users visualize and better understand what their data means, without having to plot the data in a chart. Three variations of sparklines—Line, Column, and Win/Loss—are available (as shown below). Notice that the Win/Loss sparkline simply indicates positive and negative values in the selected range, as opposed to the Column sparkline, which shows the relative weighting of values.

	A	B	C	D	E	F	G	H
1	Growth	2010	2011	2012	2013	Line	Column	Win/Loss
2	**Widgets**	10%	20%	-5%	12%			
3	**Gadgets**	15%	8%	4%	-6%			
4								

SKILLS PREVIEW

Add a sparkline to a cell or cell range	• SELECT the cell or cell range that will contain the sparkline. CLICK the INSERT tab and locate the Sparklines group, and then • CLICK the Line button (⊠) to add a line sparkline, *or* • CLICK the Column button (⊞) to add a column sparkline, *or* • CLICK the Win/Loss button (⊞) to add a win/loss (plus/minus) sparkline. SELECT the data range and target location for the sparkline.

PROJECT PRACTICE

1. After launching Microsoft Excel, locate and open the project data file **ex02b.xlsx**. On the File menu tab, use the Save As command to save the file as **ex02b-salesforecast.xlsx**.

2. To add sparkline graphics to the cells in column H, do the following:

   SELECT cell H3.

   TYPE Sparklines.

   PRESS Enter.

   SELECT the cell range H4:H9.

3. To insert line sparklines within the selected cell range:

   CLICK the INSERT tab and locate the Sparklines group.

   CLICK the Line button (⊠).

   (*Result:* The Create Sparklines dialog box appears, asking you to specify the data you want plotted.)

4 In the Create Sparklines dialog box, ensure that the cursor appears in the Data Range selection text box, and then:

SELECT the cell range B4:G9.

(*Result:* Your screen should now appear similar to Figure EX2.20.)

FIGURE EX2.20 Selecting cell ranges for sparklines

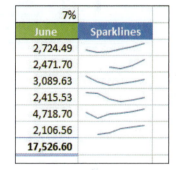

	A	B	C	D	E	F	G	H	I	J	K
1	**Gourmet Blenz Coffee Shop**										
2	The date & time:	Tue, 10-16	9:23:45 PM			5%	7%				
3	Sales ($)	Jan	Feb	Mar	Apr	May	June	Sparklines			
4	Light Roast	2,400.00	2,250.00	2,300.00	2,425.00	2,546.25	2,724.49				
5	Medium Roast			2,250.00	2,200.00	2,310.00	2,471.70				
6	Dark Roast	3,350.00	2,900.00	2,625.00	2,750.00	2,887.50	3,089.63				
7	Decaffeinated	2,700.00	2,650.00	2,300.00	2,150.00	2,257.50	2,415.53				
8	Specialty	4,325.00	3,690.00	4,150.00	4,200.00	4,410.00	4,718.70				
9	Teas		1,475.00	1,600.00	1,875.00	1,968.75	2,106.56				
10	**Total Sales**	**12,775.00**	**12,965.00**	**15,225.00**	**15,600.00**	**16,380.00**	**17,526.60**				
11											
12											
13	Results (1st Half)	Sum	Average	Median	Min	Max	Count				
14	Light Roast	14,645.74	2,440.96	2,412.50	2,250.00	2,724.49	6.00	100.00	6%		
15	Medium Roast	9,231.70	2,307.93	2,280.00	2,200.00	2,471.70	4.00	100.00	6%		
16	Dark Roast	17,602.13	2,933.69	2,893.75	2,625.00	3,350.00	6.00	293.37	6%		
17	Decaffeinated	14,473.03	2,412.17	2,357.76	2,150.00	2,700.00	6.00	100.00	6%		
18	Specialty	25,493.70	4,248.95	4,262.50	3,690.00	4,718.70	6.00	424.90	8%		

Sheet1 Sheet2 Sheet3 (+)

5 CLICK OK to complete the dialog box.
(*Result:* A Line sparkline for each row appears in the cell range, as shown here.)

7%	
June	Sparklines
2,724.49	
2,471.70	
3,089.63	
2,415.53	
4,718.70	
2,106.56	
17,526.60	

6 Insert a Column sparkline for the "Total Sales" in cell H10. Do the following:

SELECT cell H10.

7 To create a Column sparkline:

CLICK the INSERT tab and locate the Sparklines group.

CLICK the Column button ( ).

8 In the Create Sparklines dialog box, ensure that the cursor appears in the Data Range selection text box, and then:

SELECT the cell range B10:G10.

CLICK OK to complete the dialog box.
(*Result:* Your worksheet should now appear similar to Figure EX2.21.)

TIP

To delete sparklines, you cannot simply select the cell and press Delete. Instead, you must select the cell range containing the sparklines and click the DESIGN tab under Sparkline Tools. Then, locate the Group group and click the Clear button (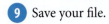).

9 Save your file.

FIGURE EX2.21 Displaying Line and Column sparklines in a worksheet

	A	B	C	D	E	F	G	H	I	J	K
1	**Gourmet Blenz Coffee Shop**										
2	The date & time:	Tue, 10-16	9:23:45 PM			5%	7%				
3	Sales ($)	Jan	Feb	Mar	Apr	May	June	Sparklines			
4	Light Roast	2,400.00	2,250.00	2,300.00	2,425.00	2,546.25	2,724.49				
5	Medium Roast			2,250.00	2,200.00	2,310.00	2,471.70				
6	Dark Roast	3,350.00	2,900.00	2,625.00	2,750.00	2,887.50	3,089.63				
7	Decaffeinated	2,700.00	2,650.00	2,300.00	2,150.00	2,257.50	2,415.53				
8	Specialty	4,325.00	3,690.00	4,150.00	4,200.00	4,410.00	4,718.70				
9	Teas		1,475.00	1,600.00	1,875.00	1,968.75	2,106.56				
10	**Total Sales**	**12,775.00**	**12,965.00**	**15,225.00**	**15,600.00**	**16,380.00**	**17,526.60**				
11											
12											
13	Results (1st Half)	Sum	Average	Median	Min	Max	Count	Commission	Rate		
14	Light Roast	14,645.74	2,440.96	2,412.50	2,250.00	2,724.49	6.00	100.00	6%		
15	Medium Roast	9,231.70	2,307.93	2,280.00	2,200.00	2,471.70	4.00	100.00	6%		
16	Dark Roast	17,602.13	2,933.69	2,893.75	2,625.00	3,350.00	6.00	293.37	6%		
17	Decaffeinated	14,473.03	2,412.17	2,357.76	2,150.00	2,700.00	6.00	100.00	6%		
18	Specialty	25,493.70	4,248.95	4,262.50	3,690.00	4,718.70	6.00	424.90	8%		

Sheet1 Sheet2 Sheet3

Customizing Sparklines

LESSON OVERVIEW

Several options are available for customizing the presentation of sparklines within your worksheet. Besides changing the type of sparkline displayed, you can show low- and high-point markers, change the color and style of elements, and display axes within cells. Several of these customization options are accessible from the DESIGN tab under Sparkline Tools, as shown below.

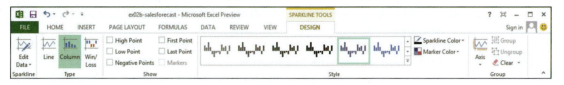

SKILLS PREVIEW

Toggle the display of point markers on a sparkline	• SELECT the cell or cell range that contains a sparkline. CLICK the DESIGN tab under Sparkline Tools. SELECT the desired check box options in the Show group.
Change the appearance and color of a sparkline	• SELECT the cell or cell range that contains a sparkline. CLICK the DESIGN tab under Sparkline Tools, and then • SELECT the desired Style option from the Style gallery, *or* • SELECT colors from the Sparkline Color drop-down button (🖊️), *or* • SELECT colors for the desired markers from the Marker Color drop-down button 9 (🎨).
Clear a sparkline from a cell	• SELECT the cell or cell range that contains a sparkline. CLICK the DESIGN tab under Sparkline Tools. CLICK the Clear button (🧹).

PROJECT PRACTICE

1 Ensure that **ex02b-salesforecast.xlsx** is open.

2 To modify the sparklines created in column H, do the following:
SELECT the cell range from H4:H10.

3 You can add markers to these sparklines:
CLICK the DESIGN tab under Sparkline Tools and locate the Show group.

4 To view point markers in the cell range:
CLICK the High Point check box in the Ribbon.
CLICK the Low Point check box in the Ribbon.
(*Result:* Notice that point markers appear on each sparkline in the range.)

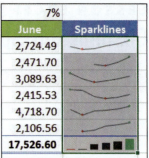

5 To apply a new style to these sparklines:

CLICK the Style drop-down gallery button.

SELECT the Sparkline Style Colorful #1 option (in the bottom left-hand corner of the gallery list box).

(*Note:* Remember to roll your mouse pointer over the gallery boxes to see the style names appear in the tooltips. Your sparklines should now appear similar to the image presented here.)

6 To see what the Win/Loss sparkline tells you, do the following:

CLICK the Win/Loss button (⊞) in the Type group.

(*Result:* The sparkline is converted to the Win/Loss type, which doesn't provide very much information since there are no negative values in the range.)

7 SELECT cell H3 to remove the range highlighting.

(*Result:* Your screen should now appear similar to the worksheet shown in Figure EX2.22.)

8 Save your file.

FIGURE EX2.22 Customizing the sparkline graphics in a worksheet

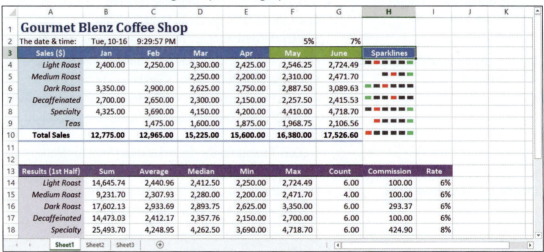

Creating an Embedded Chart

LESSON OVERVIEW

There are two approaches to creating a chart in Excel, differing primarily in the way the chart is stored and printed. First, you can create a **chart sheet** as a new, separate sheet in a workbook. This method works well for printing full-page charts and for creating computer-based presentations or electronic slide shows. Second, you can create an **embedded chart** that is stored on the worksheet itself. You can add as many embedded charts to your worksheet as your computer's memory allows. Like using sparklines, embedding a chart allows you to display a visual representation alongside your worksheet data. In the accompanying graphic, for example, two embedded charts are positioned next to one another below the data from which they were created.

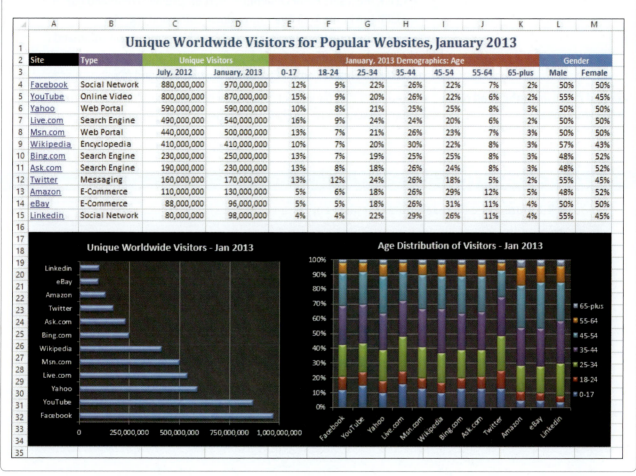

	Site	Type	Unique Visitors		January, 2013 Demographics: Age							Gender	
			July, 2012	January, 2013	0-17	18-24	25-34	35-44	45-54	55-64	65-plus	Male	Female
4	Facebook	Social Network	880,000,000	970,000,000	12%	9%	22%	26%	22%	7%	2%	50%	50%
5	YouTube	Online Video	800,000,000	870,000,000	15%	9%	20%	26%	22%	6%	2%	55%	45%
6	Yahoo	Web Portal	590,000,000	590,000,000	10%	8%	21%	25%	25%	8%	3%	50%	50%
7	Live.com	Search Engine	490,000,000	540,000,000	16%	9%	24%	24%	20%	6%	2%	50%	50%
8	Msn.com	Web Portal	440,000,000	500,000,000	13%	7%	21%	26%	23%	7%	3%	50%	50%
9	Wikipedia	Encyclopedia	410,000,000	410,000,000	10%	7%	20%	30%	22%	8%	3%	57%	43%
10	Bing.com	Search Engine	230,000,000	250,000,000	13%	7%	19%	25%	25%	8%	3%	48%	52%
11	Ask.com	Search Engine	190,000,000	230,000,000	13%	8%	18%	26%	24%	8%	3%	48%	52%
12	Twitter	Messaging	160,000,000	170,000,000	13%	12%	24%	26%	18%	5%	2%	55%	45%
13	Amazon	E-Commerce	110,000,000	130,000,000	5%	6%	18%	26%	29%	12%	5%	48%	52%
14	eBay	E-Commerce	88,000,000	96,000,000	5%	5%	18%	26%	31%	11%	4%	50%	50%
15	Linkedin	Social Network	80,000,000	98,000,000	4%	4%	22%	29%	26%	11%	4%	55%	45%

Create an embedded chart as recommended by Excel	• SELECT the cell range containing data that you wish to plot in a chart. CLICK the INSERT tab and locate the Charts group. CLICK the Recommended Charts button (▮). SELECT an option from the Insert Chart dialog box.
Create an embedded chart by selecting a chart type	• SELECT the cell range containing data that you wish to plot in a chart. CLICK the INSERT tab and locate the Charts group, and then select the desired chart option from the following buttons: • CLICK the Insert Column Chart drop-down command (▮ ▾). • CLICK the Insert Bar Chart drop-down command (▬ ▾). • CLICK the Insert Line Chart drop-down command (〰 ▾). • CLICK the Insert Pie or Doughnut Chart drop-down command (◕ ▾). • CLICK the Insert Area Chart drop-down command (◭ ▾). • CLICK the Insert Scatter (X, Y) or Bubble Chart drop-down command (⦂⦂ ▾). • CLICK the Insert Stock, Surface, or Radar Chart drop-down command (✪ ▾). • CLICK the Insert Combo Chart drop-down command (▮ ▾).
Size and move an embedded chart on the worksheet	• DRAG the sizing handles on the border of the embedded chart to size it. • DRAG anywhere else on the chart border to move it around the worksheet.

PROJECT PRACTICE

1 Ensure that **ex02b-salesforecast.xlsx** is open.

2 In the following steps, you will create and insert an embedded chart below the current worksheet data. To begin, select the data to plot in the embedded chart:

SELECT the cell range A3:G9.
(*Note:* Do not select the "Total Sales" row or the "Sparklines" column. Notice that you include the row and column labels in the selection.)

3 To view the charting options recommended by Excel:

CLICK the INSERT tab and locate the Charts group.

CLICK the Recommended Charts button (▮).
(*Result:* The Insert Chart dialog box appears with a preview of the first selection, as shown in Figure EX2.23.)

FIGURE EX2.23 Displaying chart options in the Insert Chart
dialog box

④ Click some of the other charting options in the list box to preview their appearance. When you are
ready to proceed, return to the Clustered Column option.

⑤ To insert the selected chart into the worksheet as an embedded chart:

SELECT the Clustered Column option in the list box.

CLICK OK.

(*Result:* The chart is placed over top of the worksheet area, as shown in Figure EX2.24.)

FIGURE EX2.24 Inserting an embedded chart

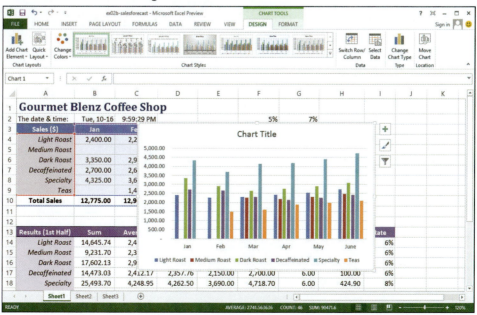

6 To modify the chart title:

CLICK once on the "Chart Title" text within the chart area.

TYPE Gourmet Blenz Sales Results.

PRESS Enter.

7 Using the mouse, move the embedded chart below the worksheet data, as shown in Figure EX2.25, by dragging its borders or by dragging on a blank area within the chart graphic. (*Note:* The mouse pointer changes shape when positioned properly over the chart border.)

8 Using the mouse, size the embedded chart to appear as shown in Figure EX2.25 by dragging its sizing boxes at each corner or near the middle of the horizontal and vertical borders.

MORE INFO

You will learn how to customize and format a chart in the next chapter. This lesson simply practices how to select a worksheet range, plot the data using a recommended charting option, and then size and position the embedded chart on the worksheet.

---

9 Save your file.

FIGURE EX2.25 Moving and sizing an embedded chart

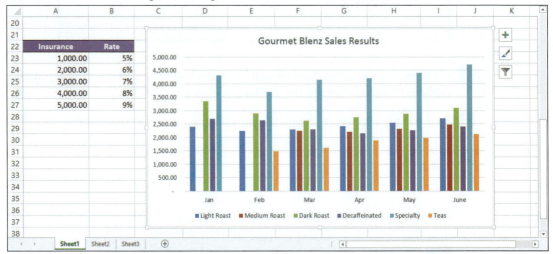

Changing the Chart Type

LESSON OVERVIEW

Once you have created a chart, Excel provides a variety of tools for customizing and formatting each element of the chart. In the next chapter, you will dive into each of these tools, but for this lesson we focus on modifying the chart type. Many types of charts are available for presenting your worksheet data to engineers, statisticians, business professionals, and other audiences. Some of the more popular charts include line charts, column charts, pie charts, and XY scatter plot diagrams. However, Excel provides many other categories from which you can select the perfect option for representing your data.

SKILLS PREVIEW

Change the type of chart used for plotting your data	• SELECT the embedded chart on the worksheet. CLICK the DESIGN tab under Chart Tools. CLICK the Change Chart Type command in the Type group. SELECT the desired Chart Category in the dialog box. SELECT the desired chart type.
Switch the row and column data to pivot the chart	• SELECT the embedded chart on the worksheet. CLICK the DESIGN tab under Chart Tools. CLICK the Switch Row/Column command in the Data group.

PROJECT PRACTICE

1. Ensure that **ex02b-salesforecast.xlsx** is open.

2. To get a better sense of the total sales for each month, you can choose to display a stacked column chart instead. Do the following:

   SELECT the embedded chart by clicking on it once.

   CLICK the DESIGN tab under Chart Tools and locate the Type group.

3. To display the Change Chart Type dialog box:

   CLICK the Change Chart Type command.

4 In the dialog box, ensure that the Column category is selected and then do the following:

CLICK the Stacked Column option, next to the Clustered Column option previously selected.
(*Result:* Your screen should now appear similar to Figure EX2.26.)

FIGURE EX2.26   The Change Chart Type dialog box

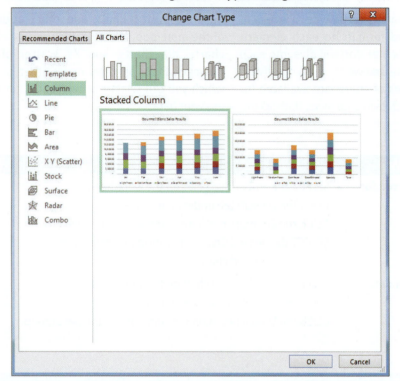

5 Position your mouse over the two preview options. (*Result:* The two images zoom larger so that you can see how your data would appear if the row and column data were switched between the X- and Y-axis. You can also use the Switch Row/Column command in the Data group to toggle back and forth between the row and column layout.)

6 With the leftmost option selected, showing the months across the horizontal X-axis:

CLICK OK to proceed.
(*Result:* Your embedded chart should now appear similar to Figure EX2.27.)

FIGURE EX2.27   Changing from a Clustered Column chart to
a Stacked Column chart

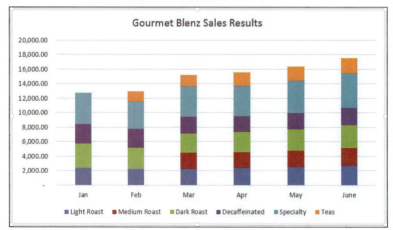

7 You can create a pie chart that shows the breakdown of total sales among products. Do the following:

SELECT the cell range A13:B19.

CLICK the INSERT tab in the Ribbon.

CLICK the Insert Pie or Doughnut Chart drop-down command (▼).

8 In the 2-D Pie gallery:

CLICK the Pie option.

9 To change the title of the chart:

CLICK once on the "Sum" chart title within the chart area.

TYPE **Sales Distribution**.

PRESS Enter .

10 Using the Change Chart Type command, change the chart type from Pie to 3-D Pie using the steps described previously.

11 Move and size both the Pie and Stacked column charts to appear next to one another, as shown in Figure EX2.28. Notice that the pie chart is covering the Insurance Rate table, which is fine for this exercise.

12 Save your file.

FIGURE EX2.28 Positioning two embedded charts side by side

Printing an Embedded Chart

LESSON OVERVIEW

One of the primary reasons for embedding a chart on a worksheet is to view and print it alongside its worksheet data. You must ensure, however, that the print area (or worksheet range) includes the entire chart object. As you would when printing a worksheet by itself, you can manipulate various page setup options, including margins, headers, and footers. Remember also that you can preview your worksheet in Page Layout view before sending it to the printer, as shown in the accompanying example.

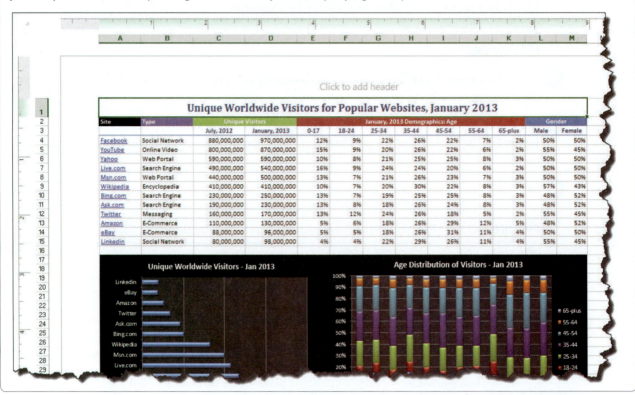

SKILLS PREVIEW

Change the display to Page Layout view	• CLICK the VIEW tab and locate the Workbook Views group. CLICK the Page Layout command.
Set the desired cell range for printing	• SELECT the cell range that includes both the worksheet data and embedded chart. CLICK the PAGE LAYOUT tab and locate the Page Setup group. CLICK the Print Area drop-down command. CHOOSE Set Print Area.
Adjust the print selection area to print on a single page	• CLICK the PAGE LAYOUT tab on the Ribbon. CLICK the Page Setup dialog box launcher (⬓). CLICK the Page tab, if it is not already selected. CLICK the Fit to option button, and then choose 1 page(s) wide by 1 tall.
Print an embedded chart, alongside its worksheet data	• CLICK the FILE tab on the Ribbon. CHOOSE the Print tab from the menu. CLICK the Print command in Backstage view.

1 Ensure that **ex02b-salesforecast.xlsx** is open.

2 To prepare for printing, select the worksheet area you want to print. To begin:

CLICK in the Name box.

TYPE **A1:I37** (or the range on your worksheet that covers the data and charts).

PRESS `Enter` to select the range.

(*Result:* The entire range should now appear highlighted in the worksheet.)

3 To assign the selected range as the print area:

CLICK the PAGE LAYOUT tab and locate the Page Setup group.

CLICK the Print Area drop-down command.

CHOOSE the Set Print Area command.

(*Result:* You may have noticed that Excel adds dashed vertical and horizontal lines in your worksheet to signify where the page will break. The location of these page breaks will, however, depend on the printer that you have selected.)

4 To print the worksheet in wide Landscape mode (instead of narrow Portrait mode):

CLICK the Orientation drop-down command.

CHOOSE the Landscape option.

5 To view the worksheet in Page Layout view mode:

CLICK the VIEW tab and locate the Workbook Views group.

CLICK the Page Layout command.

6 Scroll down the page to determine if the print area will fit on a single page. As shown in Figure EX2.29, this particular selection splits across onto page 2.

FIGURE EX2.29 Viewing a page break in Page Layout view

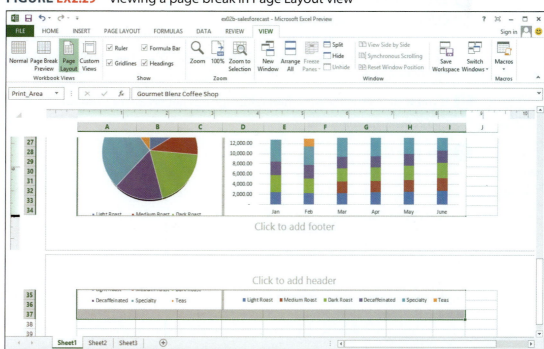

7 While you could attempt to reduce the height of the embedded charts or rows, there is an easier way to fit the print area onto a single page. Do the following:

CLICK the PAGE LAYOUT tab and locate the Page Setup group.
CLICK the Page Setup dialog box launcher (⬚).

8 In the Page Setup dialog box, ensure that the Page tab is selected and then:
CLICK the Fit to option button.

9 As shown in Figure EX2.30, ensure that the Fit to options read 1 page(s) wide by 1 tall.

FIGURE EX2.30   Page Setup dialog box

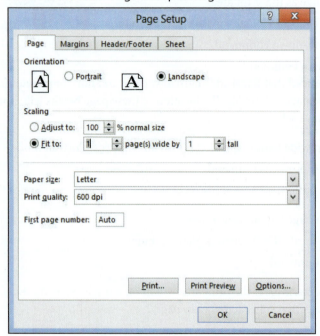

10 To preview the worksheet as it will now print:
CLICK the Print Preview button.
(*Result*: Notice that you are taken to Backstage view for the Print tab, and that the worksheet and embedded charts now appear on a single, landscape page. Your screen should appear similar to Figure EX2.31.)

11 If you wish to print the worksheet (although it is not necessary to do so):
CLICK the Print command.

12 Save your file.

FIGURE EX2.31   The Print tab in Backstage view

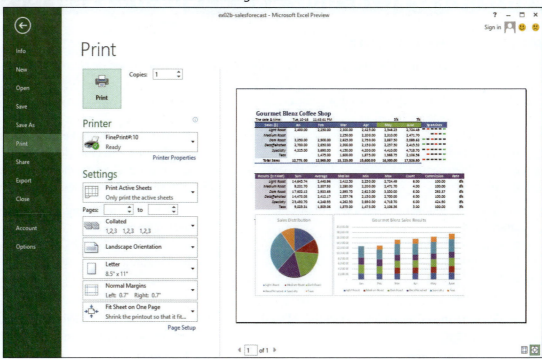

PROJECT EXCEL 2B: QUIZ AND HANDS-ON EXERCISES

MULTIPLE-CHOICE QUIZ

Select the best choice in the following questions to review the project concepts. Good luck!

1. The tiny, word-sized chart lines that you can place within cells are called
   a. plotlines.
   b. sparklines.
   c. embedded charts.
   d. column charts.

2. Which of the following is not a type of in-cell, chart line?
   a. Line
   b. Column
   c. Pie
   d. Win/Loss

3. To delete an in-cell, chart line, select the cell and
   a. PRESS Del.
   b. PRESS Ctrl + Del.
   c. CLICK Clear on the DESIGN tab.
   d. CLICK Delete on the DESIGN tab.

4. Which is not an option in the Show group that you can highlight on an in-cell, chart line?
   a. High point
   b. Low point
   c. Negative points
   d. Positive points

5. How many embedded charts can you add to a single worksheet?
   a. 1
   b. 2
   c. 64
   d. Only limited by your computer's resources

6. What are the two approaches for creating charts in Excel?
   a. Sparklines and embedded charts
   b. Plotlines and embedded charts
   c. Embedded charts and chart sheets
   d. Embedded charts and worksheets

7. Which of the following is not a chart type available in Excel?
   a. fritter
   b. doughnut
   c. radar
   d. bubble

8. To see how an embedded chart aligns with worksheet data for printing, you can switch to what view mode?
   a. Outline
   b. Page Layout
   c. Page Design
   d. Chart Layout

9. Which page orientation allows you to use the long side of a page for the printing width?
   a. Portrait
   b. Embedded
   c. Page Layout
   d. Landscape

10. The Fit to page option for printing is accessible from which of the following dialog boxes?
    a. Page Layout
    b. Page Design
    c. Page Setup
    d. Print Setup

In this exercise, you will practice creating an embedded column chart. You will then print out this chart alongside its worksheet data. The final worksheet is shown in Figure EX2.32.

FIGURE EX2.32 Work It Out EX-2B-E1: completed

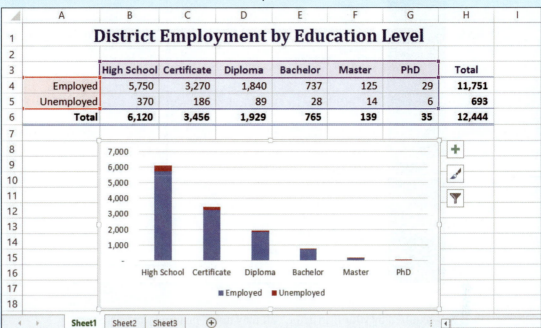

1 Locate and open the exercise data file **ex02b-ex01.xlsx**. Save the file as **ex02b-hw01.xlsx**.

2 To plot the worksheet data in a chart:
SELECT the cell range from A3:G5.
(*Note:* You do not include the total row or column in the range selection.)

3 Using the Recommended Charts command, create an embedded Clustered Column chart.

4 Remove the chart's title by selecting it and pressing Delete .

5 Modify the chart to display using the Stacked Column chart type.

6 Using the mouse, size and move the chart to cover the same area of the chart in Figure EX2.32.
(*Result:* Your screen should now appear similar to Figure EX2.32.)

7 Specify a print area from A1:H19 to print both the worksheet and the embedded chart.

8 Ensure that the print area will print on a single page and then preview the worksheet.
(*Result:* Your screen should now appear similar to Figure EX2.33.)

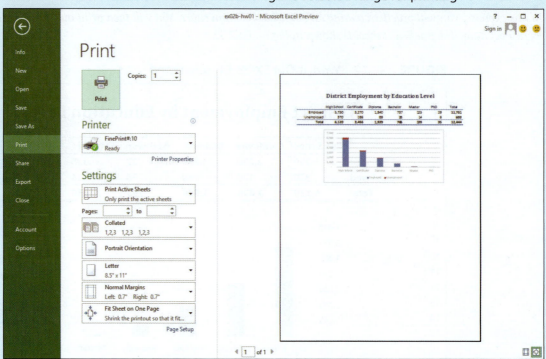

9 If required by your instructor, you may finish printing the worksheet.

10 Save and then close the workbook file.

In this exercise, your objective is to enhance a worksheet's presentation by embedding sparklines and an embedded line chart alongside and below the data. The final worksheet is shown in Figure EX2.34.

FIGURE EX2.34 Work It Out EX-2B-E2: completed

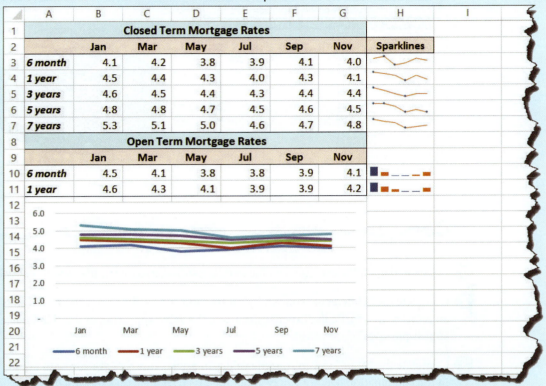

1. Locate and open the exercise data file **ex02b-ex02.xlsx**. Save the file as **ex02b-hw02.xlsx**.

2. In cell H2, enter the column title **Sparklines** and add a cell border as shown in Figure EX2.34.

3. Add a Line sparkline to the cell range H3:H7.

4. Add a Column sparkline to the cell range H10:H11.

5. Add High and Low Point markers to both sets of the sparklines.

6. Using the Style area of the DESIGN tab under Sparkline Tools, apply the Sparkline Style Accent 6, Darker 25% option to the cell range from H3:H11.

7. Insert an embedded line chart below the worksheet data area that plots the data for closed term mortgage rates only. Remove the Chart Title from displaying on the chart.

8. Size and position the chart to appear similar to Figure EX2.34.

9. Save and then close the workbook file.

In this exercise, you will open an existing workbook and then revise and modify it to appear similar to Figure EX2.35.

FIGURE EX2.35   Work It Out EX-2B-E3: completed

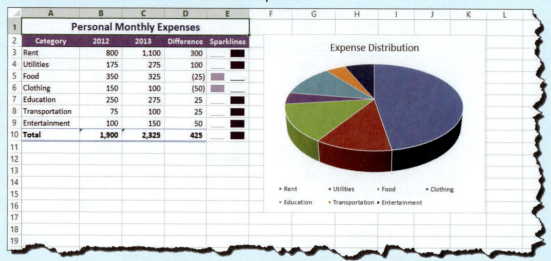

1. Locate and open the exercise data file **ex02b-ex03.xlsx**. Save the file as **ex02b-hw03.xlsx**.

2. Complete the "Difference" column by subtracting 2012 values from 2013 values. In other words, if an increase in a particular expense occurred, the value appearing in the "Difference" column should appear positive.

3. Complete the "Total" row to sum the values in each column. Make sure you do not include the year in the computation. Do not worry about the green triangle that appears in the top left-hand corner of the cell to warn you that you may have missed the year in the sum function.

4. Add a title called **Sparklines** to column E and then insert Column sparklines to the cells for years 2012 and 2013. Do not include the "Difference" results. Format the sparklines so that the first value appears different from the last value, and select an appropriate style.

5. Plot the distribution of expenses for 2013 in an embedded 3-D pie chart. To do this, first select the cell range A3:A9 and then press and hold the **Ctrl** key as you select C3:C9. You may now create the embedded pie chart using the Insert Pie or Doughnut Chart command on the INSERT tab.

6. Modify the chart title to read **Expense Distribution**.

7. Size and position the pie chart, as shown in Figure EX2.35.

8. Print the worksheet and embedded pie chart on a single, landscape-orientation page.

9. Save and then close the workbook file.

Chapter Summary

Excel provides powerful tools for analyzing and summarizing data. The ability to name cells and ranges for use in constructing expressions and navigating the worksheet increases accuracy and efficiency. You can also create formula expressions using either relative or absolute cell references. Specifying an absolute cell address by adding dollar signs ($) serves to anchor a cell reference to an exact location on the worksheet. The default, however, is to use relative cell addresses, which Excel can adjust automatically when you copy formulas to new locations in the worksheet.

Built-in functions, such as SUM and AVERAGE, are used as shortcuts to perform complex or lengthy calculations. Excel provides hundreds of functions, sorted into descriptive categories for your convenience. You enter a function by typing directly into a worksheet cell, selecting the command from the Ribbon, or by displaying the Insert Function dialog box and then selecting the desired function.

Sparklines and charts help you to present data and to convey meaning for the users of your worksheets. Most people agree that it is easier to infer trends and patterns from a line graph or column chart than from a table of numerical data. Excel makes it easy to produce and format a variety of sparkline and chart types. For reports and other professional documents, you can embed and print your charts alongside the data stored in a worksheet.

Chapter Key Terms

Absolute cell address, p. E-69
Arguments, p. E-72
AVERAGE, p. E-75
Chart sheet, p. E-99
Comparison operators, p. E-83
Conditional expressions,
  p. E-83
COUNT, p. E-78
COUNTA, p. E-79

Embedded chart, p. E-99
Functions, p. E-72
HLOOKUP, p. E-86
IF, p. E-83
MAX, p. E-78
MEDIAN, p. E-75
MIN, p. E-78
Mixed cell address, p. E-69

NOW, p. E-81
Range name, p. E-64
Relative cell address, p. E-69
Sparklines, p. E-94
SUM, p. E-72
Syntax, p. E-72
TODAY, p. E-81
VLOOKUP, p. E-86

On Your Own Exercise EX-2C-E1

This exercise provides an opportunity to practice several important skills covered in this chapter, including entering functions and creating a chart. Specifically, you will summarize the client data stored in a workbook used by a weight-loss center. To begin, open the exercise data file **ex02c-ex01.xlsx** and save it as **ex02c-hw01.xlsx**. Your screen should appear similar to Figure EX2.36.

FIGURE EX2.36   Opening the Slimmer Quicker Weight-Loss Center workbook

	A	B	C	D	E	F	G	H
1	**Slimmer Quicker Weight-Loss Center**							
2	Pounds (Lbs.) Lost per Week							
3	Client	Week 1	Week 2	Week 3	Week 4	Trend		
4	Bob	2	-2	5	-1			
5	Ted	1	0	2	3			
6	Carol	3	1	0	0			
7	Alice	2	-2	1	2			
8	Jenn	3	2	3	-1			
9	Tim	5	1	1	4			
10	Scott	3	2	-1	2			
11	Ben	0	1	2	1			
12	Susan	1	0	3	4			
13	Tessa	-1	1	-2	3			
14	Summary Statistics							
15		Week 1	Week 2	Week 3	Week 4	Trend		
16	Total							
17	Average							
18	Median							
19	Min							
20	Max							

Complete the following tasks to summarize the data in the worksheet:

- To facilitate entering functions in the Summary Statistics area of the worksheet, create range names using the row and column text labels from the cell range A3:E13.

- In the Summary Statistics area of the worksheet, use the SUM, AVERAGE, MEDIAN, MIN, and MAX functions to summarize the data for each week. You may either use the range names or the cell references to complete the functions.

- In the cell range F4:F13, insert a Win/Loss sparkline to display which weeks experienced gains versus losses. In the cell range F16:F20, insert a Column sparkline to display the magnitude of the results from one week to the next. Choose to display the High Point for these sparklines and then select an appropriate style.

- Create an embedded stacked bar chart for the client results. Size and position the results to appear similar to Figure EX2.37. Add the title **Pounds Lost by Clients** to the chart.

- Select a worksheet range containing the content and embedded chart, and then specify the range as the desired print area. Choose to print the worksheet using a landscape orientation, and then specify that it should fit on a single page. Display the worksheet in Print Preview mode and then send it to the printer

- Make any other changes that you see fit in order to match the workbook shown in Figure EX2.37. Save and then close the workbook file.

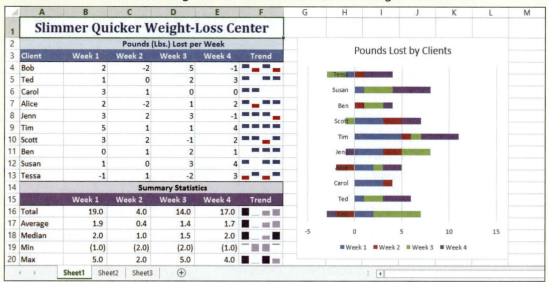

On Your Own Exercise EX-2C-E2

This exercise uses a Student Grade Tracking workbook to practice entering formulas and functions. You will use absolute cell references in your formulas, along with IF and VLOOKUP functions. To begin, open the exercise data file **ex02c-ex02.xlsx** and save it as **ex02c-hw02.xlsx**. Your screen should appear similar to Figure EX2.38.

FIGURE EX2.38 Opening the Student Grade Tracking workbook

	A	B	C	D	E	F	G	H	I	J
1	Student Grade Tracking									
2	*Weighting*	20%	30%	50%						
3	Student	Assignments	Mid-Term	Final Exam	Final Grade	Letter Grade		Score	Letter	
4	Bill	66	61	55				0	F	
5	Ted	47	58	55				50	D	
6	Juanita	82	85	78				55	C-	
7	Samuel	100	98	90				60	C	
8	Percy	79	93	92				64	C+	
9	Jennifer	68	70	73				68	B-	
10	Sima	72	62	61				72	B	
11	Joon-hae	68	54	77				76	B+	
12	Wayne	56	46	46				80	A-	
13	Garth	75	75	89				85	A	
14	Rosanne	79	84	91				90	A+	
15	Luce	99	54	77				100	Perfect	
16	**Average**									
17	**Class Advice**									
18										

Complete the following tasks to summarize the data in the worksheet:

- In cell E2, enter a SUM function to sum the Weighting percentages in the cell range B2:D2.

- In cell E4, enter a formula expression that multiplies a student's grade by the weighting factor for each activity. Because you will copy this formula down the column, you also need to specify absolute cell addresses for the weighting factors. To begin, the formula for cell E4 would be: =(B4*$B$2)+(C4*$C$2)+(D4*$D$2).

- Copy the formula in cell E4 to the cell range E5:E15. Then, format the results in the Final Grade column to appear with a single decimal place.

- In the cell range B16:E16, enter the AVERAGE function using the AutoSum button (Σ ▾). Format the results to appear with a single decimal place.

- In column F, use the VLOOKUP function to retrieve the Letter Grade from the lookup table for a student's final grade.

- In cell B17, enter an IF function that states "Good work!" if the average for the activity is greater than 72 points. If the average is less than or equal to 72, then enter "Time to study." Copy this formula to the cell range C17:E17.

- In the cell range G4:G15, enter a column sparkline to visualize the student results displayed in columns B through E. Show the Last Point marker formatted differently in the sparkline.

- Make any other changes that you see fit in order to match the workbook shown in Figure EX2.39. Save and then close the workbook file.

FIGURE EX2.39 The completed Student Grade Tracking workbook

	A	B	C	D	E	F	G	H	I	J
1	Student Grade Tracking									
2	Weighting	20%	30%	50%	100%					
3	Student	Assignments	Mid-Term	Final Exam	Final Grade	Letter Grade		Score	Letter	
4	Bill	66	61	55	59.0	C-		0	F	
5	Ted	47	58	55	54.3	D		50	D	
6	Juanita	82	85	78	80.9	A-		55	C-	
7	Samuel	100	98	90	94.4	A+		60	C	
8	Percy	79	93	92	89.7	A		64	C+	
9	Jennifer	68	70	73	71.1	B-		68	B-	
10	Sima	72	62	61	63.5	C		72	B	
11	Joon-hae	68	54	77	68.3	B-		76	B+	
12	Wayne	56	46	46	48.0	F		80	A-	
13	Garth	75	75	89	82.0	A-		85	A	
14	Rosanne	79	84	91	86.5	A		90	A+	
15	Luce	99	54	77	74.5	B		100	Perfect	
16	Average	74.3	70.0	73.7	72.7					
17	Class Advice	Good work!	Time to study	Good work!	Good work!					
18										

3 Advanced Formatting and Presenting Data in Excel

Excel Chapter 1 introduced basic formatting procedures used in Microsoft Excel 2013. In many cases, these basic formatting techniques are sufficient for most Excel users who simply need to format and present data. This chapter includes more advanced techniques used to format one cell or a range of cells. For example, using **conditional formatting** in your worksheets makes certain data stand out so data trends are easy to see. Other features such as **background bitmaps** can personalize worksheets with images.

When reports contain charts and other graphics, Excel offers options to provide you with control over the way data is displayed, either for precision or to make the data presentation more eye-catching. These options include inserting and customizing draw objects, clip art, and pictures in a worksheet.

When you work with charts in Microsoft Excel 2013, you can clarify data in a number of ways. You can change or modify how you present data on a **chart sheet** and modify **chart elements** to assist in data analysis. Examples of such modifications include changing chart scales and adding data labels to already existing charts. As with data sheets, adding draw objects and graphics to charts enhances the data presentation.

PROJECT

Working with Educational Data

In this project, you will use Microsoft Excel 2013 to format data and prepare a worksheet for printing while making statistical data more meaningful and eye-catching. You will apply conditional formatting to cells to highlight some data, apply a background bitmap, and insert and format graphics to stylize both worksheets and chart sheets.

While this project applies specifically to educational data, the techniques shown for conditional formatting, using background bitmaps, and inserting and manipulating graphics can be used in any spreadsheet, no matter what the discipline.

THE SITUATION

Work-Study Statistical Assignment

To help with the cost of college, you recently took a work-study position for a professor in the Biology Department. You proved your competence early by completing several small assignments, and the professor just gave you a major assignment that involves formatting and analyzing test data from one of his classes. He provided you with general instructions for the analysis but left the detail to you. After analyzing the data, you see that your experience with Microsoft Excel 2013 gives you the tools to successfully complete the project.

Using Conditional Formatting and Graphics in a Worksheet

In this project, you will work with educational statistical data to format it for presentation and printing. You will use conditional formatting to highlight exceptional data, use a background bitmap to personalize a worksheet, and insert and format worksheet graphics such as drawing objects, clip art, and pictures.

PROJECT FILE: *Available at* **www.mhhe.com/office2013projectlearn**

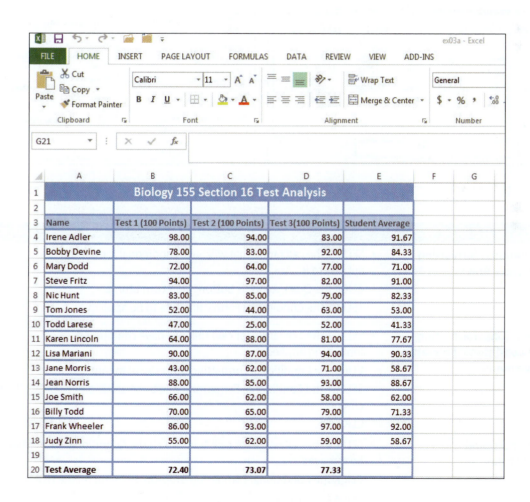

Applying Conditional Formatting

LESSON OVERVIEW

The formatting that was described and applied in Excel Chapter 1 was based on the needs and desires of the person creating and updating the workbook. Another type of formatting that can be applied to cells is conditional formatting. Conditional formatting is based on the value in the cell. For example, conditional formatting could be used to shade cells of students' test scores that are less than 60 percent. The conditional formatting is applied only if the value in the cell meets the condition (value, etc.) specified. In Excel 2013, only cells that contain text, number, date, or time values can have conditional formatting applied to them.

Apply conditional formatting with the **Quick Analysis button** or the Conditional Formatting drop-down menu in

the Styles group on the HOME tab. A number of preset conditional formatting options are available. You can delete conditional formatting rules from any data display.

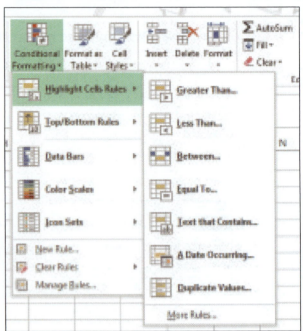

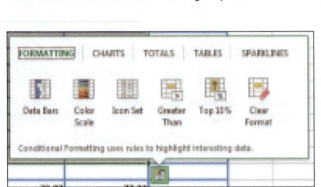

SKILLS PREVIEW

Apply conditional formatting using the Quick Analysis button	• SELECT the cell range that will have conditional formatting applied to it. CLICK the Quick Analysis button, then Formatting. SELECT the Conditional Formatting rule to be applied.
Apply conditional formatting using the Conditional Formatting drop-down menu	• SELECT the cell range (or cell) that will have conditional formatting applied to it. CLICK the Conditional Formatting drop-down menu. SELECT the Conditional Formatting rule to be applied and specify the rule criteria. CLICK OK.
Delete a Conditional Formatting rule	• SELECT the cell range (or cell) from which the Conditional Formatting rule will be removed. CLICK the Conditional Formatting drop-down menu on the HOME tab. CLICK Clear rules. CLICK the Clear option desired.

1. Locate and open the project data file **ex03a.xlsx**. On the FILE tab, use the Save As command to save the file as **ex03a-format.xlsx**. You may need to choose a place to store the file (e.g., SkyDrive or computer), and browse to the desired location.

2. Begin working with conditional formatting using the Quick Analysis button.

   SELECT the cell range of test scores and apply conditional formatting.

   SELECT the cell range B4:E18.

   CLICK the Quick Analysis button and then CLICK FORMATTING to see the conditional formatting options available.

   (*Result:* The file appears with the cell range B4:E18 highlighted and the Formatting options on the Quick Analysis button visible, as shown in Figure EX3.1.

FIGURE EX3.1 Excel project file showing Quick Analysis Conditional Formatting options

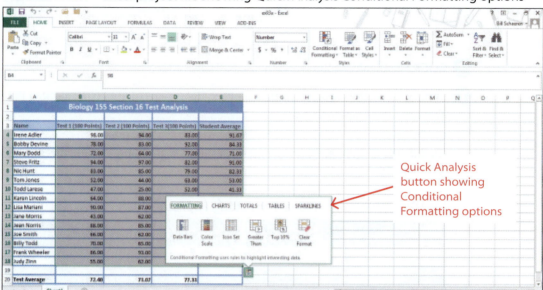

3. CLICK the Data Bars formatting option and view the display of data bars representing the test scores.

4. CLICK the Quick Analysis button again and CLICK Clear Format. This removes the conditional formatting Data Bars from the selected cell range.

5. Notice the four other Conditional Formatting options available on the Quick Analysis button. Practice using these options to view the effect the different Conditional Formatting options have on the selected cell range. Remember that conditional formatting is determined by the content of the cells.

6 A second method to apply conditional formatting to a range of cells is found in the Conditional Formatting drop-down menu in the Styles group on the HOME tab.

Display the cells containing test scores of less than 60% (passing) with a color shading and a color font. The Student Average in Column E will not be included.

SELECT the cell range B4:D18 and CLICK the Conditional Formatting drop-down menu in the Styles group on the HOME tab.

(*Result:* The Conditional Options display is shown.)

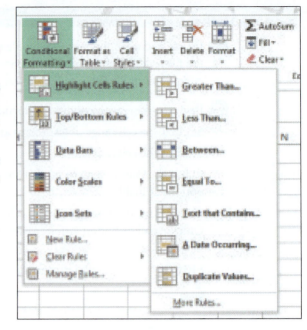

7 CLICK Highlight Cell Rules and then Less Than.

8 TYPE **60.00** in the Format cells that are Less Than area and SELECT Light Red Fill with Dark Red Text from the drop-down list.

CLICK OK.

(*Result:* The Conditional Formatting rules should appear similar to Figure EX3.2 with all test scores less than 60% highlighted.)

FIGURE EX3.2   Conditional Formatting applied

Biology 155 Section 16 Test Analysis				
Name	Test 1 (100 Points)	Test 2 (100 Points)	Test 3(100 Points)	Student Average
Irene Adler	98.00	94.00	83.00	91.67
Bobby Devine	78.00	83.00	92.00	84.33
Mary Dodd	72.00	64.00	77.00	71.00
Steve Fritz	94.00	97.00	82.00	91.00
Nic Hunt	83.00	85.00	79.00	82.33
Tom Jones	52.00	44.00	63.00	53.00
Todd Larese	47.00	25.00	52.00	41.33
Karen Lincoln	64.00	88.00	81.00	77.67
Lisa Mariani	90.00	87.00	94.00	90.33
Jane Morris	43.00	62.00	71.00	58.67
Jean Norris	88.00	85.00	93.00	88.67
Joe Smith	66.00	62.00	58.00	62.00
Billy Todd	70.00	65.00	79.00	71.33
Frank Wheeler	86.00	93.00	97.00	92.00
Judy Zinn	55.00	62.00	59.00	58.67
Test Average	**72.40**	**73.07**	**77.33**	

Conditional formatting shown in spreadsheet

9 Save the file.

Displaying a Background Bitmap

LESSON OVERVIEW

A **background** is an image placed in a worksheet that appears on the screen when the worksheet is in use. It is important to remember that background images do not print; they only appear on the worksheet on screen. However, a background image *does* show when the worksheet is displayed on the web. Generally, a background image is used to enhance the appearance of the worksheet and make it stand out on the web. Choose a background image carefully because some images detract from, rather than add to, the appearance of the worksheet and can make the data difficult to read.

Any graphic format may be used for a background, but bitmap images are most common. When the background image is inserted onto the worksheet, it fills the entire worksheet. This is known as **tiling**. Background images are available from the web, Microsoft, or the image files maintained on your computer.

SKILLS PREVIEW

Insert a background picture	• CLICK the PAGE LAYOUT tab.
	CLICK the Background button.
	Navigate to the background picture desired and DOUBLE-CLICK the picture.
Remove a background picture	• CLICK the PAGE LAYOUT tab.
	CLICK the Delete Background button.

PROJECT PRACTICE

1. Ensure that the **ex03a-format.xlsx** workbook is open in Excel.

2. Add a background image to the worksheet.

   CLICK the Background button on the PAGE LAYOUT tab.
   (*Result:* The Insert Pictures box appears that gives options where the background image may be found, as shown.)

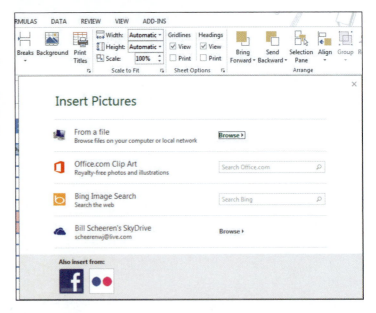

TIP

Background graphics can be procured from any online source as well as the Bing and Microsoft Corporation sites shown in the Insert Pictures box. Procedures for using images from the Internet are discussed in the Word section of the book and are discussed again later in this chapter.

3 CLICK the Browse button in the Insert Pictures box and locate the bitmap image **background_1**.

DOUBLE-CLICK the **background_1** image.

(*Result:* A scientific type background is tiled across the worksheet as shown in Figure EX3.3.)

FIGURE EX3.3 Scientific background bitmap inserted

	A	B	C	D	E	F	G	H	I	J
1			Biology 155 Section 16 Test Analysis							
2										
3	Name	Test 1 (100 Points)	Test 2 (100 Points)	Test 3(100 Points)	Student Average					
4	Irene Adler	98.00	94.00	83.00	91.67					
5	Bobby Devine	78.00	83.00	92.00	84.33					
6	Mary Dodd	72.00	64.00	77.00	71.00					
7	Steve Fritz	94.00	97.00	82.00	91.00					
8	Nic Hunt	83.00	85.00	79.00	82.33					
9	Tom Jones	52.00	44.00	63.00	53.00					
10	Todd Larese	47.00	25.00	52.00	41.33					
11	Karen Lincoln	64.00	88.00	81.00	77.67					
12	Lisa Mariani	90.00	87.00	94.00	90.33					
13	Jane Morris	43.00	62.00	71.00	58.67					
14	Jean Norris	88.00	85.00	93.00	88.67					
15	Joe Smith	66.00	62.00	58.00	62.00					
16	Billy Todd	70.00	65.00	79.00	71.33					
17	Frank Wheeler	86.00	93.00	97.00	92.00					
18	Judy Zinn	55.00	62.00	59.00	58.67					
19										
20	Test Average	72.40	73.07	77.33						

4 As it appears now, this background image is too busy and makes the data on the spreadsheet difficult to read. You should delete the background_1 image.

CLICK the Delete Background button ( ) in the Page Setup group on the PAGE LAYOUT tab.

5 Insert a more appropriate background image into the spreadsheet.

CLICK the Background button on the PAGE LAYOUT tab.

CLICK the Browse button in the Insert Pictures box and locate the bitmap image **background_2**.

DOUBLE-CLICK the **background_2** image.

(*Result:* A more appropriate background is tiled across the worksheet as shown in Figure EX3.4.)

FIGURE EX3.4 Appropriate tiled bitmap background inserted

	A	B	C	D	E	F	G	H	I	
1			Biology 155 Section 16 Test Analysis							
2										
3	Name	Test 1 (100 Points)	Test 2 (100 Points)	Test 3(100 Points)	Student Average					
4	Irene Adler	98.00	94.00	83.00	91.67					
5	Bobby Devine	78.00	83.00	92.00	84.33					
6	Mary Dodd	72.00	64.00	77.00	71.00					
7	Steve Fritz	94.00	97.00	82.00	91.00					
8	Nic Hunt	83.00	85.00	79.00	82.33					
9	Tom Jones	52.00	44.00	63.00	53.00					
10	Todd Larese	47.00	25.00	52.00	41.33					
11	Karen Lincoln	64.00	88.00	81.00	77.67					
12	Lisa Mariani	90.00	87.00	94.00	90.33					
13	Jane Morris	43.00	62.00	71.00	58.67					
14	Jean Norris	88.00	85.00	93.00	88.67					
15	Joe Smith	66.00	62.00	58.00	62.00					
16	Billy Todd	70.00	65.00	79.00	71.33					
17	Frank Wheeler	86.00	93.00	97.00	92.00					
18	Judy Zinn	55.00	62.00	59.00	58.67					
19										
20	Test Average	72.40	73.07	77.33						

6 Save the file before proceeding to the next lesson.

Inserting and Manipulating Text Boxes

LESSON OVERVIEW

Working with and adding **shapes** to your worksheets is another way to add visual emphasis with formatting options. Available shapes include lines, arrows, circles, rectangles, and triangles. Microsoft Excel's library of shapes is extensive, with more than 150 choices. Create these shapes by clicking and dragging the mouse.

Once you draw a shape, there are many options to display it. You can fill it with color, shading, or words, or the fill can be removed. Move a shape around your worksheet. You can **flip a shape** to face another direction or use the Size dialog box to add or modify it. Options for customizing your shape are similar to those for text boxes and include the use of **outline colors, fill colors, outline width,** and **precise size and positioning**.

SKILLS PREVIEW

Insert a shape into a Microsoft Excel spreadsheet	• CLICK the INSERT tab and then CLICK the Shapes drop-down list to show a palette of shapes. (See Figure EX3.5.) Choose the desired shape. DRAG the crosshair cursor to draw the shape.
Add text to a shape in a Microsoft Excel spreadsheet	• With the shape selected, TYPE the desired text. SELECT the text and format it using WordArt styles or other text formatting options.

FIGURE EX3.5 File with drop-down Shapes palette

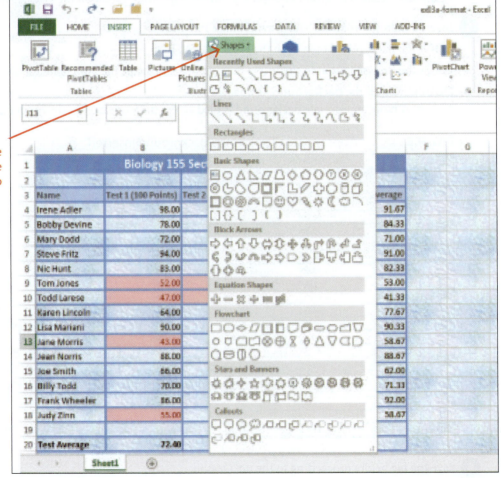

Shapes palette from the INSERT tab

TIP

When drawing a shape, you can force Excel to make the shape symmetrical by holding down the **Shift** button while you drag your mouse. For example, drawing a rectangle while holding the **Shift** button would produce a square. While drawing an oval, holding the **Shift** button would create a circle.

PROJECT PRACTICE

1 To highlight failing grades in the test analysis, you want to add a shape that points to each poor grade so your supervisor can see these quickly. Ensure that the **ex03a-format.xlsx** workbook is open in Excel.

2 CLICK the Shapes drop-down menu in the Illustrations group on the INSERT tab to display a palette of shapes, as shown in Figure EX 3.5.

In the Rectangles area, CLICK Snip Same Side Corner Rectangle (the fourth rectangle shape from the left).

(*Result:* The Shapes palette disappears and the pointer becomes a crosshair image.)

3 DRAG the crosshair down to draw a rectangular shape similar to Figure EX3.6.

DRAG the middle-left sizing handle left to widen the image (if necessary).

FIGURE EX3.6 Rectangle shape inserted on spreadsheet

	A	B	C	D	E	F	G	H	I
1		Biology 155 Section 16 Test Analysis							
2									
3	Name	Test 1 (100 Points)	Test 2 (100 Points)	Test 3(100 Points)	Student Average				
4	Irene Adler	98.00	94.00	83.00	91.67				
5	Bobby Devine	78.00	83.00	92.00	84.33				
6	Mary Dodd	72.00	64.00	77.00	71.00				
7	Steve Fritz	94.00	97.00	82.00	91.00				
8	Nic Hunt	83.00	85.00	79.00	82.33				
9	Tom Jones	52.00	44.00	63.00	53.00				
10	Todd Larese	47.00	25.00	52.00	41.33				
11	Karen Lincoln	64.00	88.00	81.00	77.67				
12	Lisa Mariani	90.00	87.00	94.00	90.33				
13	Jane Morris	43.00	62.00	71.00	58.67				
14	Jean Norris	88.00	85.00	93.00	88.67				
15	Joe Smith	66.00	62.00	58.00	62.00				
16	Billy Todd	70.00	65.00	79.00	71.33				
17	Frank Wheeler	86.00	93.00	97.00	92.00				
18	Judy Zinn	55.00	62.00	59.00	58.67				
19									
20	Test Average	72.40	73.07	77.33					

4 If needed, CLICK the rectangular shape to make it active.

TYPE **Failing Grades Contain Reddish Conditional Formatting**

CLICK the Center icon (▤) in the Alignment group of the HOME tab.

CLICK the Bold icon in the Font group of the HOME tab and then increase the font size to 12.
(*Result:* The rectangular shape should appear as in Figure EX3.7.)

Failing Grades Contain Reddish Conditional Formatting

5 Add arrows to direct the viewer to the failing grades on the spreadsheet.

CLICK the Shapes drop-down menu in the Illustrations group on the INSERT tab to open a palette of shapes.

In the Lines area, CLICK Arrow (the second line shape from the left).

(*Result:* The Shapes palette disappears and the pointer becomes a crosshair image.)

6 DRAG the crosshair from the rectangular shape to one of the failing grades. Repeat the step to draw more lines to other failing grades using Figure EX3.7 as a guide.

Hold the ⎡Shift⎤ key and CLICK to select each arrow.

On the FORMAT tab, SELECT Automatic from the Shape Outline drop-down menu.

(*Result:* The rectangular shape and arrows appear as in Figure EX3.7.)

FIGURE EX3.7   Rectangular shape with text and arrows added

Rectangular shape with text and arrows added

7 Save the file before proceeding to the next lesson.

Inserting Clip Art and Pictures

LESSON OVERVIEW

While the Office.com clip art library can be used to search for pictures and illustrations, often you will have pictures on your computer that are applicable to your project. Excel allows you to add pictures to any spreadsheet. After clicking Pictures in the Illustrations group, a dialog box opens and you can browse your computer to find the correct picture file.

In chapters in the Microsoft Word portion of the book, you used the techniques to locate clip art for your documents. In this chapter we will use clip art that is already on your computer for use in an Excel worksheet. Clip art, like a cartoon or drawing, is generally regarded as an illustration. The clip art that is part of the Office.com clip art library is royalty-free and available to anyone. You are already familiar with the techniques used to search for, insert, resize, drag, and position clip art because they are the same ones used for photographs.

SKILLS PREVIEW

Insert a graphic (photograph or clip art) from your computer	• CLICK the INSERT tab and locate the Illustrations group. CLICK Pictures as shown in Figure EX3.8. Locate the image on your computer. CLICK Insert.
Modify pictures using Layout Options	• CLICK on an image to select it. CLICK the Layout Options button (🖼). Set the text wrapping of the image, anchor it to neighboring text, or fix its position on the page or CLICK See more… to activate the Layout dialog box.
Crop an image	• CLICK the image to select it. CLICK the top half of the Crop button. DRAG the cropping handles to remove the unneeded portion of the picture. CLICK outside the picture to complete the crop.

FIGURE EX3.8   Insert Picture dialog box showing Pictures library

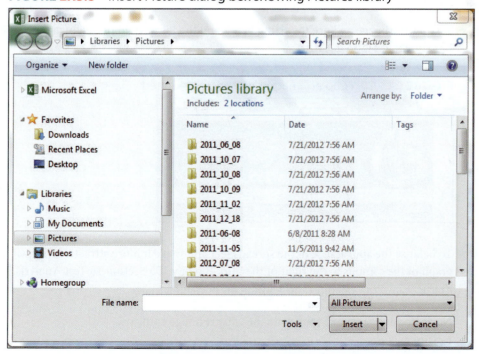

1 You want to add both a clip art image that represents Biology 155 and a photograph of the campus at the top of the spreadsheet. Ensure that the **ex03a-format.xlsx** workbook is open in Excel.

2 Prepare the spreadsheet for the two images you will insert.

RIGHT-CLICK row 1 of the **ex03a-format.xlsx** workbook.

CLICK Row Height.

TYPE **60** and CLICK the OK button.

3 CLICK the Pictures button in the Illustration group on the INSERT tab.

Navigate your files until you locate the clip art image **microscope**.

DOUBLE-CLICK it.

Use the ⊕ mouse pointer to move the clip art image to the upper left as shown in Figure EX3.9.

FIGURE EX3.9 Spreadsheet with unformatted clip art image added

4 SELECT the image and use the sizing handle on the lower right of the image to size it so it fits in row 1 as shown in Figure EX3.10.

FIGURE EX3.10 Clip art image sized and positioned

5 To balance the appearance of the spreadsheet and make it more attractive, you will insert a photograph of the campus to the right of the title "Biology 155 Section 16 Test Analysis."

CLICK Pictures in the Illustration group on the INSERT tab.

Navigate your files until you locate the clip art image **campus**.

DOUBLE-CLICK it.

Use the ✛ mouse pointer to move the clip art image to the upper right as shown in Figure EX3.11.

FIGURE EX3.11   Spreadsheet with unformatted picture inserted

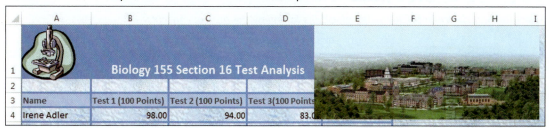

6 More of the campus is showing than is needed, so you want to crop the picture.

CLICK the Crop drop-down menu in the Size group of the FORMAT tab under Picture Tools.

SELECT Crop. The picture shows six crop marks. When you place the mouse pointer on the crop marks, the pointer appears as a T or L, depending on which crop mark was active. This pointer allows you to crop the picture.

Use the crop tool to remove portions of the picture so it appears as shown in Figure EX3.12.

CLICK outside the picture to complete the crop.

FIGURE EX3.12   Picture cropped

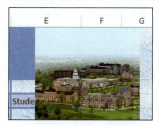

7 SELECT the image and use the sizing handle on the lower right of the image to size it so it fits in column E of row 1 as shown in Figure EX3.13.

FIGURE EX3.13   Completed worksheet with pictures sized and positioned

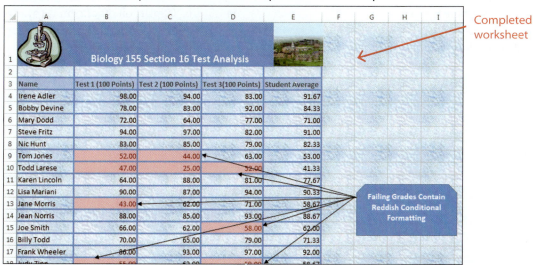

8 Save the workbook file and exit Excel.

MULTIPLE-CHOICE QUIZ

Select the best choice in the following questions to review the project concepts.

1. Conditional formatting is applied to cells containing
   a. formulas.
   b. functions.
   c. numbers.
   d. sparklines.

2. Which of the following conditional formatting options is used to highlight cells based on a specified rule?
   a. Icon sets
   b. Color scales
   c. Data bars
   d. Highlight Cell rules

3. Which of the following is true for a background in Excel 2013?
   a. It prints.
   b. It is generally a bitmap.
   c. It always tiles.
   d. It is also called a watermark.

4. How many sizing handles are there on a drawing object?
   a. 2
   b. 4
   c. 6
   d. 8

5. Which of the following is NOT used to enhance a shape added to a worksheet?
   a. Flip shape
   b. Crop shape
   c. Outline width
   d. Fill colors

6. Use _____ to enhance the overall appearance of a worksheet.
   a. charts
   b. forms
   c. clip art
   d. queries

7. When the mouse pointer changes to a _____ shape, you can move a clip art image to a new position.
   a. ✛
   b. ✜
   c. ▨
   d. ✛

8. You have marketing reps with sales greater than $1,000,000. Which conditional format in a spreadsheet would best emphasize sales?
   a. Highlight cell rules
   b. Top/Bottom rules
   c. Data bars
   d. Icon sets

9. Sizing handles will display when which of the following is selected?
   a. An embedded chart
   b. The title of a chart
   c. A text box or drawing object
   d. All of these are correct.

10. Which of the following is true for clip art?
    a. Clip art is installed with Microsoft Office 2013.
    b. Clip art on office.com is royalty-free.
    c. Clip art is exclusively photographs.
    d. Clip art is seldom color illustrations.

In this exercise, you are a student conducting a work-study project in the science department. In this task, you will finalize temperature data that your supervisor gathered for an extended climate study. You will create a worksheet similar to Figure EX3.14. The final worksheet is shown in Figure EX3.14.

FIGURE EX3.14 Work It Out EX-3A-E1: completed

	A	B	C	D	E	F
1		Quarterly Temperature Averages(in degrees Farenheit)				
2	Month	January	April	July	October	
3						
4	Albany, N.Y.	22.20	46.60	71.10	49.30	
5	Albuquerque, N.M.	35.70	55.60	78.50	57.30	
6	Anchorage, Alaska	15.80	36.30	58.40	34.10	
7	Asheville, N.C.	35.80	54.10	73.00	55.20	
8	Atlanta, Ga.	42.70	61.60	80.00	62.80	
9	Atlantic City, N.J.	32.10	50.60	75.30	55.10	
10	Austin, Texas	50.20	68.30	84.20	70.60	
11	Baltimore, Md.	32.30	53.20	76.50	55.40	
12	Baton Rouge, La.	50.10	66.60	81.70	68.10	
13	Billings, Mont.	24.00	46.10	72.00	48.10	
14						
15	Lowest temperature noted.					
16						
17						

1 Locate and open the exercise data file **ex03a-ex01.xlsx**. Save the file as **ex03a-hw01.xlsx**.

2 Your supervisor asks you to highlight temperatures less than 50 degrees. You decide to apply a Conditional Formatting rule to cells B4:E13 that shows cells that meet those criteria with green fill with dark green text.

3 Insert the rounded rectangle shape below the worksheet with an arrow pointing to the January temperature in Anchorage, Alaska, with the text "Lowest temperature noted." in the shape.

4 Resize the shape and format the text as shown in Figure EX3.14.

5 Insert the **hw01 background** in the worksheet.

6 Insert the picture **weather pix** into the spreadsheet, size it, and place it to the right of the title as shown in Figure EX3.14.

7 Insert the clip art image **snow clip** into the spreadsheet, size it, and place it to the left of the title as shown in Figure EX3.14.

8 Save and close the workbook file.

In this exercise you are working with a local automobile dealer. The dealership asks you to prepare data showing sales data for the top 10 brands of cars sold in the United States. You will use an Excel spreadsheet to present the data and to highlight significant trends in car sales. The final worksheet is shown in Figure EX3.15.

FIGURE EX3.15   Work It Out EX-3A-E2: completed

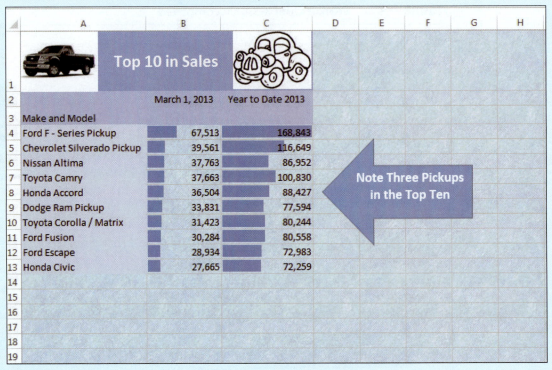

1. Locate and open the exercise data file **ex03a-ex02.xlsx**. Save the file as **ex03a-hw02.xlsx**.

2. Your supervisor at the dealership asks you to make sales for the top 10 sellers stand out. Use the Quick Analysis button to apply Conditional Formatting data bars to cells B4:C13.

3. Insert the Left arrow shape from the Block Arrows group on the right of the data. Place the words "Note Three Pickups in the Top Ten" in the shape.

4. Resize the shape and format the text as shown in Figure EX3.15.

5. Insert the **hw02 background** in the worksheet.

6. Insert the picture **pickup_truck** in the spreadsheet, size it, and place it to the left of the title as shown in Figure EX3.15.

7. Insert the clip art image **clip_car** in the spreadsheet, size it, and place it to the right of the title as shown in Figure EX3.15.

8. Save and close the workbook file.

HANDS-ON EXERCISE: WORK IT OUT EX-3A-E3 (*Available at* www.mhhe.com/office2013projectlearn)

Enhancing a Report with Charts and Graphics

In this project you will continue modifying the formatting in the worksheet from Project 3A. In addition, you will create a chart to present data graphically. The chart will initially be embedded on the worksheet and later will be moved to a separate chart sheet. First, you will plot data into a chart. Then you will create a chart sheet. Next, you will add, remove, and modify chart elements such as legends and data labels. You will also format chart elements to make them more attractive and further add to a chart's look and utility by adding and manipulating draw objects. Last, you will create headers and footers in the workbook and print the complete workbook.

PROJECT FILE: *Available at* **www.mhhe.com/office2013projectlearn**

PROJECT OBJECTIVES

After completing this project, you will be able to:

- Plot data in a chart on a separate chart sheet.

- Add, modify, and remove elements from charts.

- Format chart elements to best display the data expressed in the chart.

- Use drawing objects to enhance a chart.

- Place headers and footers in workbooks.

- Print the completed workbook to include the chart sheet.

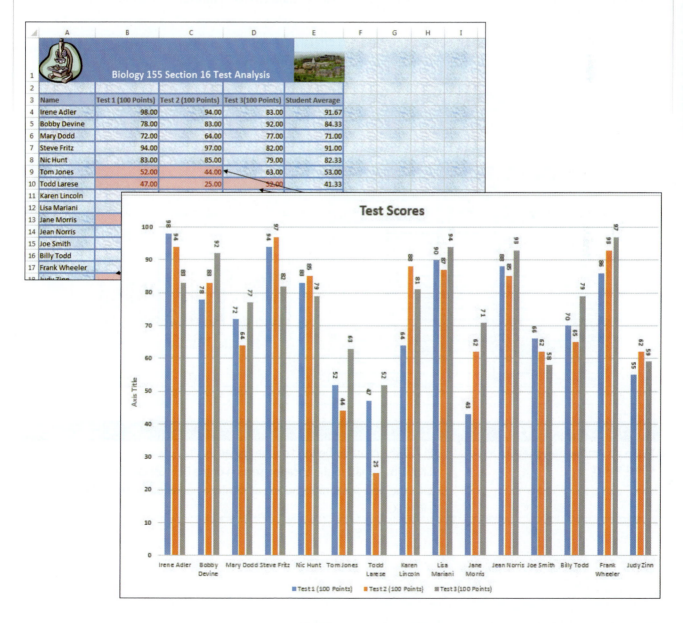

Plotting a Chart in a Chart Sheet

LESSON OVERVIEW

Chapter 2 introduced the concept of charting in Excel. A chart is simply a visual representation of the data contained in one or more spreadsheets. The creation of charts is the primary way data is displayed in Excel and can assist in the interpretation of data. Over the various versions of Excel, the creation and modification of charts has changed, generally making it easier for the user to create meaningful, easy-to-understand displays. The primary change to charting in Microsoft Excel

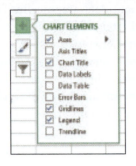

2013 is the **Chart Elements button** that appears to the right of a chart, **embedded,** or placed on a separate chart sheet. The Chart Elements button is the charting equivalent of the Quick Analysis button that appears when you select data on a spreadsheet.

In Excel 2013, the default chart location is embedded on the spreadsheet. This places all data near the spreadsheet but sometimes limits the size and how you can view a chart. In this lesson, you will place a chart on a separate sheet in the workbook, called a **chart sheet.** This placement does not change the data itself but gives you more space to add chart elements and modify them. Figure EX3.16 shows a chart embedded on a spreadsheet.

FIGURE EX3.16   Spreadsheet with embedded chart

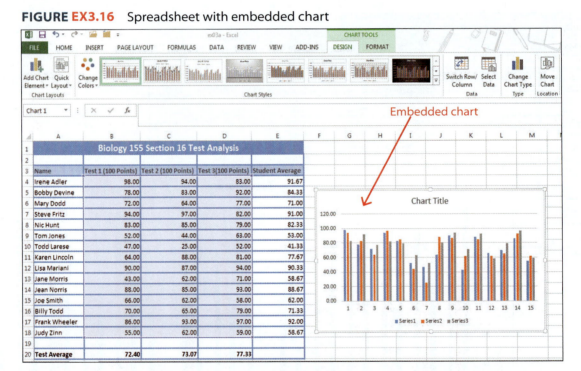

SKILLS PREVIEW

Move an embedded chart to a chart sheet	• SELECT the chart embedded on the spreadsheet. CLICK Move Chart in the Location section of the DESIGN tab under Chart Tools. CLICK the New sheet radio button and enter a name for the chart sheet. CLICK OK.

1. Locate and open the project data file **ex03a.xlsx**. On the FILE tab, use the Save As command to save the file as **ex03b-chartsheet.xlsx**. You may need to choose a place to store the file (e.g., SkyDrive or Computer), and browse to the desired location.

2. Create the chart as an embedded chart.

   SELECT cells A3:D18.

   CLICK the Quick Analysis button and CLICK Charts.
   (*Result:* This shows the recommended charts for the range of data selected.)

3. Move your mouse over the different types of charts to preview the chart with the data displayed.

   CLICK Clustered Column.
   (*Result:* This places a clustered column chart on the spreadsheet. If the chart were to be embedded, it would be moved and then formatted.)
   Ensure that the chart is selected.

   CLICK the Move Chart button in the Location group of the DESIGN tab under Chart Tools.

   CLICK the New sheet radio button and TYPE **Chart Sheet 1**.

   CLICK OK.
   (*Result:* The chart appears on a separate chart sheet titled Chart Sheet 1 as shown in Figure EX3.17.)

FIGURE EX3.17   Chart sheet with chart

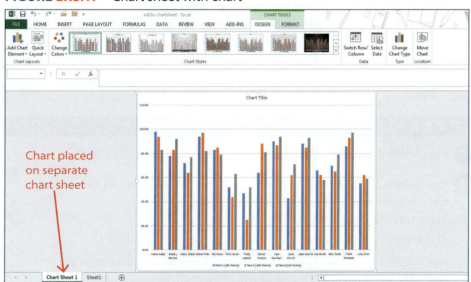

Chart placed on separate chart sheet

4. Save the file before proceeding to the next lesson.

Adding and Removing Chart Elements

LESSON OVERVIEW

You can see that this chart was created and embedded on the spreadsheet as a bare-bones chart. It is missing some chart elements and other elements are not descriptive enough to make them useful. To add chart elements, use the Chart Elements button (⊞) or the Add Chart Element drop-down menu in the Chart Layouts group of the DESIGN tab under Chart Tools. To delete an unwanted chart element, select it and then press the `Delete` key.

Chart elements that may be added or deleted are Axes, Axis Title, Chart Title, Data Labels, Data Table, Error Bars, Gridlines, Legend, and Trendlines. In this lesson we will apply some of these that are appropriate for the chart and delete those that are not suitable.

SKILLS PREVIEW

Add chart elements using the Chart Elements button	• SELECT the chart on the chart sheet. CLICK the Chart Elements button (⊞). SELECT the chart element to be added and then CLICK the right triangle for the options available for the chart element. SELECT the option of the chart element to be used.
Add chart elements using the Chart Element drop-down menu	• SELECT the chart on the chart sheet. CLICK the Add Chart Element drop-down menu in the Charts Layout group of the DESIGN tab under Chart Tools. SELECT the chart element to be added and then CLICK the right triangle for the options available for the chart element. SELECT the option of the chart element to be used.
Delete chart elements	• SELECT the chart element to be deleted and PRESS the `Del` key.

PROJECT PRACTICE

1 Ensure that the **ex03b-chartsheet.xlsx** workbook is open in Excel.

2 If necessary, navigate to Chart Sheet 1 in the workbook. You will add several chart elements and delete others.
Make sure the chart is selected.

CLICK the Chart Elements button (⊞) as shown in Figure EX3.18.

Notice that Axes, Chart Title, Gridlines, and Legend are currently on the chart. We will quickly delete one or two of those to see the results.

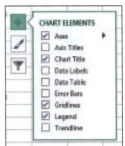

3 CLICK the right triangle to the right of Axes and then remove the check mark from Primary Vertical and Primary Horizontal.
(*Result:* Both axes are removed and the result should appear as in Figure EX3.18.)

FIGURE EX3.18 Chart with horizontal and vertical axes removed

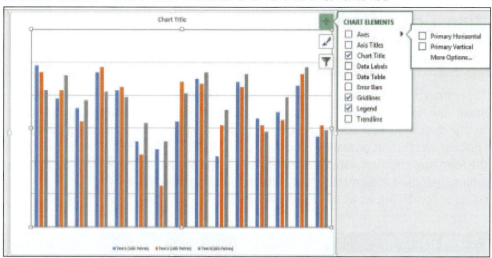

4 Place the axes back on the chart.

CLICK the Chart Elements button and place a check mark in the Axes box.
This and other commands in the Chart Elements button are toggle commands you control by removing or placing check marks in the boxes.

5 Experiment with other chart elements to observe the effect if they are removed.

6 Add the following chart elements to the chart: Axis Titles and Data Labels. These elements are typically found on charts.

CLICK the Chart Elements button and place a check mark in both Axis Title and Data Labels.
(*Result:* Default entries for these two data elements are placed in the chart as shown in Figure EX3.19. These will be formatted in the next lesson.)

FIGURE EX3.19 Chart with Axis Titles and Data Labels added

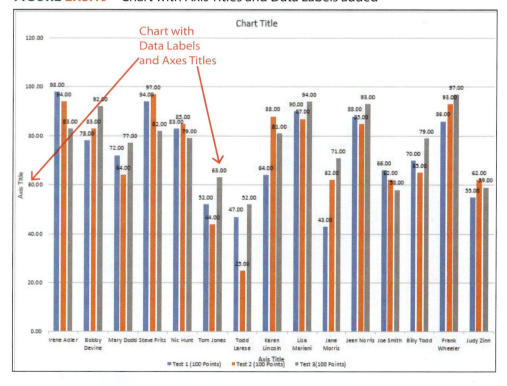

7 Save the file before proceeding to the next lesson.

Formatting Chart Elements

LESSON OVERVIEW

It is easy to see from their appearance that several of the chart elements are not appropriate for the chart or do not display the data to its best advantage. One of the strongest parts of Excel's charting feature is that you can change the format of chart elements and experiment with the chart itself once it is created. Apply different styles and color combinations to the chart with the **Chart Styles button** or eliminate data elements from the chart with the **Chart Filters button**.

In this lesson, you will experiment with both the Chart Styles and the Chart Filters buttons. First, you will restore the original setting to the chart before formatting the existing chart elements.

SKILLS PREVIEW

Change chart elements using the Chart Styles button	• SELECT the chart on the chart sheet. CLICK the Chart Styles button (a graphic of this button is shown in Figure EX3.20) CLICK the chart style to be added and the color to be changed.
Change chart elements using the Chart Filters button	• SELECT the chart on the chart sheet. CLICK the Chart Filters button (a graphic of this button is shown in Figure EX3.20) CLICK the Values or Names to delete.
Formatting chart elements	• RIGHT-CLICK the chart element to format. CLICK to choose Element from the Format shortcut menu. Make changes as appropriate to the chart element.

FIGURE EX3.20 Chart Styles and Chart Filters buttons

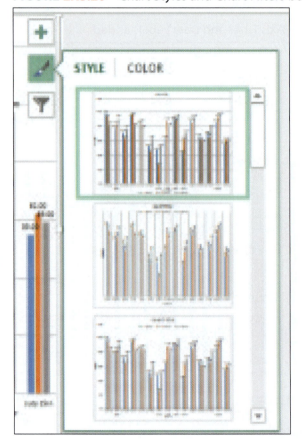
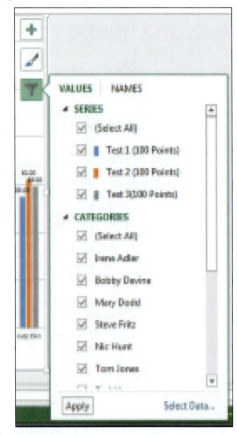

1. Ensure that the **ex03b-chartsheet.xlsx** workbook is open in Excel.

2. Change the appearance of the chart using the Chart Styles button.
   Ensure the chart on Chart Sheet 1 is selected.

   CLICK the Chart Styles button.

   CLICK Style 2.

   CLICK the Chart Styles button.

   CLICK Change Colors.

   CLICK Colorful, Color 4.
   (*Result:* The chart should appear as in Figure EX3.21.)

FIGURE EX3.21 Chart with Chart Styles formatting applied

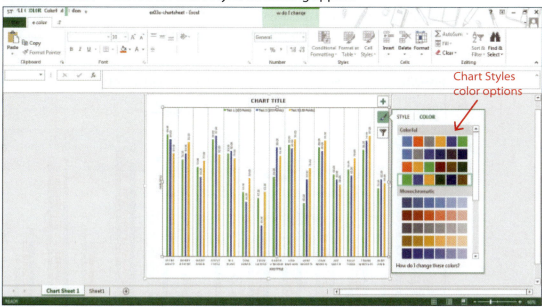

3. Experiment with different style and color combinations.

4. Restore the original chart settings (Style 2 and Colorful, Color 1).

5. Format the chart title.

   RIGHT-CLICK the Chart Title placeholder on the chart on Chart Sheet 1.

   CLICK Format Chart Title.

   TYPE **Test Scores** and PRESS Enter.
   If necessary, CLICK the Bold button (**B**) in the Font group of the HOME tab.
   Change the font size to 18 in the Font group of the HOME tab.

6. Format the vertical axis so the maximum score on the test is 100.

   RIGHT-CLICK the Vertical Axis placeholder on the chart on Chart Sheet 1.

   CLICK Format Axis.

   TYPE **100** in the Maximum Bounds text box.

   CLICK Number and TYPE **0** in the Decimal places: box.

   CLICK the Bold button (**B**) in the Font group of the HOME tab.

7 Format the data labels so they are more prominent. (It will be necessary to complete this operation three times, one for each data series, to account for all data labels.)

RIGHT-CLICK the Data Labels placeholder on the chart on Chart Sheet 1.

SELECT Format Data Labels.

CLICK the Size & Properties button.

CLICK to expand the Alignment option and then SELECT Rotate all text 90 degrees from text direction.

CLICK Number to expand the option.

SELECT Number in the Category Drop-Down list.

TYPE **0** in the Decimal places: box.

CLICK the Bold button (**B**) in the Font section of the HOME tab.

Repeat these steps for all data labels.

The final formatted chart should appear similar to Figure EX3.22.

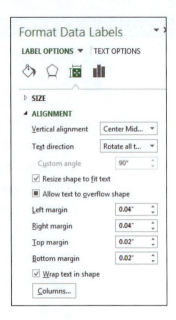

FIGURE **EX3.22**   Final formatting for chart on chart sheet

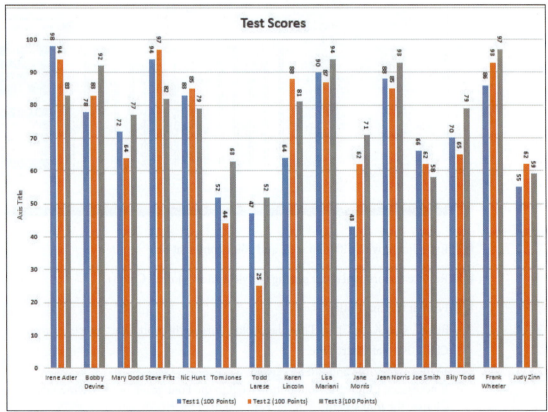

8 Save the file before proceeding to the next lesson.

Enhancing a Chart Using Drawing Objects

LESSON OVERVIEW

You were introduced to the application of shapes in the Microsoft Word section and in this chapter of Microsoft Excel where you inserted shapes into spreadsheets. You can apply the same techniques from those two discussions here. Microsoft Office 2013 provides more than 150 shapes you can use to enhance a chart and to better emphasize trends in the chart. In this lesson, you will insert a shape into the chart and add text to the shape to indicate there are no trends in student test scores.

From a design standpoint, sometimes less is more regarding formatting and including different shapes in an Excel chart. The goal of the chart is to effectively present your message; this goal is not met if your message is overwhelmed by graphic elements.

SKILLS PREVIEW

Adding a shape to a chart	• CLICK the INSERT tab and then CLICK the Shapes drop-down list to show a palette of shapes. Choose the desired shape. DRAG the crosshair cursor to draw the shape.
Add text to a shape in a chart	• With the shape selected, TYPE the desired text. SELECT the text and format it using WordArt styles or other text formatting options.

PROJECT PRACTICE

1 Ensure that the **ex03b-chartsheet.xlsx** workbook is open in Excel.

2 Create the shape and place it in an appropriate location on the chart sheet.

CLICK in the chart to ensure it is active.

CLICK the INSERT tab.

CLICK the Shapes drop-down list to display a palette of shapes.
(*Result:* The screen should appear as shown in Figure EX3.23.)

FIGURE EX3.23   Chart with Shapes palette

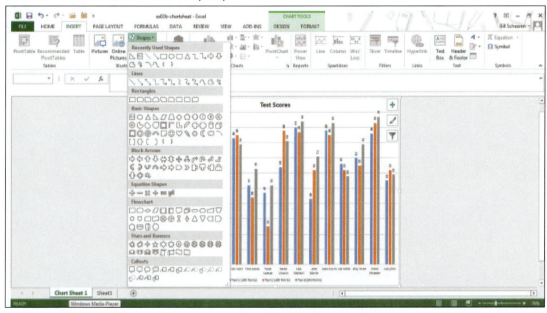

3 Go to the Block Arrows section.

SELECT Down arrow, the fourth arrow shape from the left.

Using the crosshair mouse pointer, draw the shape as shown in Figure EX3.24.

Drawing object with words added

FIGURE EX3.24 Chart with arrow shape and text

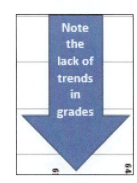

4 CLICK the arrow shape to make it active.

TYPE **Note the lack of trends in grades**

CLICK the Center icon (⬚) in the Alignment group of the HOME tab.

CLICK the Bold button (**B**) in the Font group of the HOME tab.
Increase the font size to 12.
(*Result:* The arrow shape should appear as in Figure EX3.24.)

5 Save the file before proceeding to the next lesson.

Inserting Headers and Footers

LESSON OVERVIEW

Headers and footers convey general information about the document on each page. Common header and footer elements are page numbers, the title of the document, the author, and the date. Microsoft Excel provides predefined header and footer layouts to make it easy to insert uniform header and footer information. When you use a predefined header or footer, data from the document properties and the cover page (if already created) will automatically appear in placeholders in the header or footer. You can add more information to the header and footer. Excel allows you to modify elements of a header or footer with different font styles and sizes just like text anywhere else in the spreadsheet. Changing one header or footer automatically changes all the headers or footers in your document.

SKILLS PREVIEW

Insert a header or footer using predefined headers or footers	• CLICK the INSERT tab, then CLICK the Header and Footer button in the Text group. CLICK the Header drop-down list. CLICK to select the predefined header. or CLICK the Footer button. CLICK to select the predefined footer.

PROJECT PRACTICE

1. Ensure that the **ex03b-chartsheet.xlsx** workbook is open in Excel.

2. Insert a predefined header and footer to ChartSheet1 and make a few changes.
   CLICK the INSERT tab.
   CLICK the Header and Footer button in the Text group.
   (*Result:* The Page Setup dialog box appears as shown in Figure EX3.25.)

FIGURE EX3.25   Page Setup dialog box

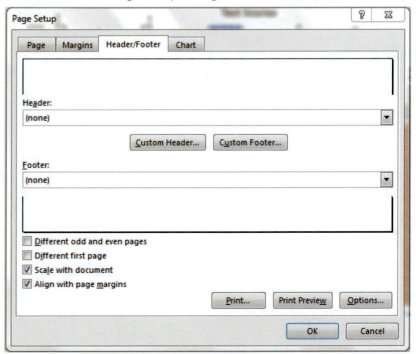

3 Add the Header and Footer elements.

SELECT Chart Sheet 1 in the Header drop-down list.

SELECT Page 1 in the Footer drop-down list.

Ensure that the options at the bottom of the Page Setup dialog box appear as shown in Figure EX3.26.

FIGURE EX3.26   Page Setup dialog box with correct options checked

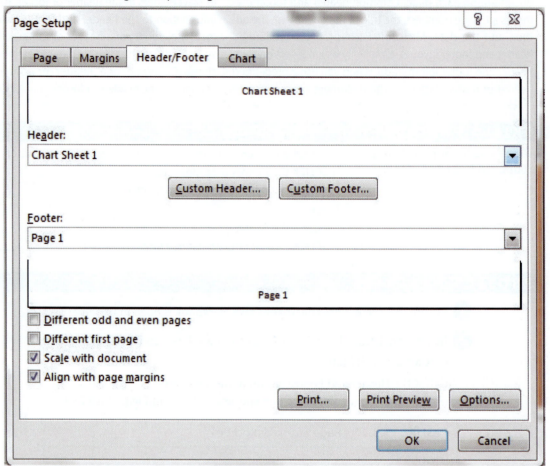

4 CLICK OK.

(*Result:* The chart sheet has both Header and Footer added, but they can only be viewed in Print Preview.)

Printing a Report with a Chart and Headers and Footers

LESSON OVERVIEW

In earlier lessons, you printed a report that included a worksheet. In this lesson, you will print an entire workbook that includes both a worksheet and a chart sheet. Printing these elements may not be the best way to display data, but it is a first step to show trends and the results of data analysis. This report also includes a header and footer that will print with the rest of the workbook.

SKILLS PREVIEW

Print a report with a worksheet, a chart sheet, and headers and footers

- CLICK the FILE tab to enter the Backstage view.
  CLICK PRINT to view the printer settings.
  SELECT the appropriate printer settings.
  CLICK the Print button.

PROJECT PRACTICE

1. Ensure that the **ex03b-chartsheet.xlsx** workbook is open in Excel. Use Figure EX-3.28 as a guide.

2. Set printer settings and view the headers and footers you created in the previous lesson.

   CLICK the FILE tab to enter the Backstage view.

   CLICK the Print menu to view the default printer settings.
   The Backstage view should be similar to Figure EX3.27.

   FIGURE EX3.27   Backstage view showing the completed chart sheet

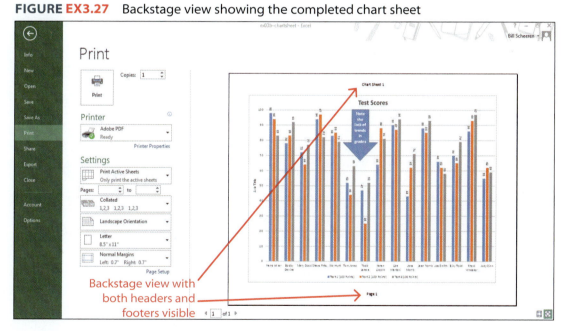

Backstage view with both headers and footers visible

3. Make the following changes to the printer settings:

   In the Printer drop-down list, select the printer that will print your file. Your instructor can help you with this.

   In the Settings drop-down list, change Print Active Sheets to Print Active Workbook.

   View the header and footer on the sheet.

   The Backstage view should appear similar to Figure EX3.28.

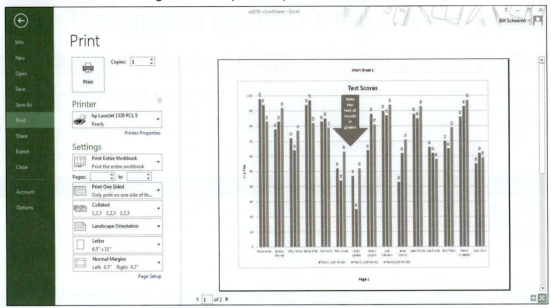

4 CLICK the Print button.

5 Save the workbook file and exit Excel.

MULTIPLE-CHOICE QUIZ

Select the best choice in the following questions to review the project concepts.

1. A workbook can contain
   a. a separate chart sheet for every workbook.
   b. a separate chart sheet for every worksheet.
   c. a separate workbook for every chart sheet.
   d. a sheet with both a workbook and a chart.

2. A workbook includes a budget worksheet with two embedded charts. The workbook also includes one chart on its own worksheet. How many files does it take to store this workbook?
   a. One
   b. Two
   c. Three
   d. Four

3. A data range is used as the basis for an embedded pie chart and a column chart in a chart sheet. Which chart(s) will change if you change the values in the data range?
   A. The column chart
   b. The pie chart
   c. Both the pie chart and the column chart
   d. Neither the pie chart nor the column chart

4. Multiple data series are selected and plotted as a clustered column chart and a stacked chart. Which of the following is true about the *y*-axis scale for the charts?
   a. The scale for the stacked columns chart contains larger values than that for the clustered chart.
   b. The scale for the clustered columns contains larger values than that for the stacked columns.
   c. The values on the scale will be the same for both charts.
   d. The values will be different, but it is not possible to tell which chart has higher values.

5. Chart elements are added to charts and may include any of the following EXCEPT
   a. axis titles.
   b. data labels.
   c. legend.
   d. chart values.

6. The following statements describe chart elements. Which statement is false?
   a. Chart elements can be formatted.
   b. Chart styles list styles and color combinations.
   c. Chart filters eliminate data elements from a chart.
   d. Formatted chart elements are deleted before reformatting.

7. Arrows and rectangle shapes can be created using this Excel feature to enhance a chart and emphasize trends in the data series.
   a. Clip art
   b. Illustrations
   c. Drawing objects
   d. Bitmap images

8. Which of the following is false for headers and footers used in Excel 2013?
   a. Common header and footer elements include page number, author, and date.
   b. One predefined header and footer layout is available for Excel.
   c. If it exists, placeholder header and footer data is copied from document properties and the cover page.
   d. Header and footer elements can be modified.

9. Which of the following is true for printing from Excel 2013?
   a. The same header and footer data is printed on all pages of a workbook.
   b. Header and footer data is not printed in chart sheets.
   c. Unique header and footer data is printed on each worksheet and chart sheet.
   d. Header and footer data must be specially formatted in order to print.

10. Charts consist of a number of _____ that are used to graphically display worksheet data.
    a. groups
    b. elements
    c. gridlines
    d. titles

You want to raise extra money for your school by selling some of your collectible baseball cards, and you need to track your earnings. In this exercise, you will prepare an Excel spreadsheet to chart the value of each card, enter the set auction minimum, and track the sale price from the auction. The final worksheet is shown in Figure EX3.29.

FIGURE EX3.29 Work It Out EX-3B-E1: completed

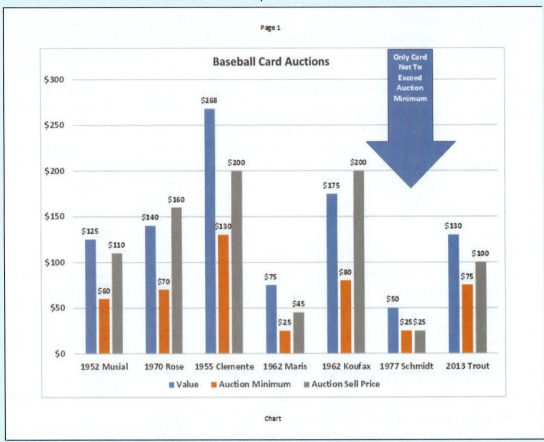

1. Locate and open the exercise data file **ex03b-ex01.xlsx**. Save the file as **ex03b-hw01.xlsx**.

2. Select the cell range A3:D10 and use the Quick Analysis button to create a Clustered Column chart embedded on the worksheet.

3. Use the Move Chart button on the **DESIGN** tab under Chart Tools to move the chart to a chart sheet. Name the chart sheet "Chart."

4. Name the chart sheet "Baseball Card Auctions" and make the title bold 14.

5. Bold both axes labels and the legend. Make the font size of these elements 14.

6. Insert data labels that are 12 point bold.

7. Insert the Down arrow shape from the Block Arrows group and place it above the 1977 Schmidt chart bars as shown in Figure EX3.29. Size the shape appropriately.

8. Type **Only Card Not To Exceed Auction Minimum** in the shape.

9. Center-align and bold the words. Make the font size 12.

10. Insert a preset header and footer as shown in Figure EX3.29.

11. Print the chart sheet.

12. Save and close the workbook file.

In this exercise, you will track the passing statistics of your favorite pro football quarterback. To help you track the statistics, you will prepare an Excel spreadsheet and chart several important statistics. The final worksheet is shown in Figure EX3.30.

FIGURE EX3.30   Work It Out EX-3B-E2: completed

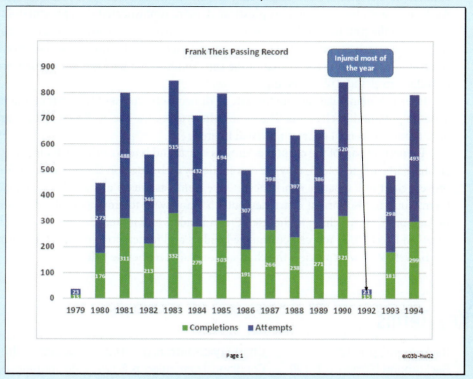

1. Locate and open the exercise data file **ex03b-ex02.xlsx**. Save the file as **ex03b-hw02.xlsx**.

2. Select the cell range A2:C17 and use the Quick Analysis button to create a Stacked Column chart embedded on the worksheet.

3. Use the Move Chart button on the **DESIGN** tab under Chart Tools to move the chart to a chart sheet. Name the chart sheet "Theis."

4. Use the Chart Style button to change the color scheme to Colorful, Color 4.

5. Name the chart "Frank Theis Passing Record" and change the font size to 16, bold.

6. Bold both axes and the legend. Make the font size of these elements 16.

7. Insert data labels that are 11 point bold White.

8. Insert a Rounded Rectangle shape from the Rectangles group and place it above the 1992 statistic chart bars as shown in Figure EX3.30. Size the shape appropriately.

9. Add an arrow shape as shown in Figure EX3.30.

10. Type **Injured most of the year** in the shape.

11. Center-align and bold the words and make the font size 14.

12. Insert a preset footer as shown in Figure EX3.30.

13. Print the chart sheet.

14. Save and close the workbook file.

HANDS-ON EXERCISE: WORK IT OUT EX-3B-E3 (*Available at* www.mhhe.com/office2013projectlearn)

Chapter Summary

Using advanced formatting techniques and deciding how to display data in Excel are important skills in any academic discipline. Presenting data in an interesting and clear way makes it easier for the audience to interpret the data and to more clearly understand the goals the preparer had for the data. As the data itself becomes more sophisticated, more sophisticated data presentation techniques must be used. In the first half of the chapter, you were introduced to advanced formatting techniques for spreadsheets such as conditional formatting and background bitmaps. In conditional formatting, the cell contents determine the format of the cell. You inserted background bitmaps into worksheets to introduce an element of ownership.

Inserting, manipulating, and formatting drawing objects assist the presenter in making key points about important data elements. The same holds true for the use of clip art and pictures, both of which have the added benefit of creating visual interest.

The second part of the chapter addresses charts and how to enhance their appearance. When you create charts in Excel 2013, they are automatically embedded on the spreadsheet. You learned how to move a chart to a separate chart sheet. Once elements are on a chart sheet, you can add or remove them. You can also format chart elements in many ways to emphasize the data on the chart and to make it more eye-catching to the user. Preset headers and footers can personalize charts and spreadsheets in Excel 2013. You can customize headers and footers to add, delete, or format elements. Use the Backstage view to preview the chart and spreadsheet before you print.

Chapter Key Terms

Background, p. E-126
Background bitmap, p. E-120
Chart elements, p. E-120
Chart Elements button, p. E-138
Chart Filters button, p. E-142
Chart sheet, pp. E-120, E-138

Chart Styles button, p. E-142
Conditional formatting, p. E-120
Embedded chart, p. E-138
Fill colors, p. E-128
Flip a shape, p. E-128
Outline colors, p. E-128

Outline width, p. E-128
Positioning, p. E-128
Precise size, p. E-128
Quick Analysis button, p. E-122
Shapes, p. E-128
Tiling, p. E-126

On Your Own Exercise EX-3C-E1

This exercise provides you an opportunity to practice the important Excel 2013 skills covered in this chapter. In this exercise, your economics professor asks you to chart the changes in the housing industry since 2005. To track the data, you will prepare an Excel spreadsheet and chart several important statistics. Open the exercise data file **ex03c-ex01.xlsx** and save it as **ex03c-hw01.xlsx**. The final screens should appear similar to Figures EX3.31 and EX3.32.

FIGURE EX3.31 Housing industry spreadsheet sample solution

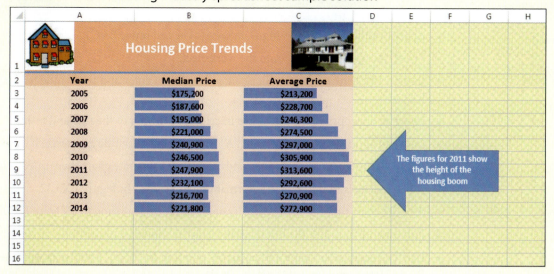

FIGURE EX3.32 Housing industry chart sample solution for chartsheet

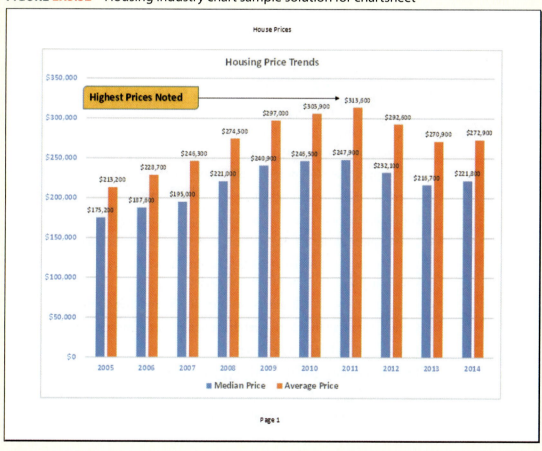

Complete the following tasks so the worksheet and chart appear similar to Figures EX3.31 and EX3.32.

- Apply Conditional Formatting Data Bars to the cell range B3:C12.
- Insert **background hwe1** onto the worksheet.
- Insert a Left arrow from the Block shapes and then enter and format the text as shown in Figure EX3.31.
- Insert an appropriate clip art image in cell A1 to the left of the title and resize it as shown.
- Insert an appropriate picture in cell A1 to the right of the title and resize it as shown.
- Create a Clustered Column chart and move it to a separate chart sheet titled "House Prices."
- Add data labels to the chart and format them as shown in Figure EX3.32.
- Add the chart title "Housing Price Trends" and format as shown in Figure EX3.32.
- Format both axes and the legend of the chart as shown.
- Insert a rectangular shape and an arrow pointing to the 2011 statistics with the words "Highest Prices Noted" and format the shape as shown.
- Insert a preset header and footer similar to that shown in Figure EX3.32.
- Print the chart sheet.
- Save and then close the workbook.

On Your Own Exercise EX-3C-E2

To practice advanced formatting and presentation of data, open the **ex03c-ex02.xlsx** file and save it as **ex03c-hw02.xlsx**. Use your knowledge of Excel 2013 and the skills you learned in this chapter to accomplish the following tasks.

- Apply appropriate Conditional Formatting rules to emphasize data.
- Insert a background bitmap image.
- Create, format, and move a predefined shape around the spreadsheet.
- Insert a piece of clip art and a picture that help to display the data effectively.
- Create a chart that is first embedded on the spreadsheet and then moved to its own chart sheet. Use an appropriate name for the chartsheet.
- Add chart elements that add to the chart display and then format them.
- Create a shape on the chart sheet that emphasizes the most important piece of data on the sheet.
- Insert a custom header and footer.
- Print the file, then save the workbook and exit Excel.

Figures EX3.33 and 3.34 are sample solutions that show both the spreadsheet and the chart sheet. These are samples only. Your solution may look different.

FIGURE EX3.33 On Your Own EX-3C-E2 sample solution

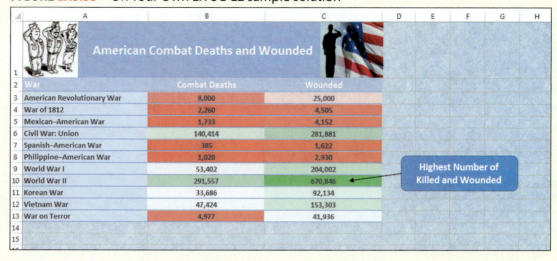

FIGURE EX3.34 On Your Own EX-3C-E2 sample solution

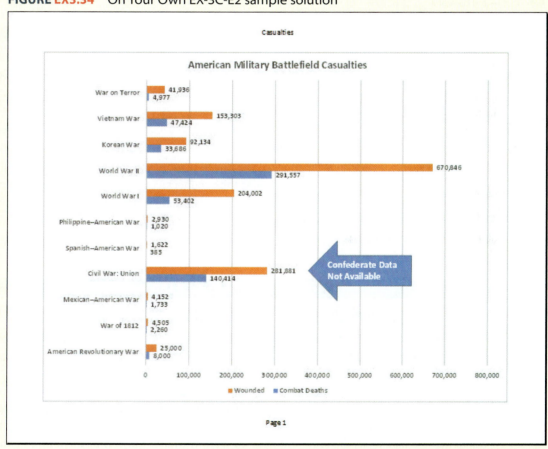

4 Working with Tables, Worksheets, and Workbooks

In this chapter about Excel, you will learn how to use larger spreadsheets and consolidate data on multiple worksheets into a summary sheet. To work with large worksheets, you can **freeze panes** so header material is visible no matter how far a user scrolls on the worksheet. You can also split the worksheet window to view different parts of the worksheet at the same time. Printing large worksheets presents some issues because you must determine what titles should print on each page and where page breaks appear so that your worksheets print exactly as you desire.

Working with **data tables** is an essential part of Excel. Knowing how to use data tables provides you with a powerful data tool that sometimes makes the use of a database application such as Access unnecessary. This chapter discusses the creation of data tables and how to format them, **sorting** and **filtering** the data to best display what is in the table and also, when the table is no longer necessary, converting the data table back to a data range.

Working with multiple worksheets or workbooks often involves consolidating data. This chapter introduces **sheet tabs** and techniques for inserting, deleting, and hiding worksheets. Grouping worksheets and creating a **summary worksheet** are necessary steps when the user must consolidate data from several worksheets. Finally, you will learn how to consolidate multiple-sheet workbooks.

PROJECT

Working with Alumni Data

In this project, you will use Microsoft Excel 2013 to manage an alumni data worksheet that is too large to view on a screen. To start, you will print the worksheet and use it to create a data table. To extract the data needed for alumni fund-raising, you will format the data table, then sort and filter it.

While this project applies specifically to alumni data, you will learn techniques to work with multiple spreadsheets such as grouping them for printing and consolidating multiple-sheet workbooks. You will also summarize data from several worksheets.

THE SITUATION

Work-Study Statistical Assignment

You completed your undergraduate degree but decided to continue your education at Greene State University. To finance this endeavor, you take a job with the school's alumni office. Your supervisor learns you have experience working with data and Excel 2013. For your first assignment, she asks you to work with one portion of the alumni database, sorting and filtering the database to determine which alumni are most likely to donate money or attend fund-raising events. Next, you will summarize alumni reports from different parts of the country and consolidate data gathered from several alumni offices.

PROJECT OBJECTIVES

Managing an Alumni Database in Excel

In this project, you will enable users to see all parts of the alumni data spreadsheet while still viewing the header material. Split worksheet windows so users view different parts of the spreadsheet at the same time. Tasks include freezing panes so users can scroll down the spreadsheet or scroll to the right while the header material remains visible.

PROJECT FILE: *Available at* www.mhhe.com/office2013projectlearn

After completing this project, you will be able to:

- Apply techniques to freeze panes and split worksheet windows to facilitate viewing large worksheets.

- Use printing options to easily print large worksheets.

- Use Find and Replace and Spelling check to refine data.

- Create a worksheet data table, then format the data table and apply style options to the formatting.

- Sort and filter data in a table.

- Convert a worksheet data table back to a data range.

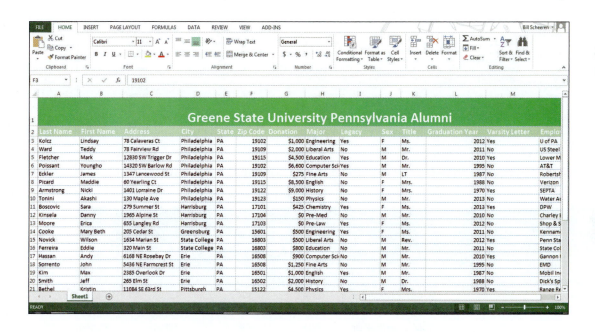

LESSON EXCEL 4A1
Viewing a Large Document

LESSON OVERVIEW

Often, users encounter spreadsheets too large to view on the screen. This may be because the spreadsheet is too large, or it may be that the user's monitor is too small or set at a resolution too low to view the complete spreadsheet. To view the data, it is necessary to freeze a pane so you can temporarily see row and column headings no matter where you scroll on the spreadsheet. Row and column headings are stationary because only the unfrozen part of the spreadsheet scrolls.

Another way to view more data in a spreadsheet is to actually split a worksheet into panes. You can split the worksheet into four panes and two scrollable windows. Figures EX4.1 and EX4.2 show a worksheet with frozen row headings and a worksheet split into panes.

FIGURE EX4.1 Excel file with row 2 frozen

Row 2 frozen

FIGURE EX4.2 Excel file showing the worksheet split at column F

Split at column F

Freeze panes using the Freeze Panes drop-down menu	• SELECT the column to the right of the one to freeze or the column below the rows to freeze. To freeze both columns and rows: CLICK the cell below and to the right of the row and column to freeze. CLICK the VIEW tab and locate the Window group. CLICK the Freeze Panes drop-down menu. SELECT the Freeze Pane option desired.
Unfreeze the window panes	• CLICK the Freeze Pane drop-down menu. SELECT Unfreeze Panes.
Split the worksheet into panes	• SELECT the row, column, or cell location where the split is to occur. CLICK the VIEW tab and locate the Window group. CLICK the Split button. Remove the split by again clicking the Split button.

PROJECT PRACTICE

1. Locate and open the project data file **ex04a.xlsx**. On the FILE tab, use the Save As command to save the file as **ex04a-alumni.xlsx**. You may need to choose a place to store the file (e.g., SkyDrive or Computer), and browse to the desired location.

2. Begin working with freezing and unfreezing columns and rows using the Freeze Panes drop-down menu

3. SELECT row 3 (Last Name Kolcz).

4. CLICK the VIEW tab.
   CLICK the Freeze Panes drop-down menu in the Window group as shown in Figure EX4.3.

FIGURE EX4.3 Freeze Panes drop-down menu

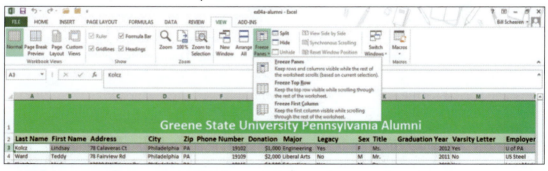

5. CLICK the Freeze Panes option.
   (*Result:* Rows 1 and 2 are frozen no matter how far you scroll down the spreadsheet, as shown in Figure EX4.4.)

FIGURE EX4.4 Excel file showing Freeze Panes applied to show row 2

	A	B	C	D
1				Gre
2	**Last Name**	**First Name**	**Address**	**City**
18	Sorrento	John	5436 NE Farmcrest St	Erie
19	Kim	Max	2385 Overlook Dr	Erie
20	Smith	Jeff	265 Elm St	Erie
21	Bethel	Kristin	11084 SE 63rd St	Pittsburgh
22	Schmidt	Joshua	11250 SW Walnut St	Pittsburgh
23	Boscovic	Laurie	11286 SW Walnut St	Pittsburgh
24	Sebastian	Kim	15500 SW Allen St	Pittsburgh

6 CLICK the VIEW tab and CLICK the Freeze Panes applied drop-down menu to unfreeze the panes.

7 CLICK Unfreeze Panes.

8 Work with splitting a worksheet pane by using the **Split button** (▱) on the VIEW tab.

9 If necessary, CLICK the VIEW tab and locate the Window group.

10 SELECT column E.

CLICK the Split button.
(*Result*: The spreadsheet shows a split bar between columns D and E. You may scroll the spreadsheet all the way to the right with columns A through D still visible, as shown in Figure EX4.5.)

FIGURE EX4.5 Excel file showing split worksheet window

	A	B	C	D	G	H	I	J	K	L	M	N
1					Gre[niversity Pennsylvania Alumni							
2	Last Name	First Name	Address	City	Donation	Major	Legacy	Sex	Title	Graduation Year	Varsity Letter	Employer
3	Kolcz	Lindsay	78 Calaveras Ct	Philadelphia	$1,000	Engineering	Yes	F	Ms.	2012	Yes	U of PA
4	Ward	Teddy	78 Fairview Rd	Philadelphia	$2,000	Liberal Arts	No	M	Mr.	2011	No	US Steel
5	Fletcher	Mark	12830 SW Trigger Dr	Philadelphia	$4,500	Education	Yes	M	Dr.	2010	Yes	Lower Merion SD
6	Poissant	Youngho	14320 SW Barlow Rd	Philadelphia	$6,600	Computer Sci	Yes	M	Mr.	1995	No	AT&T
7	Eckler	James	1347 Lancewood St	Philadelphia	$275	Fine Arts	No	M	LT	1987	No	Robertshaw
8	Picard	Maddie	60 Yearling Ct	Philadelphia	$8,500	English	No	F	Mrs.	1988	No	Verizon

11 CLICK the Split button again (known as a toggle command) to remove the split.

12 Save the file before proceeding to the next lesson.

Large Worksheet Printing Options

LESSON OVERVIEW

Printing large worksheets presents the user with several problems. Sometimes a worksheet is so large that it prints on more than one sheet, making it difficult to determine how the sheets fit together. Excel allows several printing options to solve that problem such as setting **page breaks** with an option to change them manually. This allows you to print more or less of the spreadsheet on each page.

At times, the size of the spreadsheet may make it difficult to match data after printing. Excel allows you to add Print Titles as a printing option. For example, you might want to print columns A and B on every sheet if those columns are headings for the entire spreadsheet.

SKILLS PREVIEW

Insert and remove a page break	• SELECT the Page Break location. CLICK the PAGE LAYOUT tab and locate the Page Setup group. CLICK the Breaks button and then CLICK Insert Page Break. To remove a page break, SELECT the Page Break location, CLICK the Breaks button, and then CLICK Remove Page Break.
Preview and move a page break	• CLICK the VIEW tab and locate the Workbook Views group. CLICK the Page Break Preview button. Adjust the Page Break by DRAGGING the page break line to the desired location. CLICK Normal view.
Print row or column titles on each page	• CLICK the PAGE LAYOUT tab and locate the Page Setup group. CLICK the Print Titles button. ENTER the number of the row or the letter of the column that contains the titles. CLICK OK.

PROJECT PRACTICE

1. Ensure that the **ex04a-alumni.xlsx** workbook is open in Excel. Ensure that the project is in Normal view.

2. The alumni spreadsheet currently has page breaks to print on six sheets with three of the sheets blank. Change the page breaks so there are no blank sheets.

3. CLICK row 16. This is the location of a horizontal page break.

4. CLICK the PAGE LAYOUT tab and then the Breaks button in the Page Setup group, as shown in Figure EX4.6.

FIGURE EX4.6   PAGE LAYOUT tab showing Breaks button

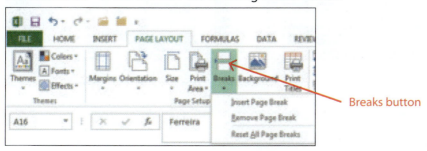

5 CLICK Insert Page Break.
(*Result*: A horizontal page break inserts between rows 15 and 16, as shown in Figure EX4.7.)

FIGURE EX4.7 Horizontal page break shown

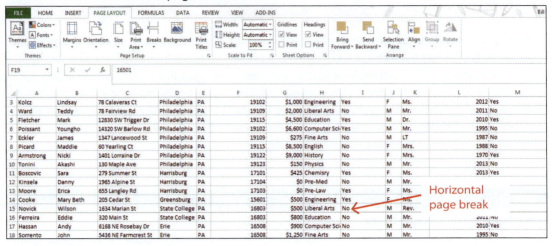

6 Preview and move a page break.

CLICK the VIEW tab.

CLICK the **Page Break Preview button**. The Page Break Preview should appear as shown in Figure EX4.8.

FIGURE EX4.8 Page Break Preview

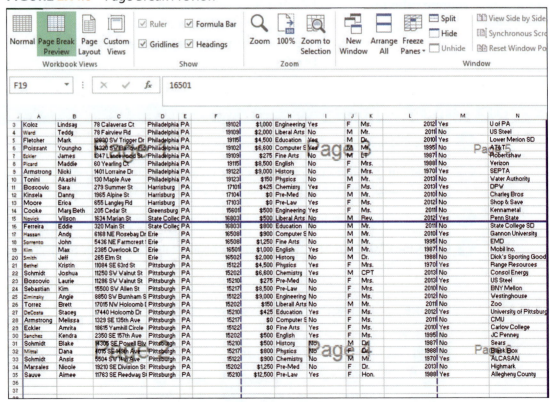

7 Use the two-headed horizontal arrow to move the page break lines as shown in Figure EX4.9. (*Result*: This balances the printing of the pages.)

FIGURE EX4.9 Page breaks adjusted

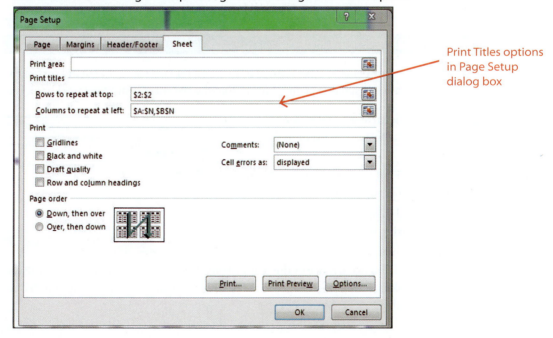

8 Print row and column titles on each page of the printout.

CLICK the PAGE LAYOUT tab and locate the Page Setup group.

CLICK the Print Titles button (▦). This opens the Page Setup dialog box.

9 TYPE $2:$2 in the Rows to repeat at top field and $A:$N,BN in the Columns to repeat at left field. The Page Setup dialog box should appear as shown in Figure EX4.10.

FIGURE EX4.10 Page Setup dialog box showing Print Titles option

10 CLICK OK. If your instructor wants printed output, you may print now.

11 Save the file before proceeding to the next lesson.

Finding, Replacing, and Spell-Checking Data

LESSON OVERVIEW

All applications within Microsoft Office use **Find and Replace** and **Spelling check** in a similar manner. This is one of the strong points of the Microsoft Office 2013 suite: If the same option is present in all applications, the feature appears in the same tab and operates the same in all applications of Microsoft Office 2013.

Using the Find and Replace feature allows the user to locate a particular piece of data in a spreadsheet and change it as needed. The Spelling check is one of the most valuable features in the Microsoft Office suite. Nothing calls into question a person's skills faster than a spreadsheet with misspellings.

SKILLS PREVIEW

Find a word(s) in a document	• CLICK the HOME tab and locate the Editing group. CLICK the Find and Select button (🔍). CLICK Find to open the Find and Replace dialog box. TYPE in the word(s) you are looking for. CLICK Find Next or Find All. The first occurrence of the word is highlighted in the text.
Replace a word(s) in a document	• CLICK the HOME tab and locate the Editing group. CLICK the Find and Select button (🔍). CLICK Replace to open the Find and Replace dialog box. TYPE the word you are looking for in the Find what field. TYPE the word that will replace the Find what word in the Replace with field. CLICK either Replace or Replace All depending on the circumstances.
Check spelling in a document	• CLICK the REVIEW tab and locate the Proofing group. CLICK the Spelling button (✓^{ABC}). CHOOSE the appropriate action for each error: Change, Change All, Ignore, Ignore All, or Add to dictionary.

PROJECT PRACTICE

1. Your supervisor believes it is essential to find and replace some shorthand text in the spreadsheet and eliminate any spelling errors. Ensure that the **ex04a-alumni.xlsx** workbook is open in Excel.

2. Find each occurrence of the word *Chemistry* to ensure the list of majors is correct.

    CLICK the Find & Select button (🔍) in the Editing group on the HOME tab.

    CLICK Find to open the Find and Replace dialog box.

    TYPE **Chemistry** and CLICK Find Next.

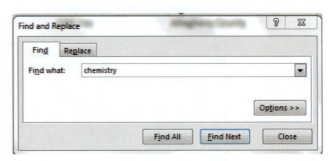

(*Result*: The first occurrence of the word *Chemistry* is highlighted in the spreadsheet.) Figure EX4.11 shows an illustration of the spreadsheet with the word *chemistry* highlighted and the Find and Replace dialog box visible.

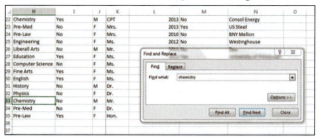

3 Replace the single letter representing sex with the word spelled out.
Select cells J3 through J35.

CLICK the Find and Select button () in the Editing group on the HOME tab.

CLICK Replace to open the Find and Replace dialog box.

CLICK the REPLACE tab.

TYPE **M** in the Find what field and **Male** in the Replace with field.

CLICK OK when the number of replacements is indicated.

Repeat the same steps to change the "F" to **Female**.

RESIZE column J so both words show fully.
(*Result*: The spreadsheet should appear as in Figure EX4.12.)

FIGURE **EX4.12** Find and Replace results

	Last Name	Femaleirst N	Address	City	State	Zip Code	Donation	Major	Legacy	Sex
1						Greene State University Pennsylvani				
3	Kolcz	Lindsay	78 Calaveras Ct	Philadelphia	PA	19102	$1,000	Engineering	Yes	Female
4	Ward	Teddy	78 Femaleairview Rd	Philadelphia	PA	19109	$2,000	Liberal Arts	No	Male
5	Femaleletcher	Mark	12830 SW Trigger Dr	Philadelphia	PA	19115	$4,500	Education	Yes	Male
6	Poissant	Youngho	14320 SW Barlow Rd	Philadelphia	PA	19102	$6,600	Computer Sci	Yes	Male
7	Eckler	James	1347 Lancewood St	Philadelphia	PA	19109	$275	Femaleine Ar	No	Male
8	Picard	Maddie	60 Yearling Ct	Philadelphia	PA	19115	$8,500	English	No	Female
9	Armstrong	Nicki	1401 Lorraine Dr	Philadelphia	PA	19122	$9,000	History	No	Female
10	Tonini	Akashi	130 Maple Ave	Philadelphia	PA	19123	$150	Physics	No	Male
11	Boscovic	Sara	279 Summer St	Harrisburg	PA	17101	$425	Chemistry	Yes	Female
12	Kinsela	Danny	1965 Alpine St	Harrisburg	PA	17104	$0	Pre-Med	No	Male
13	Moore	Erica	655 Langley Rd	Harrisburg	PA	17103	$0	Pre-Law	Yes	Female
14	Cooke	Mary Beth	205 Cedar St	Greensburg	PA	15601	$500	Engineering	Yes	Female
15	Novick	Wilson	1634 Marian St	State College	PA	16803	$500	Liberal Arts	No	Male
16	Femaleerreira	Eddie	320 Main St	State College	PA	16803	$800	Education	No	Male
17	Hassan	Andy	6168 NE Rosebay Dr	Erie	PA	16508	$900	Computer Sci	No	Male
18	Sorrento	John	5436 NE Femalearmcre	Erie	PA	16508	$1,250	Femaleine Ar	No	Male
19	Kim	Max	2385 Overlook Dr	Erie	PA	16501	$1,000	English	Yes	Male
20	Smith	JeFemaleFemale	265 Elm St	Erie	PA	16502	$2,000	History	No	Male
21	Bethel	Kristin	11084 SE 63rd St	Pittsburgh	PA	15122	$4,500	Physics	Yes	Female

4 You notice some spelling errors. Spell-check the spreadsheet to correct them.

CLICK the REVIEW tab and locate the Proofing group.

CLICK the Spelling button ( ).
Correct the words *chemisry* and *Liberall* using the suggestions box. Ignore any other words that display as misspelled.

5 Save the file before proceeding to the next lesson.

Creating and Formatting a Table

LESSON OVERVIEW

A **table** is a range of data created from the data in a spreadsheet. You can manage it separately from other rows and columns in that spreadsheet. You can filter, sort, and total data in a table separately from other data in the worksheet. Consider a table as a structured list with a row of headings to describe each column.

You may format tables in a similar fashion to other parts of the spreadsheet. The saying "less is more" applies to table formatting. Remember to use care with your formatting.

SKILLS PREVIEW

Create a table using the Quick Analysis tool	• SELECT the range of cells for the table, including the field names. CLICK the Quick Analysis button. CLICK TABLES and then CLICK the Table button.
Create a table using the Table button	• SELECT the range of cells for the table, including the field names. CLICK the INSERT tab, locate the Tables group, and then CLICK the Table button. Adjust the table size if necessary and then SELECT the My table has headers check box. CLICK OK.
Format a table	• SELECT a cell in the table. CLICK the HOME tab, locate the Styles group, and then CLICK the Format as Table button. SELECT the desired table style.
Format table elements	• SELECT a cell or cell range to be modified. CLICK the DESIGN tab under Table Tools. CLICK the appropriate check boxes to be shown or hidden.

PROJECT PRACTICE

1. You need to convert the worksheet for the alumni association to a data table so it can easily be sorted and filtered. It also needs some formatting to make it more attractive. Ensure that the **ex04a-alumni.xlsx** workbook is open in Excel.

2. Create a data table from an existing worksheet.
   SELECT the cell range A2:N35.
   CLICK the Quick Analysis tool.
   CLICK TABLES.
   CLICK Table.
   (*Result:* The data range in the spreadsheet is converted to a table as shown in Figure EX4.13.)

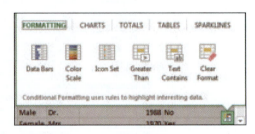

FIGURE EX4.13 Worksheet converted to a data table

Greene State University Pennsylvania Alumni

Last Name	First Name	Address	City	State	Zip Code	Donation	Major	Legacy	Sex	Title	Graduation Year
Armstrong	Melissa	1329 SE 135th Ave	Pittsburgh	PA	15217	$0	Computer Science	No	Female	Ms.	2011
Armstrong	Nicki	1401 Lorraine Dr	Philadelphia	PA	19122	$9,000	History	No	Female	Mrs.	1970
Bethel	Kristin	11084 SE 63rd St	Pittsburgh	PA	15122	$4,500	Physics	Yes	Female	Mrs.	1970
Boscovic	Laurie	11286 SW Walnut St	Pittsburgh	PA	15210	$275	Pre-Med	No	Female	Mrs.	2013
Boscovic	Sara	279 Summer St	Harrisburg	PA	17101	$425	Chemistry	Yes	Female	Ms.	2013
Cooke	Mary Beth	205 Cedar St	Greensburg	PA	15601	$500	Engineering	Yes	Female	Ms.	2011
DeCosta	Stacey	17440 Holcomb Dr	Pittsburgh	PA	15210	$425	Education	Yes	Female	Ms.	2012
Eckler	Amrita	18615 Yamhill Circle	Pittsburgh	PA	15122	$0	Fine Arts	Yes	Female	Ms.	2010
Eckler	James	1347 Lancewood St	Philadelphia	PA	19109	$275	Fine Arts	No	Male	LT	1987
Ferreira	Eddie	320 Main St	State College	PA	16803	$800	Education	No	Male	Mr.	2011
Fletcher	Mark	12830 SW Trigger Dr	Philadelphia	PA	19115	$4,500	Education	Yes	Male	Dr.	2010
Hassan	Andy	6168 NE Rosebay Dr	Erie	PA	16508	$900	Computer Science	No	Male	Mr.	2010
Kim	Max	2385 Overlook Dr	Erie	PA	16501	$1,000	English	Yes	Male	Mr.	1987
Kinsela	Danny	1965 Alpine St	Harrisburg	PA	17104	$0	Pre-Med	No	Male	Mr.	2010
Kolcz	Lindsay	78 Calaveras Ct	Philadelphia	PA	19102	$1,000	Engineering	Yes	Female	Ms.	2012
Marsales	Nicole	19210 SE Division St	Pittsburgh	PA	15202	$1,250	Pre-Med	No	Female	Dr.	2013
Mittal	Dana	4015 SE 149th Ave	Pittsburgh	PA	15217	$800	Physics	No	Female	Dr.	1988

MORE INFO

You can also create tables using the Table button in the Tables group on the INSERT tab or by clicking Format as Table in the Styles group on the HOME tab.

---

3 There are several ways to format the table to be more attractive. For the most control, use the Format as Table button in the Styles group on the HOME tab.
Ensure that the cell range A2:N35 is still selected.

CLICK Format as Table in the Styles group on the HOME tab.
(*Result*: This opens the Table Styles gallery as shown in Figure EX4.14.)

FIGURE EX4.14 Table Styles gallery

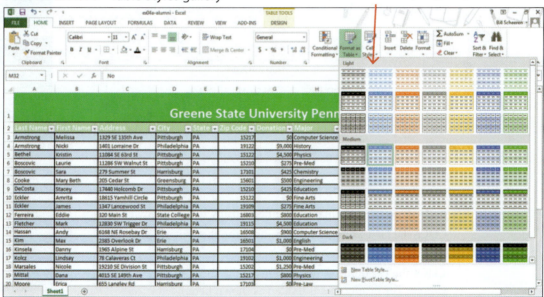

CLICK Table Style Medium 14 in the Medium section of the Table Styles gallery (last item in the second row).
(*Result*: The table appears as in Figure EX4.15.)

FIGURE EX4.15 Formatted data table

Last Name	First Name	Address	City	State	Zip Code	Donation	Major	Legacy	Sex	Title	Graduation Year
			Greene State University Pennsylvania Alumni								
Armstrong	Melissa	1329 SE 135th Ave	Pittsburgh	PA	15217	$0	Computer Science	No	Female	Ms.	2011
Armstrong	Nicki	1401 Lorraine Dr	Philadelphia	PA	19122	$9,000	History	No	Female	Mrs.	1970
Bethel	Kristin	11084 SE 63rd St	Pittsburgh	PA	15122	$4,500	Physics	Yes	Female	Mrs.	1970
Boscovic	Laurie	11286 SW Walnut St	Pittsburgh	PA	15210	$275	Pre-Med	No	Female	Mrs.	2013
Boscovic	Sara	279 Summer St	Harrisburg	PA	17101	$425	Chemistry	Yes	Female	Ms.	2013
Cooke	Mary Beth	205 Cedar St	Greensburg	PA	15601	$500	Engineering	Yes	Female	Ms.	2011
DeCosta	Stacey	17440 Holcomb Dr	Pittsburgh	PA	15210	$425	Education	Yes	Female	Ms.	2012
Eckler	Amrita	18615 Yamhill Circle	Pittsburgh	PA	15122	$0	Fine Arts	Yes	Female	Ms.	2010
Eckler	James	1347 Lancewood St	Philadelphia	PA	19109	$275	Fine Arts	No	Male	LT	1987
Ferreira	Eddie	320 Main St	State College	PA	16803	$800	Education	No	Male	Mr.	2011
Fletcher	Mark	12830 SW Trigger Dr	Philadelphia	PA	19115	$4,500	Education	Yes	Male	Dr.	2010
Hassan	Andy	6168 NE Rosebay Dr	Erie	PA	16508	$900	Computer Science	No	Male	Mr.	2010
Kim	Max	2385 Overlook Dr	Erie	PA	16501	$1,000	English	Yes	Male	Mr.	1987
Kinsela	Danny	1965 Alpine St	Harrisburg	PA	17104	$0	Pre-Med	No	Male	Mr.	2010
Kolcz	Lindsay	78 Calaveras Ct	Philadelphia	PA	19102	$1,000	Engineering	Yes	Female	Ms.	2012
Marsales	Nicole	19210 SE Division St	Pittsburgh	PA	15202	$1,250	Pre-Med	No	Female	Dr.	2013
Mittal	Dana	4015 SE 149th Ave	Pittsburgh	PA	15217	$800	Physics	No	Female	Dr.	1988

④ In the previous step, all elements of the table were formatted. In this step, certain elements of the table are modified without affecting the overall formatting.

> ℹ️ **MORE INFO**
>
> You can show or hide the following elements in a table: Header Row, Total Row, First Column, Last Column, Banded Columns, Banded Rows, and Filter Button.

Format the first column in the table.

CLICK any cell within the table area.
Place a check mark in the First Column box in the Table Style Options group of the DESIGN tab under Table Tools.
(*Result*: Column A of the table appears as shown here.)

⑤ Hide some Table Formatting elements using the Table Style Options.

CLICK the First Column box to remove the check mark. This will remove the first column formatting.

CLICK the Header Row box to remove the check mark.
(*Result*: The header row is hidden as shown here.)

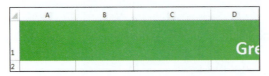

Place the check mark back in the Header Row box so the header row is restored to the table.

⑥ Save the file before going on to the next lesson.

Sorting and Filtering Data in a Table

LESSON OVERVIEW

After you create a data table, it is often advantageous to **sort** the data in the table. This allows the user to arrange the data rows in the order that displays the data for better analysis. A common sort is alphabetically by last name. Expand the sort to include more than one column so, again, the data is best displayed. An example of this would be a sort on both last and first names so individuals with the same last name are also sorted by first name. Sort by ascending (A to Z) or descending (Z to A) order.

Filtering is another step an Excel user can use to select only those data records specifically needed. For example, you can filter a data table to locate those who reside in a particular city or those who not only live in a particular city but in a specific zip code in that city.

SKILLS PREVIEW

Sort data in a table using simple sorts	• CLICK the table cell with the field to sort. CLICK the DATA tab, locate the Sort & Filter group, and then CLICK either the Sort Ascending or Sort Descending button.
Sort data using multiple criteria	• CLICK anywhere in the table. CLICK the Sort button in the Sort & Filter group of the DATA tab. CLICK the Column List area and select the first sort column. Most often leave the Sort On area as Values. SELECT the appropriate sort order from the Order drop-down list. To add additional sort levels, CLICK the Add Level button and repeat these steps. CLICK OK.
Filter a table to display selected records	• CLICK anywhere in the table. CLICK the DATA tab. Ensure that the Filter button in the Sort & Filter group is highlighted. CLICK the column header filter arrow to set the first filter criterion. SELECT the filter criteria to apply. CLICK OK. Repeat the previous steps to apply additional filter criteria. To remove a filter, CLICK the column filter arrow, then CLICK Clear Filter From (column name).

PROJECT PRACTICE

1. Sort and filter the worksheet for the alumni association to show data for selected criteria. It also needs some formatting to be more attractive. Ensure that the **ex04a-alumni.xlsx** workbook is open in Excel.

2. Sort the data table by last name.
   CLICK in cell A3.
   CLICK the DATA tab, locate the Sort & Filter group, and CLICK the ⬇️ button.
   (*Result:* The table is sorted by last name as shown in Figure EX4.16.)

	A	B	C	D	E
1					Green
2	Last Name	First Name	Address	City	Zip
3	Armstrong	Nicki	1401 Lorraine Dr	Philadelphia	PA
4	Armstrong	Melissa	1329 SE 135th Ave	Pittsburgh	PA
5	Bethel	Kristin	11084 SE 63rd St	Pittsburgh	PA
6	Boscovic	Sara	279 Summer St	Harrisburg	PA
7	Boscovic	Laurie	11286 SW Walnut St	Pittsburgh	PA
8	Cooke	Mary Beth	205 Cedar St	Greensburg	PA
9	DeCosta	Stacey	17440 Holcomb Dr	Pittsburgh	PA
10	Eckler	James	1347 Lancewood St	Philadelphia	PA
11	Eckler	Amrita	18615 Yamhill Circle	Pittsburgh	PA
12	Ferreira	Eddie	320 Main St	State College	PA
13	Fletcher	Mark	12830 SW Trigger Dr	Philadelphia	PA
14	Hassan	Andy	6168 NE Rosebay Dr	Erie	PA
15	Kim	Max	2385 Overlook Dr	Erie	PA
16	Kinsela	Danny	1965 Alpine St	Harrisburg	PA
17	Kolcz	Lindsay	78 Calaveras Ct	Philadelphia	PA
18	Marsales	Nicole	19210 SE Division St	Pittsburgh	PA
19	Mittal	Dana	4015 SE 149th Ave	Pittsburgh	PA

3 CLICK the Undo button to remove that sort.

4 Sort the table by last and first name.

CLICK anywhere in the table.

CLICK the Sort button in the Sort & Filter group on the DATA tab.

CLICK the Sort by drop-down list arrow.

SELECT Last Name.

Leave the Sort On as Values and the Order as A to Z.

CLICK the Add Level button.

SELECT First Name in the Then by field.

Again, leave the Sort On as Values and the Order as A to Z.

CLICK OK.

(*Result:* The table is sorted by last and first name as shown in Figure EX4.17.)

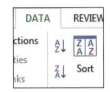

FIGURE EX4.17   Data table sorted on two criteria

	Last Name	First Name	Address	City	Zip
				Green	
3	Armstrong	Melissa	1329 SE 135th Ave	Pittsburgh	PA
4	Armstrong	Nicki	1401 Lorraine Dr	Philadelphia	PA
5	Bethel	Kristin	11084 SE 63rd St	Pittsburgh	PA
6	Boscovic	Laurie	11286 SW Walnut St	Pittsburgh	PA
7	Boscovic	Sara	279 Summer St	Harrisburg	PA
8	Cooke	Mary Beth	205 Cedar St	Greensburg	PA
9	DeCosta	Stacey	17440 Holcomb Dr	Pittsburgh	PA
10	Eckler	Amrita	18615 Yamhill Circle	Pittsburgh	PA
11	Eckler	James	1347 Lancewood St	Philadelphia	PA
12	Ferreira	Eddie	320 Main St	State College	PA
13	Fletcher	Mark	12830 SW Trigger Dr	Philadelphia	PA
14	Hassan	Andy	6168 NE Rosebay Dr	Erie	PA
15	Kim	Max	2385 Overlook Dr	Erie	PA
16	Kinsela	Danny	1965 Alpine St	Harrisburg	PA
17	Kolcz	Lindsay	78 Calaveras Ct	Philadelphia	PA
18	Marsales	Nicole	19210 SE Division St	Pittsburgh	PA
19	Mittal	Dana	4015 SE 149th Ave	Pittsburgh	PA

⑤ Apply filters to the data table to show female alumni who work as engineers.

CLICK anywhere in the table.

CLICK the drop-down arrow in the Sex field and clear the check from the Select All box and place a check mark in the Female box and CLICK OK. (*Result*: The table is filtered to show only females, as shown in Figure EX4.18.)

FIGURE EX4.18   Filtered data table

	Last Name	First Name	Address	City	State	Zip Code	Donation	Major	Legacy	Sex	Title
				Greene State University Pennsylvania Alu							
3	Armstrong	Melissa	1329 SE 135th Ave	Pittsburgh	PA	15217	$0	Computer Science	No	Female	Ms.
4	Armstrong	Nicki	1401 Lorraine Dr	Philadelphia	PA	19122	$9,000	History	No	Female	Mrs.
5	Bethel	Kristin	11084 SE 63rd St	Pittsburgh	PA	15122	$4,500	Physics	Yes	Female	Mrs.
6	Boscovic	Laurie	11286 SW Walnut St	Pittsburgh	PA	15210	$275	Pre-Med	No	Female	Mrs.
7	Boscovic	Sara	279 Summer St	Harrisburg	PA	17101	$425	Chemistry	Yes	Female	Ms.
8	Cooke	Mary Beth	205 Cedar St	Greensburg	PA	15601	$500	Engineering	Yes	Female	Ms.
9	DeCosta	Stacey	17440 Holcomb Dr	Pittsburgh	PA	15210	$425	Education	Yes	Female	Ms.
10	Eckler	Amrita	18615 Yamhill Circle	Pittsburgh	PA	15122	$0	Fine Arts	Yes	Female	Ms.
17	Kolcz	Lindsay	78 Calaveras Ct	Philadelphia	PA	19102	$1,000	Engineering	Yes	Female	Ms.
18	Marsales	Nicole	19210 SE Division St	Pittsburgh	PA	15202	$1,250	Pre-Med	No	Female	Dr.
19	Mittal	Dana	4015 SE 149th Ave	Pittsburgh	PA	15217	$800	Physics	No	Female	Dr.
20	Moore	Erica	655 Langley Rd	Harrisburg	PA	17103	$0	Pre-Law	Yes	Female	Ms.
22	Picard	Maddie	60 Yearling Ct	Philadelphia	PA	19115	$8,500	English	No	Female	Mrs.
24	Sanchez	Kendra	2350 SE 157th Ave	Pittsburgh	PA	15202	$500	English	Yes	Female	Ms.
25	Sauve	Aimee	11763 SE Reedway St	Pittsburgh	PA	15210	$12,500	Pre-Law	Yes	Female	Hon.
29	Sebastian	Kim	15500 SW Allen St	Pittsburgh	PA	15217	$8,500	Pre-Law	No	Female	Mrs.

6 CLICK anywhere in the table.

CLICK the drop-down arrow in the Major field and clear the check from the Select All box.

Place a check mark in the Engineering box and CLICK OK.

(*Result*: The table is filtered to show only female engineers, as shown in Figure EX4.19.)

FIGURE EX4.19 Data table filtered on two criteria

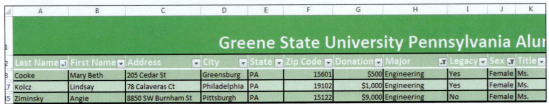

	Last Name	First Name	Address	City	State	Zip Code	Donation	Major	Legacy	Sex	Title
Cooke	Mary Beth	205 Cedar St	Greensburg	PA	15601	$500	Engineering	Yes	Female	Ms.
Kolcz	Lindsay	78 Calaveras Ct	Philadelphia	PA	19102	$1,000	Engineering	Yes	Female	Ms.
Ziminsky	Angie	8850 SW Burnham St	Pittsburgh	PA	15122	$9,000	Engineering	No	Female	Ms.

7 Clear filters from the table.

CLICK the drop-down list arrow on the Major field.

CLICK Clear Filter From "Major" to clear the Engineering filter.

CLICK the drop-down list arrow on the Sex field.

CLICK Clear Filter From "Sex" to clear the Female filter.

Save the file before going to the next lesson.

Converting a Data Table to a Range

LESSON OVERVIEW

While there are many uses for a spreadsheet that was converted to a table, it is sometimes necessary to change the data table back to a **range**. This allows you to use the full power of Microsoft Excel, including charting and data analysis capabilities.

SKILLS PREVIEW

Convert a data table to a range	• CLICK any cell in the table.
	CLICK the DESIGN tab under Table Tools.
	CLICK the Convert to Range button.
	CLICK Yes to confirm the conversion.

PROJECT PRACTICE

1. You need to change the worksheet for the alumni association from a table back to a range. Ensure that the **ex04a-alumni.xlsx** workbook is open in Excel.

2. Change the alumni table back to a range.

   CLICK in any cell in the table.

   CLICK the DESIGN tab under Table Tools.

   CLICK the **Convert to Range button**.

   CLICK Yes to confirm the change.
   (*Result:* The table is converted back to a range.)

MULTIPLE-CHOICE QUIZ

Select the best choice in the following questions to review the project concepts.

1. What command is the best to view and change page breaks in a large worksheet?
   a. Normal view
   b. Page Break Preview
   c. Print Preview
   d. Normal Preview

2. Which of the following commands specifies the order of rows in a worksheet?
   a. Filter
   b. Sort
   c. Arrange
   d. Reorder

3. Which of the following is true of the Freeze Panes command?
   a. It hides rows.
   b. It splits columns.
   c. It filters columns by an outside criterion.
   d. It allows more columns to be displayed.

4. What is the most efficient way to change several pieces of data in a spreadsheet?
   a. Find and Replace command.
   b. Spelling check.
   c. Find command.
   d. Scroll the document and change each one individually.

5. Which of the following techniques is used to format data tables?
   a. Format as Table
   b. Cell Styles
   c. Both of these are correct.
   d. None of these is correct.

6. What command is used to perform a multilevel sort in a data table?
   a. Sort
   b. Sort using the Sort dialog box
   c. Filter
   d. Convert

7. Which of the following techniques isolates data in a spreadsheet that meets only select criteria?
   a. Filter
   b. Filter drop-down arrows
   c. Sort and Filter
   d. All of these are correct.

8. After completing work on a data table, what command returns the data table to a spreadsheet?
   a. Table to Text
   b. Table to Range
   c. Convert to Range
   d. It cannot be done once a spreadsheet has been converted to a data table.

9. If you spell-check a document, which of the following options is available?
   a. Ignore
   b. Ignore All
   c. Change Once
   d. Dictionary

10. On which tab do you find the Sort & Filter command?
    a. DATA
    b. HOME
    c. INSERT
    d. VIEW

HANDS-ON EXERCISE: WORK IT OUT EX-4A-E1

In this exercise, you have a job working with a large bakery to assist in an analysis of products and sales data. The previous employee created a large Excel workbook that needs some modification to be more meaningful. You will work with some of the large worksheet functions in Excel such as find, replace, spell-check, create a table, format a table, and convert the table back to a data range. You will also sort and filter the data. The final worksheet is shown in Figure EX4.20.

FIGURE EX4.20 Work It Out EX-4A-E1: completed

	A	B	C	D	E	F
1	Sale #	Date	Item Description	Qty	Price	Order
86	11014	3/8/2014	Carrot Cake	24	$ 18.75	Mail Order
87	15866	5/15/2014	Carrot Cake	20	$ 18.95	Mail Order
88	14574	4/27/2014	Carrot Cake	18	$ 18.95	Online
89	14094	4/22/2014	Carrot Cake	12	$ 18.95	Domestic
90	10026	2/19/2014	Carrot Cake	12	$ 18.75	Mail Order
91	10450	2/25/2014	Carrot Cake	12	$ 18.75	Domestic
92	12710	3/29/2014	Carrot Cake	12	$ 18.75	Domestic
93	12378	3/25/2014	Carrot Cake	3	$ 22.00	Mail Order
94	15754	5/14/2014	Carrot Cake	3	$ 22.00	Domestic
95	11234	3/9/2014	Carrot Cake	2	$ 22.00	Domestic
96	12534	3/26/2014	Carrot Cake	2	$ 22.00	Domestic
97	12942	4/1/2014	Carrot Cake	2	$ 22.00	Mail Order
98	14642	4/28/2014	Carrot Cake	2	$ 22.00	International
99	16014	5/18/2014	Carrot Cake	2	$ 22.00	Domestic
100	10218	2/23/2014	Carrot Cake	1	$ 22.00	Online
101	10350	2/23/2014	Carrot Cake	1	$ 22.00	Mail Order
102	11330	3/10/2014	Carrot Cake	1	$ 22.00	Domestic
103	11774	3/16/2014	Carrot Cake	1	$ 22.00	Mail Order
104	12254	3/23/2014	Carrot Cake	1	$ 22.00	Domestic
105	12750	3/30/2014	Carrot Cake	1	$ 22.00	Online
106	13826	4/15/2014	Carrot Cake	1	$ 22.00	Domestic
107	14026	4/21/2014	Carrot Cake	1	$ 22.00	Domestic
108	14254	4/23/2014	Carrot Cake	1	$ 22.00	Domestic
109	16138	5/19/2014	Carrot Cake	1	$ 22.00	Domestic

1. Locate and open the exercise data file **ex04a-ex01.xlsx**. Save the file as **ex04a-hw01.xlsx**.

2. Your supervisor asks you to make all the entries in the workbook visible but with the column heading visible no matter how far down you scroll. Select row 2 and freeze the rows. Unfreeze the rows. Split the worksheet pane after column B and then remove the split.

3. Insert page breaks after rows 25, 50, 75, and 100.

4. Use the Page Break Preview to move each of the inserted page breaks down five rows and then print the row titles on each page.

5. Use the Find and Replace command to replace each occurrence of the words "Fat Free" with "Low Calorie," then spell-check the worksheet.

6. Convert the worksheet into a data table and then, for practice, convert it back to a range. (Remove the custom format from row 1 of the file.) Format the table again so it appears as shown in Figure EX4.20.

7. Sort the table by item, description, quantity, and price.

8. Filter the table to show only the entries for carrot cake.

9. Save and close the workbook file.

In this exercise, you work with the college athletic department. The athletic director asks you to refine the school's football roster. You will use an Excel spreadsheet to show these refinements. The final worksheet is shown in Figure EX4.21.

FIGURE EX4.21 Work It Out EX-4A-E2: completed

	Student ID	Last Name	First Name	Height (ft.)	Height (in.)	Weight (lb.)	Position	Class	Scholarship Amount
5	451	Bethala	Jason	5	10	190	Guard	Senior	$4,670
7	541	Bradford	Kenneth	6	0	185	Tackle	Senior	$4,860
13	423	Costello	James	5	8	186	End	Senior	$4,660
21	535	Johnson	Blair	6	2	246	Tackle	Senior	$4,840
22	480	Johnson	Nate	5	10	185	Quarterback	Senior	$4,690
23	494	Leva	Joe	5	7	160	Back	Senior	$4,750
25	516	Martin	Grandville	6	2	220	Guard	Senior	$4,760
29	546	Mitchell	Rodney	6	2	220	Guard	Senior	$4,870
30	456	Morris	Taj	5	7	185	Back	Senior	$4,680
35	483	Pluta	Michael	5	11	175	Back	Senior	$4,740
40	521	Stairker	Evan	5	10	160	Back	Senior	$4,820
45	520	Viaud	Marlon	5	5	164	Kicking Specialist	Senior	$4,770

1. Locate and open the exercise data file **ex04a-ex02.xlsx**. Save the file as **ex04a-hw02.xlsx**.

2. Your supervisor asks you to make all the entries in the workbook visible, leaving the column heading visible as users scroll. Select row 2 and freeze the rows. Unfreeze the rows. Split the worksheet pane after column C, then remove the split.

3. Insert page breaks after rows 10, 20, 30, 40, and 50.

4. Use the Page Break Preview to move each of the inserted page breaks down two rows and then print the row titles on each page.

5. Use the Find and Replace command to replace each occurrence of the word *Punter* with "Kicking Specialist" and then spell-check the worksheet. (Be sure to resize columns as needed.)

6. Convert the worksheet into a data table and, for practice, convert it back to a range. (Remember to remove all formatting remaining before proceeding.) Format the table again and modify the format so it appears as shown in Figure EX4.21.

7. Sort the table by last name, first name, and class.

8. Filter the table to show only senior football players.

9. Save and close the workbook file.

HANDS-ON EXERCISE: WORK IT OUT EX-4A-E3 (*Available at* www.mhhe.com/office2013projectlearn)

Consolidating Alumni Association Worksheet Data

PROJECT OBJECTIVES

After completing this project, you will be able to:

- Navigate, rename, and format sheet tabs.

- Insert, delete, and hide worksheets in a workbook.

- Consolidate a multiple-sheet workbook using a summary worksheet.

- Add a documentation worksheet to a workbook.

- Group worksheets for easy formatting and printing.

In this project, you will modify information from a workbook containing worksheets for each of the Greene State University Alumni Association chapters. You will navigate, rename, and format the sheet tabs. You will also add, delete, and hide worksheets, then group a series of worksheets for easier formatting and printing. You will add a documentation worksheet to the workbook and finally consolidate the multiple-sheet workbook using a summary worksheet.

PROJECT FILE: *Available at* www.mhhe.com/office2013projectlearn

	A	B	C	D	E	F	G
1			Greene State University Ohio Alumni				
2							
3	Monthly Alumni Income						
4	Month	Income					
5	January	$400					
6	February	$550					
7	March	$350					
8	April	$300					
9	May	$560					
10	June	$320					
11	July	$220					
12	August	$250					
13	September	$460					
14	October	$190					
15	November	$250					
16	December	$650					
17							
18							
19							
20							
21							
22							
23							

Sheet1 | Sheet2 | Sheet3 | (+)

Navigating, Renaming, and Formatting Sheet Tabs

LESSON OVERVIEW

Sheet tabs display at the bottom of the Excel window. They indicate what sheets are available in a workbook and which worksheet is currently active. When you open a workbook in Excel, the default is three worksheets, named with sheet tabs: Sheet1, Sheet2, and Sheet3. To move from one sheet to another, click the appropriate sheet tab. You can create as many sheets as you need within the limits of your computer's memory and rename them as necessary. Excel offers some limited formatting for sheet tabs.

SKILLS PREVIEW

Navigate from one sheet to another	• CLICK the sheet tab to view.
Rename a sheet tab	• RIGHT-CLICK the sheet tab to rename. CLICK Rename. TYPE the new sheet tab name.
Format sheet tabs using the right-click method	• RIGHT-CLICK the sheet tab to format. CLICK Tab Color. SELECT the Standard Color, Theme Color, or More Colors for the sheet tab.
Format sheet tabs using the Format button	• CLICK the sheet tab to format. CLICK the Format button in the Cells group on the HOME tab. CLICK Tab Color. SELECT the Standard Color, Theme Color, or More Colors for the sheet tab.

PROJECT PRACTICE

1. Locate and open the project data file **ex04b.xlsx**. On the FILE tab, use the Save As command to save the file as **ex04b-consolidate.xlsx**. You may need to choose a place to store the file (e.g., SkyDrive or Computer), and browse to the desired location.

2. When you open the file, Sheet1 is the active sheet.

   CLICK on the Sheet2 sheet tab to make it the active sheet. (*Result:* Sheet2 is now the active worksheet.)

   CLICK on other sheet tabs to move from one worksheet to another.

3. Rename a sheet tab to more accurately represent the sheet's contents.

   RIGHT-CLICK the Sheet1 sheet tab to open the sheet tab context menu.

   CLICK Rename.

   TYPE Ohio

   PRESS Enter.
   Repeat the steps for Sheet2 and Sheet3 and name them "Maryland" and "New York," respectively.

4 Add color to the sheet tabs.

RIGHT-CLICK the Ohio sheet tab.

CLICK Tab Color to display the color palette.

SELECT Standard Color Green.

CLICK the Maryland sheet tab and, while holding the **Ctrl** key, CLICK the New York sheet tab.
(*Result*: Both the Maryland and New York sheets are active.)

CLICK the Format button in the Cells group of the HOME tab.

CLICK Tab color to display the color palette.
Select Standard Color Green.
(*Result*: All three sheet tabs are now Standard Color Green, as shown in Figure EX4.22.)

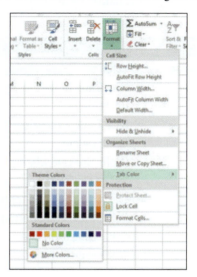

FIGURE EX4.22 Formatted sheet tabs

	A	B	C	D	E	F
1			Greene State University Ohio Alumni			
2						
3	Monthly Alumni Income					
4	Month	Income				
5	January	$400				
6	February	$550				
7	March	$350				
8	April	$300				
9	May	$560				
10	June	$320				
11	July	$220				
12	August	$250				
13	September	$460				
14	October	$190				
15	November	$250				
16	December	$650				
17						
18						
19						
20						
21						
22						
23						

Ohio   Maryland   New York   ⊕

5 CLICK the Ohio sheet tab. Save the file.

Inserting, Deleting, and Hiding Worksheets

LESSON OVERVIEW

When you work with Excel, you may find that three worksheets, the default, are too few or too many worksheets. Adding worksheets in Excel 2013 is slightly different than in previous versions of Excel, but the principle remains the same. Exercise care when you delete worksheets because once you delete a worksheet, the data is lost forever.

Hiding worksheets is a valuable technique to protect sensitive or classified data. In this lesson, you will hide a worksheet using one technique and unhide a worksheet using another.

SKILLS PREVIEW

Insert a new worksheet	• CLICK the `Ohio` `Maryland` `New York` ⊕ button to the right of the existing sheet tabs. NAME and move the new sheet tab as appropriate. (Note: The new sheet tab appears to the right of the active sheet tab.)
Delete a sheet tab	• RIGHT-CLICK the sheet tab for the spreadsheet to delete. CLICK Delete. (Note: Use care when you delete sheet tabs because once you delete a sheet tab, it is not recoverable.)
Hide worksheets	• CLICK the sheet tab for the worksheet to be hidden. CLICK the Format button in the Cells group on the HOME tab. CLICK Hide & Unhide. CLICK Hide Sheet, or • RIGHT-CLICK the sheet tab of the worksheet to hide. CLICK Hide on the shortcut menu.
Unhide worksheets	• CLICK the Format button in the Cells group on the HOME tab. CLICK Hide & Unhide. CLICK Unhide Sheet. DOUBLE-CLICK the worksheet to unhide in the Unhide dialog box, or • RIGHT-CLICK a sheet tab of the worksheet. CLICK Unhide on the shortcut menu. DOUBLE-CLICK the worksheet to unhide in the Unhide dialog box.

PROJECT PRACTICE

1. Ensure that the **ex04b-consolidate.xlsx** workbook is open in Excel.

2. Navigate to the New York sheet tab in the workbook.

3. Insert a new worksheet.
   CLICK the plus sign to the right of the New York sheet tab (`Ohio` `Maryland` `New York` ⊕).
   (*Result*: A new sheet tab with a default name, e.g., Sheet4, appears to the right of the New York sheet tab as shown in Figure EX4.23.)

FIGURE EX4.23 Worksheet with new sheet tab inserted

⬩	A	B	C	D	E	F	
1							
2							
3							
4							
5							
6							
7							
8							
9							
10							
11							
12							
13							
14							
15							
16							
17							
18							
19							
20							
21							
22							
23							

◂ ▸ | Ohio | Maryland | New York | **Sheet4** | ⊕

4 Delete the new sheet tab you inserted.

RIGHT-CLICK the Sheet4 sheet tab to show the Sheet Tab shortcut menu.

CLICK Delete.

(*Result*: Sheet4 is deleted.)

5 Hide and unhide a worksheet.

RIGHT-CLICK the New York sheet tab.

CLICK Hide.

(*Result*: The New York worksheet is hidden.)

To unhide the New York worksheet,

CLICK the Format button in the Cells group of the HOME tab.

CLICK Hide & Unhide.

CLICK Unhide Sheet.

CLICK OK.

(*Result*: The New York worksheet is unhidden.)

6 Save the file.

Consolidating a Multiple-Sheet Workbook Using a Summary Worksheet

LESSON OVERVIEW

The first two lessons in Project B covered a workbook containing multiple worksheets. Each worksheet showed the income for a Greene State University Alumni Association chapter in Ohio, Maryland, and New York. The head of the association asks that you total the dona- tions for each chapter to show the combined income for the three chapters.

There are two ways to do this: using range names with a summary sheet and using **3-D Reference Formulas**. The lesson presents both methods.

SKILLS PREVIEW

Create a summary sheet using range names	• INSERT a new worksheet in the workbook. CLICK the cell where the total will appear. TYPE **=sum(** TYPE the first range name. TYPE a comma (**,**). TYPE the second range name. TYPE a comma (**,**). Continue typing range names with a comma after them until you enter them all. Rather than typing a comma after the last range name, TYPE **)** PRESS [Enter]. Format the total on the summary sheet as appropriate.
Create a summary sheet using 3-D Reference Formulas	• INSERT a new worksheet in the workbook. CLICK the cell where the total will appear. TYPE **=sum(** CLICK the first sheet tab to include. HOLD the [Shift] key and select the final sheet tab. Using the [Shift] key selects all sheet tabs included in the calculation. SELECT the range on the active worksheet to total. TYPE **)** and PRESS [Enter]. Format the total on the summary sheet as appropriate.

PROJECT PRACTICE

1. Ensure that the **ex04ab-consolidate.xlsx** workbook is open in Excel.

2. Insert a summary worksheet to show total donations for the three Greene State University alumni chapters.

   | Ohio | Maryland | New York | ⊕ |

   With New York as the active worksheet,

   CLICK the New Sheet button.

   RIGHT-CLICK the newly inserted sheet tab.

   CLICK Rename.

   TYPE **Summary**

   PRESS [Enter].

   RIGHT-CLICK the Summary sheet tab.

   CLICK Tab Color.

SELECT Standard Colors Green so the sheet tab matches the others.
(*Result*: The Summary sheet tab appears as shown here.)

3 CLICK and DRAG the Summary sheet tab so it is to the left of the Ohio sheet.

4 Create the Summary sheet for the total.

CLICK cell A1.

TYPE **Greene State University Alumni Association Donations Summary**

CLICK cell B3.

TYPE **Chapter Donations Total**.

(*Result*: The Summary sheet appears as shown in Figure EX4.24.)

FIGURE EX4.24 Summary sheet

5 Range names are already created for the three worksheets. View them.

CLICK the Down arrow in the Name Box, located on the left of the formula bar.

CLICK the Summary tab to ensure the Summary worksheet is active.

CLICK cell E3 to make it the active cell. This is where the donations total will appear.

TYPE **=SUM(Ohio,Maryland,NewYork)**

PRESS Enter.

Note that Excel requires no space be entered between *New* and *York*.

RIGHT-CLICK cell E3.

CLICK Format Cells.

CLICK the NUMBER tab, if necessary, and CLICK Currency and change the number of decimal places to 0.

CLICK OK.

(*Result*: The currency formatted total of donations from the three chapters appears in cell E3, as shown in Figure EX4.25.)

Range names in Name box

FIGURE EX4.25 Summary sheet with formatted donations total

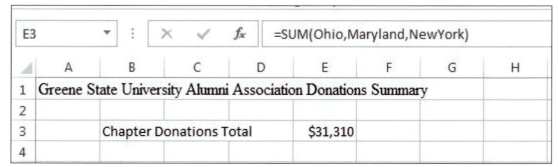

6 Use the alternative method to enter a total on the Summary sheet.

DELETE the formula in cell E3.

Ensure Cell E3 is still selected.

TYPE =SUM(

CLICK the Ohio Sheet tab.

HOLD the [Shift] key and CLICK the New York tab.

Because of Excel's requirements, remove the space between *New* and *York* in the Formula bar. The formula should appear as shown.

=SUM('Ohio:NewYork'!

With Ohio as the active worksheet,

SELECT the cell range B5:B16.

TYPE)

PRESS [Enter].

If necessary, format cell E3 as Currency with 0 decimal places.

(*Result*: The same total appears as shown in Figure EX4.25.)

7 Save the file.

Adding a Documentation Worksheet

LESSON OVERVIEW

Often, users create Excel workbooks in isolation and no description for the purpose or other important information about the workbook exists. Creating a **documentation worksheet** solves this issue by describing or annotating the workbook. A documentation worksheet describes the purpose of the workbook and the contents of each worksheet within the workbook.

SKILLS PREVIEW

Adding a documentation worksheet to an Excel workbook	• INSERT a new worksheet in the workbook. Enter the documentation information needed. Format the worksheet.

PROJECT PRACTICE

1 Ensure that the **ex04b-consolidate.xlsx** workbook is open in Excel.

With Summary as the active worksheet,

CLICK the New Sheet button.

RIGHT-CLICK the newly added sheet tab.

CLICK Rename.

TYPE Documentation

PRESS Enter .

RIGHT-CLICK the Documentation sheet tab.

CLICK Tab Color.

Select Standard Colors Green so the sheet tab matches the others.

Move the Documentation sheet tab to the left so it is the first sheet tab.

2 TYPE the following:

Cell	Text
A1	Greene State University Alumni Donations
A3	Author
B3	Student Name
A4	Date of Creation
B4	Today's Date
A5	Last Modified
B5	Tomorrow's Date
A7	Description of Workbook
B7	The Greene State University Donations workbook contains the total of donations for all chapters and a breakdown of donations by chapter
A9	Sheets in the Book
A10	Documentation
B10	Describes the school's alumni donations
A11	Summary
B11	Summary totals for each alumni chapter

3 Format the Documentation sheet.

Size columns A and B using the techniques learned in earlier chapters.

CLICK cell range A1:B1.

CLICK Merge and Center in the Alignment group of the HOME tab.

CLICK cell A1.

CLICK Bold in the Font group of the HOME tab.

CLICK the Font Size drop-down list. Change the font to 24.

SELECT cells A2:A11.

CLICK Bold in the Font group of the HOME tab.

With A2:A11 still selected, hold the **Ctrl** key and CLICK cell A1 to add cell A1 to the selection.

CLICK the Fill Color drop-down list.

CLICK Standard Colors Green.

Ensure that cells A1:A11 remain selected.

CLICK the Font color drop-down list.

CLICK Theme Color White, Background 1.

CLICK cell B7 and CLICK the Wrap Text button in the Alignment group on the Home tab.
(*Result:* The worksheet should appear as shown in Figure EX4.26.)

FIGURE EX4.26   Completed Documentation sheet

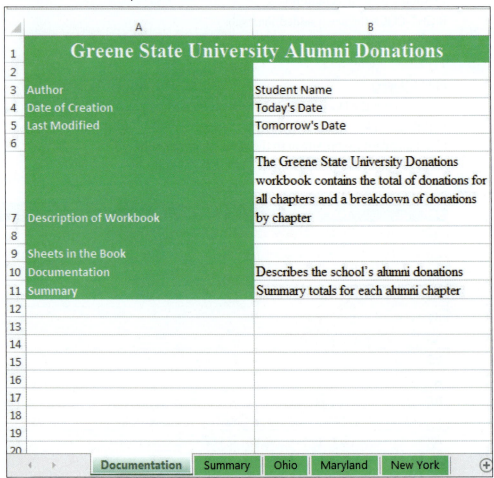

4 Save the file.

Grouping Worksheets for Formatting and Printing

LESSON OVERVIEW

The final lesson in Excel uses some of the techniques discussed previously but with new results. In an Excel workbook with multiple worksheets, worksheets may be **grouped** to simplify formatting and printing. You can then format each sheet of the workbook by applying formatting to one worksheet. When you group worksheets, the formatting is applied to each worksheet at the same time. The same principle applies to printing. By grouping the worksheets to be printed, it is not necessary to print each worksheet individually.

SKILLS PREVIEW

Group worksheets for formatting	• CLICK the first sheet tab of the worksheets to be grouped. Use **Shift** + CLICK to select contiguous worksheets or **Ctrl** + CLICK to select noncontiguous worksheets. Apply the appropriate formatting.
Group worksheets for printing	• CLICK the first sheet tab of the worksheets to be grouped. Use **Shift** + CLICK to select contiguous worksheets or **Ctrl** + CLICK to select noncontiguous worksheets. Print the grouped worksheets.

PROJECT PRACTICE

1 Ensure that the **ex04b-consolidate.xlsx** workbook is open in Excel.

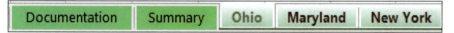

CLICK the Ohio sheet tab and then, while holding down the **Shift** key, CLICK the New York sheet tab.

CLICK cell A1 on the Ohio worksheet.

CLICK the Bold button in the Font group on the HOME tab.

CLICK the Font Size drop-down list and change the font size to 20.

CLICK the Fill Color drop-down list.

CLICK Standard Colors Green.

CLICK the Font color drop-down list.

CLICK Theme Color White, Background 1.

CLICK the Summary sheet tab to ungroup the worksheets.
(*Result*: The Ohio, Maryland, and New York worksheets contain the same formatted heading.)

2 Group worksheets for printing.

CLICK the Ohio sheet tab and then, while holding down the **Shift** key, CLICK the Documentation sheet tab.

CLICK FILE and then Print to enter the Backstage Print view, as shown in Figure EX4.27.

SELECT the appropriate printer settings as directed by your teacher and print if directed.
(*Result*: By grouping the worksheets, you can print all worksheets at one time.)

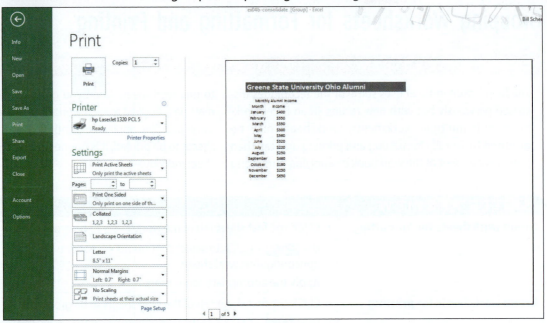

3 CLICK the Maryland sheet tab to ungroup the worksheets.

4 Save the workbook file and exit Excel.

MULTIPLE-CHOICE QUIZ

Select the best choice in the following questions to review the project concepts.

1. When you create a new Excel workbook, how many sheets does it include?
   a. One
   b. Two
   c. Three
   d. Four

2. What command is used to change the name of a sheet tab?
   a. Change
   b. Update
   c. Rename
   d. Name

3. What click technique do you user to group noncontiguous sheets in a workbook?
   A. Click each tab in turn
   b. **Ctrl** +Click
   c. **Shift** +Click
   d. **Alt** +Click

4. A sheet in a workbook that contains information about the worksheet, who prepared it, and the worksheet's purpose is called:
   a. Summary sheet
   b. Worksheet
   c. Page Preview sheet
   d. Documentation sheet

5. Which of the following are techniques used in the creation of a workbook summary sheet?
   a. 3-D Reference Formulas
   b. Data ranges
   c. Neither of these is correct.
   d. Both of these are correct.

6. What is the correct syntax to begin a formula for a workbook summary sheet?
   a. =SUM
   b. =SUMMARY
   c. =RANGE
   d. =3-D

7. =SUM(Wisconsin!B12:E12) is an example of
   a. Data range.
   b. Cell Related Formula.
   c. 3-D Reference Formula.
   d. Multilevel Summary Formula.

8. Which of the following functions can you accomplish when worksheets are grouped?
   a. Print
   b. Save
   c. Merge and Center
   d. All of these are correct.

9. Your company wants you to consolidate data from different worksheets. What is your first step?
   a. Create a summary sheet.
   b. Create a documentation sheet.
   c. Rename all sheets to ensure uniformity.
   d. Go back to your supervisor. This cannot be accomplished in Microsoft Excel.

10. How many worksheets can you include in an Excel workbook?
    a. 256
    b. 900
    c. Limited only by available memory
    d. Unlimited

In this exercise, you work for a restaurant chain in Pennsylvania. Previously, accounting for each location was done separately. You and your manager decide to summarize the data from the three sites and consolidate the workbook. To help you keep track, the financial data documentation is added to the workbook. The final worksheet is shown in Figure EX4.28.

FIGURE EX4.28 Work It Out EX-4B-E1: completed

	A	B	C	D	E	F	G
1				Erie Location			
2							
3	Category	1st Quarter	2nd Quarter	3rd Quarter	4th Quarter	Total	
4	Dine-In	$40,000	$34,000	$29,000	$22,000	$125,000	
5	Pick-up	$62,000	$63,000	$62,000	$63,000	$250,000	
6	Delivery	$22,000	$26,000	$35,000	$42,000	$125,000	
7	Total	$124,000	$123,000	$126,000	$127,000	$500,000	

Sheet tabs: Documentation | Summary | **Erie** | Pittsburgh | Harrisburg | ⊕

1 Locate and open the exercise data file **ex04b-ex01.xlsx**. Save the file as **ex04b-hw01.xlsx**.

2 Rename the three sheet tabs "Erie," "Pittsburgh," and "Harrisburg." Format the sheet tabs Dark Blue as shown in Figure EX4.28.

3 Delete Sheet4 from the workbook and hide the Pittsburgh sheet, then unhide the Pittsburgh sheet.

4 Insert a new sheet to the left of the Erie sheet, name it Summary, and format the sheet tab as shown in Step 2.

	A	B	C	D
1	Summary			
2				
3			Total Sales: All Locations	
4				
5				

5 Fill in the information on the Summary sheet as shown here.

6 Use the Range Name technique to summarize the Total Sales from the Erie, Pittsburgh, and Harrisburg sheets into cell C3 on the Summary sheet. Adjust the column widths on the Summary sheet. Format cell C3 as Currency, no decimals.

7 Insert a new sheet to the left of the Summary sheet and name it "Documentation."

8 Enter the information and formatting on the Documentation sheet as shown in Figure EX4.29.

FIGURE EX4.29 Documentation sheet

	A	B	C
1		Davis Restaurant	
2			
3	Author	Student Name	
4	Date of Creation	Today's Date	
5	Last Modified	Tomorrow's Date	
6			
7	Description of Workbook	The Davis Restaurants workbook contains the total of sales for all locations and a breakdown of sales by location	
8			
9	Sheets in the Book		
10	Documentation	Describes the restaurants' sales	
11	Summary	Total sales for all locations	
12			
13			
14			
15			
16			
17			
18			
19			

Sheet tabs: **Documentation** | Summary | Erie | Pittsburgh | Harrisburg

9 Group the Summary, Erie, Pittsburgh, and Harrisburg sheets and format them as shown in the sample solution (Figure EX4.28).

10 Print the grouped worksheets if desired by your instructor.

11 Save and close the workbook file.

In this exercise, you will summarize the financial data for Cosmo Industries. To assist you, a spreadsheet is manipulated to include a summary and documentation. The final worksheet is shown in Figure EX4.30.

FIGURE EX4.30 Work It Out EX-4B-E2: completed

	A	B	C	D	E	F	G
1	**New Jersey Operating Budget**						
2							
3		Qtr 1	Qtr 2	Qtr 3	Qtr 4	Total	
4	**Bottles Sold:**						
5	**Cranberry Drink**	$ 214,710	$ 106,205	$ 113,055	$ 104,843	538,813	
6	**AllBerry Quencher**	33,195	29,672	36,908	36,456	136,231	
7	**Total Bottles**	247,905	135,877	149,963	141,299	675,044	
8							
9	**Revenues:**						
10	**Cranberry Drink**	$ 469,477	$ 231,851	$ 246,852	$ 228,868	$ 1,177,048	
11	**AllBerry Quencher**	135,032	120,306	150,552	178,663	584,553	
12	**Total Sales**	$ 604,509	$ 352,157	$ 397,404	$ 407,531	$ 1,761,601	
13							
14	**Cost of Sales**	7,914	4,802	5,360	5,115	23,191	
15	**Gross Profit**	$ 596,595	$ 347,355	$ 392,044	$ 402,416	$ 1,738,410	
16							
17	**Expenses:**						
18	**Advertising**	$ 20,577	$ 12,407	$ 14,027	$ 13,315	$ 60,326	
19	**Benefits**	27,710	16,537	18,695	17,747	80,689	
20	**Communication**	27,710	16,537	18,695	17,747	80,689	
21	**Electronic Equipment**	19,138	11,574	13,085	12,421	56,218	
22	**Insurance**	16,261	9,908	11,202	10,634	48,005	

1 Locate and open the exercise data file **ex04b-ex02.xlsx**. Save the file as **ex04b-hw02.xlsx**.

2 Rename the two sheet tabs "New Jersey" and "Wisconsin." Format the sheet tabs Red as shown in Figure EX4.30.

3 Delete Sheet3 from the workbook and hide the New Jersey sheet, then unhide the New Jersey sheet.

4 Insert a new sheet to the left of the New Jersey sheet, name it "Summary," and format the sheet tab as shown in Step 2.

5 Fill in the information on the Summary sheet as shown here.

	A	B	C	D
1	Cosmo Industries Consolidated Sales			
2				
3				
4		Sales Total		
5				
6				
7				

6 Use the 3-D Reference Formula technique to summarize the total sales from the New Jersey and Wisconsin sheets into cell C4 on the Summary sheet. Adjust the column widths on the Summary sheet. Format cell C4 as Currency, no decimals.

7 Insert a new sheet to the left of the Summary sheet and name it "Documentation."

8 Enter the information and formatting on the Documentation sheet as shown in Figure EX4.31.

FIGURE EX4.31 Documentation sheet

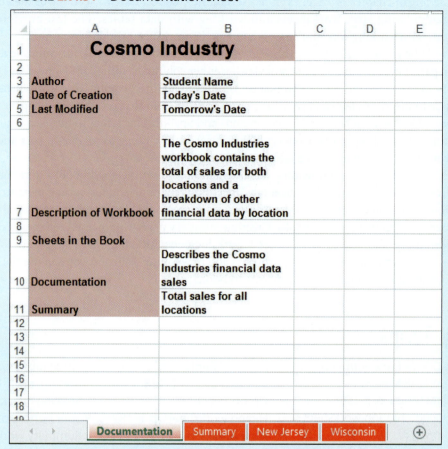

9 Group the New Jersey and Wisconsin sheets, then format them as shown in the sample solution in Figure EX4.30.

10 Print the grouped worksheets if desired by your instructor.

11 Save and close the workbook file.

HANDS-ON EXERCISE: WORK IT OUT EX-4B-E3 (*Available at* <u>www.mhhe.com/office2013projectlearn</u>)

Chapter Summary

The fourth chapter of Excel explored several new concepts. Two sections of the chapter discussed manipulating large worksheets and working with data tables. The last portion of the chapter addressed working with and consolidating multi-worksheet workbooks.

When you work with worksheets with a large number of records, it is valuable to be able to view all parts of the workbook while still viewing either column headings or row headings or both. You can use freeze panes and split the worksheet window to do this. Printing large worksheets often forces the user to insert or change page breaks or to print titles so that column titles appear on each printed page. Use the Find and Replace commands and Spelling check tool to make changing data easy and eliminate spelling errors. Convert a worksheet from a range to a table to sort and filter data in a worksheet. You can convert a table back to a range if necessary.

Consolidating and providing documentation to multisheet workbooks were the final topics addressed. You can manipulate sheet tabs, including renaming and formatting them to make identification of the sheets much easier. Adding, deleting, and hiding worksheets are also important in managing multisheet workbooks. Creating summary pages with named cell ranges or 3-D Reference Formulas makes data analysis easier. Create documentation pages in a large workbook to permit users to see what the workbook's purpose is and how to use it. Finally, you can use the group operation to easily format and print multisheet workbooks.

Chapter Key Terms

3-D Reference Formulas, p. E-184

Data tables, p. E-158

Documentation worksheet, p. E-187

Filtering, pp. E-158, E-171

Find and Replace, p. E-166

Freeze panes, p. E-158

Group, p. E-189

Hiding worksheets, p. E-182

Page breaks, p. E-163

Range, p. E-175

Sheet tabs, pp. E-158, E-180

Sorting, pp. E-158, E-171

Spelling check, p. E-166

Split button, p. E-162

Summary worksheet, p. E-158

Table, p. E-168

On Your Own Exercise EX-4C-E1

This exercise provides a chance to practice the important Excel 2013 skills covered in this chapter. In this exercise, you have a contract with Acco Inc. to analyze its sales force using Excel 2013 and the skills learned in this chapter. Open the exercise data file **ex04c-ex01.xlsx** and save it as **ex04c-hw01.xlsx**. The final screen should be similar to Figure EX4.32.

FIGURE EX4.32 On Your Own Exercise EX-4C-E1: sample solution

	A	B	C	D	E	F	G	H
1				Acco, Inc Sales Employees				
2								
3	Employee ID	Last Name	First Name	Gender	Title	Salary	Location	Performance
9	29034	Beamer	Courtny	F	Store Manager	$ 70,000	Miami	Excellent
15	12797	Bocholis	Ashley	F	Store Manager	$ 76,300	Boston	Good
28	28888	Crowder	McClendon	M	Store Manager	$ 77,100	Detroit	Good
51	10398	Foerster	Gwen	M	Store Manager	$ 74,200	New York	Excellent
72	11935	Jones	Wendy	F	Store Manager	$ 70,900	Cleveland	Good
39	16424	Titley	Ben	M	Store Manager	$ 84,400	Miami	Good

Complete the following tasks so the worksheet is similar in appearance to Figure EX4.32.

- Freeze the rows to view the column titles. Unfreeze the rows. Split the worksheet pane after column B and then remove the split.

- Insert page breaks to make printing easier.

- Move each of the page breaks to facilitate printing, and print the row titles on each page.
- Use the Find and Replace function to replace each occurrence of the word *Trainee* with *Probationary,* and spell-check the worksheet.
- Convert the worksheet into a formatted data table.
- Sort the table by last name, first name, and location.
- Filter the table to show only store managers.
- Save and close the workbook file.

On Your Own Exercise EX-4C-E2

To practice working with consolidating department store data, open the **ex04c-ex02.xlsx** file and then save it as **ex04c-hw02.xlsx**. Accomplish the following tasks using your knowledge of Excel and the skills you learned in this chapter.

- Rename and format the sheet tabs "Quarters 1 through 4."
- Delete Sheet5.
- Insert a Summary sheet to summarize the total for the four quarters.
- Format the Summary sheet.
- Insert and format a Documentation sheet.
- Group the four quarter sheets and format them.
- Print the workbook if required by your instructor.
- Save the file, then save the workbook and exit Excel.

Figure EX4.33 is a sample solution. Your solution may be different.

FIGURE EX4.33   On Your Own Exercise EX-4C-E2: sample solution

ProjectLearn
Microsoft
Access 2013

1

Introduction to Access

Microsoft Access is a database software program that enables you to enter, store, analyze, and present data. For end users, power users, and software developers alike, Access provides easy-to-use yet powerful tools most often associated with higher-end **database management systems (DBMS)**. In fact, Access offers scalability never before seen in desktop database software to meet needs ranging from simple to complex. At the desktop level, Access can help you manage your personal information or collect data for a research project. At the enterprise level, Access can retrieve and display data stored on servers located throughout the world. Access also enables you to publish web-based lists, forms, and reports for delivery over the Internet.

Although this is not a database theory tutorial, a familiarity with some basic terms will help you become more productive using Access. The word **database**, for example, refers to a collection of related information, such as a company's accounting data. The primary object in a database for storing data is called a **table**. In Access, a table is commonly viewed in a **datasheet** using the **Datasheet view**, which organizes data into rows and columns similar to a spreadsheet. Each individual entry in a table (for example, a person's name and address) is called a **record** and appears as a horizontal row in a datasheet. Furthermore, each record in a table is composed of one or more fields, columns in a datasheet. A **field** holds a single piece of data, such as a phone number or e-mail address. If you are familiar with using Excel, you will find Access datasheets easy to learn and understand.

In this chapter, you will be introduced to Microsoft Access, open and view database objects, learn how to manipulate table data, and then create new tables for adding and storing information.

PROJECT

Exploring and Maintaining a School Database

In this project, you will load Microsoft Access and tour the various objects that may be stored within a database file. You will also practice navigating, adding, deleting, and editing table data, as well as formatting and customizing the Datasheet window.

This chapter will introduce you to the core skills required to use Access productively. These core skills will continue to be developed and expanded in later projects.

THE SITUATION

Administrative Duties at Ridgemont College

As one of the campus administrative personnel at Ridgemont College, you have been asked to review data that have been exported and compiled by IT Services in a Microsoft Access database. Unfortunately, you have never used Access and have had only limited experience using Excel. You hope that your Word skills can help carry you through this next set of tasks. To begin, you've secured a copy of the Access database and plan to practice with the data on your own time. Let's go explore!

PROJECT OBJECTIVES

Maintaining the School Database

This project will introduce you to Microsoft Access, as well as the various objects that may be created and stored in a local Access database file. You will take a user's perspective in this project, and learn how to navigate, add, edit, and delete table data.

PROJECT FILE: *Available at www.mhhe.com/office2013projectlearn*

After completing this project, you will be able to:

- Identify the components of the Microsoft Access application window, as well as the objects that may be stored within a single, local Access database file.

- Navigate and select table data within a datasheet.

- Add, edit, and delete both field and record data.

- Format the Datasheet window using fonts, colors, and borders.

- Customize the Datasheet window by sorting records into ascending or descending order.

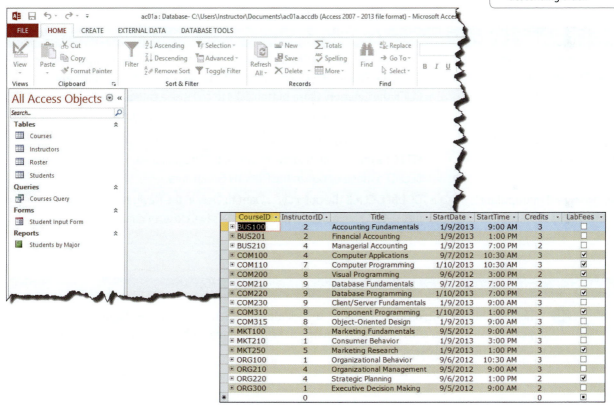

Touring an Access Database

LESSON OVERVIEW

Within a single, local Access 2013 **database file** (appearing in Windows Explorer with a *.accdb* file extension), you create and work with individual database objects, including tables, queries, forms, reports, macros, and modules. There are **database objects** for storing data (tables), entering and editing data (forms), retrieving data (queries), displaying or printing data (reports), and automating your work flow (macros and modules). In this project, you will open an existing database file, tour the features of the Access application window, and familiarize yourself with the various objects.

Once a database is opened, the **Navigation pane** appears along the left border of the application window (as shown here) and becomes your command control center within Access. The Navigation pane provides a categorical listing of the database objects contained therein, but also allows you to group and search for objects. Most of your time in Access will be spent working with the objects listed in the Navigation pane. When you are more familiar with Access, you can customize the Navigation pane and define your own object groups.

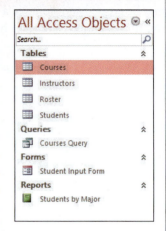

SKILLS PREVIEW

Collapse and expand the Navigation pane, as well as categories within the pane	• CLICK the Shutter Bar Close button (≪) to collapse the Navigation pane, *or* • CLICK the Shutter Bar Open button (≫) to expand the Navigation pane, *or* • CLICK the Category Close button (⌃) to collapse a category, *or* • CLICK the Category Open button (⌄) to expand a category.
Group and filter objects in the Navigation pane	• CLICK the drop-down category button (⊙) for the Navigation pane. SELECT a menu option in the Navigate to Category area. SELECT a menu option in the Filter by Group area.
Open, close, and manipulate object windows	• DOUBLE-CLICK the object you want to view in the Navigation pane, *or* • RIGHT-CLICK an object's window tab to save, close, or change the View mode for an object.

PROJECT PRACTICE

1 When you launch Microsoft Access 2013, an opening or welcome screen (see Figure AC1.1) appears, showing you a list of recently opened databases, along with several template options to use in creating new database applications.

FIGURE AC1.1   The Access 2013 welcome screen

Recently opened databases will appear in a list

To open an existing database file, click this command option

To start a new database, double-click on a template

2 To begin, open the database project file named **ac01a.accdb**. Do the following:

CLICK the Open Other Files command, located on the left side of the screen as shown in Figure AC1.1.

3 When the Open pane of the Backstage view appears:

CLICK the Computer command ( ) in the Open area.

CLICK the Browse button ( ) in the Computer area.

4 Using the Open dialog box, locate and then open the **ac01a.accdb** database project file on your local computer.

HEADS UP

The security warning shown below may appear, as a precautionary measure. If you are confident that you have selected the correct project data file, click the Enable Content button to proceed with this lesson.

(*Result:* Your screen should now appear similar to Figure AC1.2. Notice the variety of objects listed in the Navigation pane at the left of the window.)

FIGURE AC1.2 The Access 2013 application window

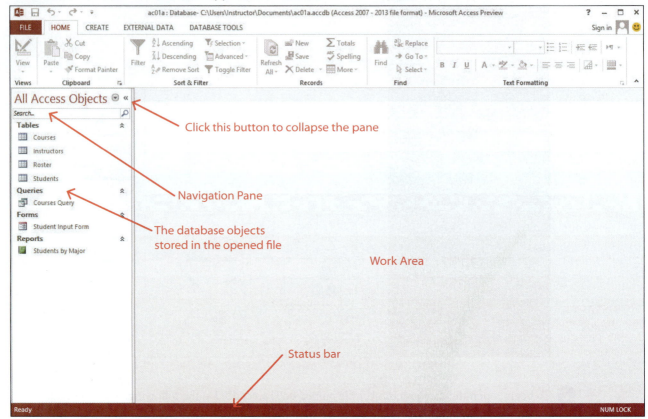

5. To hide and then display the Navigation pane:

CLICK the Shutter Bar Close button (⟪) to collapse the pane.

CLICK the Shutter Bar Open button (⟫) to expand the pane.

6. To change the arrangement of objects being displayed in the Navigation pane:

CLICK the drop-down menu button (⊙) in the Navigation pane.

SELECT the Tables and Related Views command.

(*Result:* Notice that the pane is divided into four areas, with headings that reference the table names, as shown here.)

7. To switch back to the Object Type view:

CLICK the drop-down menu button (⊙) in the Navigation pane.

SELECT the Object Type command.

(*Result:* The categories revert to Tables, Queries, Forms, and Reports.)

8. You may have noticed that many of the Ribbon commands are dimmed, because no object has been opened in the work area. Open a table object to display the data stored in Datasheet view mode and see how that impacts the Ribbon. Do the following:

DOUBLE-CLICK Courses in the Tables group of the Navigation pane.

(*Result:* The Courses Datasheet window opens and fills the work area, as shown in Figure AC1.3. Notice that the commands for manipulating a table are dynamically added to the Ribbon and displayed under Table Tools.)

FIGURE AC1.3 Opening a table in a Datasheet window

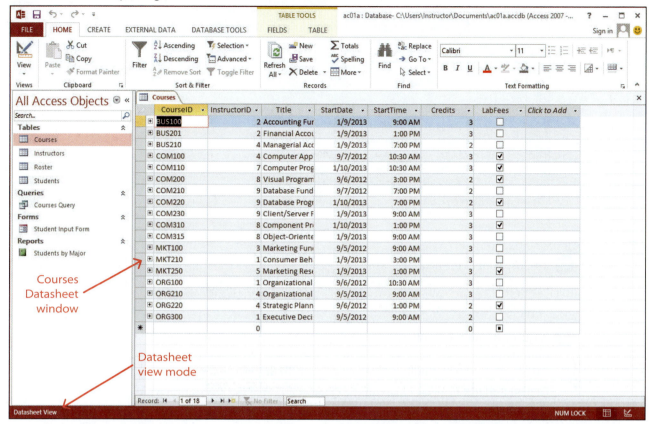

9 To display another table's datasheet:

DOUBLE-CLICK Instructors in the Tables group.
(*Result:* The Instructors datasheet appears, with its tab placed next to the Courses datasheet tab.)

10 Click the Courses and Instructors datasheet tabs to switch back and forth between the two datasheets. When you are ready to proceed, ensure that the Instructors tab is selected.

11 You may have noticed that there are plus sign symbols (+) in the leftmost column of the Instructors (and Courses) datasheet. When two or more tables are related or joined (in this database, the Instructors and Courses tables are related), Access can retrieve related data from another table and display its contents in a **subdatasheet**. To display the related course assignments for a particular instructor:

CLICK the plus sign symbol (+) next to Mindy Neumann's row (also known as a record).
(*Result:* The subdatasheet with Mindy's assigned courses appears, as shown in Figure AC1.4.)

FIGURE AC1.4 Displaying related records in a subdatasheet

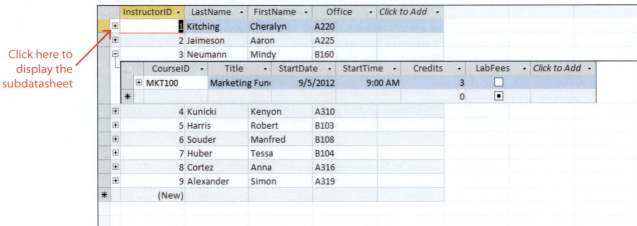

Click here to display the subdatasheet

12 To close both of the datasheet windows:

RIGHT-CLICK the Instructors tab to display the menu shown here.

CHOOSE the Close All command.

- Save
- Close
- Close All
- Design View
- Datasheet View

13 A **query** is a question you ask of your database. The answer, which may draw data from more than one table in the database, typically displays a datasheet of records, similar to the table object. To display a query:

DOUBLE-CLICK Courses Query in the Queries group of the Navigation pane.

(*Result*: Although the datasheet appears similar to the previous table objects, notice that data from both the Courses table (CourseID and Title) and the Instructors table (LastName and FirstName) are represented in a single datasheet window.)

14 Unlike a datasheet's column and row layout, a **form** generally displays one record at a time and is used for adding and editing record data. To display a form:

DOUBLE-CLICK Student Input Form in the Forms group.

(*Result*: A form object is displayed in its own window, as shown in Figure AC1.5.)

FIGURE AC1.5 Displaying a form object

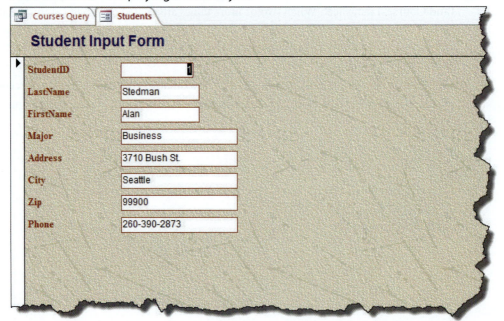

15 Whereas you use datasheets and forms to input and modify data, you create **reports** to present, summarize, and print data. To view a report as it will appear when printed:

DOUBLE-CLICK Students by Major in the Reports group.
(*Result:* Your screen should now appear in Print Preview mode, similar to Figure AC1.6.)

FIGURE AC1.6 Displaying a report object

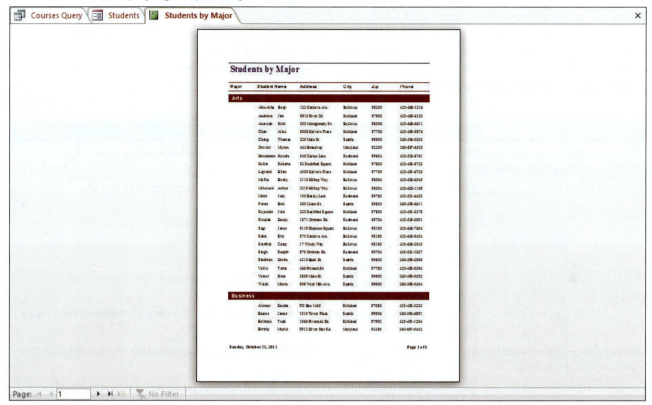

16 You should close all the open windows before proceeding to the next lesson. Do the following:

RIGHT-CLICK the Students by Major tab.
CHOOSE the Close All command.

17 Keep the database open and proceed to the next lesson.

Navigating and Selecting Table Data

LESSON OVERVIEW

Much like an electronic worksheet, a table object stores data in a series of rows and columns called a datasheet. Each row represents an individual record and each column represents a field. The intersection of a row and column is called a **cell**. The Datasheet view mode lets you display many records at once, as well as add, edit, and remove records from a table. Learning how to navigate, customize, and print datasheets is fundamental to working effectively with Access. In this lesson, you will learn how to navigate a datasheet and how to select records using the mouse in the **Record Selection area**, sometimes called the Row Selector buttons.

SKILLS PREVIEW

Navigate a table in Datasheet view using the following keyboard commands	• PRESS ↑ , ↓ , ← , and → to move to the next and previous record or field. • PRESS Ctrl + ↓ and Ctrl + ↑ to move to the bottom or top of a field column. • PRESS PgUp and PgDn to move up or down one screen. • PRESS Home to move to the leftmost (first) field. • PRESS End to move to the rightmost (last, empty) field. • PRESS Ctrl + Home to move to the top of the datasheet (first record and field). • PRESS Ctrl + End to move to the bottom of the datasheet (last record and table field).
Select data in a datasheet using the following methods	• CLICK the desired selector button in the Record Selection area to select an entire record. • CLICK and DRAG across the desired selector buttons to select a group of records, *or* CLICK the first selector button and then Shift + CLICK the last selector button in a record group. • CLICK the column title in the field header to select an entire field column. • CLICK the border of a cell using the cross mouse pointer (✛) to select the entire cell. • CLICK in a cell using the i-beam mouse pointer (Ⅰ) to select a cell's contents.

PROJECT PRACTICE

1 Ensure that the **ac01a.accdb** is open and that no windows appear in the work area. (*Note:* If there are windows open in the work area, right-click on one of the window tabs and choose the Close All command.)

2 To display the Students datasheet:

DOUBLE-CLICK Students in the Tables group of the Navigation pane.

(*Result:* Currently, the flashing cursor appears in the leftmost field of the first record. Notice that the **Record Navigation bar** just above the Status bar shows record 1 of 65, as seen here.)

3 To move through records using the Record Navigation bar:

CLICK the Next Record button (▶) twice to move to record 3 of 65.

CLICK the Last Record button (▶|) to move to record 65 of 65.

CLICK the First Record button (|◀) to move to record 1 of 65.

4 To move the cursor around the datasheet using the keyboard, do the following:

PRESS **End** to move the cursor to the last column in the datasheet.

PRESS **←** to move the cursor into the Phone field column.

PRESS **↓** four times to move the cursor to the fifth record (see the Record Navigation bar).

PRESS **PgDn** twice to move the cursor down two screens.

PRESS **Ctrl** + **Home** to return to the top left-hand corner of the Datasheet window.

5 Position the mouse pointer over the scroll box on the vertical scroll bar and then drag the scroll box downward. Notice that a Scroll Tip appears, identifying the record number that appears first in the window. Release the mouse button when you see "Record: 25 of 65" in the Scroll Tip.

MORE INFO

Scroll Tips: Although the window pans the Datasheet window when the vertical scroll bar is dragged up and down, this method does not move the cursor. Looking into the Record Navigation bar, you will notice that the active or current record remains as "1 of 65."

6 To edit a cell's contents, you click the i-beam mouse pointer (I) inside the desired cell. However, to select an entire cell for formatting or deletion, you position the cross mouse pointer (✚) over a cell's border and then click once. Practice selecting text inside a cell using the i-beam mouse pointer (I) and then practice selecting an entire cell using the cross mouse pointer (✚).

7 To select an entire field column:

Move the mouse pointer to the Major column and CLICK the "Major" column title (⬇) appearing in the field header area to select the column, as shown here.

	StudentID ▾	LastName ▾	FirstName ▾	Major ▾	Address ▾	City ▾	Zip ▾	Phone ▾	Click to Add ▾
⊞	25	Williams	Richard	Business	298 Primore St.	Kirkland	97780	425-499-1223	
⊞	26	Arston	Jane	Science	1201 Broadway	Maryland	92250	260-887-3454	
⊞	27	Schuler	Presley	Business	190 Greer Rd.	Seattle	99900	260-394-1245	

8 Now scroll the window up, if necessary, and select the 10th record:

CLICK the Selector button (☐) in the Record Selection area (➡) for StudentID 10, Sue Finklestein.

	StudentID ▾	LastName ▾	FirstName ▾	Major ▾	Address ▾	City ▾	Zip ▾	Phone ▾	Click to Add ▾
⊞	9	Rinaldo	Sandy	Arts	1871 Orrinton F	Redmond	99704	425-535-0001	
⊞	10	Finklestein	Sue	Business	888 Burrard St.	Seattle	99904	260-390-9273	
⊞	11	Mortimer	Bruce	Science	235 Johnston S	Redmond	99704	425-531-9309	

9 To select multiple records at once:

CLICK the Selector button (☐) for StudentID 15, Eric Sakic, and hold down the mouse button.

DRAG the mouse pointer downward to StudentID 21, Bruce Towne.

(*Result:* When you release the mouse button, your selection of seven records should appear similar to the screen shown in Figure AC1.7.)

10 Now that you know how to select records and move around the datasheet, close the Students Datasheet window, but keep the **ac01a.accdb** open in preparation for the next lesson.

FIGURE AC1.7 Selecting multiple records in Datasheet view

StudentID	LastName	FirstName	Major	Address	City	Zip	Phone	Click to Add
9	Rinaldo	Sandy	Arts	1871 Orrinton F	Redmond	99704	425-535-0001	
10	Finklestein	Sue	Business	888 Burrard St.	Seattle	99904	260-390-9273	
11	Mortimer	Bruce	Science	235 Johnston S	Redmond	99704	425-531-9309	
12	Jung	Chris	Science	1005 West 9th	Redmond	99780	425-531-8100	
13	Abu-Alba	Benji	Arts	122 Cordova A\	Bellevue	98200	425-660-1216	
14	Stockton	Gretta	Arts	4210 Bush St.	Seattle	99900	260-390-2909	
15	Sakic	Eric	Arts	875 Cordova A\	Bellevue	98180	425-640-9454	
16	Modano	Joey	Science	36 Primore St.	Kirkland	97780	425-491-1256	
17	Francis	Mike	Business	875 Broadway	Maryland	92250	260-887-9872	
18	Hillman	Frances	Business	29 Redmond R	Redmond	99850	425-531-1998	
19	Brewski	Randy	Science	190 Greer Rd.	Seattle	99890	260-394-0778	
20	Walsh	Moira	Arts	909 West 18th	Seattle	99900	260-390-5454	
21	Towne	Bruce	Business	818 East 8th Av	Seattle	99950	260-304-4403	
22	Adams	Cecilia	Science	1091 Panorama	Maryland	92340	260-887-5433	
23	Henderson	Kendra	Arts	540 Cactus Lan	Redmond	99804	425-535-8761	
24	Edsell	Camilla	Science	7000 Union St.	Seattle	99890	260-390-5535	
25	Williams	Richard	Business	298 Primore St.	Kirkland	97780	425-499-1223	
26	Arston	Jane	Science	1201 Broadway	Maryland	92250	260-887-3454	
27	Schuler	Presley	Business	190 Greer Rd.	Seattle	99900	260-394-1245	
28	Yap	Steve	Business	1799 West 16th	Seattle	99904	260-390-2232	
29	Azavedo	Kirk	Arts	550 Montgome	Bellevue	98008	425-660-6611	
30	Andrews	Jim	Arts	9910 River Dr.	Kirkland	97900	425-493-6120	
31	Trimarchi	Valerie	Business	7981 Shannon S	Bellevue	98100	425-640-0012	
32	Matson	Lisa	Science	14489 3rd Ave.	Seattle	99890	260-390-4432	

LESSON ACCESS **1A3**
Adding, Editing, and Deleting Data

LESSON OVERVIEW

You can edit information in Datasheet view either by typing over an existing cell entry or by modifying the contents as you would in a word processor. Unlike other applications in Office, you do not choose the Save command to save your work once you are finished. Instead, your editing changes are saved automatically when you move the cursor to another record. Fortunately, the **Undo command** allows you to reverse mistakes during editing.

In Datasheet view, you typically add new records to the blank row appearing at the bottom of a datasheet.

However, you can also use the right-click shortcut menu to insert a new entry between records in the datasheet. If the text "(AutoNumber)" appears in a cell, you can ignore its contents for now and press Enter, Tab, or → to bypass the cell and move to the next field. Any cell containing an AutoNumber field is incremented automatically by Access when a new record is added to the table. Access also provides several methods for removing records from a table.

SKILLS PREVIEW

Edit data within a datasheet cell	• PRESS F2 to enter and exit Edit mode for the selected cell. • You can use common editing keys, such as Del and BackSpace, for editing data within a cell. • CLICK the Undo button (↶ ▾) to undo an operation.
Add a record to the current datasheet	• CLICK the New Record button (▶*) in the Record Navigation area. • PRESS Ctrl + End to move to the bottom of the Datasheet window, and then PRESS Enter to begin entering a new record. • CLICK the HOME tab and locate the Records group. CLICK New command (🗒).
Delete a record from the current datasheet	• SELECT the desired record, and then CLICK the HOME tab and locate the Records group. CLICK Delete Record command (✕), *or* • RIGHT-CLICK the selector button (▭) for the desired record. CHOOSE Delete Record from the shortcut menu.

PROJECT PRACTICE

1. Ensure that the **ac01a.accdb** is open and that no windows appear in the work area.

2. To update office numbers for instructors, open the Instructors datasheet:
DOUBLE-CLICK Instructors in the Tables group.

3. To edit Cheralyn Kitching's office number:
PRESS → three times to highlight the "A220" cell entry.
TYPE B113.
(*Result:* The new entry replaces the existing entry and a pencil icon 🖉 appears in the record selection area to signify that you are working in Edit mode. While in Edit mode, your changes have not yet been saved to disk.)

4. To save your changes and move the cursor to the next record:
PRESS Enter.

5 Rather than retyping an entire cell's contents, you can modify individual characters in a cell. To illustrate, let's modify the last name spelling of an instructor. Do the following:

CLICK the i-beam mouse pointer (⌶) to the right of "Kunicki" in the LastName field column for record 4.

PRESS **BackSpace** to remove the letter "i."

TYPE y.

(*Result:* You have just corrected the spelling of Kenyon Kunicki's surname to "Kunicky.")

6 To save your changes using the Quick Access toolbar, without leaving the row:

CLICK the Save button (💾).

7 You can add a new record to the table:

CLICK the HOME tab and locate the Records group.

CLICK the New command (▦).

(*Result:* Access moves you to a blank row at the bottom of the datasheet. Notice the asterisk ✳ appearing in the record selection area to signify that this is a new entry.)

8 The InstructorID AutoNumber field is the first entry. To bypass this field and let Access increment the ID number:

PRESS **Tab** to move to the LastName field.

9 To enter the remaining information:

TYPE Melville.

PRESS **Tab** to move to the FirstName field.

TYPE Herman.

PRESS **Tab** to move to the Office field.

TYPE C230.

PRESS **Tab** to move to the next row.

(*Result:* Notice that the AutoNumber entry for the InstructorID field is calculated and entered automatically. Your screen should now appear similar to Figure AC1.8.)

⚠ **HEADS UP**
To delete a record, you should first ensure that any related records have been updated or removed. For this practice session, the only record that does not have any related records from other tables is the "Herman Melville" record that you just entered. Therefore, for the purposes of this practice, we will not perform a record deletion.

10 Close the Instructors Datasheet window, but keep the **ac01a.accdb** open for use in the next lesson.

FIGURE AC1.8   Adding a new record to the table

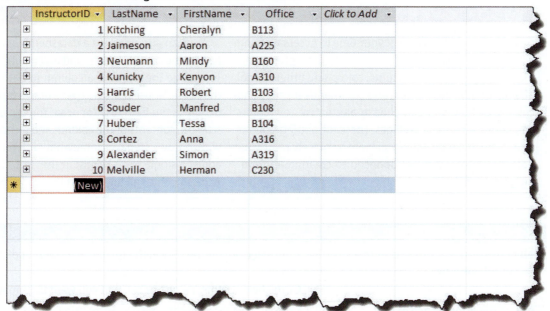

	InstructorID	LastName	FirstName	Office	Click to Add
⊞	1	Kitching	Cheralyn	B113	
⊞	2	Jaimeson	Aaron	A225	
⊞	3	Neumann	Mindy	B160	
⊞	4	Kunicky	Kenyon	A310	
⊞	5	Harris	Robert	B103	
⊞	6	Souder	Manfred	B108	
⊞	7	Huber	Tessa	B104	
⊞	8	Cortez	Anna	A316	
⊞	9	Alexander	Simon	A319	
⊞	10	Melville	Herman	C230	
✳	(New)				

Formatting the Datasheet Window

LESSON OVERVIEW

Given that you spend a lot of your time in Access working with Datasheet windows, you may find it helpful to format the appearance using fonts, colors, and other special effects. Besides text formatting commands for font and color selection, you can choose alternative row colors and apply or hide cell gridlines. These formatting options also come in handy when you want to quickly print your datasheets for review, as opposed to creating and running a report.

You can also enhance a datasheet's appearance by adjusting the column widths and row heights in a datasheet. To change the width of a column in Datasheet view, use the sizing mouse pointer (⟷) to drag a field column's borderline in the **field header area**. You can also have Access scan the contents of the column and recommend the best width. Rows behave somewhat differently. When you adjust a single row's height in the Record Selection area, Access updates all the rows in the datasheet.

SKILLS PREVIEW

Select the desired contents of the Datasheet window	• CLICK the Select All button (☐) in the top left-hand corner of the Datasheet window, *or* • SELECT the field column, record, or cell that you want to format.
Format the appearance of the Datasheet window	• CLICK the HOME tab and locate the Text Formatting group. CLICK the desired formatting commands.
Adjust column widths	• DOUBLE-CLICK a field's column border to size it to the best fit, based on the length of data currently stored in the column. • DRAG a field's column border using the horizontal sizing mouse pointer (⟷) to increase or decrease its width. • CLICK the HOME tab and locate the Records group. CLICK the More drop-down menu command. CHOOSE the Field Width command to adjust the column spacing.
Adjust row heights	• DRAG a record's row border using the vertical sizing mouse pointer (⬍) to increase or decrease the height of all rows in the datasheet. • CLICK the HOME tab and locate the Records group. CLICK the More drop-down menu command. CHOOSE the Row Height command to adjust the row spacing.

PROJECT PRACTICE

1 Ensure that the **ac01a.accdb** is open and that no windows appear in the work area.

2 Open a Datasheet window to practice formatting:

DOUBLE-CLICK Courses in the Tables group to open its Datasheet window.

3 To make changes to the entire datasheet at one time, select all the cells:

CLICK the Select All button (☐) in the top left-hand corner of the Datasheet window.
(*Result:* The entire datasheet should now appear highlighted. Although this step is not necessary to format the datasheet, you should develop the habit of first selecting what you want to format before issuing commands.)

4 Now change the font typeface that is used to display the cell contents:

CLICK the HOME tab and locate the Text Formatting group.

CLICK the Font drop-down menu box (Calibri ⌄).

SELECT Verdana.

(*Result:* The datasheet appears with the new font typeface.)

5 You may have noticed that the column size is too narrow to show the course title. Increase the width of the column before proceeding:

CLICK the Title column heading in the field header area.

6 Using the horizontal sizing mouse pointer (↔), position the pointer over the Title column's right borderline in the field header area. When you have positioned the mouse properly:

DOUBLE-CLICK the right border of the Title column heading.

(*Result:* The column's width automatically sizes to fit the longest course title entry, as shown in Figure AC1.9.)

> **TIP**
>
>
>
> You can also change a column width by right-clicking on the field name header and then choosing the Field Width command.

FIGURE AC1.9 Formatting and sizing columns in a datasheet

CourseID ⌄	Instructor ⌄	Title	StartDate ⌄	StartTime ⌄	Credits ⌄	LabFees ⌄
⊞ BUS100	2	Accounting Fundamentals	1/9/2013	9:00 AM	3	☐
⊞ BUS201	2	Financial Accounting	1/9/2013	1:00 PM	3	☐
⊞ BUS210	4	Managerial Accounting	1/9/2013	7:00 PM	2	☐
⊞ COM100	4	Computer Applications	9/7/2012	10:30 AM	3	☑
⊞ COM110	7	Computer Programming	1/10/2013	10:30 AM	3	☑
⊞ COM200	8	Visual Programming	9/6/2012	3:00 PM	2	☑
⊞ COM210	9	Database Fundamentals	9/7/2012	7:00 PM	2	☐
⊞ COM220	9	Database Programming	1/10/2013	7:00 PM	2	☑
⊞ COM230	9	Client/Server Fundamentals	1/9/2013	9:00 AM	3	☐
⊞ COM310	8	Component Programming	1/10/2013	1:00 PM	3	☑
⊞ COM315	8	Object-Oriented Design	1/9/2013	9:00 AM	3	☐
⊞ MKT100	3	Marketing Fundamentals	9/5/2012	9:00 AM	3	☐
⊞ MKT210	1	Consumer Behavior	1/9/2013	3:00 PM	3	☐
⊞ MKT250	5	Marketing Research	1/9/2013	1:00 PM	3	☑
⊞ ORG100	1	Organizational Behavior	9/6/2012	10:30 AM	3	☐
⊞ ORG210	4	Organizational Management	9/5/2012	9:00 AM	3	☐
⊞ ORG220	4	Strategic Planning	9/6/2012	1:00 PM	2	☑
⊞ ORG300	1	Executive Decision Making	9/5/2012	9:00 AM	2	☐
✱	0				0	▣

7 To continue formatting the datasheet:

CLICK the InstructorID column heading in the field header area.

CLICK the Center button (≡) in the Text Formatting group.

Widen the Instructor ID column.

(*Result:* The InstructorID values now appear centered in the column.)

8 Repeat the previous step for the Credits field column.

9 PRESS Ctrl + Home to return to the top left-hand corner of the datasheet.

10 Continue the formatting with a new row color selection:

CLICK the Alternate Row Color drop-down button (⊞ ▾) in the Text Formatting group.

SELECT Tan, Background 2, Darker 10% in the first row beneath the primary Theme Colors.

11 To better see the formatting results, remove the cell gridlines:

CLICK the Gridlines drop-down button (⊞ ▾) in the Text Formatting group.

SELECT the Gridlines None option.

(*Result:* Your screen should now appear similar to Figure AC1.10.)

12 Close the datasheet window and save changes to the layout by clicking the Yes command button when asked in the dialog box shown.

13 Keep the database open and proceed to the next lesson.

FIGURE AC1.10   Selecting a new row color with no gridlines

CourseID ▾	InstructorID ▾	Title ▾	StartDate ▾	StartTime ▾	Credits ▾	LabFees ▾
⊞ BUS100	2	Accounting Fundamentals	1/9/2013	9:00 AM	3	☐
⊞ BUS201	2	Financial Accounting	1/9/2013	1:00 PM	3	☐
⊞ BUS210	4	Managerial Accounting	1/9/2013	7:00 PM	2	☐
⊞ COM100	4	Computer Applications	9/7/2012	10:30 AM	3	☑
⊞ COM110	7	Computer Programming	1/10/2013	10:30 AM	3	☑
⊞ COM200	8	Visual Programming	9/6/2012	3:00 PM	2	☑
⊞ COM210	9	Database Fundamentals	9/7/2012	7:00 PM	2	☐
⊞ COM220	9	Database Programming	1/10/2013	7:00 PM	2	☑
⊞ COM230	9	Client/Server Fundamentals	1/9/2013	9:00 AM	3	☐
⊞ COM310	8	Component Programming	1/10/2013	1:00 PM	3	☑
⊞ COM315	8	Object-Oriented Design	1/9/2013	9:00 AM	3	☐
⊞ MKT100	3	Marketing Fundamentals	9/5/2012	9:00 AM	3	☐
⊞ MKT210	1	Consumer Behavior	1/9/2013	3:00 PM	3	☐
⊞ MKT250	5	Marketing Research	1/9/2013	1:00 PM	3	☑
⊞ ORG100	1	Organizational Behavior	9/6/2012	10:30 AM	3	☐
⊞ ORG210	4	Organizational Management	9/5/2012	9:00 AM	3	☐
⊞ ORG220	4	Strategic Planning	9/6/2012	1:00 PM	2	☑
⊞ ORG300	1	Executive Decision Making	9/5/2012	9:00 AM	2	☐
*	0				0	▪

Sorting Records in a Datasheet

LESSON OVERVIEW

Records in a datasheet are displayed in the order in which they are originally entered in a table, unless a primary key has been assigned (discussed further in the next project). With a primary key, records are arranged and displayed according to the contents of the primary key field. Even so, Access allows you to rearrange records appearing in a datasheet into ascending (0 to 9; A to Z) or descending (Z to A; 9 to 0) order by the contents of any field. A field chosen to sort by is referred to as a **sort key**. Sorting is often your first step in extracting information from raw data. It allows you to organize records and makes it easier to scan a datasheet for specific information.

SKILLS PREVIEW

Sort records in a datasheet using the Ribbon	• SELECT the desired field column to sort. CLICK the HOME tab and locate the Sort & Filter group. CLICK the Ascending command (⬆) to sort alphabetically from A to Z, or CLICK the Descending command (⬇) to sort in reverse order from Z to A.
Sort records in a datasheet using the shortcut menu	• CLICK the Sort & Filter button (▾) attached to the field column heading you want to sort. CHOOSE the desired sort command for ascending or descending order. (*Note:* You can also use the right-click shortcut menu to display the sort commands.)

PROJECT PRACTICE

1. Ensure that the **ac01a.accdb** is open and that no windows appear in the work area.

2. Open the Students datasheet to practice sorting:

   DOUBLE-CLICK Students in the Tables group to open its Datasheet window.

3. Currently, the datasheet is sorted in numeric order by StudentID. To sort the datasheet alphabetically by surname (last name), first select any cell in the column you wish to sort by:

   PRESS `Tab` to move to the LastName field column.

4. To issue the sort command using the Ribbon:

   CLICK the HOME tab and locate the Sort & Filter group.

   CLICK the Ascending command (⬆).
   (*Result:* The datasheet is now sorted by student surname. Note that you are not affecting the underlying table data with the sort command. You are merely changing the record display order in the Datasheet window.)

5. To sort the list into descending order by major:

   CLICK the Sort & Filter button (▾) attached to the Major column heading.
   (*Result:* Your screen should now appear similar to Figure AC1.11.)

	StudentID	LastName	FirstName	Major	Address	City	Zip	Phone	Click to Add
⊞	13	Abu-Alba	Benji	Arts			0	425-660-1216	
⊞	22	Adams	Cecilia	Science			0	260-887-5433	
⊞	6	Alomar	Sandra	Business			0	425-493-3233	
⊞	30	Andrews	Jim	Arts			0	425-493-6120	
⊞	26	Arston	Jane	Science			0	260-887-3454	
⊞	29	Azavedo	Kirk	Arts			8	425-660-6611	
⊞	42	Barnes	James	Business			6	260-394-6891	
⊞	61	Boltman	Todd	Business			2	425-491-1204	
⊞	37	Bowman	Victoria	Science			0	260-887-9110	
⊞	19	Brewski	Randy	Science			0	260-394-0778	
⊞	57	Britzky	Muriel	Business			9	260-887-5432	
⊞	40	Brown	Ibrahim	Science			0	260-390-8763	
⊞	4	Buggey	Diana	Science			4	425-531-1177	
⊞	54	Chan	Alice	Arts			0	425-493-9876	
⊞	35	Chang	Thomas	Arts			0	260-394-0333	
⊞	36	Clifford	Karen	Business			0	425-640-3312	
⊞	59	Davis	Julie	Science	1321 Cordova A	Bellevue	98200	425-660-1090	
⊞	52	Delaney	William	Science	111 Union St.	Seattle	99850	260-394-9898	
⊞	58	Drexler	Myron	Arts	444 Broadway	Maryland	92250	260-887-6520	
⊞	24	Edsell	Camilla	Science	7000 Union St.	Seattle	99890	260-390-5535	
⊞	7	Fernandez	Rosa	Science	151 Greer Rd.	Seattle	99890	260-394-7645	
⊞	10	Finklestein	Sue	Business	888 Burrard St.	Seattle	99904	260-390-9273	
⊞	17	Francis	Mike	Business	875 Broadway	Maryland	92250	260-887-9872	
⊞	47	Garros	Roland	Science	3109 East 5th A	Seattle	99900	260-392-9012	

Drop-down menu items shown: Sort A to Z; Sort Z to A; Clear filter from Major; Text Filters; (Select All); (Blanks); Arts; Business; Science; OK; Cancel

6 From the drop-down menu that appears above:

CHOOSE the Sort Z to A command.

(*Result:* The Science major is listed first, followed by the Business and Arts majors. Notice that surnames of students remain sorted alphabetically from A to Z within each of the majors.)

7 To sort the datasheet by city:

RIGHT-CLICK the City column heading in the field header area.

CHOOSE Sort A to Z from the shortcut menu.

(*Result:* Within each city, the datasheet records are then sorted by descending major, and then lastly by ascending surname. As shown in Figure AC1.12, you will notice arrows attached to the Sort & Filter buttons for the columns used in the current sort order.)

8 Close the Datasheet window, but do not save the layout changes.

9 To close the ac01a.accdb:

CLICK the FILE tab in the Ribbon.

CHOOSE the Close command.

10 At this point, you have learned how to open and display the objects stored within a database, navigate and edit a table's datasheet, format the Datasheet window, and order the display of records within a datasheet. When you are ready to proceed, you can exit Microsoft Access.

FIGURE AC1.12 Sorting the datasheet by three fields

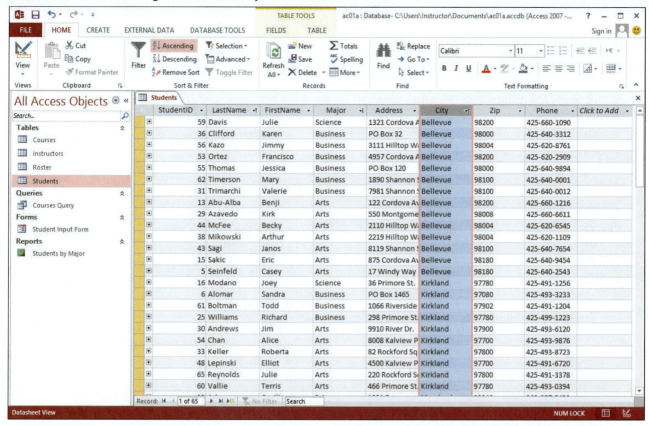

MULTIPLE-CHOICE QUIZ

Select the best choice in the following questions for review of the project concepts. Good luck!

1. Which of the following object categories does not appear in the Navigation pane?
   a. Forms
   b. Queries
   c. Programs
   d. Reports

2. Which database object do you use to focus the display of information on one record at a time?
   a. Table
   b. Form
   c. Query
   d. Report

3. In a datasheet, the intersection of a row and column is called a
   a. cell.
   b. cursor.
   c. form.
   d. record.

4. In a datasheet, what does each column represent?
   a. Database
   b. Table
   c. Record
   d. Field

5. In a datasheet, what does each row represent?
   a. Database
   b. Table
   c. Record
   d. Field

6. In a datasheet, which mouse pointer do you use to select a cell by clicking on its border gridline?
   a. ⊕
   b. ⬉
   c. ⌛
   d. I

7. In a datasheet, which icon appears at the left-hand side of a record while it is being edited?
   a. Asterisk (✳) 
   b. Pencil (✎) 
   c. Pointer (▷) 
   d. Selector (☐)

8. When editing a record, which keystroke allows you to save the changes without leaving the record?
   a. `Ctrl` + `Enter`
   b. `Ctrl` + `Alt`
   c. `Alt` + `Enter`
   d. `Shift` + `Enter`

9. Any cell containing this type of field is incremented automatically by Access when a new record is added:
   a. AutoElevate.
   b. AutoIncrement.
   c. AutoNumber.
   d. AutoValue.

10. The Row Selector buttons in a datasheet are located in the
    a. Column Selection area.
    b. Record Selection area.
    c. Field Selection area.
    d. Table Selection area.

In this exercise, you will practice formatting a datasheet by selecting a new display font, adjusting column widths, and choosing an alternating row color. The final Datasheet window is shown in Figure AC1.13.

FIGURE AC1.13 Work It Out AC-1A-E1: completed

Customer	Username	Address	City	Zip	Phone	Amount	Billing Typ	Click to
Ann Harris	ahariss	123 W. Rose	Lodi	95240	339-1997	$19.95	CK	
Bo Bailey	bbailey	1 Merriwether	Victor	95244	367-3665	$24.95	DD	
Bonnie Mar	bmar	7855 "E" St.	Victor	95244	367-5443	$24.95	DD	
G. T. Morris	gmorris	P.O. Box 9844	Ripon	95336	264-5221	$19.95	DD	
Jose Cuervo	jcuervo	56 Mar Vista Dr	Ripon	95336	264-1489	$19.95	CC	
Kaley Lewis	klewis	St. John's Clinic	Lodi	95240	339-6552	$24.95	CK	
Liz Schuler	lschuler	599 W. Walnut	Lodi	95240	367-6548	$24.95	CC	
Sam Yee	syee	944 E. Fifth St.	Victor	95244	267-3125	$19.95	CK	
Tom Sawyer	tsawyer	5065 Villa Arroyo	Ripon	95336	264-9552	$19.95	CC	
Vu Nguyen	vnguyen1	P.O. Box 3992	Lodi	95242	339-9254	$24.95	CK	
Van Nguyen	vnguyen2	11 N. Weber	Victor	95244	367-2114	$19.95	DD	

1 After launching Microsoft Access, locate and open the exercise data file **ac01a-ex.accdb**. (*Note:* If a security warning appears, click the Enable Content button before proceeding.)

2 Open the "E1 Internet Accounts" table in a Datasheet window:

DOUBLE-CLICK E1 Internet Accounts in the Tables group.

3 To change the font typeface and font size for the datasheet, first select the entire datasheet:

CLICK the Select All button ( ) in the top left-hand corner of the Datasheet window.

4 Using the HOME tab on the Ribbon, select the Text Formatting options to change the Font to Cambria and the Font Size to 12 points.

5 PRESS Ctrl + Home to remove the highlighting.

6 Adjust the column width for the Customer field to 12 characters by dragging its border gridline.

7 To have Access calculate the "best-fit" width for the Address field column, position the horizontal sizing mouse pointer ( ) over the Address column's right borderline in the field header area. When you have positioned the mouse properly:

DOUBLE-CLICK the right border of the Address column heading.

8 Lastly, use the Alternate Row Color drop-down menu ( ) in the Text Formatting group to change the color to Orange, Accent 6, Lighter 80% (in the first row beneath the primary Theme Colors row).

9 PRESS Ctrl + Home to remove any highlighted selections.

(*Result:* Your screen should now appear similar to Figure AC1.13.)

10 Close the Datasheet window and save the layout changes. Then, close the database file, unless you are proceeding to the next exercise.

In this exercise, you will edit data in an existing datasheet and practice using the Undo command. The final datasheet is shown in Figure AC1.14.

FIGURE AC1.14   Work It Out AC-1A-E2: completed

ProductCode	Species	Size	Grade	Finish	Category	Click to Add
B12	BIRCH	0.5	Cab.	G2S	Plywood	
DF14	DFIR	1 X 4	Ungraded	RGH	Board	
DF16	DFIR	1 X 6	Ungraded	RGH	Board	
DF210	DFIR	2 X 10	Standard	S4S	Dim.	
DF242	DFIR	2 X 4	2+	S4S	Dim.	
DF24S	DFIR	2 X 4	Standard	S4S	Dim.	
DF24U	DFIR	2 X 4	Utility	S4S	Dim.	
DF26	DFIR	2 X 6	Standard	S4S	Dim.	
DF28	DFIR	2 X 8	Standard	S4S	Dim.	
P12	SPF	0.50	Constr.	G1S	Plywood	
P12U	SPF	0.5	Utility	RGH	Plywood	
P14	SPF	0.25	Constr.	G1S	Plywood	
P34	SPF	0.75	Constr.	G1S	Plywood	
P34T	SPF	0.75	Constr.	T&G	Plywood	
P38	SPF	0.375	Constr.	G1S	Plywood	
P58	SPF	0.625	Constr.	G1S	Plywood	
P58T	SPF	0.675	Constr.	T&G	Plywood	
P58U	SPF	0.625	Utility	RGH	Plywood	
SP14	SPF	1 X 4	Ungraded	S4S	Board	
SP14R	SPF	1 X 4	Ungraded	RGH	Board	
SP16	SPF	1 X 6	Ungraded	S4S	Board	
SP18	SPF	1 X 8	Ungraded	S4S	Board	
SP210	SPF	2 X 10	Standard	S4S	Dim.	

1. Locate and open the exercise data file **ac01a-ex.accdb**, if it is not already open in Access.

2. Open the "E2 Products" table for display in Datasheet view.

3. Using the keyboard, position the cursor in the Species column of the third record.

4. Change the cell value, D.FIR, to match the standard abbreviation, **DFIR**.

5. Save the changes by moving the cursor to the next record.

6. Edit the product code for record 4, DF210S, so that it reads **DF210**.

7. Delete records 10 and 11 for the ROAK Species.

8. Select the Grade field cell (Cab.) for record 1, and change it to **Utility**.

9. Undo the change in Step 8 using the Undo button (↶ ▾) on the Quick Access toolbar. Your screen should now appear similar to Figure AC1.14.

10. Close the Datasheet window and save any changes. Then, close the database file, unless you are proceeding to the next exercise.

HANDS-ON EXERCISE: WORK IT OUT AC-1A-E3

In this exercise, you will practice adding and deleting records, and formatting the Datasheet window to match the one shown in Figure AC1.15.

FIGURE AC1.15 Work It Out AC-1A-E3: completed

ID	Volunteer Group	Contact	Address	City	Phone 1	Phone 2	Click
50	Silverdale Community Pow-Wov	Alberta Snyder	P.O. Box 4531	Silverdale	953-4017	953-4803	
51	Boy Scout Troop 16	Anelise Krause	4590 Pine Valley Circle	Silverdale	476-0637		
52	Boy Scout Troop 425	Mike Lehr	680 Aurora Ct	Manteca	823-7634	823-0260	
53	S.J. Co. Sheriff Aux.	Lt Fred Meyer	7000 Michael N. Cannily 1	French Cam	473-8005	468-4172	
54	North Silverdale Rotary	James Hulstrom	555 W. Benjamin Holt Dr.	Silverdale	952-5850	951-7470	
55	Silverdale Metropolitan Kiwis	Steve Shelby	P.O. Box 1002	Silverdale	464-4505	477-8762	
56	St. Joseph's Spirit Club	Brad Singer/P.Halligan	3240 Angel Dr.	Silverdale	467-6374	474-8350	
57	Beta Sigma Phi/Xi Omicron	Patty Tealdi	2251 Piccardo Circle	Silverdale	951-3553	948-6802	
58	Blind Center	Mimi Eberhardt		Silverdale	951-3554	948-6803	
59	Alan Short Gallery	Yvonne Sotto	1004 N. Grant St.	Silverdale	948-5759	462-5052	
60	Julie Mulligan/Cathi Schuler	Julie Mulligan	9119 Casterbridge Dr	Silverdale	952-2460	946-5230	
62	Volunteer Center	Peggy Hazlip	265 W. Knolls Way	Silverdale	943-0870	944-0152	
63	Delta Valley Twins Group	Debbie Hunt	P.O. Box 691316	Silverdale	474-0662	948-6802	
64	Library & Literacy Foundation	Dr. Mary Ann Cox	605 N. El Dorado St.	Silverdale	937-8384		
65	Hospice Of San Joaquin	Sherry A. Burns	2609 E. Hammer Lane	Silverdale	957-3888	474-0534	
66	National Restaurant Assn. Scho	Peter T. Valets	9617 Enchantment Lane	Silverdale	483-3548	951-3548	
67	Silverdale Search and Rescue	Amy McTell	P.O. Box 1359	Silverdale	474-9636		
68	Historical Society	Craig Burns	3528 Pacific Ave.	Silverdale	945-6621		
*	(New)						

1. Locate and open the exercise data file **ac01a-ex.accdb**, if it is not already open in Access.

2. Open the "E3 Contacts" table for display in Datasheet view.

3. Collapse the Navigation pane, if you need more room to view the datasheet.

4. Add the following two records to the table:

   Volunteer Group: **Silverdale Search and Rescue**   Volunteer Group: **Historical Society**
   Contact: **Amy McTell**   Contact: **Craig Burns**
   Address: **P.O. Box 1359**   Address: **3528 Pacific Ave.**
   City: **Silverdale**   City: **Silverdale**
   Phone 1: **474-9636**   Phone 1: **945-6621**

5. Remove the record for ID 61, which is a duplicate of the record for ID 60.

6. Format the datasheet by selecting a Times New Roman italic font, with an 11 point font size.

7. For an alternative row color, select the Olive Green, Accent 3, Lighter 80% option, appearing in the first row under the Primary Theme Colors, and then choose to display horizontal gridlines only.

8. Adjust the column widths to their best fit and then choose a row height of 18. (*Result:* If you scroll to the bottom of the datasheet, it should now appear similar to Figure AC1.15.)

9. Close the Datasheet window and save any changes. Then, close the database file and exit Microsoft Access.

Adding a Table to the School Database

An Access database file is simply a container for storing database objects. In this project, you will learn how to populate a database with table objects and how to modify and print datasheets and a table documentation report.

PROJECT FILE: *Available at* **www.mhhe.com/office2013projectlearn**

PROJECT OBJECTIVES

After completing this project, you will be able to:

- Create a new table object using Datasheet view.

- Create a new table object using Design view.

- Assign a primary key to a table object and define indexes.

- Modify a table's structure by inserting, deleting, and renaming fields.

- Send a table's datasheet and other database information to the printer.

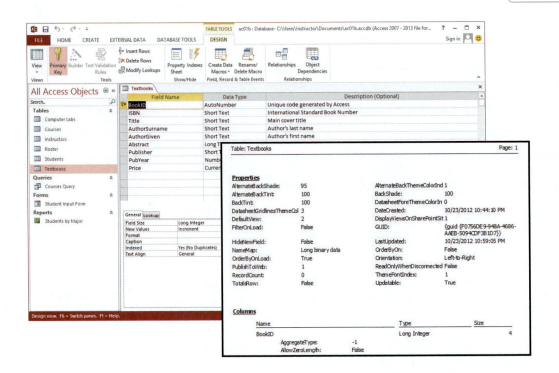

Creating a Table Using Datasheet View

LESSON OVERVIEW

The quickest method for creating a new table in Access is to type information into a blank datasheet, just as you would enter data into an Excel worksheet. When you save the datasheet, Access creates the table structure for you and assigns the proper data types to each field based on the information entered. The benefit of using the Datasheet view method for creating a table is that it lets novice users create table structures without an in-depth understanding of fields and data types.

SKILLS PREVIEW

Create a new table using Datasheet view	• CLICK the CREATE tab and locate the Tables group. CLICK the Table command. TYPE *your data* into the Datasheet window. When you save the datasheet, enter a name for the new table.
Add a new field in Datasheet view	• CLICK the FIELDS tab under Table Tools and then locate the Add & Delete group. CLICK the desired field type.
Delete a field in Datasheet view	• CLICK the FIELDS tab under Table Tools and then locate the Add & Delete group. CLICK the Delete command to remove the selected field column.
Rename a field in Datasheet view	• DOUBLE-CLICK a column title in the field header area. TYPE *a new name* for the field column. PRESS Enter.

PROJECT PRACTICE

1. Launch Microsoft Access and open the database file named **ac01b.accdb**. (*Note:* If a security warning appears, click the Enable Content button before proceeding.)

2. To create new database objects, you use the **CREATE** tab in the Ribbon. In this session, you will create a new table object using the Datasheet view method. Do the following:

   CLICK the **CREATE** tab and locate the Tables group.

   CLICK the Table command.

   (*Result:* Your screen should now appear similar to Figure AC1.16. Notice that Access gives the table a temporary name of "Table1" and inserts an AutoNumber field named "ID.")

FIGURE AC1.16 Creating a new table in Datasheet view

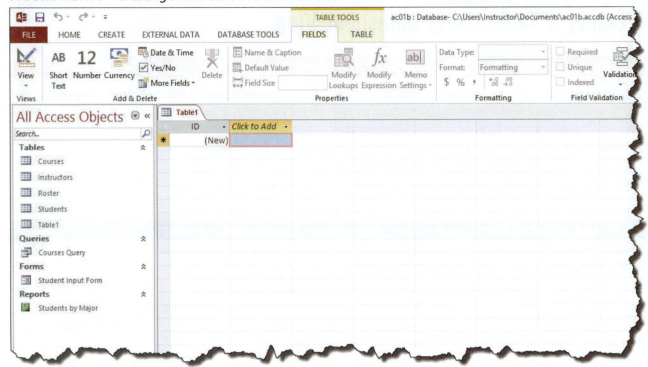

③ At this point, you have the option of simply typing in sample data and having Access figure out the appropriate data types, or you can select the data type by clicking the Click to Add column title in the field header area. To create a table for storing information about the computer labs on campus, do the following:

CLICK the shaded box and then TYPE Lab 101.

PRESS Tab.

(*Result:* Notice that Access gives the field a name of "Field1" in the field header area.)

④ While you could continue entering information at this point, go back and customize your new field with a more descriptive name:

DOUBLE-CLICK "Field1" in the field header area, so that the text appears highlighted.

TYPE Lab Name.

PRESS Enter.

(*Result:* Notice that the column title is renamed and the next field column is selected. Rather than letting Access figure out the data type, you can now choose an option from the menu that appears in Figure AC1.17. Although this menu is shown automatically here, you would typically have to click the Click to Add column title in the field header area to specify a data type.)

FIGURE AC1.17 Defining fields and data types

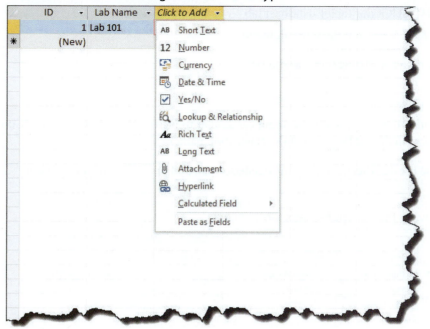

5 From the field data type menu:

CHOOSE Short Text.

TYPE **Building**.

PRESS [Enter].

(*Result:* Notice that you are no longer typing data into the datasheet, but defining fields using the column titles in the field frame area.)

6 To define the third column's data type and field name:

CHOOSE Number.

TYPE **Workstations**.

PRESS [Enter].

7 Now go back and complete the record entry:

CLICK in the Building field cell for record 1.

TYPE **Stafford Hall**.

PRESS [Tab].

TYPE **40**.

PRESS [Enter].

8 Enter a second record with the following data:

Lab Name: **Lab A90**.

Building: **Student Services**.

Workstations: **45**.

9 Customize the datasheet so that the each column displays its best fit width.

10 Now it's time to save the table object. Do the following:

RIGHT-CLICK the Table1 datasheet tab.

CHOOSE Save from the shortcut menu.

11 In the Save As dialog box that appears:

TYPE Computer Labs.

CLICK OK.

(*Result:* Your screen should now appear similar to Figure AC1.18. Notice that "Computer Labs" now appears in the Tables group of the Navigation pane.)

12 Close the datasheet, but keep the database open and proceed to the next lesson.

FIGURE AC1.18   Saving the Computer Labs table object

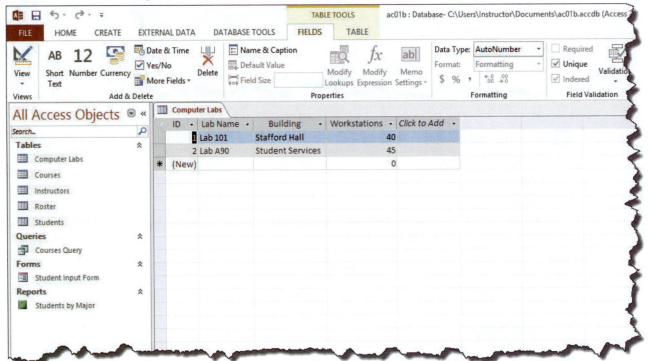

Creating a Table Using Design View

LESSON OVERVIEW

The table **Design view** allows you to get down to the nuts and bolts of designing and constructing a table. In Design view, you create the table structure manually, specifying the field names, data types, and indexes. After some practice, you will find that this method affords the greatest power and flexibility in designing and modifying table objects. This lesson introduces table Design view, but further details and practice are provided in the next chapter.

SKILLS PREVIEW

Create a new table using table Design view	• CLICK the CREATE tab and locate the Tables group. CLICK the Table Design command. In the **field grid area** of Design view, enter the desired field names, descriptions, and data types for the new table.
Select a data type for a new field in the field grid area	• Short Text, for short alphanumeric data, such as names, zip codes, and telephone numbers. • Long Text, for long blocks of plain or formatted alphanumeric data, such as descriptions. • Number, for numeric data on which you may want to perform mathematical calculations. • Date/Time, for dates and times. • Currency, for monetary values that you want to display with a leading dollar sign. • AutoNumber, for implementing a numeric value that increments automatically. • Yes/No, for logical or Boolean values that have two states that you will toggle either on or off. • OLE Object, for storing embedded data created in other applications. • Hyperlink, for creating hyperlinks from alphanumeric entries. • Attachment, for storing attached images, files, documents, and other files. • Calculated, for composing a text, numeric, or other type of calculated expression. • Lookup & Relationship, for establishing linkages between two or more tables.

PROJECT PRACTICE

① Ensure that the ac01b.accdb is open and that no windows appear in the work area.

② Use Design view to create a new table object for storing textbook information:
CLICK the CREATE tab and locate the Tables group.
CLICK the Table Design command.
(*Result:* Your screen should now appear similar to Figure AC1.19. Before proceeding, locate the field grid area and the **Field Properties area** in the Design view screen image.)

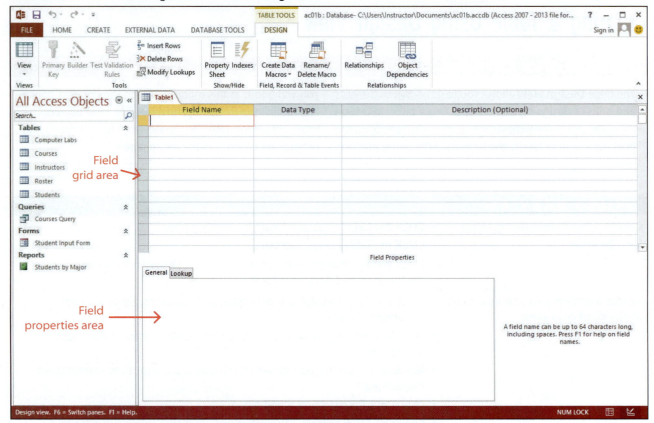

3 To define the first field in the table, ensure that the insertion point appears in the "Field Name" column and then:

TYPE **BookID**.

PRESS Tab to move to the Data Type column.

TIP

Access provides specific rules for naming fields in a table. First, names cannot exceed 64 characters. Second, names should not contain special symbols or punctuation, such as a period or exclamation point. Third, names cannot begin with a space and, in our opinion, should not contain spaces. Descriptive single-word names are best.

---

4 By default, Access inserts Short Text as the data type for the BookID field. The data type you select determines the kind of values that you will be able to enter into the field. For this field, you want Access to number each record sequentially. Therefore:

CLICK the Data Type drop-down arrow attached to the grid cell.

SELECT AutoNumber as the data type.

PRESS Tab .

5 The Description column allows you to store helpful comments, called **metadata**, for describing the contents of the field. Simply stated, metadata is data about the data. To proceed:

TYPE **Unique code generated by Access**.

PRESS Enter to move to the next row.

6 Complete the field grid area as displayed in Figure AC1.20. Notice that the longer field names, such as "AuthorSurname," contain mixed case letters to enhance their readability. This is a common practice when defining field names.

FIGURE AC1.20 Completing the table definition in the field grid area

Field Name	Data Type	Description (Optional)
BookID	AutoNumber	Unique code generated by Access
ISBN	Short Text	International Standard Book Number
Title	Short Text	Main cover title
AuthorSurname	Short Text	Author's last name
AuthorGiven	Short Text	Author's first name
Publisher	Short Text	Publisher's name
PubYear	Number	Year published (e.g., 2013)
PageCount	Number	Total number of pages
Price	Currency	Retail purchase price of the book

MORE INFO

Besides the Access rules for naming fields, some naming conventions are used by programmers to convey specific information about fields and database objects. For example, the prefix "str" is often used to denote a text or string data type (such as strName), and the prefix "bln" is used to name a Boolean yes/no field (such as blnMailingList). Furthermore, a group of database objects may be named tblBooks (table), qryBooks (query), frmBooks (form), and rptBooks (report) to denote the different types of objects using a three-letter prefix. The important concept here is to remain consistent in whatever naming scheme you select.

7 Before saving your new table object, proceed to the next lesson and assign a primary key. Keep the table Design view open and displayed in the work area.

Assigning a Primary Key and Defining Indexes

LESSON OVERVIEW

In creating a table structure, you need to specify a field (or fields) that will uniquely identify each and every record in the table. This field, called the **primary key**, is used by Access in searching for data and in establishing relationships between tables. Once a field is defined as the primary key, its datasheet is automatically indexed, or sorted, into order by that field. Access will also prevent you from entering a duplicate value or a **null value** (nothing) into a primary key or index field. Because fields based on the **AutoNumber** data type automatically increment sequentially as each new record is added to a table, this data type is one of the best choices for a primary key.

SKILLS PREVIEW

Assign a primary key to a field in Design view	• SELECT the desired field to designate as the primary key. CLICK DESIGN tab under Table Tools and locate the Tools group. CLICK the Primary Key command.
Open the Indexes window to define an index in Design view	• SELECT the desired field on which to base the new index. CLICK DESIGN tab under Table Tools and locate the Show/Hide group. CLICK the Indexes command.
Specify index parameters in the Indexes window	• TYPE *a name* for the new index in the "Index Name" column. SELECT a field name from the Field Name drop-down list box. SELECT Ascending or Descending from the Sort Order drop-down list box.

PROJECT PRACTICE

1. Ensure that the table Design window is still open from the previous lesson and that the field grid area appears similar to Figure AC1.20.

2. To select a field for the primary key:

   CLICK the Row Selector button (☐) for BookID.

3. To assign a primary key for the table:

   CLICK the DESIGN tab under Table Tools and locate the Tools group.

   CLICK the Primary Key command.
   (*Result:* A key icon should now appear in the row selector area, as shown below. Notice in the field properties area that the field is now indexed and does not allow duplicate entries, which is a requirement for a primary key field.)

	Field Name	Data Type	Description (Optional)
🔑▶	BookID	AutoNumber	Unique code generated by Access

4. While the table is now indexed and sorted automatically by the BookID primary key, most people search for a book based on its title and author. Therefore, you should add two indexes to help Access perform more efficient searches. To begin:

   CLICK the Row Selector button (☐) for Title.

5. In the field properties area for the Title field:

   CLICK in the Indexed drop-down text box.

   CLICK the drop-down arrow attached to the text box.

   SELECT Yes (Duplicates OK) from the list.

(*Result:* Your screen should now appear similar to Figure AC1.21. Notice that you chose to allow duplicates, as you do not want to limit the possibility of searching for two different books having the same title.)

FIGURE AC1.21 Setting an index

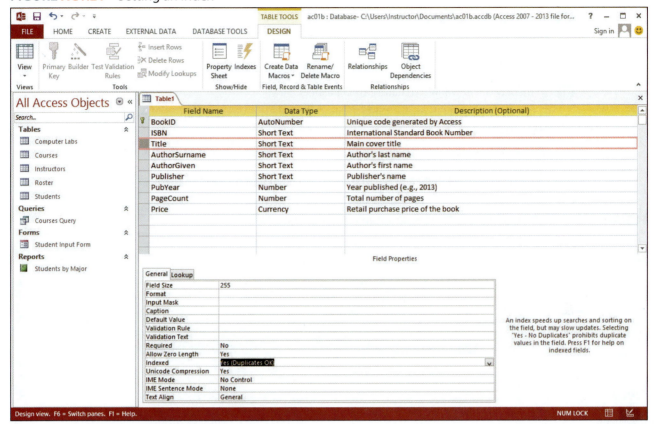

6 To define an author index for the table:

CLICK the Row Selector button (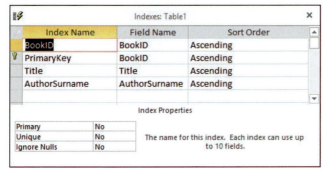) for AuthorSurname.

CLICK in the Indexed text box in the field properties area.

SELECT Yes (Duplicates OK) from the drop-down list.

7 To see the indexes that you have now created and stored in the database:

CLICK the DESIGN tab under Table Tools and locate the Show/Hide group.

CLICK the Indexes command.
(*Result:* The Indexes dialog window, shown in Figure AC1.22, lists the indexes created by both you and Access, based on the primary key field setting.)

FIGURE AC1.22 Indexes dialog window

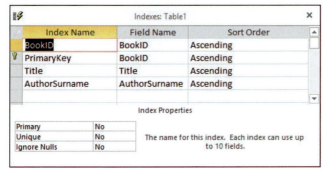

8 Close the Indexes window by clicking its Close button.

9 To save the table structure, along with its primary key and index settings:
CLICK the Save button (💾) in the Quick Access toolbar.

10 In the Save As dialog box:
TYPE Textbooks.
CLICK OK.

11 To display the new table structure in Datasheet view:
CLICK the DESIGN tab under Table Tools and locate the Views group.
CLICK View - Datasheet View command.
(*Result:* The empty table structure appears in a Datasheet window, as shown in Figure AC1.23.)

12 Close the datasheet, but keep the **ac01b.accdb** open and proceed to the next lesson.

FIGURE AC1.23   Displaying the Textbooks table object in Datasheet view

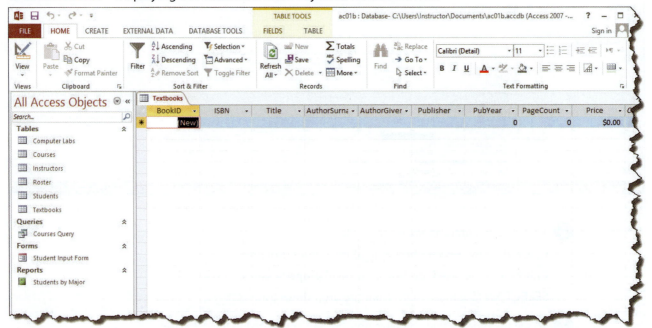

Modifying a Table's Structure

LESSON OVERVIEW

A database is a dynamic entity. It is not uncommon for the initial design requirements to change once a database is set in front of users. Fortunately Access enables you to modify a table's structure quickly and efficiently. Adding, deleting, and changing field specifications in table Design view are similar to editing records in a datasheet. Nonetheless, you should not perform structural changes hastily. When you modify a table's structure, you may unintentionally affect the forms and reports that are based on the table.

After displaying a table structure in Design view, you can easily add a field by entering the desired field's name and data type on a blank row in the field grid area. Removing an existing field deletes the field entry from the Field Grid pane but also deletes all the data stored in the field. Therefore, you must be extra careful when deleting existing fields! Renaming and moving fields in Design view also affects the display of a datasheet. You may have noticed that the columns in Datasheet view follow the field names and display order appearing in Design view.

SKILLS PREVIEW

Display a table's structure in Design view	• If the table's datasheet is open: CLICK the HOME tab and locate the Views group. CLICK the View - Design View command. • If the table's datasheet is not open: RIGHT-CLICK the table name in the Navigation pane. CHOOSE Design View from the shortcut menu.
Modify a table's structure using the field grid area	• To insert and delete fields in the field grid area using the DESIGN tab on the Ribbon: SELECT the desired field. CLICK Insert Rows or Delete Rows commands in the Tools group. • To insert and delete fields in the field grid area using the shortcut menu: RIGHT-CLICK the row selector of the field you want to insert or delete. CHOOSE Insert Rows or Delete Rows from the menu.

PROJECT PRACTICE

1. Ensure that the **ac01b.accdb** is open and that no windows appear in the work area.

2. In the previous two lessons, you created a table object named "Textbooks." To modify the Textbooks table structure using Design view:

   RIGHT-CLICK Textbooks in the Tables group of the Navigation pane.

   CHOOSE Design View from the shortcut menu.
   (*Result:* You should now see the field grid area for the Textbooks table object.)

3. Assume you no longer need the PageCount field because you have learned that there is no method of collecting information on a book's page count without actually opening each book. Therefore, you have decided to remove the field from the table. To do so:

   RIGHT-CLICK the Row Selector button (☐) for PageCount.

   CHOOSE Delete Rows from the shortcut menu.
   (*Note:* You can right-click on any part of the field, but the Row Selector button is preferred.)

4 Now add a new field after the author's first name. To begin:

RIGHT-CLICK the Row Selector button () for Publisher.

CHOOSE Insert Rows from the shortcut menu.
(*Result:* A new empty field row appears in the field grid area.)

5 To enter the new field information:

CLICK in the Field Name cell of the new row.

TYPE **Abstract**.

PRESS `Tab`.

SELECT Long Text as the data type.

PRESS `Tab`.

TYPE **Summary written by the author or publisher**.

6 In the Field Properties area for the new Abstract field:

CLICK in the Text Format text box.

SELECT Rich Text from the drop-down list box.
(*Result:* Your screen should now appear similar to Figure AC1.24.)

> **TIP**
>
> By selecting the Rich Text property for a Long Text data type field, you can enter and store formatted text in the field, including a selection of fonts, font styles, colors, and other formatting characteristics.

FIGURE AC1.24 Modifying the table structure

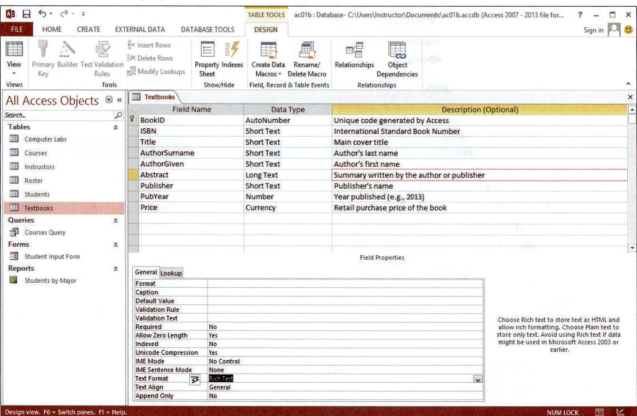

7 To save the changes:

CLICK the Save button () in the Quick Access toolbar.

8 To view the results in Datasheet view:

CLICK the DESIGN tab under Table Tools and locate the Views group.

CLICK View - Datasheet View command.

(*Result:* Notice that the new Abstract field appears in the same order as shown in the field grid area, between the author's given name and the publisher's name, as shown here.)

BookID	ISBN	Title	AuthorSurn:	AuthorGiver	Abstract	Publisher	PubYear	Price
(New)							0	$0.00

9 Close the datasheet, but keep the **ac01b.accdb** open and proceed to the next lesson.

Printing a Table's Datasheet and Structure

LESSON OVERVIEW

Before sending a datasheet to the printer, you can preview it using a full-page display that resembles the printed output. In Print Preview mode, you can move back and forth through the pages, zoom in and out on desired areas, and modify page layout options such as print margins and page orientation. Once you are satisfied with your datasheet's appearance, you may then print it with a single mouse click.

Access also provides a special tool called the **Documenter** that allows you to preview and print various design characteristics of your database objects, including a table's structure and field properties. This tool is especially useful when you are planning or revising a table's field specification or when you require documentation to assist other users in working with your database.

SKILLS PREVIEW

Print a table's datasheet	• CLICK the FILE tab in the Ribbon. CLICK the PRINT tab. CHOOSE either the Quick Print, Print, or Print Preview commands.
Print a table's structure	• CLICK the DATABASE TOOLS tab and locate the Analyze group. CLICK the Database Documenter command. SELECT the database objects that you want included in the documentation report. CLICK OK.

PROJECT PRACTICE

1 Ensure that the **ac01b.accdb** is open and that no windows appear in the work area.

2 Using the Navigation pane, open the Students table in Datasheet view.

3 To send the datasheet to the printer:

CLICK FILE tab in the Ribbon.

CLICK PRINT command in the Backstage view menu.
(*Result:* Your screen should now appear similar to Figure AC1.25. Notice the three options for printing that are provided.)

FIGURE AC1.25 Print options in Backstage view

4 To preview the datasheet before printing:

CLICK the Print Preview button.

5 Move the magnifying mouse pointer over the page area and click once to zoom in on the page. Your screen should now appear similar to Figure AC1.26.

FIGURE AC1.26 Print Preview mode for a datasheet

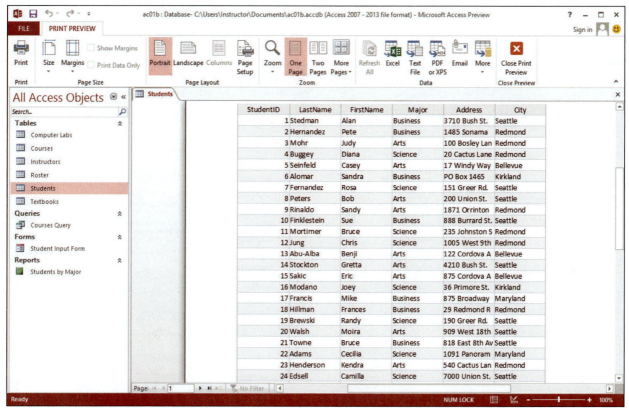

6 If you have a printer connected and are ready to print, you can click the Print command in the Print group of the Ribbon. Otherwise, close the preview by clicking the Close Print Preview command in the Close Preview group.

7 Close the Students datasheet.

8 To print a documentation report for all of your database objects, Access provides the Database Documenter tool. To run this report:

CLICK the DATABASE TOOLS tab and locate the Analyze group.

CLICK the Database Documenter command.

(*Result:* The Documenter dialog box appears, as shown in Figure AC1.27.)

FIGURE AC1.27 Database Documenter dialog box

9 To run the Documenter report for all of the table objects:

CLICK the Select All command button.

CLICK OK.

10 Move the magnifying mouse pointer over the page area and click once to zoom in on the report. Your screen should now appear similar to Figure AC1.28.

FIGURE AC1.28 Database Documenter report preview

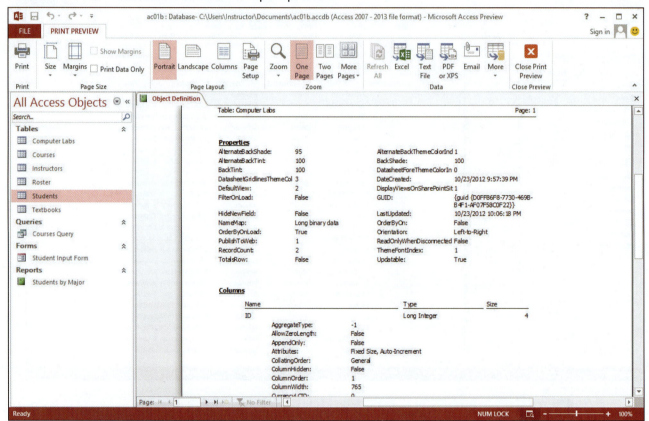

11 If you have a printer connected and want to print the report (over 20 pages), you can click the Print command in the Print group of the Ribbon. Otherwise, close the preview by clicking the Close Print Preview command in the Close Preview group.

12 When you are ready to proceed, close the ac01b.accdb and exit Microsoft Access.

MULTIPLE-CHOICE QUIZ

Select the best choice in the following questions for review of the project concepts. Good luck!

1. Which data type would you use to store the price of an item within an inventory table?
   a. AutoNumber
   b. Currency
   c. Number
   d. Short Text

2. Which data type would you use to store a phone number?
   a. AutoNumber
   b. Currency
   c. Number
   d. Short Text

3. Which data type would you use to specify whether a person was an active customer?
   a. AutoNumber
   b. Lookup Wizard
   c. Yes/No
   d. Long Text

4. Which determines a table's default sort order in a datasheet?
   a. AutoNumber field
   b. Field order
   c. Index field
   d. Primary key

5. In table Design view, the Primary Key command is located in which group of the DESIGN tab?
   a. Views
   b. Tools
   c. Show/Hide
   d. Relationships

6. To delete a field in Design view, right-click the Field Selector button and choose
   a. Delete Field.
   b. Delete Rows.
   c. Remove Field.
   d. Remove Rows.

7. To rename a field when creating a table using Datasheet view,
   a. Double-click the column title.
   b. Press `F2`.
   c. Press `Ctrl` + `F2`.
   d. You cannot rename a field in Datasheet view.

8. A field name can be up to how many characters long, including spaces?
   a. 32
   b. 64
   c. 128
   d. 256

9. Which of the following is not one of the print options for printing a datasheet?
   a. Quick Print
   b. Print
   c. Layout view
   d. Print Preview

10. What tool do you use to generate a report of a table's structure?
    a. Analyzer
    b. Documenter
    c. Designator
    d. Generator

HANDS-ON EXERCISE: WORK IT OUT AC-1B-E1

In this exercise, you will practice creating two new table objects in an existing database. These tables appear in Figures AC1.29 and AC1.30—the first in Datasheet view and the second in Design view.

FIGURE AC1.29 Work It Out AC-1B-E1: completed (Datasheet view)

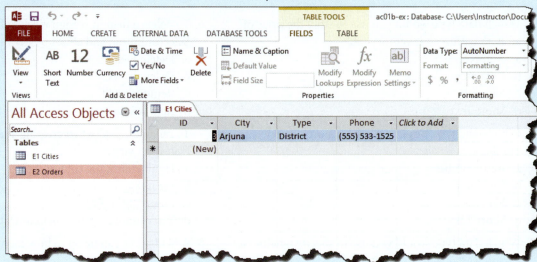

FIGURE AC1.30 Work It Out AC-1B-E1: completed (Design view)

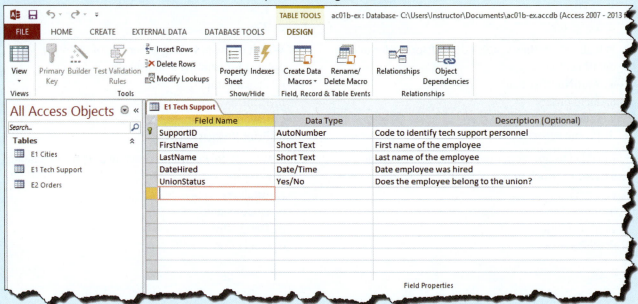

1. After launching Microsoft Access, locate and open the exercise data file **ac01b-ex.accdb**. (*Note:* If a security warning appears, click the Enable Content button before proceeding.)

2. Create a new table object in Datasheet view.

3. Start by entering a record of data:

   TYPE **Arjuna**.

   PRESS **Tab**.

   TYPE **District**.

   PRESS **Tab**.

   TYPE **(555) 533-1525**.

   PRESS **Shift** + **Enter** to save the record.

4 Now rename the fields:

DOUBLE-CLICK Field1 in the field header area.

TYPE **City**.

PRESS [Enter].

DOUBLE-CLICK Field2 in the field header area.

TYPE **Type**.

PRESS [Enter].

DOUBLE-CLICK Field3 in the field header area.

TYPE **Phone**.

PRESS [Enter].

5 If the Data Type menu appears for the next field column, click anywhere in the Datasheet window to remove it from displaying.

6 Save the table object and name it **E1 Cities**. (*Result:* Your screen should now appear similar to Figure AC1.29.)

7 Close the E1 Cities datasheet.

8 Create a second table object using Design view.

9 Define the table fields in the field grid area to match Figure AC1.30.

10 Save the table object as **E1 Tech Support**.

11 When prompted, click Yes to let Access define a primary key for the new table. Your screen should now appear similar to Figure AC1.30.

12 Close all open windows in the work area and save your changes. Then, close the database file, unless you are proceeding to the next exercise.

In this exercise, you will add a primary key to an existing table object and then modify its indexes. The final table Design window is shown in Figure AC1.31.

FIGURE AC1.31 Work It Out AC-1B-E2: completed

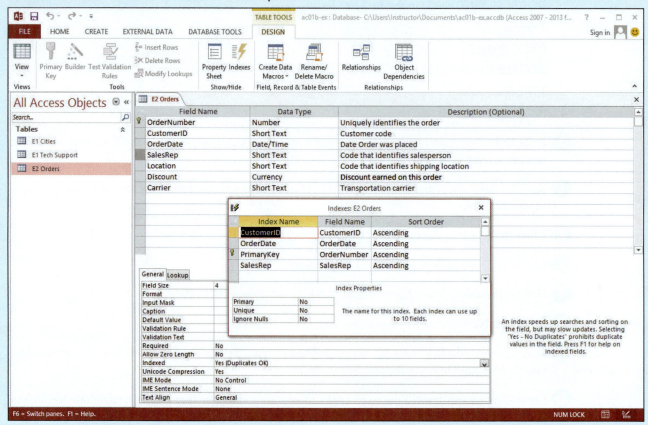

1. Locate and open the exercise data file **ac01b-ex.accdb**, if it is not already open in Access.

2. Open the E2 Orders table object in Datasheet view.

3. Switch to Design view using the Ribbon command.

4. In Design view, assign the OrderNumber field as the primary key for the table. When completed, a key icon should appear in the field's Row Selector button.

5. Insert a new field named **Discount** between "Location" and "Carrier." Select a Currency data type for the new field and enter the text **Discount earned on this order** in the "Description" column.

6. To speed up operations for finding a particular salesperson, create an index for the SalesRep field that allows for duplicate values.

7. Display all the indexes for the table using the Indexes window, as shown in Figure AC1.31.

8. Close the Indexes window and save the table structure. Then, close the Design window.

9. Close the database file, unless you are proceeding to the next exercise.

HANDS-ON EXERCISE WORK IT OUT AC-1B-E3

In this exercise, you will use the table Design view to create a new table object. The completed Design view and Documenter preview are provided in Figures AC1.32 and AC1.33.

FIGURE AC1.32 Work It Out AC-1B-E3: completed (Design view)

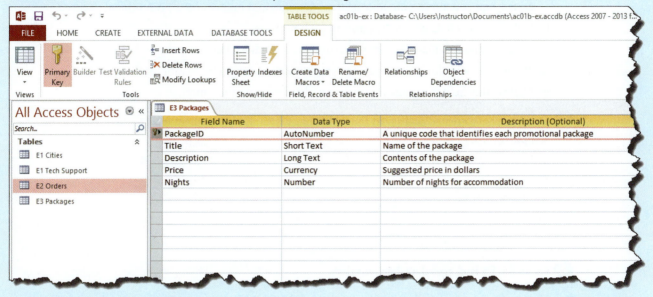

FIGURE AC1.33 Work It Out AC-1B-E3: completed (Documenter Preview)

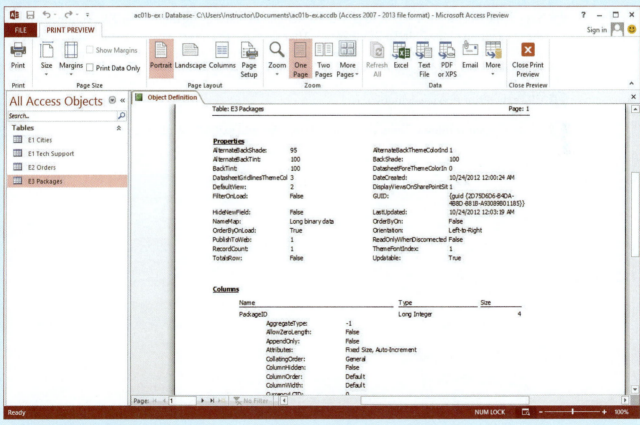

1. Locate and open the exercise data file **ac01b-ex.accdb**, if it is not already open in Access.

2. Use table Design view to create a new table object titled **E3 Packages**. The table should include the following fields to describe the vacation packages being offered by a travel agent.

   a. PackageID: This primary key field automatically increments by one each time a new record is added, and contains a unique code that identifies and indexes each promotional package.

   b. Title: This text field stores the name of each package.

   c. Description: This field describes the contents of each package in paragraph form.

   d. Price: This field stores the suggested price in dollars for each vacation package.

   e. Nights: This field stores the number of nights for accommodation.

3. Once you have created and saved the table object, switch to Datasheet view and enter the following sample record:

   Title: **Bermuda Getaway**

   Description: **This exciting adventure will thrill you and your loved ones. Escape the winter doldrums and run your toes through the sands of our exquisite all-inclusive resort.**

   Price: **$1,800.00**

   Nights: **4**

4. Close the E3 Packages datasheet window.

5. Use the Documenter tool to preview and print the E3 Packages table structure, as shown in Figure AC1.33.

6. Export the Documenter report to an Adobe Acrobat PDF file using the PDF or XPS command in the Data group of the PRINT PREVIEW tab. After selecting the directory where you would like to store the report, name the file **E3Packages.pdf** and click the Publish command button. When prompted, click the Close button without saving the export steps.

7. Close the Print Preview window.

8. Close all open windows. Then, close the database file and exit Microsoft Access.

Chapter Summary

Microsoft Access is a full-featured database management application for desktop computers. Database software enables you to store and manipulate large amounts of data, such as inventory items and customer mailing lists. When you first open a database using Access, you are presented with the main control center for accessing database objects called the Navigation pane. Using the Navigation pane and Ribbon commands, you can create and display a variety of database objects, including tables, forms, queries, and reports. The main type of object used for storing and manipulating data is the table, or datasheet. In Datasheet view, you can enter, edit, and delete field and record data. With the Undo command, you can immediately reverse your previous action.

In this chapter, you used both the Datasheet view and Design view for creating a new table object. Table Design view is especially important for modifying an existing table's structure, specifying field properties, and setting indexes. Access also lets you preview and print a table's contents as they are displayed in Datasheet view, as well as a table's structure using the Documenter tool.

Chapter Key Terms

AutoNumber, p. A-34
Cell, p. A-10
Database, p. A-2
Database file, p. A-4
Database management
 system (DBMS), p. A-2
Database objects, p. A-4
Datasheet, p. A-2
Datasheet view, p. A-2
Design view, p. A-31

Documenter, p. A-40
Field, p. A-2
Field grid area, p. A-31
Field header area, p. A-16
Field properties
 area, p. A-31
Form, p. A-8
Metadata, p. A-32
Navigation pane, p. A-4
Null value, p. A-34

Primary key, p. A-34
Query, p. A-8
Record, p. A-2
Record Navigation bar, p. A-10
Record Selection area, p. A-10
Report, p. A-9
Sort key, p. A-19
Subdatasheet, p. A-7
Table, p. A-2
Undo command, p. A-13

On Your Own Exercise AC-1C-E1

In this exercise, you will help Samson Trucking manage an Access database for its fleet of trucks. One view of the finished database appears in Figure AC1.34.

FIGURE AC1.34   Formatted Drivers datasheet

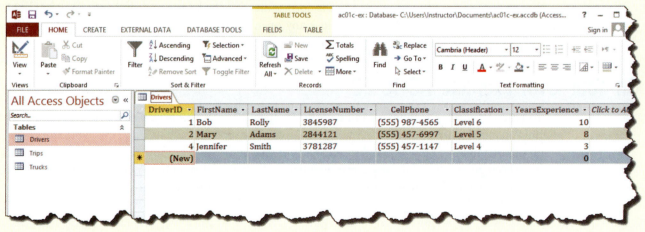

To begin, locate and open the exercise data file **ac01cp1.accdb**. This database currently contains a single table object for the company's drivers. Your first task is to create two additional tables to store information regarding the company's trucks and trips. Review the field grid areas in Figures AC1.35 and AC1.36 and then replicate them in your database.

FIGURE AC1.35 Trucks table object in Design view

Field Name	Data Type	Description (Optional)
TruckID	AutoNumber	Uniquely identifies each truck
TruckDescription	Short Text	Description of the truck
Make	Short Text	Manufacturer's make of the truck
Model	Short Text	Manufacturer's model information
ModelYear	Number	Model year (e.g., 2013)
AssetTag	Number	Company's asset tag number
PurchasePrice	Currency	Purchase price of truck
PurchaseDate	Date/Time	Purchase date of truck

FIGURE AC1.36 Trips table object in Design view

Field Name	Data Type	Description (Optional)
TripID	AutoNumber	Uniquely identifies each trip
TruckID	Number	Identifies the truck used in the trip (from the Trucks table)
DriverID	Number	Identifies the driver used in the trip (from the Drivers table)
DeliveryDate	Date/Time	Date of the delivery trip
Destination	Short Text	Location of the delivery trip
Miles	Number	Number of miles between depot and delivery location
LoadWeight	Number	Weight in pounds of the delivery

Open the Drivers table in Design view and create an index that allows duplicate values for the driver's LastName field. Switching over to Datasheet view, add a new driver record for **Jennifer Smith**, license **3781287**, and cell phone **(555) 457-1147**. She is a novice driver with a classification of **Level 4**. While you are in the Drivers table, delete Jerry Pintovski's record, as he has been let go from the company. Also, add a new field to the Drivers table object that will store each driver's number of years of experience. Select a suitable name and data type for the field and then enter sample data in the datasheet for each driver. Lastly, format the worksheet to appear similar to Figure AC1.34.

Once you are finished, save and close any open windows. Then, close the database file. Exit Microsoft Access, unless you are proceeding to the next exercise.

On Your Own Exercise AC-1C-E2

To practice working with tables and datasheets, open the **ac01cp2.accdb** database file and display the Personnel table in a Datasheet window. As you can see in Figure AC1.37, this table stores data about a company's employees. As a new hire in the company's administration department, you have been given a list of database management tasks to perform on the Personnel table. Once you have completed these tasks, your screen should appear similar to Figure AC1.37. Good luck in your new job!

FIGURE AC1.37 Maintaining and formatting the Personnel table

ID	Surname	Given	Title	Department	Hired	Salary	Gender	Vacation	Education
1	Kitching	Cheralyn	Researcher	Research	8/3/2003	22,800	F	10	B.Sc.
2	Jaimeson	Aaron	Clerk	Marketing	7/23/2002	21,700	M	10	B.Com.
3	Neumann	Kenyon	Operator	Production	8/1/1988	34,900	M	25	B.Sc.
4	Kunicki	Barbara	Clerk	Administration	11/6/1996	17,500	F	15	
5	Killian	Connie	Manager	Management	8/4/1984	37,500	F	25	B.Admin.
6	Turgeon	Luce	Librarian	Administration	11/23/1996	18,500	F	15	
7	Buggey	Diana	Salesperson	Marketing	9/4/1992	40,000	F	20	B.Admin.
8	McRae	Gail	Secretary	Management	4/21/1981	24,800	F	15	
9	Alexander	Mandy	Manager	Administration	1/31/2002	29,000	F	10	B.A.
10	Harris	Mindy	Researcher	Research	1/19/1986	29,500	F	20	B.Sc.
11	Souder	Robyn	Salesperson	Marketing	3/19/1999	34,000	F	15	B.Com.
12	Stedman	Simon	Salesperson	Marketing	5/29/1997	36,000	M	15	B.Admin.
13	Huber	Tessa	Foreman	Production	3/4/1979	39,000	F	20	
14	Cortez	Anna	Controller	Finance	2/15/2001	54,000	F	25	B.A.
15	Bradley	Brenda	Accountant	Finance	11/4/1995	32,000	F	20	
16	Strange	Douglas	Technician	Research	6/2/1997	29,200	M	15	
17	Palfrey	Ernie	Operator	Production	3/25/1995	34,000	M	15	B.A.
18	Hildebrand	Robert	Researcher	Research	2/3/1987	32,000	M	20	B.A.
19	Alomar	Sandra	Salesperson	Marketing	12/1/1993	42,000	F	20	B.Com.

Complete the following tasks to reproduce the formatted Datasheet window for the Personnel table.

- The company has decided to remove the bonus plan from the company remuneration package. Therefore, remove the Bonus field from the Personnel table using table Design view.

- You have noticed that the table's design lacks metadata about each of the fields. On your own, enter a brief description for each field, based on your understanding of the table's contents.

- Create two indexes for Surname and Department, allowing duplicate values for both fields. Then, display the Indexes window to check your work.

- Save your work and return to the Datasheet view. Ensure that the Bonus field has been deleted.

- Format the datasheet to appear with an italicized, 12 point, Trebuchet MS font typeface. Then, adjust each column's width to its best fit. Format the alternating row color and vertical gridline selection to match Figure AC1.37 as closely as possible.

- Add your own information (i.e., name, gender, desired job title, and future education level) to the bottom of the Personnel table.

Once you are finished, save and close any open windows. Then, close the database file and exit Microsoft Access.

2

Organizing and Retrieving Data

CHAPTER OBJECTIVES

After completing this chapter, you will be able to:

2.1 Customize a Data Sheet

2.2 Find and Replace Table Data

2.3 Filter Records in Datasheet View

2.4 Create Advanced Custom Filters

2.5 Create a Query Using the Query Wizard

2.6 Create a Query Using Query Design View

2.7 Modify and Sort a Select Query

2.8 Design Queries with Custom Criteria

2.9 Add Simple Calculated Fields

Microsoft Access provides several tools, features, and methods to organize and retrieve information from a database. Besides reordering columns in a datasheet, you can sort records using the Sort Ascending and Sort Descending commands. To locate data quickly, the Find command enables you to search an entire table for records containing a few characters or words. Access also provides two powerful filtering methods (Filter By Selection and Filter By Form) to limit the display of records in a datasheet. Understanding the strengths and weaknesses of these features is especially important when learning to design, modify, and apply queries in Access. A query is an Access database object that lets you ask a question of your database, such as "How many customers live in Chicago?" or "What is the average age of employees in XYZ Corporation?" Using queries, you can prepare, view, analyze, and summarize your data, as well as perform advanced updating routines. The results of a query are displayed in a Datasheet window and may also be used when presenting data in forms and reports.

In this chapter, you will use Microsoft Access to organize and retrieve data from your database.

PROJECT

Asking Questions of Your Database

In this project, you will learn how to search your database for answers. Microsoft Access provides several methods to find and retrieve data, replace and update data, filter and sort information in a datasheet, and build a select query to perform calculations and to provide custom search results in a datasheet.

This chapter will help you master working in Datasheet view and create query objects using both the Simple Query Wizard and the query Design view, powerful tools for all levels of Microsoft Access users.

THE SITUATION

The Registrar's Office at Ridgemont College

The Registrar's Office at Ridgemont College is experiencing unusually high volumes of requests for information from the various schools within the college, not to mention the college's Board of Governors. While the data are stored securely in the database management system, you know that it should not take this long to retrieve information. Rather than wading through folders and files of data, you decide to learn how to retrieve and organize information using the tools available in Microsoft Access. After witnessing your gains in productivity, you look forward to sharing these skills with your co-workers as soon as possible!

Working in the Datasheet Window

This project will introduce you to the primary tools and techniques to organize and retrieve data from a Microsoft Access database. In addition to modifying the appearance of a datasheet, you will be introduced to the filtering options to locate and restrict the display of records.

PROJECT FILE: *Available at* www.mhhe.com/office2013projectlearn

PROJECT OBJECTIVES

After completing this project, you will be able to:

- Customize the display of a datasheet.

- Find a record and replace data using search criteria.

- Filter the records displayed in a datasheet using Filter By Selection.

- Create multi-criteria custom filters using Filter By Form.

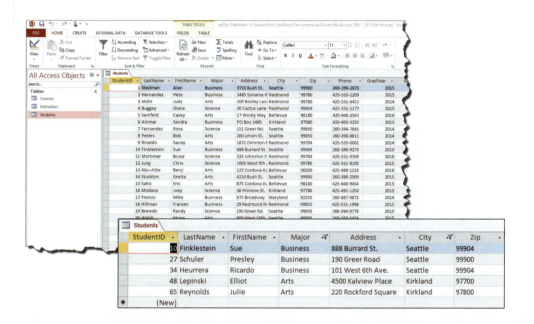

Customizing the Datasheet

LESSON OVERVIEW

Microsoft Access provides numerous options for customizing the appearance, or layout, of a datasheet. Because a datasheet is only a tool for viewing the data stored in an underlying table, you can manipulate the datasheet's column widths, row heights, and field order without affecting the table structure itself. Exceptions to this rule are when you rename or delete a column. These changes flow through to the structure of the table. Once you customize the table to your satisfaction, remember to save the layout changes by clicking the Save button (🖫) on the Quick Access toolbar. Otherwise, you will discard the modifications when you close the Datasheet window.

SKILLS PREVIEW

Change the field column order in Datasheet view	• SELECT the desired column in the field header area. DRAG the column heading to its new location.
Hide or unhide field columns in Datasheet view	• SELECT the desired column in the field header area. CLICK the More button (▦) on the HOME tab. CHOOSE the Hide Fields command to hide the selection, *or* CHOOSE the Unhide Fields command to unhide field columns. • RIGHT-CLICK the desired column in the field header area. CHOOSE the Hide Fields command to hide the selection, *or* CHOOSE the Unhide Fields command to unhide field columns.
Freeze or unfreeze field columns in Datasheet view	• SELECT the desired column in the field header area. CLICK the More button (▦) on the HOME tab. CHOOSE the Freeze Fields command to freeze the selection, *or* CHOOSE the Unfreeze All Fields to unfreeze the selection. • RIGHT-CLICK the desired column in the field header area. CHOOSE the Freeze Fields command to freeze the selection, *or* CHOOSE the Unfreeze All Fields to unfreeze the selection.

PROJECT PRACTICE

1. After launching Microsoft Access, open the project data file **ac02a.accdb**. Three table objects will appear in the Navigation pane: Courses, Instructors, and Students.

2. To begin, display the Courses table in Datasheet view:
   DOUBLE-CLICK the Courses table in the Navigation pane.

3. Now modify the column placement to display certain fields side by side, which is especially useful for performing multiple-field sort operations. If necessary, use the horizontal scroll bar to scroll the window so that the "Faculty" and "DeptHead" field columns are visible. Then:
   CLICK the "DeptHead" field column header.

4. Position the white arrow mouse pointer (⇘) over the field name. Then:
   DRAG the "DeptHead" field column to the left and release the mouse button so that the bold vertical gridline appears between the "Faculty" and "MaxStudents" columns, as shown in Figure AC2.1.

FIGURE AC2.1   Moving the "DeptHead" field column

CourseID	Title	StartDate	StartTime	Credits	LabFees	Faculty	MaxStudent	MinStudent:	DeptHead	Instructorl
BUS100	Accounting Fur	1/10/2013	9:00 AM	3	☐	Business	120	40	Abernathy	
BUS201	Financial Accou	1/10/2013	1:00 PM	3	☐	Business	60	30	Abernathy	
BUS210	Managerial Acc	1/10/2013	7:00 PM	2	☐	Business	30	10	Bowers	
COM100	Computer App	9/9/2012	10:30 AM	3	☑	Science	150	75	Rhodes	
COM110	Computer Prog	1/11/2013	10:30 AM	3	☑	Science	60	30	Rhodes	
COM200	Visual Program	9/8/2012	3:00 PM	2	☑	Science	30	15	Greer	
COM210	Database Fund	9/9/2012	7:00 PM	2	☐	Science	60	30	Williamson	
COM220	Database Progi	1/11/2013	7:00 PM	2	☑	Science	30	15	Williamson	
COM230	Client/Server F	1/10/2013	9:00 AM	3	☐	Science	30	15	Rhodes	

> **ⓘ MORE INFO**
>
> Access determines the initial column order displayed in a Datasheet window from the field order in the underlying table structure. When you move a field in the datasheet, you do not affect the underlying table structure.

5 Now try moving two fields at the same time:

CLICK the "Faculty" field column header.

PRESS and hold **Shift**.

CLICK the "DeptHead" field column header.

Remember to release the **Shift** key after you click "DeptHead."
(*Result:* Both columns should now appear highlighted.)

6 To reposition the two field columns, position the mouse pointer (⯭) on one of the selected column headings. Then:

DRAG the "Faculty" (or "DeptHead") column heading to the left so that the bold vertical gridline appears between "Title" and "StartDate."

7 After releasing the mouse button:

PRESS **Home** to remove the highlighting.

CLICK the Save button (🖫) to save the layout changes.
(*Result:* Your Datasheet window should now appear similar to Figure AC2.2.)

FIGURE AC2.2   Moving two field columns

CourseID	Title	Faculty	DeptHead	StartDate	StartTime	Credits	LabFees	MaxStudent	MinStudent:	Instructorl
BUS100	Accounting Fur	Business	Abernathy	1/10/2013	9:00 AM	3	☐	120	40	
BUS201	Financial Accou	Business	Abernathy	1/10/2013	1:00 PM	3	☐	60	30	
BUS210	Managerial Acc	Business	Bowers	1/10/2013	7:00 PM	2	☐	30	10	
COM100	Computer App	Science	Rhodes	9/9/2012	10:30 AM	3	☑	150	75	
COM110	Computer Prog	Science	Rhodes	1/11/2013	10:30 AM	3	☑	60	30	
COM200	Visual Program	Science	Greer	9/8/2012	3:00 PM	2	☑	30	15	
COM210	Database Fund	Science	Williamson	9/9/2012	7:00 PM	2	☐	60	30	
COM220	Database Progi	Science	Williamson	1/11/2013	7:00 PM	2	☑	30	15	
COM230	Client/Server F	Science	Rhodes	1/10/2013	9:00 AM	3	☐	30	15	

8 You can hide columns that you do not want displayed in a particular printout or that you are thinking about deleting permanently. In this step, you will hide the last three columns of administrative data. To begin:

PRESS **End** to move to the last field column.

9 Fortunately, the three columns, "MaxStudents," "MinStudents," and "InstructorID," appear next to one another in the datasheet. To select the three columns:

CLICK the "MaxStudents" field column header.

PRESS and hold **Shift**.

CLICK the "InstructorID" field column header.
Remember to release the **Shift** key after you click "InstructorID."

10 To hide the selected field columns:

CLICK the More button () in the Records group of the HOME tab.

CHOOSE the Hide Fields command.

(*Result:* The columns disappear from the Datasheet window display, as shown in Figure AC2.3, although the data remains safely in the table object.)

FIGURE AC2.3   Hiding columns in Datasheet view

CourseID	Title	Faculty	DeptHead	StartDate	StartTime	Credits	LabFees	Click to Add
BUS100	Accounting Fun	Business	Abernathy	1/10/2013	9:00 AM	3	☐	
BUS201	Financial Accou	Business	Abernathy	1/10/2013	1:00 PM	3	☐	
BUS210	Managerial Acc	Business	Bowers	1/10/2013	7:00 PM	2	☐	
COM100	Computer App	Science	Rhodes	9/9/2012	10:30 AM	3	☑	
COM110	Computer Prog	Science	Rhodes	1/11/2013	10:30 AM	3	☑	
COM200	Visual Program	Science	Greer	9/8/2012	3:00 PM	2	☑	
COM210	Database Fund	Science	Williamson	9/9/2012	7:00 PM	2	☐	
COM220	Database Progr	Science	Williamson	1/11/2013	7:00 PM	2	☑	
COM230	Client/Server F	Science	Rhodes	1/10/2013	9:00 AM	3	☐	

> **TIP**
>
> Hiding columns in a datasheet is also useful for temporarily restricting the display of sensitive data, such as salaries or commissions.

11 To unhide the columns:

RIGHT-CLICK the "LabFees" field header column.

CHOOSE the Unhide Fields command.

(*Result:* The dialog box shown in Figure AC2.4 appears.)

FIGURE AC2.4   Unhide Columns dialog box

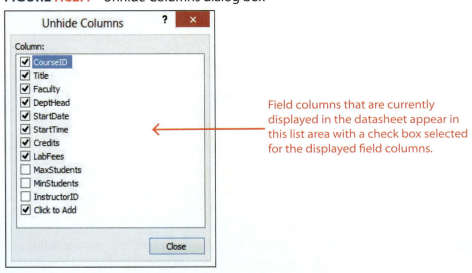

Field columns that are currently displayed in the datasheet appear in this list area with a check box selected for the displayed field columns.

12 In the Unhide Columns dialog box:

SELECT the MaxStudents check box.

SELECT the MinStudents check box.

SELECT the InstructorID check box.

CLICK Close.

(*Result:* The field columns reappear in the Datasheet window.)

13 When you navigate a large table with many columns, the Datasheet window scrolls automatically to accommodate your cursor movements. To more easily identify the current record, you can freeze or lock in place one or more columns, such as a company name or product number, along the left edge. To demonstrate:

RIGHT-CLICK the "CourseID" field column header.
(*Result:* The shortcut menu shown in Figure AC2.5 appears.)

FIGURE AC2.5 Displaying a field column's shortcut menu

14 To freeze this column in place so it does not scroll:

CHOOSE the Freeze Fields command.

PRESS `End` to move to the last field column.
(*Result:* The first column, "CourseID," remains at the left-hand side of the window, as shown in Figure AC2.6. (Your display may not exactly match depending on your screen size.) This command is especially useful for displaying datasheets that contain many fields.)

15 Save the layout changes and then close the Courses Datasheet window. If proceeding to the next lesson, keep the database open.

FIGURE AC2.6 Freezing a field column

First column in the datasheet

Fourth column in the datasheet

Finding and Replacing Data

LESSON OVERVIEW

Access provides some simple commands to help you find and manipulate data within Datasheet view. The Find command lets you search an entire table for the existence of a few characters, a word, or a phrase. With large tables, this command is especially useful for moving the cursor to a particular record for editing. Most commonly, the Find command is used to locate a single record, while filters are best suited to locate groups of records matching a specific criteria.

The Replace command lets you perform a global find-and-replace operation to update the contents of an entire table. Replace is an excellent tool to correct spelling mistakes and update standard fields, such as telephone area codes. Lastly, you can specify several options to control how a search is performed using the Find and Replace commands, including using **wildcard characters** to help locate words for which you are unsure of the spelling or the form of the word.

SKILLS PREVIEW

Find text, dates, or values in a datasheet	• SELECT a cell in the field column you want to search. CLICK the Find command (🔍) on the HOME tab. Specify the desired text and search options.
Search for data using wildcard characters	• Use the question mark (?) in place of a single character. For example, the search pattern ??S? matches ROSI and DISC. • Use the number symbol (#) in place of a single number. For example, the search pattern ##9 matches 109 and 349. • Use the asterisk (*) to represent a group of characters. For example, the search pattern Sm* yields entries beginning with "Sm," such as Smith, Smythe, and Smallwood.
Find and replace text, dates, or values in a datasheet	• SELECT a cell in the field column you want to search. CLICK the Replace command (🔤) on the HOME tab. Specify the desired text and search options.

PROJECT PRACTICE

1 Ensure that the **ac02a.accdb** is open and that no windows appear in the work area.

2 Open the Students table in Datasheet view.

3 To find the record for "Jimmy Kazo" in the datasheet:
CLICK any cell in the "LastName" field column.
CLICK the Find command (🔍) in the Find group on the HOME tab.

>
> **TIP**
> You can also display the Find tab in the Find and Replace dialog box by pressing `Ctrl`+f.

4 In the Find and Replace dialog box, the "Current field" selection is already selected in the Look In drop-down box. For this search, do the following:

TYPE **Kazo** in the Find What combo box.

SELECT Whole Field in the Match drop-down box, if it does not already appear.
(*Result:* Your screen should now appear similar to Figure AC2.7.)

FIGURE AC2.7   Find and Replace dialog box

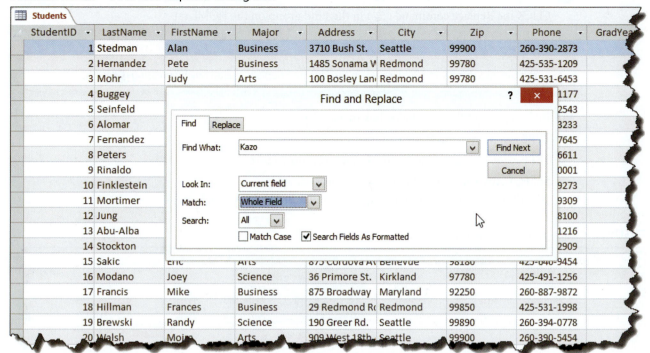

5 To proceed with the search:

CLICK the Find Next command button.

(*Result:* The cursor moves down the column and stops on the first occurrence of "Kazo" in StudentID record 56.)

6 To see if there are any other Kazos in the datasheet:

CLICK the Find Next command button.

CLICK the OK command button when the dialog box below appears to explain that no additional records were found.

7 To close the Find and Replace dialog box:

CLICK the Cancel command button.

8 To move to the top of the datasheet:

PRESS Ctrl + Home .

9 You will now change all occurrences of the abbreviation "Rd." in the "Address" field column to "Road." To begin, increase the width of the "Address" column and then select it:

DOUBLE-CLICK the right border of the "Address" field column header for its best-fit width.

CLICK the "Address" field column header to select the column.

10 To begin the find and replace operation:

CLICK the Replace command (ab/ac) in the Find group on the HOME tab.

TIP

You can also display the Replace tab in the Find and Replace dialog box by pressing Ctrl + h.

---

11 In the Find and Replace dialog box that appears:

TYPE **Rd.** in the Find What combo drop-down box.

TYPE **Road** in the Replace With combo drop-down box.

SELECT Any Part of Field in the Match drop-down box.
(*Result:* Your screen should now appear similar to Figure AC2.8.)

FIGURE AC2.8 Replacing "Rd." with "Road"

12 If you want to check the values you are about to replace, you can click the Replace command button to proceed one change at a time. For this step, however, change all the values in a single step:

CLICK the Replace All command button.

CLICK the Yes command button to accept the following confirmation dialog box.

13 To close the Find and Replace dialog box:

CLICK the Cancel command button.
(*Result:* You should now see that the "Rd." entries have been modified in the datasheet, as shown in Figure AC2.9.)

14 Close the Students datasheet window, saving the layout changes. If proceeding to the next lesson, keep the **ac02a.accdb** open.

> **ⓘ MORE INFO**
>
> Similar to how you would perform a spelling check in other Microsoft Office applications, you can check the spelling of entries in a datasheet. With the Datasheet window displayed, click the Spelling command (ABC✓) in the Records Group of the HOME tab. A dialog box appears for each word that the spelling checker does not recognize or believes to be misspelled. You can correct the spelling, ignore the entry, or add the word to a custom dictionary and then proceed to the next flagged entry.

FIGURE AC2.9 Finding and replacing data in the Students datasheet

StudentID	LastName	FirstName	Major	Address	City	Zip	Phone	GradYe
1	Stedman	Alan	Business	3710 Bush St.	Seattle	99900	260-390-2873	
2	Hernandez	Pete	Business	1485 Sonama Way	Redmond	99780	425-535-1209	
3	Mohr	Judy	Arts	100 Bosley Lane	Redmond	99780	425-531-6453	
4	Buggey	Diana	Science	20 Cactus Lane	Redmond	99804	425-531-1177	
5	Seinfeld	Casey	Arts	17 Windy Way	Bellevue	98180	425-640-2543	
6	Alomar	Sandra	Business	PO Box 1465	Kirkland	97080	425-493-3233	
7	Fernandez	Rosa	Science	151 Greer Road	Seattle	99890	260-394-7645	
8	Peters	Bob	Arts	200 Union St.	Seattle	99850	260-390-6611	
9	Rinaldo	Sandy	Arts	1871 Orrinton Road	Redmond	99704	425-535-0001	
10	Finklestein	Sue	Business	888 Burrard St.	Seattle	99904	260-390-9273	
11	Mortimer	Bruce	Science	235 Johnston St.	Redmond	99704	425-531-9309	
12	Jung	Chris	Science	1005 West 9th Ave.	Redmond	99780	425-531-8100	
13	Abu-Alba	Benji	Arts	122 Cordova Ave.	Bellevue	98200	425-660-1216	
14	Stockton	Gretta	Arts	4210 Bush St.	Seattle	99900	260-390-2909	
15	Sakic	Eric	Arts	875 Cordova Ave.	Bellevue	98180	425-640-9454	
16	Modano	Joey	Science	36 Primore St.	Kirkland	97780	425-491-1256	
17	Francis	Mike	Business	875 Broadway	Maryland	92250	260-887-9872	
18	Hillman	Frances	Business	29 Redmond Road	Redmond	99850	425-531-1998	
19	Brewski	Randy	Science	190 Greer Road	Seattle	99890	260-394-0778	
		Meira		909 West 18th A	eattle	99 0	26 20 5454	

Filtering Records in Datasheet View

LESSON OVERVIEW

A **filter** is a tool that limits the display of records in a table using a simple matching criterion. Similar to a pasta strainer that lets water through but not the pasta, a filter allows only some records to pass through for display. Filtering is an excellent way to find a subset of records that match a particular value or range of values. Using the **Filter By Selection** method, you apply a filter based on a selected value from the datasheet. The selection may be an entire cell's contents or only a portion of the entry.

SKILLS PREVIEW

Use Text, Date, and Number filters to filter a datasheet	• CLICK the Sort & Filter button (▪) attached to the field column heading you want to sort. CHOOSE the desired filter command (Text, Date, or Numbers), *or* SELECT or DESELECT the check boxes appearing beside each category data group.
Use Filter By Selection to filter a datasheet	• SELECT the data you wish to use as a filter in Datasheet view. CLICK the HOME tab and locate the Sort & Filter group. CLICK the Selection command (▾) to display the filtering options. (*Note:* You can also use the right-click shortcut menu to display the Selection filter options.)
Toggle a filter on and off to apply and remove a filter	• CLICK the HOME tab and locate the Sort & Filter group. CLICK the Toggle Filter command (▼).

PROJECT PRACTICE

1. Ensure that the **ac02a.accdb** is open and that no windows appear in the work area.

2. Open the Students table in Datasheet view.

3. To display only those students living in the city of Redmond:
   SELECT "Redmond" in the "City" field column of the second record.
   CLICK the Selection command (▾) in the Sort & Filter group on the HOME tab.
   CHOOSE "Equals Redmond" from the drop-down menu.
   (*Result:* A subset of 10 records is displayed in the Datasheet window, as shown in Figure AC2.10.)

FIGURE AC2.10 Filtering a datasheet by selection

StudentID ▾	LastName ▾	FirstName ▾	Major ▾	Address ▾	City ▾	Zip ▾	Phone ▾
2	Hernandez	Pete	Business	1485 Sonama Way	Redmond	99780	425-535-1209
3	Mohr	Judy	Arts	100 Bosley Lane	Redmond	99780	425-531-6453
4	Buggey	Diana	Science	20 Cactus Lane	Redmond	99804	425-531-1177
9	Rinaldo	Sandy	Arts	1871 Orrinton Road	Redmond	99704	425-535-0001
11	Mortimer	Bruce	Science	235 Johnston St.	Redmond	99704	425-531-9309
12	Jung	Chris	Science	1005 West 9th Ave.	Redmond	99780	425-531-8100
18	Hillman	Frances	Business	29 Redmond Road	Redmond	99850	425-531-1998
23	Henderson	Kendra	Arts	540 Cactus Lane	Redmond	99804	425-535-8761
50	Maynard	Elaine	Business	15201 Johnston Road	Redmond	99702	425-535-3481
51	Singh	Ranjitt	Arts	870 Orrinton Road	Redmond	99704	425-531-1827
*	(New)						

4 To demonstrate how you can move between filtering states, toggle the filter off, on, and off again. Watch the datasheet records as you do the following:

CLICK the Toggle Filter command (▼) in the Sort & Filter group on the HOME tab three times.

5 To display only those students who are *not* taking Arts as their major:

CLICK the Sort & Filter button (▾) for the "Major" field column heading.

CHOOSE the Text Filters command.

CHOOSE the Does Not Equal command.
(*Result*: The Custom Filter dialog box shown below should now appear.)

6 In the Custom Filter dialog box:

TYPE **Arts**.

CLICK the OK command button.
(*Result*: Notice that there are no "Arts" majors now displayed in the datasheet of 42 records and that the field column heading has a filter icon attached to its Sort & Filter button.)

7 To display only those non-Arts majors whose GradYear is 2015 and later (more recent):

RIGHT-CLICK on "2015" in the "GradYear" column of StudentID 1.

CHOOSE Greater Than or Equal To 2015.
(*Result*: As shown in Figure AC2.11, a filter icon appears on the "GradYear" field column heading to denote that it has an active filter applied, and the display of records is now limited to 24 non–Arts majors whose graduation year was 2015 or later.)

FIGURE AC2.11   Applying a filter to display non–Arts majors whose graduation year is 2015 or later

StudentID	LastName	FirstName	Major	Address	City	Zip	Phone	GradYear	GPA	Click
1 Stedman	Alan	Business	3710 Bush St.	Seattle	99900	260-390-2873	2015	3.25	
2 Hernandez	Pete	Business	1485 Sonama V	Redmond	99780	425-535-1209	2015	3.75	
	Diana	Science	20 Cactus Lane	Redmond	99804	425-531-1177	2015	3.15	
	Sue	Business	888 Burrard St.	Seattle	99904	260-390-9273	2015	3.75	
	Bruce	Science	235 Johnston S	Redmond	99704	425-531-9309	2016	3.50	
	Chris	Science	1005 West 9th	Redmond	99780	425-531-8100	2015	3.00	
	Joey	Science	36 Primore St.	Kirkland	97780	425-491-1256	2015	2.85	
18 Hillman	Frances	Business	29 Redmond R	Redmond	99850	425-531-1998	2015	2.75	
19 Brewski	Randy	Science	190 Greer Rd.	Seattle	99890	260-394-0778	2015	3.00	
27 Schuler	Presley	Business	190 Greer Rd.	Seattle	99900	260-394-1245	2015	3.75	
28 Yap	Steve	Business	1799 West 16th	Seattle	99904	260-390-2232	2016	3.00	
31 Trimarchi	Valerie	Business	7981 Shannon S	Bellevue	98100	425-640-0012	2015	3.00	
32 Matson	Lisa	Science	14489 3rd Ave.	Seattle	99890	260-390-4432	2015	2.75	
34 Heurrera	Ricardo	Business	101 West 6th A	Seattle	99904	260-394-1214	2015	3.50	
37 Bowman	Victoria	Science	110 Glen Vista	Maryland	92300	260-887-9110	2015	3.00	
39 Koh	Audrey	Science	903 Panorama	Maryland	92340	260-887-9091	2016	3.50	
46 Wong	Chuck	Business	6144 Silver Star	Maryland	92289	260-887-0199	2015	3.75	
	Red	Science	89 Bush St.	Seattle	99950	260-390-2281	2015	3.50	
	Elaine	Business	15201 Johnstor	Redmond	99702	425-535-3481	2015	3.00	
	William	Science	111 Union St.	Seattle	99850	260-394-9898	2015	3.85	
	Todd	Business	1066 Riverside	Kirkland	97902	425-491-1204	2015	2.65	
	Mary	Business	1890 Shannon S	Bellevue	98100	425-640-0001	2015	3.15	
63 Raggio	Jacob	Science	5521 Greer Rd.	Seattle	99890	260-394-3342	2015	3.75	
64 Kaplanoff	Mitch	Science	1234 West 23rd	Seattle	99900	260-390-0119	2015	3.50	
(New)							0	0.00	

This icon denotes which columns are used in the current filter

This indicator shows that the datasheet is currently filtered

Record: 1 of 24   Filtered   Search

8 To remove the filters and return to normal Datasheet view with all records displaying:
CLICK the Advanced command (⊞) in the Sort & Filter group on the HOME tab.
CHOOSE the Clear All Filters command.

9 PRESS `Ctrl` + `Home` to move to the top left-hand corner of the datasheet.

10 Keep the Students Datasheet window open in the Access work area and proceed to the next lesson.

Creating Advanced Custom Filters

LESSON OVERVIEW

For more detailed filtering operations, use the **Filter By Form** method to set multiple criteria. Unlike Filter By Selection, a blank datasheet row appears in which you can enter or select the desired criteria. Another key difference is that you can define criteria using logical AND and OR relationships. Once you have defined a filter, Access enables you to save it as a query object in the Database window.

SKILLS PREVIEW

Use Filter By Form to filter a datasheet	• CLICK the HOME tab and locate the Sort & Filter group. CLICK the Advanced command (⬚). CHOOSE the Filter By Form command. Specify the criteria to use in the filter. CLICK the Toggle Filter command (▼) to apply the filter.

PROJECT PRACTICE

1 Ensure that the **ac02a.accdb** is open and that the Students Datasheet window appears in the work area.

2 To use the Filter By Form method for filtering a datasheet:

CLICK the Advanced command (⬚) in the Sort & Filter group on the HOME tab.

CHOOSE the Filter By Form command.

(*Result:* Your screen should now appear similar to Figure AC2.12.)

FIGURE AC2.12 The Filter By Form window

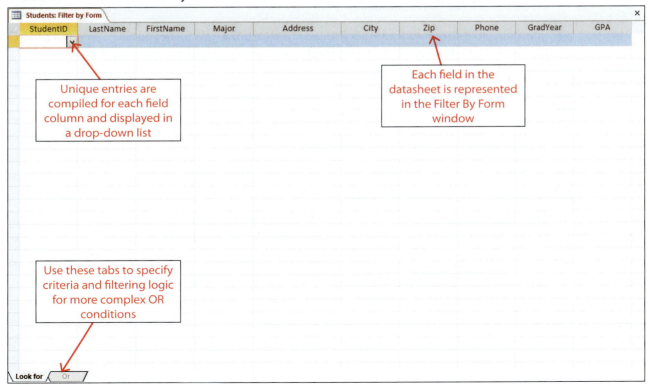

3 To display only those students taking Arts as their major:

CLICK in the row below the Major field and then CLICK the down arrow.

SELECT Arts from the list of values.
(*Result:* Notice that Access places quotes [e.g., "Arts"] around text-based criteria.)

4 To display only those Arts students who live in Kirkland:

CLICK in the row below the City field and then CLICK the down arrow.

SELECT Kirkland from the list of values.

5 To display only those Arts students from Kirkland with over a 3.25 GPA:

CLICK in the GPA cell on the first row.

TYPE **>3.25**.
(*Result:* The first row of your Filter By Form window should appear similar to the image shown here.)

Students: Filter by Form									
StudentID	LastName	FirstName	Major	Address	City	Zip	Phone	GradYear	GPA
			"Arts"		"Kirkland"				>3.25

6 Now you are ready to apply the filter and view the results:

CLICK the Toggle Filter command (🔽) in the Sort & Filter group on the HOME tab.
(*Result:* Your screen should now display the two records shown here.)

Students									
StudentID	LastName	FirstName	Major	Address	City	Zip	Phone	GradYear	GPA
48	Lepinski	Elliot	Arts	4500 Kalview P	Kirkland	97700	425-491-6720	2014	3.80
65	Reynolds	Julie	Arts	220 Rockford S	Kirkland	97800	425-491-3378	2014	3.50
* (New)								0	0.00

7 Now revise the filtering criteria. To return to Filter By Form:

CLICK the Advanced command (⧉) in the Sort & Filter group on the HOME tab.

CHOOSE the Filter By Form command.

8 In addition to the Arts students from Kirkland who earned a GPA higher than 3.25, you will add to the display those Business students from Seattle who also have a GPA higher than 3.25. To begin:

CLICK the Or sheet tab at the bottom of the window.

9 In the new "Or" Filter By Form sheet:

SELECT "Business" from the "Major" field column.

SELECT "Seattle" from the "City" field column.

TYPE **>3.25** into the "GPA" field column.

10 To apply the filter and view the results:

CLICK the Toggle Filter command (🔽) in the Sort & Filter group on the HOME tab.
(*Result:* Your screen should now display five records, as shown in Figure AC2.13.)

11 Save and close the Students Datasheet window. (*Note:* When you return to this datasheet, you simply need to click the Toggle Filter command (🔽) on the HOME tab to reapply the filter.)

12 When you are ready to proceed, you may close the **ac02a.accdb** and exit Microsoft Access.

FIGURE AC2.13 Applying a Filter By Form to the Students datasheet

Only Arts majors from Kirkland and Business majors from Seattle who have earned a GPA of greater than 3.25 are now displayed.

MULTIPLE-CHOICE QUIZ

Select the best choice in the following questions for review of the project concepts. Good luck!

1. Which of the following is not an option to customize a Datasheet window?
   a. Freeze one column
   b. Hide one column
   c. Change one row's height
   d. Change one column's width

2. Which of the following is not a command that is selectable from a field column's right-click menu?
   a. Hide Fields
   b. Freeze Fields
   c. Find
   d. Replace

3. Which of the following is not an option in the Find and Replace dialog box for matching the Find What criteria in a field column?
   a. Any Part of Field
   b. Whole Field
   c. Start of Field
   d. End of Field

4. The process of restricting the display of records in a table to those matching a particular criterion is called
   a. filtering.
   b. sorting.
   c. restricting.
   d. sifting.

5. Which of the following allows you to right-click in a cell and filter a datasheet by its contents?
   a. Filter By Example
   b. Filter By Selection
   c. Filter By Form
   d. Filter For Input

6. Which of the following allows you to specify multiple criteria, as well as perform logical OR and AND operations, in a filter?
   a. Filter By Example
   b. Filter By Selection
   c. Filter By Form
   d. Filter For Input

7. Which of the following criterion returns the name "Jones" as a match?
   a. *ne*
   b. J??nes
   c. J#s
   d. ?ne*

8. Which of the following criterion returns all prices greater than $12.50?
   a. >12.50
   b. <12.50
   c. >=12.50
   d. <=12.50

9. Which of the following criteria is the best choice for returning city names beginning with the letter "B"?
   a. =B
   b. B*
   c. B?
   d. B#

10. Which of the following statements is false?
    a. A filter operation limits records displayed in a datasheet.
    b. A sort operation modifies the natural order of data in a table.
    c. A find operation that is successful moves the cursor to the record.
    d. A replace operation cannot be used to correct common spelling mistakes in a table.

HANDS-ON EXERCISE: WORK IT OUT AC-2A-E1

You will now practice customizing a datasheet by moving a field column, using the Freeze and Hide commands, and formatting and sorting the data. The final result is shown using Print Preview mode in Figure AC2.14.

FIGURE AC2.14 Work It Out AC-2A-E1: completed

E1 Internet Accounts

Username	Customer	Address	City	Zip	Billing Type
vnguyen1	Vu Nguyen	P.O. Box 3992	Lodi	95242	CK
lschuler	Liz Schuler	599 W. Walnut	Lodi	95240	CC
klewis	Kaley Lewis	St. John's Clinic	Lodi	95240	CK
ahariss	Ann Harris	123 W. Rose	Lodi	95240	CK
tsawyer	Tom Sawyer	5065 Villa Arroyo	Ripon	95336	CC
jcuervo	Jose Cuervo	56 Mar Vista Dr	Ripon	95336	CC
gmorris	G. T. Morris	P.O. Box 9844	Ripon	95336	DD
vnguyen2	Van Nguyen	11 N. Weber	Victor	95244	DD
syee	Sam Yee	944 E. Fifth St.	Victor	95244	CK
bmar	Bonnie Mar	7855 "E" St.	Victor	95244	DD
bbailey	Bo Bailey	1 Merriwether	Victor	95244	DD

1 After launching Microsoft Access, open the exercise data file **ac02a-ex.accdb**.

2 Open the E1 Internet Accounts table object for display in a Datasheet window.

3 Move the UserName field to the first column.

4 Freeze the "Username" field column in the datasheet so it is always visible when you scroll the window.

5 Move the "Billing Type" field column to appear between the "Phone" and "Amount" field columns.

6 Center the column entries for the "Billing Type" field column.

7 Adjust the width of the "Address" column to its best-fit width by double-clicking the borderline between the "Address" and "City" columns.

8 Hide the "Phone" field column from displaying in the Datasheet window. (Note: Hidden columns are temporarily hidden in the Datasheet window, but they are not removed from the table object.)

9 Sort the records in ascending order by the contents of the "City" field column.

10 Preview what the datasheet will look like when printed.

11 Use the magnifying glass mouse pointer to zoom in on the Print Preview window, as shown in Figure AC2.14. Once previewed, return to the table Datasheet view.

12 CLICK the Save button (🖫) to save the layout changes and then close the Datasheet window.

13 If you are not proceeding to the next exercise, close the database file and exit Microsoft Access.

In this exercise, you will sort data using more than one column and practice using the Find and Replace commands. The final result is shown in Figure AC2.15.

FIGURE AC2.15 Work It Out AC-2A-E2: completed

Category	ProductCode	Species	Size	Grade	Finish	Click to Add
Board	DF14	DFIR	1 X 4	Ungraded	RGH	
Board	DF16	D.FIR	1 X 6	Ungraded	RGH	
Board	SP14	SPF	1 X 4	Ungraded	S4S	
Board	SP14R	SPF	1 X 4	Ungraded	RGH	
Board	SP16	SPF	1 X 6	Ungraded	S4S	
Board	SP18	SPF	1 X 8	Ungraded	S4S	
Board	WP110	WPINR	1 X 10	Utility	RGH	
Board	WP13	WPINE	1 X 3	Utility	RGH	
Board	WP14	WPINE	1 X 4	Utility	RGH	
Board	WP16	WPINE	1 X 6	Utility	RGH	
Board	WP18	WPINE	1 X 8	Utility	RGH	
Dimension	DF210S	DFIR	2 X 10	Standard	S4S	
Dimension	DF242	DFIR	2 X 4	2+	S4S	
Dimension	DF24S	DFIR	2 X 4	Standard	S4S	
Dimension	DF24U	DFIR	2 X 4	Utility	S4S	
Dimension	DF26	DFIR	2 X 6	Standard	S4S	
Dimension	DF28	DFIR	2 X 8	Standard	S4S	
Dimension	SP210	SPF	2 X 10	Standard	S4S	
Dimension	SP212	SPF	2 X 12	Standard	S4S	
Dimension	SP242	SPF	2 X 4	2+	S4S	
Dimension	SP243	SPF	2 X 4	3+	S4S	
Dimension	SP24U	SPF	2 X 4	Utility	S4S	
Dimension	SP26S	SPF	2 X 4	Standard	S4S	

1. Open the exercise data file **ac02a-ex.accdb**.

2. Open the E2 Products table for display in Datasheet view.

3. Move the "Category" field column to appear as the first column at the left-hand side of the datasheet.

4. Perform a sort operation that displays the table in ascending order by Category and then by the ProductCode stored within each category. Sort the ProductCode field first and then the Category field. Your screen should now appear similar to Figure AC2.16.

FIGURE AC2.16 Sorting by two field columns

Category	ProductCode	Species	Size	Grade	Finish	Click to Add
Board	DF14	DFIR	1 X 4	Ungraded	RGH	
Board	DF16	D.FIR	1 X 6	Ungraded	RGH	
Board	SP14	SPF	1 X 4	Ungraded	S4S	
Board	SP14R	SPF	1 X 4	Ungraded	RGH	
Board	SP16	SPF	1 X 6	Ungraded	S4S	
Board	SP18	SPF	1 X 8	Ungraded	S4S	
Board	WP110	WPINR	1 X 10	Utility	RGH	
Board	WP13	WPINE	1 X 3	Utility	RGH	
Board	WP14	WPINE	1 X 4	Utility	RGH	
Board	WP16	WPINE	1 X 6	Utility	RGH	
Board	WP18	WPINE	1 X 8	Utility	RGH	
Dim.	DF210S	DFIR	2 X 10	Standard	S4S	
Dim.	DF242	DFIR	2 X 4	2+	S4S	
Dim.	DF24S	DFIR	2 X 4	Standard	S4S	
Dim.	DF24U	DFIR	2 X 4	Utility	S4S	
Dim.	DF26	DFIR	2 X 6	Standard	S4S	
Dim.	DF28	DFIR	2 X 8	Standard	S4S	

5 Now find all the products made from birch wood. Use the Find command in the "Species" field column to find "birch." (Note: By default, the Find command is not case sensitive.) What product category does the cursor stop on first?

6 Use the Find Next command button to determine if any of the other products are made from birch. When you finish, close the Find and Replace dialog box.

7 You will now use the Replace command to replace all occurrences of the code "Dim." in the "Category" field column with the word "Dimension." Move to the top leftmost corner in the table and then open the Find and Replace dialog box.

8 On the REPLACE tab of the Find and Replace dialog box:

TYPE **Dim.** in the Find What combo box.

PRESS [Tab].

TYPE **Dimension** in the Replace With combo box.
(*Result:* The Find and Replace dialog box should now appear as shown in Figure AC2.17.)

FIGURE AC2.17 Find and Replace dialog box

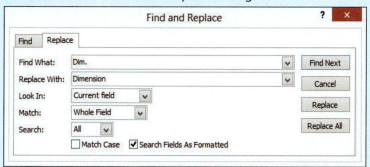

9 Proceed with the Find and Replace operation. When Access asks you to confirm the replacement, click the Yes command button. When you are ready to return to the datasheet, close the Find and Replace dialog box.

10 You may now close the Datasheet window and save your layout changes.

11 If you are not proceeding to the next exercise, close the database file and exit Microsoft Access.

Filtering provides an excellent method for displaying only those records that match a specific criterion. In this lesson, you will practice using the Filter By Selection and Filter By Form methods. The final result is shown in Figure AC2.18.

FIGURE AC2.18   Work It Out AC-2A-E3: completed

ID	Volunteer Group	Contact	Address	City	Phone	Phone 2	Click to Add
33	Junior Aide	Judi T. White	19343 Wilderness	Woodbridge	369-0878	957-8740	
48	Boy Scout Troop 421	Bruce René	504 Curry Court	Manteca	239-8816	481-2707	
52	Boy Scout Troop 425	Mike Lehr	680 Aurora Ct	Manteca	823-7634	823-0260	
* (New)							

1. Open the exercise data file **ac02a-ex.accdb**, if it is not already open in Access.

2. Open the E3 Contacts table for display in Datasheet view.

3. Apply a filter so that only the records containing the word *Club* in the "Volunteer Group" field column are displayed. How many groups have *Club* as part of their name?

4. Remove the current filter from displaying and then use Filter By Selection to extract those groups based in the city of Pinawa. How many groups contain *Pinawa* in the "City" field column?

5. Remove the current filter and use the Filter By Form method to display only those groups from either Woodbridge or Manteca. How many groups contain *Woodbridge* or *Manteca* in the "City" field column? Your screen should now appear similar to Figure AC2.18.

6. You may now close the Datasheet window and save your design changes.

7. Close the database file and exit Microsoft Access.

Creating and Modifying Queries

This project introduces the use of queries to retrieve and display a subset of records. Queries allow you to display data from multiple tables, to control which fields display and in what order they appear, and to perform calculations on selected field values. In addition, whereas filters typically provide a temporary view of a subset of records, queries are saved as independent database objects. In fact, you can summarize the operations in this chapter with the following statement: You *find* a record, *filter* a table, and *query* a database.

PROJECT FILE: *Available at* www.mhhe.com/office2013projectlearn

After completing this project, you will be able to:

- Create a simple query using a wizard-driven approach.

- Modify and customize a query object in Design view.

- Sort the results from a query.

- Filter, or restrict, the results from a query.

- Perform basic calculations using table data.

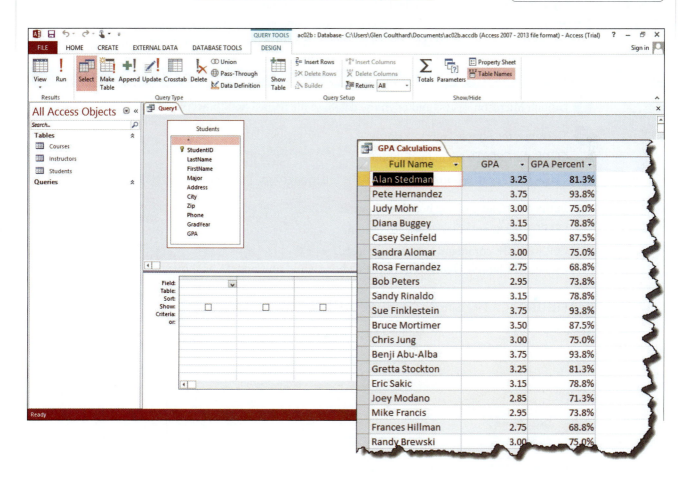

Creating a Query Using the Query Wizard

LESSON OVERVIEW

The **Simple Query Wizard** is a step-by-step tool that helps you retrieve data from one or more tables in a database. While the wizard does not allow you to specify search criteria or sort parameters, it is especially useful when you need to select fields from various tables to display in a single Datasheet window. The type of query object created by the wizard is known as a **select query**, because you use it to select data for display. The results of the query are listed in a Datasheet window.

SKILLS PREVIEW

Create a new query using the Simple Query Wizard	• CLICK the CREATE tab in the Ribbon. CLICK the Query Wizard command in the Queries group. SELECT the Simple Query Wizard in the New Query dialog box.

PROJECT PRACTICE

1. Launch Microsoft Access and open the database file named **ac02b.accdb**.

2. To launch the Simple Query Wizard:

   CLICK the CREATE tab in the Ribbon.

   CLICK the Query Wizard command in the Queries group.

3. In the New Query dialog box that appears:

   SELECT the Simple Query Wizard option.

   CLICK the OK command button to proceed.

   (*Result:* The Simple Query Wizard dialog box should now appear, as shown in Figure AC2.19.)

FIGURE AC2.19 Simple Query Wizard dialog box

The table or query object that was selected in the Navigation pane before you launched the wizard is shown here.

Use this area to select the fields you want displayed in the query.

4 To display a listing of courses along with their appointed instructor's name, you must select fields from two tables. To begin:
SELECT "Table: Courses" from the Table/Queries drop-down list box.

5 In the Available Fields list box:
SELECT the CourseID field.
CLICK the Include button (>).
SELECT the Title field.
CLICK the Include button (>).

6 You must now display fields from the Instructors table. To do so:
SELECT "Table: Instructors" from the Table/Queries drop-down list box.

7 You can use a shortcut to add fields from the Available Fields list box:
DOUBLE-CLICK the LastName field to include it.
DOUBLE-CLICK the FirstName field to include it.
(*Result:* Your dialog box should now appear similar to Figure AC2.20.)

FIGURE AC2.20   Selecting fields for display in the query

8 To proceed to the next step in the wizard:
CLICK the Next command button.

9 To name the query:
TYPE **Course Listing with Instructor** in the text box provided.

10 Ensure that the Open the Query to View Information option button is selected, and then:
CLICK the Finish command button.

11 On your own, size the "Title" field column in the datasheet to its best-fit column width.
(*Result:* Your screen should now appear similar to Figure AC2.21. Data in the first two columns is taken from the Courses table, and data in the last two columns is taken from the Instructors table.)

12 Close the Datasheet window and save the layout changes. You should now see the new query object appear in the Navigation pane. If proceeding to the next lesson, keep the database open.

FIGURE AC2.21 Displaying the results of a query

Course Listing with Instructor

CourseID	Title	LastName	FirstName
COM200	Visual Programming	Kitching	Cheralyn
ORG100	Organizational Behavior	Kitching	Cheralyn
ORG300	Executive Decision Making	Kitching	Cheralyn
BUS100	Accounting Fundamentals	Jaimeson	Aaron
BUS201	Financial Accounting	Jaimeson	Aaron
COM100	Computer Applications	Neumann	Mindy
BUS210	Managerial Accounting	Kunicki	Kenyon
COM210	Database Fundamentals	Kunicki	Kenyon
ORG210	Organizational Management	Kunicki	Kenyon
ORG220	Strategic Planning	Kunicki	Kenyon
COM110	Computer Programming	Harris	Robert
COM220	Database Programming	Huber	Tessa
COM230	Client/Server Fundamentals	Cortez	Anna
MKT210	Consumer Behavior	Cortez	Anna
MKT250	Marketing Research	Cortez	Anna
COM310	Component Programming	Alexander	Simon
COM315	Object-Oriented Design	Alexander	Simon
MKT100	Marketing Fundamentals	Alexander	Simon

Creating a Query Using Query Design View

LESSON OVERVIEW

The Simple Query Wizard makes it easy to start creating queries. Modifying an existing query, however, requires that you use the query Design window. Like other database objects, you can create, modify, and save query objects in Design view and then copy, rename, delete, and print them from the Navigation pane. The query Design window uses a graphical **query-by-example (QBE)** layout called the **query Design grid** that lets you select field columns for display, enter criteria statements, specify sort orders, and perform calculations.

SKILLS PREVIEW

Create a new query using Query Design view	• CLICK the CREATE tab in the Ribbon. CLICK the Query Design command in the Queries group. Complete the query Design grid to define your query.
Add a field to the query Design grid	• DOUBLE-CLICK the desired field in the table's field list, *or* • CLICK in an empty Field cell to display its drop-down arrow. SELECT the desired field from the drop-down field list, *or* • DRAG the desired field from the table's field list and drop it on the next available column in the "Field" row of the grid.
Run a query	• CLICK the Run command on the DESIGN tab, *or* • DOUBLE-CLICK a query object in the Navigation pane, *or* • RIGHT-CLICK a query object in the Navigation pane. CHOOSE the Open command.

PROJECT PRACTICE

1. Ensure that the **ac02b.accdb** is open and that no windows appear in the work area.

2. To create a new query object in Design view:

   CLICK the CREATE tab in the Ribbon.

   CLICK the Query Design command in the Queries group.
   (*Result:* The Show Table dialog box appears.)

3. The first step to create a query is to identify the table or tables required for specifying criteria and extracting data for display. In this project, you will create a single table query. Do the following:

   SELECT the Students table.

   CLICK the Add command button.

   CLICK the Close command button.
   (*Note:* You can also double-click a table object in the Show Table dialog box to add it to the query Design window. If you make a mistake such as choosing the wrong table, RIGHT-CLICK the table and SELECT Remove Table.)

4 On your own, size the Students table object so it displays all of its fields. Notice that the window is divided into a **Table pane**, which identifies the source data tables, and the query Design grid, which contains the fields for display, filter criteria, and sort order selections. Drag the split bar separating the two panes to adjust the shared space. Take a few minutes to familiarize yourself with the various parts of the query Design window shown in Figure AC2.22.

FIGURE AC2.22   Query Design window

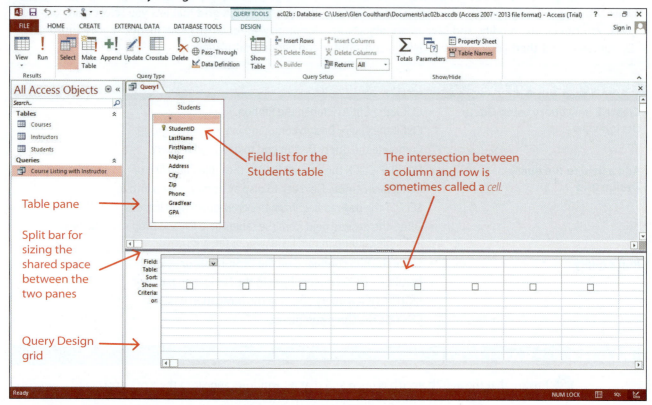

5 At this point, the query does not perform any function. To select data to display or to use a field in specifying criteria, you must add fields to the "Field" row in the query Design grid by dragging or double-clicking its name in the Table pane. To illustrate:

DOUBLE-CLICK the LastName field in the Students field list.
(*Result:* The LastName field is placed in the first column of the Design grid.)

6 To add the FirstName field to the grid by dragging:

DRAG the FirstName field from the Students field list and drop it on the next available column in the "Field" row of the grid.

7 Finally, add the Phone and GradYear fields to the grid:

DOUBLE-CLICK the Phone field in the Students field list.

DOUBLE-CLICK the GradYear field in the Students field list.
(*Result:* Notice that the fields add to the grid in the order they are selected. Your screen should now appear similar to Figure AC2.23.)

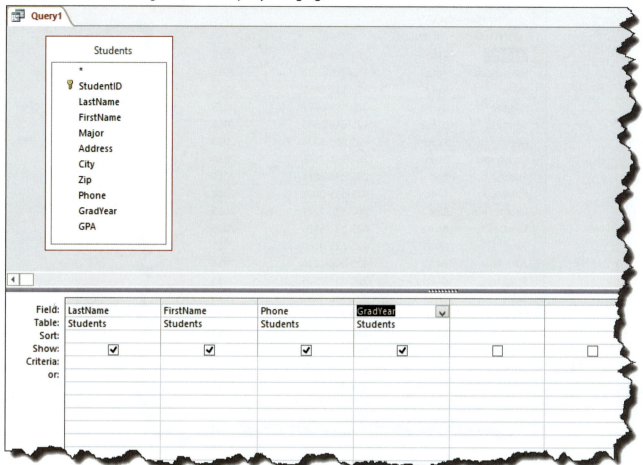

8 Before running a query, save the query object. To do so:

CLICK the Save button () on the Quick Access toolbar.

TYPE **Student Phone List** in the Save As dialog box.

CLICK the OK command button.
(*Result:* The query object should now appear in the Navigation pane.)

9 To view the results of your query:

CLICK the Run command in the Results group on the DESIGN tab.
(*Result:* Your screen should now appear similar to Figure AC2.24.)

> ⚠ **HEADS UP**
>
> If you edit or make changes to the data in a query's Datasheet window, the underlying table object(s) also change. Therefore, you can use a query to edit, delete, and maintain data in your tables.

10 Close the Datasheet window and, if necessary, save the layout changes. If proceeding to the next lesson, keep the database open.

FIGURE AC2.24 Query results displayed in a datasheet

LastName	FirstName	Phone	GradYear
Stedman	Alan	260-390-2873	2015
Hernandez	Pete	425-535-1209	2015
Mohr	Judy	425-531-6453	2014
Buggey	Diana	425-531-1177	2015
Seinfeld	Casey	425-640-2543	2016
Alomar	Sandra	425-493-3233	2013
Fernandez	Rosa	260-394-7645	2014
Peters	Bob	260-390-6611	2014
Rinaldo	Sandy	425-535-0001	2014
Finklestein	Sue	260-390-9273	2015
Mortimer	Bruce	425-531-9309	2016
Jung	Chris	425-531-8100	2015
Abu-Alba	Benji	425-660-1216	2016
Stockton	Gretta	260-390-2909	2015
Sakic	Eric	425-640-9454	2015
Modano	Joey	425-491-1256	2015
Francis	Mike	260-887-9872	2014
Hillman	Frances	425-531-1998	2015
Brewski	Randy	260-394-0778	2015
Walsh	Moira	260-390-5454	2015
Towne	Bruce	260-304-4403	2014
Adams	Cecilia	260-887-5433	2014

MORE INFO

In addition to select queries, Access provides action, parameter, and crosstab queries. An **action query** performs mass changes to the data it retrieves. The four types of action queries include (1) **update query**, which modifies the data in a table; (2) **append query**, which adds data from one or more tables to another table; (3) **delete query**, which deletes records from one or more tables; and (4) **make table query**, which creates a new table from a query's results. Moreover, a **parameter query** displays a dialog box and accepts input from the user before proceeding. Use parameter queries to enter customized search criteria at run-time. Mainly used for analysis, a **crosstab query** summarizes numerical results in a spreadsheet-like datasheet. Similarly, you can display your queries using PivotTable and PivotChart view modes.

Modifying and Sorting a Select Query

LESSON OVERVIEW

You create and modify a query in the query Design window. The results of the query are displayed in a Datasheet window. Identical to working with tables, use the View button to toggle between Datasheet view and Design view. Ways that you can modify a query include inserting and removing tables, adding and deleting fields, widening and reordering columns, and specifying search criteria. You can also change the sort order for displaying records in both Datasheet view and Design view. In Design view, you use the "Sort" row of the query Design grid. In addition to specifying ascending or descending sort order, you can create multi-key sorts by selecting more than one field in the grid. The leftmost field column becomes the primary sort key, while the remaining columns sort according to their column order. This feature enables you to perform complex sort operations, such as listing records alphabetically by country, then by state, and lastly by city. If you choose not to specify a sort order, the resulting records display in the same order that governs the underlying table.

SKILLS PREVIEW

Modify an existing query object using Design view	• RIGHT-CLICK the desired query object in the Navigation pane. CHOOSE Design view, *or* • Open the query object to display its Datasheet window. CLICK the View – Design View command on the HOME tab.
Sort a query's datasheet results using Design view	• CLICK in the Sort text box for the desired field column. CLICK the down arrow attached to the cell. SELECT Ascending, Descending, or (not sorted).
Delete a field column in the query Design grid	• SELECT the desired field column by clicking in it. CLICK the Delete Columns command ( ) on the DESIGN tab, *or* • CLICK the header area of the desired field column. PRESS Delete .

PROJECT PRACTICE

1. Ensure that the **ac02b.accdb** is open and that no windows appear in the work area.

2. In the next few steps, you will add and delete field columns to the Student Phone List query:
   RIGHT-CLICK the Student Phone List query in the Navigation pane.
   CHOOSE Design View.
   (*Result:* The query Design window appears for the Student Phone List query.)

3. To remove the "GradYear" field column from the Design grid:
   CLICK in the Field cell for "GradYear."
   CLICK the Delete Columns command ( ) in the Query Setup group on the DESIGN tab.
   (*Result:* The field column is removed from the Design grid.)

4. To add the "City" field column to the grid:
   SELECT the City field from the drop-down field list, as shown in Figure AC2.25.

FIGURE AC2.25 Deleting and adding fields in the Design grid

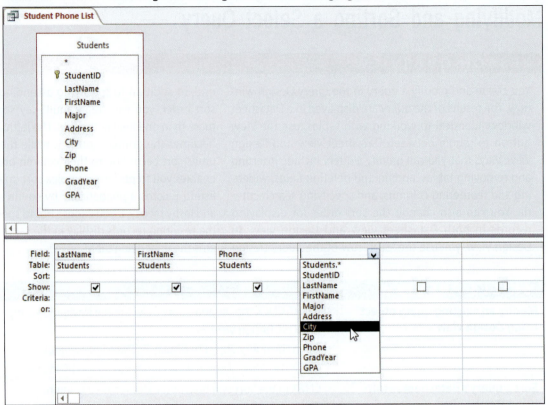

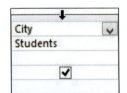

5 You will now move the "City" field column to appear to the left of the "LastName" field column. To begin, position the mouse pointer over the column header for the City field, as shown here, and then click once to select the column.

6 Using the arrow mouse pointer ( ), as shown here, drag the field column to the left of the "LastName" field column and then release the mouse button.

7 To sort the query results by city and then by student last name:

SELECT Ascending in the "Sort" row for the "City" field column.

SELECT Ascending in the "Sort" row for the "LastName" field column.
(*Result:* Your query Design grid should now appear similar to Figure AC2.26.)

FIGURE AC2.26 Moving field columns and selecting sort orders

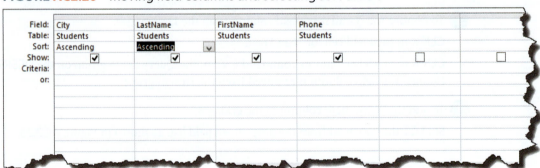

8 To save and then run the query:

CLICK the Save button (🖫) on the Quick Access toolbar.

CLICK the Run command in the Results group on the DESIGN tab.
(*Result:* The results of your modified query appear in Figure AC2.27. Notice that the column order impacts how the results are displayed and sorted.)

9 Close the Datasheet window. If proceeding to the next lesson, keep the database open.

FIGURE AC2.27   Displaying the results of the modified query

The primary sort order is by City

The secondary sort order is by LastName

City	LastName	FirstName	Phone
Bellevue	Abu-Alba	Benji	425-660-1216
Bellevue	Azavedo	Kirk	425-660-6611
Bellevue	Clifford	Karen	425-640-3312
Bellevue	Davis	Julie	425-660-1090
Bellevue	Kazo	Jimmy	425-620-8761
Bellevue	McFee	Becky	425-620-6545
Bellevue	Mikowski	Arthur	425-620-1109
Bellevue	Ortez	Francisco	425-620-2909
Bellevue	Sagi	Janos	425-640-7654
Bellevue	Sakic	Eric	425-640-9454
Bellevue	Seinfeld	Casey	425-640-2543
Bellevue	Thomas	Jessica	425-640-9894
Bellevue	Timerson	Mary	425-640-0001
Bellevue	Trimarchi	Valerie	425-640-0012
Kirkland	Alomar	Sandra	425-493-3233
Kirkland	Andrews	Jim	425-493-6120
Kirkland	Boltman	Todd	425-491-1204
Kirkland	Chan	Alice	425-493-9876
Kirkland	Keller	Roberta	425-493-8723
Kirkland	Lepinski	Elliot	425-491-6720
Kirkland	Modano	Joey	425-491-1256
Kirkland	Reynolds	Julie	425-491-3378

Designing Queries with Custom Criteria

LESSON OVERVIEW

Querying a table involves more than limiting a datasheet's display to specific fields. Select queries can also extract and organize data that meet a set of conditions, which can be used in generating reports. When you base a report on a query instead of a table, you can print mailing labels for a range of zip codes, monthly statements for customers with overdue accounts, and emergency contact sheets for specific employees. To limit the records that display in a datasheet, enter a **conditional** **statement** in the "Criteria" row of the query Design grid. A conditional statement can take one of several forms. First, you can enter an example of the value that you are looking for, such as "Toronto" or "Seattle." Second, you can use the question mark (?) and asterisk (*) wildcard characters to represent one or more alternative characters in a conditional expression. Finally, you can use mathematical operators, such as < and >, to limit records between a given range of values or dates.

SKILLS PREVIEW

Enter text criteria and wildcards to limit results to specific entries	• TYPE *"text"* to retrieve entries that match the "text" exactly.
	• TYPE **Not** *"text"* to retrieve entries not matching the "text."
	• TYPE **Like** *"A*"* to retrieve entries beginning with the letter "A."
	• TYPE **Like** *"*text*"* to retrieve entries containing the "text."
	• TYPE **Like** *"*text"* to retrieve entries ending with the "text."
	• TYPE **"USA" Or "Canada"** to retrieve entries containing either of the values specified.
	• TYPE **In("USA", "Canada", "Mexico")** to retrieve entries containing one of the values in the list.
Enter date criteria (enclosed in # symbols) to limit results to specific dates	• TYPE **>#10/31/2013#** to retrieve entries after 31-Oct-2013.
	• TYPE **Between #1/1/2013# And #3/31/2013#** to retrieve entries occurring in the first quarter of 2013.
	• TYPE **<Date()** to retrieve entries earlier than the current date.
Enter numeric criteria to limit results to specific values	• TYPE **>=98000** to retrieve zip code entries of 98000 and higher.
	• TYPE **In(100,200,300)** to retrieve entries containing one of the values in the list.
Enter logical criteria to evaluate and limit results	• TYPE **Is Null** to retrieve entries that have missing field values.
	• TYPE **Is Not Null** to retrieve only those entries with no missing field values.

PROJECT PRACTICE

1. Ensure that the **ac02b.accdb** is open and that no windows appear in the work area.

2. To add some criteria to limit the records retrieved by the Student Phone List query:

   RIGHT-CLICK the Student Phone List query in the Navigation pane.

   CHOOSE Design View.
   (*Result:* The query Design window appears for the Student Phone List query.)

3. To add additional fields to the query Design grid:

   DOUBLE-CLICK "Major" in the Students field list.

   DOUBLE-CLICK "GradYear" in the Students field list.

4 Now you will limit the display of records to Business majors who will graduate after 2014:

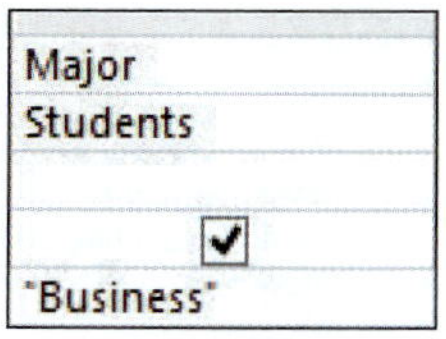

CLICK in the Criteria text box in the "Major" column.

TYPE **Business**.

PRESS `Tab`.

(*Result:* As shown here, double quotes add to the entry automatically. In fact, Access will evaluate and modify, if necessary, all entries you make in the Criteria field. Therefore, you can type text expressions using a variety of formats, including Business, "Business", =Business, and ="Business".)

| Major |
| Students |
| |
| ☑ |
| "Business" |

5 In the Criteria Row, in the "GradYear" field column:

TYPE **>2014**.

PRESS `Tab`.

6 To execute the query:

CLICK the Run command in the Results group on the DESIGN tab.

(*Result:* The query retrieves 12 records, as shown in Figure AC2.28.)

FIGURE AC2.28 Executing a query containing custom criteria

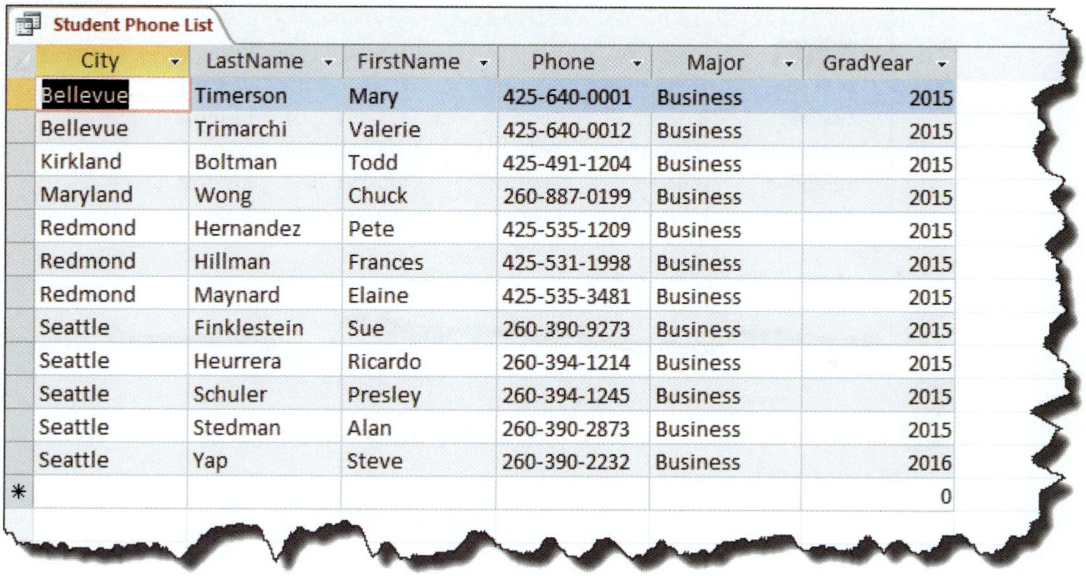

City	LastName	FirstName	Phone	Major	GradYear
Bellevue	Timerson	Mary	425-640-0001	Business	2015
Bellevue	Trimarchi	Valerie	425-640-0012	Business	2015
Kirkland	Boltman	Todd	425-491-1204	Business	2015
Maryland	Wong	Chuck	260-887-0199	Business	2015
Redmond	Hernandez	Pete	425-535-1209	Business	2015
Redmond	Hillman	Frances	425-531-1998	Business	2015
Redmond	Maynard	Elaine	425-535-3481	Business	2015
Seattle	Finklestein	Sue	260-390-9273	Business	2015
Seattle	Heurrera	Ricardo	260-394-1214	Business	2015
Seattle	Schuler	Presley	260-394-1245	Business	2015
Seattle	Stedman	Alan	260-390-2873	Business	2015
Seattle	Yap	Steve	260-390-2232	Business	2016
*					0

Student Phone List

7 Return to Design view to continue modifying the query object.

8 To further limit the display to only those students who live in the 425 area code:

CLICK in the Criteria text box in the "Phone" column.

TYPE **Like "425*"**.

PRESS `Tab`.

(*Note:* Using the "*" wildcard tells Access to ignore the remaining characters after the "425" area code portion of the field contents. Your query Design grid should now appear similar to the one shown in Figure AC2.29.)

FIGURE AC2.29   Entering criteria in the query Design grid

Field:	City	LastName	FirstName	Phone	Major	GradYear	
Table:	Students	Students	Students	Students	Students	Students	
Sort:	Ascending	Ascending					
Show:	☑	☑	☑	☑	☑	☑	☐
Criteria:				Like "425*"	"Business"	>2014	
or:							

9 To save and then run the query:

CLICK the Save button (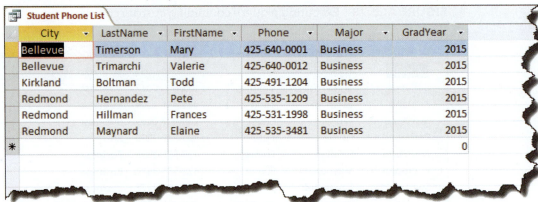) on the Quick Access toolbar.

CLICK the Run command in the Results group on the DESIGN tab.
(*Result:* The results from the query are displayed in Figure AC2.30.)

FIGURE AC2.30   Final query results

Student Phone List

City	LastName	FirstName	Phone	Major	GradYear
Bellevue	Timerson	Mary	425-640-0001	Business	2015
Bellevue	Trimarchi	Valerie	425-640-0012	Business	2015
Kirkland	Boltman	Todd	425-491-1204	Business	2015
Redmond	Hernandez	Pete	425-535-1209	Business	2015
Redmond	Hillman	Frances	425-531-1998	Business	2015
Redmond	Maynard	Elaine	425-535-3481	Business	2015
*					0

10 Close the Datasheet window. If proceeding the next lesson, keep the database open.

Adding Simple Calculated Fields

LESSON OVERVIEW

A **calculated field** enables you to draw data from other field columns and perform a mathematical calculation on a row-by-row basis. Generally, if a value can be calculated for display, you should not store it permanently in the database. For example, you can multiply the contents of a Price field by a Quantity field to yield a result titled Amount. Rather than defining a field named Amount to store the calculation's result, this information may be calculated on the fly.

You can perform simple and complex calculations using calculated fields in queries. To create a calculated field, enter an **expression** into the "Field" row of the query Design grid. Expressions may contain table and field names (which are enclosed in square brackets), mathematical operators (+, −, /, and *), the comparison operators (< and >), logical operators (AND and OR), concatenate operator (&), and constants (True, False, and Null). There are two parts to an expression entered into the query Design grid: the name of the resulting field (e.g., Amount) and the expression itself. You separate the field name and expression using a colon. To further customize the resulting datasheet, you can hide the display of unnecessary fields by removing the ✓ from the check box in the "Show" row of the grid.

SKILLS PREVIEW

Create a calculated field in the query Design grid	• CLICK in an empty Field cell in the query Design grid. TYPE *field name: expression* for example, **Amount: [Price]*[Quantity]**.

PROJECT PRACTICE

1 Ensure that the **ac02b.accdb** is open and that no windows appear in the work area.

2 In this project practice, you will use calculated fields to combine each student's first and last name, and to calculate their GPA percent average. To begin:

CLICK the CREATE tab in the Ribbon.

CLICK the Query Design command in the Queries group.
(*Result:* The Show Table dialog box appears.)

3 To add the Students table to the Tables pane:

DOUBLE-CLICK the Students table.

CLICK the Close command button.

4 On your own, size the Students field list box and use the split bar to distribute the area evenly between the Tables pane and the Design grid.

5 Position the mouse pointer over the right-hand border line in the field header of the first column. When placed properly, the mouse pointer changes shape (⟷). To increase the width of the first field column, drag the border line to the right, as shown here, and then release the mouse button.

6 To create a calculated field that displays students' full names:

CLICK in the Field cell of the first column, if it is not already selected.

TYPE **Full Name: [FirstName]&" "&[LastName]**.

PRESS `Tab`.

(*Note:* Field names from the Students table object must appear within square brackets. Also, notice that the ampersand symbol is used to join an empty string (blank space) between students' first names and last names.)

7 To add the GPA field to the grid:

DOUBLE-CLICK the GPA field in the Students field list.

8 Save the query before proceeding:

CLICK the Save button (🖫) on the Quick Access toolbar.

TYPE **GPA Calculations**.

PRESS `Enter`.

9 To execute the query:

CLICK the Run command in the Results group on the DESIGN tab.

10 On your own, increase the width of the "Full Name" field column, so it appears similar to Figure AC2.31.

FIGURE AC2.31 Displaying the results of a calculated field

Full Name	GPA
Alan Stedman	3.25
Pete Hernandez	3.75
Judy Mohr	3.00
Diana Buggey	3.15
Casey Seinfeld	3.50
Sandra Alomar	3.00
Rosa Fernandez	2.75
Bob Peters	2.95
Sandy Rinaldo	3.15
Sue Finklestein	3.75
Bruce Mortimer	3.50
Chris Jung	3.00
Benji Abu-Alba	3.75
Gretta Stockton	3.25
Eric Sakic	3.15
Joey Modano	2.85
Mike Francis	2.95

Rather than appearing in two separate columns, the student names now appear in a single calculated column.

11 Return to Design view to continue modifying the query object.

12 As before, increase the width of the third column in the Design grid. Now enter a formula to calculate the GPA percent average by dividing the GPA by a perfect score of 4.0. To begin:

CLICK in the Field cell of the third column, if it is not already selected.

TYPE **GPA Percent: [GPA]/4**.

PRESS `Enter`.

13 Run the query.

14 To format the results of this new calculated field as a percentage value:

Switch back to Design view and then CLICK the Property Sheet command (🗒) in the Show/Hide group on the DESIGN tab to display the Property Sheet pane.

CLICK in the text box for the "Format" row (in the Property Sheet pane).

SELECT Percent from the drop-down list box.

CLICK in the text box for the "Decimal Places" row.

SELECT 1 from the drop-down list box.
(*Result*: The query Design window should now appear similar to Figure AC2.32.)

FIGURE AC2.32   Entering calculated fields in the query Design grid

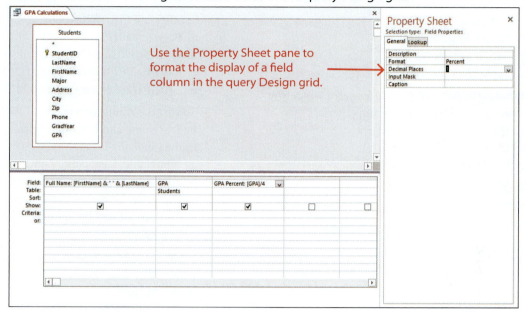

15 To save and then run the query:

CLICK the Save button (💾) on the Quick Access toolbar.

CLICK the Run command in the Results group on the DESIGN tab.
(*Result*: The results from the query are displayed in Figure AC2.33.)

FIGURE AC2.33   Final query results

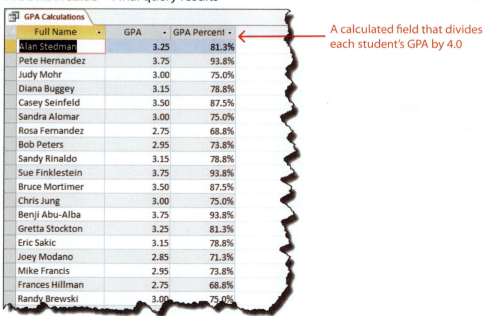

16 Close the GPA Calculations Datasheet window. Then, exit Microsoft Access.

MULTIPLE-CHOICE QUIZ

Select the best choice in the following questions for review of the project concepts. Good luck!

1. What is the name of the Access tool that simplifies the process of creating a query object?
   a. Database Filter Wizard
   b. Simple Filter Wizard
   c. Simple Query Wizard
   d. Table Query Wizard

2. What is the name of the window area where you build query objects by entering criteria?
   a. Query Design worksheet
   b. Query Design grid
   c. Query Design table
   d. Query Design datasheet

3. What is the most common type of query you build using query Design view?
   a. Append query
   b. Search query
   c. Select query
   d. Update query

4. To answer the question "Which employees earn more than $50,000 annually?" you use what type of query?
   a. Append query
   b. Search query
   c. Select query
   d. Update query

5. To compute employees' annual bonuses as a percentage of salary, you could use what type of field in a query?
   a. Compensation
   b. Calculated
   c. Conditional
   d. Logical

6. To list all of the company names ending with "Inc." type the following into the appropriate *Criteria* text box:
   a. *inc.
   b. "*inc."
   c. Like "*inc."
   d. All of these are correct.

7. To list all of the records entered between January 1 and March 31, 2013, type the following into the appropriate *Criteria* text box:
   a. Between #01/01/2013# And #03/31/2013#
   b. From #01/01/2013# To #03/31/2013#
   c. <#01/01/2013# And >#03/31/2013#
   d. >#01/01/2013# Or <#03/31/2013#

8. To sort the results of a query by ZipCode and then by LastName and FirstName, place the field columns in the following order:
   a. FirstName, LastName, ZipCode
   b. ZipCode, LastName, FirstName
   c. ZipCode, FirstName, LastName
   d. You cannot sort by multiple field columns.

9. Which of the following criterion retrieves all of the records that have a blank value in the field column?
   a. Is Null
   b. Is Not Null
   c. Is Empty
   d. Is Blank

10. In a calculated field, what is the portion of the expression that appears to the left of the colon?
    a. The expression to be evaluated
    b. The name of the field and column
    c. The name of an existing field in the table
    d. A placeholder for a field stored in the table

HANDS-ON EXERCISE: WORK IT OUT AC-2B-E1

In this exercise, you will practice using the Simple Query Wizard to retrieve specific field information from a table. You then will add a calculated field to the query to introduce a price increase. The final datasheet result is shown in Figure AC2.34.

FIGURE AC2.34   Work It Out AC-2B-E1: completed

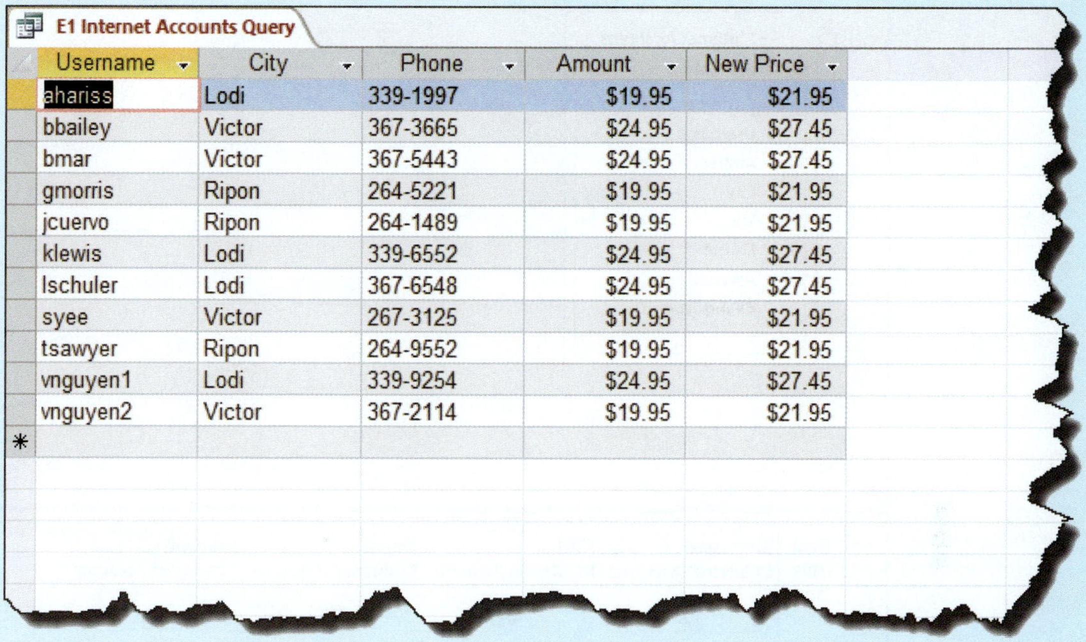

Username	City	Phone	Amount	New Price
ahariss	Lodi	339-1997	$19.95	$21.95
bbailey	Victor	367-3665	$24.95	$27.45
bmar	Victor	367-5443	$24.95	$27.45
gmorris	Ripon	264-5221	$19.95	$21.95
jcuervo	Ripon	264-1489	$19.95	$21.95
klewis	Lodi	339-6552	$24.95	$27.45
lschuler	Lodi	367-6548	$24.95	$27.45
syee	Victor	267-3125	$19.95	$21.95
tsawyer	Ripon	264-9552	$19.95	$21.95
vnguyen1	Lodi	339-9254	$24.95	$27.45
vnguyen2	Victor	367-2114	$19.95	$21.95

1 After launching Microsoft Access, open the exercise data file **ac02b-ex.accdb**.

2 Launch the Query Wizard using the CREATE tab on the Ribbon.

3 Select the Simple Query Wizard and ensure that "Table: E1 Internet Accounts" is selected.

4 Add the following fields to the query: Username, City, Phone, and Amount.

5 In the next step of the wizard, accept the default selection for a detail query type and then proceed to the next screen.

6 In the final step, accept the default title "E1 Internet Accounts Query" and choose to "Modify the query design" before clicking the Finish command button. (*Result:* Your screen should now appear similar to Figure AC2.35.)

FIGURE AC2.35 Displaying the query Design window

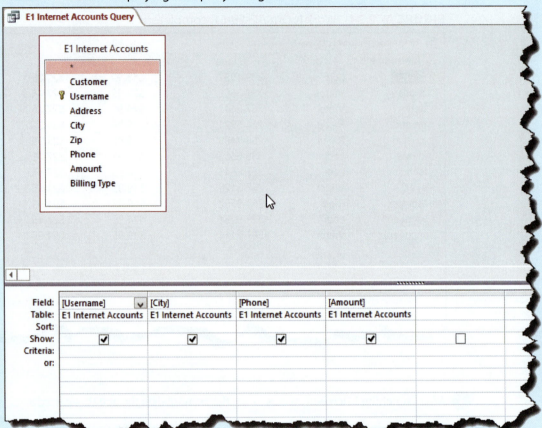

7 In the fifth column of the Design grid, just to the right of [Amount], enter a calculated field named "New Price" that computes a 10% increase in the amount charged. (*Hint:* Enter the formula expression as **New Price: [Amount]*1.10** into the text box of the "Field" row.)

8 Run the query.

9 In the Property Sheet pane for the new calculated field, select the currency format.

10 Save and then run the query. (*Result:* Your screen should now appear similar to Figure AC2.34.)

11 Close the Datasheet window. Then, close the database file, unless you are proceeding to the next exercise.

HANDS-ON EXERCISE: WORK IT OUT AC-2B-E2

You will now practice sorting a datasheet, entering criteria statements, and using AND and OR logic. The final result is shown in Figure AC2.36.

FIGURE AC2.36 Work It Out AC-2B-E2: completed

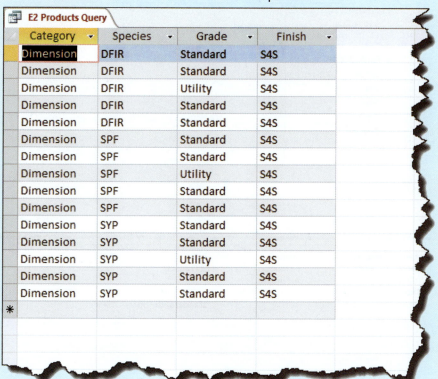

① Open the exercise data file **ac02b-ex.accdb**, if it is not already open in Access.

② Create a new query using query Design view. Using the Show Table dialog box, add the E2 Products table to the Table pane of the query Design window.

③ On your own, adjust the size and placement of the table's field list and the shared area between the Table pane and query Design grid.

④ Add the following fields to the Design grid: Category, Species, Grade, and Finish.

⑤ Sort the query's results so that the records are listed in alphabetical order by Category and then by Species.

⑥ Save the query as **E2 Products Query** and then run the query to display its results in a Datasheet window. After checking your work, return to Design view.

⑦ Now limit the display of records to only those with "Standard" or "Utility" grades. Check your work in Datasheet view and then return to Design view.

8 Further limit the display of records to only those "Standard" and "Utility" grade products with an "S4S" finish (on both rows). (*Result:* Your screen should now appear similar to Figure AC2.37.)

FIGURE AC2.37 Building a Select query in query Design view

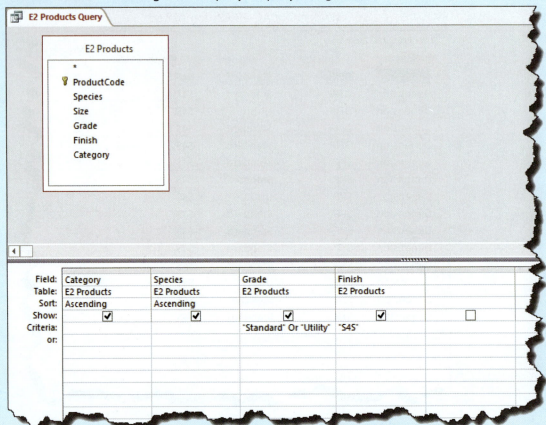

9 Save and then execute the query. (*Result:* Your screen should now appear similar to Figure AC2.36.)

10 Close the Datasheet window. Then, close the database file, unless you are proceeding to the next exercise.

In this exercise, you will practice concatenating or joining field information using calculated fields. The final result is shown in Figure AC2.38.

FIGURE **AC2.38** Work It Out AC-2B-E3: completed

Contact Info	Mailing Address
A.B. Coleman, Kids On Track	P.O. Box 645, Silverdale
Alberta Snyder, Silverdale Community Pow-Wow	P.O. Box 4531, Silverdale
Anelise Krause, Boy Scout Troop 16	4590 Pine Valley Circle, Silverdale
Art Sera/D. Robertson, Last Chance Recovery	P.O. Box 1020, Silverdale
Bill Convey, Convey, Bill	3014 Country Club Blvd., Silverdale
Bill Fuser, Lilliput Children's Svcs	130 E. Magnolia St., Silverdale
Bob Harley, Secty, St. Lukes Knights Of Colum.#4784	5815 Morgan Place #8, Silverdale
Brad Singer/P.Halligan, St. Joseph's Spirit Club	3240 Angel Dr., Silverdale
Bruce René, Boy Scout Troop 421	504 Curry Court, Manteca
Carl & Frau Nelson, Nelson, Carl - Golf Game	8323 Rothesay, Silverdale
Cherrie Newell, Bear Creek Athletic Boost.	9644 Apple Blossom Way, Silverdale
CHP: Larry Burlingame, Designated Driver Taskforce	3330 No. Ad Art Rd, Silverdale
Chris Mc Chaffers, Serra Club	3203 W. March Lane, Silverdale
Cindy Scott, No. Silverdale Rotary	5837 Morgan Pl. #81, Silverdale
Connie Wyman, Silverdale Police Youth Activ.	22 E. Market St., Silverdale
Dave Burley, Pinawa High Class Of '99	3 S. Pacific Ave, Pinawa
David Sandstorms, Sandstorms, Mary & David	3255 W Swain Rd., Silverdale
Debbie Hunt, Delta Valley Twins Group	P.O. Box 691316, Silverdale
Don Bryan, Sundance Running Club	14999 Comstock Road, Centerville
Dr. Mary Ann Cox, Library & Literacy Foundation	605 N. El Dorado St., Silverdale
Gary Giovanetti, Delta Rotary	318 E. Vine Street, Silverdale
Jackie Soupe, Pinawa B.P.W.	P.O. Box 2324, Pinawa
James Hulstrom, North Silverdale Rotary	555 W. Benjamin Holt Dr., Silverdale
Jan Moore, CookBook Coordinator	4565 Quail Lakes Dr. A-1, Silverdale

1 Open the exercise data file **ac02b-ex.accdb**, if it is not already open in Access.

2 Create a new query using query Design view and add the E3 Contacts table to the Table pane. On your own, adjust the size and placement of the query Design window and field list object.

3 In the query Design grid, enter a calculated field that concatenates or joins data from the Contact and Volunteer Group fields for display in the first column. The result should display as "Contact, Volunteer Group." To begin, increase the width of the first column in the Design grid and then enter the expression **Contact Info: [Contact] &", "& [Volunteer Group]**.

4 Using a similar process, join data from the Address and City fields for display in the second column of the Design grid. The result should display as "Address, City" and the column heading should read "Mailing Address."

5 Sort the query alphabetically by the Contact Info field.

6 Save the query as **E3 Contacts Mailing Query**. (*Result:* The query Design window should now appear similar to Figure AC2.39.)

FIGURE AC2.39 Concatenating fields in the Design grid

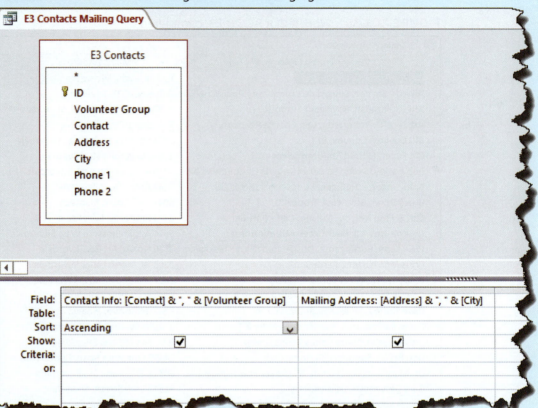

7 Run the query to display the Datasheet window.

8 Size the columns in the datasheet to display to their best-fit width. (*Result:* Your screen should now appear similar to Figure AC2.38.)

9 Close the Datasheet window and save the layout changes.

10 Close the database file and exit Microsoft Access.

Chapter Summary

One of the primary advantages of using a computerized database is the ability to manipulate, retrieve, and display information quickly and easily. Making your information pleasing to read requires the further ability to format and customize the results. Besides applying fonts, styles, and special effects to a datasheet window, you can move, hide, and freeze field columns. To help you turn raw data into information, the Sort, Find and Replace, and Filter commands enable you to organize, locate, and highlight records in a table. You can also use filters to limit the display of records in a table and use queries to ask questions of your database. In addition to being able to draw data from multiple tables, Access query objects enable you to specify complex search criteria, perform calculations, and aggregate data for summary reporting. Queries are arguably the most powerful database objects in Access.

Chapter Key Terms

Action query, p. A-80	Filter, p. A-62	Query Design grid, p. A-77
Append query, p. A-80	Filter By Form, p. A-65	Select query, p. A-74
Calculated field, p. A-87	Filter By Selection, p. A-62	Simple Query Wizard, p. A-74
Conditional statement, p. A-84	Make table query, p. A-80	Table pane, p. A-78
Crosstab query, p. A-80	Parameter query, p. A-80	Update query, p. A-80
Delete query, p. A-80	Query-by-example (QBE), p. A-77	Wildcard characters, p. A-58
Expression, p. A-87		

On Your Own AC-2C-E1

You will now create a query object using the Simple Query Wizard and then use filters to limit the display of records even further. The objective of using a query in this exercise is to display data from two tables in the database. Once you have completed these tasks, your screen should appear similar to Figure AC2.40.

FIGURE AC2.40 Displaying query results

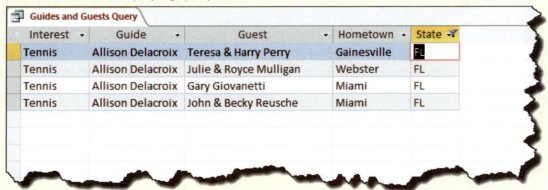

To begin, open the **ac02cp1.accdb** database file and then launch the Simple Query Wizard. From the Guides table, include the Guide field. From the Patrons table, include the Guest, Hometown, State, and Interest fields. In the next step of the wizard, save the query as "Guides and Guests Query" and then open the query to view the initial results.

Using query Design view, modify the query to display only those records where the State field is not empty (or Is Not Null). Move the "Interest" field column to the leftmost column in the Design grid and then choose ascending for its sort order. Your query Design grid should appear similar to Figure AC2.41.

FIGURE AC2.41   Displaying the Design grid

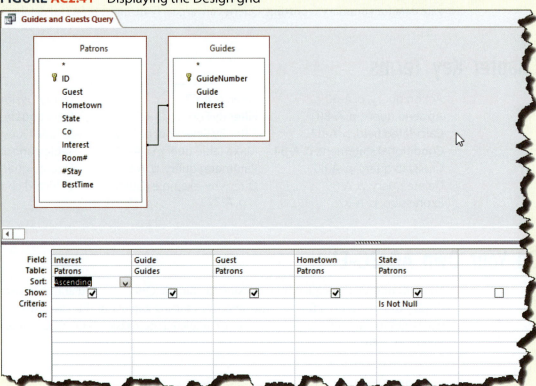

Save and then run the query to view the results. In the Datasheet window that appears, use the Filter By Selection method to filter the records displayed to only those guests who live in Florida (FL). Your screen should now appear similar to Figure AC2.40. When you are ready, close the Datasheet window and save any changes. Then close the database file. Exit Microsoft Access, unless you are proceeding to the next exercise.

On Your Own AC-2C-E2

To practice entering calculated expressions, you will now analyze the on-hand quantity, cost, and retail price data for an inventory listing. Open the **ac02cp2.accdb** database file to start. Once you complete the tasks appearing below, your screen should appear similar to Figure AC2.42.

FIGURE AC2.42 Displaying calculated fields

Description	Total Value	Profit Per Unit	Markup
0.5 mm pencil lead	$39.69	$0.76	155.10%
0.7 mm pencil lead	$22.88	$0.83	159.62%
1" Binder	$63.36	$1.27	64.14%
1.5" Binder	$29.37	$1.82	68.16%
2" Binder	$56.52	$1.85	58.92%
2" Deluxe Binder	$92.53	$1.12	23.00%
3" Binder	$236.60	$2.94	64.62%
Copy Paper - economy	$170.85	$2.44	95.69%
Copy Paper - legal	$184.22	$3.47	114.90%
Copy Paper - regular	$95.04	$3.11	107.99%
Deluxe Disposable Pen - black	$38.76	$0.81	119.12%
Deluxe Disposable Pen - blue	$21.76	$0.81	119.12%
Deluxe mech pencil	$59.66	$0.92	58.60%
Disposable Pen - black	$10.81	$0.52	110.64%
Disposable Pen - blue	$113.27	$0.52	110.64%
Disposable Pen - blue, fine	$76.61	$0.52	110.64%
Disposable Pen - red	$69.56	$0.52	110.64%
Disposable Pen - red, fine	$35.25	$0.52	110.64%
Dividers - clear tab	$46.55	$0.54	56.84%
Dividers - colored tab	$43.70	$0.54	56.84%
Economy mech pencil	$37.96	$0.47	90.38%
Elastic - medium	$28.77	$0.62	45.26%
Elastic - narrow	$79.54	$0.52	53.61%

Complete the following tasks to reproduce the Datasheet results shown in Figure AC2.42.

- Create a new query object in Design view based on the Inventory table.
- Add the Description field to the first column of the Design grid and then specify an ascending sort order for the field column.
- To display the inventory value for each product, create a calculated field named "Total Value" that multiplies together the [OnHand] and [Cost] fields.
- To display the potential profit earned per product, create a second calculated field named "Profit Per Unit" that subtracts [Cost] from [Retail].
- To display the markup percentage, create a third calculated field named "Markup" that computes the following expression: ([Retail]−[Cost])/[Cost].
- Format the Markup field to display using a Percent format.

Save the query as "Inventory Analysis Query" and then run the query to display its Datasheet window. Adjust the column widths so that your screen appears similar to Figure AC2.42. Lastly, close the Datasheet window and save the layout changes. Once you finish, close the database file and exit Microsoft Access.

Presenting and Managing Data

This chapter introduces you to four Access tools that allow for efficient presentation and management of data. These tools are form creation, tool creation, working with database objects, and management of the database. The chapter also presents a practical use of reports with the creation of a mailing labels report.

In an earlier chapter, you learned a technique to add records to a database. In this chapter, you will create forms to make adding records to a database easier. Create forms with the **Form wizard** and learn how to use the Form button. Both techniques perform the same action. You will edit the form in the **Form Layout view** and **Design view** and modify Form controls.

Similarly, in an Excel chapter, you use basic techniques to create reports. Chapter 3 expands on this knowledge with the **Report wizard**. Modify reports in the **Report Layout view** and Design view and edit Form controls. Prepare a mailing labels report as a practical application of the Report function.

The final portion of the chapter addresses working with database objects. Remember that database objects are such things as tables, reports, forms, and queries. Finally, you will examine management of a database, including how to compact and repair a database.

PROJECT

Presenting and Managing a College Database

In this chapter's projects, you will use Microsoft Access 2013 to create forms and reports from a college database. Both the forms and the reports are created using a wizard and modified using two different views. The correct use depends on the complexity of the data needed.

The final portion of the chapter addresses a practical application of the report creation process, working with database objects. You will also use database management techniques to compact and repair the database.

THE SITUATION

Work-Study Statistical Assignment

As part of your ongoing duties in the Registrar's Office at Ridgemont College, you are asked to work with the school's database to easily add records to existing data tables. Your supervisor also asks you to apply your Microsoft Access skills to create reports, in general, and to create a mailing labels report from the student data stored in the database. Finally, the supervisor noticed some anomalies in the database. Your experience with Access indicates that the database needs to be compacted and repaired.

Working with Forms and Tables in a College Database

In this project, you will use college data to simplify adding records to the student database. You will create and use forms from the college student database and create simple reports. Finally, your supervisor asks you to take over management of the database, so you will compact the database and repair it.

PROJECT FILE: *Available at* **www.mhhe.com/office2013projectlearn**

PROJECT OBJECTIVES

After completing this project, you will be able to:

- Create a simple form using the Form wizard.

- Use both Form Layout view and Design view to modify, align, and size Form controls.

- Create and print simple reports using the Report wizard.

- Use both Report Layout view and Design view to modify, align, and size Report controls.

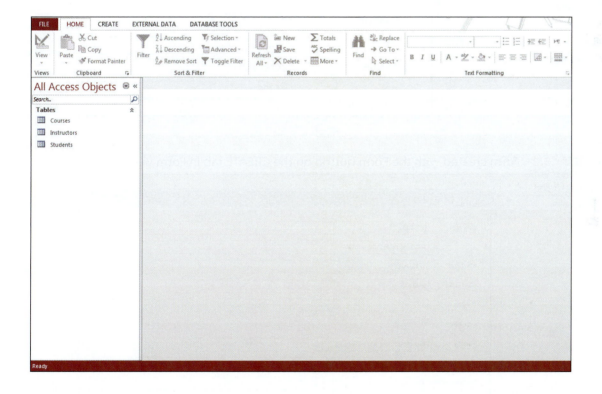

Creating and Using a Simple Form

LESSON OVERVIEW

As mentioned earlier, an Access user can add or modify information in a table just by opening the table in Datasheet view and adding the record at the bottom of the table or, to modify the table, click the cell to modify and make the necessary changes. While this works well in small databases, a user often wants to perform the same actions in a larger database.

In this lesson, you will use the Form wizard to create a simple form to add information to a table. Note that the Form button also performs the same function. Refer to Figures AC3.1 and AC3.2.

FIGURE AC3.1   Form created with Form wizard shown in Form view

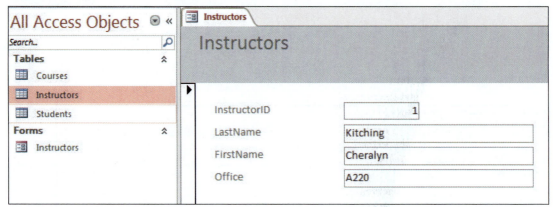

FIGURE AC3.2   Form created with the Form button on the CREATE tab in Form view

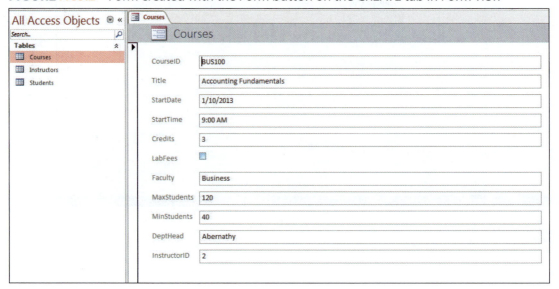

Create a form using the Form wizard	• CLICK the Form wizard button in the Forms group on the CREATE tab. SELECT the Table (or Query) from the Table/Queries list the form is based on. ADD the fields to include in the form to Selected Fields. CLICK Next. SELECT the most appropriate layout and then CLICK Next. ENTER a name for the form and indicate the view to display. CLICK Finish.
Create a form using the Form button	• CLICK the table the form is to be based on in the Tables bar of the Navigation pane. CLICK the CREATE tab and locate the Forms group. SELECT the appropriate form button to create the form. (The Form Wizard is also available here.)

PROJECT PRACTICE

1. Locate and open the project data file **ac03a.accdb**. Notice there is no Save command until you add another piece to the database.

2. Create a form to enter new data into the students table.

3. CLICK the Form Wizard button to display the Form Wizard dialog box as shown in Figure AC3.3.

FIGURE AC3.3 Form Wizard dialog box

4 SELECT Table: Students from the Tables/Queries drop-down list.

ADD all the fields from the Available Fields to the Selected Fields by CLICKING the [>] button. (*Result:* The Form Wizard dialog box should appear as shown in Figure AC3.4.)

FIGURE AC3.4 Form Wizard dialog box with fields selected

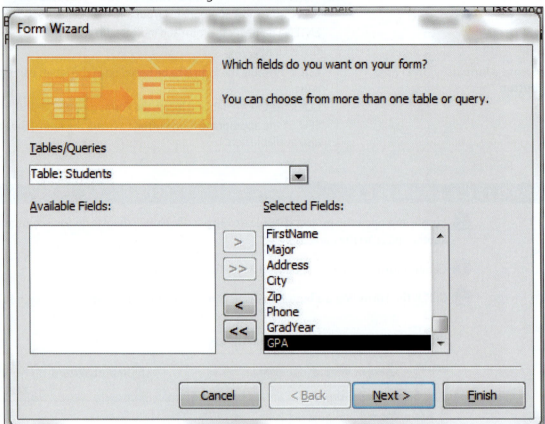

5 CLICK Next and SELECT the best layout for your form.

Clicking the different radio buttons shows a preview of the format of the form.

6 Generally forms use the Columnar format.

CLICK Next.

TYPE a name for the form in the title box.

SELECT the option to open the form. (*Result:* The Form window should now appear as shown in Figure AC3. 5.)

7 CLICK Finish and the completed form appears in Form view as shown in Figure AC3.5.

FIGURE AC3.5 Completed form in Form view

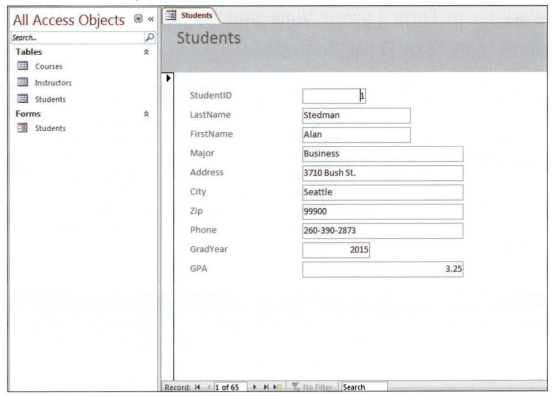

8 ENTER a new record.

CLICK the New (blank) Record button (▶※).

TYPE the following information for the new record:

Student ID: No typing—the ID is automatically generated

LastName: **Smith**

FirstName: **Joe**

Major: **Science**

Address: **62 Wistful Vista**

City: **Seattle**

Zip: **99900**

Phone: **260-390-9876**

GradYear: **2015**

GPA: **3.15**

9 Close the Students form window to enter the new record and save the database. Keep the **ac03a.accdb** database open to proceed to the next lesson.

Working in Form Layout View and Design View to Modify, Align, and Size Form Controls

LESSON OVERVIEW

When the Access user created the form using the Form wizard, it created a very basic form. In this lesson, you will use the Form Layout view and Design view to modify parts of the form, change the alignment of some Form controls, and change the size of other form controls. You will apply Themes, Theme Colors, and Theme Fonts.

Your goal, when making Form control modifications, is to make the form easier to use and more interactive. The basic form created allows addition and modification of records as the user scrolls down a columnar list. When you change the appearance of the form, it not only makes the form more attractive but also makes it more user-friendly.

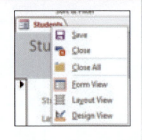

SKILLS PREVIEW

Format the form	• OPEN the form, RIGHT-CLICK the FORM tab, and SELECT Layout view.
	CLICK the Themes button in the Themes group on the DESIGN tab under Form Layout Tools.
	To assign a background color to the form:
	CLICK the Back Color button from the ALL tab on the Property sheet and select an appropriate background color.
Modify a control	• OPEN the form, RIGHT-CLICK the FORM tab, and SELECT Design view.
	CLICK the appropriate Form control, either in the Label section or the Text Box section.
	To resize the control:
	CLICK the control and use the sizing handles to resize the control.
	To remove a control:
	CLICK the control and press Delete.
	To edit a control:
	CLICK the control and place the insertion in the area to modify.
	Use any of the standard Text control devices to modify the control.
	To modify a control:
	CLICK the control and use the four-headed pointer to move the control to the desired location.

PROJECT PRACTICE

1. Ensure the **ac03a.accdb** file is open in Access.

2. The first task is to format the Students form.
   DOUBLE-CLICK the Students form to open it.
   CLICK Layout view from the View button in the Views group on the HOME tab.
   CLICK the Themes button in the Themes group on the DESIGN tab under Form Layout Tools.
   (*Result:* The Themes palette is shown in Figure AC3.6.)

FIGURE AC3.6   Themes palette

3 SELECT Ion Boardroom (the first theme on the left in the second row under Office). The form with the theme applied is shown in Figure AC3.7.

FIGURE AC3.7   Form with theme applied

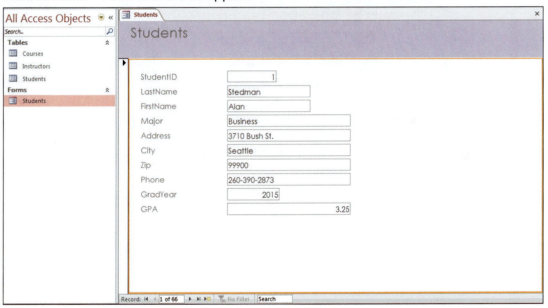

4 Insert a background color on the form.

CLICK in the white space of the form before opening the Property Sheet.

Open the Property Sheet.

CLICK the ⊡ button in the Back Color of the ALL tab on the Property Sheet (found in the Tools group of the DESIGN tab under Form Layout Tools).

(*Result:* This opens the color palette for Background Colors, as shown in Figure AC3.8.)

FIGURE AC3.8 Color palette for Background colors

CLICK Lavender, Accent 5, Lighter 80% under Lavender in the Theme Colors (first color down).

Close the Property sheet.

(*Result:* The form appears as shown in Figure AC3.9.)

FIGURE AC3.9 Form with background color

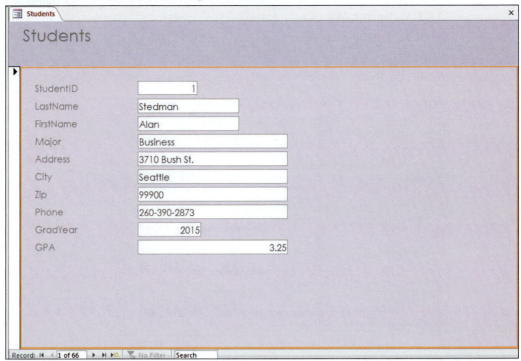

5 You can modify, align, and size Form controls. (It is also possible to delete Form controls, but you should take extreme care before you delete controls as the action can affect the database as well as the form.)

To modify a Form control:

RIGHT-CLICK the STUDENTS tab and SELECT Design View.

The form in Design view appears as shown in Figure AC3.10.

FIGURE AC3.10 Form in Design view

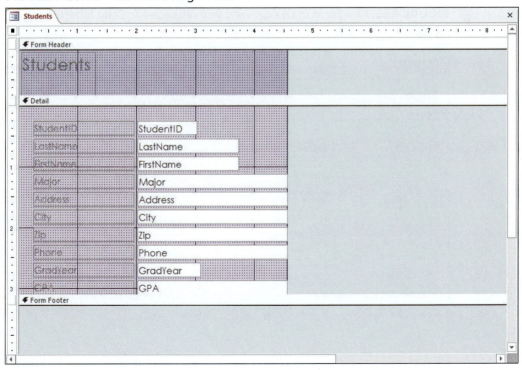

SELECT all Control labels by CLICKING StudentID and then holding the **Shift** key and CLICKING the rest of the Control labels.

CLICK Bold in the Text Formatting section of the HOME tab.

CHANGE the font to Arial 12.

(*Result:* The form in Design view with changes appears as shown in Figure AC3.11.)

FIGURE AC3.11   Form in Design view with changes made

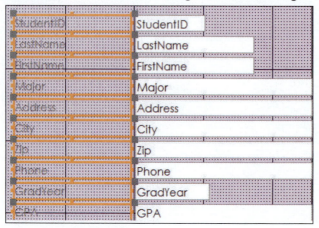

6 Some of the text boxes on the form are too big for efficient data entry. Select all the labels, RIGHT-CLICK and CHOOSE Size to fit. The form should appear as shown in Figure AC3.12 after resizing the following labels:

StudentID

Major

Zip

GPA

Use the same technique to resize the labels as shown. The form width may vary depending on your computer settings.

FIGURE AC3.12   Form in Design view with changes to Data labels made

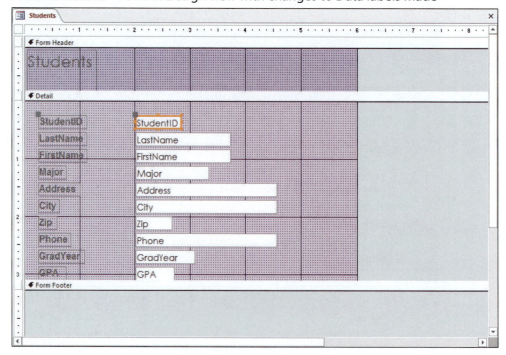

7 The final task in this lesson is to move and align the Form controls to make the form more user-friendly.

CLICK Design view, if necessary, in the Students form drop-down list as seen above.

SELECT all Control text boxes by CLICKING StudentID and then holding the **Shift** key and CLICKING the rest of the Text Box labels.

CLICK the Align button on the **ARRANGE** tab, then CLICK Left.
(*Result:* The form in Design view appears as shown in Figure AC3.13.)

FIGURE AC3.13   Completed form in Design view

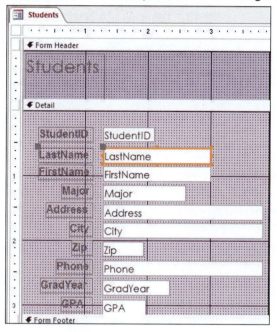

The completed form appears as shown in Figure AC3.14.

FIGURE AC3.14   Final form

8 Close and save the Students form. Keep the **ac03a.accdb** database open to proceed to the next lesson.

Creating and Printing a Simple Report

LESSON OVERVIEW

In an earlier chapter, you created a simple report using Access data. However, Access users and those viewing Access reports often need to create and manipulate reports that are more complex and therefore use the actual Report creation tools.

In this lesson, you will create a simple report to show information from a table using the Report wizard, as shown in Figure AC3.15. You will also use the Table button in the Tables group of the CREATE tab to create a table, as shown in Figure AC3.16. You will then print the report.

FIGURE AC3.15   Report created with Report wizard shown in Report view

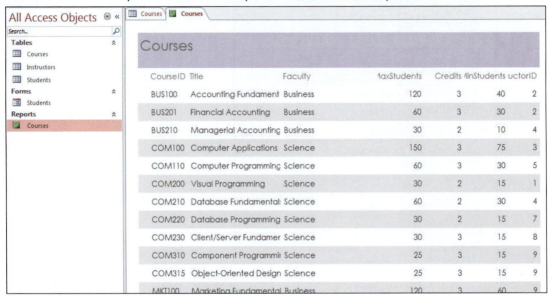

FIGURE AC3.16   Report created with the Report button shown in Report view

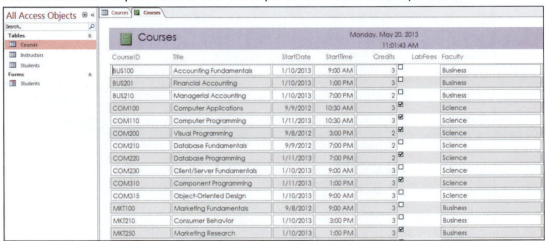

Create a report using the Report wizard	• CLICK the CREATE tab. CLICK the  button in the Reports group. CLICK the list arrow to choose the table on which to base the report and then CLICK the appropriate table. ADD the fields to include in the form to the Selected Fields. CLICK Next. SPECIFY groupings of records if necessary and CLICK Next. SPECIFY the order of the records and CLICK Next. SELECT the layout for the report and CLICK Next. Name your report and CLICK Finish.
Create a report using the Report button	• CLICK the table in the Tables bar of the Navigation pane on which to base the report. CLICK the CREATE tab. CLICK the Report button in the Reports group. CLICK the Save button, name the report, and CLICK OK.
Print a report	• Go to Backstage view, CLICK Print, and CLICK Print Preview. SELECT the appropriate setting for the printed report. CLICK the Print button, prepare the necessary settings, and CLICK OK to print the report.

PROJECT PRACTICE

1 In this lesson, you will create and print a report in Access. Ensure that the file **ac03a.accdb** is open in Access.

Create a report using the Report wizard.

CLICK the CREATE tab and then the [Report Wizard] button in the Reports group.

SELECT Table: Courses from the Table/Queries drop-down list.

ADD the following fields to include in the report to the Selected Fields list:

    CourseID

    Title

    Credits

    Faculty

CLICK Next.

Specify groupings of records if necessary. In this case, none are selected.

CLICK Next.

Select CourseID as the only sort criteria for data in the report.

CLICK Next.

CLICK the appropriate radio button to select Tabular for the layout for the report and Landscape as the orientation.

CLICK Next.

Name your report "Courses."

CLICK Finish.

(*Result:* The completed report should appear as shown in Figure AC3.17.)

FIGURE AC3.17 Report created using the Report wizard

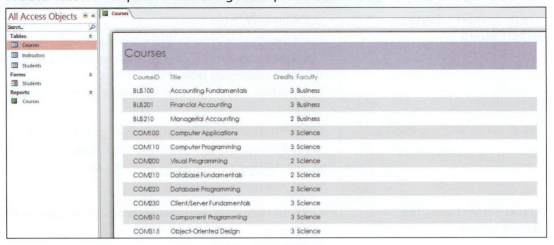

2 Print the report.

Notice that when the report finishes using the Report wizard, it appears in Print Preview view, as shown in Figure AC3.18.

FIGURE AC3.18 Report created using the Report wizard shown in Print Preview view

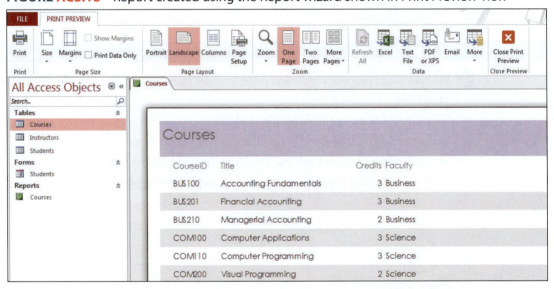

CLICK the Portrait button in the Page Layout group to change the page orientation.

CLICK the Page Setup button in the Page Layout group to open the Page Setup dialog box (see Figure AC3.19).

FIGURE AC3.19 Page Setup dialog box

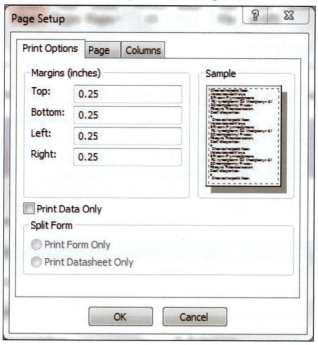

Ensure that the Page Setup settings are the same as Figure AC-3.19.

If you are to turn in a printed copy, CLICK the Print button, change the settings for your printer, and print the report.

CLOSE and save the COURSE report.

Working in Report Layout View and Design View to Modify, Align, and Size Report Controls

LESSON OVERVIEW

Using the Report wizard created a very basic report. In this lesson, you will use the Report Layout view and Design view to modify parts of the report, change the alignment of some Report controls, and change the size of other Report controls.

When making Report control modifications, your goal is to make the report more attractive and to present the data in the most understandable way. Changing the appearance of the report can not only make the report more attractive but also make it more user-friendly.

SKILLS PREVIEW

Change the Report view	• RIGHT-CLICK the Courses report tab. CLICK the desired view.
Modify a control	• OPEN the report and RIGHT-CLICK Design view. CLICK the appropriate Report control, either in the Label section or the Text Box section. To resize the control: CLICK the control and use the sizing handles to resize the control. To remove a control: CLICK the control and press Delete . To edit a control: CLICK the control and place the insertion point in the area to modify. Use any of the standard text control devices to modify the control. To modify a control: CLICK the control and use the four-headed pointer to move the control to the desired location.

PROJECT PRACTICE

1 Ensure that the ac03a.accdb file is open in Access.

2 Modify a Report control.

DOUBLE-CLICK the Courses report to open it.

RIGHT-CLICK the COURSE INFORMATION tab.

CLICK the report's Layout view.

CLICK twice on the CourseID label and change the title to "ID."

SELECT the words in the label.

TYPE ID

RIGHT-CLICK the COURSE INFORMATION tab.

CLICK Report view.

(*Result:* Your report should appear as shown in Figure AC3.20.)

FIGURE AC3.20 Modification of a Report control

Courses

Courses

ID	Title	Credits	Faculty
BUS100	Accounting Fundamentals	3	Business
BUS201	Financial Accounting	3	Business
BUS210	Managerial Accounting	2	Business
COM100	Computer Applications	3	Science
COM110	Computer Programming	3	Science
COM200	Visual Programming	2	Science
COM210	Database Fundamentals	2	Science

3 Align and size Report controls in Design view.

RIGHT-CLICK the COURSES tab.

CLICK Design view.

The report should appear as shown in Figure AC3.21.

FIGURE AC3.21 Report shown in Design view

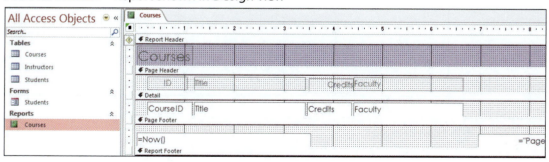

Resize the fields in the Page Header as shown in Figure AC3.22.

FIGURE AC3.22 Report shown in Design view with resized fields

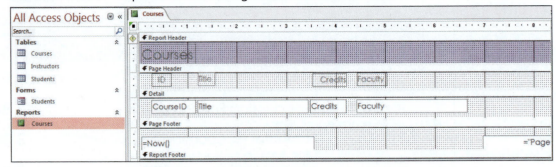

RIGHT-CLICK the COURSES tab.

CLICK Report Layout view.

CLICK the ID label.

SELECT the text.

CLICK the Bold button in the Text Formatting group of the HOME tab.

Repeat the process for each label.
(*Result:* The completed report should appear as shown in Figure AC3.23.)

FIGURE AC3.23 Completed report

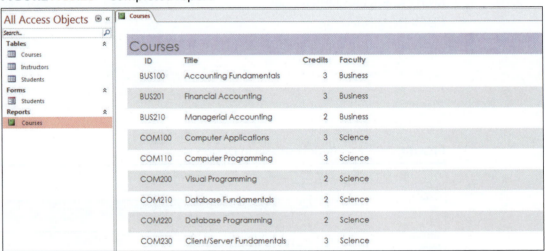

4 Save the report.

MULTIPLE-CHOICE QUIZ

Select the best choice in the following questions to review the project concepts

1. What is a feature of Access 2013 that takes the user through the steps of a process?
   a. Button
   b. Wizard
   c. Pull-down menu
   d. Task pane

2. When creating a form using the Form wizard, which type of layout vertically arranges data to the left of the field data with a field label?
   a. Justified
   b. Stacked
   c. Columnar
   d. Tabular

3. How do Microsoft Access forms relate to a data table?
   a. Contingent on
   b. Independent of
   c. Reliant on
   d. Dependent on

4. What determines how data is displayed in a form?
   a. Tab order
   b. Design styles
   c. Controls
   d. Layouts

5. Which report layout allows the Access user to view the data in the report and also modify the report design?
   a. Layout view
   b. Print Preview view
   c. Report view
   d. Design view

6. Which tab contains the Report Wizard button?
   a. HOME
   b. CREATE
   c. REPORTS
   d. FORMAT

7. Which of the following techniques is NOT a view available for a report?
   a. Design
   b. Report
   c. Layout
   d. Forms

8. What key allows an Access user to select all control objects in Layout view?
   a. Ctrl
   b. Alt
   c. Shift
   d. Insert

9. What view does a form display in if the form is created using the Form button?
   a. Print Preview
   b. Layout
   c. Design
   d. Form

10. What is the simplest way to create a form?
    a. Form wizard
    b. Form button
    c. Form design
    d. Blank form

In this exercise, you will work in Microsoft Access to create simple data entry forms in a couple of views to modify, align, and size Form controls. In the second portion of the exercise, you will create and print a simple report and work in Design view to modify, align, and size Report controls.

1 Locate and open the exercise data file **ac03a-ex1.accdb**.

2 Open the E3 Contacts table. Create a form using the Form wizard based on data from the E3 Contacts table. The form should be columnar and titled "Contacts Form."

3 Add a record with the following information:

ID: (Leave blank: the ID will be automatically added.)

Volunteer Group: **Silverdale Lions**

Contact: **Lee Lyons**

Address: **72 Whipple St**

City: **Silverdale**

Phone1: **478-1645**

Phone2: **577-7838**

4 Work in either Design or Form Layout view to resize the Form controls and add both a theme and a background color to the form.

5 Change the font on all controls on the form to bold.

6 The form should appear as shown in Figure AC3.24.

FIGURE AC3.24 Work It Out AC-3A-E1: form

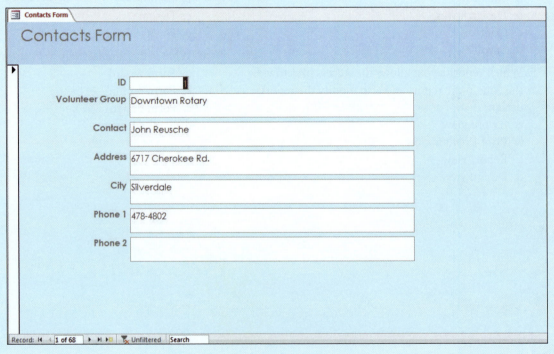

7 Create a report using the Report wizard. Base the report on the E2 Products table and include the following fields:

>   ProductCode
>   Species
>   Finish
>   Category

Sort the report on Species and make it a tabular report.

8 Change the name of the report to "Products."

9 Bold the items in the Page Header and space them as shown in the sample report in Figure AC3.25.

10 Use Print Preview to set the printing parameters as your instructor requires and print the report as needed.

FIGURE AC3.25   Work It Out AC-3A-E1: completed

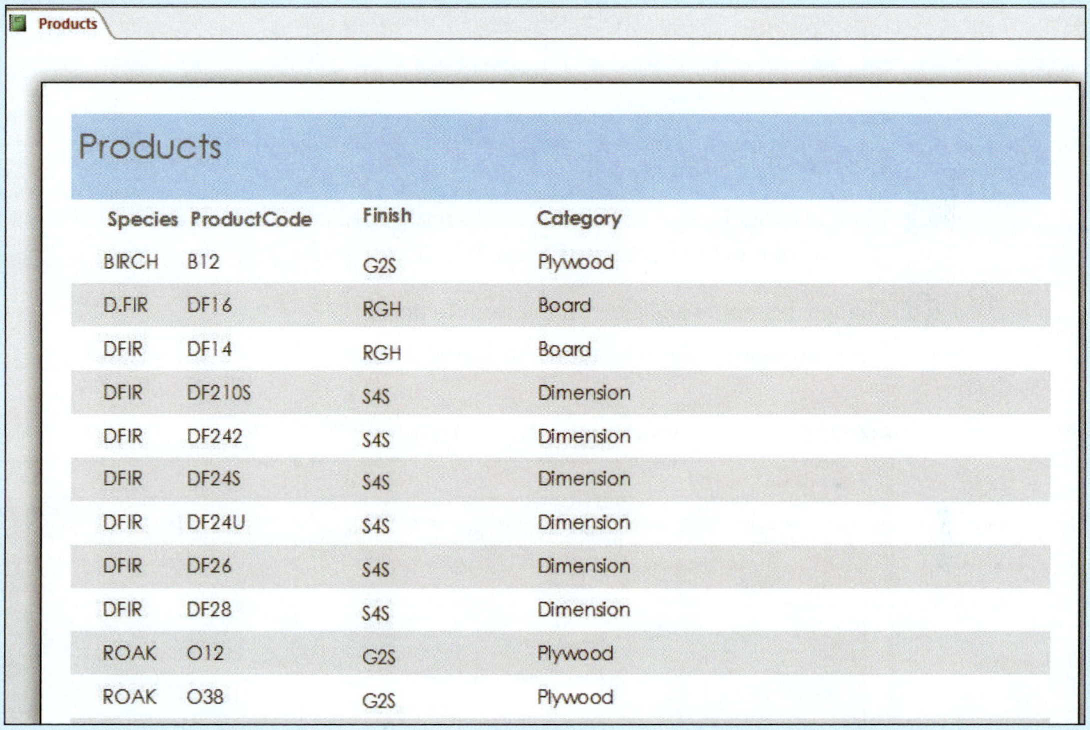

Species	ProductCode	Finish	Category
BIRCH	B12	G2S	Plywood
D.FIR	DF16	RGH	Board
DFIR	DF14	RGH	Board
DFIR	DF210S	S4S	Dimension
DFIR	DF242	S4S	Dimension
DFIR	DF24S	S4S	Dimension
DFIR	DF24U	S4S	Dimension
DFIR	DF26	S4S	Dimension
DFIR	DF28	S4S	Dimension
ROAK	O12	G2S	Plywood
ROAK	O38	G2S	Plywood

11 Save and close the database file.

In this exercise, you will work with a report. You will use an Access database to create simple data entry forms and use a couple of views to modify, align, and size Form controls. In the second portion of the exercise, you will create and print a simple report and work in Design view to modify, align, and size Report controls.

1 Locate and open the exercise data file **ac03a-ex2.accdb**.

2 Open the Patrons table and create a form using the Form wizard, adding patrons to the table. The form should be columnar. Insert the title as "New Patrons."

3 Add a record with the following information:

ID: (Leave blank: the ID will be automatically added.)

Guest: **Jack & Fran Tepsky**

Hometown: **Pittsburgh**

State: **PA**

Co: **US**

Interest: **Golf**

Room#: **D156**

#Stay: **3**

BestTime: **11:00 AM**

4 Work in either Design or Layout view to resize the Form controls and add both a theme and a background color to the form. Use Figure AC3.26 as a guide.

5 Change the font of all labels on the form to bold.

The form should appear as shown in Figure AC3.26.

FIGURE AC3.26 Work It Out AC-3A-E2: form

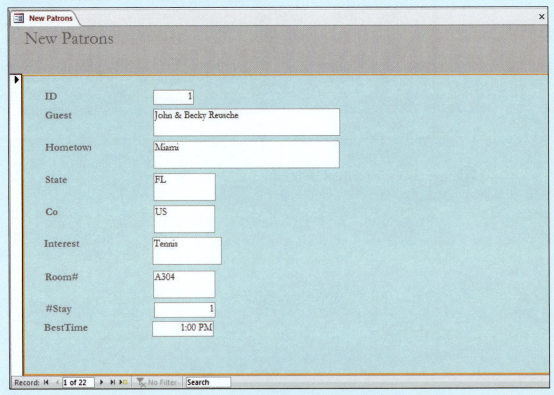

6 Create a report using the Report wizard. Base the report on the Guides table and include the following fields:

Guide

Interest

Use the resizing handles to change the size of the text boxes.

7 Sort the report on Guide and make it a tabular report.

8 Change the name of the report to "Available Guides."

9 Bold the items in the Page Header and space them as shown in the sample report in Figure AC3.27.

Use Print Preview to set the printing parameters as your instructor requires and print the report, if needed.

FIGURE AC3.27 Work It Out AC-3A-E2: completed

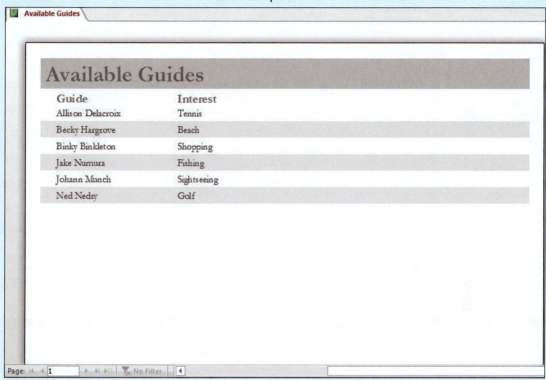

10 Save and close the database file.

HANDS-ON EXERCISE: WORK IT OUT AC-3A-E3 (*Available at* www.mhhe.com/office2013projectlearn)

Creating Mailing Labels and Managing Database Objects

In this project, you will accomplish four tasks. First, you will create a **mailing labels report**. This is a continuation of the report functions started in Project A. Second, once you create the mailing label report, you will perform some basic customization and formatting actions. Third, you will rename, copy, and delete database objects. Finally, you will **compact** and **repair** the database file.

PROJECT FILE: *Available at* <u>www.mhhe.com/office2013projectlearn</u>

PROJECT OBJECTIVES

After completing this project, you will be able to:

- Create a mailing labels report.

- Customize and format mailing labels.

- Rename, copy, and delete database objects.

- Compact and repair the database.

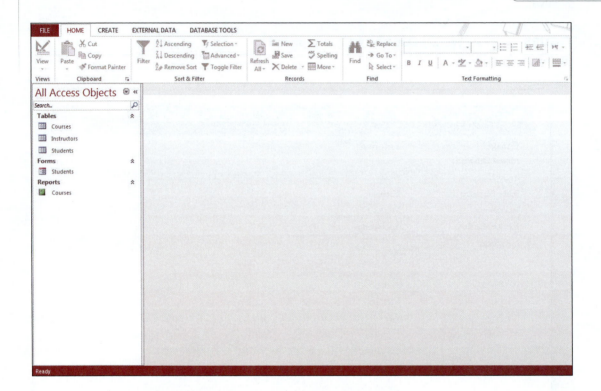

Creating a Mailing Labels Report

LESSON OVERVIEW

In the previous project, you created both forms and reports that are useful, but you did not generate a practical report. In this lesson, you will create a mailing labels report to generate labels from a mailing list that is in table. While this is, by definition, a report, it is created differently from other reports. A mailing labels report uses the Labels button.

SKILLS PREVIEW

Create a mailing labels report	• CLICK the table in the Navigation pane that is the basis of the mailing labels report.
	CLICK the Labels button (⊞) on the CREATE tab in the Reports group.
	SELECT the Product number for the labels the report creates.
	CLICK Next and SELECT fonts and colors.
	CLICK Next and DOUBLE-CLICK each item to place in the mailing labels report. When these choices are made, you will space the items as they should appear on the label.
	CLICK Next and SELECT the sorting fields.
	CLICK Next and then CLICK Finish.
	The default name for a mailing labels report is "Labels" followed by the name of the table on which you based the report.

PROJECT PRACTICE

1 Locate and open the project data file **ac03b.accdb**.

2 Create a mailing labels report from the Students table.

CLICK the Students table on the Navigation pane to select it (see Figure AC3.28).

FIGURE AC3.28   Student table

StudentID	LastName	FirstName	Major	Address	City	State	Zip	Phone	GradYear
1	Stedman	Alan	Business	3710 Bush St.	Seattle	WA	99900	260-390-2873	2015
2	Hernandez	Pete	Business	1485 Sonama Way	Redmond	WA	99780	425-535-1209	2015
3	Mohr	Judy	Arts	100 Bosley Lane	Redmond	WA	99780	425-531-6453	2014
4	Buggey	Diana	Science	20 Cactus Lane	Redmond	WA	99804	425-531-1177	2015
5	Seinfeld	Casey	Arts	17 Windy Way	Bellevue	WA	98180	425-640-2543	2016
6	Alomar	Sandra	Business	PO Box 1465	Kirkland	WA	97080	425-493-3233	2013
7	Fernandez	Rosa	Science	151 Greer Rd.	Seattle	WA	99890	260-394-7645	2014
8	Peters	Bob	Arts	200 Union St.	Seattle	WA	99850	260-390-6611	2014
9	Rinaldo	Sandy	Arts	1871 Orrinton Rd.	Redmond	WA	99704	425-535-0001	2014
10	Finklestein	Sue	Business	888 Burrard St.	Seattle	WA	99904	260-390-9273	2015

CLICK the Labels button in the Reports group on the CREATE tab.

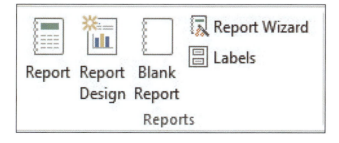

CLICK C2160 in the Product number list box. Ensure the other settings in the Label wizard dialog box are as shown in Figure AC3.29.

FIGURE AC3.29 Label Wizard dialog box

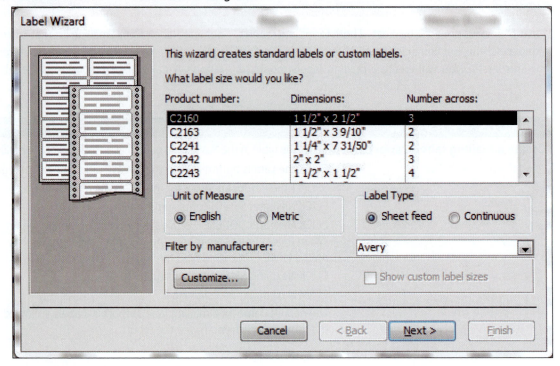

CLICK Next.

CLICK Times New Roman in the Font name drop-down list. CLICK 10 in the Font size drop-down list.

3 CLICK Next.

DOUBLE-CLICK FirstName and tap the space bar to add a space after FirstName.

DOUBLE-CLICK LastName and press Enter to move to the second line.

DOUBLE-CLICK Address and press Enter.

DOUBLE-CLICK City and tap the space bar.

DOUBLE-CLICK State and press Enter.

DOUBLE-CLICK Zip.

4 CLICK Next.

DOUBLE-CLICK LastName as the sort field.

5 CLICK Next and accept the suggested name in the text box of the Label wizard.

6 CLICK Finish.

(*Result:* The mailing labels report appears as shown in Figure AC3.30. The report appears in Print Preview view.)

FIGURE AC3.30 Mailing labels report

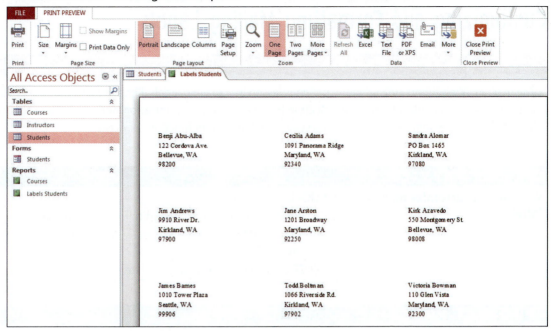

7 Save the report but keep it open before you proceed to the next lesson but do not close Access.

Customizing and Formatting Mailing Labels

LESSON OVERVIEW

The mailing labels report created in the previous lesson is basic. It does not include formatting or effects in the mailing labels. In this lesson, you will format and customize the mailing labels. Keep in mind that the available formatting and customization options are less robust than in some other functions of Access.

SKILLS PREVIEW

Format and customize mailing labels	• CLICK Design view.
	CLICK the placeholder in the report to format or customize.
	CLICK the FORMAT tab under Report Design Tools and apply the desired formatting effects.
	RESIZE the placeholders as appropriate.

PROJECT PRACTICE

1. Ensure project data file **ac03b.accdb** is open in Access.

2. RIGHT-CLICK the Labels Students report on the Navigation pane.
   CLICK Design view as shown in Figure AC3.31.

FIGURE AC3.31 Mailing labels report shown in Design view

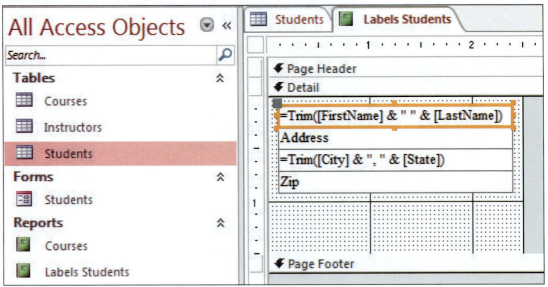

3. CLICK each placeholder field while the Shift key is held down so all four fields are selected.

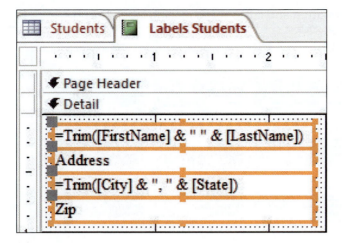

4 CLICK the Shape Fill drop-down list in the Control Formatting group on the FORMAT tab under Report Design Tools.

Change the Theme to Slice.

CLICK Blue, Accent 1, Lighter 80% (second row top item under Theme Color, Blue Accent 1).

CLICK the Line Thickness option in the Shape outline group.

SELECT the second line thickness as shown in Figure AC3.32.

FIGURE AC3.32 Line Thickness options in Shape Fill drop-down list

5 CLICK the Bold button in the Font group on the FORMAT tab under Report Design Tools.
(*Result:* The formatted and customized mailing label report appears as shown in Figure AC3.33.)

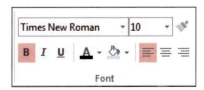

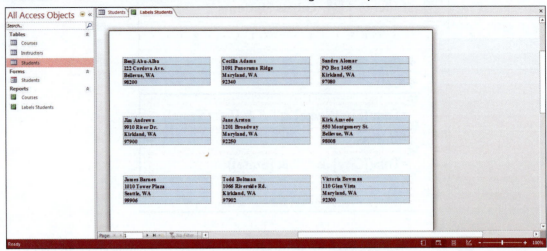

6 View the report in Print Preview view.

7 Save and close the Labels Students mailing labels report before you proceed to the next lesson.

Renaming, Copying, and Deleting Database Objects

LESSON OVERVIEW

Database objects include tables, forms, reports, and queries. These objects and macros and modules are the sum of the complete Access database. You can rename, copy, or delete each of these objects. It cannot be overemphasized that you should use great caution when deleting a database object. When you delete an item, you cannot recover it. Further, deleting a database object can adversely affect the entire database.

SKILLS PREVIEW

Rename a database object	• RIGHT-CLICK the database object to rename in the Navigation pane. CLICK Rename. TYPE the new name you will use for the database object. PRESS Enter .
Copy a database object	RIGHT-CLICK the database object to copy in the Navigation pane. CLICK Copy. CLICK anywhere in the Navigation pane. CLICK Paste. ENSURE the table name is correct and CLICK OK.
Delete a database object	RIGHT-CLICK the database object to delete in the Navigation pane. CLICK Delete. Verify the deletion and CLICK Yes.

PROJECT PRACTICE

1 Ensure project data file **ac03b.accdb** is open in Access.

2 Rename a database object.

RIGHT-CLICK the Courses table in the Tables area of the Navigation pane.

CLICK Rename.

TYPE **College Courses**.

PRESS Enter .

(*Result*: The Navigation pane should appear as shown in Figure AC3.34.)

FIGURE AC3.34 Access Objects Navigation pane

3 Copy a database object.

RIGHT-CLICK the Students table in the Tables section of the Navigation pane.

CLICK Copy.

RIGHT-CLICK the mouse anywhere in the Navigation pane.

CLICK Paste.

Verify that the name of the table is "Copy of Students."
(*Result:* The Paste Table As dialog box is shown.)

CLICK OK.
(*Result:* The Navigation pane appears as shown in Figure AC3.35 with the new table.)

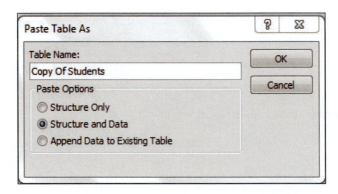

FIGURE AC3.35   Access Objects Navigation pane with copied object

4 Delete a database object.

RIGHT-CLICK the Copy of Students table in the Navigation pane.

CLICK Delete.

CLICK Yes to verify the deletion.

Compacting and Repairing a Database

LESSON OVERVIEW

Compacting and repairing an Access database helps you recognize parts of the database that you can eliminate. These two procedures (done in one step) also ensure data integrity. You can compact and repair an Access database at any time or set an option to do it automatically when you close the database.

SKILLS PREVIEW

Compact and repair an Access database	• With the database open, CLICK the FILE tab. CLICK Compact & Repair Database. (The function is performed in the background; you will not notice any change to the database.)
Compact and repair the Access database on closing	• With the database open, CLICK the FILE tab. CLICK Options in the Backstage view. CLICK the Current Database category. CLICK the Compact on Close check box. CLICK OK twice.

PROJECT PRACTICE

1 Ensure project data file **ac03b.accdb** is open in Access.

2 Compact and repair the database.

CLICK the FILE tab.

The Backstage view should be as shown in Figure AC3.36.

FIGURE AC3.36 Backstage view showing Compact & Repair Database button

CLICK the Compact & Repair Database button.

(*Result:* The database compacts and repairs and the Backstage view closes.)

3 Compact the database when you close the database.

CLICK the FILE tab.

CLICK Options.

CLICK Current Database (see options in Figure AC3.37).

FIGURE AC3.37 Access options showing Compact on Close check box

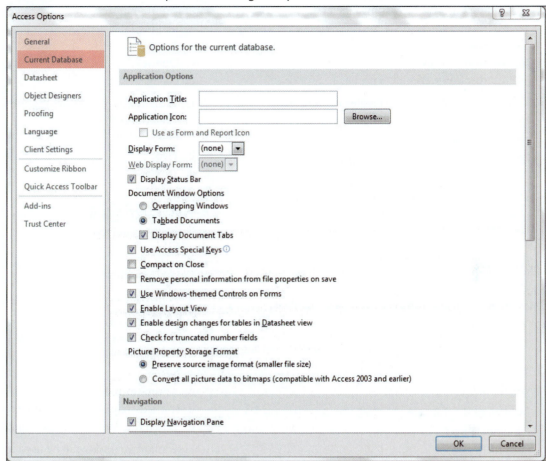

CLICK the Compact on Close check box.

CLICK OK.

CLICK OK a second time to acknowledge that the database must be closed and reopened for that change to take effect.

Close the database.

MULTIPLE-CHOICE QUIZ

Select the best choice in the following questions to review the project concepts.

1. Which Microsoft Office application does not have a procedure for creating mailing labels?
   a. Microsoft Word
   b. Microsoft Excel
   c. Microsoft Access
   d. Microsoft PowerPoint

2. What tool most efficiently creates mailing labels?
   a. Report
   b. Form wizard
   c. Report wizard
   d. Labels

3. What area of the CREATE tab contains the Labels button?
   a. Tables
   b. Reports
   c. Forms
   d. Queries

4. Which of the following are good uses for labels created in Access?
   a. Mailing labels
   b. Name tags
   c. Inventory labels
   d. All of these are correct.

5. Which of the following options provides data for mailing labels?
   a. Form
   b. Report
   c. Data range
   d. Table

6. Which of the following is not a type of database object used in Access?
   a. Mailing labels
   b. Tables
   c. Queries
   d. Forms

7. How many commands are required to copy a database object?
   a. One
   b. Two
   c. Three
   d. Four

8. Which Microsoft Access tab contains the Compact & Repair Database button?
   a. FILE
   b. HOME
   c. CREATE
   d. FORMAT

9. When an Access user compacts and repairs the database, when are changes evident in the data and the structure of the database?
   a. Never
   b. Always immediately
   c. Immediately only if there are modifications made
   d. When the database is saved and reopened

10. How many methods can be used to compact a database?
    a. One
    b. Two
    c. Three
    d. Four

HANDS-ON EXERCISE: WORK IT OUT AC-3B-E1

In this exercise, you will create a mailing labels report based on the Internet Accounts table. You will customize and format the report, then work with database objects. Finally, you will compact and repair the database. The final mailing labels report is shown in Figure AC3.38.

1 Locate and open the exercise data file **ac03a-ex1.accdb**.

2 With the Labels button, create a mailing labels report based on the E1 Internet Accounts table. Use the C2160 product number and leave the font items as they appear. The fields on the mailing label will be:

> Customer
>
> Address
>
> City, State, Zip

Sort the labels by Customer.

Name the labels report Internet Accounts.

Customize the report labels so they appear as shown in Figure AC3.38.

FIGURE AC3.38 Work It Out AC-3B-E1: customized report labels

3 Rename the E2 Products table "Instock."

4 Copy the Instock table and paste it using the name suggested by Access.

5 Delete the Copy of Instock table.

6 Compact and repair the **ac03a-ex1.accdb** database.

7 Close the database file.

In this exercise, you will create labels to make resort guest name tags based on the Patrons table. You will customize and format the labels and work with database objects. Finally, you will compact and repair the database. The final name tag labels report is shown in Figure AC3.39.

1. Locate and open the exercise data file **ac03a-ex2.accdb**.

2. Use the Labels button to create a name tag labels report based on the Patrons table. Use the C2160 product number and leave the font items as they appear. The fields on the mailing label will be:

   Guest

   Hometown, State

   Interest

   Room#

   Sort the labels by State.

   Name the labels report Guests.

   Customize the report labels so they appear as shown in Figure AC3.39.

FIGURE **AC3.39**   Work It Out AC-3B-E2: customized report labels

3. Rename the Guides table "Resort Guides."

4. Copy the Resort Guides table and paste it using the name suggested by Access.

5. Delete the Copy of Resort Guides table.

6. Compact and repair the **ac03a-ex02.accdb** database.

7. Close the database file.

HANDS-ON EXERCISE: WORK IT OUT AC-3B-E3 (*Available at* www.mhhe.com/office2013projectlearn)

Chapter Summary

Chapter 3 of Access introduced you to new tools in Access that allow you to create forms and reports. You learned a practical application of the report feature, creating a mailing labels report. Creating reports and forms lies at the heart of Access. A sophisticated database with numerous tables and queries has its place, but unless you can easily enter the data using a form and then parse and display in a report, it is useless.

In this technological age, most retail shops track customers and their purchases. Retailers use databases similar to Access, usually on a larger scale. In Project B, you created a mailing labels report. Creating this report in Access provides flexibility that you would not have if you created a similar report in Word.

Finally, you worked with database objects to rename them, make copies of them, and delete those you do not need. Compacting and repairing a database are essential steps to maintain data integrity.

Chapter Key Terms

Compact, A-124	Form wizard, p. A-100	Report Layout view, p. A-100
Design view, p. A-100	Mailing labels report, p. A-124	Report wizard, p. A-100
Form Layout view, p. A-100	Repair, p. A-124	

On Your Own Exercise AC-3C-E1

This exercise provides a chance to practice the important Access 2013 skills covered in this chapter. You will work with a simple Access database to create and customize forms and reports in the exercise. Open the exercise data file **ac03cp-ex.accdb**. Two figures will show a sample form and a sample report.

Complete the following tasks so the database form is similar in appearance to Figure AC3.40.

- Use the Form wizard to create an input form for the Personnel table.

- Format the form using Figure AC-3.40 as a guide.

- Add another record to the table.

- The completed form should appear as shown in Figure AC3.40.

FIGURE AC3.40 Personnel Input form

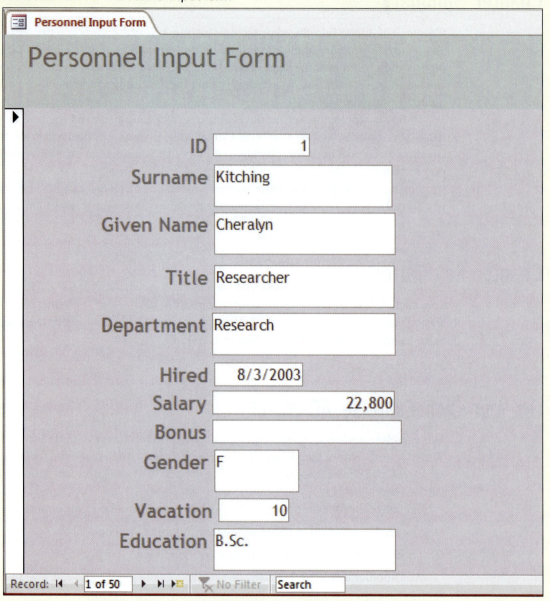

- Create a report using the Report button.
- Manipulate report controls so the report appears as shown in Figure AC3.41.

Personnel				

Personnel

Surname	Given	Title	Department	Education
Akelaitis	Eric	Vice President	Management	MBA
Alexander	Mandy	Manager	Administration	B.A.
Alomar	Sandra	Salesperson	Marketing	B.Com.
Beaver	Geoffrey	Clerk	Administration	
Bouchard	Guy	Foreman	Production	B.A.
Bradley	Brenda	Accountant	Finance	
Buggey	Diana	Salesperson	Marketing	B.Admin.
Chong	Tony	Operator	Production	B.A.
Chow	Tina	Operator	Production	
Cortez	Anna	Controller	Finance	B.A.
Fernandez	Rosa	Salesperson	Marketing	B.A.
Fuller	Tony	Clerk	Administration	
Harris	Mindy	Researcher	Research	B.Sc.

- Practice working in both Layout and Design views.
- Print the report (if desired by your instructor).
- Save and close the report and close the database file.

On Your Own Exercise AC-3C-E2

This exercise provides a chance to practice the more important Access 2013 skills covered in this chapter. You will work with a simple Access database to create and modify a labels report that employees will use for a new hires event. You will manipulate database objects and compact and repair the database. Open the exercise data file **ac03cp-ex.accdb**.

- Create a labels report for the company to use as name tags for employees at a new hires event.
- Customize and format the labels as shown in Figure AC3.42.

FIGURE AC3.42   Labels to be used at a company mixer

- Rename the Personnel table "Current Personnel."
- Make a copy of the Personnel Input form and paste it using the name suggested by Access.
- Delete the Copy of Personnel Input form from the database.
- Compact and repair the database.
- Save and close the labels report and exit Access.

ProjectLearn
Microsoft
PowerPoint 2013

Introduction to PowerPoint

Microsoft PowerPoint is all about adding "power" to your "point." When you make a presentation, it provides the ability to emphasize and accentuate the point or points you try to share with others. PowerPoint combines the strengths of many other presentation tools and gives you the control. It can be the simplicity of a flip chart or the emotional impact of a photograph. It can be the entertainment of a slide show or the involvement of a video. PowerPoint can work as any one of these, or as all of these at the same time.

The true power of the program comes from its flexibility. Use PowerPoint to inform others with data and charts. Use PowerPoint to persuade your audience about the need for action or a specific plan. Make PowerPoint fun and interesting to engage your viewers. Done properly, PowerPoint can do all three to maximize the impact of each moment you have the attention of your audience.

This chapter will show you how to control your slide show with a click of a button. Learn how to edit and add your own words to a show. Revise existing presentations so they are complete with the speaker's notes and handouts. It is easy to add pictures, clip art, video, and sound to your slide show to craft an interesting and professional production to connect with your audience at both an intellectual and emotional level.

PROJECT

Enhancing a Marketing Presentation

In this project, you will enhance a number of existing presentations and improve them by adding your own special touches. These touches include controlling the flow and timing, adding elements such as photographs and illustrations, and video and sound.

Although this chapter will provide you with the technical skills to make a powerful presentation, it will also begin to unlock your creativity as you experiment with the many tools you can use over and over again.

THE SITUATION

Presenting How to Make a Presentation

You have a new job with a small marketing company. The company has many varied clients and has asked you to review and update some of the marketing presentations from their clients. You realize that many of these presentations have good information in them, but they need some extra work. First you build some slide shows meant to help your clients improve their presentations. Then you help a construction company build a presentation to show to its investors.

Enhancing a Marketing Presentation

The first project in PowerPoint will focus on two slide shows created to help marketers teach some of the most important concepts to their clients. You will control the flow of the slides, edit the content, and print the show, the speaker's notes, and audience handouts. While the lessons emphasize editing and presenting skills, do not overlook the content of the slide shows. Each is full of tips and suggestions to improve both the effectiveness of the slide show and the presentation of the speaker.

PROJECT FILE: *Available at* **www.mhhe.com/office2013projectlearn**

PROJECT OBJECTIVES

After completing this project, you will be able to:

• Select views, themes, gridlines, and guides and control zoom.

• Run and control the delivery of a presentation.

• Edit slides by adding or changing text and text color, and using copy, paste, and Format Painter.

• Create and print notes and handouts.

• Promote, demote, edit, and work in outline view.

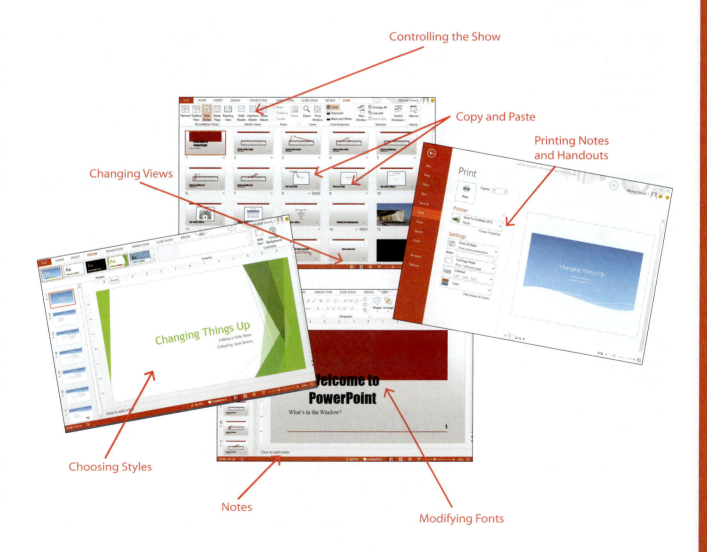

Controlling the Show

Copy and Paste

Printing Notes and Handouts

Changing Views

Choosing Styles

Notes

Modifying Fonts

What's in the Window

LESSON OVERVIEW

The design of the window or screen in PowerPoint is consistent with the other members of the Microsoft Office family. Word, Excel, and PowerPoint have similar designs with tabs that reveal ribbons and buttons arranged into groups. PowerPoint has the HOME, INSERT, REVIEW, and VIEW tabs that you see in other programs, but it also has tabs specific to PowerPoint such as TRANSITIONS, ANIMATIONS, and SLIDE SHOW. Because PowerPoint is a program for creating effective presentations, the layout of the screen and the arrangement of buttons are designed to make those common features readily available.

A PowerPoint show is a series of slides. Each **slide** can contain text, pictures, images, graphs, and more that can be arranged in almost any manner. Slide shows can use a **theme** that will tie the design and colors of the slides together throughout the slide show. Use **placeholders** to hold text, pictures, and graphs so each one can be controlled independently. Clicking on any element on a slide will display the placeholder. There are different ways to **view** the slide show. The **main editing window** allows you to see one slide close up so you can make changes on the slide. The **Slide Sorter view** lets you see all the slides side by side for easy reorganizing.

Other ways to view a slide show include the zoom factor and running the show on your computer monitor. The **zoom** factor allows you to magnify or demagnify the image on the monitor. This is ideal for detailed work or getting a broader view of the slide. Zooming in or out does not change the actual size of the presentation or the printing size. Zoom buttons reside on the VIEW tab or along the **Status bar** at the bottom of the screen.

To help you in the design of your slides, PowerPoint provides access to a **ruler** that displays the actual size of the page and elements on it. Other useful tools for aligning elements are the guides and gridlines that you can superimpose on the slide, but will not print. The **guides** consist of one perfectly vertical dotted line and one perfectly horizontal dotted line that intersect to separate the slide into quadrants. The **gridlines** are a series of dotted lines that overlay a grid on the slide to provide more detailed alignment.

SKILLS PREVIEW

Display a placeholder	• CLICK anywhere in the text or image.
Move to another slide for editing	• CLICK the desired slide from the thumbnails on the left, or • CLICK and HOLD the mouse on the slider on the right-hand margin of the screen. DRAG the slider to the desired slide.
Preview a theme	• CLICK the DESIGN tab and locate the Themes group. HOVER over the thumbnails of the themes.
Insert a new theme into a slide show	• CLICK the DESIGN tab and locate the Themes group. CLICK on the thumbnails of the desired theme.
Undo any action or change made	• CLICK the Undo button, or • PRESS Ctrl + Z .
Change the view of the slide show	• CLICK the VIEW tab and locate the Presentation Views group. CLICK the desired view, or • CLICK the desired view from the Status bar.
Change the zoom factor	• CLICK the VIEW tab and locate the Zoom group. CLICK the Zoom button to open the Zoom dialog box. CHOOSE from the preset zoom factors, or • CLICK the desired zoom from the Status bar shortcut: CLICK the plus sign to zoom in. CLICK the minus sign to zoom out. DRAG the Zoom indicator along the Zoom line. CLICK the zoom factor percentage to open the Zoom dialog box.

Activate the ruler	• CLICK the VIEW tab and locate the Show group. CLICK Ruler to turn on the rulers.
Activate alignment lines	• CLICK the VIEW tab and locate the Show group. CLICK Gridlines to show the slide's alignment grid. CLICK Guides to show vertical and horizontal lines.
View in grayscale or black and white	• CLICK the VIEW tab and locate the Color/Grayscale group. CLICK Grayscale or Black and White.

PROJECT PRACTICE

1 When opening PowerPoint, you will see a screen similar to Figure PP1.1. When you locate and open the project data file **pp01a1.pptx**, you will see a screen similar to Figure PP1.2.

CLICK the FILE tab to open the Backstage view.

CLICK SaveAs.

DOUBLE-CLICK Computer to store the file locally on your computer.

TYPE **pp01a1-welcome.pptx** in the File Name window to save the file.

FIGURE PP1.1   Opening screen of PowerPoint

TIP

When you open PowerPoint as shown in Figure PP1.1, you can open a blank presentation, take a tour of what PowerPoint has to offer, choose from preset slide designs, or open recent PowerPoint files. It is great advice for the novice to take the tour. This screen will not appear if, instead of opening the PowerPoint program, you open a PowerPoint file. If you open a PowerPoint file, it automatically opens PowerPoint, but it will send you to the Normal view and look similar to Figure PP1.2.

FIGURE PP1.2   Normal view of PowerPoint

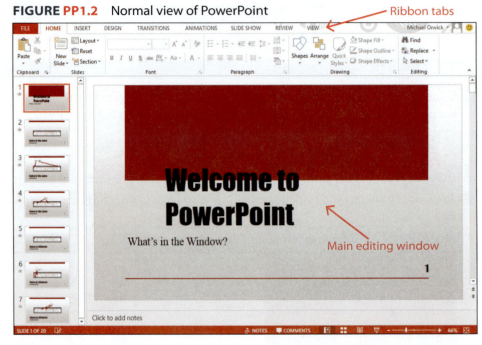

2   The main part of the screen displays the first slide of the show. This is the **main editing window** of the Normal view (Figure PP1.2).

CLICK anywhere on the words "Welcome to PowerPoint" to show the placeholder around the text.

CLICK anywhere on the words "What's in the Window?" to show the placeholder for that text.

Almost everything in PowerPoint is held inside a placeholder.

3   The left side of the screen is the **slide pane** (Figure PP1.2), which provides thumbnails of each slide in the show.

CLICK on slide 2 to bring that slide into the main editing window.

Slide 2, although similar in pattern to slide 1, has a slightly different structure. Slide 1 used a large red block to catch attention; slide 2 allows more room for you to add images and text.

4   CLICK the DESIGN tab and locate the Themes group.

HOVER the mouse over any of the thumbnails to preview the new theme.

CLICK on one of the thumbnails to change all the slides in the show to the new theme.

CLICK the Undo button to return to the original style.

5   CLICK the VIEW tab and locate the Presentation Views group.

CLICK Slide Sorter to show all the slides laid out side to side (Figure PP1.3).

This view is easier for sorting, rearranging, and adding transitions.

FIGURE PP1.3 Slide Sorter view

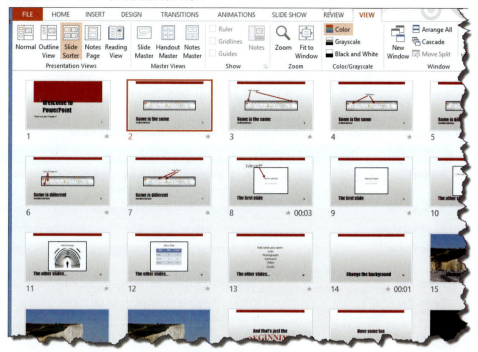

6 In the Zoom group, there are options to set the zoom factor.
CLICK **Zoom** (🔍) to display a menu of preset zoom factors.
CLICK the 50% button.
CLICK OK.
(*Result:* The slides in the sorter view shrink to 50% zoom factor. This makes it easier to see more slides at a time.)

7 Move the mouse to the bottom right of the Status bar to locate shortcut buttons for view and zoom controls (see Figure PP1.4).

FIGURE PP1.4 View and Zoom controls in the Status bar

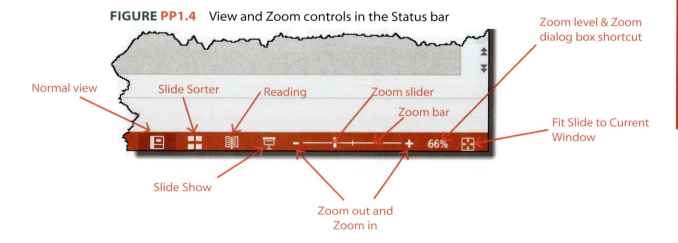

CLICK Normal View to return to Normal view.

CLICK the plus sign at the end of the Zoom control to increase the zoom factor.

CLICK the plus sign three more times.

CLICK the Fit slide to current window button.

(*Result*: The slide in the main editing window adjusts to fit the window.)

See Table PP1.1 for details on the controls in the Status bar.

TABLE PP1.1 View and Zoom buttons available in the Status bar

Status Bar Buttons	Results
Normal	Most common view including the main editing window in the center and the slide pane down the left.
Slide Sorter	All the slides are shown side by side, in order from left to right.
Reading View	Runs a preview of the slide show within the program window.
Slide Show	Starts the slide show in full-screen mode from the current slide in the main editing window.
Zoom Out	Reduces the zoom factor by 10% each time it is clicked.
Zoom Bar	Shows the current zoom factor on a sliding scale. The scale can be clicked to quickly adjust the zoom factor.
Zoom Slider	This can be dragged left and right to adjust the zoom factor of the main editing window.
Zoom In	Increases the zoom factor by 10% each time it is clicked.
Zoom level	Indicates the current zoom factor as a percentage. Clicking it will open the Zoom dialog box.
Fit slide to current window	Clicking this will automatically zoom the slide in or out to fill the main editing window.

8 CLICK the VIEW tab and locate the Show group.

CLICK Ruler, if necessary, to turn on the rulers across the top and down the left-hand side of the screen.

CLICK Gridlines, if necessary, to show the slide's alignment grid.

CLICK Gridlines again to turn them off.

CLICK Guides, if necessary, to show movable vertical and horizontal lines.

CLICK Guides again to remove them from the screen.

TIP

While the guides will always remain perfectly vertical and horizontal, you can move them around the slide to suit your purposes. Just position your mouse right on top of a guide, then drag it to the desired position. Guides and gridlines will not show when printing.

9 CLICK the VIEW tab and locate the Color/Grayscale group.

CLICK Grayscale to view the slide as it would appear in Grayscale (for printing without color).

CLICK Back To Color View to return to full color (and the ribbon automatically returns to the HOME tab).

CLICK the VIEW tab and locate the Color/Grayscale group.

CLICK Black and White to see the slide in true black and white.

CLICK Back To Color View.

10 Return to Slide Two. While you moved around the presentation in many different ways, the file itself did not change and should appear similar to Figure PP1.5. Save the **pp01a1-welcome.pptx** file.

FIGURE PP1.5   Completion of Lesson PowerPoint 1A1

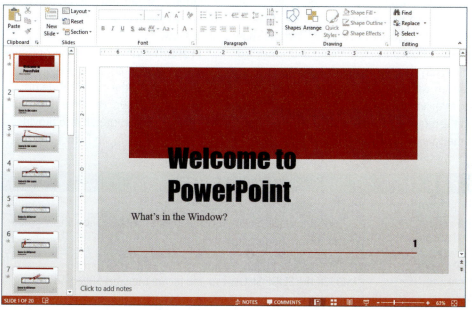

Running and Navigating a Presentation

LESSON OVERVIEW

PowerPoint is all about presentation. When it enters the **Slide Show** mode, PowerPoint fills the entire computer screen to show you exactly what the viewers would see. While that makes a strong impact on the audience and removes any distractions, it also removes the tabs, ribbons, and icons. This can make controlling the presentation and navigating the show difficult. PowerPoint has many different ways to start, pause, replay, and advance the show.

The SLIDE SHOW tab provides buttons to start the show from the first slide or from the slide currently in the main editing window. You can also use keyboard shortcuts for these. When you want to pause a show, you can turn the screen white or black, as that may produce the best effect based on the lighting in the room. You can reverse one slide at a time, or you can immediately access a certain slide number.

Right-click in PowerPoint to display a shortcut menu (even during the actual slide show). **Shortcut menus** are context sensitive so that the options displayed are related to the area of the screen that your mouse was in when activated. When you are working on a slide, right-clicking will display a menu related to the text or object beneath the mouse. When you are running a show, right-clicking displays a menu of options available to you for running the slide show.

Presenter view allows the presenter to view a split screen while the audience views only the current slide. This view shows the current slide displayed to your audience, the next slide, the time (both running and actual), and any speaker's notes. It also provides shortcuts to highlighters, pens, zoom, and other features.

SKILLS PREVIEW

Start slide show from the beginning	• PRESS **F5** , or • CLICK the SLIDE SHOW tab and locate the Start Slide Show group. CLICK From Beginning.
Start slide show from current slide	• PRESS **Shift** + **F5** , or • CLICK the SLIDE SHOW tab and locate the Start Slide Show group. CLICK From Current Slide.
Advance slide show one slide at a time	• CLICK the mouse, or • PRESS **Enter** , or • PRESS the space bar, or • PRESS the **→** or **↓** key.
Reverse a slide show one slide at a time	• CLICK the **←** or **↑** key.
Pause a show by turning the screen black or white	• PRESS the **B** key to turn the screen black. • PRESS the **W** key to turn the screen white.
Move directly to a specific slide	• PRESS the slide number key (e.g. **2**) and **Enter** to move to slide number 2.
Bring up the shortcut menu	• RIGHT-CLICK anywhere on the slide show screen. CHOOSE your desired option.
Enter Presenter view	• While the show is running, RIGHT-CLICK anywhere on the screen. CHOOSE Show Presenter View.
End a slide show before it is over	• PRESS **Esc** .

1. You can view a slide show on your computer screen exactly as it will appear when projected or shared with others. There are some great ways to navigate within the show once it starts. To begin, ensure that **pp01a-welcome.pptx** is open.

2. PRESS the Slide Show button on the PowerPoint Status bar to start the show from the first slide.

   The entire screen fills with the slide show. After the slide fades in, the slide show stops.

MORE INFO

There are many ways to launch a slide show. You can go to the SLIDE SHOW tab and choose to start the show From Beginning or From Current Slide (meaning the slide that is currently in the main editing window). You can go to the bottom right of the screen and click the Slide Show icon. This starts the show from the slide shown in the main editing window. You can also PRESS `Shift`+`F5` to start the show from the slide currently shown in the main editing window.

---

3. To move the show forward one slide at a time:

   CLICK the mouse to move to the next slide (the slide number at the bottom right of each slide).

   PRESS the `Enter` key to move to the next slide.

   PRESS the space bar.

   PRESS the `→` or `↓` key.

   To move the show backward one slide at a time:

   CLICK the `←` or `↑` key to move back one slide.

TIP

Clicking the mouse is the least preferred way to advance slides. All it takes is a slight movement of the mouse and the cursor appears on the slide. Unless you want to point to something with the cursor, this is very distracting to the viewer. After the cursor appears, you can make it disappear by either advancing to the next slide using one of the other methods, or just wait—the cursor will eventually disappear.

---

4. To pause the show:

   PRESS the `B` key to turn the screen black.

   PRESS any alphabetic key to bring the slide back on the screen.

   PRESS the `W` key to turn the screen white.

   PRESS any alphabetic key to bring the slide back on the screen.

5. To move directly to a specific slide:

   PRESS `2` and `Enter` to move to slide number 2.

   PRESS `6` and `Enter` to move to slide number 6.

6. To find a slide if you do not know the slide number:

   RIGHT-CLICK anywhere on the slide show screen to display a shortcut menu.

   CHOOSE See All Slides to display Slide Sorter view.

   CLICK on the desired slide (e.g., slide 11) to go directly to slide 11.

   RIGHT-CLICK anywhere on the slide show screen to display the Options menu.

   SELECT Last Viewed to return to slide 6.

7 PowerPoint provides a Presenter view that allows you to see the current slide as well as the next slide—without affecting what the audience sees through a projector.

To activate the Presenter view:

RIGHT-CLICK anywhere on the slide show screen to display the Options menu.

CHOOSE Show Presenter View to display the Presenter view.

This view shows the next slide and any notes attached to it. It also provides easy access to the taskbar, markup tools, blacking the show, and zoom controls (see Figure PP1.6).

To hide the Presenter view:

RIGHT-CLICK anywhere on the slide show screen to display the Options menu.

CLICK Hide Presenter View to return to the full slide show view.

FIGURE PP1.6   Presenter view

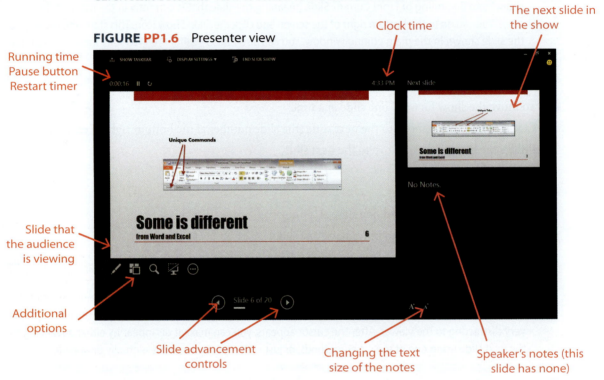

8 RIGHT-CLICK anywhere on the slide show screen to display the shortcut menu.

CHOOSE Help to display the help tabs.

These tabs display shortcut keys for use in the slide show including many of the shortcuts we just reviewed.

CLICK OK to close the Help window.

9 At times, you might want to zoom in a small section of a slide to help the viewers see detail.

To zoom in a portion of the screen:

RIGHT-CLICK anywhere on the slide show screen to display the shortcut menu.

CHOOSE Zoom In and a lightened box appears on the screen.

MOVE your mouse (do not click the mouse) to some part of the screen.

CLICK the mouse to zoom that portion.

The mouse now looks like a hand and can be used to move the zoom around the slide just by dragging the mouse any direction.

RIGHT-CLICK to turn the zoom feature off.

10 Often, when editing, you do not want to start the show from the first slide. You can start from any slide you wish.

PRESS the **Esc** button to exit the show.

CLICK Slide 13 from the slide pane.

To start the show from the current slide:

CLICK the Slide Show button in the Status bar (or PRESS **Shift** + **F5**). Your screen should appear similar to Figure PP1.7.

Press **Esc** to return to the edit screen.

11 Save and close the **pp01a1-welcome.pptx** file.

FIGURE PP1.7   Completion of Lesson PowerPoint 1A2

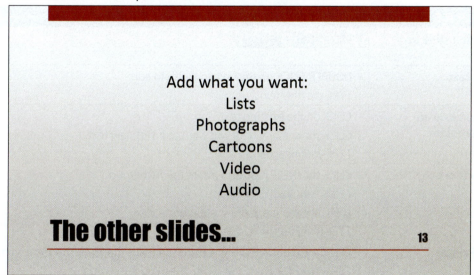

LESSON OVERVIEW

Creating text or editing existing text is very easy to do in PowerPoint. Most of the elements in a PowerPoint slide are contained inside placeholders. This includes text, pictures, videos, tables, graphs, and more. This allows the designer to effortlessly move elements around the screen; layer one element in front or behind another; and format the font, style, color, and size of text without affecting the other elements. It also makes it simple to copy one element and paste it onto another slide.

A **text box** is the placeholder for text. Clicking on any element on a slide displays the placeholder and its **sizing handles.** These allow you to change the size and proportions of a placeholder or image. You can control the typeface, size, alignment, and all other aspects of the text without affecting other elements on the slide. Text boxes are controlled separately so even other text boxes are not affected. Of course, the positioning of text boxes is as easy as dragging them around the slide.

The **Copy and Paste** function not only saves time, but in PowerPoint it can provide improved alignment. When you copy something from one slide and paste it on another slide, it appears in precisely the same position on the new slide as it was on the original slide. This is usually what is desired, and it avoids the tedious nudging to get it just right so it does not appear to hop when you move from one slide to the next.

When you want to use the same effects on more than one element, use the **Format Painter**. This tool allows you to copy the formatting of one element and paint it onto another element. If you have one text box with text that is bold, green, 18 point, and italic, and you would like to do the same to the text in other text boxes, click the Format Painter and with a mouse click you transfer the bold, green, 18 point, and italic attributes to as many text boxes as you like.

SKILLS PREVIEW

Move to the first slide in Normal view	• PRESS `Ctrl` + `Home`.
Edit existing text	• DOUBLE-CLICK on the text you wish to edit. TYPE the new text.
Insert new text into an existing placeholder	• CLICK on the existing text. CLICK the cursor where you want to insert new text. TYPE your new text.
Create a new text box	• CLICK the INSERT tab and locate the Text group. CLICK Text Box. DRAG the mouse to draw a text box. TYPE text into the text box.
Use Format Painter	• CLICK the mouse into the text that contains the formatting you want to copy. CLICK the HOME tab and locate the Clipboard group. CLICK the Format Painter button. DRAG the "paintbrush" over the text you want to adopt the formatting.
Copy selected text	• CLICK the HOME tab and locate the Clipboard group. CLICK the Copy button, or • PRESS `Ctrl` + `C`.
Paste copied text	• CLICK the HOME tab and locate the Clipboard group. CLICK the Paste button, or • PRESS `Ctrl` + `V`.
Change the color of selected text	• CLICK the HOME tab and locate the Font group. CLICK the Font Color drop-down arrow. SELECT from the color palette.

1 Locate and open file **pp01a3.pptx**. Save it as **pp01a3-fun.pptx**.

2 PRESS the [F5] key to begin the show from slide 1.

View the show. Be patient and wait until you are sure the show is paused before you advance. When complete, return to the Normal view. Now make some changes to an existing show.

3 PRESS [Ctrl]+[Home] to move to the first slide of the show.

CLICK anywhere on the words "Editing a Slide Show" to open the placeholder (see Figure PP1.8).

CLICK the mouse after the word *Show*.

PRESS the [Enter] key once to move to another line.

TYPE **By Your Name** (using your first and last names).

PRESS the [F5] key to review your changes.

PRESS the [Esc] key to return to Normal view.

FIGURE PP1.8   Adding text in a placeholder

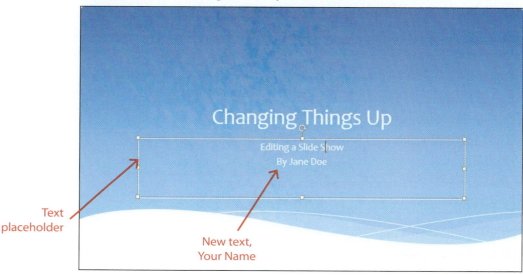

Text placeholder

Changing Things Up

Editing a Slide Show
By Jane Doe

New text, Your Name

4 CLICK on slide 3 in the slide pane on the left-hand side of the screen to display it in the main editing window.

CLICK the mouse under the third bullet in the right text placeholder.

TYPE **Say them out loud**.

DRAG the bottom-center sizing handle up until the dotted placeholder of the text box fits nicely around the text (see Figure PP1.9).

FIGURE PP1.9 Editing text in a placeholder

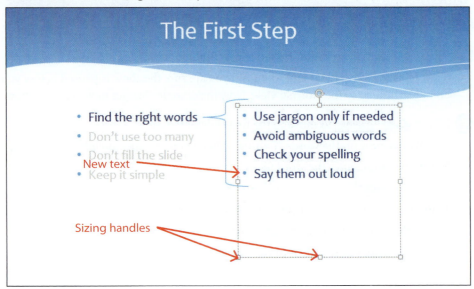

5 CLICK on slide 5 in the slide pane to display it in the main editing window.

SELECT the word *Blank*.

TYPE White.

If necessary, PRESS the space bar to insert a space before the next word.

CLICK away from the text box to deselect it.

6 CLICK on slide 6 in the slide pane.

SELECT the word *graphs*.

TYPE graphics.

If necessary, PRESS the space bar.

CLICK away from the text box to deselect it.

7 CLICK on slide 7 in the slide pane.

SELECT the word *Next* in the title area.

TYPE Second.

If necessary, PRESS the space bar.

CLICK away from the text box to deselect it.

8 CLICK on slide 11 in the slide pane.

To create a text box placeholder:

CLICK the INSERT tab and locate the Text group.

CLICK on Text Box to change your cursor to a text box crosshair.

DRAG to draw a text box about 4 inches long (using the ruler as a guide) just below the blue shape across the top of the slide (see Figure PP1.10).

TYPE Consider the background.

FIGURE PP1.10 Drawing a text box

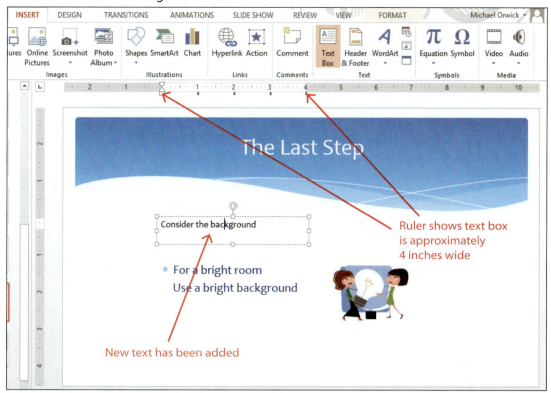

9 It would be better if the new text box matched the style of the others.

To use Format Painter:

CLICK the mouse in the existing text box that says "For a bright room."

CLICK the HOME tab and locate the Clipboard group.

CLICK the Format Painter button ( ).

DRAG the paintbrush I-beam over the text "Consider the background."
(*Result:* This "paints" the formatting from the preexisting text box to the newly created one.)

TIP

It does not matter where you draw the text box; you can always move it. If it is not the right size, you can use the sizing handles to make it larger or smaller. If you leave a text box too large, it will not affect how the slide looks, but it might make it difficult to select another element directly behind it. For that reason, we recommend resizing placeholders to match the content they hold.

---

10 To avoid a placeholder from appearing to jump when advancing from one slide to another, use copy and paste.

CLICK on the dotted placeholder around the text box containing "Consider the background."

CLICK the HOME tab and locate the Clipboard group.

CLICK the Copy button (or PRESS **Ctrl** + **C**).

CLICK on slide 12 in the slide pane.

CLICK the Paste button (or PRESS **Ctrl** + **V**).
(*Result:* The copied text box appears on the new slide in the identical position it was on the original slide, although the font appears invisible because it is blue.)

11 SELECT the text (although invisible) in the newly pasted text box.

CLICK the HOME tab and locate the Font group.

CLICK the Font Color drop-down arrow.

SELECT White, Background 1 from the color palette.
(*Result:* This font turns to white and is now visible against the blue background, as shown in Figure PP1.11.)

12 To review the changes you just made:

CLICK on slide 11 in the slide pane.

CLICK on the Slide Show icon in the Status bar to start the show from slide 11.

The new text box you created is on slide 11. When you click to advance the show, the text box appears not to move, but to change font color against the blue background of slide 12.

13 Start the show from the beginning and see all your changes.

14 Save the **pp01a3-fun.pptx** file.

FIGURE PP1.11   Completion of Lesson PowerPoint 1A3

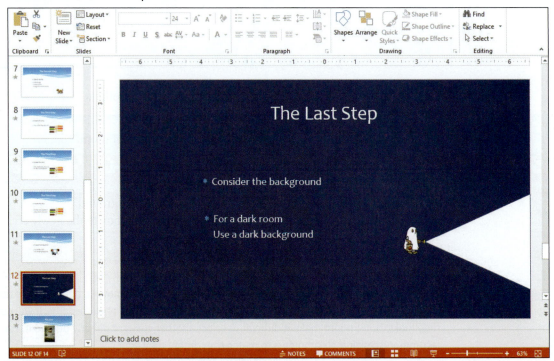

Adding Notes and Printing Handouts

A good presentation is not just about what appears on the screen. A skilled presenter brings the message and the visuals together to form a persuasive and interesting event. PowerPoint has ways to improve the presenter's and the audience's ability to follow the show.

Type **notes** directly under the corresponding slide so they are kept in order with the slide. Only presenters can see them. Printing notes allows the presenter to keep certain notes with specific slides.

To save files, find print controls, and set PowerPoint options, use the **Backstage view**. From here, presenters can print **handouts** so the audience can follow the flow, take notes about the slide show, or keep a small-scale copy of the presentation. Printing options allow for handouts to include as many as nine slides per page.

The **Print page** provides options for what is printed, how many are printed, and which printer you use. Because many presentations use photos and other colorful images, the Print page offers choices for printing in color, black and white, or grayscale. The Print page also displays the **Print Preview** pane so you can see ahead of time exactly what your printing will look like.

SKILLS PREVIEW

Add notes to a slide	• CLICK into the bottom of the screen on the words Click to add notes. TYPE your notes.
Show or hide notes	• CLICK the Notes button in the Status bar on the bottom of the screen.
Enlarge the notes area	• DRAG the line between the main editing window and the Notes box up or down, as desired.
Add bullets to notes	• CLICK into the Notes box. CLICK the HOME tab and locate the Paragraph group. CLICK the Bullets button.
Print a slide show	• CLICK the FILE tab. SELECT Print to enable the Print page (and Print Preview pane). CLICK the Print button.
Print notes	• CLICK on the Full Page Slides button. CHOOSE Notes Pages from Print Layout options. CLICK Print.
Print an outline of a slide show	• CLICK on the Full Page Slides button. CHOOSE Outline from Print Layout options. CLICK Print.
Print handouts	• CLICK on the Full Page Slides button. CHOOSE from Handouts options. CLICK Print.

PROJECT PRACTICE

1 Storing your slide show and your speaker notes separately can lead to problems. PowerPoint keeps them together for you. To begin, ensure that **pp01a3-fun.pptx** is open.

2 CLICK on slide 1.

To add notes to a slide:

CLICK the mouse at the bottom of the screen on NOTES to add speaker notes (see Figure PP1.12)

TYPE **Welcome to my talk on creating a PowerPoint presentation. My name is (add your name) and I am happy to have a few minutes of your time to discuss a few things that can improve a slide show.**

CLICK anywhere away from the notes area to disable the typing.

FIGURE PP1.12 Adding notes to a slide

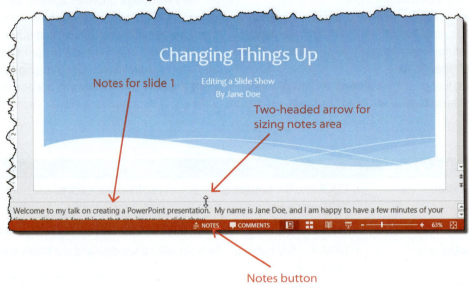

3 CLICK on slide 2.

CLICK into the notes area.

TYPE **We will discuss four main ideas: The importance of finding the right words. And the importance of not using too many words. We will also warn against filling each slide with too much content. Finally, we will stress the value of keeping it simple.**

CLICK anywhere away from the notes area to disable the typing.

TIP

To see more of the notes area on the screen, move the cursor down to the line between the notes and the main editing window. When the cursor changes to the two-headed arrow sizing image (Figure PP1.12), you can drag the window up or down to provide a better view. The size of the slide in the editing window adjusts automatically.

---

4 CLICK on slide 3 and notice that notes are already there.

DRAG the Notes window larger until the zoom factor of the main editing window is around 50 percent.

CLICK on slide 4.

Here the notes are separated into bullets related to the bullets on the screen. Usually bullets are much easier to read than one big paragraph.

CLICK the Notes button (▲ NOTES) in the Status bar to close the Notes window.

CLICK the Notes button again to open the Notes window.

5 To print the slide show:

CLICK the FILE tab.

SELECT Print to enable the Print page (see Figure PP1.13).

CLICK the Print button (🖶) if your instructor wants you to print the presentation.

FIGURE PP1.13   The Print page in PowerPoint

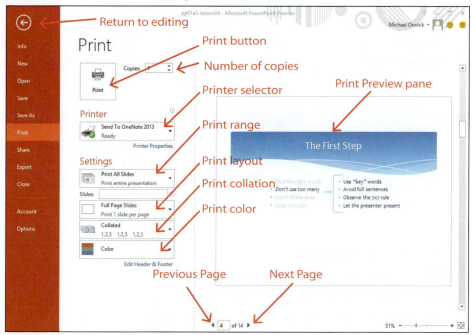

6 To send the print job to a different printer:

CLICK the **Printer button** (Figure PP1.13) to view a list of the printers that are available.

This list will vary depending on your computer and network.

SELECT the printer you desire.

CLICK Print to send your choices to the printer if your instructor wants you to print the presentation.

See Tables PP1.2 and PP1.3 for the available print options.

TABLE PP1.2   Print All Slides drop-down options

Print Range Options	Result
Print All Slides	Print every slide in the presentation.
Print Selection	Select slides and print only those selected.
Print Current Slide	Print the slide currently displayed in the Print Preview pane.
Custom Range	Enter specific slide numbers for printing. You can choose a range with a hyphen, such as 4-7 to print slides 4, 5, 6, and 7. Or you can use a comma to select nonconsecutive slides, such as 4, 7-8 to print slides 4, 7, and 8.

TABLE PP1.3 Other Settings options available

Print Layout, Collation, and Color Options	Result
Collated	Four copies of the slide show would print as pages 1,2,3,4, then 1,2,3,4, and so on.
Uncollated	Four copies of the slide show would print as pages 1,1,1,1, then 2,2,2,2, and so on.
Color	Print the slides in full color.
Grayscale	Print the slides using shades of gray to show color variations.
Pure Black and White	Print slides without showing large colored objects to save printer ink or toner.

> ⚠ **HEADS UP**
>
> The names of the buttons on the Print page change to reflect the last choice made. This provides you with a clear idea of which options are chosen for the print job, but it can be confusing because the name on the button might be different than when you started. Refer to Figure PP1.13 if needed.

7 To print notes:

CLICK the **Print Range button** (currently titled: "Full Page Slides").

SELECT Notes Pages to display in the Print Preview pane.

Ensure the Print Range button says Print All Slides.

CLICK the Print button if your instructor wants you to print the presentation.

8 To print just the outline of the slide show:

CLICK on the Print Range button (which likely now says "Notes Pages").

CHOOSE Outline to enable the Print Preview pane to display the Outline view.

CLICK Print if your instructor wants you to print the presentation.

9 To print a handout for the audience:

CLICK on the Print Range button (which likely now says "Outline").

CLICK 3 Slides to enable the Print Preview pane to display that option.

10 To print these handouts in color is costly, so you can print them without color.

To print in grayscale:

CLICK the **Print Color button**.

CHOOSE Grayscale to enable the Print Preview pane to display the grayscale printing.

CLICK the **Next Page button** in the taskbar to preview the other pages in grayscale.

11 If the grayscale preview is fine, you could print the handouts, but perhaps the Pure Black and White option might use less print toner.

To print in Pure Black and White:

CLICK the Print Color button (now likely called "Grayscale").

Preview the slides using the Next Page and Previous Page buttons in the taskbar.

You decide the Pure Black and White is the best choice, so:

CLICK the Print button if your instructor wants you to print the presentation. Refer to Figure PP1.14 to view these settings.

12 Save the pp01a3-fun.pptx file.

FIGURE PP1.14 Completion of Lesson PowerPoint 1A4

Working in Outline View

LESSON OVERVIEW

Because PowerPoint is built on slides, it can be distracting to work slide by slide if the idea on each slide is not fully developed. The **Outline view** (different from printing an outline of your slide show) allows you to enter your ideas and text without having to position text boxes and placeholders. You can easily move text from one place to another (including one slide to another) by dragging up and down on the outline. You also can reorder bullets and insert new slides. The Outline view helps you plan a slide show by allowing you to organize your thoughts. You can create slides with as little text as a title to organize your ideas before you add a lot of content.

The Outline view also allows you to instantly **collapse** the view so just the slide titles show. You can then expand your current slide to keep distractions to a minimum. You can expand or collapse all slides at once or one at a time.

Slides in Outline view are structured by levels. The title is the top level. The next level is a text box (often bulleted). There are lower levels within the text box, so text can appear as bullets below a bullet. Moving text up and down these levels is called **promoting** and **demoting**. This is easy to do in Outline view.

SKILLS PREVIEW

Activate Outline view	• CLICK the VIEW tab and locate the Presentation Views group. CHOOSE Outline View.
Reorder slides in Outline view	• DRAG the slide from its current position above or below another slide.
Edit directly in Outline view	• CLICK the mouse in the text of the Outline view. Make your changes.
Resize placeholders	• CLICK on the text on the slide to display the placeholder. DRAG the sizing handles to the desired size.
Collapse or expand a slide in Outline view.	• DOUBLE-CLICK the box next to the slide number. If the slide is expanded, this will collapse it. If the slide is collapsed, this will expand it.
Collapse or expand all slides in Outline view	• RIGHT-CLICK on any slide to display the shortcut menu. CHOOSE Collapse All to collapse all slides. CHOOSE Expand All to expand all slides.
Insert a new slide into Outline view	• RIGHT-CLICK on a slide (the new slide will appear after the selected slide). CHOOSE New Slide.
Demote text one level	• CLICK inside the bullet you wish to demote. PRESS `Tab`.
Promote text one level	• CLICK inside the bullet you wish to demote. PRESS `Shift` + `Tab`.
Remove a slide using Outline view	• RIGHT-CLICK on the slide to display the shortcut menu. CHOOSE Delete Slide, or • CLICK on the slide. PRESS `Delete`.

PROJECT PRACTICE

1 Working on your slide show one slide at a time is great for design. But, when it comes to working on just the ideas or text for each slide, the Outline view may be best. Ensure that **pp01a3-fun.pptx** is open.

2 To activate the Outline view:

CLICK the VIEW tab and locate the Presentation Views group.

CHOOSE Outline view.

(*Result:* The slide pane now changes to the Outline view.)

3 In the Outline view, each slide has a number, a box, the title of the slide in bold, and bullet points below it (see Figure PP1.15).

CLICK on slide 2 in the Outline view.

SELECT the text of the last bullet ("Keep it simple").

DRAG it above the first bullet and RELEASE the mouse (see Figure PP1.15).

(*Result:* The selected text moves above the other text. Notice the image in the main editing window instantly shows the change.)

FIGURE PP1.15 Slide pane in Outline view

Drag selected bullet here

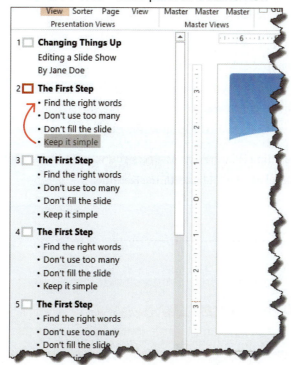

4 CLICK in front of the word *Keep* in the new first bullet.

TYPE KISS:

PRESS the space bar.

CLICK after the word *simple*.

PRESS the space bar.

TYPE students.

(*Result:* The slide in the editing window inserts our changes and reads "KISS: Keep it simple students.")

5 CLICK on the text in the main editing window to display the placeholder box.

DRAG the sizing handles to resize the box so the first bullet fits on one line.

CLICK after the third bullet in the editing window ("Don't use too many").

PRESS the space bar.

TYPE words.

(*Result:* The typing is added to the slide in the editing window and to the text in the Outline view.)

6 One of the big advantages of working in the Outline view is that you can concentrate on different perspectives by expanding and collapsing the outline.

To collapse the slides in the Outline view:

DOUBLE-CLICK on the box next to slide 4 to collapse the text on that slide.

DOUBLE-CLICK again on the box to expand the text on slide 4.

7 RIGHT-CLICK on slide 6 to bring up a shortcut menu.

HOVER the mouse over the Collapse option until a submenu appears.

CHOOSE Collapse All.
(*Result:* All the text in the slides have collapsed to leave just the slide titles.)

8 To change the order of slides:

CLICK and HOLD on slide 7.

DRAG it up to just below slide 2 and RELEASE the mouse.
(*Result:* Slide 7 has now become slide 3.)

9 CLICK Undo to return the slides to their original order.

RIGHT-CLICK on slide 1 to bring up the shortcut menu.

CHOOSE New Slide to insert a new slide immediately after slide 1.

The mouse becomes active in the Outline view.

TYPE **Thanks for your time** to make the words appear in the title of the new slide.

10 PRESS `Enter` to move to the next line (PowerPoint assumes you want to create another slide).

To demote a slide down to the level of a bullet beneath the last title:

PRESS `Tab` once.

TYPE **Great presentations are about ideas**.

PRESS `Enter` once.

TYPE **Don't let poor techniques ruin things**.

PRESS `Enter` once.

TYPE **Anyone can create great presentations**.

TIP

If you want to type a second line in the title placeholder, PRESS `Shift` + `Enter` after typing the first line. This moves your cursor down to the next line, but keeps the text inside the title placeholder.

---

11 Outline view allows you to demote bullets to lower levels quickly.

To demote a bullet, while the cursor is still in the last bullet:

PRESS `Tab` once to demote (indent) the bullet one level.

PRESS `Tab` again to demote the bullet another level (see Figure PP1.16).

FIGURE PP1.16   Levels of text in the Outline view

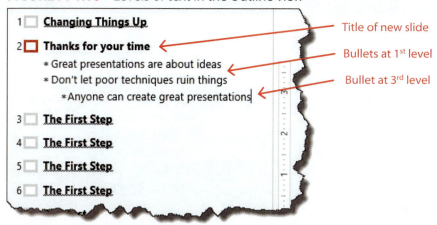

Title of new slide

Bullets at 1st level

Bullet at 3rd level

12 Promote bullets just as quickly.

To promote a bullet, while the cursor is still in the last bullet:

PRESS [Shift] + [Tab] to promote the bullet one level.

13 You can promote bullets right up to the level of a new slide.

With the cursor still in the last bullet:

PRESS [Shift] + [Tab] twice to promote it past the level of the other bullets.
(*Result:* The final bullet now becomes its own slide with the bulleted text moving up into the title of the slide.)

14 To remove a slide using the Outline view:

RIGHT-CLICK on slide 2 to display the shortcut menu.

CHOOSE Delete Slide (🗙) to remove it completely.

There is another way to delete a slide using the Outline view:

CLICK on the new slide 2.

PRESS [Delete] on the keyboard to remove the slide completely. Refer to Figure PP1.17.

15 Save the document and exit PowerPoint.

FIGURE PP1.17   Completion of Lesson PowerPoint A5

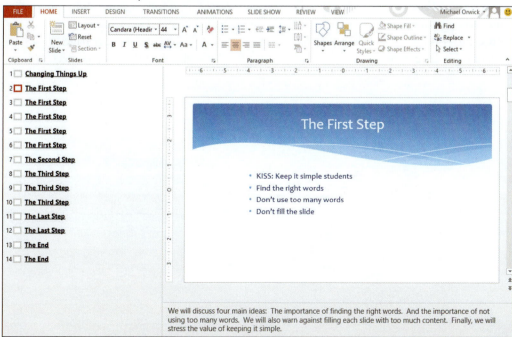

MULTIPLE-CHOICE QUIZ

Select the best choice in the following questions to review the project concepts. Good luck!

1. When editing a slide in Normal view, to ensure it fits best into the editing window:
   a. double-click the slide.
   b. right-click and select Fit to window.
   c. click Fit slide to current window.
   d. All of these are correct.

2. To start a slide show from its beginning, you can
   a. click slide 1 and click Slide Show button.
   b. click From Beginning in the Start Slide Show group.
   c. press the F5 button.
   d. All of these are correct.

3. Holding down the Shift button and pressing F5 will
   a. start the slide show from the beginning.
   b. exit from the slide show.
   c. bring up the slide show control panel.
   d. None of these is correct.

4. While in the middle of a slide show, pressing the Esc key will
   a. stop the show.
   b. bring up the Help menu.
   c. fade the screen to white.
   d. None of these is correct.

5. To advance a slide show presentation to the next slide, you can
   a. press the ↑ key.
   b. press the ↓ key.
   c. press the + key.
   d. All of these are correct.

6. If you need to go back a slide during a presentation, you can
   a. press the ↑ key.
   b. press the ↓ key.
   c. press the space bar.
   d. press the PgDn key.

7. Notes can be
   a. added at the bottom of each slide in Normal view.
   b. added along the left-hand margin of each slide in Slide Sorter view.
   c. seen during the show at the bottom of the slide.
   d. All of these are correct.

8. To edit text in a text box:
   a. double-click the word.
   b. right-click the word.
   c. you must delete the text box and create another.
   d. None of these is correct.

9. To apply the formatting of one text box to another, you can
   a. right-click, select Format, and choose Re-do.
   b. click on the first text box, hold Ctrl, then click the other text box.
   c. click the Format Painter, then click the text box.
   d. None of these is correct.

10. PowerPoint shows can be printed with
    a. a full page per slide.
    b. notes showing.
    c. three slides per page.
    d. All of these are correct.

In this exercise, you will open an existing presentation, make changes to complete it, and prepare it for printing. You will be provided with specific tasks, but not step-by-step instructions. The final document is shown in Figure PP1.18.

FIGURE **PP1.18**   Work It Out PP-1A-E1: completed

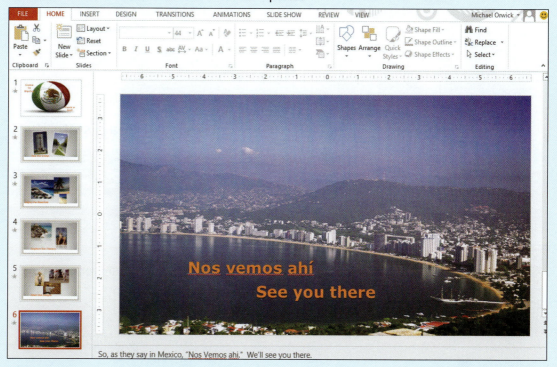

① After launching Microsoft PowerPoint, locate and open the project data file **pp01a-ex01.pptx**. Save it as **pp01a-hw01.pptx**.

② View the show from the beginning. Some of the action runs automatically. When it pauses, use at least three different ways to advance. When the show is complete, return to the Normal view.

③ Change the word "Visit" to "Enjoy" on slide 3.

④ Check your changes by starting the show from the current slide (slide 3). Close the show after slide 4.

⑤ Add the following notes to slide 1:
I would like to invite you to visit the land of sun and sand—Mexico.

⑥ Add the following notes to slide 6:
So, as they say in Mexico, "Nos vemos ahi." We'll see you there.

⑦ Copy the text box on slide 6. Paste it somewhere else on the slide.
Drag the newly pasted text box below and to the right of the existing text box.
Replace the text in the new text box with **See you there**.

⑧ Print the notes pages of the current slide.

⑨ Set the Print page to print handouts of three slides per page. Print both pages of these handouts.

⑩ Watch the new show with all your changes. Save and then close the file.

HANDS-ON EXERCISE: WORK IT OUT PP-1A-E2

In this exercise, you will open an existing presentation and make changes to complete it and prepare it for printing. You will be provided with specific tasks, but not step-by-step instructions. The final document is shown in Figure PP1.19.

FIGURE PP1.19 Work It Out PP-1A-E2: completed

1. Locate and open the exercise data file **pp01a-ex02.pptx**. Save it as **pp01a-hw02.pptx**.

2. Watch the presentation. Some of the action runs automatically. When it pauses, advance using a method other than clicking the mouse. When the show is complete, return to the Normal view.

3. Make the following corrections:
   On slide 2, change "Laura" to "Lara."
   On slide 2, change "year" to "Year."
   On slide 4, change "Averge" to "Average."

4. Add a text box in slide 3 that says **We live in your neighborhood**. Move the text box into the open area below the slide title above the photo on the left. Use the Format Painter to give your new text box on slide 3 the same formatting as the text box on slide 2.

5. Add the following notes:
   Slide 2: **Lara and Turner Handover are a husband and wife team of real estate agents. They have over 30 years of combined experience in real estate. Both were raised in the same Ventula Valley that they work in. This has helped them win the Agent of the Year award 3 times. In effect, you get two agents working for you, for the price of one.**
   Slide 4: **The average price of homes in the Ventula Valley has increased steadily the past 30 years. From about $580,000 in 1990 to just below $660,000 in 2013.**

6. On the final slide (slide 6), insert a text box below the picture with the company phone number: **(888) 555-7355**. Change the font size to 28 and the font color to red.

7. Print a handout that has all six slides on one sheet.

8. Set the Print page to print the Outline view for your reference. Print the outline.

9. Print the note pages for slides 1, 2, and 3.

10. Watch the show from the beginning. Save and close the file.

In this exercise, you will open an existing presentation and make changes to complete it and prepare it for printing. You will be provided with specific tasks, but not step-by-step instructions. The final document is shown in Figure PP1.20.

FIGURE PP1.20 Work It Out PP-1A-E3: completed

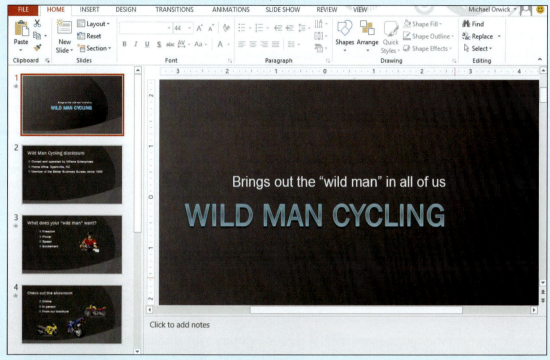

1. Locate and open **pp01a-ex03.pptx**.

2. Change to the Outline view. On slide 3, move the bullet "In person" from the third position to the second position.

3. On slide 5, add a title (using the Outline view) that says **Head out on the highway...**

4. On slide 5, drag the picture on the top left, down a bit so it is just below the new title you added.

5. Add the following notes to slide 6:
   Wild Man Cycling does not endorse dangerous driving. All stores provide a Safe and Defensive Driving course that is available to anyone for a nominal fee. The course is free with the purchase of any new motorcycle from the store.

6. On slide 2, add two more bullets using the Outline view. Add: **Speed** and **Excitement**.

7. Using the Outline view, insert a new slide after slide 1. In the title, type: **Wild Man Cycling disclosure**.

8. Using the Outline view, create three bullets below the title:
   Owned and operated by Millans Enterprises
   Home office: Sparkville, NC
   Member of the Better Business Bureau since 1988

9. Print the handouts three per page in black and white.

10. Save the file as **pp01a-hw03.pptx** and then close the file.

Placeholders and Media Buttons

Now that you know how to run and control a PowerPoint presentation, you can learn ways to add impact to the marketing presentation. You will start with nothing but a Title slide and ideas provided by the client. Use PowerPoint's predesigned slide layouts to quickly add slides that are already constructed to provide optimum appeal to the audience. These layouts contain placeholders that empower users to easily add pictures from their own sources as well as from online sources. Placeholders make it simple to include video and audio, aligning precisely and quickly.

PROJECT FILE: *Available at* **www.mhhe.com/office2013projectlearn**

After completing this project, you will be able to:

- Insert various slide layouts, pictures from your computer, and clip art.

- Locate and align pictures using online searches and alignment guides.

- Insert video from your computer and from online sources.

- Control video playback, trim the video, and fade in and out.

- Insert and control sound clips and music settings: looping and playing across slides.

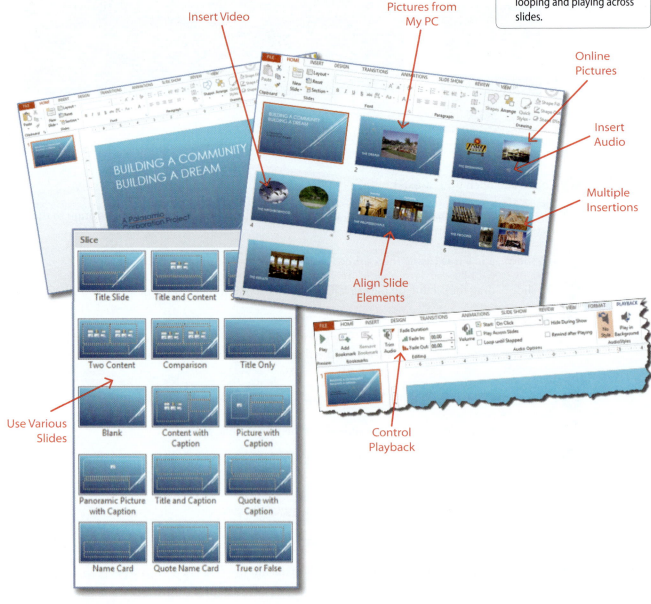

Insert Video

Pictures from My PC

Online Pictures

Insert Audio

Multiple Insertions

Align Slide Elements

Use Various Slides

Control Playback

Exploring the Placeholders

LESSON OVERVIEW

The placeholders in PowerPoint allow you to control each element separately, but more than that is included in a placeholder. When you use the predesigned **slide layouts**, many of the placeholders contain shortcuts to most of the images and media you would want to use in a slide show. These are called **content placeholders**. Not only do these shortcuts make it easier to locate pictures, video, and music, but once you have inserted them into the show, the placeholders also keep the elements nicely centered and aligned.

The **New Slide button** allows you to choose from any of the slide layouts so new slides provide the layout that suits your needs. If you wish to change the slide layout, select the slide, click the Layout button, and select the layout you want. PowerPoint instantly changes the slide to the new layout.

PowerPoint provides two sources for pictures. Find **Online pictures** on the Internet to insert into a slide show. Add your own pictures to a slide in a placeholder. The Picture button in a placeholder allows you to access Office .com's massive library of clip art. This collection of images includes illustrations, drawings, cartoons, and photos, all royalty-free.

Once you insert an image, PowerPoint provides a special set of commands, called **Picture tools,** to format and size the image accurately, so you can customize it to match your presentation. Almost every group along a tab ribbon has a **Launch button** to open a dialog box with all the possible settings for that group. Use these for more precise controls.

SKILLS PREVIEW

Insert a new slide (default layout)	• CLICK the HOME tab and locate the Slides group. CLICK the New Slide button (▨).
Insert a new slide (choose the layout)	• CLICK the HOME tab and locate the Slides group. CLICK the New Slide drop-down button (▨ New Slide). CHOOSE the desired layout.
Insert a picture into a placeholder	• CLICK on the Pictures button (▨) in the placeholder. Locate the image file. CLICK on the file. CLICK the Insert button, or • CLICK on the Pictures button in the placeholder. Locate the image file. DOUBLE-CLICK on the file.
Resize a picture while keeping the aspect ratio	• SELECT the image to activate Picture tools. CLICK the FORMAT tab and locate the Size group. Adjust the height and width as required.
Search and insert clip art	• CLICK the Online Pictures button (▨) in the placeholder to open the Office .com Clip Art window. TYPE what you are looking for into the search window. PRESS Enter . DOUBLE-CLICK the image you desire.
Insert an image from your computer	• CLICK the Pictures button placeholder. Locate the file on your computer. DOUBLE-CLICK on the file.
Open a group's dialog box	• CLICK the Dialog box launcher button (▨) in the bottom right-hand corner of the group.

1 Locate and open file **pp01b1.pptx**. Save it as **pp01b1-construction.pptx**.

2 By default, PowerPoint starts with a title slide. Table PP1.4 provides an overview of the most common slide layouts and their uses.

To insert a new slide:

CLICK the HOME tab and locate the Slides group.

CLICK the New Slide button ( ) to add a new slide below the existing one.
(*Result*: By default, after a Title slide, PowerPoint inserts a Title and Content slide. It is easily the most common slide layout.)

TABLE PP1.4 Common predesigned slide layouts

Slide Layout	Purpose of Design
Title Slide	Offers a main title placeholder and a smaller subtitle placeholder.
Title and Content	Provides a slide title placeholder and a content placeholder.
Section Header	Similar to the Title slide, but separates the following slides into a different section from the slides before it.
Two Content	Similar to the Title and Content layout, but includes two content placeholders, side by side.
Comparison	Identical to the Two Content slide, but includes separate subtitle placeholders above each of the content placeholders.
Blank	Provides the same design as the current slide show but has no placeholders.
Other Layouts	Provide larger areas for specific media. One may offer a larger placeholder for a picture or perhaps a panoramic picture.

3 CLICK into the title placeholder that says "Click to add title."

TYPE **The Dream** (the current settings will change the font to uppercase).

MORE INFO

The content placeholder has seven possible entries. Click on the Click to add text area. The six images in the center of the placeholder include shortcut buttons to insert a table, chart, and SmartArt. These are not part of this project. Instead, concentrate on the three buttons below: Pictures, Online Pictures, and Insert Video.

4 CLICK on the Pictures button ( ) in the large placeholder (the content placeholder).

Locate the file of media that accompanies this lesson.

CLICK on **pp01b1-dream.jpg**.

CLICK the Insert button to bring the picture onto the slide.

5 CLICK on the picture to ensure it is selected (sizing handles will appear around the image).

Once selected, the Picture tools will appear.

CLICK the FORMAT tab under Picture Tools and locate the Size group as shown in Figure PP1.21.

As long as the picture is selected, this Ribbon remains. If the Ribbon is lost, simply select the picture again.

CLICK the arrowhead (spinner) in the Shape Height window until it reads 4.2".

The picture is larger, and it retained its proper proportions.

FIGURE PP1.21 Picture Tools: Size and Arrange groups

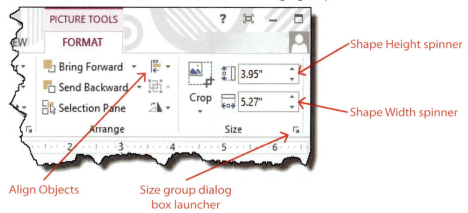

Shape Height spinner

Shape Width spinner

Align Objects

Size group dialog box launcher

⑥ CLICK the HOME tab and locate the Slides group.

CLICK the New Slide drop-down button (📄).

Rather than automatically inserting a Title and Content slide, this opens a palette of choices.

SELECT Two Content.

CLICK into the title placeholder.

TYPE **The Beginning**.

⑦ CLICK the Online Pictures button (🖼) in the left content placeholder to open the Office.com Clip Art window.

TYPE **under construction** into the search window.

PRESS Enter .

DOUBLE-CLICK the image with the Under Construction sign and the red light.

Adjust the size of the image height to 3".

> **TIP**
>
> When using the Online Pictures search window, we first clicked on the image to select it, and then clicked the Insert button to insert it into the slide show. In this last step, we double-clicked the image to insert it directly into the placeholder. Both ways work. While the double-click method is quickest, the first method is handy when you wish to insert more than one image at a time.

⑧ CLICK the Pictures button (🖼) in the right placeholder.

Locate the media file that accompanies this lesson.

CLICK on **pp01b1-beginning.jpg**.

CLICK the Insert button to bring it into the slide show.

⑨ Ensure the Picture tools are active.

CLICK the FORMAT tab under Picture Tools and locate the Size group (Figure PP1.22).

CLICK the Launch button (🖼) to open the Format Picture pane.

Here we see detailed control settings for the picture. Notice the Lock aspect ratio command has a check mark next to it. This is the default setting and that is why when we adjust the height of an image, the width adjusts accordingly to stay in proportion.

CLICK the Height spinner to adjust the image to 3".

CLICK the Close button (❌) to close the Format Picture pane.

FIGURE PP1.22 Format Picture pane

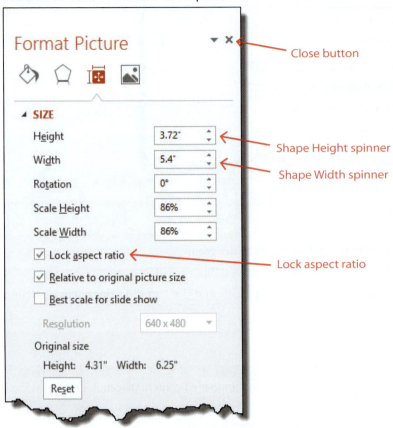

10 Your screen should look similar to Figure PP1.23. Before proceeding, save the **pp01a1-construction.pptx** file.

FIGURE PP1.23 Completion of Lesson PowerPoint 1B1

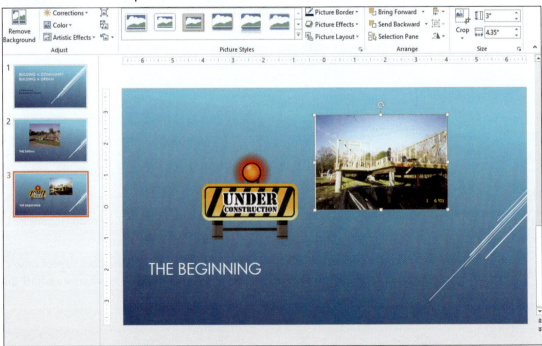

Using Online Searches

LESSON OVERVIEW

To make a presentation effective, we often include pictures from our files. But if we lack the most effective images, we can use the power of the Internet to bring images to our fingertips (and to our slide shows). PowerPoint's online searches provide direct access with a minimum of effort.

When you insert an image in a slide, dragging the image activates **automatic alignment guides** (faint dotted lines) when your image moves into obvious positions such as the center of the slide or straight across from another image. The automatic alignment guides vary depending on the elements on the slide.

Online searches allow you to add more than one image at a time. These **multiple insertions** save time. Hold the

`Ctrl` button down and click on different images to select more than one. Now one click on the Insert button brings them into your slide show all at once.

You can also save time with the **Align Objects** commands. They provide you the power to align objects into absolute positions on the slide with just a click. The positioning can be as simple as centering an image on a slide or matching images to the positioning of another image.

Once you have a slide just the way you like it, rather than create another slide just like it (or based on some of the same elements), use the **duplicate slide** feature to copy the entire slide, so you can start a new slide with all the same settings and elements in place—just waiting for your changes.

SKILLS PREVIEW

Search for and insert online pictures	• CLICK the Online Pictures button in the placeholder. CLICK into the Bing Image Search window. TYPE what you are looking for. PRESS `Enter`. DOUBLE-CLICK the desired image.
Activate automatic alignment guides	• DRAG the selected image across the slide. Automatic alignment guides will appear when the image touches obvious placements such as center of placeholder and aligned with another image.
See a larger image of an online picture search result	• CLICK the View Larger button (🔍) in the bottom right-hand corner of the picture. CLICK the X in the upper right-hand corner to close the larger view.
Center text in a placeholder	• CLICK in the text. CLICK the HOME tab and locate the Paragraph group. CLICK the Center button.
Insert more than one search result at a time	• HOLD the `Ctrl` button. CLICK on each image you desire. RELEASE the `Ctrl` button. CLICK Insert to insert all images at once.
Align objects in relation to each other	• HOLD the `Ctrl` button and select images to activate the Picture tools. CLICK the FORMAT tab under Picture Tools and locate the Arrange group. CLICK the Align Objects button (⬚▾). SELECT the alignment option you desire.

1 Ensure that **pp01b1-construction.pptx** is open.

2 CLICK the HOME tab and locate the Slides group.

PowerPoint inserts a new slide directly below the slide that is in the main editing window.

CLICK on slide 3.

CLICK the New Slide drop-down button (New Slide▾).

CLICK on Comparison to bring that slide layout into the main editing window.

3 CLICK into the title placeholder of the new slide.

TYPE **The Professionals**.

4 CLICK the Online Pictures button in the left content placeholder.

CLICK into the Bing Image Search box.

TYPE **framing a house**.

PRESS Enter .

DOUBLE-CLICK the first image shown in Figure PP1.24.

Resize the picture to a height of exactly 3".

FIGURE PP1.24 Suggested images

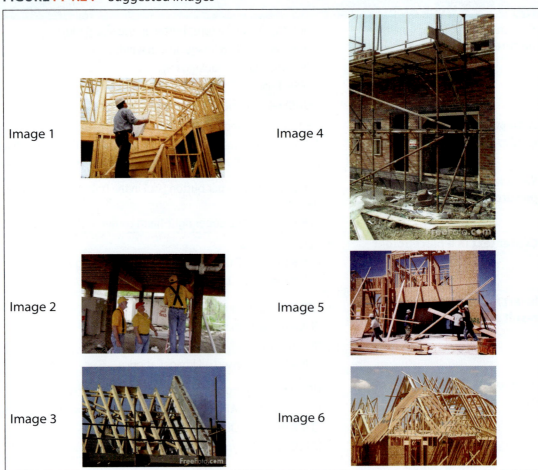

Image 1

Image 2

Image 3

Image 4

Image 5

Image 6

5 While the image is a good height, it no longer fits into the center of the placeholder. Use the automatic alignment guides to put it back where it belongs.

DRAG the picture into the center of the left placeholder.

Move it until you see dotted guidelines that center the picture both horizontally and vertically as shown in Figure PP1.25.

RELEASE the mouse.

FIGURE PP1.25 Automatic alignment guides: Vertical and Horizontal

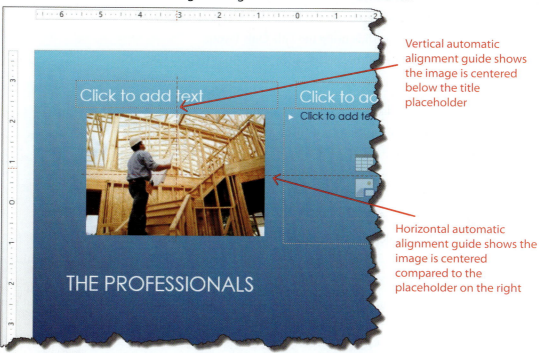

Vertical automatic alignment guide shows the image is centered below the title placeholder

Horizontal automatic alignment guide shows the image is centered compared to the placeholder on the right

6 CLICK the Online Pictures button in the right content placeholder.

CLICK into the Bing Image Search window.

TYPE **plumbing a house**.

CLICK on four images similar to the last four images shown in Figure PP1.24.

CLICK the View Larger button (🔍) in the bottom right-hand corner of the picture.

The larger picture shows this is a good image.

CLICK the X in the upper right-hand corner to close the larger view.

DOUBLE-CLICK the image to insert it into the placeholder.

7 Using the skills for resizing and aligning, set this picture to 3" high and centered horizontally and vertically into the right-hand placeholder.

8 CLICK into the title of the left-hand text placeholder (above the framing picture).

TYPE **Framing**.

CLICK the HOME tab and locate the Paragraph group.

CLICK Center to center the title over the image in the left-hand placeholder.

CLICK into the title of the right-hand text placeholder (above the plumbing picture).

TYPE **Plumbing**.

Center this text over the image in the right-hand text placeholder.

9 Now add a slide with four pictures. Because none of the preset layouts are designed for this, you will create your own.

CLICK on slide 4.

Insert a new slide using the Title Only layout.

CLICK into the title placeholder.

TYPE **The Process**.

10 Without placeholders, inserted pictures appear in the center of the slide.

To insert pictures without using placeholder buttons:

CLICK the INSERT tab and locate the Images group.

CLICK Online Pictures.

CLICK into the Bing Image Search window.

TYPE **house construction**.

PRESS Enter.

If the license warning appears, click the X on the right side of the yellow warning to bypass it.

HOLD the Ctrl button.

CLICK on four images similar to the last four images shown in Figure PP1.24. (You may need to scroll down in the selection window to find all four images.)

RELEASE the Ctrl button.

CLICK Insert to insert all four pictures at once.

11 All the pictures are centered on the slide (on top of each other). They are also all selected.

CLICK a blank area of the slide to deselect the images.

DRAG each picture to a different part of the slide.

Resize each image to 3" high.

12 DRAG one picture to a spot in the top left-hand corner of the slide (see Figure PP1.26).

HOLD the Ctrl button so you can select more than one image at a time.

SELECT a second picture from the bottom right of the slide to activate the Picture tools.

CLICK the FORMAT tab under Picture Tools and locate the Arrange group.

CLICK the Align Objects button (⊞ ▾).

SELECT Align Top to align both pictures with the one that is on top (highest on the slide).

13 DRAG one of the other pictures to a spot in the bottom right-hand corner of the slide.

HOLD the Ctrl button.

SELECT the remaining picture to activate the Picture tools.

CLICK the FORMAT tab under Picture Tools and locate the Arrange group.

CLICK the Align Objects button (⊞ ▾).

SELECT Align Bottom to align both pictures with the one that is on bottom (lowest on the slide).

14 Your screen should look similar to Figure PP1.26. Save and close the **pp01b1-construction.pptx** file.

FIGURE PP1.26 Completion of Lesson PowerPoint 1B2

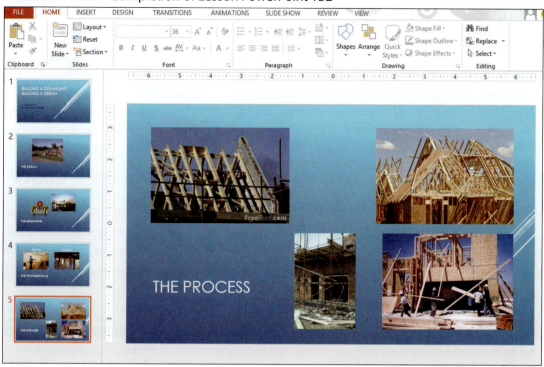

Adding Video

LESSON OVERVIEW

While you can have a great presentation with pictures and text, sometimes a little video can make a big impression on your audience. Videos come from various sources, including online. With the predesigned slide layouts and the placeholders, PowerPoint provides a quick and simple way to include video in your slide show.

Even without a specific placeholder layout, PowerPoint provides a simple way to insert video through the **Media group**. This feature provides quick access to video stored on your computer. Also through the Media group, you can access Internet searches for videos.

Video on My PC takes you to your local computer and automatically narrows the search for only video files. Even if your folder has documents, spreadsheets, and other file types, only the usable video files appear. This reduces clutter and confusion to help you quickly locate the files you can use.

The **online video** feature uses the power of Microsoft's Bing search engine to locate video based on your search request. You can also specify a search of YouTube.com directly from this feature. If you store files on SkyDrive, you can search there as well. Searching is also offered through the Video Embed Code window. Paste in the embed code to add the video to your slide.

SKILLS PREVIEW

Align an image using the rulers	• CLICK and HOLD your mouse in the center of the image. DRAG the image in the desired direction and watch the dotted line move across the top and side rulers. RELEASE the mouse when the image is in the correct location.
Insert video from your computer	• CLICK the INSERT tab and locate the Media group. CLICK the Video button. CHOOSE Video on My PC. Locate the media file on your computer. DOUBLE-CLICK the file to insert it.
Search and insert a video online	• CLICK the INSERT tab and locate the Media group. CLICK the Online Video button. Use the Bing Video Search to locate videos. DOUBLE-CLICK the video thumbnail and then CLICK the Insert button to insert the video.
Preview a video in the main editing window	• CLICK the image of the video to activate the controls. CLICK the Play button below the image.

PROJECT PRACTICE

1. Ensure that **pp01b1-construction.pptx** is open.

2. During the first two lessons, you used a couple of techniques for aligning images. Now you can clean up the only slide that has some alignment issues.

   CLICK on slide 3 in the slide pane.

   Using the rulers across the top and down the left-hand side of the slide:

   CLICK and HOLD your mouse in the center of the right-hand picture.

   DRAG the image to the (approximately) 3" mark right of center on the top ruler and the 1" mark above center on the left-hand ruler (see Figure PP1.27).

   DRAG the "under construction" image to the 3" mark left of center on the top ruler, and let the automatic alignment guides show you when it is properly aligned with the right-hand picture.

   RELEASE the mouse.

FIGURE PP1.27 Using the rulers to align images

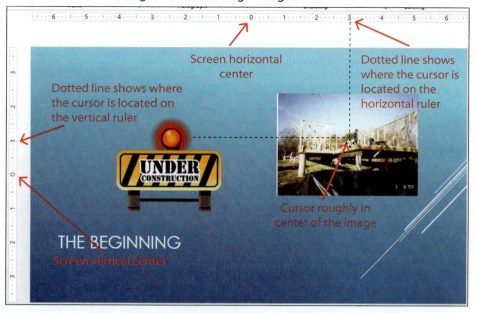

3 CLICK on the last slide.

CLICK the New Slide drop-down button (New Slide).

CHOOSE Title and Content.

CLICK in the title placeholder.

TYPE **The Results**.

CLICK the Pictures button in the content placeholder.

Locate the media files for this lesson.

DOUBLE-CLICK **pp01b3-view** to insert the picture onto the screen.

Resize the picture to a height of 4" and position as you wish.

⚠ HEADS UP

Although the clip art library is a part of Microsoft's services and remains a stable source of images, online searches vary greatly. By their very nature, online searches for video, pictures, and audio are dynamic and will likely not return the same results as when these lessons were created. When you are asked to insert a specific image, audio, or video, you may use any appropriate substitute.

---

4 CLICK on slide 3 in the slide pane.

Insert a Title and Content slide so that the new slide is slide 4.

CLICK into the title placeholder.

TYPE **The Neighborhood**.

5 CLICK the INSERT tab and locate the Media group.

CLICK the Video button.

CHOOSE Video on My PC.

Locate the media files associated with this lesson.

DOUBLE-CLICK on **pp01b3-deer.wmv** to insert it into the slide.

6 Once inserted, the Video tools become active.

CLICK the FORMAT tab under Video Tools and locate the Arrange group.

CLICK the Align button.

CHOOSE Align Center to center the image across the slide.

7 CLICK the Play button (see Figure PP1.28) to preview the video in the main editing window.

CLICK the Slide Show button in the Status bar to start the show from the current slide.

CLICK anywhere on the video image to start the video.

PRESS Esc to stop the video and again to end the slide show.

FIGURE PP1.28   Inserted video and controls

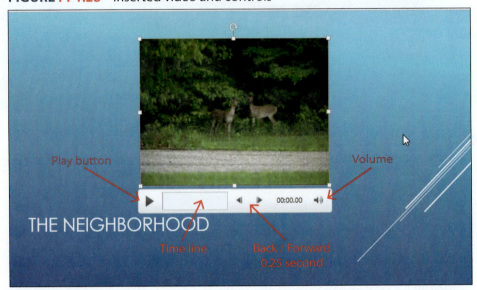

8 You are not limited to videos stored on your computer. While still on slide 4, search online. Deselect the video image. **Note: Steps 8, 9, and 10 may not work for all students on all computers.**

CLICK the INSERT tab and locate the Media group.

CLICK the Online Video button.

Use the Bing Video Search box to locate videos for birds in flight.

DOUBLE-CLICK the first choice to bring the video into the slide.

9 SELECT the deer video and resize it to 3.5" high.

SELECT the bird video and do the same.

DRAG the deer video so the center is approximately 3" right of center and 1" above center.

SELECT the deer and bird videos.

CLICK the HOME tab and locate the Drawing group.

CLICK the Arrange button.

Pause at the Align command until a submenu appears.

SELECT Align Top.

10 PRESS Shift + F5 to start the show from the current slide.

CLICK on both videos to run them.

PRESS Esc to end the slide show.

11 Your screen should look similar to Figure PP1.29. Save the **pp01b1-construction.pptx** file.

FIGURE PP1.29   Completion of Lesson PowerPoint 1B3

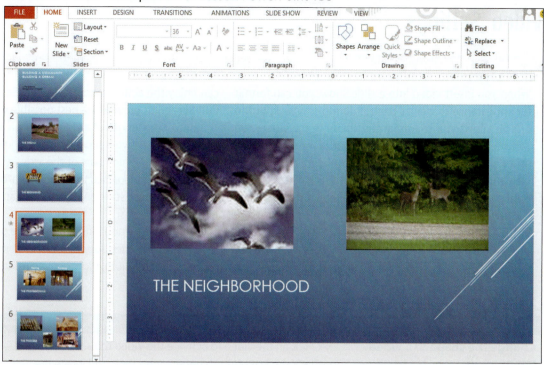

Video Settings

LESSON OVERVIEW

When you insert video into a slide show, you can format for appearance as well as control during playback. **Video Shape** allows you to format the shape of the video. You can present a video in a circle, a star, a triangle, or any other shape. When an action is completed on one slide element, use the **Repeat button** in the Quick Access toolbar to duplicate that action on another element of the slide.

Playback settings offer a series of controls for the video. Under **Video Options**, you can set the video to begin with a mouse click or automatically as the slide appears. Set videos to **Loop until Stopped** so the audience can enjoy the action more than once. Set a video to **Play Full Screen** to provide the best possible view.

Control the length of a video through **Trim Video**. This allows you to move a slide across the video time line and decide exactly which part of the video you would like to show. Set the video itself to **Fade In** and/or **Fade Out** for a smoother, softer start and end. You can also adjust the length of the fades.

Sometimes a good video might have poor sound quality or even unwanted sound. You can set the volume of the video to low, medium, high, or even mute.

SKILLS PREVIEW

Change the shape of a video image	• CLICK on the video to activate the Video tools. CLICK the FORMAT tab under Video Tools and locate the Video Styles group. CLICK the Video Shape button to drop down a palette of shapes. CHOOSE the shape you desire.
Set a video to start automatically	• CLICK on the video to activate the Video tools. CLICK the PLAYBACK tab under Video Tools and locate the Video Options group. CLICK the Start drop-down arrow. SELECT Automatically.
Control the volume of a video	• CLICK on the video to activate the Video tools. CLICK the PLAYBACK tab under Video Tools and locate the Video Options group. CLICK the Volume button in the Video Options group. SELECT the level (including mute).
Trim the length of a video	• CLICK on the video to activate the Video tools. CLICK the PLAYBACK tab under Video Tools and locate the Editing group. CLICK the Trim Video button. DRAG the green handle to adjust the start and end times of the video. CLICK OK.
Set a video to repeat	• CLICK on the video to activate the Video tools. CLICK the PLAYBACK tab under Video Tools and locate the Video Options group. CLICK the Loop until Stopped box to place a check mark in it.
Fade a video in or out	• CLICK on the video to activate the Video tools. CLICK the PLAYBACK tab under Video Tools and locate the Editing group. CLICK the Fade In spinner to desired length. CLICK the Fade Out spinner to desired length.

1 Ensure that **pp01b1-construction.pptx** is open.

⚠️ **HEADS UP**

If you closed this file, you may see a security warning upon reopening the file. This is because of the online content added in the previous lesson. If someone else created this file, you should be wary of the content. Since you created this file yourself, click the [Enable Content] button.

---

2 CLICK on slide 4.

CLICK on the deer video to activate the Video tools.

CLICK the FORMAT tab under Video Tools and locate the Video Styles group.

CLICK the Video Shape button to drop down a palette of shapes.

CHOOSE Oval (first item in Basic Shapes).

CLICK the bird video.

CLICK the Repeat button (🔃) in the Quick Access toolbar.

Now both videos appear as though they are being viewed through binoculars.

3 CLICK on the deer video to activate the Video tools.

CLICK the PLAYBACK tab under Video Tools and locate the Video Options group.

CLICK the Start drop-down arrow.

SELECT Automatically to make this video start as soon as the slide appears.

4 CLICK the Volume button in the Video Options group.

SELECT High.

CLICK the Reading View button in the Status bar to preview this slide.

PRESS Esc twice to return to the Normal view.

5 CLICK on the bird video.

CLICK the PLAYBACK tab under Video Tools and locate the Video Options group.

CLICK the Start drop-down arrow.

SELECT Automatically to make this video start as soon as the slide appears.

6 CLICK the Volume button in the Video Options group.

CLICK Mute so the audio from this video does not interfere with the other video.

7 The deer video is 27 seconds long. The bird video is more than a minute long. You can make them closer in length. **Note: Steps 7, 8, and 9 may not work for all students on all computers.**

CLICK on the bird video to activate the Video tools.

CLICK the PLAYBACK tab under Video Tools and locate the Editing group.

CLICK the Trim Video button to bring up the Trim Video dialog box (see Figure PP1.30).

DRAG the green slider (on the left of the time line) to about the 5-second mark to move it past the loud noise heard at the start of the video.

DRAG the red slider (on the right of the time line) to about the 35-second mark.

A timing above the time line should show about 30 seconds of total time.

CLICK OK.

FIGURE PP1.30 Trim Video control box

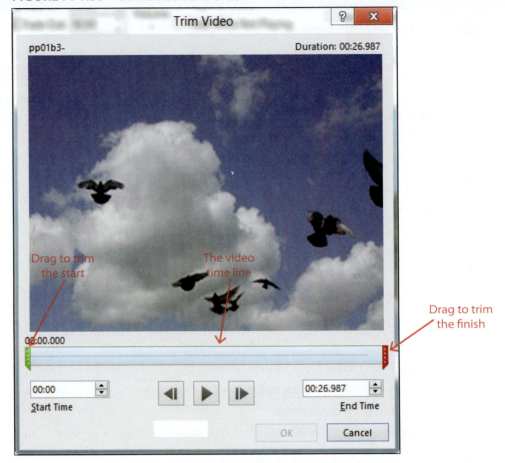

8 It is possible that during a presentation, this slide may remain longer than the 30 seconds of video. Set the video to repeat automatically.

CLICK on the bird video to activate the Video tools.

CLICK the PLAYBACK tab under Video Tools and locate the Video Options group.

CLICK the Loop until Stopped box to place a check mark in it.

Do the same to the deer video so both videos will repeat until you advance to the next slide.

9 To provide a graceful fade in for both videos, set the Fade duration.

CLICK on the bird video to activate the Video tools.

CLICK the PLAYBACK tab under Video Tools and locate the Editing group.

CLICK the Fade In spinner to 00.50.

CLICK the Fade Out spinner to 01.00.

Do the same to the deer video. Now both videos will gently fade in, fade away, and then start over automatically. Since they are not identical in length, this creates a nice effect.

10 Your screen should look similar to Figure PP1.31. Save the **pp01b1-construction.pptx** file.

FIGURE PP1.31   Completion of Lesson PowerPoint 1B4

Adding Sound

LESSON OVERVIEW

One of the most overlooked aspects of a presentation is sound. PowerPoint makes it easier to include and control sound in a slide show. A video often has accompanying sound, but the addition of music or background ambience increases the sensory experience of the presentation.

Online audio uses a similar search model as online video to find audio clips online to match your search request. For example, type in **construction** and the search results will be sounds related to construction. If you have sounds files or music on your computer, add them quickly through the **Audio on My PC** command. When you add to a slide, PowerPoint inserts an audio icon on the slide. During the slide show, click on that icon and the audio begins. You can also set the audio to start automatically as soon as the slide appears.

Control the volume of each audio file separately to ensure a good mix. Set it to **Play Across Slides** so one audio clip continues to play throughout the slide show, even if you introduce other audio. Set audio to **Play in Background** or use other options such as **Hide During Show** so the audio icon does not appear on the slide (to help reduce distraction).

SKILLS PREVIEW

Insert audio from your computer	• CLICK the INSERT tab and locate the Media group. CLICK the Audio button. CHOOSE Audio on My PC. Locate the audio file you desire. CLICK the file.
Insert audio from online sources	• CLICK the INSERT tab and locate the Media group. CLICK the Audio button. CHOOSE Online Audio. Enter your search words. DOUBLE-CLICK one of the results to insert it.
Set audio to start automatically	• CLICK the audio icon to activate the Audio tools. CLICK the PLAYBACK tab under Audio Tools and locate the Audio Options group. CLICK the Start drop-down arrow. CHOOSE Automatically to start the audio when the slide is presented.
Control the playback of audio	• CLICK the audio icon to activate the Audio tools. CLICK the PLAYBACK tab under Audio Tools and locate the Audio Options group. Select from: Volume, Play Across Slides, Loop until Stopped, Hide During Show, and Rewind after Playing.
Set audio to play in background	• CLICK the audio icon to activate the Audio tools. CLICK the PLAYBACK tab under Audio Tools and locate the AudioStyles group. CLICK Play in Background to use preset controls.
Remove all audio options	• CLICK the audio icon to activate the Audio tools. CLICK the PLAYBACK tab under Audio Tools and locate the AudioStyles group. CLICK No Style.

PROJECT PRACTICE

 Ensure that **pp01b1-construction.pptx** is open.

2 When there is only one image on a slide, you can still align it automatically.

CLICK on slide 2.

CLICK on the picture to activate the Picture tools.

CLICK on the FORMAT tab under Picture Tools and locate the Arrange group.

CLICK the Align button.

CHOOSE Distribute Horizontally to center the picture horizontally.

CLICK the Align button.

CHOOSE Distribute Vertically to center the picture vertically.

The picture is now in the very center of the slide.

3 CLICK on slide 3.

CLICK the INSERT tab and locate the Media group.

CLICK the Audio button.

CHOOSE Online Audio.

TYPE **construction**.

DOUBLE-CLICK one of the results to enter it on the center of the slide (some results cannot be downloaded, and you will see an error message).

4 DRAG the audio icon (◀) out of the way to the lower right-hand side of the screen.

Preview the slide in the slide show.

CLICK the start arrow in the audio icon to start the audio.

PRESS Esc to end the show.

5 Starting the audio with a click allows you to control it, but the mouse on the screen can be awkward and distracting.

To set the audio to start automatically:

CLICK the audio icon to activate the Audio tools.

CLICK the PLAYBACK tab under Audio Tools and locate the AudioStyles group.

CLICK Play in Background to change the settings in the Audio Options.

6 The change in settings makes some changes you do not want. Turn some of them off.

CLICK Play Across Slides to disable it.

CLICK Loop until Stopped to disable it.

Leave the Hide During Show on and the Rewind after Playing off (see Figure PP1.32).
(*Result:* Now when you preview the slide, the construction sounds play in the background until the audio ends or you advance to the next slide.)

FIGURE PP1.32 Audio tools: The Playback ribbon

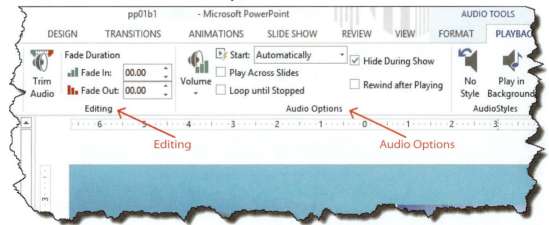

7 CLICK on slide 2 in the slide pane.

CLICK the INSERT tab and locate the Media group.

CLICK the Audio button.

CHOOSE Audio on My PC.

Locate the media files associated with this lesson.

CLICK on **pp01b5-adrenaline.mp3**.

CLICK Insert to place the audio icon in the center of the slide.

8 DRAG the audio icon away from the picture to avoid confusion.

CLICK the Play arrow to preview the music.

CLICK the Pause button to stop the music.

9 CLICK the audio icon to activate the Audio tools.

CLICK the PLAYBACK tab under Audio Tools and locate the Audio Options group.

CLICK the Start drop-down arrow.

CHOOSE Automatically so the music starts as soon as slide 2 is presented.

CLICK Play in Background and accept all the presettings.

10 Play the slide show from the beginning to see how the music blends with the other audio. Notice that the construction sound is too loud and drowns out the music.

CLICK on slide 3.

CLICK on the audio icon to activate the Audio tools.

CLICK the PLAYBACK tab under Audio Tools and locate the Audio Options group.

CLICK the Volume button.

SELECT Low.

Run the show again and see how the sounds mix.

 MORE INFO

The Audio on My PC button also offers a Record Audio option. You need a microphone connected to your computer, but you can record sounds directly into a slide show. This should not be confused with recording narration. That is handled through the SLIDE SHOW tab and is not part of this lesson.

11 Your screen should look similar to Figure PP1.33. Save the document.

FIGURE PP1.33 Completion of Lesson PowerPoint 1B5

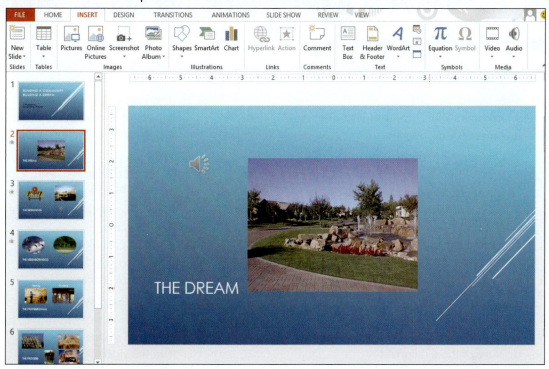

MULTIPLE-CHOICE QUIZ

Select the best choice in the following questions to review the project concepts. Good luck!

1. Slide layouts provide
   a. an overview of all your slides.
   b. a main editing window.
   c. predesigned slide formats.
   d. All of these are correct.

2. To insert clip art you must/can click
   a. online pictures.
   b. pictures.
   c. insert clip art.
   d. All of these are correct.

3. The Launch button ( )
   a. opens a detailed dialog box.
   b. starts the slide show from that slide.
   c. starts the slide show from the beginning.
   d. None of these is correct.

4. Automatic alignment guides
   a. sit along the top of the slide.
   b. appear when an image is inserted.
   c. appear when an image is double-clicked.
   d. None of these is correct.

5. To insert more than one photograph at a time, you must
   a. hold the `Shift` button while selecting.
   b. right-click while selecting.
   c. press the `Alt` button before each selection.
   d. hold the `Ctrl` button while selecting.

6. To duplicate a slide
   a. right-click and select Duplicate slide.
   b. click New Slide and select Duplicate Selected Slides.
   c. press `Ctrl`+`D`.
   d. All of these are correct.

7. Online video searches can include
   a. YouTube.com.
   b. your personal SkyDrive.
   c. Bing video search.
   d. All of these are correct.

8. Video Options allows you to
   a. play a video across all slides.
   b. loop until stopped.
   c. trim the video.
   d. All of these are correct.

9. The audio of a video can be set to
   a. play in background.
   b. fade in at a certain time.
   c. rewind after playing.
   d. None of these is correct.

10. Which of these is NOT an audio setting?
    a. No Style
    b. Play in Background
    c. Loop until Stopped
    d. Send Backward

HANDS-ON EXERCISE: WORK IT OUT PP-1B-E1

In this exercise, you will open an existing presentation and make changes to complete it and prepare it for printing. You will be provided with specific tasks, but not step-by-step instructions. The final document is shown in Figure PP1.34. Also remember that online searches will change quickly and not always return the same images, videos, or audio. If there is a change in the search results from the time this lesson was created and the time you perform it, feel free to substitute any appropriate image, video, or audio when completing this exercise.

FIGURE PP1.34   Work It Out PP-1B-E1: completed

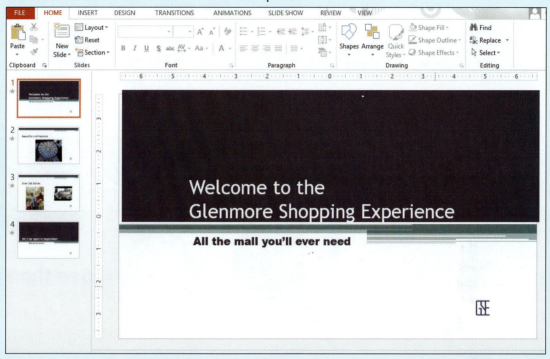

1. After launching Microsoft PowerPoint, locate and open the project data file **pp01b-ex01.pptx**. Save it as **pp01b-hw01.pptx**.

2. This presentation has only opening and closing slides. Add a Title and Content slide after slide 1. In the slide title placeholder, Type **Beautiful Architecture**.

3. Locate the media files associated with this lesson and use the placeholder to insert **pp01b-ex01.jpg** into the main placeholder.

4. Add a two content slide after slide 2. Type **Over 200 Stores** into the slide title placeholder.

5. In the left-hand placeholder, insert a clip art image by searching Office.com for the word *mall*. See Figure PP1.34 for an example.

6. In the right-hand placeholder, insert any video found by searching for "shopping mall exterior." (Because online searches change constantly, any appropriate video will do.) **Note: Steps 6, 7, 8, and 9 may not work for all students on all computers.**

7. Format the video to 3" high and align it with the top of the picture you inserted into the left-hand placeholder.

8. Format the video to fit into a Video Shape of Round Diagonal Corner Rectangle (last icon in Rectangles).

9. Set the video to start automatically.

10. Save and close the file.

In this exercise, you will open an existing presentation and make changes to complete it and prepare it for printing. You will be provided with specific tasks, but not step-by-step instructions. The final document is shown in Figure PP1.35. Also remember that online searches will change quickly and not always return the same images, videos, or audio. If there is a change in the search results from the time this lesson was created and the time you perform it, feel free to substitute any appropriate image, video, or audio when completing this exercise.

FIGURE PP1.35   Work It Out PP-1B-E2: completed

1 Locate and open **pp01b-ex02.pptx**. Save it as **pp01b-hw02.pptx**.

2 Insert a new title only slide after slide 1. Type **See the Sights** into the slide title placeholder.

3 Using the INSERT tab, search Office.com Clip Art for the three photos of San Francisco that you see in Figure PP1.35.

4 Using the rulers, drag the cityscape picture to approximately 3.5" right of center and 1.5" top of center.

5 Resize the picture of the cable car to be 5" high.

6 Using the automatic alignment guides, align the cable car picture with the top of the cityscape picture.

7 Using the automatic alignment guides, align the remaining picture with the bottom of the cable car picture.

8 Locate the media files associated with this lesson. Return to slide 1 and insert the audio file **pp01b-ex02.mp3**.

9 Trim the audio to start at 9:00 seconds and end at 44:00 seconds.

10 Set the audio to Play in Background.

11 Save and close the file.

In this exercise, you will open an existing presentation and make changes to complete it and prepare it for printing. You will be provided with specific tasks, but not step-by-step instructions. The final document is shown in Figure PP1.36. Also remember that online searches will change quickly and not always return the same images, videos, and audio. If there is a change in the search results from the time this lesson was created and the time you perform it, feel free to substitute any appropriate image, video, or audio when completing this exercise.

FIGURE PP1.36 Work It Out PP-1B-E3: completed

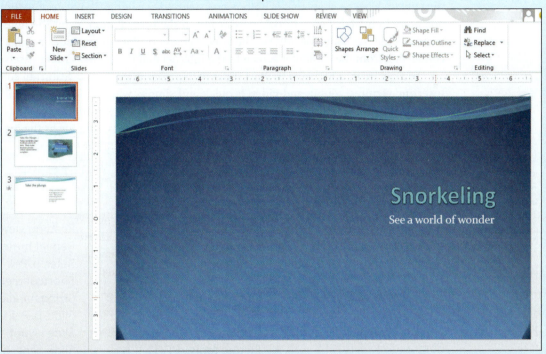

1. Locate and open **pp01b-ex03.pptx**. Save it as **pp01b-hw03.pptx**.

2. Insert a new slide after slide 1 with a Content with Caption layout.

3. In the title placeholder, type **Take the Plunge**. Increase the font size to 40 point.

4. In the caption placeholder, type **Today, snorkelers come in all ages and in all sizes. Many warm locations provide unique opportunities to explore**. Increase the font size to 28 point.

5. In the content placeholder, make an Online Video search for "snorkeling." Insert a short video from any appropriate source. **Note: Steps 5 and 6 may not work for all students on all computers.**

6. Set the size of the video to 4" high.

7. Using the automatic alignment guides, align the video with the bottom of the title placeholder.

8. Format the video to appear in a Flowchart: Document shape (printout).

9. Set the video to start on a mouse click.

10. Save and close the file.

Chapter Summary

PowerPoint is one of the most recognized and widely used presentation programs in the world. And no wonder. The ability to combine pictures, drawings, video, and sound along with text can make every presentation impactful. Very few programs are as truly intuitive as PowerPoint. You can learn most of the skills by experimenting. This makes PowerPoint more than just a tool for high-level presentations. Individuals can create mini shows to share with others.

This chapter begins by showing you how to run and control existing shows. This gives you the capacity to deliver a show that is both persuasive and engaging. The Notes function provides the opportunity to include your speaker notes right in the presentation, print the notes for yourself, and provide slide handouts for others. The latest version of PowerPoint does a great job of making the connection from the computer screen to the Internet and the immeasurable assets available there.

You can easily add media to your slides with predesigned layouts featuring content placeholders. Inserting pictures, sound, and video is quick and simple, whether it is from your own computer or from the Internet. Controlling the length, volume, and display of this content has never been easier. Blending these assets makes the creation of the slide show as fascinating as the presentation itself.

Chapter Key Terms

Align Objects, p. P-37
Audio on My PC, p. P-50
Automatic alignment guides, p. P-37
Backstage view, p. P-19
Collapse, p. P-24
Content placeholders, p. P-33
Copy and Paste, p. P-14
Demoting, p. P-24
Duplicate slide, p. P-37
Fade In, Fade Out, p. P-46
Format Painter, p. P-14
Gridlines, p. P-4
Guides, p. P-4
Handouts, p. P-19
Hide During Show, p. P-50
Launch button, p. P-33
Loop until Stopped, p. P-46
Main editing window, p. P-4
Media group, p. P-42

Multiple insertions, p. P-37
New Slide button, p. P-33
Notes, p. P-19
Online audio, p. P-50
Online pictures, p. P-33
Online video, p. P-42
Outline view, p. P-24
Picture tools, p. P-33
Placeholder, p. P-4
Play Across Slides, p. P-50
Play Full Screen, p. P-46
Play in Background, p. P-50
Playback, p. P-46
Presenter view, p. P-10
Print Color button, p. P-22
Print page, p. P-19
Print Preview, p. P-19
Print Range button, p. P-22
Printer button, p. P-21
Promoting, p. P-24

Reading view, p. P-8
Repeat button, p. P-46
Ruler, p. P-4
Shortcut menu, p. P-10
Sizing handles, p. P-14
Slide, p. P-4
Slide layout, p. P-33
Slide pane, p. P-6
Slide Show, p. P-10
Slide Sorter view, p. P-4
Status bar, p. P-4
Text box, p. P-14
Themes, p. P-4
Trim Video, p. P-46
Video on My PC, p. P-42
Video Options, p. P-46
Video Shape, p. P-46
View, p. P-4
Zoom, p. P-4

On Your Own Exercise PP-1C-E1

In this exercise, you will combine the skills you learned into a final PowerPoint project. This exercise allows you the freedom to add your own touches to an existing show to make it truly your own. This project can become part of your own portfolio of work. Figure PP1.37 is only an idea of how the final presentation may look.

Take some ideas from Conners-Weibe Investors and make improvements for a big presentation.

FIGURE PP1.37   Investment presentation: finished version

Locate and open **pp01cp1.pptx**. Save the slide show as **pp01cp1-hw01.pptx**.

Type the following notes to slide 1: **Thank you for taking the time to be part of this presentation. On behalf of Conners-Weibe Investors, let me welcome you and promise that "your money is our business."**

Insert a new slide after slide 1 using a content with caption layout. Title the slide **Services Offered**. In the caption add four bulleted points: **Investing**, **Monitoring**, **Reporting**, **Strategizing**. In the content placeholder, search Office.com Clip Art for "penny on graph chart." Insert, size, and align it appropriately.

Insert a new slide after slide 2 using the two content layout. In the title placeholder type **Knowledge and Experience**. In the left-hand content placeholder use an online search for something related to a bear or bull market. Size the image and align it appropriately.

In the right-hand content placeholder add the following bullet points: **50 years' experience**, **Testimonials**, **Proven results**, **Monthly reporting**. Position the two content placeholders appropriately.

Add a new slide after slide 3 using the Title and Content layout. Title it **Great Investing**. Insert an online video with "Warren Buffett" as the search request. Size the video to 5" high and center it both horizontally and vertically on the slide. Set it to start automatically. **Note: This step may not work for all students on all computers.**

Print slide show handouts with three slides per page.

Save and close the presentation. Exit Microsoft PowerPoint.

On Your Own Exercise PP-1C-E2

In this exercise, you will combine the skills you learned into a final PowerPoint project. This exercise allows you the freedom to add your own touches to an existing show to make it truly your own. This project can become part of your own portfolio of work. Figure PP1.38 is only an idea of how the final presentation may look.

Use a concept by Claptene Green, a company that specializes in helping organizations become more environmentally friendly, and add some impact.

FIGURE PP1.38   Claptene Green: finished version

Perform the following steps to complete this comprehensive chapter project.

Locate and open **pp01cp2.pptx**. Save the slide show as **pp01cp2-hw02.pptx**.

Insert a new slide after slide 1 using the Comparison layout. Title the slide **Environmental Advantage**. In the title for the left-hand placeholder type **Our future?** Center the title across the placeholder. In the title for the right-hand placeholder type **Our future!!** Center this title across the placeholder. In the left-hand content placeholder, search online for an image showing "waste disposal." In the right-hand content placeholder, search online for an image of "environmentally friendly action."

Insert a new slide after slide 2 using the Blank layout. Create a text box across the top and type in **Are you with us?** Use the Format Painter to apply the same formatting to the new text box as exists in the title placeholder on slide 2. Use the Media group to insert a video showing solar or some other alternate energy source. Size the video to 4.4" high. Align the title directly atop the center of the video.

Set the video to play full screen when it is clicked. **Note: Steps concerning the use of videos may not work for all students on all computers.** Trim the video to about 30 to 40 seconds in length. Set the volume to low.

Add the following notes to the following slides:

Slide 1: **Almost seven years ago, Jermaine Claptene and Emma Green formed a company that was determined to make a difference. Today Claptene Green has helped over 50 national and international companies improve their operations and improve the world.**

Slide 2: **When we look back at what has been accomplished with our partner companies, we realize even little changes can have a big effect.**

Slide 3: **The partnership is not just you and me and your people. The sun, the wind, the water, and the entire Earth are our partners, too**.

Locate the files associated with this lesson and add the audio **pp01cp2.mp3**. Set the audio to medium volume, play across slides, hide during show. Trim the audio to start at 48 seconds. Fade the audio in for 00.50 second.

Insert a slide after slide 3 using the content with caption layout. In the slide title, type the company name, **Claptene Green**. Make up contact information for the placeholder below the title. In the content placeholder, search online for a picture of some alternate energy source. Align and size the image appropriately.

Save and close the file. Exit from PowerPoint.

2

Enhancing Your Presentations

Enhancing your presentations through a variety of tools allows you to make your presentations match the environment or your speaking style. PowerPoint gives you the power to control settings, such as the screen ratios between the standard 4:3 size and the newer wide-screen ratio of 16:9, depending on the projector being used. To complement your speaking style, you can use different animations to make your presentation suit your speech. Depending on the type of presentation you are delivering, you even have the ability to create interactive PowerPoint shows that integrate hyperlinks within the presentation or to external content!

Setting the right mood for your presentation is important. In this chapter, you will learn how to use and modify themes to create your own unique templates to use in your presentations.

This chapter will empower you to create presentations from scratch. You will learn how easy it is to insert elements, transitions, animations, interactivity, and themes. You will also learn how to easily finalize your presentation for your specific venue.

PROJECT

Preparing a Sales Pitch

In this project, you will build a sales slide show for Bocher & Sons from a blank presentation. You will learn how to insert elements such as images, transitions, animations, and hyperlinks to augment your presentation.

This project will provide you with a concrete example of implementing technical skills, which you will be able to use in your future presentations. Your creativity is the driving force behind the presentations you create.

THE SITUATION

Bocher & Sons

Jim Bocher, owner of Bocher & Sons, is thinking about hiring a company to manage his information technology services. He wants to be sure he can rely on one company for all of his technology needs and has requested proposals from a number of computer firms. Your company, TechGem Computers, wants you to produce a sales pitch for Jim. You realize this presentation needs to be unique and concise. Therefore, you start a presentation from scratch and decide to make a three-slide presentation with the significant points.

Creating an Informational Presentation

This project will focus on the creation of a presentation for a sales pitch. You will learn about making presentations from scratch and enhancing them to match your presentation style and audience. As you will see, there are many different ways to enhance presentations. It will be up to you to determine how best to match your purpose, presentation style, and audience.

PROJECT FILE: *Available at* **www.mhhe.com/office2013projectlearn**

After completing this project, you will be able to:

- Create a new presentation.
- Insert and modify transitions.
- Add animations to elements.
- Synchronize and time transitions and animations.
- Add interactivity through hyperlinks.

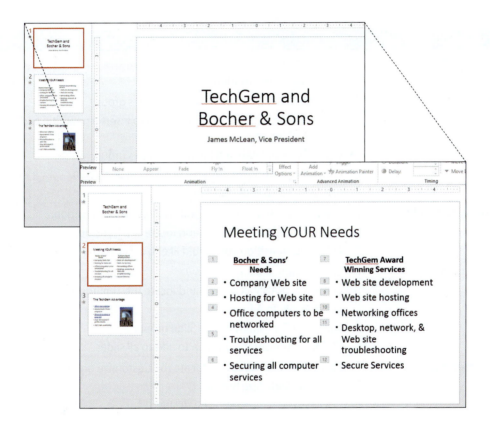

Creating a New Presentation

LESSON OVERVIEW

You typically use PowerPoint to develop a presentation for a specific purpose. In the previous chapter, you learned how to present and edit an existing presentation. This lesson will focus on building a powerful slide show starting from a blank presentation.

Creating a blank presentation is just the start. You can fill it with different **elements** and work with them on the slides. Elements refers to the different types of slide content, such as graphics, texts, and shapes. These slide elements allow you to truly customize your presentation to fit your needs. You can insert **transitions** to control how one slide changes into the next slide. Transitions can add a feeling of flow to your presentation.

You will also learn how to save your presentation in different **file formats** and change the **screen ratio** to match the ratio of your presentation venue.

SKILLS PREVIEW

Create a blank presentation	• Launch PowerPoint. CLICK Blank Presentation.
Insert a new slide	• CLICK the HOME tab and locate the Slides group. CLICK the top of the New Slide button to insert a new Title and Content slide (default slide), or • CLICK the HOME tab and locate the Slides group. CLICK the drop-down arrow of the New Slide button. CHOOSE the style of slide you desire.
Apply a transition to a slide	• CLICK on the slide to which you want to add a transition. CLICK the TRANSITIONS tab and locate the Transitions to this Slide group. CLICK the Transition you would like to apply to the slide.
Apply the same transition to all slides	• CLICK on any slide in the show. CLICK the TRANSITIONS tab and locate the Timings group. CLICK Apply To All. Locate the Transition to This Slide group. CLICK the transition you wish to add to all slides.
Set different screen ratios	• CLICK the DESIGN tab and locate the Customize group. CLICK the Slide Size button. CHOOSE the screen ratio you desire.

PROJECT PRACTICE

 Start Microsoft PowerPoint to open the welcome page.

CLICK on Blank Presentation.

CLICK the FILE tab and use the Save As command to save the file to your computer as **pp02a1-salespitch.pptx**. Your presentation should appear similar to Figure PP2.1 before proceeding.

FIGURE PP2.1 Starting a blank presentation

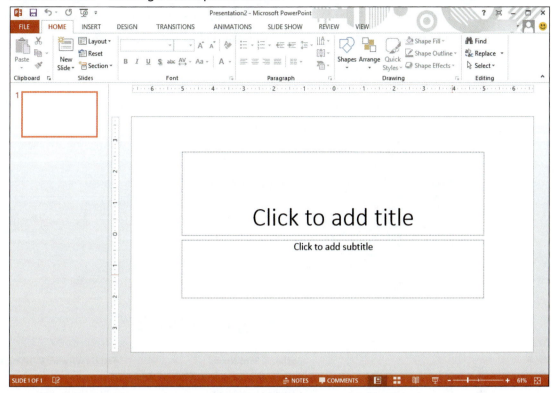

2 CLICK in the Click to add title placeholder to enter text there.

TYPE TechGem and Bocher & Sons

CLICK the mouse before the text "Bocher."

PRESS Enter.

CLICK in the subtitle placeholder.

TYPE Your Name, Vice President

3 Locate the Slides group on the HOME tab.

CLICK the drop-down arrow on the New Slide button.

CHOOSE Comparison.

Edit this slide in the following manner:

TYPE Meeting YOUR Needs in the title placeholder.

CLICK into the upper-left placeholder.

TYPE Bocher & Sons Needs

CLICK into the lower-left placeholder.

TYPE the following pressing Enter between each line:

- Company Web site
- Hosting for Web site
- Office computers to be networked
- Troubleshooting for all services
- Securing all computer services

4 Move to the placeholders on the right-hand side and add the following:

TYPE **TechGem Award Winning Services** in the upper-right placeholder.

Add the following into the lower-right placeholder (see Figure PP2.2):

- **Web site development**
- **Web site hosting**
- **Networking offices**
- **Desktop, network, and Web site troubleshooting**
- **Secure services**

FIGURE PP2.2 Text on a Comparison slide

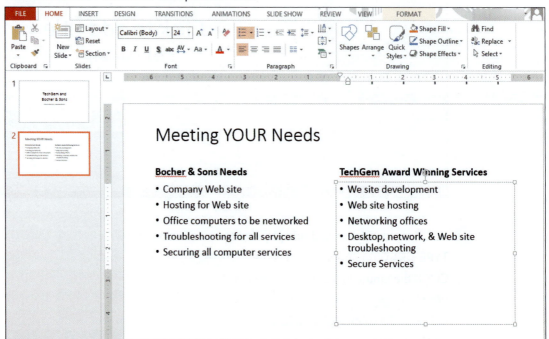

5 CLICK the New Slide button.

CHOOSE Two Content.

CLICK into the title placeholder.

TYPE **The TechGem Advantage**

CLICK into the text placeholder on the left.

TYPE the following:

- **All-in-one solution**
- **Guaranteed 2 hour response**
- **Physical location in your city**
- **Over 30 trained IT professionals**
- **24/7/365 availability**

6 CLICK the On-line Pictures button (⬛) in the right-hand placeholder.

CLICK in the Office.com Clip Art search box.

TYPE computer

CLICK Enter.

CLICK on an image that will complement the slide.

CLICK the INSERT button.

7 Transitions control how one slide changes into the next slide.

Apply a transition to this slide:

CLICK the TRANSITIONS tab and locate the Transitions to This Slide group.

CLICK the More button to reveal more transitions (see Figure PP2.3).

CLICK the Fade transition to apply it to this slide.

FIGURE PP2.3 The palette of Transitions after clicking the More button

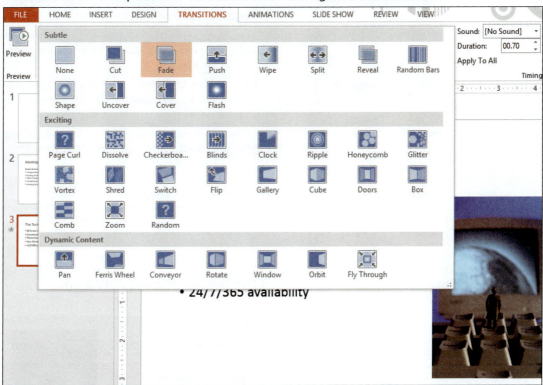

8 PRESS F5 to start the presentation.

PRESS Enter to move to the second slide (notice there is no transition from slide to slide).

PRESS Enter to move to the third slide (notice how it fades in).

Exit the presentation.

9 Although you can add a different transition to each slide, since this transition works well, add it to all the slides at once.

CLICK on slide 3 (which has the desired transition).

CLICK the TRANSITIONS tab (if not already showing) and locate the Timing group.

CLICK the Apply To All button to apply slide 3's transition to all the slides.

Start the show again and notice that even the first slide fades in.

10 You found out that Bocher & Sons' presentation room has a projector with a 4:3 ratio.

PowerPoint defaults to the high-definition 16:9 ratio.

To match the presentation with the projector:

CLICK the DESIGN tab and locate the Customize group.

CLICK the Slide Size button.

CHOOSE Standard (4:3) to adjust the show to suit the projector.

CHOOSE Ensure Fit so nothing is lost on the slide.

11 Your screen should look similar to Figure PP2.4. Save the **pp02a1-salespitch.pptx** file. You can use many formats to save a PowerPoint presentation. Table PP2.1 explains the various formats and their use.

TABLE PP2.1 File formats for PowerPoint

Status Bar Commands	Result
PowerPoint Presentation	PowerPoint's default file format is .pptx. Some features may not be available if opened in earlier formats.
PowerPoint 97-2003 Presentation	This file type (.ppt) will save the show in a format that is compatible with older versions of Microsoft Office. Some features of the newer formats will be lost.
PowerPoint Template	You can save your presentation as a template (.potx) so it can be used again. This is a great idea if you created a unique look or feel to the show.
PowerPoint Show	When you open the show in this format (.ppsx), it opens directly into the show itself and not into the editing view.

FIGURE PP2.4 Completion of Lesson PowerPoint 2A1

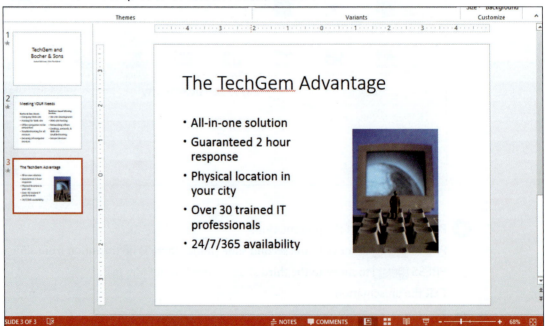

Transition Timing, Sounds, and Effects

LESSON OVERVIEW

PowerPoint allows you to control how transitions work, adding to the impact of the show. The way a presentation moves from one slide to the next can really add to the feel of the presentation. For example, if you want to build a little anticipation with your audience between slides, choose a transition that moves slowly as it displays the contents of the next slide. While transitions can add much to the show, be certain they are appropriate, and do not overdo them. Too many can detract from the overall look and feel.

The three types of transitions are Subtle, Exciting, and Dynamic Content. While you may not agree with the classification (what is exciting to one may not be to another), it provides a quick way to locate your favorite transitions. You can alter the duration of each transition so it takes longer or shorter for the effect to occur. You can also add sound to the transition if it suits your show. Because each transition has its own effect, you can also adjust the **Effect Options**, depending on which transition you choose.

You will also learn to use the **Slide Sorter view** to quickly modify transitions and to preview each slide separately.

SKILLS PREVIEW

Open Slide Sorter view	• Move to the Slide Sorter button (⊞) on the PowerPoint Status Bar, or • CLICK the VIEW tab and locate the Presentations Views group. CHOOSE Slide Sorter.
Preview a transition	• In the Slide Sorter view, CLICK the tiny star below the slide (Preview button). The preview appears in the slide thumbnail.
Change the duration of a transition	• CLICK the TRANSITIONS tab and locate the Timing group. CLICK the Duration spinner to the desired timing.
Add a sound to a transition	• CLICK the TRANSITIONS tab and locate the Timing group. CLICK the Sound drop-down. CHOOSE the desired sound.
Change the effects of a transition	• CLICK the TRANSITIONS tab and locate the Transition to This Slide group. CLICK Effect Options. CHOOSE the desired effect.

PROJECT PRACTICE

1. In the previous lesson, you applied the Fade transition to all slides. In this presentation, you will use the first two slides to build to the final slide. In this way, Bocher & Sons executives will leave the presentation knowing that you matched your services to their needs. Open the **pp02a2.pptx** file. Save it as **pp02a2-salespitch.pptx**.

2. CLICK the TRANSITIONS tab and locate the Transition to This Slide group.

   CLICK the More button.

   CLICK Vortex from the Exciting category.

   After a short delay, a preview of the transition will display in the main editing area.

3 Move to the Slide Sorter button ( ) on the PowerPoint Status Bar.

This view provides an overview of all the slides in the show.

Slides that have transitions applied to them have tiny stars (Preview buttons) below the slide.

CLICK the Preview button below slide 1 to see the current transition in the slide thumbnail (see Figure PP2.5).

FIGURE PP2.5 Preview of transition in the Slide Sorter view

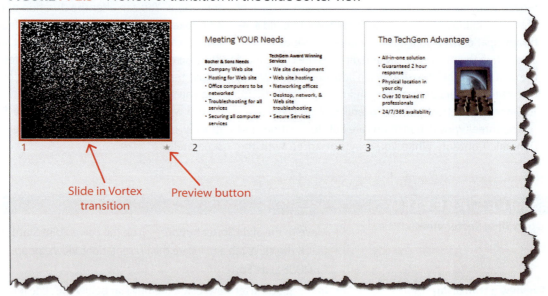

Slide in Vortex transition

Preview button

TIP

The Slide Sorter view (and all other views) can be accessed by clicking the VIEW tab and locating the Presentation Views group.

---

4 CLICK on slide 2 to select it.

The ribbon shows that this slide has a Fade transition.

CHOOSE the Reveal transition.

The slide transition will display in the main editing window.

5 The transition is quite slow and should work faster.

Locate the Timing group.

CLICK the down arrow on the Duration spinner to read 1.50 (see Figure PP2.6).

Preview the transition (click the transition star) to see that it works much faster.

FIGURE PP2.6 The Timing group

Sound drop-down

Duration spinner

Timing

6. CLICK on slide 3 to select it.

   Apply the Blinds transition (in the Exciting group) to slide 3.

   Preview the slide.

7. Locate the Timing group.

   CLICK the Sound drop-down (see Figure PP2.6).

   CHOOSE Chime.

   Ensure the computer volume is loud enough to hear the sound.

   Preview the slide to see how the sound enhances the transition to show a "solution" for the client.

 HEADS UP

As you can imagine, sounds need to be used very carefully. Sounds that are sent through a large sound system can jolt the audience if they are not expecting it. The sound must match not only the transition itself, but also the mood you are trying to convey. Overusing sounds quickly makes the audience start to ignore them, and they lose effectiveness.

8. CLICK on slide 1 to select it.

   The Vortex transition is applied to it, but you can change how it appears.

   Locate the Transition to This Slide group.

   CLICK Effect Options.

   CHOOSE From Bottom.

   See in the preview how the Vortex starts at the bottom and solidifies from the top down.

9. CLICK on slide 2 to select it.

   CLICK Effect Options.

   CHOOSE Smoothly from the left.

   Preview the effect.

   Run the show from the beginning to see how the transitions work.

   CLICK on Slide 1 to select it.

10 Your screen should appear similar to Figure PP2.7. Save the **pp02a2-salespitch.pptx** file.

FIGURE PP2.7 Completion of Lesson PowerPoint 2A2

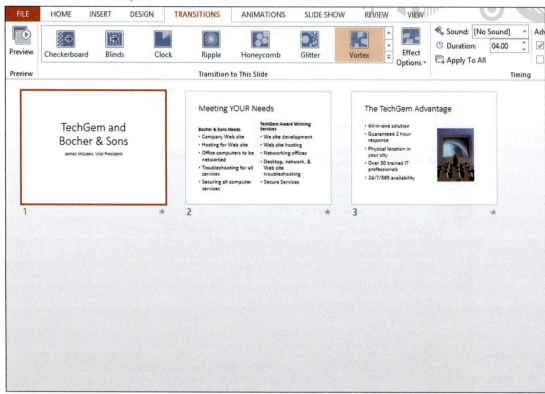

Adding Animations

LESSON OVERVIEW

While transitions allow you to control the way one slide moves to another, animations provide a way to bring things to life on each slide. **Animations** include the ability to control how elements enter a slide (**Entrance effects**), how they exit a slide (**Exit effects**), and what happens while they are on the slide (**Emphasis effects**).

Probably the most commonly used function in PowerPoint, animations can make a presentation more fun and exciting. But the main purpose is to allow you to control the amount of information that appears on the slide at any time. By bringing your points up one at a time, you can explain each point before moving to the next one. This makes it easier for the audience to follow and provides time for you to make your point in a logical manner.

While animations are important, they can easily be overused and must be chosen to suit the flow of the presentation.

SKILLS PREVIEW

Add animations	• Select the element you wish to animate. CLICK the ANIMATIONS tab and locate the Animation group. CHOOSE the animation you want to apply. To see more animations, CLICK the More button or CLICK the Add Animation button in the Advanced Animation group.
Apply animations to more than one element at a time	• CLICK the first element. PRESS and hold Shift. CLICK the other elements. Release the Shift button. CLICK the ANIMATIONS tab and locate the Animation group. CHOOSE the animation you want to apply to the elements.
Locate more animation effects	• CLICK the ANIMATIONS tab and locate the Animation group. CLICK the More button. CLICK More Entrance (Emphasis, Exit) Effects.

PROJECT PRACTICE

1. Slide 2 of the presentation contains a lot of information. On the left-hand side, it lays out needs of the client point by point. Then, on the right-hand side, it states how TechGem meets each one of those needs point by point. This slide would be much more effective if the points were presented one at a time. Open the file **pp02a3.pptx**. Save it as **pp02a3-salespitch.pptx**.

2. Adjust a few placeholders to accommodate the 4:3 ratio.

   CLICK the VIEW tab and locate the Presentation Views group.

   CLICK the Normal button to return to the main editing window.

   CLICK slide 2 from the thumbnails on the left.

   CLICK the placeholder that says "Bocher & Sons' Needs."

   DRAG the right-hand edge of the placeholder to the left until the word *Needs* moves to its own line.

   Select the text in that placeholder and center it.

   CLICK into the placeholder that says "TechGem Award Winning Services."

Resize the placeholder until the words "Winning Services" appear on the second line. Select the text in that placeholder and center it (see Figure PP2.8).

FIGURE PP2.8   Sizing handles on placeholders

3 CLICK the placeholder that says "Bocher & Sons' Needs."

Be sure to select the placeholder, not the text.

CLICK the ANIMATIONS tab and locate the Animation group.

CHOOSE Fly In (see Figure PP2.9).

CLICK the Preview button in the ribbon to see how that placeholder animates from the bottom.

Do the same to the placeholder that says "TechGem Award Winning Services."

FIGURE PP2.9 The transitions group: the Fly In transition

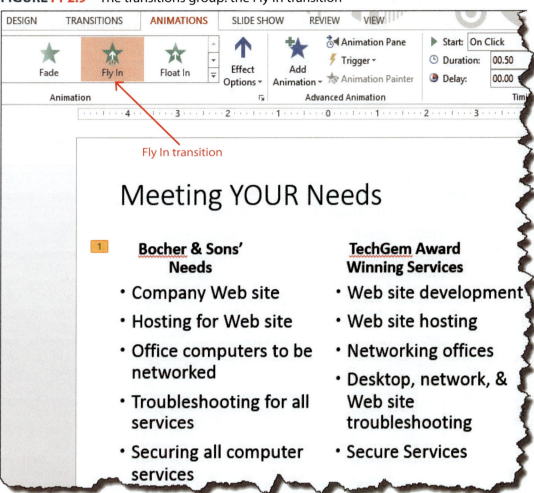

Fly In transition

 MORE INFO

There are three types of animations. Entrance animations control how the element "enters" the slide. Emphasis animations control what the element does once it is on the slide. Exit animations control how the element leaves the slide.

---

4 You can apply a different animation to any element on a slide. If you want to apply the same animation to a number of elements, you can do it all at once.

CLICK the lower placeholder on the left-hand side.

PRESS and hold Shift.

CLICK the lower placeholder on the right-hand side.

Both placeholders are now selected and the same animation can be applied to both.

CLICK the More button in the Animation group to drop down the palette of animations.

CLICK Zoom from the Entrance animations.

The preview of the new animation occurs automatically on the slide.

CLICK the Preview button on the ribbon to see a preview of the entire slide.

5 CLICK on slide 3.

CLICK in the Title placeholder.

CLICK the More button in the Animation group to drop down the palette of animations.

CHOOSE Bounce.

6 CLICK on the image on the right-hand side of the slide.

CLICK the More button in the Animation group.

CHOOSE More Entrance Effects (see Figure PP2.10).

Locate the Exciting category.

CHOOSE Float.

CLICK OK.

FIGURE PP2.10 The Transition palette

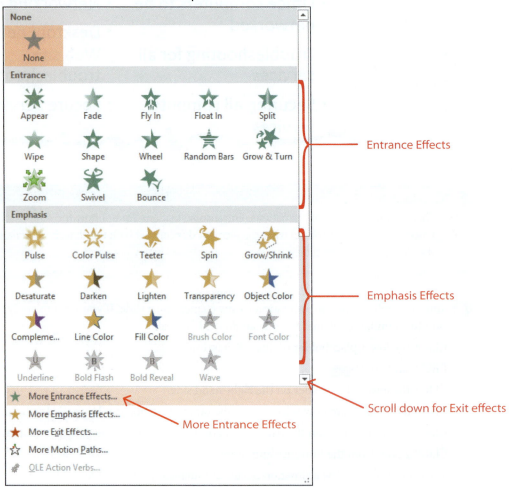

7 CLICK the text placeholder on the left of the slide.

Open the Animation palette.

Apply the Grow & Turn animation.

8 You decide to add another effect to the image on this slide for emphasis.

To add more than one effect to an element:

CLICK the image to select it.

Locate the Advanced Animation group.

CLICK Add Animation.

CHOOSE Teeter in the Emphasis group.

Notice this action is number 8 and will occur after all the others.

Preview the slide.

> **MORE INFO**
>
> Copy an animation from one element to another with the Animation Painter. Simply click on the element that currently has the animation you want. Click the Animation Painter in the Advanced Animation group. Then click on the element that does not have an animation. The animation from the first element is "painted" onto the second element.

9 CLICK on slide 1.

CLICK in the slide title.

CLICK Add Animation.

Locate the Emphasis category.

CLICK Wave.

See the preview.

CLICK on slide 3.

> **MORE INFO**
>
> After you add the "wave" effect, you will notice an unusual arrow pointing straight up from the title. These types of arrows are specific to the action of the effect. In this case, the green arrowhead shows the original position of the middle of the text; the red arrowhead shows how much the text will "jump" when it waves. The arrows appear when you click in another location on the slide. Drag the red arrowhead up or down to adjust the amount.

10 Your screen should appear similar to Figure PP2.11. Save and close the **pp02a3-salespitch.pptx** file.

FIGURE PP2.11 Completion of Lesson PowerPoint 2A3

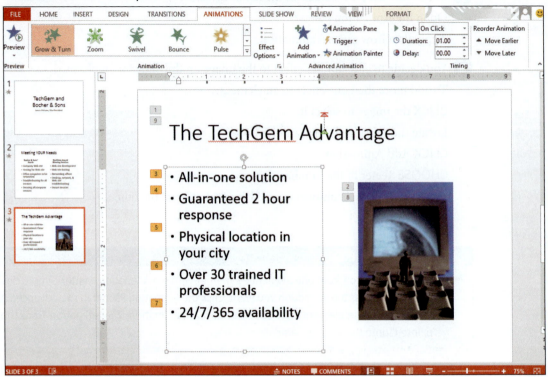

Timing and Synchronizing Actions

LESSON OVERVIEW

When you work with animations and transitions, Power-Point allows you to control when and how each of these occur. By modifying the **timing options**, you can set a slide transition or animation to occur when you advance the show (**Start On Click**), or the action can happen at the same time as another action (**Start With Previous**). You can even delay one action to occur a specific time after an earlier action by adjusting the **Start**, **Duration**, and **Delay** controls.

PowerPoint orders the animations based on the one you apply first to a slide. You can easily **reorder animations** later to suit your needs. **Remove animations** from a slide by clicking on the action order number and deleting it.

You can also control each animation by adjusting the **Effect Options**. These options are different depending on the characteristics of the specific animation.

SKILLS PREVIEW

Open the Animation pane	• CLICK the ANIMATIONS tab and locate the Advanced Animation group. CLICK Animation pane. CLICK the expand arrows (⌄) to see all the animations.
Reorder animations	• Open the Animation pane. Drag the action up or down to the desired location.
Set animation timings	• CLICK the ANIMATIONS tab and locate the Timing group. CLICK on the element you wish to adjust. Adjust the Start, Duration, and/or Delay options as desired.

PROJECT PRACTICE

1 Adjust the timing or the elements to match your presentation to improve your slide show. Open the **pp02a4.pptx** file. Save it as **pp02a4-salespitch.pptx**.

2 CLICK on slide 2.

CLICK the ANIMATIONS tab and locate the Advanced Animation group.

CLICK Animation pane to open the pane on the right-hand side of the screen.

CLICK the expand arrows (⌄) to see all the animations on the slide (they are numbered).

3 You can reorder the placeholder titles so "TechGem Award Winning Services" doesn't appear until the "Bocher & Sons' Needs" is complete.

The title of the second column "TechGem Award Winning Services" is action number 2 on the Animation pane.

DRAG it down just below action number 7 (see Figure PP2.12).

Preview the slide.

FIGURE PP2.12 Reordering actions on the Animation pane

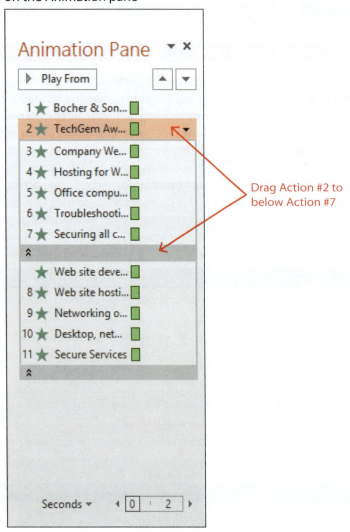

Drag Action #2 to below Action #7

④ While the left-hand placeholder works fine, the right-hand placeholder has the title flying in at the same time as the first bullet appears (they are both action number 7). You can control that. Return to the Animation pane.

CLICK on the action "Web site development."

CLICK the drop-down arrow next it (see Figure PP2.13).

CLICK Start On Click to delay the animation until you want to advance it.

Notice that the action is now number 8 and the other actions are renumbered to follow.

Preview the slide.

FIGURE PP2.13 The Timings menu

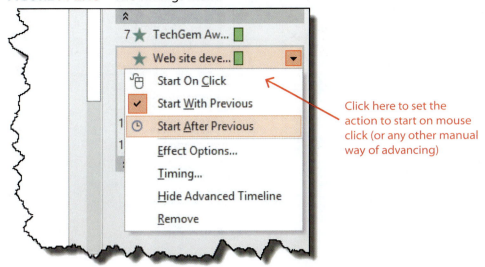

Click here to set the action to start on mouse click (or any other manual way of advancing)

5 CLICK on slide 3.

To make the image on the right appear at the same time as the title bounces into place:

CLICK on the image to select it.

This highlights it on the Animation pane.

CLICK on Action 2 in the Animation pane.

CLICK the drop-down next to Action 2 on the Animation pane.

CHOOSE Start With Previous so the title and the image both are given number 1.

Preview the slide.

6 Notice the image floats onto the screen before the title bounces in. This is because the two effects simply have different durations (found in the Timing group). This is also shown graphically in the Animation pane (see Figure PP2.14).

You can drag the green bars showing the duration of the action either longer or shorter.

You can also use the Duration spinner to ensure precise timing.

CLICK on the image to highlight its two actions in the Animation pane.

CLICK on the first action.

Locate the Duration spinner in the Timing group.

CLICK the spinner to 2.00 to match the duration of the title's duration.

Preview the slide.

FIGURE PP2.14 Duration of elements in Animation pane

The duration of the action is shown by the length of the colored bar. The first action is about twice as long as the second action.

7 Notice the title is still a little delayed in appearing on the slide. That is just a characteristic of the animation. You can delay the image, ever so slightly, so they appear on the screen at the same time.

CLICK on the image to select it.

Locate the Delay spinner in the Timing group.

Set it to 00.50.

Preview the slide.

Now the timing is almost perfect.

8 As a final touch, you want the teeter action on the image to occur at the same time as the wave animation on the title.

CLICK the action number 8 on the slide (this is the wave animation for the title).

Locate the Start control in the Timing group.

CLICK the drop-down arrow.

CHOOSE With Previous.

Now both actions are numbered 7.

Preview the slide.

9 There are options specific to each type of animation.

CLICK into the bulleted list.

Locate the Animation group.

CLICK Effect Options.

CLICK All at Once.

The preview runs to show each bullet in its own animation, but appearing at the same time.

10 CLICK the ANIMATIONS tab and locate the Animation group.

CLICK Effect Options.

CLICK As One Object.

The preview runs to show all the bullets animating as one object.

CLICK Effect Options.

CHOOSE By Paragraph to return it to the original action.

11 Your screen should appear similar to Figure PP2.15. Save and close the pp02a4-salespitch.pptx file.

FIGURE PP2.15 Completion of Lesson PowerPoint 2A4

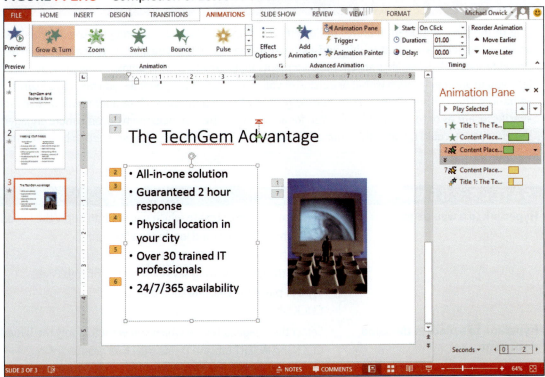

Hyperlinks and Interactivity

LESSON OVERVIEW

One of the most important features of PowerPoint is its ability to **hyperlink** content within and external to the presentation itself. Hyperlinks are clickable elements that lead you to another location within or outside of your presentation. This feature allows you to quickly go back to specific locations or to the World Wide Web for additional details that you could not fit within your presentation.

When considering the use of hyperlinks, you need to be sure that you analyze your audience to determine how you might use hyperlinks in the presentation. Even though you can add hyperlinks, you need to be sure the addition serves a purpose, such as adding interactivity for your audience. This can help them become more engaged in the presentation, but also requires you to be a little more flexible.

SKILLS PREVIEW

Hyperlink to a web page	• Select the image or text to which you want to apply the hyperlink. CLICK the INSERT tab and locate the Links group. CLICK the Hyperlink button. Ensure the Link to setting says Existing File or Web Page. Type or paste the URL into the Address box. CLICK OK.
Hyperlink to a place in the same document	• Select the image or text to which you want to apply the hyperlink. CLICK the INSERT tab and locate the Links group. CLICK the Hyperlink button. Ensure the Link to setting says Place in This Document. CLICK on the desired slide in the Select a place in this document window. CLICK OK.
Edit or remove a hyperlink	• CLICK on the image or text that is hyperlinked. CLICK the INSERT tab and locate the Link group. CLICK the Hyperlink button. CLICK the Remove Link button, or • RIGHT-CLICK on the image of text that is hyperlinked. CHOOSE Remove Hyperlink from the short-cut menu.
Activate a hyperlink during a slide show	• CLICK on the hyperlinked image or text. Close the Internet page when completed.

PROJECT PRACTICE

1 Locate and open the file **pp02a5.pptx**. Save it as **pp02a5-salespitch.pptx**.

2 CLICK on slide 3.

Select the text "Physical location in your city."

CLICK the INSERT tab and locate the Links group.

CLICK the Hyperlink button.

TYPE http://maps.google.com/ in the Address field as shown in Figure PP2.16.

CLICK OK.

FIGURE PP2.16   The Hyperlink window

3 You can test the web address while on the main editing window.

RIGHT-CLICK on the hyperlinked text.

CHOOSE Open Hyperlink.

If you are connected to the Internet, the Google maps home page should open in a new window.

Close the new window.

> **MORE INFO**
>
> When you are actually running the slide show, the hyperlink can be activated by simply clicking on the hyperlinked text. The Internet will open in a new window. When you are finished with it, simply close the window to return to your PowerPoint slide show.

4 RIGHT-CLICK the image on slide 3.

CHOOSE Hyperlink.

The same Hyperlink window appears.

Type the website of any company into the Address window.

CLICK OK.

The image, although it does not appear changed, is now hyperlinked to that site.

5 Start the slide show on slide 3.

Notice the hyperlinked text shows the usual blue color (purple if the site has been recently visited) and underline of a hyperlink.

CLICK on the text to open the Google maps site.

CLOSE the window.

HOVER the mouse over the image to see the hyperlink address.

CLICK the image to open the site you inserted.

Close the window to return to the slide show.

6 RIGHT-CLICK on the image.

CHOOSE Edit Hyperlink to open the hyperlink window.

Enter a different company website into the Address window.

CLICK OK.

Open that link to see if your "editing" worked.

Close the window to return to the show.

7 You can also hyperlink to other documents or other slides within the same slide show.

SELECT the text "All-in-one solution."

RIGHT-CLICK on the text.

CHOOSE Hyperlink.

Locate the Link to section of the Insert Hyperlink dialog box.

CLICK Place in This Document (see Figure PP2.17).

CLICK Meeting YOUR Needs in the Select a place in this document window.

A thumbnail appears to show which slide has been selected (slide 2).

CLICK OK.

FIGURE PP2.17 Hyperlinking to a place in the same document

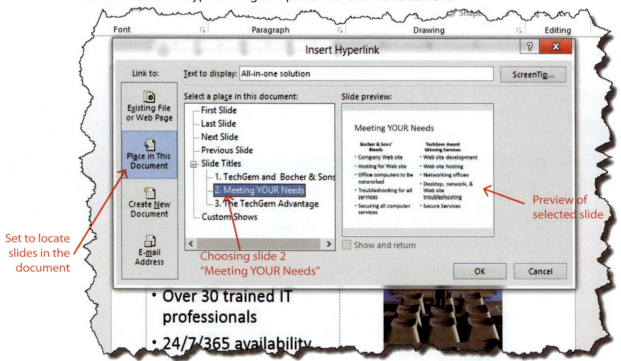

8 Start the show from slide 3.

Advance until the first bullet is displayed (All-in-one solution).

CLICK the bullet.

The slide show moves to slide 2.

You can link back and forth across slides throughout a slide show.

RIGHT-CLICK on a blank area of the screen.

CHOOSE Last Viewed to return to the last slide viewed.

You should be returned not only to slide 3, but to the same place on the slide as when you left.

9 End the slide show and return to slide 3.

CLICK the image to select it.

On the **INSERT** tab, locate the Links group.

CLICK Hyperlink.

CLICK the Remove Link button.

Try to activate the hyperlink on the image.

It has been removed.

TIP

You can also remove hyperlinks by right-clicking and choosing Remove Hyperlink. There are many uses for hyperlinking within a slide show. Perhaps one slide contains the sources used in researching the presentation. Clicking on a statistic or a chart can hyperlink to the source slide for reference. Instructors can post questions on a slide and hyperlink to the correct answer, then back to the slide of questions.

---

10 Your screen should appear similar to Figure PP2.18. Save and close the **pp02a5-salespitch.pptx** file. Exit PowerPoint.

FIGURE PP2.18 Completion of Lesson PowerPoint 2A5

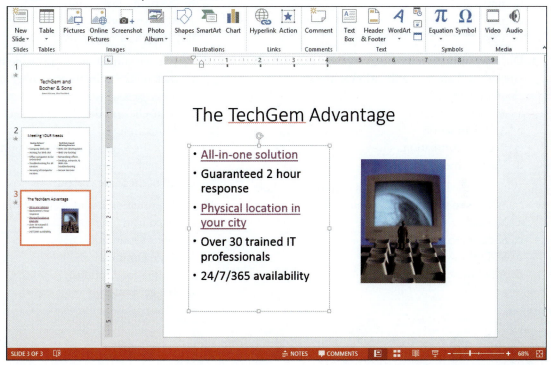

MULTIPLE-CHOICE QUIZ

Select the best choice in the following questions to review the project concepts. Good luck!

1. To apply the same transition to all slides in a show, select the transition and
   a. click each slide.
   b. your computer.
   c. click Apply To All.
   d. None of these is correct.

2. Which of the following ratios is typically used by high-definition televisions?
   a. 3:2
   b. 4:3
   c. 16:10
   d. 16:9

3. Which of the following formats automatically starts in PowerPoint when the file is opened?
   a. .pptx
   b. .ppt
   c. .pdf
   d. .ppsx

4. Once an animation has been applied to an element, you can add another animation to the same element using
   a. Animation pane.
   b. Add Animation.
   c. Reorder Animation.
   d. None of these is correct.

5. Which of the following views is best to apply slide transitions to several slides at once?
   a. Normal
   b. Slide Sorter
   c. Slide Show
   d. All of these are correct.

6. Which of the following animations would be the best to demonstrate an important concept?
   a. Entrance
   b. Emphasis
   c. Exit
   d. None of these is correct.

7. Hyperlinks to external websites are used to allow the presenter to
   a. review concepts before presentation.
   b. move the presentation online.
   c. add more content within the presentation.
   d. showcase more information if needed.

8. Animations can be "copied" from one element to another using
   a. Animation Painter.
   b. the right-click menu.
   c. Add Animation.
   d. All of these are correct.

9. To remove animations from elements,
   a. click on the animation number and press `Delete`.
   b. right-click on the element and choose Remove Animation.
   c. click the Remove Animation button in the Animation group.
   d. All of these are correct.

10. Each animation has its own settings that can be adjusted using the
    a. Effect Options.
    b. Paste Options.
    c. Animation Options.
    d. Trigger button.

HANDS-ON EXERCISE: WORK IT OUT PP-2A-E1

In this exercise, you will animate and add transitions to a PowerPoint presentation. You will adjust the timings and change the order of animations. The final document is shown in Figure PP2.19.

FIGURE PP2.19 Work It Out PP-2A-E1: completed

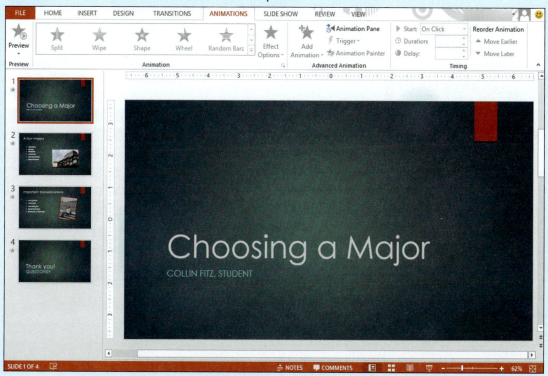

1. Locate and open the exercise data file **pp02a-ex01.pptx**. Save the file as **pp02a-hw01.pptx**.

2. On slide 1, replace the text **YourName** with **your name**.

3. On slide 2, set the bullets to the Entrance Wheel animation.

4. Set the duration of the animation to 0.75 second.

5. Paint the animation to the bulleted list on slide 3.

6. Animate the image on slide 2 to Wheel.

7. Set the duration of this animation to 1.00 second.

8. Reorder the animation so that the image animates first on that slide.

9. Apply the Push upward transition to all slides.

10. Change the duration of slide 1's transition to 2.00 seconds.

11. Save the **pp02a-hw01.pptx** file. Close PowerPoint.

In this exercise, you will create a presentation from a blank document. You will add a minimum of text, but you will apply animations and hyperlinks to the slide show. The final document is show in Figure PP2.20.

FIGURE PP2.20 Work It Out PP-2A-E2: completed

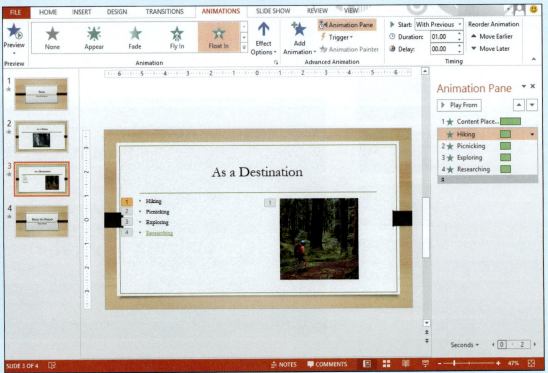

1. Open a blank PowerPoint document. Save it as **pp02a-hw02.pptx**.

2. Using the DESIGN tab, apply the Organic design to the presentation.

3. TYPE **Trees** for the title and **A Forest Full of Miracles** in the text placeholder.

4. Add a Title and Content slide for slide 2. Title it **As a Home**.

5. Insert an online photo using the keyword "forest."

6. Hyperlink that photo to the Wikipedia page for "forest." Hint: Locate the page online, copy the URL of the page, then paste it into the Hyperlink Address window using **Ctrl** + **V**.

7. Add a Two Content Slide and title it **As a Destination**.

8. In the left-hand text placeholder, type the following bullets:

Hiking

Picnicking

Exploring

Researching

9. Insert an online photo using the keywords "Hiking Trail" in the right-hand place holder.

10 Hyperlink the word *Researching* to the US Forest Service website: www.fs.fed.us/.

11 Insert a Title slide at the end of the show. Type **Enjoy the Forests** for the title and **Respect for Nature** in the text placeholder below it.

12 Set the transitions for all slides to Pan. Change the transition for the first slide to Zoom. Adjust the timing of the Zoom transition to 2.00 seconds.

13 On slide 2, set the image to animate using Split with a Vertical Out effect.

14 Animate the text on slide 3 using Float In.

15 Animate the image to Swivel. Adjust the image's animation to occur at the same time as the first bullet (Hiking).

16 Save the **pp02a-hw02.pptx** file. Close PowerPoint.

In this exercise, you use internal hyperlinks, transitions, animations, and timings to create a game for skill-testing knowledge regarding World Series winners. The final document appears in Figure PP2.21.

FIGURE PP2.21 Work It Out PP-2A-E3: completed

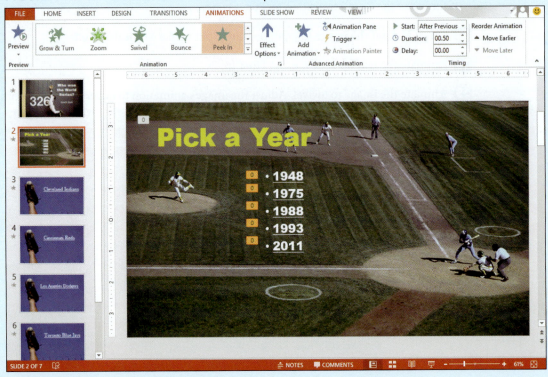

1. Locate and open the exercise data file **pp02a-ex03.pptx**. Save the file as **pp02a-hw03.pptx**.

2. On slide 2, hyperlink the following text to the following slides:

   1948 to slide 3

   1975 to slide 4

   1988 to slide 5

   1993 to slide 6

   2011 to slide 7

3. On slide 3, hyperlink the text "Cleveland Indians" to slide 2.

4. On slide 4, hyperlink the text "Cincinnati Reds" to slide 2.

5. On slide 5, hyperlink the text "Los Angeles Dodgers" to slide 2.

6. On slide 6, hyperlink the text "Toronto Blue Jays" to slide 2.

7. On slide 7, hyperlink the text "St. Louis Cardinals" to slide 2.

8. Apply the Whip animation to each of the baseball team names on slides 3 through 7. Set the timing of the Whip animation so that it occurs automatically after the slide starts. Hint: You can paint the animation from one slide to the next.

9 Give slide 1 a Split transition. Give slide 2 a Cube transition. Give slides 3 through 7 the Ripple transition.

10 On slide 1, animate the Title text to Zoom from the Slide Center. Animate the "Quick Quiz" text to Fly In from the right. Set the timing so the title animates 1 second after the transition is complete. Set the "Quick Quiz" to animate immediately after.

11 Animate the slide 2 title "Pick a Year" to Dissolve In right after the transition is complete. Animate the dates to Peek In immediately after the title animation.

12 Run the show and click a year to select it. Click the name of the team to return to slide 2, so you can pick another.

13 Save the file and exit PowerPoint.

Setting the Mood

In this project, you will experiment with PowerPoint themes. These preset themes allow you to use professional designs and fully coordinated colors for a great show. You will also learn how to customize these themes to suit your own needs. You will modify clip art, including learning how to group and ungroup objects to help you design your own images. This project includes creating your own slide backgrounds and adjusting the transparency. By adding footnotes to your slideshow, you can provide better references for you and for your audience. Add headers and footers to handouts to make them more useful. You will also be introduced to templates for thousands of PowerPoint shows.

PROJECT OBJECTIVES

After completing this project, you will be able to:

• Use slideshow themes.

• Modify clip art to suit the presentation.

• Design slide backgrounds.

• Insert headers and footers.

• Locate and use templates.

PROJECT FILE: *Available at* www.mhhe.com/office2013projectlearn

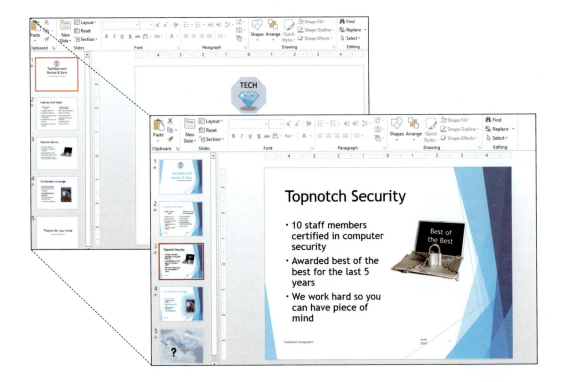

Using Slide Show Themes

LESSON OVERVIEW

One of the quickest ways to create a new show is to type your information and worry about the slide design later. That is even easier with PowerPoint's Design **Themes**. Each of the many predesigned themes has its own family of **Variants** that will instantly change your show to the new theme. The colors, fonts, background design, and placement of elements are professionally coordinated to provide an eye-pleasing layout.

Before changing to a new theme, PowerPoint's **Live Preview** can show you what the slides would look like by hovering over the themes. The slide in the main editing window will transform to the new theme. Once you decide, you can click on the theme and the rest of the slides will change to the new theme.

While the variants generally offer all the choices you need, you can find more color and font choices by opening the **Slide Master view**. From here you can choose from many more color and font options that are still fully coordinated for professional presentation.

SKILLS PREVIEW

Apply a Theme	• CLICK the DESIGN tab and locate the Themes group. Hover the mouse over the theme thumbnails to preview. CHOOSE the theme you desire.
Use a Theme Variant	• CLICK the DESIGN tab and locate the Variants group. Hover the mouse over the variant thumbnails to preview. CHOOSE the variation you desire.
Use Automatic Alignment Guides	• DRAG the desired placeholder or image across the slide. Wait for the dotted alignment guides to display the placeholder in relation to other points on the slide. Release the mouse when the placeholder is in the correct place.
Open Slide Master view	• CLICK on the VIEW tab and locate the Master Views group. CLICK Slide Master. Adjust colors and fonts for the theme from the Background group.

PROJECT PRACTICE

1. Locate the files associated with this lesson and open **pp02b1.pptx**. Save the file as **pp02b1-salespitch.pptx**.

2. This presentation has five slides with information already on them. You can add a design to instantly change the appearance of the slides quickly.

   CLICK the DESIGN tab and locate the Themes group.

   Hover the mouse over the theme thumbnails.

   PowerPoint's Live Preview feature shows how the current slide would appear (see Figure PP2.22).

   Notice that font styles, colors, text placement, and background designs change.

3 CLICK the Themes More button to display a palette of themes.

You decide the Ion design works well.

CLICK Ion and all the slides in the show change to reflect that style.

FIGURE PP2.22   Theme palette showing Live Preview

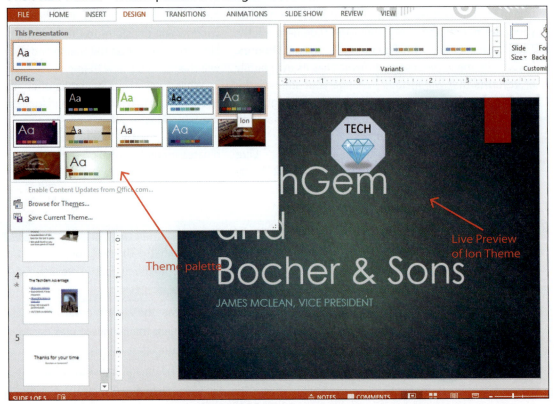

⚠ **HEADS UP**

When you apply a new design to a slide show, it will adjust the elements based on its preset style. This may (as in this case) cause some rearranging of elements on your slides. It is a good idea to check for any changes that may have occurred and correct them, if required.

---

4 CLICK slide 1.

The new style moved the placeholders around. Now the title is too close to the company logo. You could move them, but then you also remember that the presentation room you will use is rather bright, so a dark background such as this will not show up well.

On the DESIGN tab, locate the More button to select a different theme.

CLICK the Facet theme.

5 CLICK slide 1.

Change "James McLean" to your name.

CLICK slide 3.

DRAG the image so the automatic alignment guides align it with the text (see Figure PP2.23).

CLICK on slide 4.

DRAG the image so the alignment guides appear on top and on the right-hand side of the image.

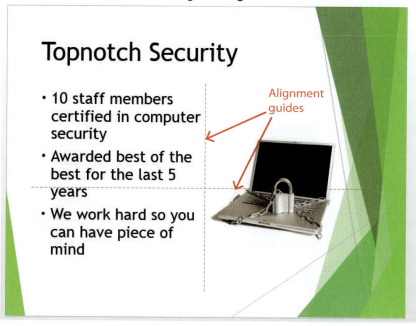

6 Locate the Variants group on the ribbon.

CLICK the second variant (blue).

The entire show changes to match the blue variant.

7 While each theme has its own family of variants with carefully coordinated color and font combinations, you can find even more choices.

CLICK the VIEW tab and locate the Master Views group.

CLICK Slide Master and locate the Background group.

CLICK on the Colors button to drop down a list of color options (see Figure PP2.24).

HOVER the mouse on the color sets to see a preview of how the colors would change.

CLICK on Yellow to change the background on all the slides in the show.

FIGURE PP2.24 The Slide Master and the Colors menu

8 CLICK the Fonts button to drop down a list of fonts.

Again, hover the mouse over the choices and Live Preview will show them to you.

CLICK Corbel to change the fonts used on all slides to the Corbel style.

9 Locate the Close Master View button in the menu.

CLICK Close Master View (see Figure PP2.24).

Upon returning to the slide show, you realize the yellow style does not suit the company logo.

CLICK the DESIGN tab and locate the Themes group.

CLICK Facet to select that style again.

CLICK the Blue variant to return to the style that works the best.

10 CLICK on slide 3.

11 Your screen should look similar to Figure PP2.25. Save the **pp02b1-salespitch.pptx** file.

FIGURE PP2.25   Completion of Lesson PowerPoint 2B1

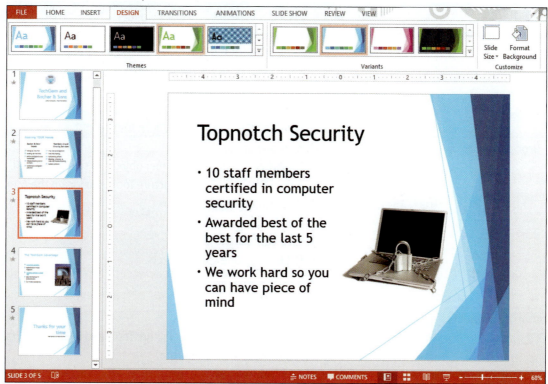

Editing Clip Art for Presentation Purposes

LESSON OVERVIEW

Adding clip art can bring so much to a presentation if it is done properly. Office.com Clip Art provides so many choices, but even then, sometimes an image isn't exactly as you want it. PowerPoint provides controls for the general color of an object. You can decide which color you would like to set as a **transparent color** to allow the background to show through. You can even set the **Artistic Effects** so an image has the preset appearance of paint strokes or being made of glass. Of course, you can also adjust an image to your own settings for the shadow, reflection, glow, soft edges, and three-dimensional formatting or rotation.

Group images or objects (such as a text box) to allow you to move, copy, and paste them as if they were one object. This is very useful when you create a logo or recurring image. Once grouped, you can **ungroup** an object for editing or adjusting. It is even possible to ungroup some clip art images and animate the elements separately.

SKILLS PREVIEW

Set Transparent Color	• CLICK on the image. CLICK the FORMAT tab and locate the Adjust group. CLICK the Color button to drop down color options. CHOOSE Set Transparent Color. Move the mouse to the image. CLICK on the color you wish to make transparent.
Group objects	• CLICK on one of the objects. HOLD Shift and click on the other objects to select them all. CLICK the FORMAT tab under Picture Tools and locate the Arrange group. CLICK the Group Objects button. CHOOSE Group, or • After selecting all the objects, RIGHT-CLICK on one of the objects. CHOOSE Group. CLICK Group
Ungroup objects	• CLICK on the grouped object. CLICK the FORMAT tab under Picture Tools and locate the Arrange group. CLICK the Group Objects button. CHOOSE Ungroup, or • RIGHT-CLICK the grouped object. CHOOSE Group. CLICK Ungroup.
Apply Artistic Effects to objects	• CLICK on the image to select it and to open the FORMAT tab under Picture Tools. Locate the Adjust group. CLICK Artistic Effects to drop down a palette of preset effects. CHOOSE Artistic Effects Options to open the Format Picture pane on the right-hand side. CHOOSE from Shadow, Reflection, Glow, Soft Edges, and more. Make the adjustments you desire.

1 Open the **pp02b2.pptx** file. Save it as **pp02b2-salepitch.pptx**.

2 CLICK on slide 3.

The image of the laptop and the lock has a white border around it that blocks out some of the background design of the slide. To edit the image to fix that:

CLICK on the image.

CLICK the FORMAT tab and locate the Adjust group.

CLICK the Color button to drop down color options.

CHOOSE Set Transparent Color if not already chosen.

CLICK the mouse on the white area around the image to make that color transparent.

(*Result:* The white area around the image becomes transparent.)

 MORE INFO

The Color command has many other controls including the Saturation, Tone, and Recolor. These are preset treatments that can quickly match an image with the general color of a slide.

3 CLICK the INSERT tab and locate the Text group.

CLICK the Text Box button.

Draw a text box on the black screen of the image (see Figure PP2.26).

Change the font color in the text box to white.

TYPE **Best of the Best**

FIGURE PP2.26   Placing the text box on the existing image

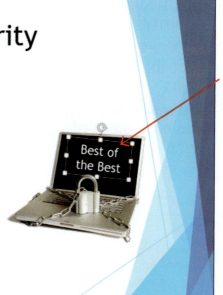

The text box has been placed and rotated to appear as if it were printed on the laptop screen

4 Center the text inside the text box.

Change the text size to 20.

Rotate the text box and move it to match the positioning in Figure PP2.26.

(*Result:* The text box appears as if it were writing on the laptop screen.)

5 CLICK away to deselect the text box.

DRAG the image up a bit on the slide.

Notice the image moves, but the text box remains in place. To group these elements so they will move around the slide as if they were one element:

CLICK Undo to return the image to the correct spot.

CLICK the text box to select it.

HOLD `Shift`.

CLICK the image to select it.

While both are selected, CLICK the FORMAT tab under Picture Tools and locate the Arrange group.

CLICK the Group Objects button.

CHOOSE Group to "group" the elements into one.

6 DRAG the grouped object up until the alignment guides appear as in Figure PP2.27.

Notice the image and the text box now move as one object.

FIGURE PP2.27 Aligning grouped object

TIP

You can group as many elements (or objects, as they are often called) as you wish. Once grouped, you can move, copy, and paste them as if they were one object. If you find you want to make an adjustment to one of the grouped objects, you may have to ungroup them all first, select the object you want, make your changes, then group them again. Some limited editing options are available while elements are grouped.

7 CLICK on slide 4.

CLICK on the image to select it and to open the FORMAT tab under Picture Tools.

Locate the Adjust group.

CLICK Artistic Effects to drop down a palette of preset effects.

CHOOSE Artistic Effects Options to open the Format Picture pane on the right-hand side.

CLICK Soft Edges to expand that option.

DRAG the marker across the Size bar to see the effect it has on the image.

Set the soft edge at 25 pt. (that is how "thick" the soft, blurry edge is on the image).

8 CLICK the Glow option to expand it.

DRAG the marker along the Size bar to set the glow to 105 pt.

See how the image tends to bleed to match the colors of the background.

Close the Format Picture pane.

9 CLICK on the final slide.

CLICK the INSERT tab and locate the Images group.

Search Office.com Clip Art for "information center."

Insert the black square with the white question mark inside it.

Resize it to 2.5" high and drag it to the approximate position shown in Figure PP2.28.

FIGURE PP2.28 Resizing an ungrouped image

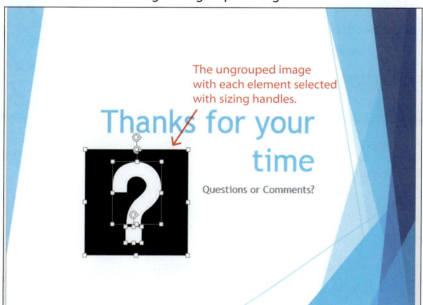

10 Rather than grouping two or more objects, we will ungroup an existing object and animate each piece separately.

RIGHT-CLICK on the new image.

CHOOSE Group.

CLICK Ungroup.

CLICK Yes to the imported picture warning to allow you to ungroup the image.

Repeat the right-clicking and ungrouping procedure.

Now the image has three elements (the black box, the white dot, and the top of the question mark) as shown in Figure PP2.28.

HEADS UP

You can only ungroup some of the inserted objects. Pictures, of course, cannot be ungrouped because they are complete images. Even some clip art cannot be ungrouped. Some clip art, when ungrouped, shows dozens or more tiny elements and images that were used to create it. It can take some practice to pull them apart and use the pieces, but if, for example, you found clip art with a car in it, you might be able to separate the elements, delete the rest of the image, and just use the car.

---

11 CLICK away to deselect the three elements of the image.

DRAG the question mark to the right so it is visible against the blue background.

DRAG the dot to the right so it is visible against the blue background.

CLICK the black box.

Animate it to zoom from the slide center.

Set the timing to start After Previous.

12 CLICK the dot to select it.

DRAG it back onto the black square.

Set the animation of the dot to Fly In from the top.

Set the timing to start After Previous.

13 CLICK the question mark.

DRAG it into place above the dot.

Set the animation of the question mark to Fly In from the bottom.

Set the timing to start With Previous.

14 CLICK the text box that says "Questions or Comments?"

Animate it to Float In.

Set the timing to start After Previous.

Run the final slide to see how the individual elements of the question mark are animated separately.

15 Your document should appear similar to Figure 2.29. Save the **pp02b2-salepitch.pptx** file.

FIGURE PP2.29   Completion of Lesson PowerPoint 2B2

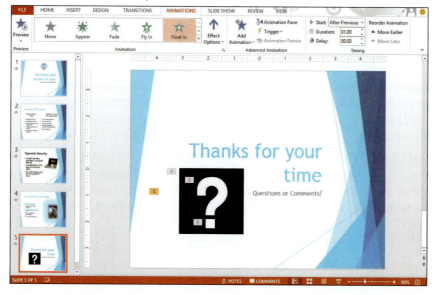

Designing Backgrounds

LESSON OVERVIEW

While PowerPoint offers many outstanding designs for slide backgrounds, sometimes you need something unique. The **Format Background** controls allow you to change a slide background whether you have started with a plain, white slide or used one of the preset designs. **Solid fill** allows you to fill the entire background with any color. **Gradient fill** allows you to merge one color (or more) into another.

You can use more than just colors to create a background. The **Picture or texture fill** allows you to fill the entire slide background with a picture (from your computer or from an online search) or to use a predesigned texture in the background. You have control over the color of the background and also what **Artistic Effects** you would like to apply, choosing from more than 20 preset effects that adjust the picture to appear in a range of treatments from Pencil Grayscale to Glow Edges and Plastic Wrap.

Adjusting the **transparency** of a background can fade the background to help emphasize text or images on the slide. Creating your own background can provide a customized slide or entire slide show that suits the purpose of your presentation.

SKILLS PREVIEW

Format a slide background as a solid color	• CLICK the DESIGN tab and locate the Customize group. CLICK Format Background to open the Format Background pane. CLICK Solid fill. CHOOSE the color from the drop-down palette.
Apply slide background to all slides in a presentation	• After making the selection of background, CLICK the Apply to All button.
Hide background graphics	• Open the Format Background pane. CLICK the check box next to Hide background graphics.
Insert a picture as a background	• Open the Format Background pane. CLICK the check box next to Hide background graphics. CLICK Picture or texture fill. CLICK File to locate an image on the computer. CLICK Insert.
Set the transparency of a background	• Open the Format Background pane. DRAG the marker along the Transparency line, or • CLICK the spinner control to adjust the transparency.
Adjust the effects of a background	• Open the Format Background pane. CLICK the Effects button (⬠). CLICK the Artistic Effects button. CHOOSE the effect you desire.
Adjust the color of a background	• Open the Format Background pane. CLICK the Picture button (🖼). CLICK Picture Color to expand that option. CLICK the Recolor button. CHOOSE the color treatment you desire.

1 The background of a slide includes the colors and the shapes. The current Facet background uses shades of blue and straight triangular shapes on a white backdrop. See what happens when you change the white to something else. Open the pp02b3.pptx file. Save it as pp02b3-salepitch.pptx.

2 CLICK on slide 1 if necessary.

CLICK the DESIGN tab and locate the Customize group.

CLICK Format Background to open the Format Background pane on the right-hand side (see Figure PP2.30).

Currently it is set to a Solid fill (that being white).

CLICK the Color button in the Format Background pane to see the color palette.

CLICK on Green to see what part of the slide changes.

While this color clashes with the blue, it emphasizes the part of the background that is affected.

FIGURE PP2.30   Format Background pane

3 CLICK on Turquoise, Accent 1, Darker 25%.

This color is part of the colors that are used in the Facet design, so this is not effective.

CLICK Blue, Accent 2, Lighter 60%.

This color works well with the background, but not with the font colors.

CLICK Blue, Accent 2, Lighter 80%.

This color works better with the current design.

CLICK the Apply to All button in the Format Background.

(*Result:* All the slides in the show now display that color.)

4 CLICK the Gradient Fill in the Format Background pane. (See Table PP2.2 for a listing of the fill options.)

See how this creates a gradual blending of the color.

CLICK Apply to All so each slide has the gradient fill.

CLICK on slide 4.

See how well the gradient fill blends with the image, but notice that the turquoise color of the font (especially the hyperlinked text) does not stand out very well on this background.

TABLE PP2.2 Format Background options

Option	Results
Solid fill	• Changes the background of a slide to a solid color of your choice.
Gradient fill	• Changes the background to a gradient color, which is typically one color merging into another.
Picture or texture fill	• Changes the background to a picture of your choice or to a preset texture.
Pattern fill	Changes the background to a preset pattern.

5 CLICK the Solid fill button.

CLICK the color drop-down.

CHOOSE White, Background 1.

CLICK Apply to All.

6 CLICK on slide 5.

Move to the Format Background pane.

CLICK the check box next to Hide background graphics to hide the design on this slide.

CLICK Picture or texture fill (see Figure PP2.31).

CLICK File to locate an image on the computer.

Locate the files associated with this lesson.

CLICK Blurred_timepiece.png.

CLICK Insert.

(*Result:* That image now sits in the background of the final slide.)

FIGURE PP2.31   Inserting a picture or texture as a background

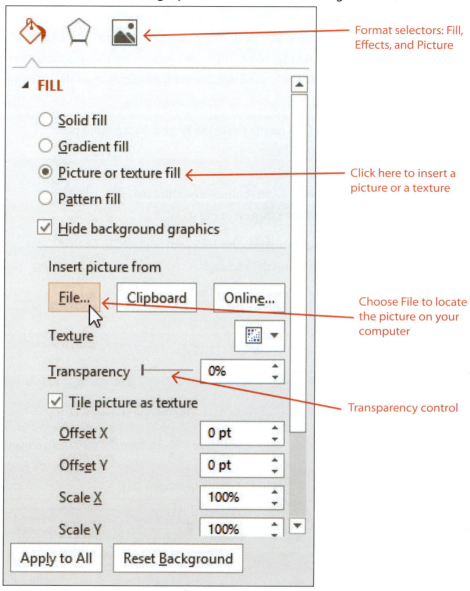

Format selectors: Fill, Effects, and Picture

Click here to insert a picture or a texture

Choose File to locate the picture on your computer

Transparency control

7   Locate the Transparency control in the Format Background pane (see Figure PP2.31).
DRAG the marker to 50% to fade the image (use the spinner for precise control).
CLICK the check box to turn on the Tile picture as texture command.
This is ideal if the original image is not shaped the same as the slide.
CLICK the check box to turn the feature off.

8 CLICK the Effects button (⬠) on the top of the Format Background pane.

CLICK the Artistic Effects button to drop down a palette of choices.

CLICK Light Screen (third row, first item) to see how that changes the background.

CLICK Paint Strokes (second row, second item) to see how that changes the background.

CLICK Pencil Grayscale (first row, third item) to see how that changes the background.

CLICK None to return the background to its previous setting.

9 CLICK the Picture button (🖼) on the top of the Format Background pane.

CLICK Picture Color to expand that option.

CLICK the Recolor button.

CHOOSE Blue, Accent color 2 Light (bottom row, third item).

Now the background color suits the rest of the show.

10 The black box with the question mark now looks out of place. To fix that:

CLICK the top of the question mark to select it.

Locate the FORMAT tab under Drawing Tools.

CLICK Shape Fill to open the color palette.

Change the color of it to black.

Do the same to the white dot (change it to black).

CLICK the black box to select it.

Delete the box.

(*Result:* Only the question mark remains. The elements are still animated.)

11 Your document should appear similar to Figure PP2.32. Save the **pp02b3-salespitch.pptx** file.

FIGURE PP2.32 Completion of Lesson PowerPoint 2B3

Headers and Footers for Slides

LESSON OVERVIEW

Adding headers and footers to a PowerPoint document is very easy. PowerPoint controls the amount of information and the placement so they do not get in the way of the slide show. In fact, the actual presentation slides permit only footers, **slide numbers**, and **date and time**. Headers are available only on printed material.

The date and time feature allows you to quickly add a date that automatically updates or to type in a fixed date.

Slide numbers help keep the presenter on track and allow viewers to refer to slides by numbers when asking questions or looking at a handout.

Handouts and Notes pages can have their own headers and footers, slide numbers, and date and time settings. Entering text into a header or footer is simple and can add a final touch of customization to the presentation for both the presenter and the viewing audience.

SKILLS PREVIEW

Insert date and time to a slide	• CLICK the INSERT tab and locate the Text group. CLICK Header and Footer. CLICK the check box to activate the Date and time. CLICK Update automatically. Drop down the menu to choose the format of the date (and/or time), or CLICK Fixed and type in a date.
Insert slide numbers	• CLICK the INSERT tab and locate the Text group. CLICK Header and Footer. CLICK the check box to activate the Slide number.
Insert a footer on a slide	• CLICK the INSERT tab and locate the Text group. CLICK Header and Footer. CLICK the check box to activate the Footer. Type your text into the Footer text window.
Prevent the header or footer from appearing on the title slide	• CLICK the INSERT tab and locate the Text group. CLICK Header and Footer. CLICK the check box for Don't show on title slide.
Insert a header or footer on a printout of Notes or Handouts	• CLICK the INSERT tab and locate the Text group. CLICK Header and Footer. CLICK the Notes and Handouts tab. Turn on and type in the options you desire to display when notes or handouts are printed.

PROJECT PRACTICE

1. Open the **pp02b4.pptx** file. Save it as **pp02b4-salepitch.pptx**.

2. CLICK on slide 1.
   CLICK the INSERT tab and locate the Text group.
   CLICK Header and Footer to open the Header and Footer window (see Figure PP2.33).
   CLICK the check box to activate the Date and time.

CLICK the Fixed button.

TYPE the month and year into the Fixed text window (e.g., **June 2014**).

CLICK Apply to All.

The date appears at the bottom of all the slides.

FIGURE PP2.33   The Header and Footer window

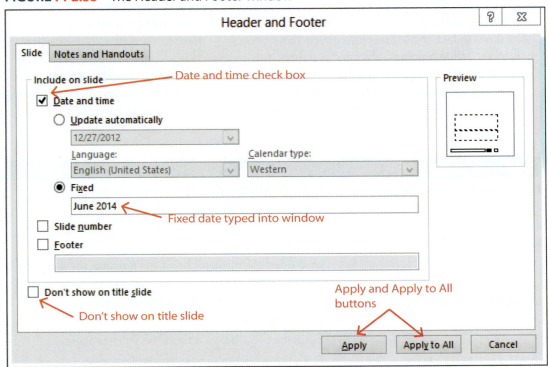

3 CLICK the INSERT tab and locate the Text group.

CLICK Header and Footer.

CLICK the Slide number check box.

Notice on the Preview where the page number will appear.

CLICK the Don't show on title slide check box.

CLICK Apply to All.

4 Run the show to see where the date and slide number show up on the slides.

The date and slide number do not appear on the first or the final slide because both of those slides used the "title" slide for their design. Neither slide needs that information.

5 CLICK on slide 2 (or any slide that is not a title slide).

Open the Header and Footer window.

CLICK to check the Footer check box.

TYPE **TechGem Computers** into the Footer text window.

CLICK Apply to All.

The footer appears on all but the first and last slides.

6 Open the Header and Footer window again.

CLICK on the NOTES AND HANDOUTS tab.

CLICK the Date and time check box on (leave the Update automatically button on).

Leave the Page number check box on.

CLICK the Header check box on.

TYPE **A Presentation for Bocher & Sons** (see Figure PP2.34).

CLICK Apply to All.

FIGURE PP2.34   NOTES AND HANDOUTS tab of the Header and Footer window

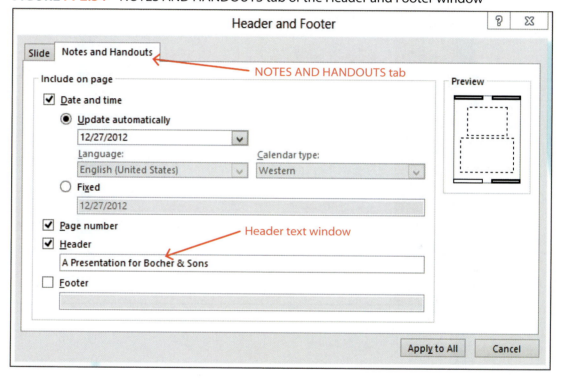

7 CLICK the FILE tab.

CLICK Print.

CLICK the Full Page Slides button (this button will change its name to match its last setting).

CLICK Note Pages to see a preview of the note pages with the header and date.

8 CLICK the Note Pages button (this is same button that previously read Full Page Slides).

CLICK 3 Slides to see a preview of that page with the header and date showing.

9. CLICK the back arrow to return to the normal view.

Open the Header and Footer window.

CLICK the NOTES AND HANDOUTS tab.

CLICK the Footer check box.

TYPE **Created by TechGems Computers**

CLICK Apply to All.

10. Return to the Print Preview window to see that the footer will appear on the handouts when you print them. Your document should appear similar to Figure PP2.35. Save the **pp02b4-salepitch.pptx** file.

FIGURE PP2.35 Completion of Lesson PowerPoint 2B4

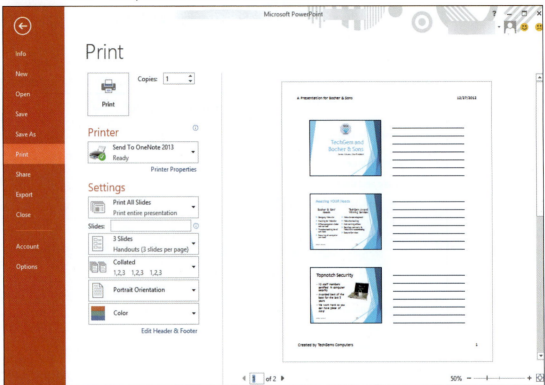

Templates

LESSON OVERVIEW

This lesson will not add to the current project, but rather show alternative ways to start a PowerPoint presentation by using a theme or template. Themes are presented as predesigned slides with coordinated colors and layouts. **Templates** are predesigned as well but include suggested content slides with placeholders already positioned throughout the presentation.

PowerPoint has thousands of predesigned themes and templates you can search to find the right one for your slide show. Once you download a template or theme (using the Create button), you can customize it to suit your presentation.

SKILLS PREVIEW

Locate a template	• If you have not opened PowerPoint: Open PowerPoint. Enter your search word into the search window, or • If you are already working in PowerPoint: CLICK the FILE tab. CLICK New. Enter your search word into the search window.
Filter template search	• CLICK the filter you desire from the right-hand menu of the New (or welcome) page.
Preview a template	• CLICK on the thumbnail of the template. Use the More Images buttons to move back and forth through the slide previews.
Download a template	• CLICK on the thumbnail of the template. CLICK the Create button.

PROJECT PRACTICE

1. Open PowerPoint. The welcome page (see Figure PP2.36) offers recent files on the left-hand side and thumbnails on the right. The thumbnails display designs you can choose before you add any text to the show. This is also the way to locate templates and themes. You can type what you are looking for into the search window, or use the suggested searches.

   CLICK on Business to limit the selection to business-related templates.

   Locate the Category by column on the right-hand side of the screen.

   CLICK 4:3 (because you know the projector at Bocher & Sons has that ratio).

FIGURE PP2.36 Welcome page

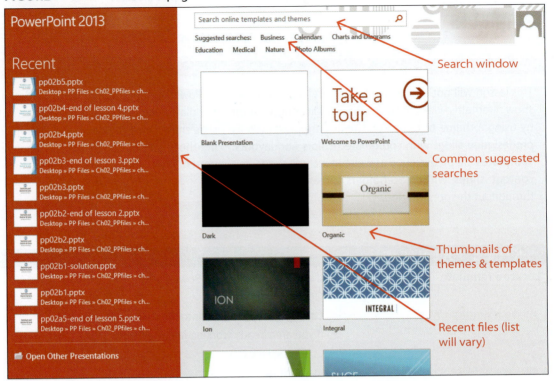

2 CLICK on the first thumbnail to open a Preview window.

CLICK the More Images arrows to move back and forth through the slides (see Figure PP2.37).

CLICK the X in the top-right corner of the Preview window to close the preview.

FIGURE PP2.37 Theme and Template preview

3 Scroll down and locate the Light streams business presentation thumbnail.

CLICK to open the preview.

CLICK Create to download the theme into your PowerPoint document (see Figure PP2.37).

TIP

Although you can search templates by their screen ratio, that does not have to limit you. It is just as easy to switch a 16:9 template to 4:3 (using the DESIGN tab and Slide Size button) as long as you remain aware that when PowerPoint changes its ratio, there are likely changes in the way elements are positioned on the slides. You can manually adjust elements to suit the new ratio.

4 This theme is now loaded into PowerPoint.

CLICK the DESIGN tab and notice that the thumbnail appears in the Themes palette.

Click through the slides to see the style of each slide. Notice that text placeholders are already in place and are filled with random writing. You can insert your own by simply replacing the random text with your own text (see Figure PP2.38).

FIGURE PP2.38   Placeholders temporarily filled with random words

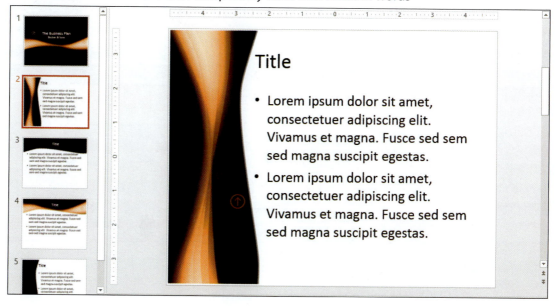

5 CLICK the FILE tab.

CHOOSE New from the menu.

This opens a window similar to the welcome page (without the recent files list). You can access templates and themes this way, too.

TYPE **business** into the Search Online window.

PRESS [Enter].

This brings you back to the same page as before.

6 CLICK 4:3 in the Filter by menu.

CLICK on the Business Plan thumbnail.

CLICK Create.

Another PowerPoint document opens. This one is more than a theme; it is a template. Click through the 25 slides and see how each one is specially designed to suit a presentation of a business plan.

CLICK the Close button to exit the Business Plan template and return to the original PowerPoint.

MORE INFO

While a theme provides coordinated colors and design for all slides, a template also provides an actual "outline" of what to include in such a presentation. In this case, slide 2 is an agenda for the rest of the slides (see Figure PP2.39). You could hyperlink the agenda to the appropriate slide to allow quick reference during a presentation.

FIGURE PP2.39 Slide sorter view of Business Plan template

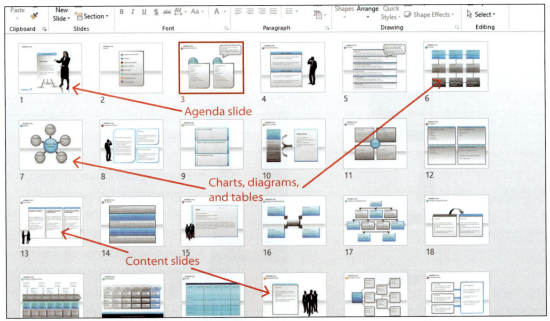

7 CLICK the FILE tab.

CLICK New and locate the Suggested searches.

CLICK Calendars.

CLICK on one of the calendars.

CLICK Create to open it in a new PowerPoint document.

Notice that each slide represents a month. When you click on a certain date, you can add text. This would be useful when showing an advertising campaign plan.

Close the document.

8 Open the New page again.

CLICK Education.

DOUBLE-CLICK on Academic presentation for college course (globe design) to load it directly into a document.

The slides provide a template for course information, schedules, and required texts.

Close the document.

9 Open the New page again.

So far, all the templates and themes you looked for were among the suggested searches. Now try something that is not.

TYPE **science** into the search window and press Enter.

CLICK and create the Medical design presentation.

This provides placeholders for charts, tables, and graphics (see Figure PP2.40).

10 With thousands of predesigned themes and templates available, it may save you a lot of time to download one of them. It is easy to customize.

11 Close PowerPoint.

FIGURE PP2.40 Placeholders in Medical design template

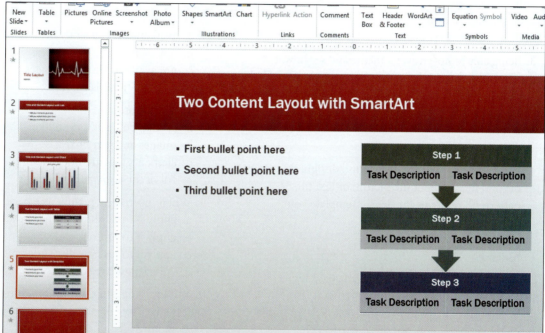

MULTIPLE-CHOICE QUIZ

Select the best choice in the following questions to review the project concepts. Good luck!

1. Each PowerPoint Theme includes
   a. variants of colors.
   b. slight variations of shapes.
   c. a different set of layouts.
   d. All of these are correct.

2. Clip art is made up of
   a. many smaller images.
   b. one image.
   c. realistic photos.
   d. ungrouped images.

3. Being able to hover over a theme and see how it affects the slide in the main editing window is called a
   a. mouseover effect.
   b. context-sensitive menu.
   c. preview pane.
   d. live preview.

4. When modifying the background design, the choice of solid fill, gradient fill, picture or text fill, or pattern fill removes the design template you previously applied.
   a. True
   b. False

5. If you set a color as a transparent color, it will
   a. allow the image behind it to show.
   b. allow the image in front to cover it.
   c. remain white no matter what covers it.
   d. None of these is correct.

6. Which of the following is a reason to include slide numbers on your slides?
   a. To allow the audience to refer to slide numbers when asking questions.
   b. To ensure your audience knows how far along you are in a presentation.
   c. To keep the slides organized.
   d. To add additional content to your slides.

7. Headers are
   a. available on any slide.
   b. not available on title slides.
   c. not available on Notes pages.
   d. None of these is correct.

8. You can group
   a. as many objects as you like.
   b. images and text boxes.
   c. elements that are not touching.
   e. All of these are correct.

9. When inserting a picture as a background, you can
   a. apply it to all slides in the show.
   b. apply it to just one slide.
   c. apply it to just specific slides.
   d. All of these are correct.

10. You can fade a background picture so that it appears less sharp by adjusting the
    a. picture fill.
    b. transparency.
    c. gradient effects.
    d. None of these is correct.

HANDS-ON EXERCISE: WORK IT OUT PP-2B-E1

In this exercise, you will apply a theme to an existing presentation. You will use one of the variants of the theme, change the font style of the theme, insert footnotes, and add a transparent color to a clip art image. The final presentation is shown in Figure PP2.41.

FIGURE PP2.41   Work It Out PP-2B-E1: completed

1. Locate and open the exercise data file **pp02b-ex01.pptx**. Save the file as **pp02b-hw01.pptx**.

2. Replace the text "YourName" with your name.

3. Apply the Slice design template to all slides.

4. Add a footer to the slides that does not show on the title page. The footer should include the slide number and this text: **MyTech Instruments: Sound Quality**.

5. Change the design of all slides to the reddish-brown variant.

6. On slide 3, set the white that surrounds the picture of drums to a transparent color.

7. Go to the Master slide and change the font theme of the slides to the Arial Black-Arial style.

8. Save the file and close PowerPoint.

In this exercise, your objective is to edit a clip art image to better match the presentation. The final presentation is shown in the Print Preview mode in Figure PP2.42.

FIGURE PP2.42   Work It Out PP-2B-E2: completed

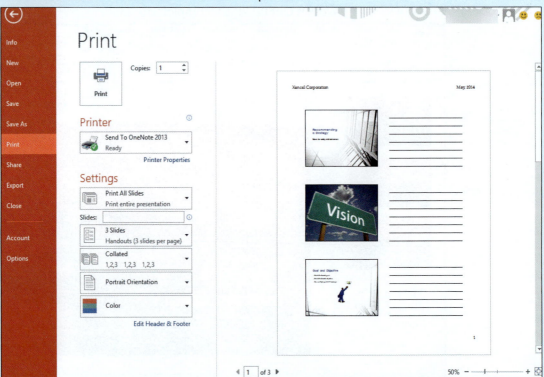

1. Locate and create a new template under the Industry category called Business strategy presentation. Save the file as **pp02b-hw02.pptx**.

2. Change the ratio to 4:3 and ensure the fit to the new slide size.

3. Change the background of slide 2 by using a picture (search Office.com Clip Art for "vision"). Delete the placeholders on this slide.

4. On slide 3, insert the clip art image shown here using the keyword *desires*.

5. Resize the image to 3" high.

6. Ungroup the image. Separate the yellow and the black colors of the star.

7. Animate the black color of the star to fly in from the bottom of the slide. Animate the yellow color of the star to fly in from the top of the slide. Animate each black "glow" line to fly in from the appropriate area of the slide. Set the timing so all these animations happen at the same time.

8. Insert a footer on all handouts that contains the page number and today's fixed date of month and year.

9. Insert a header on all handouts that reads: **Xencel Corporation**.

10. Save the file and close PowerPoint.

HANDS-ON EXERCISE: WORK IT OUT PP-2B-E3

In this exercise, you will take an existing presentation and alter the colors using the Slide Master. You will also insert a background picture and adjust the transparency of a background image. You will animate and set a transparent color on a clip art image. You will also insert a footer into the slide show. The completed project is shown in Figure PP2.43.

FIGURE PP2.43 Work It Out PP-2B-E3: completed

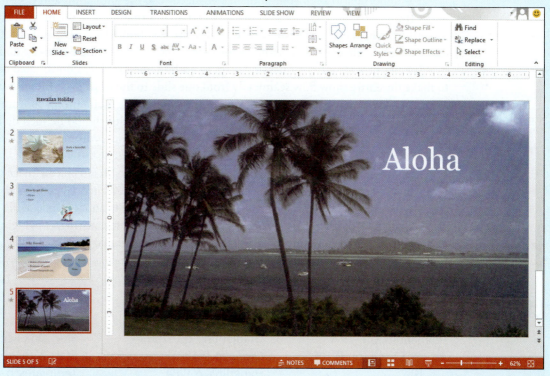

1. Open **pp02-ex03.pptx**. Save it as **pp02-hw03.pptx**.

2. Using the Slide Master, change the color of the theme to Blue II.

3. Go to slide 4 and change the background to a picture. Locate the files associated with this exercise and use the Hawaii_beach image. Hide the background graphics on this slide.

4. On slide 3, set the white bordering on the image to transparent.

5. Set the image of the ocean liner to Fly In from the left with a duration of 2:00 seconds.

6. Set the timing of the ocean liner to occur at the same time as the bullet "Plane" appears. Delay the bullet "boat" to start 1:00 second after the first bullet.

7. Create a footer with slide number, date, and the text: **My Perspective**.

8. On slide 5, set the transparency of the background to 16%.

9. Save the file and close PowerPoint.

Chapter Summary

PowerPoint 2013 provides you with many tools to enhance your presentation. It allows you to change your presentation to match your specific venue, such as using a 4:3 projector or a 16:9 high-definition system. All of these tools empower you to make your presentation technically sound and match your needs.

It is important to keep your audience engaged. Use the animation and transition effects to enhance the focus of the viewer and emphasize certain information. Tie the movement of these features directly into the mood you wish to create in the presentation. The timing and duration of transitions and animations allow you to customize the flow of the show to suit the message and the audience.

Themes provide quick professionalism as each theme provides coordinated colors and designs to make the entire show flow seamlessly from one slide to the next. Each theme has a family of variants that allow you to change the coloring of the slides while maintaining continuity. Thousands of templates are also available to provide a sample of what slides should be included in specific topic presentations. Although templates include specific suggestions, you can always customize them for your purpose.

Any element in a slide show can be hyperlinked. This allows you to link an image or text to a website for further information or an existing video to share with the audience. Hyperlinks also work within the slides themselves, allowing you to link an element on one slide to another slide of the same show.

Elements on a slide can be grouped to become one object for moving, copying, and pasting. Many clip art images can be ungrouped to alter or animate the individual pieces separately. Add headers and footers to handouts and include them on slides to provide information such as date and slide number.

Chapter Key Terms

Animations, p. P-73
Artistic Effects, pp. P-100, P-106
Date and time, p. P-111
Delay, p. P-79
Duration, p. P-79
Effect Options, pp. P-69, P-79
Elements, p. P-64
Emphasis effects, p. P-73
Entrance effects, p. P-73
Exit effects, p. P-73
File formats, p. P-64
Format Background, p. P-106

Gradient fill, p. P-106
Group, p. P-100
Hyperlink, p. P-84
Live Preview, p. P-95
Picture or texture fill, p. P-106
Remove animations, p. P-79
Reorder animations, p. P-79
Screen ratio, p. P-64
Slide Master view, p. P-95
Slide numbers, p. P-111
Slide Sorter view, p. P-69
Solid fill, p. P-106
Start, p. P-79

Start On Click, p. P-79
Start With Previous, p. P-79
Templates, p. P-115
Themes, p. P-95
Timing options, p. P-79
Transitions p. P-64
Transparency, p. P-106
Transparent color, p. P-100
Ungroup, p. P-100
Variants, p. P-95

On Your Own Exercise PP-2C-E1

This exercise provides an opportunity to practice several important skills covered in this chapter. A file is provided for you. Apply the following to make the show practically run itself. Open the file **pp02cp1.pptx**. *Save it as* **pp02cp-hw01.pptx**. *An example of how the final project may look can be seen in Figure PP2.44.*

FIGURE PP2.44 On Your Own PP-2C-E1: completed

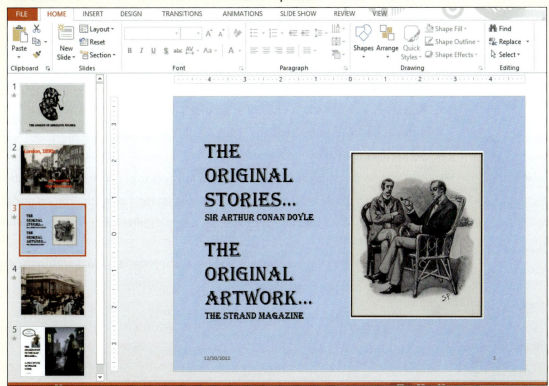

Complete the following tasks to adapt this presentation to your own style.

- Remove the white outline surround the image on slide 1 and the two identical images on slide 4.
- Add transitions to each slide. The same can be used for slides 2 to 5, but the opening slide transition should be different.
- Ensure your presentation is in 4:3 ratio.
- Animate the text and images throughout the show to allow the presentation to flow.
- Set the timings so that text and images appear in a mixture of "with previous" and "after previous."
- Change the duration of at least two of the animations.
- Insert a picture of London, England, in the 1890s as a background on slide 2.
- Hyperlink one of the images to a website that relates to the topic.
- Add the slide number and date to the footer of the slide show.
- Save the file and exit PowerPoint.

On Your Own Exercise PP-2C-E2

This exercise provides you with the opportunity to be creative with a presentation.

To begin, open a new PowerPoint presentation and save it as **pp02cp-hw02.pptx**.

Create a six-slide presentation on any topic of interest. The following guidelines ensure this project uses the skills you learned in this chapter.

- Open a template (no matter the size, you can delete extra slides).
- Be sure the show has a title slide (as the first slide) and an agenda slide.

- Ensure this show is in the 16:9 ratio.
- Ensure all text is large enough to be seen from the back of a presentation room.
- Modify the colors of the theme to match your presentation.
- Use at least three different transition styles in the presentation.
- Include a background picture from an online search.
- Add either a solid background color, gradient, picture, or pattern to your template.
- Apply at least five animations—at least two of them should occur at the same time.
- Adjust the duration of a transition.
- Add footers to your slides to improve the audience's experience in a presentation.
- Add a clip art image. Add a text box next to the image. Group the clip art and the text box.
- Create handouts for the audience based on your presentation. Include the appropriate header and footer information.
- Hyperlink the bullets on the agenda slide to the appropriate slides within the show.
- Save the file and exit PowerPoint.

Working with Objects

PowerPoint has a variety of uses. While it is typically seen as a tool to create presentations for business, it can also be used for fun, such as creating presentations about your vacation for friends and family. This type of presentation is very different from those used for business, as your audience is looking to experience your vacation. Therefore, the way you design your presentation must meet this need.

Understanding the purpose of a vacation presentation is a good start. Next, you need to learn how to work with objects to impart the look and feel of your vacation. You can even modify vacation pictures to help your family and friends understand how much fun you had while traveling.

This chapter will enable you to create a vacation presentation based on a number of preselected pictures. You will learn how easy it is to edit photographs to give them just the right feel for your family and friends. You will learn how to add charts and tables with their own animations. Plus, you will also learn how to create your own unique shapes and edit them to create a vacation presentation that will impress your family and friends.

PROJECT

Creating a Vacation Presentation

In this project, you will build a vacation presentation for your family and friends. You will learn how to insert and edit objects such as photographs, SmartArt, charts, and tables. You will learn how to use animations that are specific to them.

This project will provide you with an example that allows you to use your technical skills, plus you will be able to develop your own vacation presentations. Depending on your inspiration, you will be able to create presentations that engage your viewers and keep them interested in your travels.

THE SITUATION

John's Vacation

John Bowler is a businessman who likes traveling with his family. Even though he enjoys vacations, he is so busy at work and home that he rarely has the opportunity to share his vacation photos with his family and friends. They constantly ask John what his vacations were like and he always answers, "It was…you know… fun!" He wishes he had a better answer and could share his experiences with his family and colleagues. He finally decides to sit down with PowerPoint and create a vacation presentation that will help his friends feel like they experienced vacation with his family.

PROJECT OBJECTIVES

After completing this project, you will be able to:

- Insert and adjust photographs from your computer.
- Insert and edit SmartArt objects.
- Add and edit charts and tables.
- Apply and control animations for charts and tables.

Designing a Vacation Presentation

In this PowerPoint project, you will design a vacation presentation. You will use John's PowerPoint file with his vacation images and make it engaging for his family and friends. There are many ways to tell a vacation story, so it will be up to you to determine how to tell **your** story.

PROJECT FILES: *Available at* www.mhhe.com/office2013projectlearn

Inserting and Editing Photographs

LESSON OVERVIEW

This lesson presents a few ways that PowerPoint does the editing work for you. It is easy to manually adjust the size and position of an image, but it is difficult to get it precise. Using the controls in the Size and Arrange groups, you can ensure accurate and specific settings for an image.

The **Shape Height** and **Shape Width** controls allow you to either spin the number up or down or enter a specific size directly into the control. If you enter a new width or a new height, PowerPoint automatically adjusts the corresponding ratio to maintain the image's proper proportion.

PowerPoint allows you to add **borders** around images to make them look sharper. You can change the color and the weight (thickness) of the borders. You can apply these borders to more than one image at a time.

The **Rotate Objects** button can flip images either horizontally or vertically to suit the design and the focal point of your slide. And, while you can always drag images to where you want them, you can use the **Align Objects** button to center them perfectly on the slide both vertically and horizontally.

SKILLS PREVIEW

Insert an image	• CLICK the INSERT tab and locate the Images group. CLICK the Pictures button. Locate the file(s) you desire. CLICK the Insert button.
Adjust image size	• CLICK the image to select it. CLICK the FORMAT tab and locate the Size group. CLICK the Shape Height or Width window. Spin the button to the size or type the size directly into the window. PRESS `Enter`.
Apply image borders	• CLICK the image to select it. CLICK the FORMAT tab under Picture Tools. Locate the Picture Styles group. CLICK the Picture Border button. CHOOSE the color you wish the border to be.
Align automatically	• CLICK the FORMAT tab under Picture Tools and locate the Arrange group. CLICK the Align Objects button. CHOOSE the alignment you desire.
Flip an image	• CLICK the image to select it. CLICK the FORMAT tab under Picture Tools and locate the Arrange group. CLICK the Rotate Objects button. Select Flip Horizontal or Flip Vertical.

PROJECT PRACTICE

1. Locate the files associated with this lesson and open the project data file **pp03a1.pptx**. Save the file as **pp03a1-vacation.pptx**.

2. CLICK the INSERT tab and locate the Images group.

   CLICK the Pictures button.

   Locate the files associated with this lesson and open the **familymontage.png** file.

   CLICK the Insert button.

3 CLICK the image to select it.

CLICK the FORMAT tab under Picture Tools and locate the Size group.

CLICK the Shape Height text window (currently says 4.21").

TYPE **4.35"**

PRESS Enter.

MORE INFO

In this case, you set the precise height of the image using the Size group. PowerPoint automatically adjusts the width of the image to maintain its proportions. You could adjust the width and let PowerPoint adjust the height automatically. If you clicked the Size group Launch button, the Format Picture pane opens to provide more in-depth controls of height, width, rotation, and scale, relative to the original image. Here you will find the check box for **Lock aspect ratio**. That is the control that forces PowerPoint to automatically adjust the image to maintain the proportion (ratio) of height to width.

4 Drag the image so that the leftmost picture is above the word *The*.

See Figure PP3.1 for an example of the location of the image.

FIGURE PP3.1   Moving the family picture above the title

5 CLICK the FORMAT tab under Picture Tools (if it is not already selected) and locate the Arrange group.

CLICK the Align Objects button.

Select Align Center.

(*Result:* The images align horizontally across the slide.)

6 CLICK in the text box for "The Bowler's Hawaiian Adventure."

Move the cursor before the text *Bowler's*.

7 Press the `Tab` key four times.

Your presentation should look similar to Figure PP3.2.

FIGURE PP3.2   Manually wrapping the title around the image

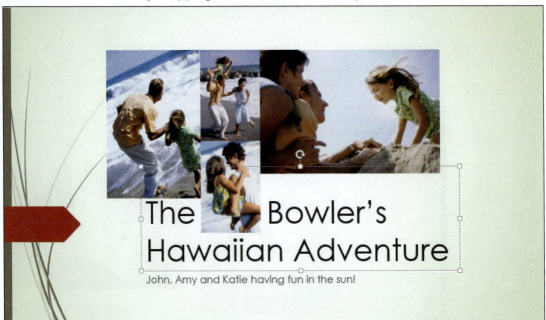

8 CLICK slide 4.

CLICK the image on the left.

CLICK the FORMAT tab under Picture Tools and locate the Arrange group.

CLICK the Rotate Objects button.

Select Flip Horizontally.

TIP

It is good practice to face your images toward the middle of the slide. This concept, called focal point, helps your viewers keep their eyes on the presentation. When images face toward the outside of the slide, audience members may look away from your slide.

9 PRESS and HOLD ⇧ Shift and click the other two images to select them both.

Locate the Picture Styles group.

CLICK the Picture Border button.

CLICK Black.

CLICK away from the images to show that all selected images now have black borders.

10 PRESS and HOLD ⇧ Shift and click all three of the images on slide 4.

Locate the Picture Styles group.

CLICK the Picture Border button.

CLICK the Weight (thickness of the line) button.

It is currently ¾ pt.

Hover the mouse over 3 pt. and then over 6 pt.

Notice how the weight of the line around all three images would change.

CHOOSE 1½ pt. to apply that weight border to all the images.

11 Your screen should appear similar to Figure PP3.3. Save and close the **pp03a1-vacation.pptx** file.

FIGURE PP3.3   Completion of Lesson PowerPoint 3A1

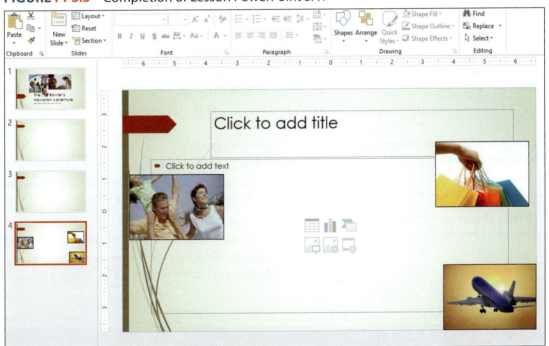

SmartArt Objects

LESSON OVERVIEW

PowerPoint (and other Office applications) includes hundreds of professionally designed graphics called **SmartArt**. These include sophisticated graphics that allow you to quickly add your own text and information into models specifically designed for maximum impact on a PowerPoint slide.

Office organizes SmartArt into categories to suit the purpose of your information, such as List, Process, Cycle, Hierarchy, Relationship, Matrix, and more. Within each category are a number of designs, and within each design are a number of layouts, color formats, and styles you can apply instantly.

One of the most useful features of SmartArt is that once you enter information into a graphic, if you choose a different layout, the information you entered is automatically redistributed into the new layout. You can preview new layouts to see which best suits your needs.

It is easy to add new shapes to existing SmartArt because the graphics immediately adjust font size and internal margins to include the new shape.

SKILLS PREVIEW

Insert SmartArt	• CLICK the INSERT tab and locate the Illustrations group. CLICK SmartArt. CHOOSE from the SmartArt graphics. Type directly into the placeholders.
Add a shape to an existing SmartArt graphic	• CLICK on the SmartArt graphic. Locate the DESIGN tab under SmartArt Tools and locate the Create Graphic group. CLICK Add Shape (click the drop-down to choose to add shapes before, after, above, or below).
Change the layout of an existing SmartArt graphic	• CLICK the SmartArt graphic. Locate the DESIGN tab under SmartArt Tools and locate the Layouts group. CLICK the desired layout (hover the mouse over a choice to see a preview of the current slide changing to the new layout).
Change the style of an existing SmartArt graphic	• CLICK the SmartArt graphic. Locate the DESIGN tab under SmartArt Tools and locate the SmartArt Styles group. CLICK the desired style (hover the mouse over a choice to see a preview of the current slide changing to the new style).

PROJECT PRACTICE

1. Locate the files associated with this lesson and open the project data file **pp03a2.pptx**. Save the file as **pp03a2-vacation.pptx**.

2. CLICK slide 2.

   CLICK into the title placeholder.

   TYPE **The Process**

   CLICK the INSERT tab and locate the Illustrations group.

   CLICK SmartArt to see the palette of SmartArt graphics.

   CLICK List from the menu on the left of the palette to filter the choices to list graphics.

   CLICK the Vertical Chevron List.

   CLICK OK to insert the SmartArt.

3 CLICK into the first Chevron Text placeholder.

TYPE **Plan**

CLICK into the placeholder below it.

TYPE **Save**

CLICK into the placeholder below it.

TYPE **Enjoy** (see Figure PP3.4 for a complete view of slide 2 with steps 3, 4, and 5 completed).

4 CLICK into the first Text placeholder bullet next to "Plan."

TYPE **Decide "where" to go**

CLICK onto the next bullet.

TYPE **Decide "when" to go**

5 Using the same process, complete the next two sets of bullets with the following:

Next to Save:

TYPE **Determine how much you need**

Start putting it away

Next to Enjoy:

TYPE **Buy the tickets**

Sit back and relax

FIGURE PP3.4 Slide 2 with completed information

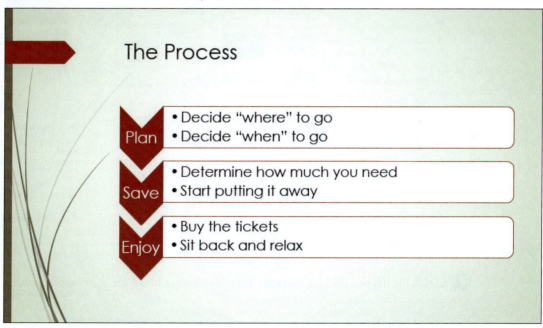

6 Ensure the SmartArt graphic is selected.

CLICK the DESIGN tab under SmartArt Tools and locate the Layouts group.

CLICK the More button.

Hover the mouse over the various layouts and the slide will preview the layout.

CHOOSE the Hierarchy List layout.

7 Use SmartArt for a different purpose.

CLICK slide 3.

CLICK the INSERT tab and locate the Illustrations group.

CLICK SmartArt to open the palette of SmartArt graphics.

Select Picture from the menu on the left-hand side of the palette.

CHOOSE Bending Picture Caption (see Figure PP3.5).

CLICK OK.

FIGURE PP3.5 SmartArt graphics: choosing the bending picture caption

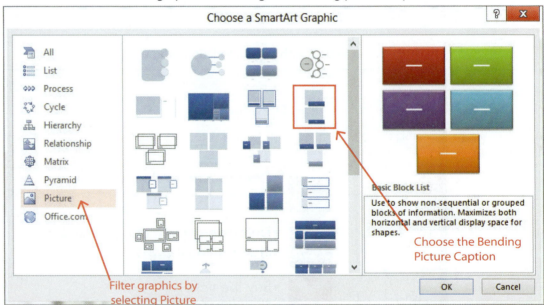

8 CLICK the left placeholder that says Text. (See Figure PP3.6 for the complete slide 3.)

TYPE **Beach**

PRESS `Enter` to create a new line of text within the placeholder.

PRESS `Tab` to create a bullet beneath the first line. Input the text directly on image/flow.

TYPE **Flying a kite**

FIGURE PP3.6   Slide 3 with text and pictures inserted

FIGURE PP3.6   Slide 3 with text and pictures inserted

9 CLICK the second text area.

TYPE **Shop**

PRESS [Enter].

PRESS [Tab].

TYPE **Hat stand**

10 You can create additional shapes within a SmartArt shape. You will insert a shape identical to the existing ones. The DESIGN tab under SmartArt Tools should be open. If not, open it and locate the Create Graphic group (while your cursor is still in the placeholder that says "Shop, Hat Stand").

CLICK Add Shape.

(*Result:* A third shape appears on the slide, and all the shapes readjust to fit the slide.)
See Figure PP3.6.

TIP

When adding more shapes to a SmartArt graphic, depending on the design of the graphic, you can add a shape before or after the shape containing the cursor. If available, you can add shapes above and below, too. The option for the Text pane allows you to enter and arrange text in a more conventional manner.

11 CLICK into the new text placeholder of the new shape.

TYPE **Cruise**

PRESS the [Enter] key.

PRESS the [Tab] key.

TYPE **Our ship**

12 CLICK the Picture button (🖼) in the first placeholder.

CLICK Browse.

Locate the files associated with this lesson.

CLICK familykite.jpg.

CLICK the Insert button.

13 Using the same process, add handstand.jpg to the second picture placeholder and cruise.jpg to the third picture placeholder. (See Figure PP3.6.)

14 CLICK the DESIGN tab under SmartArt Tools and locate the Layouts group.

CLICK the Captioned Pictures button to change the formatting of the picture captions.

Locate the SmartArt Styles group.

CLICK the More button.

CHOOSE Intense Effect and see how it changes the formatting of the SmartArt.

15 Your document should appear similar to Figure PP3.7. Save and close the pp03a2-vacation.pptx file.

FIGURE PP3.7   Completion of Lesson PowerPoint 3A2

Charts and Tables

LESSON OVERVIEW

Charts and **tables** are powerful ways to represent data in PowerPoint. Inserting and editing charts and tables is quick and easy in PowerPoint. When inserted, both are automatically sized and colored to match the slide and style of the presentation.

Charts allow you to visually display data in a variety of ways including column, line, bar, and pie charts. These help the audience better understand the data and allow you to focus on the point you want to make.

Tables enable you to organize data in a tabular format. This ensures the audience can see what major headings exist in tables and what information falls under each heading.

The right chart or table can summarize an important point or collection of information in a way that is not only easier for the audience to see, but also appealing and interesting.

SKILLS PREVIEW

Insert a chart	• CLICK the INSERT tab and locate the Illustrations group. CLICK Chart to open the Insert Chart window. CHOOSE the chart type from the menu on the left. CLICK OK, or • CLICK the Insert Chart button ( ) in the content placeholder. CHOOSE the chart type from the menu on the left. CLICK OK.
Edit chart data	• Once the chart is created, the Edit Data window appears. CLICK into the cells and change the data. Close the window by clicking the X in the top right corner of the window, or • If the chart is already created, the Edit Data window can be opened by: RIGHT-CLICKING on the image of the chart. CHOOSE Edit Data. CLICK into the cells and change the data. Close the window by clicking the X in the top right corner of the window.
Insert a table	• CLICK the INSERT tab and locate the Tables group. CLICK Table. Move the mouse to select the columns and rows of the table. CLICK on the square to insert the table, or • Insert a Table and Content slide. CLICK the Insert Table button ( ) in the content placeholder. Use the spinner buttons to set the number of columns and rows. CLICK OK.
Edit data in tables	• CLICK in the Table to select it. Type directly into each cell.

1 Locate the files associated with this lesson and open the project data file **pp03a3.pptx**. Save the file as **pp03a3-vacation.pptx**. Refer to Table 3.1 for Chart types and their use.

2 CLICK slide 4.

This is a Title and Content slide, so there are two ways to insert content. You can click directly onto the content you desire in the placeholder on the slide (in this case a chart). Now try another way.

CLICK the INSERT tab and locate the Illustrations group.

CLICK Chart to open the Insert Chart window (see Figure PP3.8).

CLICK Pie from the menu on the left of the Insert Chart window.

CLICK OK.

FIGURE PP3.8 The Insert Chart window showing the pie chart choices

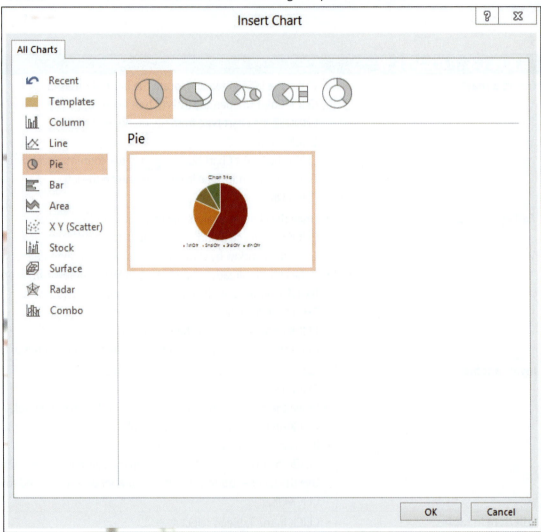

TABLE 3.1 Chart types and their usage

Chart Type	Usage
Column	Used to compare categorical data using a similar scale shown in a vertical manner
Bar	Used to compare categorical data using a similar scale shown in a horizontal manner
Line	Used to demonstrate a trend over time
Pie	Used to demonstrate the proportion of different categories

3 A chart with filler information is now inserted onto the slide. You can edit this filler information.

Edit the data in the spreadsheet as follows (you can move from one cell of the spreadsheet to the next by pressing Tab, or you can click directly into the cell). See Figure PP3.9 for details.

Cell A2: **Beach**

Cell A3: **Shopping**

Cell A4: **Traveling**

Cell B1: **Time spent…**

Cell B2: **60%**

Cell B3: **25%**

Cell B4: **15%**

FIGURE PP3.9 The Edit Data window

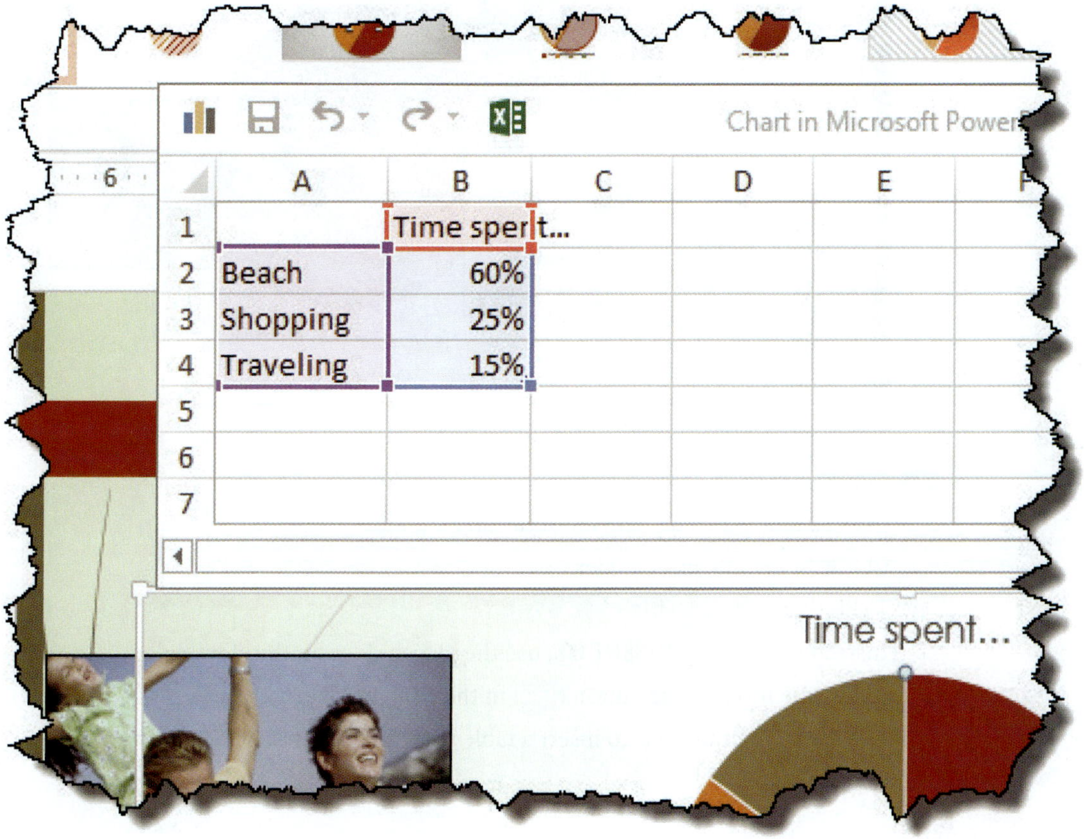

④ RIGHT-CLICK on the fifth row (4ᵗʰ Qtr) to open a short-cut menu.

CHOOSE Delete to remove the extra row from the spreadsheet.

CLICK the X in the right-hand corner of the Edit Data window to close it.

TIP

To open the editing feature of the chart, right-click on the chart image and choose Edit Data. This works on any type of chart. It also gives you the option of opening Excel 2013 to edit with all additional features available in that application. To close the Edit Data window, click the X in the top right-hand corner of the window.

⑤ DRAG the images next to the appropriate pie slices as shown in Figure PP3.10.

FIGURE PP3.10 Slide 4 with the pictures dragged into the proper spots

⑥ CLICK slide 2.

Insert a new Title and Content slide after slide 2.

CLICK in the title placeholder.

TYPE **Planned Activities**

Instead of using the INSERT tab, use the placeholder on this new slide.

CLICK the Insert Table button (⊞) in the content placeholder.

Use the spinner buttons to insert a table with three columns and one row.

CLICK OK.

7 The cursor should be flashing in the first cell.

TYPE **Day**

Use **Tab** to move to the next cell.

TYPE **Activity**

Move to the final cell.

TYPE **Location**

PRESS **Tab** to create another row in the table.

8 Fill out the rest of the table as follows, pressing **Tab** to create a new row when needed (see Figure PP3.11):

Day	Activity	Location
Sunday	Traveling	Honolulu Airport
Monday	Beach	Ala Moana Beach Park
Tuesday	Shopping	Ala Moana Shopping Center
Wednesday	Beach	Waikiki Beach
Thursday	Dinner Cruise	Star of Honolulu
Friday	Beach	Haleiwa
Saturday	Traveling	Honolulu Airport

9 Your document should appear similar to Figure PP3.11. Save and close the **pp03a3-vacation.pptx** file.

FIGURE PP3.11 Completion of Lesson PowerPoint 3A3

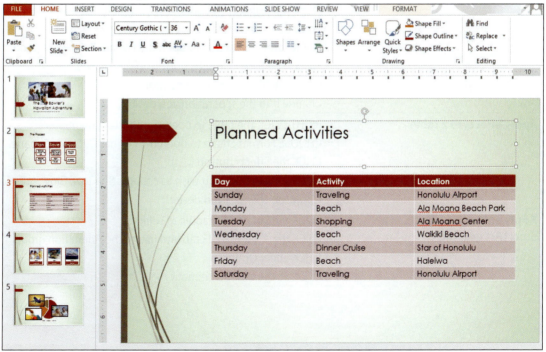

Editing and Animating Charts and Tables

LESSON OVERVIEW

When using a chart or table to present data, you run the risk of losing the audience as you suddenly present a lot of information. Focusing attention on what is important is one of the great features of PowerPoint.

Charts provide you with a number of ways to animate an image. These **Effect options** allow you to present one set of data at a time—providing an opportunity to explain each point.

You can modify charts and tables to insert new information as it is available. This is quick and easy with the **edit data** controls. As you enter new data, the chart rearranges itself to display the material.

You can also animate tables to enter and exit on your command. However, tables do not allow the specific animations for each component.

SKILLS PREVIEW

Format a chart	• CLICK the chart to select it. CLICK the FORMAT tab under Chart Tools and locate the Current Selection group. CLICK Format Selection to open the Format Data Point pane. Make the changes you desire to the Fill & Line, Effects, or Series options.
Apply animation effect options	• Select the object and animate normally. CLICK the Effect Options button. CHOOSE the option and/or sequence you desire.
Explode a slice from a pie chart	• CLICK the pie chart to select it. CLICK one of the pie slices again to select it separately from the other slices. CLICK the FORMAT tab under Chart Tools and locate the Current Selection group. CLICK Format Selection to open the Format Data Point pane. Ensure the Series Options button (▮▮) is clicked. Locate the Point Explosion control. Change it to the separation you desire.
Apply effects to a table	• RIGHT-CLICK the table to open the shortcut menu. CHOOSE Format Shape to open the Format Data Series pane. CLICK the Effects button (⬠). CLICK the category you wish to change: Shadow, Glow, Soft Edges, 3-D Format. Apply the changes you desire.
Apply animation effects to a SmartArt graphic	• CLICK the SmartArt graphic to select it. CLICK the ANIMATIONS tab and locate the Animation group. CLICK Effect Options. CHOOSE the desired animation effect.

1 Locate the files associated with this lesson and open the project data file **pp03a4.pptx**. Save the file as **pp03a4-vacation.pptx**.

2 Complete the titles for your slides.

CLICK slide 4.

CLICK into the title placeholder.

TYPE **Our Photos**

CLICK slide 5.

CLICK into the title placeholder.

TYPE **Our Time**

3 CLICK the chart to select it.

CLICK the Beach pie slice to select it separately from the other slices.

CLICK the FORMAT tab under Chart Tools and locate the Current Selection group.

CLICK Format Selection to open the Format Data Point pane.

Ensure the Series Options button (▮▮) is clicked.

Locate the Point Explosion control.

Change it from 0% to 5% (see Figure PP3.12).

(*Result*: This "explodes" the pieces of the pie apart from each other by 5 percent.)

FIGURE PP3.12   Setting the Point Explosion to 5%

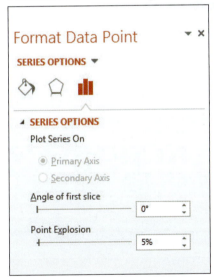

4 While the Beach slice of the pie is still selected:

CLICK the Fill & Line button (◈) in the Format Data Point pane.

CLICK Fill.

CLICK the Color button.

CHOOSE Light Blue to fill the selected slice with a new color.

5 Deselect the pie slice by clicking elsewhere on the slide.

CLOSE the Format Data Point pane.

CLICK the Chart to select all three slices at the same time.

Apply the Zoom animation to the chart.

6 Locate the Advanced Animation group.

CLICK Animation Pane to open the Animation pane.

CLICK the down arrow next to the animation in the Animation pane.

CHOOSE Effect Options.

CLICK the CHART ANIMATION tab.

CLICK the drop-down menu for Group chart.

SELECT By Category.

CLICK OK.

(*Result:* The chart is now animated slice by slice as each slice represents one category of the chart.)

7 CLICK and hold (**Shift**) on all three pictures to select them all.

APPLY the Float In animation.

CLICK the expand arrow in the Animation pane to reveal all the animations.

DRAG to reorder the animations as shown in Figure PP3.13.

Ensure the picture of the airplane is set to Start With Previous.

Close the Animation pane.

FIGURE PP3.13 Final order of animation for slide 4

8 CLICK slide 3.

RIGHT-CLICK the table.

CHOOSE Format Shape.

CLICK the Effects button ( ).

CLICK Shadow.

CLICK the drop-down next to Presets.

Hover the mouse to see the names of the effects.

CHOOSE Inside Diagonal Bottom Right to add a shadow to the table.

9 Close the Format Shape pane.

CLICK the table.

CLICK the ANIMATIONS tab.

Apply the Entrance Effect of Pinwheel (located in the Exciting category).

Change the Duration of the animation to 1.00 second.

10 CLICK slide 2.

CLICK the SmartArt graphic to select it.

Apply the Grow & Turn animation.

11 Open the Animation pane.

CLICK the drop-down arrow next to the animation.

CLICK Effect Options.

CLICK the SMARTART ANIMATION tab in the Grow & Turn dialog box.

CLICK the drop-down for Group graphic.

CLICK each of the following, and click OK to watch the preview:

> By branch one by one
>
> By level at once
>
> By level one by one.

CHOOSE By level one by one.

12 Your document should appear similar to Figure PP3.14. Save and close the **pp03a4-vacation.pptx** file.

FIGURE PP3.14   Completion of Lesson PowerPoint 3A4

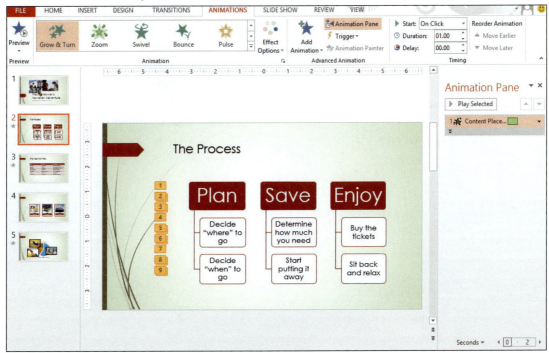

PROJECT POWERPOINT 3A: QUIZ AND HANDS-ON EXERCISES

MULTIPLE-CHOICE QUIZ

Select the best choice in the following questions to review the project concepts. Good luck!

1. For images to have the correct focal point, they should face the
   a. center of the slide.
   b. top of the slide.
   c. bottom of the slide.
   d. right of the slide.
2. To resize an image to a specific size, you should
   a. use the sizing handle.
   b. type the size into the FORMAT tab.
   c. type the percentages in the FORMAT tab.
   d. use the Select exact size.
3. SmartArt can include
   a. text.
   b. pictures.
   c. text and pictures.
   d. None of these is correct.
4. When working with SmartArt, you can add additional shapes after the last item by pressing the
   a. Add Shape button.
   b. Shift key
   c. Enter key
   d. All of these are correct.
5. To edit the design of your SmartArt, you should click on the
   a. DESIGN tab.
   b. DESIGN tab under SmartArt Tools.
   c. FORMAT tab.
   d. FORMAT tab under SmartArt Tools.
6. Which of the following charts should be used to demonstrate stock market prices over the course of a year?
   a. Bar
   b. Column
   c. Line
   d. Pie
7. Which of the following charts should be used to demonstrate the percentage of students in each grade level at a school?
   a. Bar
   b. Column
   c. Line
   d. Pie
8. When animating charts, which tab do you need to select to animate a chart by category?
   a. Chart Animation
   b. Chart
   c. Animation
   d. None of the above is correct.
9. If your cursor is in the last cell of a table, which key do you press to create a new row?
   a. Shift
   b. Enter
   c. PgDn
   d. Tab
10. You can animate tables by different cells.
   a. True
   b. False

HANDS-ON EXERCISE WORK IT OUT PP-3A-E1

In this exercise, you will insert an image from a file, add a border to it, and align it on the slide. You will also insert a chart, edit its data, and animate it to appear by series. Transitions and other animations will be included as well. The final presentation is shown in Figure PP3.15.

FIGURE PP3.15   Work It Out PP-3A-E1: completed

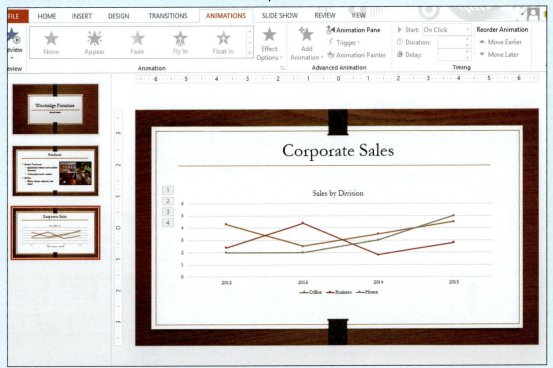

1. Locate and open the exercise data file **pp03a-ex01.pptx**. Save the file as **pp03a-hw01.pptx**.

2. On slide 1, replace the text *YourName* with your name.

3. On slide 2, insert the image **woodridge.png**.

4. Give the picture a Black Text 1 border with a weight of 1 pt. Resize the picture to be 3.4" by 4.76". Drag the picture to the right of the text placeholder.

5. Use the Align Objects button to align the picture to the middle of the slide. Resize the text placeholder to ensure all text is visible.

6. Drag the picture (using the automatic alignment guides) so the top is aligned with the top of the text placeholder.

7. Animate the picture with Random Bars and set it to appear before the text placeholder.

8. Add a Title and Content slide to the end of the show. Set its transition to Split.

9. Insert a line chart on slide 3 using the Line with Markers design.

10. Edit the data to change the Categories into the years **2012**, **2013**, **2014**, **2015**.

11. Edit the data to change the Series into **Office**, **Business**, **Home**.

12. Change the chart title to be **Sales by Division**. Do not change the numeric data. Close the edit pane.

13. Change the title of the slide to **Corporate Sales**.

14. Animate the chart to Float In and set the Chart Animation to By Series on Click.

15. Save the **pp03a-hw01.pptx** file and close it.

HANDS-ON EXERCISE WORK IT OUT PP-3A-E2

This exercise includes creating an organizational chart using SmartArt. You will populate the chart with data and adjust the layout and colors of the chart. You will animate the chart to have a pause after each level is revealed. The final presentation is shown in Figure PP3.16.

FIGURE PP3.16 Work It Out PP-3A-E2: completed

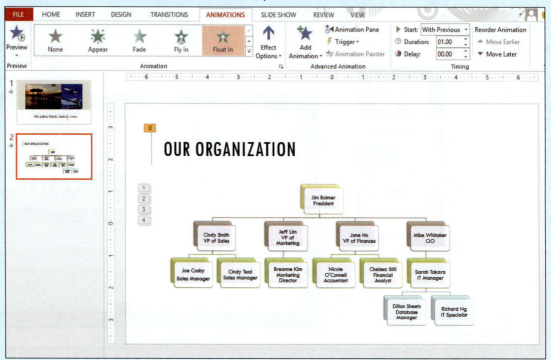

1. Locate and open the exercise data file **pp03a-ex02.pptx**. Save the file as **pp03a-hw02.pptx**.

2. On slide 1, replace the text *YourName* with your name.

3. On slide 2, insert the Organization Chart SmartArt.

4. Create the following organization chart:

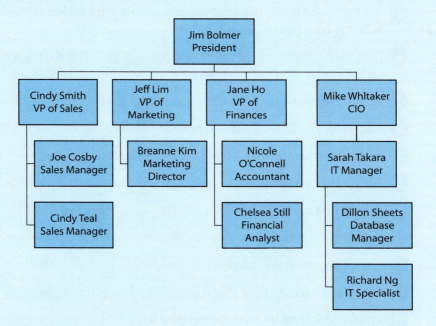

5 Change the layout of the SmartArt to Hierarchy.

6 Change the SmartArt colors to Colorful Range – Accent Colors 4 to 5.

7 Animate the organizational chart to Curve Up using the Level at Once setting.

8 Save the **pp03a-hw02.pptx** file and close it.

In this exercise, you will add tables and charts to a presentation. The completed presentation will appear similar to Figure PP3.17.

FIGURE PP3.17 Work It Out PP-3A-E3: completed

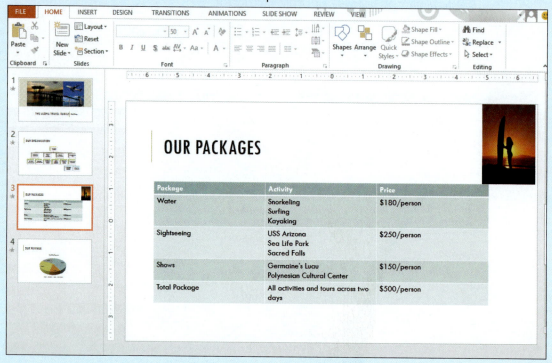

1 Locate and open the exercise data file **pp03a-ex03.pptx**. Save the file as **pp03a-hw03.pptx**.

2 On slide 1, replace *YourName* with your name.

3 On slide 3, create the following table

Package	Activity	Price
Water	Snorkeling Surfing Kayaking	$180/person
Sightseeing	USS Arizona Sea Life Park Sacred Falls	$250/person
Shows	Germaine's Luau Polynesian Cultural Center	$150/person
Total Package	All activities and tours across two days	$500/person

4 Animate the table with the Appear animation.

5 On slide 4, create a 3-D pie chart using the following data:

	Monthly Revenue
Water activities	$7,200
Sightseeing	$2,000
Shows	$5,000
Total Package	$3,000

6 Animate the chart by having each pie slice Fade in on mouse click.

7 Click the chart and use the Chart Elements shortcut on the slide to add the Data Labels.

8 On slide 3, locate the files associated with this exercise and insert surf.jpg.

9 Resize the image to 2.5" high and 1.73" wide.

10 Use the Align Objects control to align the image to the right and to the top.

11 Flip the image so the surfer faces into the slide.

12 Animate the image to Float In at the same time as the slide title.

13 Save the pp03a-hw03.pptx file and close it.

Enriching the Experience

PROJECT OBJECTIVES

After completing this project, you will be able to:

- Work with shapes.
- Enhance shapes.
- Modify shapes with Quick Styles.
- Work with drawing tools.

In this project, you will learn how to use shapes to quickly add emphasis to aspects of your presentation. You will do this by incorporating a variety of shapes in the presentation you created in the previous section. After you insert the shapes, you will learn how to modify them to meet your needs. You will also learn to connect ideas with different lines and connectors.

PROJECT FILE: *Available at* www.mhhe.com/office2013projectlearn

Working with Shapes

LESSON OVERVIEW

PowerPoint includes a variety of **shapes** you can incorporate into your presentation. Use shapes to augment your slides—to emphasize components or to enhance the appearance of other objects. For example, you may want your audience to focus on a specific photo or a certain piece of information. In either case, you can include an arrow to point to the photo or add a circle that highlights particular data.

There are many creative ways to use shapes. In this lesson, you will create a block arrow to point out a certain place on a table. You will also use curved arrows to show the flow from one column of information to the next. You will also use a shape to surround three photos to present them as part of a collection.

The use of shapes is limited only by your imagination. Be sure to try the various shapes and remember to stretch them, drag them, and resize them to explore the possibilities.

SKILLS PREVIEW

Insert shapes	• CLICK the INSERT tab and locate the Illustrations group. CLICK the Shapes button. CHOOSE the shape you want. DRAG the mouse to draw the shape on the slide.
Apply Shape Styles	• CLICK the shape to select it. CLICK the FORMAT tab under Drawing Tools and locate the Shape Styles group. CLICK the More arrow to show a palette of choices. CHOOSE the style to apply it to the current shape.
Resize shapes	• CLICK the shape to select it. DRAG the sizing handles to make the shape longer, shorter, taller, or smaller, or • CLICK the shape to select it. CLICK the FORMAT tab under Drawing Tools and locate the Size group. Adjust the height and width controls of the shape.
Apply animations to a shape	• CLICK the shape to select it. CLICK the ANIMATIONS tab and locate the Animation group. CHOOSE the animation you desire. CLICK Effect Options to choose options for each animation.

PROJECT PRACTICE

1. Locate the files associated with this exercise and open **pp03b1.pptx**. Save the file as **pp03b1-vacation.pptx**.

2. CLICK slide 3.

   CLICK the INSERT tab and locate the Illustrations group.

   CLICK the Shapes button.

   CHOOSE the Right arrow to activate the mouse crosshairs.

CLICK and DRAG the crosshairs to create an arrow next to the word *Wednesday* (see Figure PP3.18).

Set the arrow to 1.5" high and 2.5" wide.

FIGURE PP3.18   Drawing the arrow shape on the slide

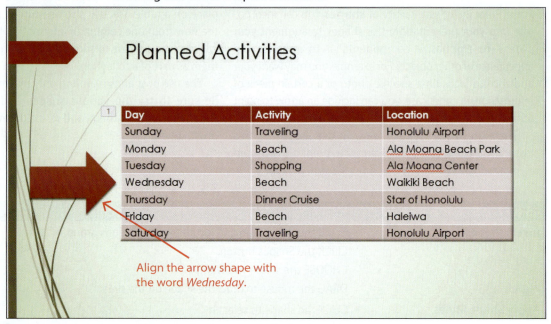

Align the arrow shape with the word *Wednesday*.

3 CLICK the arrow shape to select it.

CLICK the FORMAT tab under Drawing Tools and locate the Shape Styles group.

CLICK the More arrow to show a palette of choices.

CHOOSE Intense Effect – Dark Red Accent 1.

> **MORE INFO**
>
> When you insert shapes into PowerPoint, by default their selected color coordinates with the style of the slide show. If the slide show was not created using a style or template, the color and fill of the shape are a blue fill with a 1 pt. border of the same blue.

4 Ensure the arrow is selected.

CLICK the FORMAT tab under Drawing Tools and locate the Arrange group.

CLICK the Align Objects button.

SELECT Align Left.

(*Result:* The arrow is aligned with the far left edge of the slide.)

5 Ensure the arrow is selected.

DRAG the right-middle sizing handle until the automatic alignment guide appears to show the arrow is aligned with the edge of the table (see Figure PP3.19).

> **ⓘ MORE INFO**
>
> When you select only one object, the Align Objects control defaults to the Align to Slide setting. But if you select two or more objects, the Align Selected Objects becomes the default. For example, if you select both a picture in the top left of your slide and a text box near the bottom of the slide and then click the Align Bottom button, the highest selected object (the picture) aligns with the bottom of the lowest selected object (the text box). Experiment to see how each of the alignment options works when you use Align Selected Objects.

FIGURE PP3.19 Positioning the Right arrow using both the Align Left command and the Automatic Alignment guides

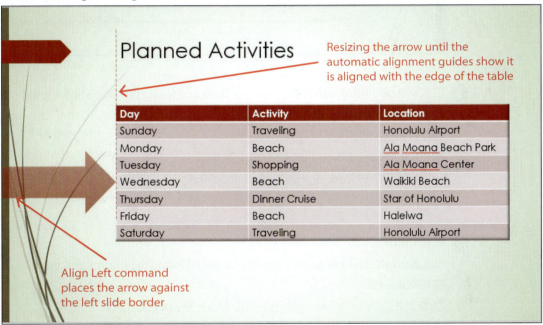

6 CLICK slide 4.

CLICK the INSERT tab and locate the Illustrations group.

CLICK Shapes.

CHOOSE Rounded Rectangle.

CLICK and DRAG to draw the rectangle around the three pictures as shown in Figure PP3.20.

FIGURE PP3.20   Placement of the Rounded Rectangle shape

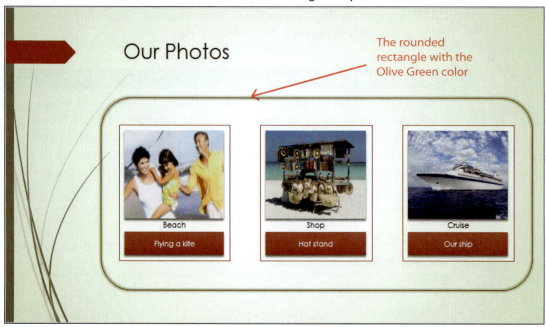

7 CLICK the **FORMAT** tab under Drawing Tools and locate the Shape Styles group.

CLICK Shape Fill.

CHOOSE No Fill.

CLICK the Shape Effects button.

CHOOSE Olive Green, 5 pt glow, Accent color 4.
(*Result:* A rounded rectangle encloses the three photographs and complements the color of the blades of grass in the background of the slide.)

8 CLICK slide 2.

CLICK the **INSERT** tab under Drawing Tools and locate the Illustrations group.

CLICK Shape.

CHOOSE Curved Down arrow from the Block Arrows category.

Drag to draw an arrow between and above the placeholders "Plan" and "Save" (see Figure PP3.21).

Copy the first arrow and place it between and above the "Save" and "Enjoy" placeholders.
(*Result:* The arrows shown are 0.47" high and 2.12" wide.)

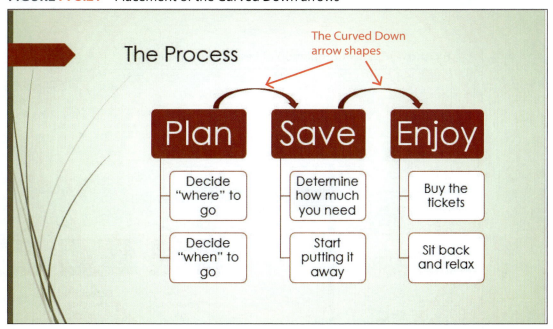

9 Animate each arrow to use the Wipe effect.

Set the Wipe Effect Options for both arrows to From Left.

Open the Animation pane and arrange the left arrow's animation order so it appears just before the "Save" placeholder is revealed.

Set the "Save" animation to Start With Previous.

Set the right arrow's animation order so it appears just before the "Enjoy" placeholder appears.

Set the "Enjoy" animation to Start With Previous.

See Figure PP3.22 for the order of animation.

FIGURE **PP3.22**   Reordering the animations

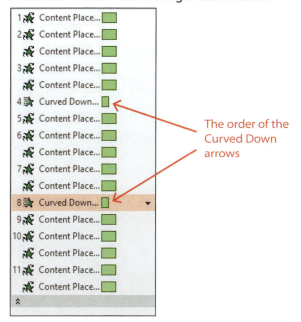

10 Your document should appear similar to Figure PP3.23. Save and close the pp03b1-vacation.pptx file.

FIGURE PP3.23 Completion of Lesson PowerPoint 3B1

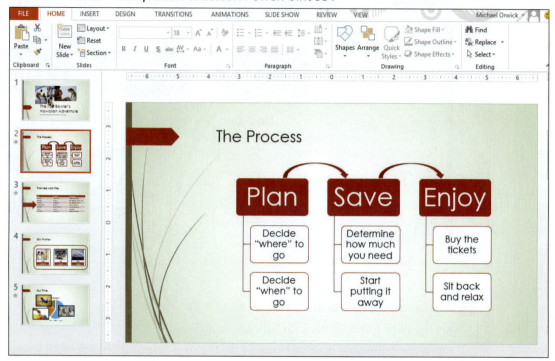

Enhancing Shapes

LESSON OVERVIEW

One of the greatest things about shapes is that you can modify them to suit your needs. When you require a perfect circle, PowerPoint can instantly create one from an oval. These **symmetrical shapes** include almost any shape.

You can fill shapes with different colors (even images and pictures) or fill them with nothing in order to show the images beneath them. Layer shapes appear behind or on top of another image through the **Send Backward** and **Bring Forward** commands.

The **Shape Effects** button applies predesigned effects such as shadow, reflection, glow, soft edges, bevel, and even 3-D rotation to a shape. Each effect has many preset options, or adjust the settings yourself from the **Format Shape** pane.

SKILLS PREVIEW

Create a symmetrical shape	• CLICK the INSERT tab and locate the Illustrations group. CLICK the Shapes button. CHOOSE the shape you desire. HOLD the **Shift** key down as you draw the shape.
Change the fill of a shape	• CLICK the shape to select it. CLICK the FORMAT tab under Drawing Tools and locate the Shape Styles group. CLICK Shape Fill. CHOOSE the desired fill (or no fill).
Copy and drag shapes to another place	• HOLD the **Ctrl** key down. CLICK on the shape. DRAG a copy of the shape to its new location. RELEASE the **Ctrl** key to place the shape there.
Send a shape behind an image	• CLICK on the shape to select it. CLICK the FORMAT tab under Drawing Tools and locate the Arrange group. CLICK the drop-down arrow next to the Send Backward button. CHOOSE Send to Back.
Format a shape	• RIGHT-CLICK the shape to open the shortcut menu. CLICK Format Shape to open the Format Shape pane. CLICK Fill or Line to expand options. CHOOSE the options you desire, or • CLICK on the image to select it. CLICK the FORMAT tab under Drawing Tools and locate the Shape Styles group. CLICK the Shape Effects button. CHOOSE the desired effect.
Use Repeat to apply formatting to another shape	• Apply the formatting changes to one shape. CLICK on the next shape to select it. CLICK the Repeat button (⟳) in the Quick Access toolbar.

1. Locate the files associated with this exercise and open **pp03b2.pptx**. Save the file as **pp03b2-vacation.pptx**.

2. CLICK slide 5.

   CLICK the INSERT tab and locate the Illustrations group.

   CLICK the Shapes button.

   CHOOSE Oval.

   HOLD the `Shift` key down.

   DRAG to draw a circle over the image on the right-hand side of the slide (see Figure PP3.24).

TIP

Holding the `Shift` key down as you draw a shape forces PowerPoint to make the shape perfectly symmetrical. This means that ovals become circles, rectangles become squares, and stars appear equal on all sides.

FIGURE PP3.24   The location of the circle shape on the slide

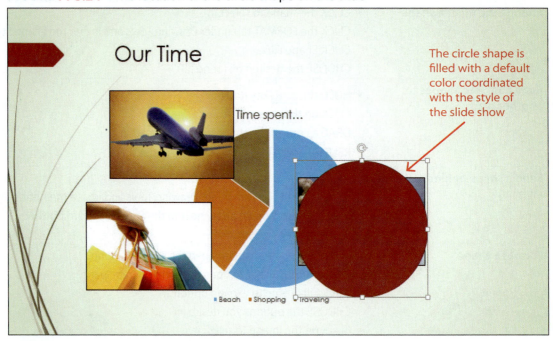

3. Ensure the shape is still selected.

   CLICK the FORMAT tab under Drawing Tools (if needed) and locate the Shape Styles group.

   CLICK Shape Fill.

   CHOOSE No Fill.

4 HOLD the [Ctrl] key down.

CLICK on the circle shape.

(*Result*: The cursor changes to a left-facing white arrow with a plus (+) sign next to it. This means a copy of the shape will move wherever you drag the mouse—as long as you hold the [Ctrl] button down.)

DRAG the new circle to the picture of the airplane.

RELEASE the [Ctrl] key to place the circle there.

5 HOLD the [Ctrl] key down.

DRAG either circle to the final picture.

RELEASE the [Ctrl] key to place the circle there (see Figure PP3.25 for the placement of the circles).

FIGURE PP3.25   The placement of the circle shapes on the slide

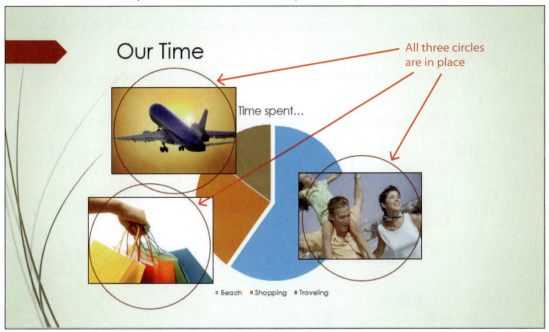

6 CLICK on one of the circles to select it.

CLICK the FORMAT tab under Drawing Tools and locate the Arrange group.

CLICK the drop-down arrow next to the Send Backward button.

CHOOSE Send to Back.

(*Result*: The circle moves behind the other images. It is layered behind them.)

Do the same to the remaining two circles.

7 CLICK slide 2.

RIGHT-CLICK the arrow between "Plan" and "Save" to open the shortcut menu.

CLICK Format Shape to open the Format Shape pane.

CLICK Fill to expand the Fill options.

CLICK Gradient fill of your choice to apply a gradient fill to the arrow.

Do the same to the second arrow.

8 CLICK on the left arrow to select it.

CLICK the Direction drop-down in the Format Shape pane.

CHOOSE the Linear Left option.

CLICK on the right arrow to select it.

CLICK the Repeat button (⟳) to repeat the last command.
(*Result:* The Linear Left option is repeated and applied to the right arrow.)

Close the Format Shape pane.

9 CLICK the "Plan" placeholder.

CLICK the FORMAT tab under SmartArt Tools and locate the Shape Styles group.

CLICK the Shape Effects button.

CHOOSE Shadow.

CHOOSE Offset Diagonal Bottom Right.

CLICK away to see that this places a slight shadow at the bottom and right of the placeholder.

10 CLICK on the "Save" placeholder.

CLICK the Repeat button (⟳) to apply the same effect to that placeholder.

CLICK on the "Enjoy" placeholder.

CLICK the Repeat button (⟳) to apply the same effect to that placeholder.

11 Your document should appear similar to Figure PP3.26. Save and close the **pp03b2-vacation.pptx** file.

FIGURE PP3.26 Completion of Lesson PowerPoint 3B2

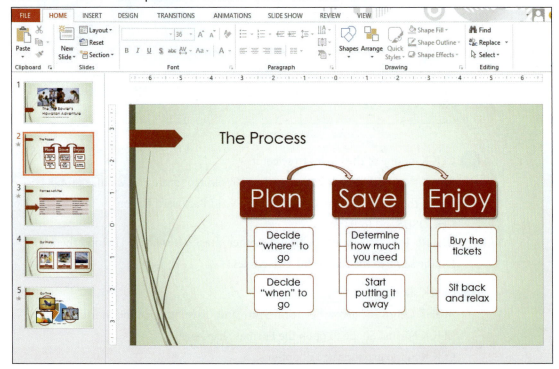

Modifying Shapes and Applying Quick Styles

LESSON OVERVIEW

You can modify shapes in many ways. Modifications include the line color, the fill, and the font color. In this lesson you will explore the power of **Quick Styles,** a very quick method of modifying shapes within PowerPoint. Quick Styles contains preset designs to instantly format a shape, picture, table, chart, and even SmartArt. To make things even faster, Quick Styles adjusts to provide choices that automatically coordinate with the theme of the slide show so fill and line colors will not clash with the rest of the presentation.

Quick Styles may also include other formatting such as shadow, reflection, flow, soft edges, and artistic effects. You can adjust these with the Format Shape pane.

While there are too many shapes to cover each one separately, this lesson adds a **callout** to the slide. Callouts serve many purposes, but some of the more common styles appear as the thought and dialog balloons often used in cartoons. Adding and adjusting text in a callout is the same as adding and adjusting text in any other shape.

SKILLS PREVIEW

Insert a callout	• CLICK the INSERT tab and locate the Illustrations group. CLICK Shapes. Locate the Callouts category. CHOOSE the shape you desire. DRAG across the slide to draw the shape.
Enter text into a shape	• CLICK the shape to select it. Begin typing as PowerPoint automatically centers the text.
Apply Quick Styles to an object	• CLICK the object (picture, table, chart, SmartArt) to select it. CLICK the FORMAT tab under the particular Tools (e.g., Picture Tools, Drawing Tools) and locate the Shape Styles group. CLICK the More button. Hover the mouse over the options to preview. CLICK the desired style to apply it.
Adjust shape characteristics	• CLICK the shape to select it. DRAG the yellow adjustment handle to alter the shape. (Some shapes have more than one adjustment handle; some have none.) Release the mouse to complete the adjustment.

PROJECT PRACTICE

1 Locate the files associated with this exercise and open **pp03b3.pptx**. Save the file as **pp03b3-vacation.pptx**.

2 CLICK slide 5.

CLICK the INSERT tab and locate the Illustrations group.

CLICK Shapes.

Locate the Callouts category.

CHOOSE Cloud Callout.

DRAG to draw Cloud Callout above the Bowler family picture (see Figure PP3.27).

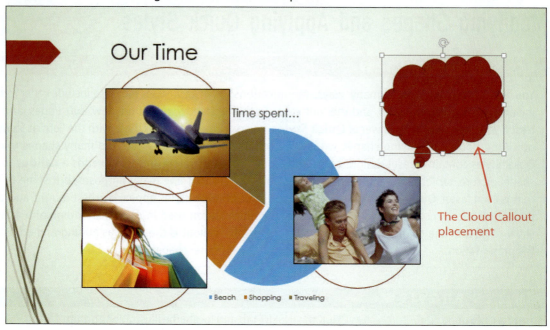

3 Ensure the Cloud Callout is selected.

TYPE **The beach was our favorite!**

The text should appear inside the callout.

Select all the text inside the callout.

Change it to Black Text 1 font color.

4 Ensure the callout is still selected.

CLICK the FORMAT tab under Drawing Tools (if required) and locate the Shape Styles group.

CLICK the More button to reveal the palette of Quick Styles options.

Each time you hover the mouse over one of the options, Live Preview shows the results on the slide. CHOOSE Colored Outline – Black, Dark 1.

(*Result:* The outline of the callout becomes black and the fill is white. See Figure PP3.28.)

TIP

Quick Styles provides a number of formatting designs based on the object that is selected at the time. If you have selected a table, the Quick Styles will present Table Styles. If you select a shape, Quick Styles is Shape Styles, and if you select a picture, Quick Styles is Picture Styles. You can be sure that all of the options provided have border colors, font colors, and (if applicable) fill colors that coordinate with the original theme of the slide show. If your presentation was not created using a slide show theme, the options are more general.

FIGURE PP3.28 Applying Quick Styles to the callout shape

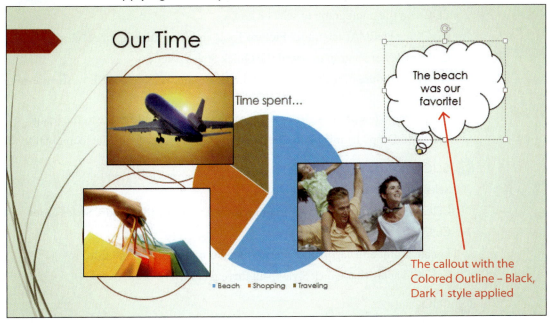

5 At the bottom of the callout is a small yellow box. Most shapes have at least one of these adjustment controls. They are used to alter the characteristics of the shape. How many and where they are located on the shape depend on the shape itself.

DRAG the adjustment handle close to the woman's head in the picture.
(*Result:* This will extend the callout's pointer to clearly indicate the proper person. It also moves the callout on top of the picture to blend them in a more natural manner. See Figure PP3.29.)

FIGURE PP3.29 Comparison of the original callout to the adjusted one

6 CLICK slide 1.

CLICK on the photograph to select it.

CLICK the FORMAT tab under Picture Tools and locate the Picture Styles group.

CLICK the More button to reveal the Quick Styles palette.

Hover the mouse over the first style (Simple Frame, White) to see how the image changes on the slide.

Hover over a few of the styles to see the changes they would make to the image.

CHOOSE Drop Shadow Rectangle (the fourth one on the first row) to apply it to the image.

7 CLICK slide 5.

Select all three pictures on the slide.

CLICK the FORMAT tab under Picture Tools and locate the Picture Styles group.

CLICK the More button.

Locate Rounded Diagonal Corner, White (second choice in the third row).

CLICK to apply that Quick Style to all three pictures.

8 CLICK slide 2.

CLICK on the "Plan" placeholder to select it.

CLICK the FORMAT tab under SmartArt Tools and locate the Shape Styles group.

CLICK the More button.

Hover the mouse over the various options to see the effects.

CHOOSE Subtle Effect – Dark Red, Accent 1 (second option, fourth row).

Apply this Quick Style to the "Save" and "Enjoy" placeholders.

9 Your document should appear similar to Figure PP3.30. Save and close the **pp03b3-vacation.pptx** file.

FIGURE PP3.30   Completion of Lesson PowerPoint 3B3

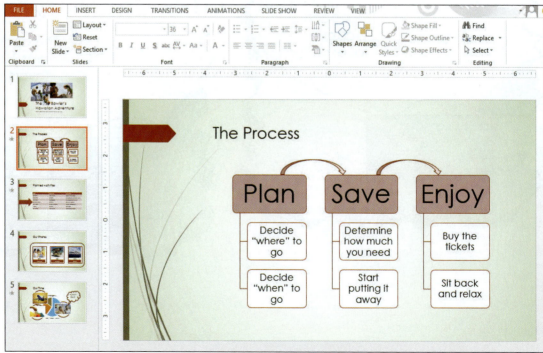

Working with Drawing Tools

LESSON OVERVIEW

This final lesson on the use of shapes focuses on the details that make a presentation strong. Adding shapes draws attention to points that you want the audience to recognize. Normally, when you complete drawing a shape, the mouse returns to its normal setting. If you want to draw another of the same shape, you have to select it again. With the **Lock Drawing mode**, you can lock the mouse into drawing the same shape again and again until you turn it off.

Group shapes to allow them to function as one object or use the Control and Drag method to instantly copy one shape and drag it across to its new location. After creating perfect copies of shapes, it is easy to add a **connector** line, arrow, or elbow connector (straight or curved) to show a relationship between two shapes.

You will also use the adjustment handle on a shape to make subtle changes to pull shapes together into an image, helping the audience follow your process.

SKILLS PREVIEW

Lock Drawing mode	• CLICK the INSERT tab and locate the Illustrations group. CLICK the Shapes button. RIGHT-CLICK on any shape. CHOOSE Lock Drawing mode. Draw the shape as many times as you wish. Press the `Esc` key to turn the Lock Drawing mode off.
Copy a shape to another location on the same slide	• HOLD `Ctrl` down and click the shape you wish to copy. DRAG the cursor (still holding the `Ctrl` button) to where you want the copy to be pasted. RELEASE the mouse to paste the copy. RELEASE the `Ctrl` button.
Draw a straight vertical or horizontal line (using a shape)	• CLICK the INSERT tab and locate the Illustrations group. CLICK Shapes. CHOOSE one of the line shapes. HOLD the `Shift` button down as you draw the line. This will create a straight line that is horizontal, vertical, or at a 45-degree angle.
Group shapes	• CLICK on the first shape. HOLD the `Shift` button down and click on the other shapes. CLICK on the FORMAT tab under Picture Tools. CLICK the Group Objects button. CHOOSE Group.

PROJECT PRACTICE

1. Locate the files associated with this exercise and open **pp03b4.pptx**. Save the file as **pp03b4-vacation.pptx**.

2. If you plan to draw the same shape more than once, PowerPoint offers the Lock Drawing mode.
   CLICK slide 3.
   CLICK the INSERT tab and locate the Illustrations group.
   CLICK the Shapes button.

RIGHT-CLICK on the Line (or any shape, but you will use the line twice here).

CHOOSE Lock Drawing mode.

Now the mouse will do nothing but draw lines until you turn it off.

DRAG a straight line above and below the arrow shape (see Figure PP3.31).

Press the key to turn the Lock Drawing mode off.

FIGURE PP3.31   The position of the line shapes above and below the arrow shape

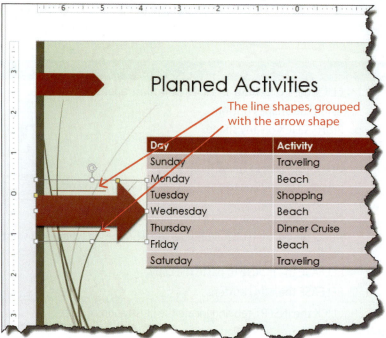

3. To ensure the arrow and the two lines act as one object, group the arrow and the two lines.

Apply a Fade entrance animation to the newly grouped shape.

4. Add a new Title and Content slide to the end of the show.

CLICK into the Title placeholder.

TYPE **Our Advice**

Delete the Content placeholder.

Insert text boxes as shown in Figure PP3.32.

TYPE **Pick a place** into the first text box.

TYPE **Set a date** into the second text box.

TYPE **Go for it** into the third text box.

FIGURE PP3.32   Placement of the three text boxes

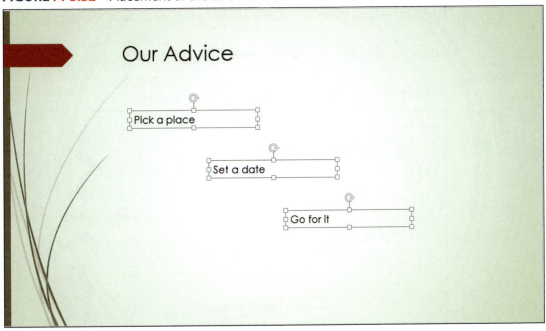

5 CLICK the INSERT tab and locate the Illustrations group.

CLICK Shapes.

RIGHT-CLICK the Elbow Arrow Connector (in the Lines category).

CHOOSE the Lock Drawing mode.

Draw the shapes as shown in Figure PP3.33.

Turn the Lock Drawing mode off.

FIGURE PP3.33   The elbow connectors added to the slide

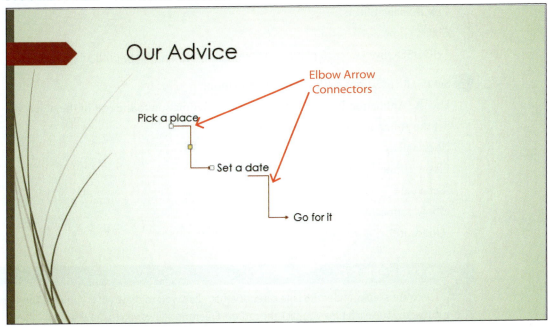

6 The top line of the elbow connectors should underline the last word in the sentence.

DRAG the yellow adjustment handle on the first elbow connector to increase the length of the top line.

Adjust the second elbow connector if needed (see Figure PP3.34).

FIGURE PP3.34 Adjusting elbow connector arrows

7 Select both elbow connectors.

CLICK one of the elbow shapes.

CLICK the FORMAT tab under Drawing Tools and locate the Shape Styles group.

CLICK Shape Effects.

CLICK Glow.

CHOOSE Olive Green, 5 pt glow, Accent color 4 to apply it to both shapes.

8 Set the first text box to the Expand animation.

Use the Animation Painter to apply the same animation to the rest of the objects.

Set the animation to the following order:

"Pick a place"

Elbow connector

"Set a date"

Elbow connector

"Go for it"

MORE INFO

There are shapes under the Line category that allow you to draw what you like. The Curve allows you to curve the line each time you click the mouse. Freeform allows you to draw straight lines while you drag the mouse and curved lines when you hold the mouse down. The Scribble allows you to draw any pattern as long as you hold the mouse button down. In all cases, when you complete your drawing, double-click the mouse to insert the shape.

9 Your document should appear similar to Figure PP3.35. Save and close the **pp03b4-vacation.pptx** file.

FIGURE PP3.35 Completion of Lesson PowerPoint 3B4

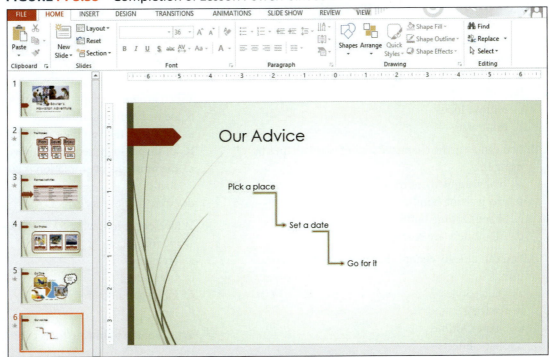

MULTIPLE-CHOICE QUIZ

Select the best choice in the following questions to review the project concepts. Good luck!

1. Shapes, such as arrows, can be used to _____ content of slides.
   a. emphasize
   b. understate
   c. remove focus
   d. minimize

2. You can alter the characteristics of many shapes by using the
   a. yellow adjustment handle.
   b. green sizing handle.
   c. Shape Outline button.
   d. All of these are correct.

3. You can quickly change the appearance of shapes using
   a. Quick Styles.
   b. SmartArt.
   c. Shape Outline.
   d. Shape Effects.

4. Quick Styles are preset formats that can include
   a. shadow.
   b. reflection.
   c. soft edges.
   d. All of these are correct.

5. Cloud _____ allow you to add thoughts or dialog to images.
   a. textboxes
   b. tables
   c. WordArt
   d. callouts

6. Shapes can take the background color of your slide.
   a. True
   b. False

7. When grouping shapes that have animations with those without animations
   a. all shapes take on the existing animation.
   b. all shapes lose their animations.
   c. the most recent animation is applied to all the shapes.
   d. None of these is correct.

8. Which of the following tools allows you to create a shape from scratch?
   a. Freeform
   b. Connector
   c. Elbow connector
   d. Line

9. Which of the following tools connects two objects together with an angled line?
   a. Scribble
   b. Quad Arrow
   c. Line
   d. Elbow connector

10. Which key do you press to quit the Lock Drawing mode?
    a. End
    b. Esc
    c. Enter
    d. BackSpace

HANDS-ON EXERICSE: WORK IT OUT PP-3B-E1

In this exercise, you will use the skills learned during the project such as inserting shapes, resizing shapes, and applying Quick Styles. You will also add a shape and use the adjustment handle to drastically change the shape's form. You can add arrows and layer the shape behind the images on the slide. You may add transitions and animations as desired. The final presentation is shown in Figure PP3.36.

FIGURE PP3.36   Work It Out PP-3B-E1: completed

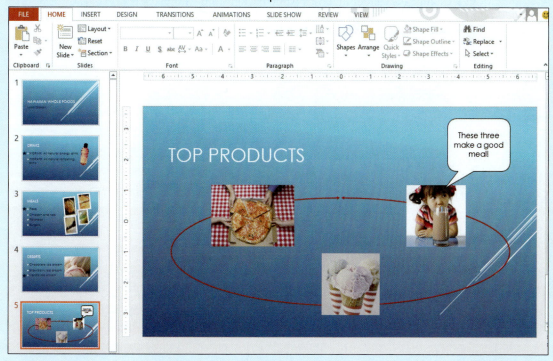

1. Locate and open the exercise data file **pp03b-ex01.pptx**. Save the file as **pp03b-hw01.pptx**

2. Replace the text *YourName* with your name.

3. On slide 2, insert a star shape to the left of the "HIDRINK" point. Set the star to 0.5" high and 0.5" wide.

4. On slide 3, insert a star shape next to the text "Pizza." On slide 4, insert a star shape next to the text "Vanilla ice cream." Set both of these stars to be identical to the star on slide 2.

5. Change the style of the stars to Colored Outline – Dark Blue, Accent 1.

6. Align each star to the left of the page.

7. On slide 3, apply the Rotated White Quick Style to all four of the pictures.

8. On slide 5, insert an arc shape. Use Quick Styles to set the shape to Intense Effect – Red, Accent 6. Make the height of the shape 3.5".

9. Use the yellow adjustment handle to adjust the arc into an oval shape (see Figure PP3.36).

10. Align the arrow to the middle of the slide. Drag it until the arc intersects all three pictures.

11 Change the Shape Outline of the arc to arrowheads on both ends of the arc.

12 Send the arc to the back so it is behind all three pictures.

13 On slide 5, insert a Rounded Rectangular Callout shape with the text **These three make a good meal!** Set the callout to 1.7" high and 2.1" wide. Move the callout above and to the right of the picture of the little girl.

14 Change the callout to have a white background with black text.

15 Save and close the presentation file.

In this exercise, you will use the skills learned during the project including inserting shapes and applying Quick Styles to them. You will also insert a shape and add text to it. You will also duplicate the same action on other slides (practicing your copying or redo skills). The final presentation is shown in Figure PP3.37.

FIGURE PP3.37 Work It Out PP-3B-E2: completed

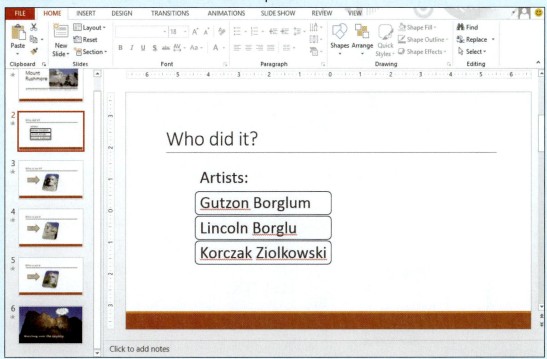

1. Locate and open the exercise data file **pp03b-ex02.pptx**. Save the file as **pp03b-hw02.pptx**.

2. Using Quick Styles, apply the Reflected Rounded Rectangle to the picture on slide 1.

3. On slide 2, draw a Rounded Rectangle around the name "Korczak Ziolkowski" (see Figure PP3.37). Set the outline of the shape to black with a 1 pt. border. Change the Shape Fill to no fill.

4. Do the same to the other two names on slide 2 (hint: you can repeat the same steps or you can use one of the copy methods to add them).

5. On slide 3, use Quick Styles to apply the Bevel Perspective to the picture. Align the picture horizontally across the slide. Insert a block arrow shape (Right arrow) on the left of the picture. Make the arrow 1.5" high and 2.4" wide.

6. Align the arrow vertically on the slide. Using Quick Styles, apply the Subtle Effect – Brown, Accent 4 to the arrow. Enter the following text into the arrow shape: **Washington**.

7. Using the Format Shape controls, apply the following preset Shadow effect to the arrow: Perspective Diagonal Lower Right.

8. Do the same to slides 4 and 5, but ensure the text added to the arrow on slide 4 says **Jefferson** and **T. Roosevelt**. On slide 5, add the text **Lincoln** to the arrow.

9. On slide 6, add a cloud callout above Lincoln's head. Add the text: **Hey, I can see my house!** Use Quick Styles to apply the Colored Outline – Green, Accent 6 formatting. Ensure the callout is clearly indicating who the words belong to.

10. Save and close the presentation file.

In this exercise, you will use the skills learned during the project such as inserting shapes and applying Quick Styles to them. You will also insert a chart and edit the data of the chart. You will use the Align Objects button after selecting more than one object to allow you to align objects in relation to each other. The final presentation is shown in Figure PP3.38.

FIGURE PP3.38 Work It Out PP-3B-E3: completed

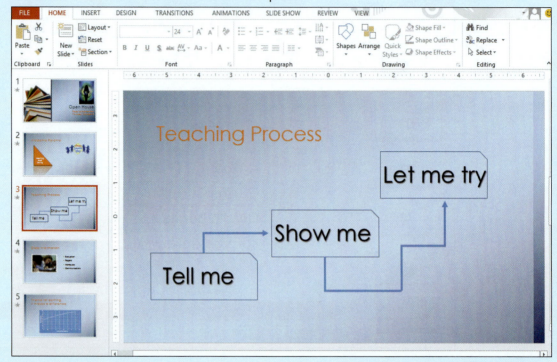

1. Locate and open the exercise data file **pp03b-ex03.pptx**. Save the file as **pp03b-hw03.pptx**.

2. On slide 1, select both the picture and the text box "Open House." Using the Align Objects button, align the picture to the right based on the current position of the text box (hint: do not Align to slide).

3. On slide 2, set the reflection for the triangle to the preset Half Reflection, touching.

4. On slide 3, insert the shape Snip Single Corner Rectangle to each of the text boxes. Set the size of the shape to 1.4" high and 3.3" wide. Set the fill to No Fill.

5. Using the Elbow Arrow Connector, insert that shape from the "Tell me" text box to the "Show me" text box. Set the connector to a weight of 4½ pt.

6. Using an Elbow Connector (no arrow) and another Elbow Arrow Connector (with an arrow), blend them to form a connection from the "Show me" text box to the "Let me try" text box (see Figure PP3.38). Set the connectors to the same weight of 4½ pt.

7. On slide 4, use Quick Styles to set the picture to Perspective Shadow, White. Using the Align Objects control, select the picture and the text box and Align Middle (in relation to each other).

8. On slide 5, insert an X Y (Scatter) Chart (Scatter with Smooth Lines and Markers). Insert the data shown in Figure PP3.39.

FIGURE PP3.39 Data for scatter chart

	A	B
1	Column1	Column2
2	0	51
3	1	65
4	2	77
5	3	89
6	4	94
7		

9 Click on the chart and use the floating Chart Styles button ( ) and select Style 8.

10 Use the floating Chart Elements button ( ):

Turn off the Chart Title.

Turn on the Axis Title.

11 Click into the Y axis (vertical) and type **Student Grades**. Click into the X axis (horizontal) and type **Parent/Teacher Meetings**.

12 Save and close the presentation file.

Chapter Summary

There are many tools in PowerPoint that allow you to customize images for your presentations. Once you insert an image, you can change the size and add borders to help your images stand out. You can even flip your image to ensure it has the right focal point. This helps you to hold your audience's attention.

SmartArt, charts, and tables allow you to quickly summarize information, which in turn makes it easier for your audience to follow your presentation. SmartArt offers many different types for different purposes. You can even add pictures to SmartArt to enhance a process or a hierarchy in your presentation. PowerPoint also lets you quickly sum up information with charts. When using charts, first understand what you want to communicate to your audience. If you do not, you may select a chart that is not quite right for your presentation. You can display a lot of information in a grid format with tables, organizing items into categories for your audience. With all of these tools at your fingertips, the most important determination to make is what information you want your audience to gain from your presentation. Once you know this, you can select the appropriate illustrations to make your point.

Shapes are a good tool to make your presentations unique. Shapes, such as arrows, can help focus your audience's attention on specific content or areas of a slide. Use other shapes with transparencies to highlight the information, making it appear more important. This technique is particularly useful in large data tables, when you need to call attention to just a few cells. Consider using connector shapes when you need to link ideas. With these shapes, you can link shapes and the cursor locks on to the different slide elements you select. This is much easier than using lines that do not automatically link to different parts of your slide elements.

Now that you know how to edit photographs, SmartArt, charts, tables, and shapes, it is important to explore their possible uses. When you test these tools in different scenarios, you are sure to learn new uses and discover the limitless possibilities of PowerPoint.

Chapter Key Terms

Align objects, p. P-130	Effect options, p. P-144	Shape Effects, p. P-161
Border, p. P-130	Format Shape, p. P-161	Shape Height, p. P-130
Bring Forward, p. P-161	Lock aspect ration, p. P-131	Shape Width, p. P-130
Callout, p. P-165	Lock Drawing mode, p. P-169	Shapes, p. P-155
Charts, p. P-139	Quick Styles, p. P-165	SmartArt, p. P-134
Connector, p. P-169	Rotate objects, p. P-130	Symmetrical shapes, p. P-161
Edit data, p. P-144	Send Backward, p. P-161	Tables, p. P-139

On Your Own Exercise PP-3C-E1

This exercise provides you with the opportunity to use all the skills learned in the projects of this chapter to complete a comprehensive exercise. Much of the steps are suggestions, but there are a few specific instructions. Feel free to add your own touches. To begin, open the exercise data file **pp03cp1.pptx** and save it as **pp03cp1-hw01.pptx**. An example of how this exercise might look is shown in Figure PP3.40.

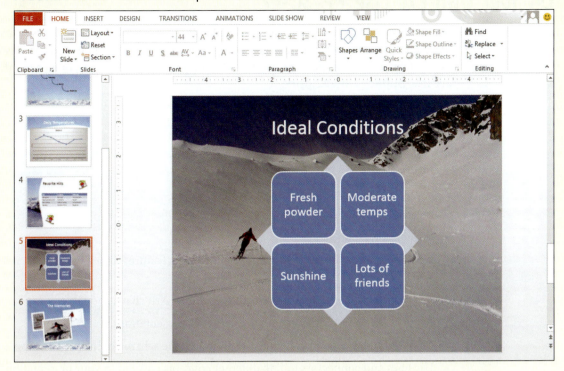

Complete the following tasks to modify your presentation.

- Slide 2: Select the four text boxes and distribute them evenly vertically and horizontally in relation to each other.

- On slide 2, add connectors between the four levels of text boxes to show the order and flow from Planning to Traveling to Skiing and to Returning. Animate it so a text box appears first, followed by an arrow and the next text box, and so on.

- Slide 3: Insert a line chart showing the temperatures over the week of skiing. Use Quick Styles to set the chart to Style 2. Animate it to appear by Category.

- Slide 4: Search for a "skiing" clip art cartoon image. Resize it to about 1.5" high. Place it at the bottom left-hand side of the slide. Copy and flip the image and place it at the top right-hand side of the slide.

- On slide 4, insert a three-column, five-row table with the Name, Location, and Difficulty (Beginner, Intermediate, or Expert) of four imaginary ski hills.

- On slide 5, insert a SmartArt graphic showing four things required to make for "Ideal Conditions." Perhaps include fresh powder, moderate temperatures, sunshine, and lots of friends. Animate the parts to appear separately.

- On slide 6, insert the following pictures from file: **ski chair lift.jpg, ski woman.jpg, ski resting. jpg**. Apply a Quick Style to each of the pictures to make them appear as real photographs. Animate so that the ski resting image appears last and sits on top of the other two images.

Save the document. Close PowerPoint.

On Your Own Exercise PP-3C-E2

This exercise will provide you with the opportunity to use all the skills learned in the projects of this chapter to complete a comprehensive exercise. There are many suggestions but no specific instructions. However, the tasks are outlined for you below. To begin, open a blank slide show and save it as **pp03cp2-hw02.pptx**.

Complete the following tasks to create your own presentation.

- Create a new presentation based on a vacation you took.

- Your presentation should be at least five slides.

- Include at least 10 pictures.

- Include at least one SmartArt.

- Include at least one chart.

- Include at least one table.

- Use the Align to Slide and Align to Select Objects features to help you set up at least one of the slides.

- Apply custom animations to your pictures, SmartArt, chart, and table.

- Insert at least two shapes to complement your presentation.

- Modify the shapes to ensure their colors match the scheme of the presentation.

- Use lines and connectors to link different concepts covered in your presentation.

- Save the document. Close PowerPoint.

appendix

Microsoft Office 2013 Shortcuts

COMMON OFFICE 2013 KEYBOARD SHORTCUTS

Action	Keyboard Shortcut
Open	Ctrl + O
Copy	Ctrl + C
Cut	Ctrl + X
Paste	Ctrl + V
Save	Ctrl + S
Close a file	Ctrl + W
Open the System Menu	Alt + spacebar

EXCEL 2013 KEYBOARD SHORTCUTS

Action	Keyboard Shortcut
Move to cell A1	Ctrl + Home
Move to a specific cell	F5
Go to the last filled cell in a column	Ctrl + ↓
Insert formula into all selected cells	Ctrl + Enter
Absolute symbol toggle	F4
Move to the next text box	Tab

WORD 2013 KEYBOARD SHORTCUTS

Action	Keyboard Shortcut
Select All	Ctrl + A
Move the cursor to the end of the document	Ctrl + End
Move the cursor to the beginning of the document	Ctrl + Home
Copy	Ctrl + C
Cut	Ctrl + X
Paste	Ctrl + V
Undo	Ctrl + Z
Bold	Ctrl + B
Italic	Ctrl + I
Underline	Ctrl + U
Center text	Ctrl + E
Justify text	Ctrl + J
Right-align text	Ctrl + R
Left-align text	Ctrl + L
Move to the next text box	Shift + Tab
Print a document	Ctrl + P
Insert page break	Ctrl + Enter
Select all the text inside a text box	Ctrl + A
Go to the previous tab	Shift + Tab
Open Spelling and Grammar task pane	F7

Appendix Microsoft Office 2013 Shortcuts **AP-1**

POWERPOINT 2013 KEYBOARD SHORTCUTS

Action	Keyboard Shortcut
Open a new blank presentation	Ctrl + N
Open an existing presentation from the Backstage view	Ctrl + O
Open an existing presentation from the Open dialog	Ctrl + F12
Undo any action or change made	Ctrl + Z
Start a presentation slide show from the beginning	F5
Start slide show from current slide	Shift + F5
Move to the first slide in normal view	Ctrl + Home
Cut	Ctrl + X
Copy	Ctrl + C
Paste	Ctrl + V
Promote text one level	Shift + Tab
Exit Slide Show view	Esc
Bold	Ctrl + B
Italic	Ctrl + I
Underline	Ctrl + U
Align text left	Ctrl + L
Center text	Ctrl + E
Align text right	Ctrl + R
Justify text	Ctrl + J
Move to first slide	Home
Move to last slide	End
Move to next slide	PgDn or ↓
Move to previous slide	PgUp or ↑
Blank the screen to black	B or .
Blank the screen to white	W or ,

ACCESS 2013 KEYBOARD SHORTCUTS

Action	Keyboard Shortcut
Go to the next field in the record	→
Go to the previous field in the record	←
Go to the next record	↓
Go to the previous record	↑
Go to the top of a field column	Ctrl + ↑
Go to the bottom of a field column	Ctrl + ↓
Move to the left-most (first) field	Home
Move to the right-most (last) field	End
Move to the top of the datasheet (first record and field)	Ctrl + Home
Move to the bottom of the datasheet (last record and field)	Ctrl + End
Navigate from field to field within a record	Tab
Navigate from the last field in the record to the first field in the next record	Tab
Save your editing changes without leaving the current record	Shift + Enter
Display the REPLACE tab in the Find and Replace dialog box	Ctrl + H
Delete a record	Del or Ctrl + -
Save a database object. If first time saving the object, opens the Save As dialog.	Ctrl + S

Glossary

OFFICE 2013

Auto-hide Ribbon This view option in Office provides an optimal screen view by eliminating the Ribbon and tabs and expanding your document to fit the entire screen.
Autosave This Office feature backs up and saves your work at regularly scheduled intervals.

Backstage view Accessed from the FILE tab, this is the place to manage files. Common commands such as Open, Close, Save, and Print are on this tab. You can add or change the properties of a document and customize the Quick Access toolbar and the ribbons to contain the commands you most often use.

Clipboard This powerful tool allows you to copy, paste, and move elements around a document.
context-sensitive menu This right-click shortcut menu contains the most common options that apply to a folder.
Copy A command that allows you to duplicate an item or document.
Cut A command that allows you to remove an item or document from its current location.

dragging Move files from folder to folder or select text by moving the computer's mouse across an item or group of items.

file Each document you create.
folder tree This feature in Office graphically displays how one folder connects to another.
folders Where all the documents you gather or produce for a project are organized.

maximize Use this Office option to view a window by moving it from the Windows taskbar at the bottom of the screen.
Mini toolbar Allows you to adjust the settings on hundreds of default options. It automatically displays when the mouse rests above text in your document.
minimize This option provides more room on the screen by moving your document to the Windows taskbar at the bottom of the screen.

Navigation pane This feature appears down the left side of the screen and contains commands for moving within your document and between applications and folders.

Paste A command that allows you to move an item to another document or place in your document after cutting or copying it from its current location.

Quick Access toolbar Allows you to add commands you use often to the toolbar so they remain on the screen no matter what ribbon is active.

Recycle bin Where your computer stores material you delete.

Save Stores your document so that you can reopen it to change it, copy it, move it, and delete it.
Save As Stores your document in a specific location of your choice.
scroll Move up or down a document quickly.
Show Tabs An option that hides the Ribbon but leaves the tabs visible.

taskbar Appears at the bottom of the screen and contains minimized documents or applications.
templates Professionally designed files for use as is or as a basis for a custom document.

view The way a document appears on the screen; for example, Word contains the Read Mode, Print Layout, and Outline view. Excel provides Normal, Page Break, and Page Layout views.

Word options This menu allows you to turn on, turn off, and adjust the settings on hundreds of default options.

Zoom A command that allows you to change the magnification level of your document.

WORD 2013

align How you position text on the page, either on the left, in the center, or on the right.
APA Stands for the American Psychological Association. This organization dictates the style of punctuation and writing used by many academic and business organizations.
Autofit This command sizes rows and columns automatically and evenly in a table.
automatic alignment guides This Office 2013 feature helps position graphics and other elements quickly and accurately.

Backstage view Accessed from the FILE tab, this is the place to manage files. Common commands such as Open, Close, Save, and Print are on this tab. You can add or change the properties of a document and customize the Quick Access toolbar and the ribbons to contain the commands you most often use.
Below text This option is available for the placement of footnotes or endnotes in a document.
bibliography A list of the sources used in the research for a document.
Bing Image Search An option to search the Internet to find an image for a document.
bold A font style used to add emphasis to text.
Border Painter button Used to apply changes to specific borders you choose, not all.

borders A design option for highlighting text boxes by placing a single line, double lines, dotted line, or other feature around it.

breaks These are the places in your document where a new page or section begins.

Bring Forward This option moves a selected image or text up, or forward, one layer.

callouts A shape in Word designed to hold text, similar to dialog and thought balloons in comics.

cell/row selection arrow Used to make formatting changes to one particular cell or row of cells.

cells The intersections of columns and rows.

center-align text This option displays text in the center of a document or in the center of a text box.

character style A document formatting option that controls where a page or section starts or stops.

Chicago style The style of punctuation and writing used by most newspapers and journalists.

citations In-line references that indicate where the specific information was taken.

Clear all tabs Clear all tabs from the HOME tab under the Paragraph group.

click This action of pressing the computer's mouse activates Ribbon options, selects text, and helps you navigate files and folders.

clip art Illustrations such as cartoons or drawings.

column break An organizational control to force text to move from one column to the next.

Column selection arrow Use this to select one or more adjacent columns to format them separately from the rest of the table.

columns (table) Vertical fields in a table.

columns (text) A space-saving measure that sets apart a section of text in a vertical field.

Columns dialog box This is where options are found to make adjustments to a column such as changing the width, margins, column breaks, or other additions.

Compress pictures An option that shrinks the file size for imported pictures and allows you to delete any cropped areas.

content of footnote This feature automatically displays information about a citation by hovering the mouse over it in the document.

Continue from previous section A command that directs page numbers to continue throughout the document.

continuous section break An option to change text from one column to multiple columns.

convert endnotes to footnotes This tool under the Footnotes Launch button quickly performs the operation of changing endnotes to footnotes in your document.

convert footnotes to endnotes This tool under the Footnotes Launch button quickly performs the operation of changing footnotes to endnotes in your document.

cover page The first page of a multiple-page document that usually includes the title, author, and date.

crop Clip areas of an image to remove what you do not need.

Crop to shape This command allows you to fit a picture inside of a shape.

custom header or footer An option to add your own text in a header or footer, found in the Header & Footer view.

Custom table of contents Word allows an option to add, remove, or modify elements such as tab leaders, levels shown, and formatting within your own table of contents.

custom tabs Word allows you to make choices in setting tabs through the Tab Selection button. Here you can apply a different set of tabs to every row of text or set a tab to more than one row.

custom template Add your own information or delete placeholders from Word's pre-designed templates. You can then save this document for repeated use.

Date & Time A Word feature that inserts date and time information into a header or footer.

Date Picker This Word feature allows you to choose a date for your cover page using a calendar, reducing errors.

default tabs These are automatic settings for tab spacing, in Word at one-half inch.

delete columns An option for tables that allows for flexibility in the number of columns presented and instantly reformats the table.

delete rows An option for tables that allows for flexibility in the number of rows presented and instantly reformats the table.

deselect An action performed by clicking away from the selected text anywhere on the screen.

dialog box These options exist for almost every Ribbon group and provide more control and adjustments than the shortcuts in each Ribbon group.

Different First Page This option allows you to have a different header or footer on the first page of a section.

Different odd and even pages A header and footer option that allows you to control what appears on odd and even pages of the document rather than repeat throughout.

distribute rows/columns evenly Right-click the Table Control button and open the shortcut menu to automatically restore symmetry to a table.

document properties General information about the document such as title, author, or date that Word automatically uses for a title or cover page.

double-click This action of pressing twice on the mouse offers additional control to select text or open menus.

drag Move files from folder to folder or select text using the computer's mouse.

drop cap An initial capital at the beginning of a paragraph that provides a professional appearance.

drop-down This menu type provides more options, opening dialog boxes for more detailed controls.

edit a footnote To make changes to a footnote, click on the note and make changes.

end of chapter An option for placement of endnotes.

end of section An option for placement of endnotes.

endnote Add information or clarification to your document without interrupting the flow of your writing. These appear at the end of your document.

Fill colors A way to enhance text boxes, shapes, and other elements by adding color from the FORMAT tab.

Find A command used to locate text quickly.

Find and Replace A command used to locate text and insert new text quickly.

font typeface The style of type used for your document. Examples include Times New Roman, Verdana, and Calibri.

footer from bottom An option to control the amount of space around your footers.

footnote Add information or clarification to your document without interrupting the flow of your writing. These appear at the bottom of the page.

Format page numbers An option for customizing the way your page numbers appear. It is found in the Header and Footer view under the DESIGN tab, in the Header and Footer group.

Formulas Allows you to apply functions such as sum, multiply, average, or count to data cells in a table.

gradient font Special formatting that allows for a faded look with your text.

Group A command to layer or connect elements in your document so they are treated as a single element.

hard page break Allows you to control when text stops on one page and begins on the next page.

Header and Footer view This view opens access to headers and footers so you can insert, delete, and format page numbers without affecting the main body of the text.

header from top An option to control the amount of space around your headers.

header row Column titles in a table.

headers and footers These document features provide guidance to the reader and convey general information about the document on each page. Common elements include the title of the document, the author, and the date.

heading styles A style option such as paragraph headings or character headings that allows a document to format automatically.

headings A section title that indicates the topic that is being discussed in the paragraphs following it.

horizontal A setting for positioning elements on your document parallel to the horizon.

hyperlink A link in an endnote, footnote, table of contents, or other place that takes you directly to where that information appears in the document.

insert row/column Word offers the flexible option to create another row or column anywhere in a table by hovering the mouse over the desired location and choosing Add Column or Add Row.

italic A font option that changes your text to appear at a slant to show emphasis.

justified columns Display straight margins down the left- and right-hand sides of each column in a table.

justify text Text appears in a straight line down the left and right margins of a document or text box.

keywords Terms typed in a search box to locate an item on the Internet.

landscape A horizontal page setup option.

layer An option to place one image in front of or behind another.

Layout dialog box Manage the precise placement and positioning of elements for your document from this dialog box.

Layout Options A feature that allows you to decide how the text and other images should wrap around an image.

leader A character that appears before a tab such as a dot or dash.

left-align text This option aligns text straight down the left margin of a document or to the left of a text box.

line between columns A Word option for tables that improves the visual separation of content for your reader.

Link to Previous An option in setting headers and footers that you can turn off for more control over the information that appears in these elements in your document. This is helpful for managing separate sections that may need to include different information.

Manage Sources A Word feature that provides shortcuts for citing material and also allows you to build a bibliography in a writing style of APA, MLA, Chicago, Harvard, or other.

margins The spaces that appear to the right and left of text on a page or text box.

Mini toolbar Displays when the mouse rests above text in your document and allows you to adjust the settings on hundreds of default options.

MLA Stands for the Modern Language Association and refers to the writing style followed by that organization and most works in the fields of literature and foreign language.

modify When referring to headers and footers, making a change to one automatically changes the rest of them throughout the document.

mouse A computer peripheral used for navigation on the screen.

Navigation pane This feature appears at the left side of the computer screen and displays information regarding a file.

New Style A button on the Ribbon used to open options to customize styles.

next page section break An option that creates a page break along with a section break within a document.

No Fill A layout option that allows you to show a document through a text box.

No Outline-22 A layout option for textboxes that removes the line around the box, so the text inside appears to hover on the page.

nonadjacent selection An option that allows you to select text or blocks of text for editing that do not appear next to one another.

Normal The default heading name assigned to the body text in a document.

nudge Used to make small changes to the positioning of an image.

number format Options in Word for displaying data in a table.

orientation The positioning of a document, either portrait or landscape.

outline colors A feature in the Layout dialog box that allows you to choose the color that surrounds a shape, text box, or other document element.

Outline width A feature in the Layout dialog box that allows you to choose the size of the line that surrounds a shape, text box, or other document element.

page borders A design option for highlighting entire pages by placing a single line, double lines, dotted line, or other feature around it.

page break Forces a new page to begin, allowing you to control what appears at the top of each page of your document.

paragraph style This heading formats the entire paragraph in which it is included.

picture watermark A logo or other image placed as a background on the pages of a document.

pictures Photos used to enhance the appearance of a document, from the computer's files or the Internet.

placeholders Elements of a document that allow for separate formatting, such as author name or title on a cover page.

precise size and positioning A feature in the Layout dialog box that allows for specific control over the placement of elements in your document.

Print A command that sends your document to the selected printing device.

Print Preview pane The place where you make custom selections for your print job.

Proofing The group that contains the Spelling and Grammar checker.

Quick Access toolbar These commands appear at the top of the screen and allow one-click access to complete tasks in Word.

Quick Tables A feature in Word with mock data and professionally designed tables, easy to customize for your use.

Read Mode The default view in Word that allows you to review your document with the fewest distractions.

readability statistics An option to review information at the end of your spelling and grammar check about your document such as word, character, and paragraph counts, and the Flesch-Kincaid data for your document.

references Works cited; a list of the actual documents used in research for a document.

remove a tab Quickly eliminate a tab from your document by dragging it off the ruler and clicking the mouse.

remove a watermark An option in the Page Background group in the DESIGN tab to remove this document element.

Ribbon The location where the most commonly used tabs are located, along the top of the computer screen.

rows (table) Horizontal fields in a table.

ruler Provides information about the margins and other elements in your document, useful for editing and positioning text and graphics.

section break Provides the ability to format an entire section of a document without affecting other sections.

select The action that needs to be completed before making changes to text in Word. Choose text with the mouse or the keyboard.

Selection bar Displays the area of your document that you chose to edit.

Send Backward Moves the selected image or text down, or back, one layer.

shading Allows the addition of color or pattern to a block of text.

shape Design options used to add visual impact. Word provides more than 150 different shapes.

Shape Fill An option to apply color inside a text box or shape.

Shape Outline A feature in the Layout dialog box that allows you to add a line to surround a shape, text box, or other document element.

Show/Hide command Displays formatting marks in your document.

size Refers in Word to the appearance of the font, measured in points, for example, 10 pt. font or 12 pt. font. You choose font size from the HOME tab.

soft break As you delete and add material to your document, Word reflows automatically, formatting your document as needed.

Source Manager A feature in Word that displays a check mark next to each source in the Current List that is cited in the document.

Source type A category identifying the type of information used as a reference in your document (a book, lecture, article from a periodical, website, report, and more) that provides Word with information to automatically and correctly format a citation.

Spelling and Grammar checker A tool in Office 2013 that helps you create clear and accurate documents free of errors, either as you type or after you complete your work.

Start at This feature helps remove mistakes and analyzes the level of writing in a document.

Status bar This list of commands appears in the bottom-right corner of the Word window, next to the zoom controls.

styles palette Accessed from the More button on the Ribbon, this feature offers additional options for adding interest to your document.

tab alignment Refers to the placement of tabs on a page: left, center, right, etc.

Tab Selection button Set custom tabs with this feature found on the horizontal ruler.

table borders These lines around a table can visually enhance your document. Word allows you to choose the color, width, and style of this element.

Table Control button This tool helps you create the appearance and attributes you desire for your table in Word.

table of contents Used to help readers find information quickly in long documents. Word can use your headings to create and update this document automatically as you edit, hyperlinking each entry to the place in the document where each corresponding heading appears.

Table Styles Predesigned looks for tables for a professional and effective appearance.

tables A way to organize information in your document to make it easy to understand and edit by moving, sorting, or adding to it.

tabs Allow you to arrange rows of text or data into straight vertical lines.

Tabs dialog box Allows for additional control and options for the appearance of your document such as tab alignment, leaders, and placement.

template A professionally designed file for use as is or as a basis for a custom document.

text box You can draw these any size and move them around a document, controlling the text inside without affecting anything else on the page.

Text effects A built-in formatting command under the HOME tab that adds instant energy to your document. Options include outline, shadow, reflection, glow, and many others.

text watermark Words, such as Draft or Confidential, placed as a background on the pages of a document.

text wrapping This feature determines how images or other elements blend with the text.

triple-click An action performed on the mouse to do things such as select an entire paragraph.

underline An option for highlighting text to show emphasis.

ungrouping Eliminates the layering created by grouping, allowing you to adjust and edit each item individually.

Update Automatically An option that allows Word to change the date in a header or footer to the current date each time the document is opened.

vertical A setting for positioning elements on your document perpendicular, or at a right angle, to the horizon.

watermark An image across the background of a page designed to show the value of a document; can be a picture or text.

width of columns Refers to the size of the document's columns horizontally.

writing style A convention for punctuation, citing, and bibliography, set by MLA, APA, Chicago, or other institution.

zoom Allows you to change the magnification level on your document.

EXCEL 2013

3-D Reference Formulas An option in Excel for creating summary sheets of data that appears on several worksheets.

Absolute cell address A cell reference that refers to an exact cell location in a worksheet, specified by preceding each cell and row number with a dollar sign ($).

Application window In Excel, acts as a container for your workbook files containing worksheets and charts. Also provides the Windows icons, FILE menu, Ribbon, Name box, Formula bar, and Status bar.

arguments Labels, values, or cell references used to enter functions into a worksheet cell.

AutoCalculate A feature in Excel used to calculate results of a selected range of values in the Status bar. For example, AVERAGE, COUNT, and SUM.

AutoFill A feature in Excel that allows you to create a data series by simply dragging the fill handle for a selected range.

AutoSum A feature in Excel that reviews the surrounding cell, guesses at the range you want to sum, and places a SUM function into the active cell.

AVERAGE An Excel function used to calculate the arithmetic mean for a range of cells.

background An image placed in a worksheet that appears on the screen when that worksheet is in use.

background bitmap An image that fills the entire worksheet behind your data on screen; used to enhance a worksheet's appearance.

Backstage view Displays a preview of how a worksheet will print.

cell The intersection of a column and a row.

cell alignment The vertical and horizontal appearance of data entered into the worksheet.

cell pointer The cursor used to select a cell in the worksheet using either the mouse or the keyboard.

cell range Can be a single cell or a rectangular block of cells; contains a beginning cell address in the top left-hand corner and an ending cell address in the bottom right-hand corner.

chart elements Features available in Excel that enhance the appearance and readability of a worksheet or chart and its data. Examples include Axes, Axis title, Chart title, Data Table, Error Bars, Gridlines, Legend, and Trendlines.

Chart Elements button A feature in Excel that allows for quick access to add enhancements to your chart. This button appears to the right of the chart, is embedded, or is placed on a separate chart sheet.

Chart Filters button An Excel feature that allows you to quickly make changes to the data elements in the chart.

Chart sheet Displays a chart graphic that is typically linked to data stored in a worksheet.

Chart Styles button An Excel feature that allows you to quickly change the styles or color combinations in the chart.

comparison operators Symbols used to direct a function of conditional expressions such as equal (=), not equal (<>), less than (<), less than or equal to (<=), greater than (>), or greater than or equal to (>=).

conditional expressions Excel functions that allow you to test for a condition and perform one of two calculations, depending on the result, using comparison operators.

conditional formatting Highlights certain data in a worksheet so that data trends are easy to see.

COUNT An Excel function that tallies cells containing numbers and dates.

COUNTA An Excel function related to the COUNT function that counts all nonblank cells and included text labels in its calculations.

data tables A way to display information in Excel that helps you manage large worksheets.

Document window Each worksheet's window contains its own scroll bars, sheet tabs, and Tab Scrolling arrows for easy navigation.

documentation worksheet Describes the purpose of the workbook and the contents of each worksheet in the workbook.

embedded chart A chart stored on the worksheet, allowing you to display a visual representation alongside your worksheet.

fill colors An Excel option to customize a shape by adding color inside the entire shape.

fill handle Use the mouse to drag this pointer to select a range of cells.

filtering An Excel feature used to select the specific data records needed.

Find and Replace This feature allows you to locate a particular piece of data in Excel and edit it as needed.

Flash Fill A feature in Excel that reviews your previous entries and predicts how you want to complete a column or row.

flipped shapes An Excel option to customize a shape by changing its orientation.

fonts Typeface styles.

Format Painter A feature in Excel used to copy formatting styles and attributes from one area of a worksheet to another, ensuring speed and consistency.

formula An expression that begins with an equal ($=$) sign and contains numbers, cell references, and/or mathematical operators.

Formula bar Appears to the right of the Name box and displays the contents of the current selected cell.

freeze panes An Excel feature that displays the header constantly while the user scrolls the worksheet.

functions Excel shortcuts used in place of formulas to calculate data.

gridlines Nonprinting lines to help you align and organize information in your worksheet.

group When working with multiple worksheets, Excel allows you to connect them so that formatting and printing options apply to all worksheets, not individual worksheets.

hiding worksheets This valuable technique protects sensitive or classified data, removing a certain worksheet or group of worksheets from view.

HLOOKUP An Excel function used to look up values in a horizontal list or cell range and then retrieve data from a row in the same column as the matching value.

IF An Excel function used to employ conditional logic in a worksheet.

in-cell editing Make changes to an existing cell by pressing F2 or double-clicking into a cell.

MAX An Excel function used to determine the highest value in a range of cells.

MEDIAN A function in Excel used to compute the middle value in a set of numbers.

MIN An Excel function used to determine the lowest value in a range of cells.

mixed cell address Locks only a portion of a cell address by inserting a dollar sign ($) before either the column or the row number.

Name box Located directly above column A, where the current selected cell address is displayed.

Normal view The most common view in Excel for entering data that displays the on-screen elements.

NOW An Excel function that returns the current date and time as provided by your computer's internal dock.

outline colors An Excel option to customize a shape by adding color to the border of the shape.

outline width An Excel option to customize a shape by customizing the border of the shape.

Page Break Preview The Excel worksheet view where you can specify print area and set page breaks.

page breaks A printing option in Excel that allows you to print more or less of your spreadsheet on a page.

Page Layout view The Excel worksheet view that displays in a full-page window with margins, page breaks, and headers and footers. Used to move through the workbook pages, zoom in and out, and modify layout options.

points The measurement of a row's height; 72 points is equal to one inch.

positioning This option on the FORMAT tab helps you customize a shape, text box, or other element in your worksheet.

precise size This option on the FORMAT tab helps you customize a shape, text box, or other element in your worksheet.

Quick Analysis An Excel feature that provides options for formatting, charting, totaling, creating tables, and inserting sparklines based on the values stored in a selected range.

Quick Analysis button A button used to apply conditional formatting to a cell or cell range.

range Displaying data in this way allows you to use all of Excel's capabilities, including charting and data analysis.

range name A nickname given to a cell range to facilitate entering formulas.

relative cell address When appearing in a formula and copied, it adjusts automatically because its reference is relative to where it sits in the worksheet. This is Excel's default.

shapes Graphics used to enhance your data. They include lines, arrows, circles, rectangles, and triangles. Microsoft Excel's library is extensive with more than 150 options.

sheet tabs An Excel navigation tool that makes it easy to move between worksheets and identify the active sheet. These display along the bottom of the Excel window and are default named Sheet1, Sheet2, Sheet3, etc. You can rename them and apply limited formatting.

sort A way to arrange data rows in the order that displays data for better analysis, often alphabetically in ascending or descending order.

sparklines Tiny, word-sized charts placed within a cell to help users visualize and better understand what the data means without plotting the data into a chart.

spelling check This feature is found in Excel under the REVIEW tab in the Proofing group and allows you to produce documents without spelling errors.

split button This button on the REVIEW tab creates a split between selected columns in your worksheet.

Status bar Displays calculated results of a selected range in AutoCalculate.

SUM An Excel function that adds values appearing in a range of cells.

summary worksheet Consolidates data from several worksheets into one place for a quick review of the data included in your worksheets.

syntax The precise order in which to enter arguments.

table A range of data created from the data in a spreadsheet.

template Preexisting workbooks with data and design elements included.

tiling When a background image fills the entire worksheet.

TODAY An Excel function that provides the current date.

VLOOKUP An Excel function that allows you to find a value in a vertical list and then retrieve data from a column on the same row as the matching value.

workbook A single file containing related worksheets and chart sheets.

worksheet A document designed to display data in an easy-to-understand format, organized with lettered vertical columns and numbered horizontal rows.

ACCESS 2013

action query A type of query that applies mass changes to data it retrieves. Types include the update query, append query, delete query, and make table query.

append query A type of action query that adds data from one or more tables to another table.

AutoNumber Any cell containing this type of field is incremented automatically by Access when a new record is added.

calculated field Enables you to draw data from other field columns and perform a mathematical calculation on a row-by-row basis.

cell The intersection of a row and a column.

compact An action in Access that identifies objects in a database you can eliminate.

conditional statement Used to limit the records that display in a data sheet by extracting only data that meets certain conditions.

crosstab query Summarizes numerical results in a spreadsheet-like table; mainly used for data analysis.

database A collection of related information.

database file The document in Access, appearing with an *.accdb* extension, used to create and work with individual database objects.

database management system (DBMS) Sophisticated programs that enable you to enter, store, analyze, and present data.

database objects The elements used for storing, editing, retrieving, and displaying data within a database file including tables, queries, forms, reports, macros, and modules.

datasheet The most common way a table is presented in Access.

Datasheet view Organizes data into rows and columns similar to a spreadsheet.

delete query A type of action query that removes records from one or more tables.

Design view An Access feature that allows you to create the table structure manually and modify reports and forms.

Documenter A tool in Access that allows you to preview and print various design characteristics of your database objects, including a table's structure and field properties.

expression Used to create a calculated field in a query; it may include table and field names, mathematical operations, comparison operators, logical operators, and constants.

field A column in a datasheet that holds a single piece of data.

field grid area In Access's Design view, this is where a user enters the desired field names, descriptions, and data types for a new table.

field header area The place on the Access window to drag the mouse pointer to change the width of a column in Datasheet view.

field properties area This display at the bottom of the Access screen, under the field grid area, shows the general datasheet properties.

filter A tool that limits the display of records in a table using simple matching criterion.

Filter By Form Used for detailed filtering operations to set multiple criteria.

Filter By Selection Used to apply a filter based on a selected value from the datasheet that may be an entire cell's contents or only a portion of the entry.

form Different from a datasheet column and row layout, this database object displays one record at a time and is used to add and edit record data.

Form Layout view An Access view in which you can modify reports and forms.

Form wizard A user-friendly way in Access to create a form.

Mailing Labels report A useful report that generates mailing labels from a list in a table.

make table query A type of action query that creates a new table from a query's result.

metadata Comments that describe the contents of the field.

Navigation pane The command control center for Access; appears along the left border of the application window. It contains a categorical listing of the database objects and allows you to group and search for objects.

null value A duplicate or nothing value.

parameter query Displays a dialog box and accepts input from the user before proceeding; used to enter customized search criteria at run-time.

primary key A field that uniquely identifies each and every record in a table; used by Access to search for data and establish relationships between tables.

query A question asked of a database.

query-by-example (QBE) A graphical layout used by the Query Design window.

Query Design grid Allows you to select field columns for display, enter criteria statements, specify sort orders, and perform calculations.

record Each individual record in a table, appearing as a horizontal row in a datasheet, composed of one or more fields.

Record Navigation bar Appears just above the Status bar in Datasheet view and shows which record is currently displayed.

Record Selection area Sometimes called the Row selector buttons used to navigate an Access datasheet.

repair An action in Access that eliminates unnecessary objects in a database.

report Created to present, summarize, and print data.

Report Layout view An Access view in which you can modify reports.

Report wizard A user-friendly way in Access to create a report.

select query The type of query object created by the Simple Query wizard.

Simple Query wizard A step-by-step tool to retrieve data from one or more tables in a database.

Sort key A field chosen to organize by.

subdatasheet Used to display related data when two or more tables are joined.

table The primary object for storing data in Access.

Table pane Divides the Access window and identifies the source data tables and Query Design grid.

Undo command Used in Access to reverse mistakes made during editing.

update query A type of action query that modifies data in a table.

wildcard characters Used to represent one or more alternative characters in a conditional expression; question mark (?) and asterisk (*).

POWERPOINT 2013

Align Objects A PowerPoint command that allows you to move objects into absolute positions with a click of the mouse, either centering an image on a slide or matching images to the positioning of other images.

animations Movements applied to slide elements to enhance the presentation.

artistic effects Options to enhance images with a preset appearance of, for example, paint strokes, glass-like appearance, soft edges, or shadow.

Audio on My PC A PowerPoint command used to add sounds stored on your computer to a slide, accessed on the slide by clicking the audio icon.

automatic alignment guides Faint dotted lines activated when you insert an image into your slide show and drag it across a slide.

Backstage view Use this view in PowerPoint to save files, find print controls, and set options.

border Lines around images that make them appear sharper. You can customize the thickness of the lines and apply them to more than one image at a time.

Bring Forward Layer a shape to appear on top of another.

callout These shapes commonly appear as the thought and dialog balloons used in cartoons. Adding and adjusting text in a callout is the same as adding and adjusting text in any shape.

charts Allow you to visually display data in a variety of ways including column, line, bar, and pie charts. These help the audience better understand the data.

Collapse A command in Outline view that allows you to see only the slide titles.

connector A line, arrow, or elbow used to show the relationship between two shapes.

content placeholders A shortcut in a slide show that connects you to images and media.

Copy and Paste In PowerPoint, this command saves time by copying an object you duplicate and placing it on another slide in exactly the same place as on the original slide.

Date and time A feature in PowerPoint that quickly allows you to insert date and time information that automatically updates or is set to a date and time you choose.

delay An animation control that allows you to control the timing of an element's appearance.

demoting Moving text down a level in Outline view.

duplicate slide Copy an entire slide.

duration The length of time an action occurs in a PowerPoint presentation.

Edit data A window that appears after you create a chart that allows you to make changes to the chart.

Effect options A place to control and make changes to animations. Options for making changes will depend on the characteristics of your chosen animation.

elements Items such as images, hyperlinks, transitions, and animations that add interest to your slide presentation.

emphasis effects An animation type that appears while you view a slide.

entrance effects An animation type that controls how elements first appear on a slide.

exit effects An animation type that controls how elements leave a slide.

fade in, fade out A smooth and soft way to start and stop a video in your presentation.

file formats PowerPoint's default format is .pptx, but other file formats exist. The format .ppt is compatible with older versions of Office, .potx is a template format that can be used again, and .ppsx opens in Show mode and not in an editable view.

Format Background These PowerPoint controls allow you to change a slide background no matter how you begin, with a plain white or a preset design.

Format Painter A tool in PowerPoint that allows you to copy the formatting of one element and apply it to another element.

Format Shape A pane in PowerPoint that allows you to adjust the settings for predesigned effects you apply to your shapes.

gradient fill Allows you to merge one or more colors into another in the background of your slide presentation.

gridlines A series of dotted lines that overlay on a grid to provide you a tool to aid in placing elements in proper alignment on a slide. These do not print.

group A way to connect elements so they act as one object for moving, copying, and pasting.

guides One vertical and one horizontal line that appear on the slide to separate it into quadrants as a tool to aid in alignment of elements. These do not print.

handouts Paper copies of your slides provided to your audience so they can take notes or follow along with a small-scale copy of your presentation. Printing options allow for as many as nine slides per printed page.

Hide During Show This option removes the audio icon so that it is not a distraction during a slide show.

hyperlink Clickable link that connects you to another location within or outside of your slide show.

Launch button Used to open dialog boxes and is contained on every group along a tab Ribbon.

Live Preview This feature allows you to see what a theme would look like on your slide by hovering over a certain theme with your mouse to see that theme applied to the currently active slide.

Lock aspect ratio This control forces PowerPoint to automatically adjust an image to maintain the proper proportions of height and width.

Lock Drawing mode You can set your mouse to draw the same shape again and again until you turn it off.

Loop until Stopped A setting in PowerPoint that allows your presentation to continue playing, repeating until it is stopped manually.

main editing window The part of the screen that displays the current slide of the show in the Normal view. Contains the slide pane on the left.

Media group A PowerPoint feature that allows access to videos stored on your computer or on the Internet for use in your slides.

multiple insertions A technique used to select and insert more than one image at a time in your presentation by holding the `Ctrl` button down while clicking on selected images.

New Slide button A command used to insert a blank slide into your presentation.

notes A function in PowerPoint that allows you to place your speaker's notes directly in your presentation so they appear for your use when presenting and on audience handouts, if you choose.

online audio Sounds found on the Internet you can use in your slide shows.

online pictures Photographic images found on the Internet you can use in your slide shows.

online video Film and video footage found on the Internet you can use in your slide shows.

Outline view The view in PowerPoint that allows you to enter your information for each slide without positioning text boxes and placeholders. You can rearrange information by dragging slides up and down a list for quick organization.

picture or texture fill Allows you to fill the entire slide background with a picture (from your computer or from an online search) or to use a predesigned texture in the background.

Picture tools A command that displays when you insert a picture into PowerPoint so you can format and size the image correctly, customizing it to match your presentation.

placeholders These elements are found in PowerPoint's predesigned slide layouts and allow for easy placement of images, video, and audio.

Play Across Slides A PowerPoint setting used to run an audio clip throughout the slide show, even if you introduce new audio.

Play Full Screen A setting in PowerPoint that allows your presentation to fill the entire computer screen from edge to edge.

Play in Background An option for audio within a PowerPoint presentation so that sound continues to play while other louder sounds are layered on top. Control volume on more than one audio source individually.

playback Video settings in PowerPoint that include Video Options for starting the video, Loop until Stopped, and Play Full Screen.

Presenter view A feature in PowerPoint that allows a split screen so the speaker can view the current slide displayed to the audience along with the next slide, time, speaker's notes, and shortcuts to presentation features such as highlighters or zoom.

Print Color button An option in the Print Preview pane that allows you to print in grayscale (black ink) or in color.

Print page In PowerPoint, the options here include what is printed, how many to print, and which printer to use to print your presentation.

Print Preview Use this option to see what your printed presentation will look like before you print.

Print Range button An option in the Print Preview pane that allows you to select which slides to print, all slides or a selection of slides.

Printer button An option on the Print page to choose a printer.

promoting Moving text up a level in Outline view.

Quick Styles Contains preset designs to instantly format a shape, picture, table, chart, and even SmartArt and adjusts to provide choices that automatically coordinate with the theme of the slide show.

Reading view This view runs a preview of the slide show within the program window.

remove animations PowerPoint orders the animations based on the one you apply first to a slide. Delete one by clicking on the action order number and deleting it.

reorder animations PowerPoint orders the animations based on the one you apply first to a slide. You can move them from the Animation pane and by dragging the action up and down to the desired location.

Repeat button A choice on the Quick Access toolbar to duplicate an action or element on another slide.

Rotate objects A button that allows you to flip images either horizontally or vertically to suit the design and the focal point of your slide.

ruler A PowerPoint design feature that displays the actual size of the page and the elements on it.

screen ratio A setting in PowerPoint that is a standard 4:3 or widescreen 16:9 that you customize depending on the presentation venue and projector.

Send Backward Layer a shape to appear behind another.

Shape Effects A button that applies predesigned effects such as shadow, reflection, glow, soft edges, bevel, and even 3-D rotation to a shape.

Shape Height This control allows you to spin the number up or down or enter a specific height. PowerPoint automatically adjusts the corresponding ratio to maintain the image's proper proportion.

Shape Width This control allows you to spin the number up or down or enter a specific width. PowerPoint automatically adjusts the corresponding ratio to maintain the image's proper proportion.

shapes Images used to augment slides—to emphasize components or to enhance the appearance of other objects. These include circles, arrows, or almost any other form.

Shortcut menu Context-sensitive options, related to specific areas on the screen, that display when you click the mouse on that area.

sizing handles Allow you to control the size and proportions of a placeholder or image without affecting other elements of the slide.

slide What is contained in a PowerPoint presentation. It can contain images, graphics, text, audio, video, and more that can be arranged in almost any manner.

Slide layout A predesigned template for your slide presentation that includes placeholders with shortcuts to media or images.

Slide Master view A view in PowerPoint that offers more color and font options than other views.

slide numbers Help keep the presenter on track and allow viewers to refer to slides by number when asking questions or looking at a handout.

Slide pane This is the left-hand side of the screen where the thumbnail images of each slide appear.

Slide Show An option in PowerPoint to begin your presentation in full-screen mode, without the tabs, ribbons, and icons.

Slide Sorter view Displays all the slides in your presentation side by side for easy reorganizing.

SmartArt Professionally designed graphics that allow you to quickly add your own text and information into models specifically designed for maximum impact on a PowerPoint slide.

solid fill This background formatting option on the DESIGN tab allows you to apply any color to the entire background of a slide.

start A timing control in PowerPoint that allows animations to begin on a click or with previous (at the same time as another action). You can also delay the start of an animation and set the duration for the action.

Start On Click This option allows you to begin an animation with the click of your mouse.

Start With Previous This option allows you to begin an animation at the same time as another animation.

Status bar Found along the top of the PowerPoint screen. Contains commands such as Zoom and View.

symmetrical shapes Create these from the INSERT tab with the Shapes button, allowing you to make an evenly proportioned shape from any starting shape.

tables Enable you to organize data in a tabular format. This ensures the audience can see what major headings exist and what information falls under each heading.

templates Predesigned slides with suggested content slides and placeholders already positioned throughout the presentation.

text box A placeholder for words on a slide.

themes Predesigned slides with coordinated colors and layouts.

timing options Allow you to control when a slide transition or animation occurs.

transitions How one slide changes to the next slide.

transparency A control that can fade the background of a slide for better viewing.

transparent color Allows the background to show through.

Trim Video This is an option to control the length of video used in your presentation by moving a slide across a video timeline to decide exactly how much of the video to use.

ungroup An option that disconnects earlier connected slide elements so you can edit them individually.

variants An option within PowerPoint's design themes that instantly changes your show to the new theme. The colors, fonts, background design, and placement of elements are professionally coordinated to provide an eye-pleasing layout.

Video on My PC An option to search your computer for video files stored there.

Video Options Allows you to select how to begin a video in your presentation, with a mouse click or automatically when the slide appears.

video shape Allows you to format a video to display in any shape: a circle, star, triangle, or other shape.

view There are many options to watch and edit your slide show, including Slide Sorter view, Zoom, or main editing window.

zoom Allows you to magnify or demagnify your monitor to see more detail or the whole slide at once.

Index